HANDBOOKS

KAUA'I

ROBERT NILSEN

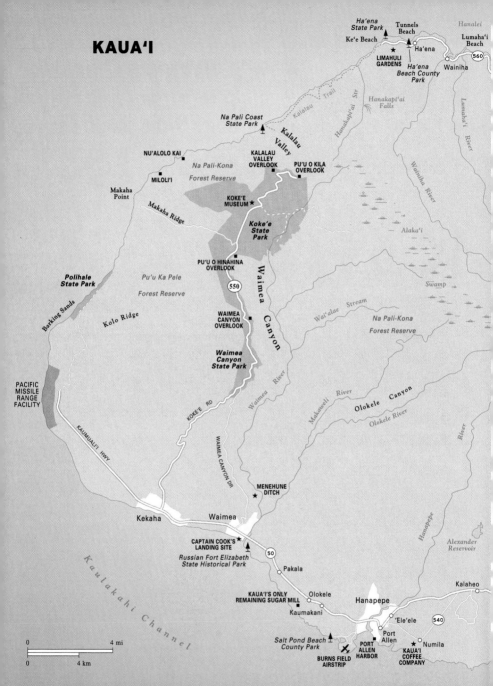

KAUA'I

Ha'ena State Park
Tunnels Beach
Ke'e Beach
Ha'ena
LIMAHULI GARDENS
Ha'ena Beach County Park
Hanalei
Lumaha'i Beach
Wainiha
560

Kalalau Trail
Hanakapi'ai Falls
Hanakapi'ai Str
Wainiha River
Lumaha'i River

Na Pali Coast State Park
Kalalau Valley

NU'ALOLO KAI
Na Pali-Kona Forest Reserve
KALALAU VALLEY OVERLOOK
PU'U O KILA OVERLOOK

MILOLI'I
KOKE'E MUSEUM
Alaka'i

Makaha Point
Makaha Ridge
Koke'e State Park
Swamp

Polihale State Park
PU'U O HINAHINA OVERLOOK
550
Pu'u Ka Pele Forest Reserve

Waimea Canyon

Barking Sands
Kolo Ridge
WAIMEA CANYON OVERLOOK

Wai'alae Stream
Na Pali-Kona Forest Reserve

PACIFIC MISSILE RANGE FACILITY
Waimea Canyon State Park

KOKE'E RD
Waimea River
Makaweli River
Olokele Canyon
River

KAUMUALI'I HWY
WAIMEA CANYON DR
Olokele River

MENEHUNE DITCH

Kekaha
Waimea

CAPTAIN COOK'S LANDING SITE
Russian Fort Elizabeth State Historical Park
50
Pakala

KAUA'I'S ONLY REMAINING SUGAR MILL
Olokele
Hanapepe
Alexander Reservoir
Kalaheo

Kaumakani
'Ele'ele
540

Salt Pond Beach County Park
PORT ALLEN HARBOR
Port Allen
KAUA'I COFFEE COMPANY
Numila

BURNS FIELD AIRSTRIP

Kaulakahi Channel

Hanapepe

0   4 mi
0   4 km

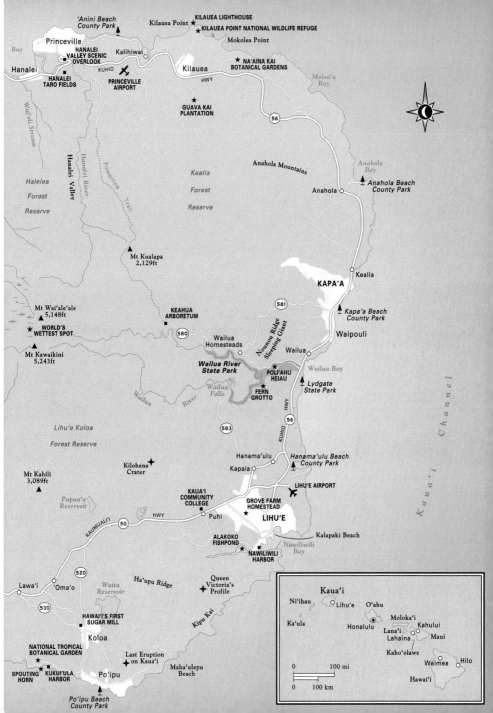

DISCOVER KAUA'I

Kaua'i is the oldest of the main Hawaiian Islands, and nature has had ample time to work sculpting Kaua'i into a beauty among beauties. Flowers and fruits burst from its fertile soil, but the "Garden Island" is much more than greenery and flora – it's the poetry of land itself! Its mountains have become rounded and smooth, and its streams tumbling to the sea have cut deep and wide, giving Kaua'i the only navigable river in Hawaii. The interior is a dramatic series of mountains, valleys, and primordial swamp. The great gouge of Waimea Canyon, called the "Grand Canyon of the Pacific," is an enchanting layer of pastels where uncountable rainbows form prismatic necklaces from which waterfalls hang like silvery pendants. These waterfalls and others on this green island are kept full by rain tickled from the underbellies of clouds passing over Mount Wai'ale'ale, one of the wettest spots on earth and the lofty center of this island. An otherworldly region of bogs and strong

Coconut Grove at the Coco Palms

winds, the Alak'ai Swamp is safe haven to many rare plants and birds, a microcosm of ancient Hawaii before human contact. The northwest encompasses the seacliffs of Na Pali, some of the mightiest in all of Oceania, looming nearly 4,000 feet above the pounding surf. Kaua'i has its share of superlatives, but the more mundane is also captivating, for it is the green mountain ridges, its necklace of sand beaches, and the surrounding blue ocean waters that capture the hearts of visitors, drawing many back again and again.

The meaning of "Kaua'i" has eluded modern scholars; no one seems to know its derivation. Some have theorized that it may have meant "Season of Abundance," because Kaua'i has always been rich in rainfall and the productive soil allows bountiful growth of native and introduced plants.

Everything seems quieter here, only 100 miles by air from Honolulu. It's rural but upbeat, with the main town being just that, a town. The pursuit of carefree relaxation is unavoidable at five-star

Sunset over Hanalei Bay and Mount Makana

hotels, where you're treated like a visiting *ali'i,* or you can camp deep in interior valleys or along secluded beaches where reality *is* the fantasy of paradise. Perhaps its greatest compliment is that Kaua'i is where other islanders come to look at the scenery.

Kaua'i is where Hollywood comes when the script calls for "paradise." The island has featured its haunting beauty as a "silent star" in dozens of major films, everything from idyllic scenes in *South Pacific* to the lurking horror of Asian villages in *Uncommon Valor.* *King Kong* tore up this countryside in search of love, and Tattoo spotted "da plane, boss" in *Fantasy Island.* In *Blue Hawaii,* Elvis's hips mimicked the swaying palms in a famous island grove, while torrid love scenes from *The Thorn Birds* were steamier than the jungle in the background.

Given an awful blow by Hurricane 'Iniki in 1992, the island has rebounded and reached a pace and scope of new development that most on the island can live with. Kaua'i has had its chance to start anew and forge ahead in a conscientiously sensitive manner. While the need to develop is clear, the need to do so without harm to

Bird's-eye view of the Na Pali coast, as seen from a helicopter

ROBERT NILSEN

the environment is also apparent. This sense of preservation runs deep, and there is community commitment not to disturb its natural beauty. The island's slower pace of life remains the norm and everyone strives to preserve this unhurried character.

Kaua'i is becoming more well known to the traveling public and, as a consequence, greater numbers of people are discovering its allure. Many first-time visitors head to the sunny southern shore to Po'ipu Beach, the first large-scale resort area on the island. Po'ipu has a good mixture of fine hotels, condominiums, and vacation rentals that accent the many fine sand beaches and rocky shoreline of this coast. Others head to the upscale planned community of Princeville, a collection of hotels, condos, and private homes that surround some of the best golf fairways on the island. Greener and wetter, Princeville is set on a bluff overlooking picture-perfect Hanalei Bay and the wide Pacific Ocean. The more economical East Shore, with its line of condominiums and time-shares set throughout the worker's communities of Wailua and Kapa'a, is once again experiencing a resurgence of development and attracting more and

The Moir Garden has an excellent collection of cacti.

more visitors. A down-home area, it offers plenty of bargains and locates visitors within easy reach of both the south and north shores. This was where early tourists first came to the island in numbers, perhaps drawn here like the early Hawaiians who also found it perfect for the island's major settlement region. No matter where you decide to stay, Kaua'i is diminutive and easy to get around. It's only a few hours there and back again to anywhere, as there is one main roadway that runs most of the way around the island with only a few major roads heading inland.

Those in the tourist industry have recognized this trend of increased visitation and have capitalized on this phenomenon by endowing Kaua'i with a new moniker: the Island of Discovery. It challenges visitors to seek not only its outward beauty and unique physical features but also its vibrant cultural soul, to enjoy its varied and exciting activities but search hard for its essence. Kaua'i is bite-sized but has as many opportunities for discovery, recreation, and enjoyment as the other Hawaiian Islands. Nothing seems to be lacking on Kaua'i, and it wouldn't matter anyway as travel is easy, food is plentiful, island residents are friendly, and the weather superb.

Hanakapi'ai Beach

Contents

MAP CONTENTS

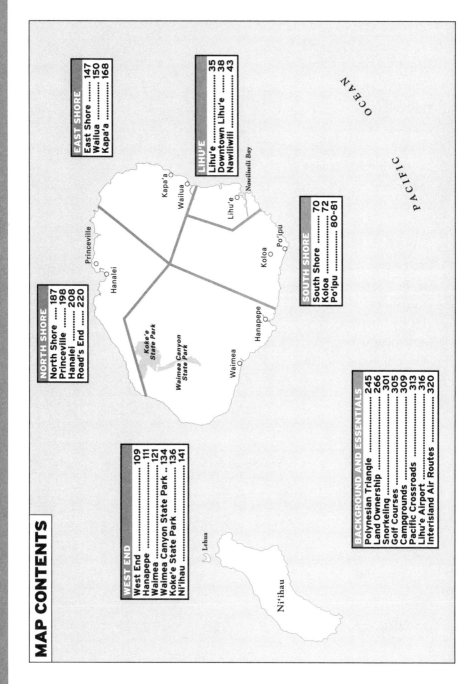

The Lay of the Land

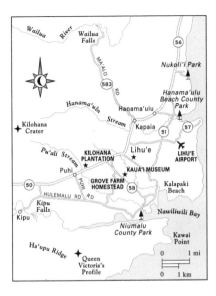

LIHU'E

Almost everyone arrives on Kaua'i at the airport in Lihu'e, the county seat and major town with a wide array of restaurants, shopping, and accommodations. Lihu'e never was a cultural center for the old Hawaiians, but the town now houses the Kaua'i Museum, where you'll learn the cultural, social, and geological history of the island, immensely enriching your visit. The legacy of Lihu'e's sugar era is encapsulated on the outskirts of town in the remarkably preserved Grove Farm Homestead, a classic Hawaiian plantation that is so intact all that seems to be missing is the workers. Several miles inland from Lihu'e is the engaging panorama of Wailua Falls, one of the most recognizable natural features of the island. The prettiest part of the Lihu'e area is Kalapaki Beach/Nawiliwili Bay with the lush and rugged backdrop of the Ha'upu Ridge coastal mountains. While it doesn't have the sexy appeal for tourists that other towns on the island have, Lihu'e does indeed have many locations worthy of a stop. It is also where you'll find the tourist office and is the place to pick up camping, hunting, and fishing permits.

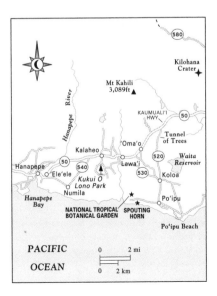

SOUTH SHORE

From Lihu'e west is a different story. Route 50 takes you past the coastal Ha'upu (Hoary Head) Ridge where Maluhia Road, famous as the Tunnel of Trees for its mile-long line of towering eucalyptus, funnels you down toward Koloa, a sugar town now rejuvenated with shops, boutiques, and restaurants, and beyond to the coast at Po'ipu Beach, the best on Kaua'i. This sunny south shore is the destination for many first-time visitors to Kaua'i, and it's easy to understand why. The great Po'ipu beaches offer everything for a perfect family outing, great snorkeling, and windswept isolation. At the west end of this resort area is **Spouting Horn,** a blowhole in the ceiling of a seaside lava tube that spouts water with each inrushing wave. An additional asset to this coastal region is the lower Lawaʻi Valley. It is here that the **National Tropical Botanical Garden** has its headquarters and is managed for the propagation and preservation of the earth's tropical plants. The largest of the inland towns is **Kalaheo,** where an island philanthropist, Walter McBride, gave the munificent land gift that has become **Kukui O Lono Park.** This hilltop location offers excellent views of the entire Poʻipu/South Shore region. The decline of sugar gave rise to a large coffee plantation here, and acre upon acre of coffee trees cover the long gradual hillside that sweeps down toward Hanapepe to the west.

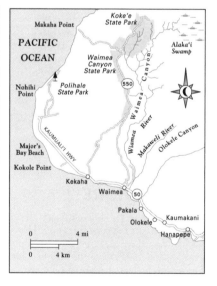

WEST END

The West End of Kauaʻi is the dry part of the island, but cutting through this region are the wet and evergreen Hanapepe and Waimea valleys. From **Hanapepe** to the end of the road is still sugar country, and the rolling lowland hillsides on both sides of the highway sway with cane. Farther to the west is **Waimea,** an important settlement where Hawaiians raised taro and some kings of Kauaʻi held residence. Historically, it's also important as the place where Captain Cook first came ashore in Hawaii, beginning the West's enchantment with the islands and their fateful and eventual domination by outside powers. Two roads branch inland, winding along the rim of **Waimea Canyon,** where scenic overlooks offer you the best views into this magnificent pastel-mottled valley. Above the canyon and encompassing the heart of the mountain is **Kokeʻe State Park.** Hiking trails and gravel roads lead the adventurous into its interior, and even the **Alakaʻi Swamp** opens up for the well prepared. This park also has several scenic overlooks, where you're king of the mountain, and 4,000 feet below is your vast domain of the Na Pali Coast.

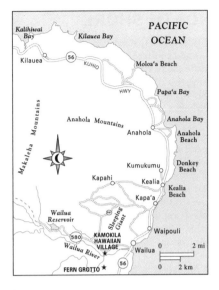

EAST SHORE

The East Shore is known as the **Coconut Coast.** Historically, the lower Wailua River valley was the center of power on the island; it was here where the *ali'i* lived and many sacred temples were built. The area is still imbued with the spirit of the people who inhabited this land, and some of their handiwork can be seen in **historical sites** and **heiau.** Today, people come to the area for many reasons, including the beautiful **Fern Grotto,** a natural riverside amphitheater. More recently, the **Kamokila Hawaiian Village** has been erected to instruct visitors about the daily life of traditional Hawaiians. Inland and above the town of **Wailua,** the squat and compact mountain ridge known as the **Sleeping Giant** lies in humble repose. Here and in the steeper mountainsides beyond are a good number of fine hiking trails. Up the coast a bit, **Kapa'a** offers numerous specialty shops, finer eateries, and affordable condos. The only town north beyond the excellent surfing spot at **Kealia Beach** is tiny **Anahola,** where Hawaiian residents sell lei strung from flowers grown in their yards. This stretch is seemingly just a pass-through for sites farther north, but those who know to look can find secluded beaches here. Two of the best are **Anahola Beach,** where the water is fine and camping is a possibility, and **Moloa'a Beach,** a perfect crescent you can have mostly to yourself.

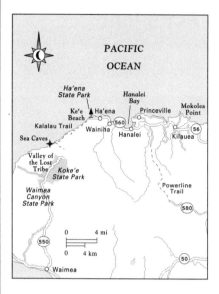

NORTH SHORE

Kilauea, the first town in the Hanalei District and a former sugarcane plantation town, begins the North Shore. It's noticeably greener along this coast, and progressively more rain falls as you travel west. The highway through this region runs above the cliff, while several side roads dip down to the coast, depositing you at secluded beaches with excellent snorkeling and wild surf. Occupying a prime spot along this cliff is **Princeville,** one of the largest planned resort communities in Hawaii. Down the narrowing lane and over a narrow, steel-strut bridge is the town of **Hanalei.** As you descend you figuratively enter another realm, one with a strong link to its traditional past. Perhaps the prettiest in the state, **Hanalei Bay** has been a safe anchorage and haven for ships ever since Westerners began coming to Hawaii. From here to the end of the road is an older and slower Hawaii. A string of beaches, uncrowded and well known for snorkeling, and tiny villages lie between Hanalei and the end of the road at **Ke'e Beach.** The domain of the **Na Pali Coast** holds emerald valleys cut off from the world by impassable 4,000-foot sea cliffs, as well as long-forgotten *heiau,* ancient village sites, caves, and lava tubes. It's also home to innumerable myths and legends, and the romantic yet authentic **Valley of the Lost Tribe** just beyond trail's end.

Planning Your Trip

The average visitor to Hawaii spends 6–8 days on his or her vacation, most often on one island but sometimes split between two. Kaua'i is relatively small and you can drive from one end of the main highway to the other in a couple of hours. The island can be "seen" in a few days, but there is much more to see and do than even a week or 10 days will give you time for. At a minimum for sightseeing, spend one day in each of the major island areas: the South Shore, West End, East Shore, and North Shore. For those with more time, a day for historical, cultural, and natural sites in and around Lihu'e would be a bonus, perhaps coupled with some shopping or an afternoon by the pool. Then there are the activities, most of which are half-day or full-day affairs. Soon you're at a full week. Remember that some activities should not be coupled with others on the same day, like scuba diving and a helicopter ride. Leave them for different days. What of food? It would take a month of Sundays to sample the best. If you spend less than a week on the island, you may leave feeling like you didn't give yourself enough time. Luckily, Kaua'i will be there singing its song of enchantment and waiting for your return trip.

WHEN TO GO

As with all of the Hawaiian Islands, the prime tourist season for Kaua'i starts two weeks before Christmas and lasts until Easter. It picks up again with summer vacation in early June and ends once more in late August. Everything is usually much more heavily booked and prices are higher. Hotel, airline, and car reservations are a must at this time of year. You can generally save substantially and it will be a lot less hassle if you travel in the "off season"—September to early December and mid-April (after Easter) until early June. Recently, the drop in numbers of tourists during the off season has not been nearly as substantial as in years past, indicating the increasing popularity of the island at all times of the year, but you'll still find the prices better and the beaches, trails, activities, and even restaurants less crowded. The local people will be happier to see you, too.

The weather in Kaua'i is moderate all year round and any time can be pleasant. Rains come and go—more so in winter—and are seldom sustained, so usually you can move a few miles down the coast to a sunny spot or wait for the warm breezes to blow away the clouds and dry things up. However, the different seasons might be a factor in when you decide to travel and what you decide to do. While most activities are available throughout the year, there are some exceptions. For instance, it's cooler and rainier during winter and therefore more problematic for comfortable mountain hiking, particularly in the Alaka'i Swamp. If you hope to see humpback whales, you must visit from late winter through spring, as these lovable giants of the sea are in Hawaiian waters only from December through May. Sea kayaking has become popular on Kaua'i; the North Shore's Na Pali Coast is its prime location. If you intend to kayak there, you must do so in the summer as wind and wave conditions make the ocean too rough along the north coast during winter. These and other activities are affected by weather and water conditions, so be conscious of these conditions during your planning.

WHAT TO TAKE

It's a snap to pack for a visit to Kaua'i. The weather is moderate and uniform on the whole, and the style of dress is delightfully casual. The rule of thumb is to pack light: few items, and clothing light in both color and weight. If you forget something at home, it won't be a disaster. You can buy everything you'll need in Hawaii. As a matter of fact, Hawaiian clothing is one of the best purchases you can make, both in comfort and style. It's quite feasible to bring only

ACCOMMODATIONS: POINTS TO CONSIDER

When it comes to places to stay, Kaua'i is blessed by a combination of happenstance and planning. The island was not a major Hawaiian destination until the early 1970s. By that time, all concerned had wised up to the fact that what you *didn't do* was build endless miles of high-rise hotels and condos that blotted out the sun and ruined the view of the coast. Besides that, a very strong grassroots movement insisted on tastefully done low-rise structures that blend into and complement the surrounding natural setting. This concept mandates "destination resorts," the kinds of hotels and condos that lure visitors because of their superb architecture, artistic appointments, and luxurious grounds. There is room for growth on Kaua'i, but the message is clear: Kaua'i is the most beautiful island of them all, and the preservation of this delicate beauty benefits everyone.

Kaua'i has roughly 8,000 accommodation units in roughly 400 properties, some 4,000 of which are condo and time-share units. There are three major resort areas on Kaua'i: the Coconut Coast, Po'ipu South Shore, and Princeville. The Coconut Coast on the eastern edge of the island is the oldest of these areas and has a concentration of condominiums and moderate-price hotels; its occupancy rate and price per room is the lowest of the three main resort areas. Po'ipu, which has the best general-purpose beach and is the most popular destination on Kaua'i, was the first big resort development on the island, and it has a good mix of hotel, condo, bed-and-breakfast, and vacation rental properties. The average price per room here and at Princeville is roughly the same. The North Shore Princeville development has mostly high-end condos and hotel rooms. In addition to these three areas, Lihu'e, which had the island's first major high-rise hotel, has two excellent destination hotels and several modest family-run motels. Vacation rentals and B&Bs along the North Shore are located primarily in Kilauea, 'Anini, Hanalei, and Ha'ena, and there is one moderate oceanside resort in Ha'ena — literally the last resort. Along the South Shore, some rooms are available in Kalaheo, but there is not much from there to the West End, except for one inn and one exceptional and relaxing cottage-type property in Waimea. Up in Koke'e State Park are a handful of cabins and camping areas. Scattered throughout the rest of the island are mostly vacation rental and B&B accommodations. Long stretches along the coast between the major centers have very little or no lodging.

one or two changes of clothing with the express purpose of outfitting yourself while there. Remember that there are self-service laundries on the island, so you can refresh your clothes rather than bring so many with you.

Even for those who have traveled to warmer climates previously, a few points are worthy of note. While shorts and T-shirts or short-sleeve shirts and blouses might be your usual daily wear, jeans or other long pants and closed-toe shoes are best and sometimes required if you plan on taking a horseback ride or dusty ATV tour. Remember to bring a billed or brimmed hat for the rain and sun, and if you forget, inexpensive baseball caps and straw or woven hats are found easily in sundry shops and clothing stores throughout the island. Only a few classy restaurants in the finest hotels require men to wear a sport coat for dinner. If you don't have one, most hotels can supply you with one for the evening. For women, a dress of the "resort wear" variety will suffice for most any occasion. By and large, "resort casual" is as dressy as you'll need to be in Hawaii.

One occasion for which you'll have to consider dressing warmly is a visit to the mountain. While elevation on Kaua'i is not as much of a factor as on Maui or the Big Island, temperatures up in Koke'e State Park will still be at least 10 degrees cooler than along the coast. If you intend to hike along the Alaka'i Swamp trails in the park, be aware that it is often windy and rainy. Bring a hooded raincoat or water-resistant windbreaker for protection, and you'll certainly appreciate the comfort of a wool or fleece sweater if you have one along. Tropical rain showers can happen at any time, so you might consider a fold-up umbrella, but the sun quickly breaks through and the warming winds blow. Nighttime winter temperatures may drop into the lower 60s or upper 50s, even along the coast, so be sure to have a sweater and long pants along just in case.

Dressing your feet is hardly a problem. You'll most often wear rubber thongs (locals call them slippahs) for going to and from the beach, leather sandals for strolling and dining, and jogging shoes or light boots for hiking and sightseeing. Teva and other types of outdoor strap sandals are good for general sightseeing and beach and water wear, plus they're great in the rain. Some people prefer *tabi,* a type of rubberized slipper, for crossing streams or wet trails. Lava, especially 'a'a, is murder on shoes, but unlike on Maui and the Big Island, the volcanic rock on Kaua'i's trails has mostly eroded to gravel and sand. Still, many backcountry trails are rugged and muddy and you may need those good old lug soles for traction and laces for ankle support. Light-duty hiking boots are sufficient. If you plan moderate hikes, jogging shoes should do.

Whether it's because the old Hawaiians didn't wear shoes, the mild climate makes people kick off their shoes, the fact that many Asian immigrants to Hawaii had the custom of removing their shoes when going indoors, or for some other reason altogether, it's a custom in Hawaii to take your shoes off when entering someone's house. This holds true for B&Bs, condos, and vacation rentals, but not for hotels. This custom, plus the weather, makes wearing rubber thongs or similar slip-on shoes most popular and piles of footwear at the door so common.

Two specialty items that you might consider bringing along are binoculars and snorkel gear. A pair of binoculars really enhances sightseeing—great for viewing birds and sweeping panoramas, and almost a necessity if you're going whale-watching. Flippers, mask, and snorkel can easily be bought in Hawaii but don't weigh much or take up much space in your luggage. They'll save you a few dollars in rental fees and you'll have them when you want them.

Explore Kaua'i

THE BEST OF KAUA'I

The Garden Island of Kaua'i holds much fascination for visitors. Everyone has an opinion on what they like best about the island and an idea about why others might want to visit. It's possible to "do" the island in a few days and it's equally possible to spend weeks upon weeks experiencing all that the island has to offer. What follows is one guy's take on an extended week's trip to this most beautiful island. As the average visitor from the Mainland spends eight days on a vacation to Hawaii, this time frame is a good choice for an all-encompassing "Best of Kaua'i Tour," while leaving plenty of time on your own for eating, shopping, and other activities.

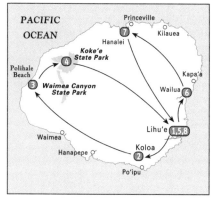

DAY 1

Fly into Lihu'e, pick up your rental car, and take a slow drive into town. Since many flights to Kaua'i arrive before mid-afternoon, make a stop at the Kaua'i Museum for your first introduction to historical and cultural information about the island. Carry on to your hotel and spend a leisurely evening at a fine restaurant followed by a stroll on the beach.

DAY 2

Head for Koloa, an old plantation town, by passing through the Tunnel of Trees and spend a few hours perusing its many unique and interesting shops. Continue down to the coast at Po'ipu for a tour at the National Tropical Botanical Garden, stopping for a few minutes on the way to watch Spouting Horn blow its stack. On your return, snorkel at Lawa'i Beach. You may be lucky enough to see turtles. Reserve some time in the afternoon for beachcombing at the more isolated Maha'ulepu Beach.

DAY 3

Head west, stopping at Kukui O Lono Park for views of the South Shore/Po'ipu area before taking a side trip down to the Kaua'i Coffee Museum to learn about coffee production and how coffee has changed the face of this part of the island. In Hanapepe, take the old main street into town and spend an hour or so making the rounds of the art galleries and studios. After lunch, drive to Waimea and check out the monuments to Captain Cook and reflect on the legacy of his fateful encounter with Hawaiians in 1778. Continue farther west to Polihale Beach to spend an afternoon on the beach (don't forget sunscreen and a hat) and stay for the colorful sunset.

DAY 4

This is the morning for your helicopter ride (arranged previously), and a time to take plenty of great pictures. Helicopter rides are usually smoother in the morning and allow you to get visuals of the island that are impossible any other way. Following your flight, drive up the mountain for ground-level views of some of what you've just seen from the air. Stop at all the overlooks along the canyon rim road and be sure to spend enough time to watch the muted pastel shades of the canyon walls change as the clouds roll in and out. Have a leisurely lunch at Koke'e Lodge. Proceed to the end of the road for a captivating view into Kalalau Valley. The cooler temperatures up at Koke'e State Park will certainly invigorate and encourage you to take a short nature hike or two. Longer hikes will require extra days.

DAY 5

Wake up early back in Lihu'e for your half-day boat tour or other water activity (arranged previously). Take it easier in the afternoon with an educational tour of the Grove Farm Homestead and then spend the rest of the day resting, shopping, or relaxing by the pool.

DAY 6

Drive north and stop in Wailua to see the many historical sites dotted along the Wailua River and beach front. Combine this with a tour boat ride up the river to the Fern Grotto. For the more adventurous, a morn-ing kayak trip and hike to a jungle water-fall is recommended, followed by a circuit of the historical sites in the afternoon. It's entertainment tonight: food, music, and dance. Enjoy the evening by attending one of the many fine lu'au the island has to offer.

DAY 7

This is your day to explore the North Shore. Make your first stop at the Kilauea Lighthouse and Kilauea Point National Wildlife Refuge. After dipping down to the coast to explore several of the north coast's less frequented beaches, head to the Princeville Hotel for views down onto Hanalei Bay and the North Shore coastline. As you leave Princeville, spend a few minutes at the Hanalei Valley Overlook, then head down into the town of Hanalei and let the slower North Shore rhythm suck you in. Eat in town, check out the bay, and stop for a tour of the Wai'oli Mission House before heading down the road to the Limahuli Botanical Gardens. Spend the afternoon snorkeling at Tunnels or Ke'e Beach and catch the sunset from the end of the road before heading back.

DAY 8

Do last-minute shopping for family and friends before packing your bags to head to the airport for your departure.

CULTURAL AND HISTORICAL TOUR

While it may be the beaches and island activities that draw most visitors to Kauaʻi today, the island does have a significant historical and cultural past. While much of the tangible evidence of this legacy is gone, most of what remains relates to pre-Western-contact stone constructions and remnants from the sugar industry. Books, chants, and stories remind us of this legacy, but it's worthwhile exploring the physical remains to learn more about the places that we visit.

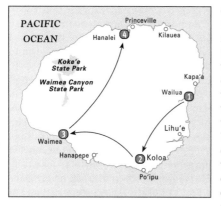

DAY 1

Start your tour by spending several hours in the Kauaʻi Museum. Pay particular attention to pre-contact displays, traditional items, and the collision of the Hawaiian culture with the West. With this information as background, your time at Wailua, the most significant and legendary of settlement sites on Kauaʻi, will be more understandable. Stop first at Lydgate Beach Park for easy access to Hauola O Honaunau (Puʻuhonua O Hauola), a temple of refuge that welcomed offending *kapu*-breakers of all social classes, and Hikina A Ka La Heiau, a site of rituals and prayers to the rising sun. Awash in the sands of the river mouth below are a few of Kauaʻi's rare petroglyphs. On the point across the bay are the remains of Kukui Heiau, a fire beacon site, thought to have been used for canoe landings and launchings.

Head a short way inland along the highway to find Holoholoku Heiau, a place of human sacrifice. A few steps away is Pohaku Hoʻo Hanau, the royal birthing stones. When babies of royal blood were born, a bell stone was struck to announce the birth; one such bell stone lies on the overgrown hillside above. Continue uphill to the partially rebuilt Poliʻahu Heiau. Although it is of unknown origin or purpose, the size of this site indicates its importance. There were once several other *heiau* that dotted this valley, and the last one crowned the mountaintop. The sheer concentration of extant ancient sites in the lower reaches of this valley is impressive, and they in microcosm encapsulate the life of the Hawaiian people, spanning the spectrum of worship, redemption, birth, and death.

As this was a heavily populated area, it seems appropriate that the Kamokila Hawaiian Village is located here. This village was constructed to illuminate aspects of the daily life of the Hawaiian people, showing various buildings and their uses, ceremonial objects, craft items, games, and plants that were important as foods and medicine.

Cap off the day by attending a luʻau, where the food, music, and dance, if not entirely traditional, at least stem from the ancient Hawaiian culture.

DAY 2

Switch gears and direction today and head west, making your first stop at Koloa. While not much remains of Kauaʻi's first commercial sugar mill, have a look at the monument to the sugar industry and its workers to learn the basics of how both radically changed the island and became integral forces behind what the state has become today. Head up through Lawa'i and on to **Olokele** for a morning **sugar mill tour.** This tour takes you into the fields and through the mill, giving you a basic overview of the milling operation, from planting cane through growth and harvest to its processing. This is the only such tour in the state and affords you an up-close look inside a sugar mill. The mill at Olokele is the only operating mill left on the island, but other mill structures, in varying states of disrepair and not open to the public, can still be seen at Lihu'e, Koloa, Waimea, and Kekaha.

In the afternoon, head back to Lihu'e and take a tour of the **Grove Farm Homestead** for an intimate look at the home of one of the island's most prosperous sugar plantation owners. This well-preserved compound offers a glimpse into the life of the Western upper class of the mid-1800s. Following your tour, head up the road and into the next century by visiting **Kilohana,** the 1930s mansion of a sugar plantation owner. This home has now been turned into shops, and perhaps you will stay for dinner at **Gaylord's restaurant** (reservations recommended), which occupies the dining room and patio of the mansion and works to bring sense of what dinner at the mansion might have been like during its occupation by sugar planters.

DAY 3

Today is the day for the **West End.** First stop is **Fort Elizabeth State Historical Park,** located on the east side of the Waimea River, just before you cross into the town of Waimea. While overgrown and rather unkempt, the tumbled walls of this former Russian fort give some sense of early foreign contact with Kaua'i. Although short-lived, this fort is emblematic of an early attempt at influence or dominance of these far-flung Pacific islands and a precursor to greater contact and the enmeshing of Hawaii with the outside world.

Cross the river and stop at the **monuments** erected to commemorate Captain Cook's first contact with Hawaii. This experienced seaman was the first known Westerner to encounter the Hawaiian Islands; following his voyage, the rest of the world began to know about Hawaii. This fateful encounter dramatically affected the Hawaiians. Their secret was out, and the continued contact with foreigners began to unravel their culture and disrupt the very foundation of their society.

Step back a bit and take a short side trip up the Waimea River to the **Menehune Ditch,** a unique creation in Hawaii. Dressed stones of irregular shape were cut to fit tightly together to create a water flume here. No one knows the origin of this ditch or how the stones were cut, as it was not a skill attributed to the ancient Hawaiians. Legends ascribe this work to the Menehune, a mythical "little people," perhaps pre-Polynesians who have been totally lost to the modern age.

Back in town, note the several old-style buildings from the late 1800s and early years of the 1900s. Not so long ago, **Waimea** was a much more vibrant and important island town than it is today. Make a quick stop at the **Faye Museum,** which has a small display of artifacts and photographs relating to the early days of sugar on this part of the island and the influential families in that industry. Occasional **mill camp walking tours** (reservations required) are offered from here to familiarize visitors with the lives of mill laborers and the importance and social role of these camp communities.

From Waimea, head up the mountain and stop at the **Koke'e Natural History Museum.** This museum is the best on the island for an introduction to the wildlife and plant communities on Kaua'i and how these have changed with the influence of humans. It also has a good section on hurricanes, and this is especially important as Kaua'i was the bull's-eye target of the last and most destructive hurricane to hit the state in living memory.

DAY 4

Head north and make your first stop at Kilauea Lighthouse and the Kilauea Point National Wildlife Refuge. This lighthouse gave safe signal for decades to ships traveling between Asia and the United States. Continue on to Hanalei for a tour of the Wai'oli Mission House Museum and a glimpse at a well-preserved home of the early missionaries. The early missionaries had, for their numbers, a disproportionate influence over the direction of Hawaiian life after the dissolution of the Hawaiian *kapu* system and weakening of the traditional Hawaiian societal norms. Be sure to stop out front for a quiet moment at the Wai'oli Church.

Head farther west to the Limahuli Botanical Gardens. Aside from its representative native flowers, the garden has preserved wetland terraces and a small traditional irrigation system, typical of what the ancient Hawaiians used for centuries to grow taro. Extensive irrigation was used in only a few places in Polynesia; Hawaiians took this technology to a high level.

To round out the day, take a short hike from Ke'e Beach at the end of the road to the sites of the ancient Kaulu Paoa Heiau and Kaulu O Laka Heiau, sacred places of hula. According to legend, it was here that the goddess Laka transferred this wonderful expression of dance and story to the ancient Hawaiians. Please be respectful of the site and know that, however ancient, hula is alive and well. This thriving culture has been radically transformed by an outside force but has also managed to protect and preserve much of its essential core.

BEST HIKES ON KAUA'I

Each of the Hawaiian Islands has excellent hiking trails, and Kaua'i is no exception. Most hiking trails on Kaua'i are up in Koke'e State Park, with another group inland of Wailua. The majority are mountain trails, but there are several valley hikes and a few worthy coastal walks. Most trails on Kaua'i can be done in one day, some in a couple of hours, but the prime hiking trail on the island, the **Kalalau Trail**—perhaps the premier hiking trail in the state—is a coastal trail that takes several days and requires that you have a permit from the state and be prepared to camp. The list of trails below is a good representation of routes for terrain and geography but is not comprehensive. The list outlines general characteristics of each hike and leaves fuller descriptions and directions for the entries in the "Explore" section of the book.

ILIAU NATURE LOOP TRAIL AND KUKUI TRAIL

The easy, nearly level Iliau Nature Loop Trail at about 3,000 feet in elevation is within **Waimea Canyon State Park.** It takes about 15-20 minutes and starts just off the highway that runs up the canyon rim. It's a good spot to stretch your legs and get your heart pumping a little for the more energetic hikes up the road, while giving you a little nature lesson to boot. Besides that, from this trail you have some pretty good views down into the middle reaches of the Waimea Canyon.

If you have lots of energy, you can head down the Kukui Trail from the Iliau Loop Trail to the floor of the canyon and **Waimea River.** The Kukui Trail drops about 2,000 feet in roughly 2.5 miles, so it's steep. Bring lots of water and a hat because much of the route is exposed to the sun until you get down to the river. You could say that the Kukui Trail is moderate going down but strenuous going up; count on at least 1.5 hours each way.

CANYON TRAIL AND EXTENSIONS

For great views of Waimea Canyon farther up the road, head for the Canyon Trail. Walk in on Halemanu Road and, if you just have a short time to hike, take Cliff Trail to the Cliff Viewpoint for a superb snapshot view of the canyon. Otherwise continue on Canyon Trail to **Waipo'o Waterfalls.** For expansive views of the canyon and the green carpet of tree cover that pushes up toward Mount Wai'ale'ale, cross the stream and continue up and around to a series of open viewpoints as the trail skirts the canyon edge, eventually ending at **Kumuwela Viewpoint.** The trail goes up and down quite a bit and is more than a moderate hike. To this point, with a return to your start, should be about three hours.

Those with more energy and greater time can extend this hike by making it a loop and in the process make this a combination canyon view and forest scenery trip. From Kumuwela Viewpoint, head up the road and follow Kumuwela and Halemanu-Koke'e trails back around to Halemanu Road, which will take you back to your start. The loop trail runs nearly eight miles, might take four hours or more, and should be considered strenuous.

PU'U KA OHELO/ BERRY FLAT TRAIL

This trail is mostly level throughout its two-mile length. An easy nature-trail hike, it should take about an hour or so. Good for bird-watching, it runs mostly through introduced forest cover, which includes sugi pine and redwoods.

NU'ALOLO/ AWA'AWAPUHI LOOP TRAIL

This 11-mile loop trail is a strenuous three-quarter-day affair that offers superb bird's-eye views of the **Na Pali Coast** and deep valleys that slice the coastal cliffs. It is a combination of two independent trails with a connector trail that runs between. The trailheads of these two trails are a couple of miles apart along the park road. As there is some 1,500 feet elevation drop going in and the same elevation gain coming out – for either trail independently or for the loop – it's tougher on the second half of the hike, so pace yourself. You can do either of these trails independently or hike from either end if you do it as a loop. When it's hiked as a loop, it's perhaps better to start at the Nu'alolo trailhead and come out via the Awa'awapuhi trail, as it's easier at the end of the day when you're tired to hike *down* the road to your parked car rather than the other way around.

PIHEA/ALAKA'I SWAMP TRAIL

This combination trail is very dependent upon the weather as the Alaka'i Swamp section tends to be windy, rainy, and stuck in clouds. You must be dressed for the weather, as you'll undoubtedly get wet and muddy. However, on a sunny or partially sunny day it can be awe-inspiring and gorgeous. This combination trail gives you expansive valley and forest views, offers great bird-watching opportunities, and lets you enter the "otherworldly" realm of a unique soggy mountaintop wetland. Luckily, much of the path over the wettest parts of the trail is on a boardwalk. This saves time, keeps you drier, and helps to preserve the integrity of the ground. The trail starts at the end of the paved park road at **Pu'u O Kila Overlook** and proceeds along the rim of **Kalalau Valley,** offering super views all along the way. The end of the trail is **Kilohana Overlook,** where, if the weather is agreeable, you can see into the deep Wainiha Valley below and to Hanalei Bay beyond. Otherwise, you might be lucky just to see 50 feet ahead of you. There is substantial elevation gain and loss, and the trail goes in and out of a number of narrow valleys. Count on five hours in and out.

NOUNOU TRAILS

While there are several trails up the **Sleeping Giant,** the shortest is the Nounou West Trail. Running up the steep back side of the hill, this trail heads up through a forest of introduced trees to the ridge, where it turns and continues over the giant's torso and chest to his face. From this promontory you are rewarded with 360-degree views of the East Shore communities and coastline, the rolling upland hills, and the sheer mountainsides in the center of the island. Elevation gain is roughly 800 feet, and the round-trip should take about two hours. If you come up the more gradual and open east side trail, the elevation gain is a little more but the hiking time about the same.

KUILAU TRAIL

The start of this trail is near the entrance to **Keahua Arboretum.** Following an old dirt track, it heads gradually up to a viewpoint and picnic area. Although good for birding, the best reward is the close-up view of the mountains in the center of the island. The trail does continue on, connecting with the Moalepe Trail, which turns and heads down the flank of the mountain to the north. If you decide to hike both, you'll have to be dropped off at one end and picked up at the other. There is moderate elevation gain on the Kuilau Trail; count on 2-3 hours for a round-trip.

POWERLINE TRAIL

This is the only well-used trail that crosses

the island. Aptly named, the Powerline Trail was built as a 4WD access road to help run an electrical power transmission line over the mountain following Hurricane 'Iniki. It runs from the **Keahua Arboretum** to a point above **Princeville.** Unless you have someone who can drop you off at one end and pick you up at the other, you are better off hiking up to the ridge and returning the way you came. The trail is about 13 miles long, so to walk the entire length or to go up to the ridge and back from either side will take at least a half day, but don't push it. This is a strenuous trail, steep in sections, gradual in others, often rutted and muddy, with an elevation gain of nearly 2,000 feet. Hike this trail for the exercise, the distance, or the distant views, which are awesome, but not for the trailside scenery, which is not always so inspiring. This trail is hot, dry, and has little shade along its length.

NORTH SHORE BEACH HIKES

Two North Shore strolls that do not really qualify as hikes are included here, nonetheless, because of their beauty and locations. The first is a walk along **Hanalei Bay,** the prettiest in the island, from the **Hanalei River** mouth to the mouth of the **Wai'oli Stream.** Second is a walk along Lumahai Beach from one end to the other. Both are easy strolls that let you get close to the water. The **Lumahai Beach** hike is about 1.5 miles long, the Hanalei Bay hike nearly twice that. Neither should take more than part of an hour, but slow down and enjoy the scenery.

HANAKAPI'AI WATERFALL TRAIL

The first part of this trail is a coastal trail, the beginning of the much longer **Kalalau Trail,** but at the first large valley along this coast, the trail turns inland and follows **Hanakapi'ai Stream** up to an archetypical tropical waterfall and pool. Although within the **Na Pali Coast State Park,** no permit is required to hike to this point. Hanakapi'ai Stream is only two miles in on the trail but there is great elevation change and the trail is often muddy. Muddier yet is the longer valley trail tha t heads up to the waterfall. This is a strenuous hike that has over 1,600 feet in elevation change and should take about five hours, more if you hang out at the pool.

KALALAU TRAIL

This trail is often considered the best that Kaua'i has to offer. It is a strenuous hike that requires a hiking/camping permit from the state, sturdy hiking shoes, waterproof gear, and a tent with sleeping bag or blanket. The trail is about 11 miles long and, while some hardy souls hike the entire length in one day, the more sensible take two days to hike in. Total elevation gain approaches 5,000 feet along the length of this trail, and the trail itself can alternately be rough and crumbly or rutted and muddy. You are permitted to spend five nights on this trail; nearly everyone spends as much time as possible at the far end relaxing on **Kalalau Beach** or cooling off in one of the stream pools. Kalalau Valley used to be permanently inhabited and farmed but is now nearly primordial in its idyllic tropical state.

BEST SIGHTSEEING SPOTS AND VISTA POINTS

While the sites mentioned below may be covered in one long day, it would be best perhaps to see them in two days and allow more time to take photographs and appreciate the beauty of the island. They are listed in the order that a visitor might logically drive, starting in Lihu'e, progressing along the South Shore to the West End, then returning to head up the East Shore and ending along the North Shore. But feel free to take them in any order that seems more convenient to you.

WAILUA FALLS

From Kuhio Highway, turn onto Rt. 583 in Kapaia and follow this rough road to the parking lot at its end. The falls can be viewed straight on from near the parking area. No walking required.

TUNNEL OF TREES

Turn off Kaumuali'i Highway onto Maluhia Road. In the first mile, towering eucalyptus trees have formed a canopy over the road. Perhaps best appreciated from the north end when the sun filters down through the leaves.

SPOUTING HORN

Take Lawa'i Road almost to its end. View this seashore "geyser" from the viewing platform. Depending upon wave action, you may have to wait for a strong rush of water.

PO'IPU COASTAL BEACHES

Head for the lawn in front of the Beach House Restaurant or the beach path in front of the Sheraton Hotel's The Point lounge for two of the best expansive, ground-level views of the coast. Alternately, try the point at Po'ipu Beach Park. Head to the lithified sandstone bluff east of the Hyatt Regency Hotel for good views of Shipwreck Beach and the coast toward Maha'ulepu Beach.

KUKUI O LONO PARK

From the pavilion on the southern edge of the golf course, you have the best views of the South Shore between the Ha'upu Ridge and Hanapepe. It's a level half-mile stroll from the parking lot.

HANAPEPE VALLEY OVERLOOK

This overlook is along Kaumuali'i Highway, halfway between Kalaheo and Hanapepe. The view here is just outside your car door.

POLIHALE BEACH

Take Rt. 56 to its end and continue on the gravel road through cane fields to the beach. The expanse of the beach is best seen from the top of the dunes, but its essential character is much better appreciated by walking its length. As a bonus, this is the best easily accessible spot to view the private island of Ni'ihau, 17 miles across the channel to the southwest; it's also a very good location for sunset.

MANA PLAIN

Stop at the first big zag as you zig-zag up Waimea Canyon Drive above the town of Waimea. From this overlook point, you have an unimpeded view of the Mana Plain as it stretches to the west toward Polihale Beach. Study the informational signage posted here relating to the land below.

WAIMEA CANYON

Arguably, the best views of the canyon are from a helicopter. However, from the ground, the best viewpoints are Waimea Canyon Overlook and Pu'u Ka Pele Overlook. Both of these are only a few steps from parking lots off Rt. 550. Superb views are also had from the Canyon Trail, but this requires a strenuous hike of several hours.

KALALAU VALLEY

For those who do not make the long Kalalau Trail hike to view the valley from the bottom, the best alternative – and actually better for getting an expansive view of the valley from the top – is to head to the Kalalau Lookout or the Pu'u O Kila Lookout at the end of the Koke'e State Park road. These lookouts are only steps from their respective parking lots. Another idea – for another day – you can get a wonderful view of this valley from watercraft that cruise the Na Pali Coast.

WAILUA RIVER

This river is best seen from a small roadside viewing area across the roadway (Highway 580) from the parking lot at Opaeka'a Falls. From this location, you see down the river to the ocean, up the river toward Fern Grotto, and all the riverboat and kayak activity. Be careful crossing the highway as there is substantial traffic. Have a look at Opaeka'a Falls while you're there.

MOUNT WAI'ALE'ALE

No roads or open trails lead to the top of this mountain; you'll have to be content to view it from a distance. As one of the wettest places on earth, Mount Wai'ale'ale is shrouded by clouds nearly every day of the year, so it's a rare surprise when you can actually see the top. Yet, the remains of its crater, the incredibly steep-walled, semi-circular mountainside that opens to the south, is usually visible. Like Waimea Canyon, the best close-up views of this spot are from a helicopter, preferably after it's rained, as innumerable threads of silver slice the mountainside with rivulets of water. From the ground, good viewpoints require some hiking. Perhaps the easiest is from the shelter and picnic table along Kuilau Trail. Spots along Powerline Trail are also good. You can get closer by following the arboretum road to its end (4WD) and hiking

in from there to a head dam or beyond to a pool at the bottom of the mountain.

EAST SHORE COASTLINE

Looking north from Lydgate Beach Park gives you a good view of this coast. However, a broader, more encompassing view is had by looking south from the pulloff lookout point just north of Kapa'a.

KILAUEA LIGHTHOUSE

This historical lighthouse is on the northernmost point of the island. Located within the Kilauea Point National Wildlife Refuge, the grounds around the lighthouse are open to the public. From the parking lot, a short walk of a couple hundred yards gets you to this flat promontory. There are good views from here along the rugged North Shore coast to the west. From Rt. 56, turn onto Kolo Road and then take Kilauea Road about one mile to the coast.

HANALEI BAY

You get the best views of the bay when you have a room at the Princeville Hotel. If you are not a guest there, see the bay from the Living Room lounge at the hotel or from the restaurant at the nearby Hanalei Bay Resort. As a bonus, multiple waterfalls running down the north face of the mountain at the back of Hanalei town during rains can also be best seen from these locations.

HA'ENA COASTLINE

Encompassing views of the Ha'ena coast are difficult because of its many bays and wandering coastline. However, a very good long-range view is from the grassy lawn to the front of the Princeville Hotel entrance, atop the Pu'u Poa bluff. Not surprisingly, this is also a wonderful spot to watch the sun set.

HANALEI VALLEY

Heavily farmed in a patchwork of taro fields and spreading out on both sides of the Hanalei River, the lower Hanalei River valley is best seen from the **Hanalei Valley scenic overlook,** a pulloff along **Rt. 56** just past the Princeville Shopping Center. Informational signboards are just steps from your door.

NA PALI COAST

Like Waimea Canyon, the full effects of the tall and long, deeply sculpted Na Pali Coast are best seen form a helicopter. From the ground, you get a fully satisfying view from **Ke'e Beach** at the end of **Rt. 560** west of Hanalei. Alternately, and for the more energetic, great views come to view as you make your way down the **Kalalau Trail.**

SEVEN-DAY ADVENTURE TOUR

While Kaua'i offers many adventure activities for visitors and residents alike, the following activity tour is a sampling of some of the most exciting the island has to offer. There are many options, so you will have to choose among tour operators for the type of tours that best fit your needs, wants, and physical abilities. Most organized tours offered by tour operators can be reserved in advance. In fact, it's encouraged and sometimes a necessity, as openings fill because of popularity or season. You may need to make some arrangements before you arrive on the island or make them on the day that you fly in. Contact numbers for various tour operators are listed in the individual travel chapters.

DAY 1

Start your adventure tour with a comprehensive **helicopter tour** over the island. While not a physical activity, this is one of the most thrilling experiences that you can have on Kaua'i, as it lets you see so much of this incredibly beautiful island that you just can't see in any other way. It gives you a sense of the "lay of the land" and will prepare you for the rest of the week. With check-in and preflight procedures, helicopter tours take about two hours, which leaves most of the rest of the day for other pursuits.

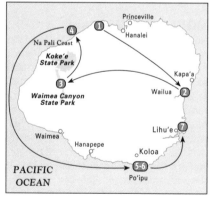

In the afternoon, head to the beach to **snorkel.** While many visitors simply make a beeline for the water outside their hotel, there are numerous recognized snorkel spots around the island, of which **Lawa'i Beach** in Po'ipu and **Tunnels Beach** on the North Shore are usually considered the best. Before you decide where to don your mask and fins, check with a water activity shop for current information on water conditions and visibility.

DAY 2

This morning is for **kayaking.** If you've done kayaking before, you may feel confident enough to rent a kayak and head off on your own. Otherwise, take an organized tour on the Hule'ia or Wailua Rivers or on Hanalei Bay. Most kayak tours combine paddling with hiking and/or snorkeling. Generally, these tours are half-day affairs, so this allows you the rest of the day to relax, shop, or sightsee.

For those who demand more physicality, full-day kayak tours are also offered that require a great deal of physical endurance. Your destination will depend on when you visit: Summer kayak tours generally run along the North Shore Na Pali Coast, while in winter, the South Shore is used.

DAY 3

Mornings are usually clear, the weather crisp in the upper elevations, and visitor traffic light in the mountains. These factors make it perfect for a morning **downhill bike tour** along the rim of Waimea Canyon. Currently, only one tour company offers this ride, so call ahead for reservations.

While you're on the West End, set aside a few hours in the afternoon for a **power hang gliding flight** from Burns Field in Hanapepe.

DAY 4

Kaua'i offers many **boating** options for a day on the water, and most boat tours head to the Na Pali Coast for sightseeing and snorkeling. Seeing this coast from water level is truly an awe-inspiring experience. Motorized boats and catamarans are the norm, while there are a few sailing catamarans. The most adventurous choose a ridged-hull raft because it's fast, skims the water, raises plenty of spray, and allows access to seaside caves.

DAY 5

Head to the corral today for a **horseback ride.** There are a handful of stables that offer rides on the island, so it's important to decide if you want to ride near the ocean, up into the forest, have time on a ranch, or trek to a waterfall. Either morning or afternoon rides allow you to be free the rest of the day for other activities.

DAY 6

Back to the water today for a **scuba tour.** Your dive locations will be selected by the tour operator based upon water conditions. If you want to dive a particular spot, like Lehua Rock, for instance, check with one of the companies ahead of time for the best opportunity. It's recommended not to travel to high elevations for 24 hours after scuba diving, so stay off the mountain and don't have a helicopter or plane ride for the rest of the day.

DAY 7

Round out your week with a morning **ATV tour.** Generally several hours long, these rides can be dusty and muddy in turn. Riding over private land, ATV tours let you experience areas of the island that not everyone can visit.

For a leisurely afternoon finale, the **mountain tubing adventure** is appropriate. Using large inner tubes, guided tour groups float through gentle irrigation flumes and a series of tunnels through the mountain lowlands and former plantation fields.

If you want to end with more of a rush, take a turn at a heart-pumping **zipline course,** where, suspended from a thin cable wire, you zip over narrow valleys, playing Tarzan in the tree tops. Each leg of the course brings you closer to your reward of a dip in a fresh mountain pool and great memories of your trip to Kaua'i.

LIHU'E

The stacks of the Lihu'e sugar mill let you know where you are: in a former plantation town on one of the world's most gorgeous islands. Lihu'e (Cold Chill) began growing cane in the 1840s, and its fields were among Hawaii's most productive. Lihu'e Plantation, a successful enterprise founded by a German firm in 1850, prospered until World War I, when anti-German sentiment forced the owners to sell out. Until 1996, when the Lihu'e mill shut down, cane from the surrounding fields was crushed here. Lihu'e, the county seat, has 5,600 residents, with an additional 7,000 in the nearby bedroom communities of Puhi and Hanama'ulu. With this strong former agricultural base and its standing as the county seat, the town has flourished and boasts all the modern conveniences, including shopping centers, a library, museum, government offices, financial businesses, the Wilcox Memorial Hospital, and the island's principal airport and commercial harbor. The feel is still somewhat of a company town now expanding its opportunities. Only a few short years ago Lihu'e had but two traffic lights; it now has nearly a dozen, with a growing rush-hour traffic problem. It isn't the geographical center of the island, but it is halfway along the coastal road that nearly encircles the island, making it a perfect jumping-off point for exploring the rest of Kaua'i. It has a concentration of long-established local restaurants, up-and-coming eateries, two major resorts, right-priced accommodations, some entertainment, and the island's most varied shopping. One of the island's best beaches and picturesque bays is

ROBERT NILSEN

HIGHLIGHTS

((**Kaua'i Museum:** This should be your first stop for the best introduction to the history and culture of the island (page 37).

((**Grove Farm Homestead:** This living representation of a sugar plantation owner's home is an exemplary bit of preservation for the bygone era of early plantation life. Access by group tour only (page 39).

((**Kilohana:** This superb manor house exemplifies the life of the well-to-do during the peak of the sugar economy on the island. The home is now an upscale restaurant and fine art shops (page 40).

((**Wailua Falls:** One of the easiest waterfalls to reach on the island, it's a "classical" tropical waterfall and an easy reminder of why the island, known to all as the Garden Island, is so lush and rich in vegetation (page 43).

((**Kalapaki Beach:** Its crescent shape, soft sand, gentle waters, and inviting surf make this one of the best all-around beaches on the island. Combined with the backdrop of Nawiliwili Bay and the Ha'upu Mountain Range, this area creates one of the most visually pleasing, and intimate, harbors in the state (page 44).

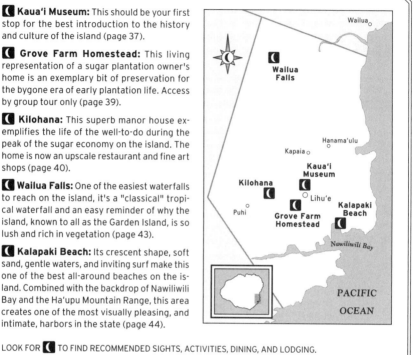

LOOK FOR ((TO FIND RECOMMENDED SIGHTS, ACTIVITIES, DINING, AND LODGING.

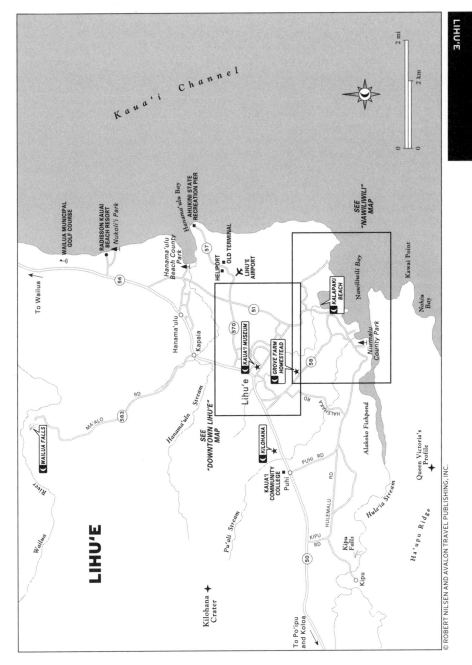

LIHU'E

© ROBERT NILSEN AND AVALON TRAVEL PUBLISHING, INC.

within a five-minute drive of downtown, with a legendary fishpond a few minutes upriver, and you can be out of town and exploring long before your shave ice begins to melt.

Lihu'e's two bedroom communities, Puhi to the west and Hanama'ulu to the north, add to the strength and importance of this area. **Puhi** has the island's only higher educational institution, Kaua'i Community College, and a growing industrial park. **Hanama'ulu,** an old sugar community, has a stronger past than present but hangs on because of its close proximity to Lihu'e. Its small center has a handful of well-established stores and a restaurant with a great reputation, and down at the coast is a beach park. Between Lihu'e and Hanama'ulu is the tiny settlement of **Kapaia,** a wide spot in the road in the Hanama'ulu Stream valley that has two additional fine shops and two churches. From Kapaia, Ma'alo Road (Rt. 583) runs up through former cane fields to Wailua Falls.

PLANNING YOUR TIME

Lihu'e is where everyone arrives in Kaua'i. Most don't spend much time here but head immediately down the highway in their rental car, leaving Lihu'e in the dust. This is a mis-take, as Lihu'e has a number of places of interest for visitors, so spend a few hours here seeing them before you leave town, or catch them on your way through from another part of the island.

Those who have the good fortune to stay at lovely **Kalapaki Beach** can use Lihu'e as a base; from here it's about equal distance around to the West End of the island or up to the North Shore. Kalapaki Beach, the adjacent Nawiliwili Harbor, and the verdant Ha'upu Range of mountains that dominate both, create one of the state's prettiest tropical harbor areas. Kalapaki Beach is a favorite for swimmers and beginning surfers because of its gentle wave action. Into the bay runs the Hule'ia River, on which kayakers paddle past the Hule'ia National Wildlife Reserve to get to waterfalls farther inland. While these waterfalls are captured by jungle and the pools below them are refreshing for a dip after a paddle on the river, one of the largest, most picturesque, and easiest to reach waterfalls on the island is **Wailua Falls.** Head inland from Kapaia through former cane fields to a spot where, almost at eye level, you can see its water tumble over the cliff's edge into a huge bowl-like pool below.

QUICK ISLAND FACTS

Kaua'i is the oldest of the main Hawaiian Islands, and hence the most "mature." For decades it has been known as "The Garden Isle," but is now being called the "Island of Discovery."

The fourth largest of the main islands, Kaua'i lies 72 miles across the Kaua'i Channel from O'ahu, and the main town of Lihu'e is 100 miles to the northwest of Honolulu. The island is about 550 square miles and has 90 miles of coastline, over half of which are beaches. With an average of about 450 inches of rain a year, Mount Wai'ale'ale in the center of Kaua'i is the wettest place on earth. At nearly 3,000 feet, Waimea Canyon, called the Grand Canyon of the Pacific, is the largest and deepest val-ley in the state. Over the ridge from Waimea Canyon is the awesome rampart of the Na Pali Coast, some 17 miles of sheer cliffs that rise out of the ocean to nearly 4,000 feet in elevation. In 1992, Kaua'i suffered the brunt of damage from Hurricane 'Iniki, the worst such storm to hit the islands in any living Hawaiian's memory.

Kaua'i is the least populous county in the state; the island has about 62,000 inhabitants, which makes about 110 per square mile.

The official island color is purple, and its lei is made from the *mokihana,* a small native citrus fruit with a slight anise fragrance that changes color from green to brown as it matures.

This is an easy one-hour jaunt and good side trip on your way up the coast.

To gain an understanding of the development of Kaua'ian history and culture you should not fail to visit the **Kaua'i Museum** in the center of town. A few hours here is time well spent and will surely enhance your visit. Economically, sugar plantations have created the most significant history of the island's past 150 years. Be sure to visit **Grove Farm Homestead,** where you'll see the restored buildings of one of the major plantation families and hear about how sugar affected life on the island for plantation owners and commoners alike. Morning and afternoon tours last about two hours. Just inland from Grove Farm is **Kilohana,** a more recent plantation estate that now has been turned into a restaurant and shops.

You can see the sights of Lihu'e in half a day by whizzing around, but you may need to spend more time. As the county seat, Lihu'e has government offices, including those for camping permits, information on state and county parks, general tourist information and brochures, and the town has the best general shopping on the island.

Sights

◖ KAUA'I MUSEUM

If you really want to enrich your Kaua'i experience, this two-building complex in downtown Lihu'e (4428 Rice St., 808/245-6931, www.kauaimuseum.org, 9 A.M.–4 P.M. Mon.–Fri. and 10 A.M.–4 P.M. Sat.; admission is $7 adults, $5 seniors 65 and older, $3 students 13–17, $1 children 6–12, free under six, with free admission for the whole family on the first Saturday of each month) is the first place to visit. Spending an hour or two here infuses you with a wealth of information regarding Kaua'i's social and cultural history. For greater enrichment, museum staff conducts one-hour

ROBERT NILSEN

Kaua'i Museum

LIHU'E

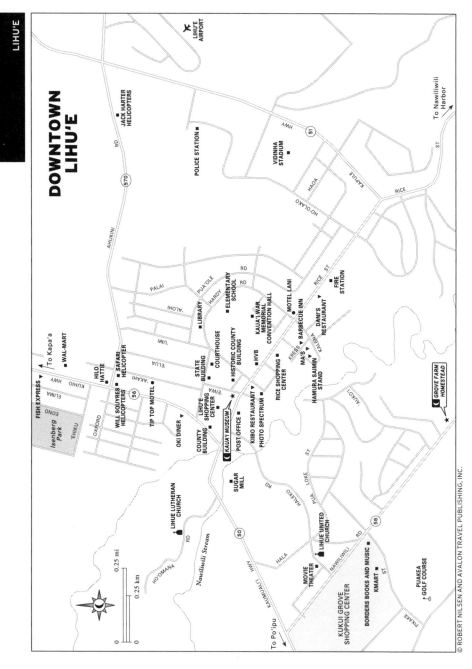

DOWNTOWN LIHU'E

To Nawiliwili Harbor

LIHU'E AIRPORT

JACK HARTER HELICOPTERS

POLICE STATION

VIDINHA STADIUM

ELEMENTARY SCHOOL

LIBRARY

MOTEL LANI

FIRE STATION

KAUA'I WAR MEMORIAL CONVENTION HALL

BARBECUE INN

DANI'S RESTAURANT

HISTORIC COUNTY BUILDING

COURTHOUSE

STATE BUILDING

HVB

KRESS

MA'S

RICE SHOPPING CENTER

HAMURA SAIMIN STAND

To Kapa'a

WAL-MART

HILO HATTIE

SAFARI HELICOPTER

WILL SQUYRES HELICOPTERS

TIP TOP MOTEL

LIHU'E SHOPPING CENTER

OKI DINER

FISH EXPRESS

Isenberg Park

COUNTY BUILDING

KAUA'I MUSEUM

POST OFFICE

KIIBO RESTAURANT

PHOTO SPECTRUM

GROVE FARM HOMESTEAD

SUGAR MILL

LIHUE LUTHERAN CHURCH

Nawiliwili Stream

LIHUE UNITED CHURCH

MOVIE THEATER

KUKUI GROVE SHOPPING CENTER

BORDERS BOOKS AND MUSIC

KMART

PUAKEA GOLF COURSE

To Po'ipu

To Nawiliwili

0.25 mi

0.25 km

RD — 570

AHUKINI

KUHIO HWY

ELIMA

EONO

EHIKU

OXFORD

56

'AKAHI

'ELUA

UMI

'EIWA

'ALOHI

PALAI

PUA'OLE

HARDY

RD

RD

RICE ST

RICE ST

AMH

51

KAPULE

HAOA

HO'OLAKO

RICE

AINKO

ALAKO

LOKE ST

PUA

HALEKO RD

HALA

HO'OMANA RD

50

NAWILIWILI

KAUMUALI'I HWY

AMH

58

PIKAKE ST

ST

© ROBERT NILSEN AND AVALON TRAVEL PUBLISHING, INC.

guided tours for $10 per person on Monday, Tuesday, and Thursday at 10 A.M. with a reservation.

Dedicated in 1924 to Albert Spencer Wilcox, son of pioneer missionaries in Hanalei, the main building has a Greco-Roman facade and was the public library until 1970. Its two floors house the main gallery, devoted to ethnic heritage and island art exhibits changed on a regular basis. Included here is a small but fascinating exhibit of calabashes, koa furniture, quilts, and feather lei. One large calabash belonged to Princess Ruth, who gave it to a local child. Its finish, hand-rubbed with the original *kukui* nut oil, still shows a fine luster. The rear of the main floor is dedicated to the Senda Gallery, with its collection of vintage photos by W. J. Senda, a Japanese immigrant from Matsue who arrived in 1906. These black-and-whites are classics, opening a window onto old Kaua'i. Upstairs in the small Oriental Art Gallery is a fine selection of art objects, mostly from China and Japan. Revolving shows, sometimes of contemporary art and crafts or children's art, are held in a second gallery on this floor.

On the far end of the first floor, the Museum Shop sells books, cards, Hawaiiana prints, a wonderful selection of Hawaiian craft items, and a fine selection of detailed U.S. Geological Survey maps of the entire island. Some inexpensive but tasteful purchases include baskets, wooden bowls, and pieces of tapa.

Kaua'i's fascinating natural and cultural history begins to unfold when you walk through the courtyard into the adjacent structure, the William Hyde Rice Building, built in 1960 to house the museum. Notice the large black iron pot used to cook sugarcane. The exhibits are self-explanatory, chronicling Kaua'i's development over the centuries. The windows of the Natural History Tunnel show the zones of cultivation on Kaua'i, along with its beaches and native forests. Farther on is an extensive collection of Kaua'i shells, old photos, and the history and genealogy of Kaua'ian royalty and the ruling class. The central first-floor area has a model of a Hawaiian village, a collection of weapons, some fine examples of adzes used to hollow canoes, and a model of the HMS *Resolution* at anchor off Waimea. An excerpt from the ship's log records Captain Cook's thoughts on the day he discovered Hawaii for the rest of the world.

As you ascend the stairs to the second floor, history continues to unfold. Missionaries stare from old photos, their countenances the epitome of piety and zeal. Most old photos record the plantation era. Be sure to see the Spalding Shell Collection, gathered by Colonel Spalding, an Ohio veteran of the Civil War who came to Kaua'i and married the daughter of Captain James Makee, owner of the Makee Sugar Company. Shells from around the world join examples of magnificent koa furniture, table settings, children's toys, dolls, and photos of Ni'ihau—about all that the outside world ever sees. Follow the stairs back to the ground floor and notice the resplendent feather capes on the wall. On the main floor, in an alcove by the front door, push the button to immerse yourself in a short video of Kaua'i. This pictorial is a treat for the eyes; soothing Hawaiian chanting in the background sets the mood.

◖ GROVE FARM HOMESTEAD

Grove Farm is a plantation started in 1864 by George Wilcox, the son of Congregational missionary teachers, who worked for the original owner of the surrounding acreage. The first owner saw no future in the parched land and sold around 500 acres to Wilcox for $12,000, which he had 10 years to repay in a lease-to-purchase arrangement. Through a system of aqueducts, Wilcox brought water down from the mountains and began one of the most profitable sugar plantations in Hawaii. During the years following, he bought additional surrounding land; at its height the property encompassed 27,000 acres. Currently it stands at slightly less than 22,000 acres—still sizable, and one of the five largest landholdings on the island.

George Wilcox never married. In 1870, his brother Sam came to live on the homestead, and in 1874, Sam married Emma, the daughter of missionaries from the Big Island. The couple had six children—three boys and three girls.

Two of the boys met with tragic early deaths, but Gaylord, the third, survived to manage the farm in his later years. Of the girls, only Etta, the oldest, married. The two other sisters, Elsie and Mabel, were single all their lives. Elsie became very involved in education and politics, while Mabel went to Johns Hopkins University and earned a degree as a registered nurse. Her parents originally didn't want her to study nursing but acquiesced when she became 25 years old and still desired that calling. She returned in 1911 and eventually opened a public health office on the grounds. The homestead was a working plantation until the mid-1930s, when George died and operations were moved nearby. His nieces, Elsie and Mabel Wilcox, both born here, continued to occupy the dwellings and care for the extensive grounds.

In 1971, Mabel Wilcox dedicated the family estate to posterity. Well advanced in years but spirited in mind, she created a nonprofit organization to preserve Grove Farm Homestead as a historical living farm. Reap the benefits of her efforts by visiting. Reservations for the tours are preferred, but staff try to accommodate drop-in visitors. (Call 808/245-3202 at least 24 hours in advance to make arrangements, Monday, Wednesday, or Thursday at 10 A.M. or 1 P.M., donation of $5 or $2 for children under 12.) Please be prompt! Reservations are accepted by mail up to three months in advance; write to Grove Farm Homestead, P.O. Box 1631, Lihu'e, HI 96766. The homestead is off Nawiliwili Road; precise directions are given when you call. Group size is limited to give full attention to detail and minimize wear and tear on the buildings. Wear comfortable shoes that can be slipped off, as shoes are not allowed inside the buildings.

The first thing you might notice when entering Grove Farm is the remains of a narrow-gauge railroad track. The tracks meant sugar, and sugar meant prosperity and change for old Hawaii. A low stone wall partially surrounds the homestead, and beyond the walls are orchards, pasture, and gardens. This is no "glass-case" museum. It's a real place with living history, where people experienced the drama of changing Hawaii. It is part of what was the oldest intact sugar plantation in Hawaii. Visitors meet at the plantation office, where you should notice the old maps on the walls showing the extent of the Wilcox landholdings. Well-informed guides take you on a two-hour walking tour of the grounds and its various buildings. The grounds are lush and fruitful, with all sorts of trees and plants, many imported, and five kinds of bamboo. At one time the workers were encouraged to have their own gardens. Vegetable and flower gardens, along with fruit and nut orchards, still grace the property. The well-kept homestead buildings include the plantation home and two cottages, the old school that was converted to a public health office for Mabel Wilcox, a fernery, a garage, and a simple but homey plantation worker's home. While on your tour, don't fail to notice that the property also extends down into the valley, an expanse that remains thickly covered with vegetation, a reminder of what it was like decades ago when the family made this their home and the island was less developed. As the tour ends you get a feeling of what Grove Farm is all about—a homestead where people lived, and worked, and dreamed.

◖ KILOHANA

The manor house at Kilohana Plantation was built in 1935 by wealthy *kama'aina* planter Gaylord Wilcox to please his wife, Ethel. She was enamored with Hollywood and its glamorous Tudor-type mansions, which were the rage of the day. Sparing no expense, Gaylord spent $200,000 building an elaborate 16,000-square-foot home; estimates are that it would cost at least $3 million in today's dollars. Inside, Gaylord's restaurant occupies the actual dining room and rear patio. Original furniture includes a huge table that seats 22 and a stout sideboard fit for a truly regal manor house. On the other end of the first floor is the huge living room, a grand room, almost museum-like, filled with period furniture, rugs, and art pieces on the walls. As you pass from room to room—some of which are occupied by fine gift

ROBERT NILSEN

horse-drawn carriage at Kilohana

boutiques and art galleries—notice the coved ceiling, wood molding, and grand staircase. A mirror from the 1930s (mirrors in Hawaii have a tough time holding up because of the moisture) still hangs just inside the tiled main entranceway. From the flagstone rear veranda, view a living tapestry of mountain and cloud, even more ethereal when mist shrouds magical Mount Wai'ale'ale in the distance.

For a small fee ($12 adults, $6 kids), a horse and carriage takes guests through part of the 35 lush acres that surround the home, which was the center of a working farm—a feeling that lingers because of the back gardens and the remaining workers' cottages. To reach Kilohana (3-2087 Kaumuali'i Hwy.), take Rt. 50 west from Lihu'e for about two miles toward the village of Puhi, and look on the mountain side for the clearly marked entrance.

LIHU'E'S OLD CHURCHES

When Rt. 56 becomes Rt. 50, just as you pass the Lihu'e Sugar Mill, look for the HVB Warrior pointing you to the **Lihue Lutheran Church.** Just before the bridge, follow Ho'omana Road up the hill through a well-kept residential area. Rebuilt following Hurricane 'Iwa in 1982, the current building is a faithful copy of the original structure built in 1885. It has everything a church should have, including a bell tower and spire, but it's all miniature. The church reflects a strong German influence that dominated Lihu'e and its plantation until World War I. The early 20th century pastor was Hans Isenberg, brother of the plantation founder and husband to Dora Rice from the old *kama'aina* family. The outside of the church is basic New England, but inside nautical influences are visible, and the more ornate altar is reminiscent of baroque Germany. Headstones in the yard to the side indicate just how old this congregation is. In fact, with an active congregation since 1881, it is the oldest Lutheran church in the islands.

Across from the Kukui Grove Shopping Center behind the car dealership along Nawiliwili Avenue is the lava stone **Lihu'e United Church,** which was mostly attended by cane workers and their families. Its cemetery is filled

ROBERT NILSEN

Lihue Lutheran Church

with simple tombstones, and plumeria trees eternally produce blossoms for the departed ones. Within the same compound is the Congregational **Lihu'e First Church,** a structure also made of stone, founded in 1840.

Two additional churches located in Kapaia are worth a stop: the 1884 Immaculate Conception Catholic Church, and Lihu'e Hongwanji Buddhist Temple. Both religious buildings, fine examples from days gone by, are well kept for present use.

ALAKOKO FISHPOND

From Nawiliwili Harbor, follow Wa'apa Road south through the little community of Niumalu, and from there continue to Hulemalu Road. Along Hulemalu Road, partway around and up the hill, is a **lookout,** below which is Alakoko (Rippling Blood) Fishpond, commonly known as Menehune Fishpond. Here, you have a sweeping view of Hule'ia Stream and the Ha'upu Ridge on the far side. This fishpond has been used to raise mullet and other commercial fish. Unlike most fishponds, which were built at the edge of the

ocean, this pond was constructed along the riverbank with a 900-foot dike, said to be the handiwork of the Menehune. Legend says that these little people built this pond for a royal prince and princess and made only one demand: that no one watch them in their labor. In one night, the indefatigable Menehune passed the stones needed for the project from hand to hand in a double line that stretched for 25 miles. But the royal prince and princess could not contain their curiosity and climbed to a nearby ridge to watch the little people. They were spotted by the Menehune, who stopped building, leaving holes in the wall, and turned the royal pair into the twin pillars of stone still seen on the mountainside overlooking the pond.

About 240 acres of river bottom land surrounding this fishpond, part of the riverbank farther on, and nearby wooded hillsides are now part of **Hule'ia National Wildlife Reserve.** This reserve has been set aside for the protection of the Hawaiian coot, stilt, moorhen, and duck, endangered water birds. No access is allowed.

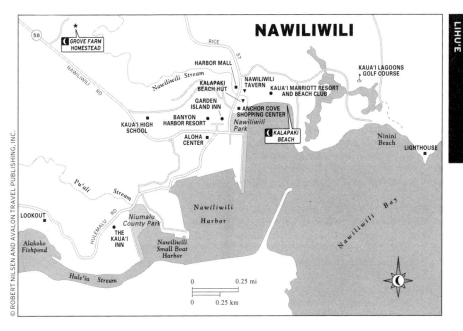

© ROBERT NILSEN AND AVALON TRAVEL PUBLISHING, INC.

(WAILUA FALLS

In Kapaia, Rt. 583 (Ma'alo Road) branches from the highway and heads north into the interior. This paved yet potholed road rises up to rolling terrain with a backdrop of lofty mountain peaks. Route 583 runs through abandoned cane fields, passes a valley overlook, and ends in a parking area about four miles up, where there are always people selling crafts. Below, Wailua Falls tumbles as two spouts, flowing 80 feet over a ledge into a large round pool, while white-tailed tropicbirds circle above. It's said that the *ali'i* would come here to dive from the cliff into the pool as a show of physical prowess; commoners were not considered to be infused with enough mana to perform this feat.

Many of the trees here are involuntary trellises for rampant morning glory. Pest or not, the blossoms are still beautiful as the weed climbs the limbs. A trail down to the falls is particularly steep and often slippery because the sun doesn't penetrate to dry the ground. Look for it about 100 feet back from the end of the guardrail, but be very careful. If you make

it down, you may have the falls to yourself, but you'll be like a goldfish in a bowl with the tourists—perhaps jealously—peering down at you. A county sign at the trailhead says "Danger, Keep Out," but the trail down is obviously well trod. This falls and the river gorge downstream from here are part of the Wailua River State Park.

BEACHES AND PARKS

Lihu'e has very convenient beaches. You can sun yourself within 10 minutes of anywhere in town, with a choice of beaches on either Nawiliwili or Hanama'ulu Bay. Few tourists head to Hanama'ulu Bay, while Nawiliwili Bay is a classic example of "beauty and the beast." There is hardly a more beautiful harbor than Nawiliwili's, with a stream flowing into it and verdant mountains all around. However, since the 1930s it has been a working harbor complete with dock storage and petrochemical tanks. It was shelled on December 31, 1941, during World War II, but there was little damage. Now, private yachts and catamarans bob at anchor with their bright colors reflecting off dappled waters, and as your eye sweeps the lovely panorama it runs into the dull tan wall of a warehouse on the hill where raw sugar used to be stored before being shipped to the Mainland to be processed. It's one of those places that separates perspectives: some see the "beauty," while others focus on the "beast."

◖ Kalapaki Beach

This most beautiful beach at Nawiliwili fronts the lavish Kaua'i Marriott Resort and Beach Club. Just follow Rice Street down until it becomes Rt. 51; you'll soon see the entrance to the hotel on your left. Park in the visitors' area at the hotel entrance, at the rear of the hotel, or at the north end of Nawiliwili Park, where a footbridge leads across Nawiliwili Stream to the hotel property and the beach. Access to the beach is open to anyone. The wave action at Kalapaki is gentle at most times, with long swells combing the sandy-bottomed beach. Kalapaki is one of the best swimming beaches on the island, only fair at best for snorkeling,

but a great place to try bodysurfing, windsurfing, or begin with a surfboard. From here there are great views of the Ha'upu Range and the bay. If you're there on the right day, you can watch cruise ships sail into or out of port on their rounds of the islands.

Nawiliwili Park

This park fronts Nawiliwili Bay, beyond the seawall to the side of Kalapaki Beach. Its lawn provides room for picnic tables, toilets, play equipment for kids, a sand volleyball court, and plenty of space for an impromptu game of football. Although it has palm trees and ironwoods for shade, it is not nearly as visually pleasing as the landscaped hotel property directly fronting the beach. A large cement-block canoe club building has been built on lawn as well, but controversy about its permitting and construction still abounds. Local swimmers and surfers come here for beach access, a few come to spearfish, and others come to drink beer and while away the hours under the trees. On occasion, turtles play off the rocks.

a cruise ship in port at Nawiliwili Harbor

ROBERT NILSEN

Follow the road out along the breakwater past the enclosed port area to the end of the breakwater for a good view of the inner harbor and Ha'upu Ridge.

Niumalu County Park
Just west of the Nawiliwili Small Boat Harbor, this flat and grassy, county-maintained park lies along the bank of the Hule'ia Stream. It's a very local park, home of the Kaiola Canoe Club, with pavilions, showers, and toilets, but no camping. People from the area use the park mostly for canoe activities, barbecues, and other such get-togethers.

Ninini Beach
Located to the harbor side of Ninini Point and the lighthouse, this small, unfrequented spot, with a narrow sandy beach backed up against the low cliff, is gentle most of the year, except when the kona winds blow in from the south. A second smaller beach is closer to the Marriott below the golf course. These secluded beaches are rarely used, but if you go to them, head past the hotel and turn right, going past the few private homes along Pali Kai Road that overlook the bay. Walk along the edge of the golf course until you see the two beaches below, both good for sunbathing. There is also access from the parking lot at the end of the road that runs past the Marriott, where a brewpub once had the best sunset scenery in the area.

To get to **Ninini Point Lighthouse,** take the paved road across from Vidinha Stadium and follow it around between the airport runways and Kaua'i Lagoons Golf Course. This road soon turns to red dirt and is used by joggers. Near the end, the right fork leads to the back of the former brewpub while the other runs out to the rocky point on which the lighthouse sits. It's about 2.5 miles. The lighthouse, now automated, has operated since 1897; the present yellow structure was built in 1932. There is shoreline access here and a few battered picnic tables.

Ahukini State Recreation Pier
As the name implies, Ahukini is simply a pier from which local people fish. And it's some of the best pole fishing around. With the airport to your right, proceed down Ahukini Road until the road ends at a large circular parking lot and breakwater. The airport flight path is directly overhead. The scenery is only fair, and the spot itself is rather unkempt and littered. A skeletal cement framework remains of the old pier, so if you're not into fishing give it a miss. On the way down, sections of train tracks cross the road, a vestige of the sugar era and the means by which cane was transported to waiting ships. Ahukini Pier was used for about 100 years as a major port to ship sugarcane from the island to be processed elsewhere, and as such played an important role in the economy of the island.

Entertainment and Events

Lihu'e is not the entertainment capital of the world, but if you have the itch to step out at night, there are a few places where you can scratch it.

EVENING MUSIC, HULA, LU'AU, AND DINNER SHOWS

At the Marriott, stop by Kukui's Restaurant or Duke's Canoe Club and Barefoot Bar for Hawaiian and contemporary music every evenings. Kukui's also hosts a free sunset hula show every Monday and a torch-lighting ceremony every Thursday evening at 6:30 P.M. Soft piano music is in store most evenings on the promenade overlooking the pool.

The Radisson also hosts a free nightly torch-lighting and hula show at the grotto in its central courtyard. This is accompanied on Sunday at 5:30 P.M. by the **Kaua'i Aloha Lu'au** (808/335-5828, $65 for adults, $62 seniors, $40 teens, and $30 for kids). Accompanied by a Polynesian revue of music and dance, the lu'au is held outdoors by the pool, weather permitting, otherwise inside the ballroom. For a less Hawaiian but still entirely entertaining evening try the **dinner show** at the Radisson, presenting music from the movie *South Pacific* (scenes of which were filmed on the island) from 6 P.M. on Monday and Wednesday, $68 adults and $50 for children 12 and under. For information and reservations, call 246-0111.

Lu'au Kilohana (808/245-9593, 5 P.M.–9 P.M. Tuesday and Thursday, adults $66, seniors and teens $56, children 4–12 $31), the second lu'au performed in the area, takes place at the Kilohana Carriage House. The evening starts with a few cultural activities and the roast pig and other goodies being taken from the *imu*. A full buffet is followed by a show of music and dance from all of Polynesia, both ancient and modern, that you may be invited to participate in.

LOCAL BAR SCENE

Enjoy a night of shared karaoke fun (free on Monday nights) and dance at **Rob's Good Times Grill** (11 A.M.–2 A.M. daily) in the Rice Street Shopping Center. A funky, dark little place with booths and Formica tables, it's become a local hangout. A would-be crooner is given the microphone and sings along with the music—the video and words to which are projected on a screen in the corner. Even if your mom used to ask you to stop singing in the shower, here you can join in the fun. Everyone gets applause, and beer and drinks are reasonably priced. Rob's Good Times Grill is one of Lihu'e's only "neighborhood bars," where you can watch sports on the big screen TVs, shoot a round of pool, hobnob with the locals, and have a reasonable meal.

The Nawiliwili Tavern (808/245-7267, 2:30 P.M.–2 A.M.), housed in the old Hotel Kuboyama building (from the early decades of the 1900s), at the bottom of Rice St. along Paena Loop Rd., is a friendly neighborhood bar and restaurant where you can mix with local people and tourists alike who are having fun playing pool or darts; music alternates with satellite sports broadcasts. Enjoy a cold beer at the long bar, or satisfy your appetite by ordering any number of plate lunches or *pu pu*, or a more filling burger, steak, or pasta dish. The grill is open until late evening, and happy hour runs weekdays 4–6 P.M.

BOWLING

If you're lucky, you can "strike out" at the **Lihue Bowling Center** (808/245-5263) in the Rice Shopping Center, the only bowling alley on the island. The lanes stay open until 11:30 P.M. on Friday and Saturday but usually close about 10:30 P.M. on weekdays depending on how busy things are. Scoring is done with an automatic system.

MOVIES AND THEATER

For movies, try the **Kukui Grove 4 Cinemas** (808/245-5055, $7 general admission), behind the gas station across Nawiliwili Road from the big Kukui Grove Shopping Center.

Since 1971, the **Kauai Community Players** (808/245-7700, www.kauaicommunityplayers.org, tickets generally $12–20) have presented the island with theatrical performances. Four times a year, this nonprofessional community theater group puts on well-known and experimental plays, usually at the War Memorial Convention Center. This is a great opportunity to catch a show—local style—so check the Internet or call for what's happening when you'll be there.

FOURTH OF JULY FIREWORKS

If you happen to be on Kaua'i on the fourth of July, don't fail to see the fireworks at Vidinha Stadium in Lihu'e. A "do not miss" event, it's reputedly one of the best light shows in the state.

Shopping

Many good selections and bargains are found in the city. Kaua'ians shop in Lihu'e, and the reasonable prices that local purchasing generates are passed on to you.

SHOPPING CENTERS

The only thing left of the old Lihu'e Shopping Center in downtown Lihu'e is the Big Save Supermarket. The rest has been converted and remodeled into county office space. This was the center from which businesses stretched to the east along Rt. 56, where you can still see the classic old Garden Island Motors Limited building dating from 1923. The remaining old in-town mall is the **Rice Shopping Center** (4303 Rice St.), which features a self-service laundry, a bowling alley, bakery, and a neighborhood bar. The real shopping now is done at the newer centers and at the huge Wal-Mart and Kmart stores; Costco is coming.

The **Kukui Grove Shopping Center** (9:30 A.M.–7 P.M. Mon.–Thurs. and Sat., until 9 P.M. on Fri., and 10 A.M.–6 P.M. on Sun.), at the intersection of Kaumuali'i Hwy. and Nawiliwili Rd., just a few minutes west of downtown Lihu'e, is Kaua'i's largest all-purpose shopping mall. Refurbished in 2004 after years of neglect, the center's main stores include Macy's and Sears, for general merchandise and apparel; Longs Drugs for sundries, sporting goods, medicines, and photo needs; and Star Market for groceries. The list of shops includes the usual apparel, jewelry, and gift stores, with a number of fast-food eateries, but specific shops that may be of interest to the traveler are the Sunglass Hut International for eyewear to keep out the tropical rays and the Kauai Products Store, which offers quality, mostly island-made goods of all sorts. Unlike the other eateries here, the more sophisticated **Deli and Bread Connection** is a kitchenware store with a deli counter and seating inside offering sandwiches and an assortment of soups and salads. Musical entertainment and hula are scheduled at various times throughout the week at the center stage. In detached buildings to the side of the main mall are Borders Books and Music and Kmart. To the rear is a Home Depot. Across Nawiliwili Rd. is a sister complex that has offices, several banks, and the Kukui Grove 4 Cinemas.

The **Anchor Cove Shopping Center,** at Kalapaki Beach, is a compact shopping mall with a great location. Among the semi-detached kiosks, you will find an ABC Store (daily 7 A.M.–10:30 P.M.), selling sundries, beachwear, groceries, film, drugs, cosmetics, and also liquor; Crazy Shirts, with well-made and distinctive T-shirts; and Honolua Surf Co. for casual clothing and resort wear. At Tropic Isle Music Company (808/245-8700, www.tropicislemusic.com) you will find CDs of classic, traditional, contemporary, and modern island music, any number of island-inspired gifts, hula supplies, and clothing. Maui Divers Jewelry stocks all sorts of ornaments for a take-home gift, and the several eateries include the well-respected JJ's Broiler restaurant. The small complex to the rear, with its bevy of gift and clothing shops and a billiard hall, has now been incorporated into Anchor Cove and is connected by a walkway. From the parking lot at the end of the short Paena Loop Rd. to the side of the mall, a footbridge over the stream connects to the Marriott hotel property and the beach.

Just up the road and across the street from the Anchor Cove is the **Harbor Mall,** landscaped and remodeled to let the breeze in. Aside from the numerous eateries, there is a used bookshop here with Internet connection and several boutiques and gift shops. Offerings

include free shuttle service from the harbor for cruise ship passengers and free hula lessons at 12:15 P.M. on Wednesday.

Kilohana

On the outskirts of Lihu'e, just west of Kukui Grove Shopping Center, Kilohana is a unique collection of shops in a unique setting. Around the time that Gaylord Wilcox moved the business office of Grove Farm from the homestead site, he had the 16,000-square-foot Kilohana plantation house built. After decades of family use, the building was renovated in 1986 and turned into shops that sell arts and crafts. Shops are open 9:30 A.M.–9:30 P.M., until 5 P.M. on Sunday.

The longest-lasting part of a journey is the memory. One of the best catalysts for recapturing your trip is an inspirational work of art or handicraft. The Country Store specializes in Hawaiian-inspired souvenirs, wind chimes, wicker picnic baskets, cutlery, pillows, vintage fabric handbags, aloha shirts, hand-blown and hand-etched glass, lovely silver jewelry, and plenty of other eye-pleasers. Master crafts from

Kilohana

ROBERT NILSEN

local artists include koa boxes, turned bowls, quilted throws, and cobalt blue hand-blown and -etched glass. Upstairs and down you will also find Sea Reflections, glimmering with glass, jewelry, coral, shells, and marine sculpture; Grande's Gems, for that impulse purchase of a gold bracelet or pearl necklace; the Kilohana Galleries Artisan's Room, offering more artwork; and Makana Gallery with painted and metal artwork. In separate buildings out back are Clayworks at Kilohana, which not only sells artists' work but is a place where you can create your own masterpiece, and Kilohana Clothing Company, which carries island-inspired alohawear.

Artwork isn't the only thing offered here, for Gaylord's restaurant serves some of the most exquisite meals on this side of the island and also presents the Lu'au Kilohana every Tuesday and Thursday evening. Appreciate the house as you wander from shop to shop, but also treat yourself to a short ride around the plantation grounds in a **horse-drawn carriage** that operates 11 A.M.–6 P.M. Just show up and stand in line near the front entrance. The cost of this 20-minute ride is $12 for adults and $6 for kids. For a more extensive look at the grounds and an introduction to the history of the plantation and culture of sugar, try the one-hour sugarcane carriage tour for $24 adults and $12 kids; call 808/246-9529 for reservations.

Specialty Shops

Don't pass up **Hilo Hattie** (3252 Kuhio Hwy., at the intersection of Ahukini Rd., 808/245-3404, 8:30 A.M.–6:30 P.M. daily), an institution of alohawear, to at least educate yourself on products and prices. Though the designs may not be one-of-a-kind, nor all made in the state, Hilo Hattie clothing is very serviceable and well made. Specials are always offered in the free tourist literature and on clearance racks at the store itself. There is a great selection of gifts and souvenirs, food items, books, and many other Hawaii-inspired products. Among the abundance of incentives to get you in is the free hotel pick-up from Po'ipu to Kapa'a, free

juice at the door, a shell lei, and free garment hemming.

In a move from Kapa'a, **Two Frogs Hugging** (3215 Kuhio Hwy., 808/246-8777, 10 A.M.–6 P.M. Mon.–Sat.) has taken up residence along Kuhio Hwy. near the intersection with Ahukini Road. Two Frogs carries a wonderfully eclectic collection of imported arts, crafts, and furniture from Indonesia, including teak outdoor furniture, mahogany chairs, rattan accessories, pottery pots, bamboo window shades, woven bags, knickknacks, and stone carvings. Look for the two hugging frogs statue out front.

You can find everything you need to try your luck in Kaua'i's waters at **Lihue Fishing Supply** (2985 Kalena St., 808/245-4930, Mon.–Sat). Its other half is a fresh fish outlet.

You knew it had to happen here as well. Both the big box stores **Kmart** (4303 Nawiliwili, 808/245-7742) and **Wal-Mart** (3-3300 Kuhio Hwy., 808/246-1599) have outlets in Lihu'e. These stores carry everything that the Mainland stores carry with the addition of island-specialty sections. Their introduction has put local stores out of business, but residents can get clothing and household items cheaper here than they were able to previously. In addition, each offers one-hour film developing and has a large sporting goods section. These stores carry basic camping supplies, mostly for the car-camping crowd and not so much for the backpack/hiker variety, but they do have reasonably inexpensive goods including dome tents, lanterns, outdoor stoves and fuel, and flannel sleeping bags.

Arts, Crafts, and Souvenirs

Kaua'i Museum Shop (808/246-2470) at the Kaua'i Museum has a limited selection of authentic souvenirs and Hawaiian items with competitive prices, which include tapa, wooden bowls, cards, prints, books, and USGS maps. Open during museum hours only.

The **Kauai Products Store** (808/246-6753) at the Kukui Grove Shopping Center is a gem. This shop carries art and crafts items, mostly made in Kaua'i, that include paintings, wooden boxes, quilts, metal sculpture, T-shirts, a smattering of jewelry, and food products. It's fine quality at reasonable prices. A good place to stop for a preview of what the island has to offer.

Down near the harbor entrance is **Aloha Center** (3371 Wilcox Rd., 808/245-6996), a two-story building housing numerous kiosks that display and sell gifts, trinkets, crafts, artwork, and souvenirs for tourists, particularly those just getting off the cruise ships. Conveniently, it has a small snack shop on premises for hungry tummies, restrooms, tourist information, and Internet connection. On occasion, music and other performance arts are staged for the enjoyment of visitors.

Kapaia Stitchery (3-3551 Kuhio Hwy., 808/245-2281, 9 A.M.–5 P.M. Mon.–Sat.) is where you'll find handmade quilts and distinctive fashions. Located along Rt. 56 in Kapaia, below the hospital in the valley, it's the best shop on the island for sewing and quilting supplies. The owner is Julie Yukimura, who, along with her grandmother and a number of very experienced island seamstresses, creates fashions, quilts, and embroideries that are beautiful, painstakingly made, and priced right. Hung from the ceiling for better display, the quilts are awe-inspiring. If you are considering purchasing a quilt while on the island, this is definitely one of the best places to start your search. Ready-made aloha shirts and dresses are mostly 100 percent cotton, and, given a couple of days, these can be made to order from most any material in the store. For those who sew, the range and quality of material is out-standing, and sewing accessories, patterns, and books are all available. You can't help but be pleased with this fine shop!

The aroma of native wood and premium cigars wafts from the small **Wailua Falls Gallery** and cigar shop (3-3601 Kuhio Hwy., 808/245-2711, 9 A.M.–5:30 P.M. Mon.–Sat.—or until they want to close) at the big dip along Rt. 56, just at the turnoff to Wailua Falls in Kapaia, next to Kapaia Stitchery. The swirl of burly koa lends natural luster to the handmade humidors and the limited number of furniture pieces and smaller wood artwork, while paintings hang on the wall and earrings on racks.

Bookshops

The only full-service bookstore on the island is **Borders Books and Music** (808/246-0862, open every day at 9 A.M., it closes at 10 P.M. Mon.–Thurs., at 11 P.M. Fri.–Sat., and at 8 P.M. Sun.), located at the Kukui Grove Shopping Center in Lihu'e. In addition to its usual assortment of fiction and nonfiction titles, Borders carries the fullest Hawaiiana sections on the island. After finding your favorite book, browse the CD racks for music or peruse the map section for guidance. Borders also carries select Mainland and international newspapers. Cafe Espresso, within the store, serves up drinks and snacks.

Another good place for books relating to Kaua'i and Hawaii is the **Kaua'i Museum Shop.** Open museum hours only.

Wal-Mart and Kmart both have book sections, but your selection is limited to generic titles.

Recreation

Lihu'e is not the recreational center of the island, but it does offer a variety of options. Aside from area-specific activities, there are several outfits based here that run activities island wide, and as the airport is located just outside town, most of the helicopter and recreational fixed-wing air tours leave from here.

Golf and Tennis

Kaua'i Lagoons Golf and Racquet Club (3351 Ho'olaulea Way, 808/241-6000 or 800/634-6400, 6:30 A.M.–6 P.M.) is one of the premier golf courses on the island, located between the Kaua'i Marriott and the airport. The fairways of its two courses are strung along 40 acres of freshwater meandering ponds. Situated closer to the runways, the older Mokihana course is a links course for recreational play; surrounding the lagoons and pushing up against the bay, the Kiele course has been designed as a more challenging championship course. While launches don't cruise these lagoons as they did during the Westin days, the water is still a pleasing backdrop for play. Greens fees run $170 for the Kiele and $120 for the Mokihana—substantially less for resort guests—with reduced afternoon fees. Golf instruction is available, and clinics are held daily at $25 per person, limit 10. Just uphill of the hotel entrance, the clubhouse (with restaurant) overlooks one of these lagoons; call ahead for tee times.

Call the golf pro shop for reservation times and check in at the golf clubhouse if you want to use the resort **tennis courts.** There are eight plexipave courts here, but no instruction, clinics, or round robin mixers are available. Except for the 600-seat stadium, these courts are not lighted, so the hours of operation run 7 A.M.–6 P.M.

The **Puakea Golf Course** (4150 Nuhou St., 808/245-8756, 6:30 A.M.–7 P.M.) has been carved from former cane fields below the green curtain of the Ha'upu Range just west of the Kukui Grove Shopping Center. Its 18 holes lie on rolling ground flanking a deep ravine and sports volcanic outcrops and other natural hazards. As the newest course on the island, it will take some time to mature, but it's getting good reviews from those who have played. Greens fees for nonresidents are $125, $65 twilight. Call for tee times. The clubhouse has a small on-site restaurant serving American standards 7 A.M.–3 P.M.

Kayaks and Sailboats

The **Kalapaki Beach Boys,** who run the Marriott hotel beach activities center, rent single- and double-seat kayaks, $10–15 per hour or $35–45 per day for use from the beach. For a guided trip up Hule'ia River, go to **Island Adventures** (808/246-6333, www.kauai-fun.com). Located at Nawiliwili Small Boat Harbor, this is the same group—different name—as the Kalapaki Beach Boys. Their longer morning trip takes you up the river past the Menehune Fishpond, to a rope swing spot, and for short hike into the jungle before heading to a 50-foot waterfall for a swim and lunch for $89 adults, $69 kids 6–12. The abbreviated afternoon paddle runs $59 and $49, respectively.

For a similar guided tour on the river ending at a different waterfall, try **Aloha Canoes and Kayak** (808/246-6804 or 877/473-5446, www.hawaiikayaks.com) at the Anchor Cove Shopping Center. Kayak tours run $70–82 with discounts for children, but an ocean kayak tour is also offered when water conditions are right and various double-hull canoe excursions on the bay and river are also options.

With an office at the Harbor Mall, the family-run **Ali'i Kayaks** (808/241-7700 or 877/246-2544, www.aliikayaks.com) puts together tours with lunch for $94 a person, as well as offering combinations tours with helicopter rides or a lu'au.

While located in Po'ipu, **Outfitters Kauai** (808/742-9667 or 888/742-9887, www.outfitterskauai.com) also offers a river trip that combines paddling a kayak upriver and riding a motorized double-hull canoe back for $90–99, discounts for children. From mid-May through mid-September, a full-day guided coastal sea kayak trip along the Kipu Kai coast goes for $119 for those in good physical condition.

Few tour boats cruise this part of the island, but **Rainbow Runner** (808/632-0202) runs its trimaran from Kalapaki Beach on various one- to three-hour rides, including its popular 90-minute sunset sails for $69 adult.

Fishing

Charter fishing boats operate out of Nawiliwili Small Boat Harbor. One of these is the 55-foot *Konane Star* run by **True Blue Charters** (808/246-6333 or 888/245-1707, www.true-bluecharters.com), which is associated with Island Adventures. When not fishing, they will do snorkeling and whale-watching trips. Other well-established fishing tour companies here include **Kai Bear Sportsfishing Charters** (808/652-4556 or 866/226-8340, www.kaibear.com); **Wild Bill's Fishing Charters** (808/822-5963); and **Lahela Ocean Adventures** (808/635-4020, www.sport-fishing-kauai.com).

Horseback Riding

A 16-acre ranch on the road up to Wailua Falls is the base for horseback rides with **Keapana Horsemanship** (808/823-9303). From the ranch, a ride to Wailua Falls is an easy one hour there and back again for $60 or at a slower speed of two hours for $120. Other trail rides include heading to upper Kapa'a and the Moalepe, Kuilau, or the Sleeping Giant trails for $145. A five-hour ride and swim near the Keahua Arboretum runs $275. Those who desire even more time on the trail should try the full-day Powerline trail exploration with swim and barbecue lunch for $375.

Adventure Van Tours

One unique tour company is **Aloha Kauai Tours** (808/245-6400 or 800/452-1113, www.alohakauaitours.com), which operates out of an office at Kilohana Plantation, where all tours start. Knowledgeable guides take you into the backcountry over dirt roads by air-conditioned, 12-passenger 4WD vans, with an informed narrative on the way. They let you see a part of Kaua'i not reached by anyone who doesn't walk or bike in. Traveling is rough, but the sights are unsurpassed. The company's guides, all local people, are excellent and have a tremendous amount of knowledge about the island's flora, fauna, and history. The eight-hour adventure costs $125 plus tax ($90 for children age 12 and under) and includes a deli/picnic lunch (vegetarian available). Also available is an excellent Kauai Backroads tour in 4WD vans through cane fields up to Kilohana Crater, with commentary about the area on the way. From the crater, the tour then heads to the east Po'ipu seashore near Maha'ulepu through the tunnel in the Ha'upu Ridge, constructed in 1946–47 by Grove Farm to transport cane to the Koloa mill from fields in the Kipu area. Virtually the whole route is on private cane land, behind locked gates, and inaccessible to those without the needed permission. Morning and afternoon tours last four hours and cost $65 for adults or $50 for children, snacks included. The Rainforest tour into the interior of the island beyond the Keahua Arboretum is a half-day 4WD and hiking trek that takes you into the very heart of the island; $70 or $50 for kids. A snorkel day trip and a moderate bike ride through former cane land to Maha'ulepu Beach are two other options.

Adventure Activities

Kauai Backcountry Adventures (3-4221 Kuhio Hwy., 808/245-2506 or 888/270-0555, www.kauaibackcountry.com) runs several adventure outings from its base in Hanama'ulu. Its first and most unusual is the Mountain Tubing Adventure where you set into an old sugar company water flume and leisurely ride a large inner tube through several miles of ditches, open spaces, and tunnels, encountering vistas that you might not be able to get any other way. The three-hour tours run $92 per person. A much faster-paced alternative is the Zipline Adventure. Sliding down seven steel cable lines strung through the treetops and across ravines, you are deposited at a forested spot for lunch and a swim in a mountain pool. All necessary instruction and equipment is provided. You must be at least 15 years old and weigh 100–250 pounds. Rates are $110 per person.

Taking advantage of the beauty and natural features of the Kipu Ranch, **Kipu Ranch Adventures** (808/246-9288, www.kiputours.com) offers ATV tours. The two outings take riders through the working ranch lands, with commentary about its history and scenes from the various movies that have been filmed here. The three-hour Ranch tour runs $105, while the four-hour Waterfall tour, which includes a hike down to a private waterfall for a picnic, is $140. All riders must be 16 years old and wear long pants and closed-toe shoes. Instruction and safety gear are provided. Those who want the adventure but don't care to drive can be chauffeured on a 4WD ATV mule to all the sights.

Motorcycle Rental

Just up from the Anchor Cove Shopping Center in Nawiliwili is **Two Wheels Rentals** (3486 Rice St., 808/246-9457 or 800/921-9457, www.kauaimotorcycle.com, 9 A.M.–6 P.M. daily). Two Wheels rents mostly Harley and Buell road bikes but also offers mopeds to get around town. The motorcycles can be rented by the hour with a two-hour minimum from $60, or $170 for 24 hours; rentals of three days or longer have a discounted rate. Renters must be 21 years old and have solid riding experience, have a motorcycle endorsement, wear closed-toe shoes, and carry a credit card to cover a $2,000 security deposit. Moped rates start at $35 for up to eight hours; $50 a day for more than two days. Moped drivers must be at least 21 years old, have a driver's license, and credit card for a $500 security deposit; no passengers.

Helicopter Tours

Of the dozen or so helicopter companies on Kaua'i, the majority operate from Lihu'e Airport, with a handful flying from Burns Field in Hanapepe and one flying from the Princeville Airport. The companies without offices adjacent

Most helicopter tours leave from the heliport at the Lihu'e Airport.

to the Lihu'e heliport shuttle guests to the tarmac in vans.

The granddaddy of them all is **Jack Harter Helicopters** (4231 Ahukini Rd., halfway between the airport and downtown Lihu'e, 808/245-3774 or 888/245-2001, www.helicopters-kauai.com). Jack, along with his wife, Beverly, literally started the helicopter business on Kaua'i and has been flying the island for over 40 years. He and his pilots know countless stories about Kaua'i and just about everywhere to go on the island. Jack Harter runs both six-passenger a/c and four-passenger open-window helicopters, and 60- and 90-minute flights for $209–290, with Internet discounts. His old slogan—Imitated by all, equaled by none—says it all.

Safari Helicopter (3225 Akahi, 808/246-0136 or 800/326-3356, www.safariair.com), is owned and operated by pilot Preston Myers, who learned to fly in the 1960s and has been flying over Kaua'i since 1987. Safari prides itself on offering a luxury tour in its state-of-the-art ASTAR helicopters with an all-seeing video camera system that records your trip for future enjoyment. Tours run $209 and a video or DVD of your personal tour costs $25. Preflight instruction takes place at Safari's Lihu'e office.

Several other companies with good reputations and competitive prices fly out of Lihu'e Airport. **Will Squyres Helicopters** (3222 Kuhio Hwy., 808/245-8881 or 888/245-4354, www.helicopters-hawaii.com), is a small operation with personalized service from an owner who loves his work. This outfit is one of the longest-running on the island and has an excellent safety record. **Island Helicopters** (808/245-8588 or 800/829-5999, www.islandhelicopters.com) has an office near the old air terminal. Also with an office near the old terminal is **Air Kauai** (808/246-4666 or 800/972-4666, www.airkauai.com), where owner and pilot Charles DiPiazza takes personal care of you in his air-conditioned AS350B with oversize and extra windows. The large and multi-island operation **Blue Hawaiian Helicopters** (3501 Rice St., in the Harbor Mall, 808/245-5800 or 800/745-2583, www.bluehawaiian.com) now offers flights here on Kaua'i as it does on Maui and the Big Island. **Heli USA** (808/828-6591 or 866/935-1234, www.heliusahawaii.com) has expanded its operation from the Princeville Airport (where it maintains its office) to also include flight departures from Lihu'e. Heli USA also offers flights on O'ahu and on the Mainland.

Fixed-Wing Air Tours

With the exception of an ultralight aircraft, all of Kaua'i's fixed-wing air tours companies leave from the Lihu'e airport, and most have desks at the small commuter air terminal. Three companies offer standard tours of the north or south shores, or of the entire island in 4-passenger aircraft: **Wings Over Kauai** (808/635-0815, www.wingsoverkauai.com); **Air Ventures** (808/651-0679, www.airventureshawaii.com); and **Kauai Aero Tours** (808/639-9893). Flights generally run 45–60 for $60–120 per person.

Perhaps a more exciting option is offered by **Tropical Biplane** (808/246-9123, www.tropicalbiplanes.com), which provides an old-fashioned open-cockpit air ride over the Garden Island, to bring you as up-close an experience as any fixed-wing aircraft can. Rides are limited to one or two passengers and run from a 30-minute tour for $178 per couple to an hour-long ride for $356 per couple.

Other Activities

When games are happening, **spectator sports** can by watched at Vidinha Stadium, which has baseball diamonds and football/soccer fields.

Ho'olaule'a Way runs past the Marriott and leads over two arching bridges. This road serves as a **jogging path** and, beyond the former brewpub at the end of the road, connects with a dirt road that runs in one direction to the Ninini Point Lighthouse and in the other direction circles around to Rt. 51. At the security gate near the highway, a road continues back through the fairways to the hotel entrance, a distance of almost four miles. Alternately, and for a jog about half that distance, take Kalapaki Circle just beyond the hotel's main entrance and proceed past the homes overlooking the bay. Continue around the lagoon to the second vehicular bridge, and then return to the hotel entrance.

Accommodations

If you like simple choices, you'll appreciate Lihu'e; it holds only two fancy resorts and two condo complexes, two small family-run hotel/motels, and a smattering of vacation rentals. In the smaller places, prices are good because Lihu'e isn't considered a prime resort town. Yet it makes an ideal base, because from Lihu'e you can get *anywhere* on the island in less than an hour. Although it's the county seat, the town is quiet, especially in the evenings, so you won't have to deal with noise or hustle and bustle.

Under $50

The pink **Motel Lani** (P.O. Box 1836, Lihu'e, HI 96766, 808/245-2965), owned and operated by Janet Naumu, offers clean, inexpensive rooms at 4240 Rice Street. There are nine units, and, although close to the road, they're surprisingly quiet. Each room has a small desk, dresser, bath, fan, and refrigerator and is cross-ventilated. Some have air-conditioning. Janet usually doesn't allow children under three years old, but she's reasonable and will make exceptions. A small courtyard with a barbecue is available to guests. Rates for two nights or more are $34–52 double, $52 and up triple, $14 for an additional person, slightly more for one night. Deposit required.

$50-100

The **Tip Top Motel** (3173 'Akahi St., 808/245-2333) is a combination motel, restaurant, and bakery popular with local folks that's been around for over 80 years. It's a functional, two-story, cinder block building painted light gray that's often used by inter-island business people. The check-in lobby/café/bakery is open 6:30 A.M.–3 P.M. and 5:30–9 P.M. Tuesday–Sunday; on Monday, hours are from 7:30 A.M. At other hours, check in at Chrissy

and Charley's Bar around the side of the building. The rooms are antiseptic in every way—a plus, as your feet stay cool on the bare linoleum floor—and there's virtually no decoration, but there is a TV in every room and all are air-conditioned. No in-room telephones. Just to add that mixed-society touch, instead of a Gideon's Bible in the dresser drawer, you get *The Teachings of Buddha,* placed by the Sudaka Society of Honolulu. Rates are $50 per room, plus a $30 refundable key deposit.

Just west of the harbor, in the tiny community of Niumalu, is **The Kaua'i Inn** (2430 Hulemalu Rd., 808/245-9000 or 800/808-2330, fax 808/245-3004, info@kauai-inn.com, www.kauai-inn.com). Originally built in Lihu'e around the turn of the 20th century and later relocated to Kalapaki Beach, this hotel was moved to its present location when the old Kauai Surf Hotel was constructed there in the 1960s. Badly damaged during Hurricane 'Iniki, this old standby has reopened and been fully modernized after six years of reconstruction, transforming it once again into a lovely lady. The 48 guest rooms surround a newly landscaped courtyard with a small swimming pool and barbecue area, and each room has a private bath, ceiling fan, refrigerator, microwave, and cable TV. Rooms run $89 for a king or queen bed, $99 for two double beds, and $109 for a suite, and that rate includes a basic continental breakfast at the pool house each morning. Quiet and a bit out of the way, the Kaua'i Inn offers clean and comfortable accommodation at reasonable prices.

$100-150

Steve and Susan Layne, owners of the attractive **Garden Island Inn** (3445 Wilcox Rd., 808/245-7227, fax 808/245-7603 or

800/648-0154, info@gardenislandinn.com, www.gardenislandinn.com), did a wonderful job of turning the once character-laden but worse-for-wear Ocean View Motel into a bright and cheery inn, with a green-on-white color scheme. Head down Rice Street toward the harbor; the inn is on a cul-de-sac across from Nawiliwili Beach Park, just a stroll from Kalapaki Beach. Each room has a/c, color cable TV, a microwave, small refrigerator, and coffeemaker with complimentary Kona-blend coffee. There is tile throughout. The inn also provides boogie boards, snorkeling gear, beach mats, and ice chests for a day's outing. The garden-view, ground-floor rooms, $90–105 double, are appointed with island prints and flowers from the garden. Second floor rooms, $95–105 double, are about the same but with a bit more of a view. The best rooms, $105–135, are on the third floor. More like mini-suites, these one- and two-room units have kitchenettes, a/c, and balconies and give you two full rooms that can easily accommodate four people comfortably. All 21 rooms are nonsmoking. In addition, a two-bedroom condo unit behind the inn with a fully furnished kitchen, cable TV, washer/dryer, and suburb views of the harbor rents from $135/day depending on the number of people (maximum of six) plus a $75 cleaning fee; four-night minimum. From the front of the inn, you can watch the goings-on in Nawiliwili Harbor and dock area. The Garden Island Inn is one of the best deals on Kaua'i.

To the side of the Garden Island Inn are the **Banyan Harbor Resort** condominiums (3411 Wilcox Rd., 808/245-7333 or 800/422-6926, fax 808/246-3687, reservations@banyanharbor.net, www.vacation-kauai.com). Stepping up the hillside in two- and three-story buildings, many of the 148 one- and two-bedroom units in this complex have views of Nawiliwili Harbor. Each is outfitted with a fully equipped kitchen and dining room, separate living room, TV and VCR, and a washer and dryer; most units have air-conditioning. Queen beds and sofa beds (double beds in some units) allow for up to four persons in the smaller units and a maximum of six in the larger. Maid service is offered every third day, and

the swimming pool, tennis courts, and barbecue grills are for guest use only. Although standard rates run $120 for the smaller units and $150 for two-bedrooms, be sure to inquire about the numerous discounts, package rates, and extended-stay deals. While not luxury, this is good value for a family at a convenient location.

$250 and Up

Midway between the airport and Kapa'a, down the tree-lined entrance road to and along a series of ponds that separate it from the adjacent Pahio time-share property, the **Radisson Kaua'i Beach Resort** (4331 Kauai Beach Dr., 808/245-1955 or 800/333-3333, fax 808/246-9085, www.radissonkauai.com, $259–359 with suites to $799) is a low-lying complex on 25 landscaped acres that's isolated from the three major resort areas on the island. Its 347 rooms lie in two- and three-story units that spread from the entrance and lobby like arms around the central garden, where tall coconut trees tower over four swimming pools, one with a sand bottom, and a "mini-mountain" with grotto and artificial waterfall. Free and open to the public, a torch-lighting ceremony with hula presentation is performed in the garden nightly. Rooms are spacious and tastefully appointed, with a full bathroom, Sleep Number beds in all rooms, entertainment centers, cable TV, a sitting area, and an ocean- or garden-view lanai. Dining amenities include the casual Naupaka Terrace restaurant, which serves up satisfying if not memorable breakfasts and dinner, and the Driftwood Sandbar and Grille by the pools for lunch options. Every evening, Shutters lobby lounge serves libations and presents soft Hawaiian music. A wide range of activities can be scheduled at the concierge desk, the Pahio spa and fitness center is there for those who want to pamper themselves, or you can head to the tennis courts for a workout. The Kauai Beach Boys activity desk near the pools can arrange any sort of water activity. Visit the lobby gift shop for sundries, reading material, and food items, view a broad selection of artwork at A Piece of Paradise Gallery, check the Internet while sipping Kaua'i-grown and -brewed coffee at Paradise Roasters, or stop in to the Remember Kauai shop for a jewelry memento of your trip. Large-group meetings and banquets can be accommodated in the function rooms, which otherwise regularly present the hotel lu'au Polynesian revue every Sunday and dinner theater shows on Monday and Wednesday. Free shuttle service to/from the airport is available, as are special packages and discounts.

The (**Kaua'i Marriott Resort and Beach Club** (3610 Rice St., Kalapaki Beach, 808/245-5050 or 800/220-2925, fax 808/246-5148, www.marriotthawaii.com, $339–454, with suites up to $2,600) is a testament to humans' perseverance coupled with the forgiving personality of Mother Nature. Kaua'i's first high-rise hotel was built on Kalapaki Beach in the 1960s as the Kauai Surf. This structure still stands as the Kilohana wing of the Marriott. In 1987, the hotel was completely refurbished and rebuilt, emerging as the Westin—at the time the most luxurious property on Kaua'i. Hurricane 'Iniki then furiously blew ashore in 1992, raking the island and mangling the hotel. Afterward, the Marriott chain purchased the property and set about restoring it to its former grandeur. The result is, once again, a fabulous 588-room hotel, where about one-third of the rooms are time-share properties. Although 10 floors tall, the Marriott doesn't seem to dominate the surroundings, as it's tucked into the bottom of the hill below town. Upon arrival, you enter through a grand foyer. Descending the escalator you emerge on a flagstone path, along the perimeter of Ka Mala O Kalapaki, a formal garden that says "Hawaii" unmistakably. This garden is surrounded by ballrooms and convention rooms. You'll soon descend a flight of marble steps on your left into the reception area. Displayed here is a lustrous original koa canoe that belonged to Prince Kuhio. In the care of a local Hawaiian family over the generations, the canoe was leased to Marriott with the understanding that funds be used in a scholarship that directly benefits a child of Hawaiian ancestry.

The beachside area of the hotel includes an extensive doughnut-shaped swimming pool (one of the largest in Hawaii and now solar heated) surrounded by five neoclassical thrust proscenium porticos bubbling with soothing whirlpools and cascades of water; greenery and small private gardens fill other spaces. Overall the hotel is decorated in muted salmon, light green, periwinkle, and island pastel colors, and the halls, walkways, and other public spaces are dotted with an extensive collection of Asian and Hawaiian artworks. Although you're surrounded by luxury at the Marriott, you experience the feeling of a quieter, more casual place. The hotel is very much like the stunning sister who decided to stay close to home instead of heading for the bright lights where her beauty would easily have dazzled everyone.

Rooms are pure luxury: each has a private lanai, and most overlook the pool or ocean. A comfy bed faces an entertainment center complete with remote-control color TV, while a writing desk, table, chairs, and floor lamps fill out the room. Each room boasts air-conditioning, a mini-fridge, tiled full bath, a steam iron and ironing board, in-room safe, and coffeemaker with complimentary Kona coffee.

The Marriott has five restaurants, one to fit your every need. Amenities include room service, an activities desk, concierge service, a fitness center, golf course and tennis center, children's program, complimentary airport shuttle, a car rental desk, and shops for gifts and sundries, jewelry, art, and fashions. Everything from hair styling to facials, body treatments, and massages is available at the full-service Alexander Day Spa. At one end of the quarter-mile-long beach promenade, the Kalapaki Beach Boys activity center has gear for all water activities and can arrange activities like scuba, sailing, kayaking, and fishing.

Vacation Rental Agencies

Kauai Vacation Rentals (3-3311 Kuhio Hwy., 808/245-8841 or 800/367-5025, fax 808/246-1161, aloha@kvrre.com, www.KauaiVacation-Rentals.com) handles condos and vacation rental homes throughout the island, including a handful of "cottages" (read: luxury homes) overlooking Kalapaki Beach next to the Marriott and a house with superb views overlooking Hule'ia Stream.

Food

Dining in Lihu'e is a treat—good to your palate and your budget. The town has many local eateries and a few fast-food chains. Stepping up in class, there are continental, Italian, and Japanese restaurants, while moderately priced establishments serve up hearty dishes of Mexican, Chinese, and good old American fare. Fancier dining is found at the big hotels and a few select restaurants around town.

In-Town Local Style

If you ask anyone in Lihu'e where you can chow down for cheap, they'll send you to **Ma's Family Inc.** (4277 Halenani St., 808/245-3142, 5 A.M.–1:30 P.M. weekdays and 5–11:30 A.M.—or until customers stop coming—Sat., Sun., and holidays), an institution operated by the family of matriarch Akiyo Honjo, a third-generation Kaua'ian. Turn off Rice Street onto Kress and follow it to the corner, where you'll find Ma's. The building is old and has seen some wear but is clean. A few tourists find it, but mostly it's local working people who come here for a hearty and filling meal. Lunches are good, but the super deals are breakfast and the Hawaiian specialties. The coffee, free with breakfast and served with condensed milk, arrives in a large pot about as soon as your seat hits the chair. The menu is posted above the kitchen window. You can start the day with The Works, which includes potatoes or fried noodles, bacon or sausage, and toast. If that's too much, ask for an omelette, French toast, or pancakes. From the Hawaiian menu, try *kalua* pork with two eggs and rice, poi, and *lomi* salmon, or Kaua'i sausage. Ma's also serves hamburgers, loco moco, noodles, and an assortment of sandwiches including teriyaki beef, most for under $6.

C **Hamura Saimin Stand** (2956 Kress St., 808/245-3271, open daily from 10 A.M., until 9:30 P.M. on Sun., until 11 P.M. Mon.–Thurs., and until 1 A.M. Fri.–Sat.) is just around the corner from Ma's, and people flock to the orange countertops and pale yellow interior of this restaurant all day long, where they perch on short stools to eat steaming bowls of saimin. To get an idea just how frequented this little shop is, have a look at the well-worn thresholds of its doors. There is no decor here (beyond the sign admonishing Please Do Not Stick Gum Under Counter), just good food. Your first time, try the Saimin Special, which gives you noodles, slivers of meat and fish, vegetables, won ton, and eggs, all floating in a golden broth. Other items on the small menu are variations on the same theme, with nothing more than $7. The bowl size determines your portion: small, medium, large, extra large, special, extra large special. On the counter sit hot sauce, mustard, and shoyu—condiments that you mix yourself in the small bowls that accompany your soup. Enjoy not only the saimin, but also the truly authentic Kaua'i experience. Also available as sides are crispy wonton, skewers of beef or chicken, *manapua,* and *liliko'i* (passion fruit) pie. **Halo Halo Shave Ice** occupies a second counter in the same building 10 A.M.–4 P.M.—use the side entrance. Here you can get some of the best throat coolers on the island.

Oki Diner (3125 Kuhio Hwy., 808/245-5899, open 21 hours a day—closed only 3–6 A.M.) just up from the county government office building, has become another favorite for locals in town. This is a spartan place, simple but pleasant. Everything on the menu is available at any time—good quality food at reasonable prices, mostly under $8. A counter at the entrance sells baked goods, so you can leave with sweets for the road or come in to pick up a cake.

Dani's (4201 Rice St., 808/245-4991, 5 A.M.–1:30 P.M. Mon.–Fri., 5 A.M.–1 P.M. Sat., closed Sun.) is located down toward Nawiliwili near the fire department. Another favorite with local people, it's been around a while and has a good reputation for giving you a hearty meal for a reasonable price. The food is American-Hawaiian-Japanese. Most

ISLAND TREATS

Certain finger foods, snacks, and island treats are unique to Hawaii. Here are some of the best and most popular.

Pronounced as in "Winnie the Pooh Pooh" and originally the name of a small shellfish, *pu pu* is now a general term that has come to mean "hors d'oeuvres" or any finger food. These can be anything from crackers to cracked crab. Often they're given free at lounges and bars and can even include chicken drumettes, fish kebabs, and tempura. At a good display of them you can have a free meal.

A sweet of Chinese origin, **crackseed** can be any number of preserved and seasoned fruits and seeds. Favorites include coconut, watermelon, pumpkin seeds, mango, plum, and papaya. Distinctive in taste, they take some getting used to but make great trail snacks.

They are available in all island markets. Also look for dried fish (cuttlefish) on racks, usually near the crackseed. Nutritious and delicious, it makes a great snack.

Shave ice, a real island institution, makes the Mainland "snow cone" melt into insignificance. Special machines literally shave ice to a fluffy consistency. It's mounded into a paper cone, and your choice of dozens of exotic island syrups is generously poured over it. Get a straw and spoon and just slurp away.

Taro chips are like potato chips but made from the taro root. If you can find them fresh, buy a bunch, as they are mostly available packaged.

Two sweets from the Portuguese, *malasadas* are holeless doughnuts and *pao dolce* is sweet bread. Sold in island bakeries, they're great for breakfast or as treats.

---

full meals range $6–10, and you have selections like *lomi* salmon, tripe stew, teriyaki beef and chicken, and fried fish. Unpretentious, the cafeteria-style interior displays Formica-topped tables and linoleum floors.

The ◖ **Barbecue Inn** (2982 Kress St., 808/245-2921, 7 A.M.–1:30 P.M. Mon.–Sat. and 5–8:30 P.M. Mon.–Thurs., and 4:30–8:45 P.M. Fri.–Sat.) has been in business and run by the Sasaki family since 1940, and if you want a testimonial, just observe the steady stream of local people, from car mechanics to doctors, heading for this restaurant. The atmosphere is "leatherette and Formica," but the service is homey, friendly, and prompt. More than 30 entrées—Japanese, American, and local—include tempura, seafood, prime rib, and a dinner plate special. The scampi is perhaps the best for the price on the island. Mostly in the $10–25 range, meals come complete with soup, salad, a beverage, and dessert. There's always a list of specials, longer than some restaurant's menus. Breakfast and lunch are at bargain prices, the homemade pies are luscious, and cocktails are available.

Japanese

Kiibo Restaurant (2991 'Umi St., just off Rice St., 808/245-2650, 11 A.M.–1:30 P.M. and 5:30–9 P.M., closed Sun. and holidays) serves authentic Japanese meals without a big price tag. Many Japanese around town come here to eat. The low stools at the counter are reminiscent of a Japanese *akachochin* or *sushiya.* The menu listing savory offerings of *udon, donburi,* teriyaki, tempura, and a variety of *bento* (simple boxed lunch) and *teishoku* (full meal with soup and rice) includes pictures showing you just what you'll get. Sushi is also served. The service is quick and friendly; most offerings are under $12. Restaurant Kiibo is *ichiban!* What it lacks in ambience and polish, it makes up for in tasty, well-presented food.

Tokyo Lobby (3501 Rice St., in Nawiliwili at the Harbor Mall, 808/245-8989, Mon.–Fri. for lunch 11 A.M.–2 P.M., dinner daily 4:30–9 P.M.) prides itself on the freshness of the food, especially the seafood. Appointed with shoji screens, a pagoda-style roof over the sushi bar, paper fans, and paper lanterns, the Tokyo Lobby creates an authentic Japanese atmosphere. Most meals are presented in small wooden boats, the signature of the restaurant. Lunch might be *nigiri* sushi or sashimi, various *donburi*, a bowl of rice with savory bits of meat, egg, and vegetables on top, or *nabeyaki*, assorted seafood with vegetables and noodles in a broth. The dinner menu includes sashimi and sushi platters, calamari steak, curried chicken, and beef teriyaki, most around $13, or combination dinners like chicken teriyaki with tempura for a bit more.

At Kalapaki Beach

Look for an anchor chain marking the two-tone blue **Kalapaki Beach Hut** (3474 Rice St., 808/246-6330, daily 7 A.M.–8 P.M.) at the bottom of Rice Street, just before Nawiliwili Harbor. This window-restaurant offers limited seating on the porch or in the upstairs "crow's nest," from where you get a view of the harbor. With a good reputation among local clientele, it serves breakfast ($4–7), like omelettes, eggs, pancakes, French toast, and loco moco, until 10:30 A.M. Lunches of fish and chips and a variety of sandwiches run $5–8. The specialty is large, juicy, flame-broiled buffalo burgers with all the fixings, but turkey burgers and traditional beef burgers are also offered. The Beach Hut is an excellent, laid-back choice for a simple meal in Nawiliwili.

Only a few steps away at the Harbor Mall is **Kauai Chop Suey** (3501 Rice St., in Nawiliwili at the Harbor Mall, 808/245-8790, Tues.–Sun. 11 A.M.–2 P.M. and 4:30–9 P.M.) The restaurant's two dining rooms, separated by a keyhole archway, are alive with plants and brightened by Chinese lanterns hanging from the open-beamed ceiling. This reasonably priced Cantonese restaurant's entrées include sizzling shrimp with lobster sauce (Mama Lau, the owner, says this is the best), boneless chicken with mushrooms, or beef or pork with tomato. House specials are Kauai Chop Suey and a variety of noodle dishes. Kauai Chop Suey also offers plate lunches and dinners to go and has a steady local clientele, a sure sign of good food at reasonable prices.

Although its location is not the best, being upstairs and around the back at the Harbor Mall, **Aroma'a** (3501 Rice St., in Nawiliwili at the Harbor Mall, 808/245-9192, 11:30 A.M.–3 P.M. and 5–9 P.M. Tues.–Sun.) is making a name for itself with its "TransPacific Mediterranean Cuisine." Lunch offers salads, wraps, sandwiches, and plates such as Moroccan grilled vegetable salad, Shaolin Curry tofu wrap, and penne rigati, most in the $11 range. Dinner is pricier at $15–27, with such selections as eggplant and tabbouleh salad, pasta primavera, honey and pecan mahimahi, and a spicy lamb chop with chutney. There is a fair wine selection to complement your meal.

JJ's Broiler (3416 Rice St., 808/246-4422, daily 11 A.M.–5 P.M. for lunch, until 10 P.M. for dinner, and from 5 P.M. for cocktails and light meals) at the Anchor Cove Shopping Center is a tradition in town. The menu offers grain-fed aged beef from the Midwest and daily choices of fish caught by local captains and delivered fresh. The living landscape of Nawiliwili Bay glistening through the huge windows creates the backdrop for the bi-level interior. The first level is more casual, with a full bar, wooden tables, and bentwood chairs, or you can dine alfresco on the veranda under large umbrellas. The upstairs offers horseshoe booths and intimate tables, along with another full bar and wraparound windows that open to cooling sea breezes. Hanging from the ceiling are replicas of 12-meter racing yachts, exactly like those entered in the America's Cup. Lunch at JJ's is soup, salad, and hearty sandwiches and wraps, mostly under $13. Aside from its famous Slavonic Steak (a thin broiled tenderloin dipped in butter, wine, and garlic sauce) at $25 or fresh fish at market price, dinner can be roasted macadamia lamb rack, New York steak, crab-stuffed shrimp, grilled salmon with cheese ravioli, or broiled chicken fettuccine, with most entrées under $27. Daily specials for both lunch and dinner are offered to help save money, but no matter what you order, large portions will arrive.

Duke's Canoe Club (808/246-9599), on Kalapaki Beach at the Kaua'i Marriott Resort, open daily 5–10 P.M. upstairs for dinner and 11:30 A.M.–11:30 P.M. for drinks, *pu pu,* and light meals at the downstairs **Barefoot Bar,** is as much a Hawaiian class act as its namesake, the legendary Duke Kahanamoku. Duke's is one of those places, with an exemplary setting just off the beach path and a lustrous wood and thatched interior illuminated by torches and moonlight, that pleasantly overwhelm you with the feeling that you're *really in Hawaii.* At the Barefoot Bar, you feel compelled to quaff a frothy brew and, well… kick off your shoes as you listen to the natural melody of wind and waves just a palm tree away. You can order sandwiches, plate lunches, pizza, burgers, and salads, most for under $10, and you can enjoy a variety of island drinks prepared at the full-service bar (open until midnight). Upstairs, still casual but elegant enough for a romantic evening, the menu offers fresh catch, prepared in your choice of five different ways. You can also order shrimp and other seafood, various steak and rib dishes, or *huli huli* chicken. Entrées start at a $17; the most expensive is the herb-roasted prime rib, Duke cut, for $30. Soft music upstairs accompanies dinner nightly, while livelier Hawaiian music fills the downstairs bar on Thursday, Friday, and Saturday. Duke's is Hawaii at its best: relaxed, charming, idyllic, and offering fine cuisine.

The Marriott has three in-house restaurants with better than average fare. **Kukui's Restaurant,** the hotel's open-air main dining room, is open for breakfast, lunch, and dinner and serves Pacific Rim cuisine by the pool. Specials include the Friday and Saturday night king crab and prime rib buffet, and a Sunday champagne brunch. Live Hawaiian music is performed here every evening, with the addition of a torch-lighting ceremony on Thursday, and a short hula show on Monday. At the far side of the pool is the **Kalapaki Grill,** which serves up broiled burgers, sandwiches, salads, sides, and drinks during the day. Overlooking the central pool from the promenade is **Aupaka Terrace.** A continental breakfast is available here in the morning; cocktails, sushi, and Hawaiian *pu pu* are offered in the evening

except Friday and Saturday, accompanied by live music.

Dining inside beyond the open shuttered windows or outside on the patio is a pleasure at the **Naupaka Terrace Steak House** at the Radisson. While open for breakfast, the Naupaka is perhaps best in the evening with a wide range of offerings that include Midwestern-raised beef. Heavy on the meats, the menu includes filet mignon, strip steak, top sirloin, or rib eye done in various taste-tempting preparations. Prime rib, pasta, and a whole assortment of fish are also on the menu, and there is always something for the vegetarian. Most meat and fish entrées run $25–35. Specials are the Prime Rib and Seafood buffet on Friday and Prime Rib and Crab buffet on Saturday. For lunch, try the Driftwood Sandbar and Grille alongside the sand-bottom pool for sandwiches and other lighter foods.

Fine Dining

The heady aroma of sautéed garlic mixed with the sweet scents of oregano and rosemary floats from the kitchens of **Café Portofino** (808/245-2121, 5–9:30 P.M.), overlooking the beach at the Marriott next to Duke's. This authentic Italian restaurant, owned and operated by Giuseppe Avocadi, is open daily for dinner only. Muted light, colorful flowers, live harp music, and gentle ocean breezes set the mood in the spacious, open-air, yet semi-formal dinning room, while the outdoor veranda is perfect for a romantic occasion. Let the dinner begin with an antipasto or a luscious soup and salad. Tempting Italian entrées, mostly in the $16–26 range, include spaghetti alla marinara, eggplant parmigiana, or pollo porcini (sautéed chicken breast in brandy with a light wild mushroom sauce), and specialties of the house like osso buco (veal shank) over fettuccine. Fish selections and preparations change nightly and are served with fresh homemade condiments. There is a full wine list, and desserts complement a cup of coffee or cappuccino. Café Portofino is an excellent choice for an evening of romance and fine dining. *Buon appetito!*

ON THE TABLE: FISH

Waters around Kaua'i produce great quantities of excellent fresh fish. Unless you know the captain of a fishing boat or have good luck on a fishing tour, you'll probably have to get your fish from a fish market. Several around the island have good selections and reputations to match. Have a good look in the deli case for the varied fish, seafood, and seaweed preparations, many that you won't find elsewhere. Still, most visitors will get their fish experience at a restaurant. Pound for pound, seafood is one of the best dining bargains on Kaua'i. You'll find it served in every kind of restaurant, and often the fresh catch-of-the-day is proudly displayed on ice in a glass case. The following is a sampling of the best.

Mahimahi is an excellent eating fish, one of the most common, most popular, and least expensive in Hawaii. It's referred to as Dorado or "dolphin fish" but is definitely a fish, not a mammal. The flesh of mahimahi is moderately firm, light, flaky, and moist. While different preparations are available, this mild-flavored fish is perhaps best seared, sautéed, baked, or broiled. You will find it served as a main course and as a patty in a fish sandwich. This fish is broadest at the head. When caught it's a dark olive color, but after a while the skin turns iridescent shades of blue, green, and yellow.

The **A'u,** a broadbill swordfish or marlin, is a true island delicacy. It's expensive even in Hawaii because the damn thing's so hard to catch. The meat is moist and light – truly superb – and the flavor is definitely pronounced. Often broiled, it can also be poached, grilled, or skewered. If it's offered on the menu, order it. It'll cost a bit more, but you won't be disappointed.

Ono means "delicious" in Hawaiian, so that should tip you off to the taste of this wahoo, or king mackerel. An open-ocean fish, ono is regarded as one of the finest eating fishes, and its mild, sweet meat lives up to its name. Its white, delicate, and lean flesh can be done in almost any preparation.

Ulua, a bottomfish and member of the jack crevalle family, has firm, white flesh with a steak-like texture. Delicious when baked, sautéed, or broiled.

Opakapaka is a pink snapper, the most preferred of the bottomfish. It has light pink, clear, and firm flesh that has a delightfully delicate flavor. Whole fish with the head on are often baked or steamed, larger fillets can be baked, poached, or sautéed.

Cousin to the *Opakapaka,* **Uku** is a gray snapper that is a favorite with local people for its moderately firm and slightly flaky flesh. It can be prepared like its relative but is often steamed.

'Ahi, a yellowfin tuna with distinctive firm, pinkish meat, is a great favorite cooked or served raw in sushi bars but can be prepared in almost any way.

Two moderately firm, open-ocean fish that sometimes appear on menus are **Opah,** or moonfish (as its shape is nearly that round when seen from the side), and **Monchong.** Opah is more moist and tender, while *Monchong* is denser, but both have full flavor.

Moi is the Hawaiian word for "king" and this fish was traditionally considered the privilege of royalty. The fish has large eyes and a shark-like head. Considered one of the finest eating fishes in Hawaii, it's best during the autumn months. It doesn't often show up at restaurants, but try it when it does.

For the uninitiated, **sushi** is a finger-size block of sticky rice, topped with a slice of (usually) raw fish or other sea creature. A delicacy in Japan, it has become very popular and much appreciated in Hawaii as a fine food.

The rear flagstone veranda and original dining room at Kilohana, the restored 1935 plantation estate of Gaylord Wilcox, have been turned into the breezy **C Gaylord's** (3-2087 Kaumuali'i Hwy., 808/245-9593, open 7:45 – 10 A.M. Mon.–Sat. for breakfast buffet; for lunch 11 A.M.–3 P.M. Mon.–Sat., dinner daily from 5 P.M., and Sun. for brunch 9:30 A.M.– 3 P.M.) Reservations are recommended. Start your day off with a full country buffet of pastries, eggs in various styles, grilled potatoes, French toast, fruits, and juices; $12 adults, $7 children. Lunch might include items like a Kilohana fruit platter, sesame chicken or Greek roasted vegetable salad, or more substantial dishes like baby-back ribs, fresh fish, or a Reuben sandwich. Dinners begin with a wide selection of appetizers, salads, and soups. Mostly in the $22–32 range, entrées include herb-crusted whole rack of lamb; chicken breast with papaya, pineapple, and macadamia nut sauce; and Greek-style linguine with grilled chicken, sun-dried tomatoes, olives, and feta cheese. Fish and game lovers will greatly enjoy the seafood rhapsody—fish, prawns, and lobster in a light creamy butter sauce; one of several choices of fresh fish (market price) that can be char-broiled, sautéed, or crusted; or Gaylord's famous farm-raised venison, which may be offered in a number of daily preparations. Save room for one of Gaylord's memorable desserts and finish your meal with a cappuccino or caffe mocha prepared on a century-old espresso machine, resplendent in its battered yet burnished glory. Gaylord's also prides itself on having one of the largest wine cellars on Kaua'i, featuring more than 100 vintages from around the world representing more than two dozen varietals. The à la carte Sunday brunch features a hearty Plantation Breakfast, strawberry French toast, Gaylord's eggs Benedict, and a vegetarian quiche. Prices for a complete brunch are $10–15 and include a fresh-baked sweet roll and fruit plate. Gaylord's is a wonderful restaurant to visit just to spend a quiet afternoon or

as a special treat for a honeymoon or anniversary. For that romantic occasion, ask for a table at the end of the portico; at one step down, it sets you off a bit by yourself. Whether outdoors on the more casual veranda or indoors in the formal dining room, with its starched linens and stemware, the feeling is one of gentility.

Supermarkets and Nutrition Centers

The two large grocers in town are **Big Save Supermarket** (7 A.M.–11 P.M. daily) next door to the county government building in the center of town and a well-stocked **Star Super Market** (6 A.M.–11 P.M. daily) at the rear of Kukui Grove Shopping Center.

For vitamins, minerals and supplements, see **General Nutrition Center** (808/245-6657) at the Kukui Grove Shopping Center or **Vim 'N Vigor** (3-3122 Kuhio Hwy., 808/245-9053, until 6 P.M. Mon.–Fri. and until 5 P.M. Sat.), which also stocks a limited selection of health foods.

Fish Markets

The Fish Express (3343 Kuhio Hwy., 808/245-9918, 10 A.M.–6 P.M., until 4 P.M. Sun.), across from Wal-Mart, is a retail sales store with a full selection of fresh and frozen fish and seafood. If you're looking for something for the road, try the lunch counter and grill for plate lunches, sandwiches, and seafood platters, mostly under $7.50. Takeout only.

Farmers Markets

If you're making your own meals while visiting Kaua'i, remember that locally grown fresh fruit and vegetables are available from vendors at the Sunshine farmers market every Friday at 3 P.M. at Vidinha Stadium parking lot in Lihu'e. There are plenty of vendors, fewer organic items.

A privately run farmers market is held every Monday at 3 P.M. at the Kukui Grove Shopping Center.

Information and Services

Government Offices

Many Kaua'i County offices are in the **Lihu'e Civic Center** complex (4444 Rice St., 808/241-6303 public information office) on the corner of Kuhio Highway and Rice Street, including that of the mayor, property tax, public works, vehicle registration, driver licensing, and county parks. A stone's throw away, the white, dignified **Historic County Building** faces Rice Street across a wide lawn between 'Eiwa and 'Umi Streets. A few county offices still occupy this structure, as does the Kaua'i Historical Society. During the Christmas/New Year season, this building is decorated inside and out in a festive holiday spirit and open for everyone's enjoyment. Directly behind is the newer three-story **State Building** (3060 'Eiwa St.) where the Land and Natural Resources office on the third floor can handle camping and hiking permits on state land, fishing licensing, and hunting permits. Next door is the

Lihu'e Courthouse. Across 'Umi Street look for the **Department of Health,** while the **fire department** is down Rice Street on the way to Nawiliwili Harbor. The main **post office** (4441 Rice St.) sits directly across from the Kaua'i Museum, and behind the post office is the **Kaua'i Chamber of Commerce** (2970 Kele, 808/245-7363).

The **Kaua'i Visitors Bureau** (4334 Rice St., Suite 101, 808/245-3971 or 800/262-1400, www.kauaivisitorsbureau.org, 8 A.M.–4:30 P.M. Mon.–Fri.) has its office on the first floor of the Watamull Plaza building.

Following Hardy Street back around past the Kaua'i War Memorial Convention Hall, you'll locate the main **library** (4344 Hardy St., 808/241-3222, 11 A.M.–7 P.M. Mon. and Wed., and 9 A.M.–4:30 P.M. Tues., Thurs., and Fri.) across the street from Wilcox Elementary School. Look for the sweep of its roof—like the sail of an outrigger canoe. In a fancy new

ROBERT NILSEN

The old Kaua'i County Building occupies a spot in the center of town.

building, the **police headquarters** (3990 Ka'ana St., 808/241-1711) is located between the airport and Vidinha Stadium.

Business Needs
As the principal population center of the island, and its county seat, Lihu'e has five major **banks,** all with main offices or branches within a few steps of each other along Rice Street near the Museum and/or along Kukui Grove street across the highway from Kukui Grove Shopping Center.

For business services, including packing, shipping, printing, copying, and Internet access, visit **Hale 'Oihana** (2970 Kele, 808/245-3442) behind the post office. The **UPS Store** (808/632-2347) at the Kukui Grove Shopping Center also has packaging and shipping services.

The **Lihu'e Laundromat** is an open-air, 24-hour, self-service laundry at the Rice Shopping Center.

Photo Needs
For film and film developing, try **Longs Drugs** (808/245-6472) or **Kmart** (808/245-7742), both at the Kukui Grove Shopping Center, or **Wal-Mart** (3-3300 Kuhio Hwy., 808/246-1599). In the center of town near Kiibo Restaurant, **Photo Spectrum** (2987 'Umi St., 808/245-7667) offers a greater selection of film, one-hour film processing, and also does studio portraits. No shop on the island does camera repair or servicing.

Around Lihu'e

PUHI
Sustaining substantial residential growth over the past decade, Puhi has become a bedroom community of Lihu'e. Its close proximity provides a convenient location for a sizable warehouse/business park. Also in Puhi is the head office for Grove Farms Co., one of the largest landowners on the island, and at the only intersection in town, a Shell station, convenience shop, terrific wine shop, and restaurant. Two road signs tip you off that you're in Puhi—one for **Kaua'i Community College** (3-1901 Kaumuali'i Hwy., 808/245-8225, www.kauai cc.hawaii.edu) and the other for the **Queen Victoria's Profile** scenic overlook turnout. It's beneficial to keep abreast of what's happening at the college by reading the local newspaper and free tourist brochures. Often, workshops and seminars concerning Hawaiian culture, folk medicine, and various crafts are offered; most are open to the general public and free of charge. The Hawaii International Film Festival and local theater groups use the college's Performing Arts Center for their performances. About 5,000 students are enrolled at this two-year community college, part of the University of Hawaii system, most in the fields of business education, health, liberal arts, and vocational technology. Call for information about registration and course offerings or visit the college's website.

Queen Victoria's Profile isn't tremendously remarkable, but a definite resemblance to the double-chinned monarch has been fashioned by nature on the ridge of the Hoary Head Mountains to the south. East and below the tallest peak is a short single rock outcrop. Along the edge of this profile you can imagine the face—the short protuberance about halfway down is the nose and the bump on top of the crown. Use your imagination.

Recreation
Located in Puhi across from Kaua'i Community College, **Street Eagle** (3-1866 Kaumuali'i Hwy., 808/241-7020 or 877/212-9253, www.streeteagle.com, 7 A.M.–6 P.M. daily) rents newer Harley-Davidsons for $169 a day with reduced daily rates for longer rentals and occasional specials. Tax, a $20 a day insurance fee, and a refundable $1,000 security deposit are additions. All riders must be 25 years old

and need a motorcycle endorsement on their driver's license. There are no clothing restrictions, but closed-toe shoes are recommended and helmets are available. While the state of Hawaii does not require a helmet, it does require eye protection.

Food

Across from the gas station at the intersection is a tiny complex with the convenience shop/deli **Puhi Store** (6 A.M.–7 P.M. Mon.–Sat., until 8 P.M. Fri.), which offers inexpensive plate lunches and sandwiches for $5–7. This place does mostly takeout, but you're welcome to eat inside at one of the tables.

To its side are the small **Hanalima Baking** (808/246-8816, 6 A.M.–2 P.M. Mon.–Fri., 7 A.M.–1 P.M. Sat.) for fresh-baked pastries and breads and sandwiches, and the even smaller **People's Market** (808/245-2210) which, despite its name, doesn't carry much except flowers, lei, and a limited supply of locally grown fruit—but they do make smoothies.

The most intriguing and unusual shop here is **The Wine Garden** (4495 Puhi Rd., 808/245-5766, 10 A.M.–6 P.M. Mon.–Sat.). Nothing but a tiny cubicle, the owner has managed to pack this store chock full of excellent and hard-to-find domestic and imported wines—all personally selected by the owner. Not your supermarket varieties, these bottles will set you back some, but you will have good breadth and depth of selection. There are always "value" selections, and you can pick up glassware, accessories, and gift baskets. Stop here for an appropriate bottle for that special occasion and don't forget to ask for help if in doubt about your choice.

The only restaurant in the community is **Paradise Seafood and Grill** (3-1878 Kaumuali'i Hwy., 808/246-4884), an easygoing eatery on the highway to the side of the shops with dining inside or out on the covered veranda at booths or tables. Quick eats for lunch include burgers and fish and chips for under $8, with a more extensive evening menu of fish, meats, chicken, and pasta, many in the $15–20 range.

HANAMA'ULU

Hanama'ulu is like a "suburb" of Lihu'e and has always been tied to sugar. It holds a tiny post office, an elementary school, a great local restaurant, gas station, and several other small shops.

Hanama'ulu Beach County Park

Although the beach here is fine and it's very accessible, few tourists spend much time here; however, local families frequent this broad grassy park, and it's particularly loved by children because they can play Tom Sawyer on the banks of the heavily forested stream that forms a small lagoon just behind the shoreline. If you're lucky, you may see dolphins jumping and spinning at the opening of the bay. There are some picnic tables, run-down showers and toilets, a pavilion, and camping (with a county permit) under the ironwood trees that front the beach. At times, homeless people stake out semi-permanent camps here, so it may not be the best for camping or the safest place to leave gear unattended. In Hanama'ulu, turn *makai* (toward the sea) off Rt. 56 onto Hanama'ulu Road at the 7-Eleven store, take the right fork onto Hehi Road, and follow it down under the highway to the park. There is no access directly off the highway.

Nukoli'i Beach Park

Between Hanama'ulu and Lydgate Beach Parks is a long and low windswept coastal area that is partially developed and occupied by the Radisson Kaua'i Beach Resort and Wailua Municipal Golf Course. Running along this coast is Nukoli'i Beach, a narrow sand strip fronted almost immediately by a shore reef. Swimming is not encouraged as the shore and near shore areas are rocky, but snorkeling is fair on days when the trade winds are not too strong. Locals sometimes come here to shore fish. On the Hanama'ulu side of the Radisson, an access road leads to the mostly undeveloped park, but you will find a paved parking lot, toilets, and showers.

Food

Clearly marked along Rt. 56 in Hanama'ulu is the **Hanamaulu Restaurant Tea House and Sushi Bar** (3-4291 Kuhio Hwy., 808/245-2511, 10 A.M.–1 P.M. for lunch Tues.–Sat. and 4:30–8:30 P.M. for dinner Tues.–Sun.—sushi Tues.–Sat. only), where they must be doing something right—they've lasted in the same location for more than 70 years! The menu, which includes sushi, *yakiniku,* and a variety of full-meal Japanese and Chinese dishes, is priced right, with most plate lunches priced under $10 and full dinners $15–17. An Oriental Buffet is served Sunday evening only, 6:30–8:30 P.M. Ho Tai, the pudgy happy Buddha, greets you as you enter the main dining room, which has shiny parquet flooring and is partitioned by shoji screens and hanging plants. Through the back and part of the same restaurant is the sushi bar, and beyond that are the elevated tatami-floored rooms (with space for your feet to dangle down) made private by sliding screens that look over a fishpond and a lovely Japanese garden. The gardens behind and to the side of the restaurant are small and wonderful and well worth a stroll. This is a local favorite—authentic food at appropriate prices.

Next door at the Hanama'ulu Plaza is **Ara's Sakanaya** (808/245-1707, 9 A.M.–7 P.M. Mon.–Sat. and 9 A.M.–5 P.M. Sun.) a much-frequented takeout deli-restaurant that offers plate lunches until 1:30 P.M., Japanese *bento,* and fresh fish daily.

In the large green Hanama'ulu Trading Co. building (built 1908) on the highway is the **Big Wheel Donut Shop** (4–11 A.M.) for a quick sugar fix. Stop early as the sweets go fast. After you fill up on donuts, you can fill your car at the Shell gas station across the street.

Services

Clearly marked at the intersection of Kuhio Highway and Hanama'ulu Road is the Hanama'ulu Plaza, a small but practical shopping center featuring a laundry and deli. Neat, tidy, and one of the best on the island, **Plaza Laundry** (7:30 A.M.–8:30 P.M. Mon.–Sat., and until 4:30 P.M. Sun.) is a full-service laundry with wash, dry, and fold service for those who don't care to do their own.

The Hanama'ulu **post office** is located in the Hanama'ulu Trading Co. building.

SOUTH SHORE

The Kaumuali'i (Royal Oven) Highway (Rt. 50) steps west from Lihu'e, with the Ha'upu Ridge (Hoary Head Mountains) adding a dash of beauty to the south and Queen Victoria's Profile winking down from the heights. Inland is Kilohana Crater, and between it and the Ha'upu Ridge are now fallow cane fields. The road rises gently over the Knudsen Gap and you enter the Koloa District, which stretches to the east bank of the Hanapepe River. Soon, Maluhia (Peaceful) Road (Rt. 520) branches to the south through an open lei of fragrant eucalyptus trees lining the route to the old sugar town of Koloa and on to the much newer resort community of Po'ipu. Continuing west on the highway, coming in quick succession, are the small inland towns of 'Oma'o, Lawa'i, and Kalaheo, way stations on the road. Here-

abouts are the remains of the area's once vibrant sugar industry, wide acres of the area's new crop, coffee, an exquisite tropical botanical garden, beautiful white-sand beaches, and two of the island's most luxurious resort hotels. It's fair to say that most people head right to the beaches or zip through to other destinations to the west, but linger awhile, travel the back roads, and learn of the historical and cultural importance of this region, particularly as it relates to sugar.

PLANNING YOUR TIME

The South Shore is where most travelers head, particularly first-time visitors. Its major draw is sunny **Po'ipu** with its inviting beaches, convenient accommodations, and varied restaurants. And it's close. You can be out of the airport,

ROBERT NILSEN

HIGHLIGHTS

◖ **Tunnel of Trees:** This inspiring green canopy of Eucalyptus parallels the road, which slides gently down through Koloa to the coast at Po'ipu (page 73).

◖ **The Great Po'ipu Beaches:** This is what drew developers to the South Shore when it began to expand as a result of the influx of tourists. Each beach has its distinct character: Lawa'i for snorkeling, Brennecke for boogie boarding, and Po'ipu and Shipwreck beaches for swimming, family fun, and the occasional basking turtle. At the end of the road, Maha'ulepu Beach is still undeveloped and draws the more adventurous, including kiteboarders (page 79).

◖ **Spouting Horn:** As consistent as Old Faithful, Spouting Horn blows a spume of water into the air through a hole in the ceiling of a lava tube when waves push water into its mouth (page 83).

◖ **National Tropical Botanical Garden:** Visit a veritable treasure trove of tropical plants, many of them endangered or threatened, at the nexus of their research, propagation, and education. Two specialty gardens in Lawa'i are open for public tours (page 83).

◖ **Kukui O Lono Park:** Along with the adjoining golf course, this is a well-tended oasis of green, but as it occupies a hilltop, it affords perhaps the best, most expansive views along the south shore of the island (page 102).

SOUTH SHORE

LOOK FOR ◖ TO FIND RECOMMENDED SIGHTS, ACTIVITIES, DINING, AND LODGING.

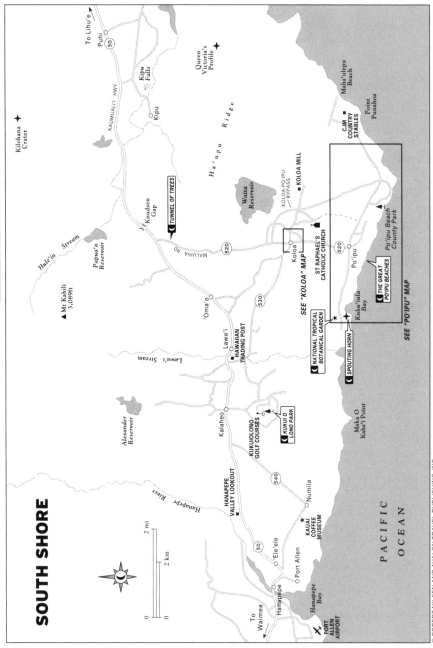

SOUTH SHORE

checked into your hotel, and on the beach in about an hour. But don't be in such a hurry: Relax, slip into island time, and begin to appreciate the beauty of the land around you, the smell of the flowers along the road, and the sight of the ocean that beckons.

On your way to Po'ipu, the **Tunnel of Trees** greets you as you turn off the highway and lets you know that you are starting your adventure. Stop at the old sugar plantation town of **Koloa** and spend a few minutes learning about how the sugar industry of Hawaii started right here and what a profound impact it had on the economy of the state. While sugar is now gone in these parts, Koloa retains its old-time charm and has hung on by transforming itself into a shopper's haven, with boutique after shop after gallery lined up along its one commercial street. Koloa is tiny, so you can spend as much or as little time as you want here, but it could occupy a real shopper for several hours with its clothing, gifts, and art.

Po'ipu itself is not a town per se but a stretch of developed coastline where most visitors find their vacation home and use it as a base from which to explore the island. Along this coast are a number of beaches, each with its own personality: Lawa'i Beach is best for snorkeling, Po'ipu Beach for families and picnics, and the beach at Maha'ulepu for great coastal scenes and its undeveloped environment. Spending time on the beach or around the hotel pool can be so relaxing, but get out and explore. Don't miss seeing the rushing spume of water at **Spouting Horn,** and be sure to spend several hours at the **National Tropical Botanical Garden** for an introduction to the gorgeous wonders of this, the Garden Island.

While not a major draw in and of itself, **Kukui O Lono Park** is a worthwhile stop on a trip to the West End. As it's set on a high hill in Kalaheo, the views over the Koloa/Po'ipu area, as well as those up and down the coast, are unsurpassed.

While you can do the accessible sights of the South Shore in a day, take your time and let the area's charm envelop you.

Koloa

The town of Koloa attracts a large number of tourists and packs them into a small area. On the site of what was the island's oldest sugar mill, Koloa has been transformed from a tumble-down sugar town to a thriving tourist community where shops, restaurants, and boutiques line its wooden sidewalks. Nearly all the old shops are remodeled plantation buildings. Dressed in red paint and trimmed with white, they are festooned with strings of lights as if decorated for a perpetual Christmas festivity. Most businesses line the town's main street, but others are found along Po'ipu Road as it heads down toward the coast. Traffic can be hectic with morning and evening mini-rush hours, and parking is always a problem. There are a few small parking lots, but you usually have to find a spot along the main drag or on one of the side streets—respect all signage.

In accord with its strong economic position, Koloa was the major population center on Kaua'i from 1835 to 1880. During this time, Koloa Landing in Po'ipu was reputedly one of the three most active whaling ports in Hawaii. Sugar and other agricultural products were shipped from the Koloa Landing, which was then one of the main ports of entry for the island. Sugar remained strong here throughout most of the last century, but the newest mill, the McBryde Sugar Co. Koloa Mill, shut down in 1996, a victim of the statewide declining sugar industry; its lifeless edifice can still be seen east of town on Maha'ulepu Road. Active cane fields in this area are now gone, replaced by limited cattle ranching, coffee, papaya, and corn production.

One of the old roads that ran from Koloa to Po'ipu was known as Hapa Road. Over

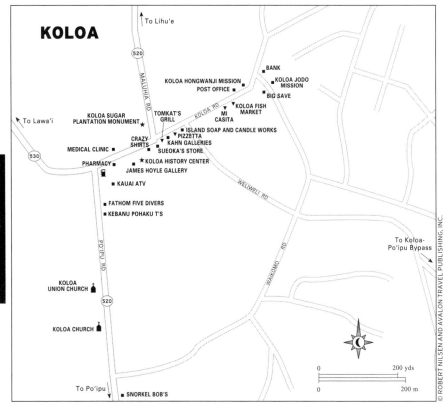

KOLOA

To Lihu'e

520

MALUHIA RD

To Lawa'i

KOLOA RD

530

PO'IPU RD

520

To Po'ipu

KOLOA HONGWANJI MISSION
POST OFFICE

BANK
KOLOA JODO MISSION
BIG SAVE

KOLOA FISH MARKET

KOLOA SUGAR PLANTATION MONUMENT

TOMKAT'S GRILL
MI CASITA

ISLAND SOAP AND CANDLE WORKS
PIZZETTA
KAHN GALLERIES

CRAZY SHIRTS
SUEOKA'S STORE

MEDICAL CLINIC

KOLOA HISTORY CENTER
PHARMACY
JAMES HOYLE GALLERY

KAUAI ATV

FATHOM FIVE DIVERS
KEBANU POHAKU T'S

WELIWELI RD

WAIKOMO RD

To Koloa-Po'ipu Bypass

KOLOA UNION CHURCH

KOLOA CHURCH

SNORKEL BOB'S

0   200 yds
0   200 m

© ROBERT NILSEN AND AVALON TRAVEL PUBLISHING, INC.

the years, it was abandoned in favor of newer routes to the coast. In response to the growing interest in the history and culture of the region, the one-mile-long Hapa Road, which now runs through overgrown and abandoned cane land from St. Raphael's Church in Koloa to the Kiahuna Swim and Tennis Club in Po'ipu, has been opened to foot and bicycle traffic. Along it are a few remnants of ancient Hawaiian habitation sites and the remains of a raised railway bed from the early sugar days.

To the east of Hapa Road, a continuation of Weliweli Road has been cut through the fields to become the **Koloa-Po'ipu Bypass,** a shortcut from just north of Koloa town to the eastern end of the Po'ipu strip, emerging near the Hyatt Regency Resort. This road eases traffic congestion in the center of Koloa as well as down Po'ipu Road and offers a second route to the burgeoning coastal community.

One meaning for *koloa* is "duck"; the area was probably so named because of the preponderance of ponds throughout the district that attract these water-loving fowl. In fact, before the development of the sugar industry, the Koloa District was known for its taro production, which employs flooded fields and necessitates much water. Today, numerous reservoirs dot the hillsides, including **Waita Reservoir** at the eastern edge of town, the largest manmade water catchment on the island and in the state.

A second meaning for *koloa* is "long sugarcane," and this seems appropriate because varieties of wild sugarcane grew throughout this area during the precontact times.

SIGHTS
◖ Tunnel of Trees

As you head down Maluhia Road, after turning off of Kaumuali'i Hwy., you immediately pass through a long stand of rough-bark *Eucalyptus robustus,* sometimes referred to as "swamp mahogany," and locally known as the Tunnel of Trees. Brought from Australia and planted by the Knudsen family, the largest landowner in this area, to help stabilize the then soggy road over the Knudsen Pass, they're well established, adding beauty, a heady fragrance, and shade to more than a mile of this country lane. Lining both sides of this road, these majestic trees form a leafy cathedral and let filtered light in through its canopy, creating a perfect spot for a photograph.

Koloa Sugar Plantation

Continue down Maluhia Road and just as you enter town, look to your right to see a weathered stone chimney standing alone in a little grassy field. Although of major historical significance, this unmarked edifice is what's left of the Koloa Sugar Plantation, established in 1835, site of the first successful attempt at refining sugar commercially in the Hawaiian Islands. On this corner lot a simple circle plot contains more than a dozen varieties of sugarcane, along with a plaque and sculpture dedicated to the sugar industry and its workers. While little remains here to see, it is important to understand the impact of what started here. Reading the plaque will give you an explanation of and appreciation for the sugar industry in Hawaii, the significance of the Koloa Sugar Plantation, and an understanding of the people who worked the fields. The bronze sculpture portrays individuals of the seven ethnic groups that provided the greatest manpower for the sugar plantations of Hawaii: Hawaiians, Chinese, Japanese, Portuguese, Puerto Ricans, Koreans, and Filipinos. (From the 1830s to about 1910, smaller numbers of Englishmen, Scots, Germans, Scandi-

ROBERT NILSEN

SOUTH SHORE

Tunnel of Trees

navians, Poles, Spaniards, African Americans, and Russians also arrived to work. All in all, about 300,000 immigrants came to Hawaii to make the sugar industry the success it has been.) Koloa is the birthplace of the Hawaiian sugar industry, the strongest economic force in the state for more than a century. More than anything else, it helped to shape the multiethnic mixture of Hawaii's population. To celebrate Hawaii's plantation life, the annual **Koloa Plantation Days Festival** takes place in late July in Koloa and the surrounding area.

Koloa History Center

While its name makes it sound more prestigious than it is, the tiny Koloa History Center does have a few small displays and pictorials. Located in a courtyard near the stream, once the site of a local hotel, it's a good place for an introduction to the historical significance of Koloa and the surrounding area. With picnic tables and a small garden, this courtyard is good for a midday rest. The courtyard, Waikomo Stream, the roadway, and nearby buildings are all shaded by the branches of a huge century-old monkeypod tree.

Koloa Churches

The tall steeple on the way to Po'ipu belongs to **Koloa Church,** locally known as the White Church. Its clapboard siding and colonial columns make it look like a transplant from New England. The congregation began in 1835, and this structure was built in 1859 and remodeled in 1929. For many years the steeple was an official landmark for many land surveys and was often used by sailors to direct their boats to shore. Next to it stands the black lava rock **Koloa Union Church,** with a heritage equally old. Across the street but close by is the **Koloa Missionary Church,** once the home of a missionary physician. Up in town near the post office and bank are the **Koloa Jodo Mission** and temple and the **Koloa Hongwanji Mission,** both founded in 1910 by Japanese immigrants to the plantation and with active congregations today. Built by Japanese woodworkers, the original Jodo temple remains but the Hongwanji temple building unfortunately burned in 1994, leaving only the mission house. If you take Weliweli Road out of town, then follow Hapa Road to the end of the pavement, you come to **St. Raphael's Catholic Church,** marking the spot where a Roman Catholic mission was first permitted in the islands, in 1841. The stone church itself dates from 1856, when it was built by Friar Robert Walsh. This is a quiet spot, and the church, with its expanded facilities, has obviously done well. The roof of the church can be seen sticking above the trees from Kiahuna Golf Club in Po'ipu and the Koloa-Po'ipu Bypass Road, both only a short distance away.

SHOPPING

In Koloa, shops and boutiques are strung along two roads in town like flowers on a lei. You can buy everything from original art to beach towels. There are shops selling jewelry, swimwear, casual clothing, gifts, and even a specialty shop for candles. Old Koloa Town packs a lot of shopping into a little area. Besides, it's fun just walking the raised sidewalks of what looks very much like an old Western town.

For casual clothing and beachwear, look for **Jungle Girl** (808/742-9649), **Progressive Expressions** (808/742-6041), and **Paradise Clothing** (808/742-1371). Much more interesting is **The Blue Orchid** (808/742-9094) at the upper end of town, a ladies' boutique selling dresses, alohawear, earrings, jewelry, and fresh-cut flowers. The owner hand-paints the dresses and T-shirts, all of which are made from cotton, rayon, or silk. Both **Christian Riso Fine Arts** (808/742-2555) and **Kahn Galleries** (808/742-2277) offer an exceptional collection of paintings and prints by some of the island's most prominent artists.

Just before the elevated walkway begins, you'll find **Hula Moon Gifts** (808/742-9298). The shelves at Hula Moon bear mostly arts and crafts made in Hawaii, with some of the gift items fashioned in Indonesia. Featured items include vests imprinted with a tapa design and antique print; lifelike Hawaiian dolls made from resin; tiles, platters, and red-dirt pottery; handmade (and numbered) ukulele; koa bowls; and less-expensive items like shark-teeth necklaces, barrettes, bracelets, mirror and comb sets, and koa bookmarks.

At the upper end of the raised walkway is **Island Soap and Candle Works** (808/742-1945, www.kauaisoap.com, 9 A.M.– 9 P.M. daily). You can't miss this shop as the strong aromas waft out of the store onto the sidewalk. It's a heady smell, and this is definitely not the place for those sensitive to fragrance. For others, head on in to an eye-popping variety of soaps, beeswax candles, lotions, gels, and oils. All handmade, these products are available at boutiques throughout Hawaii and can also be ordered by phone at 888/528-7627. A second store on Kaua'i is in Kilauea on the north shore.

Beyond the stream and the monkeypod tree on the west end of the strip is **Crazy Shirts** (808/742-7161) a Hawaiian firm selling some of the best T-shirts and islandwear available. Try **Emperors Emporium** (808/742-8377) for the usual postcards, cheap jewelry, outlet alohawear, and souvenirs, and **Koloa Country Store** (808/742-1255) for gifts. Around the corner near the Chevron gas station at **Da Life Outdoor Gear** (5330 Koloa Rd., 808/742-2925, 6:30 A.M.–6 P.M.), you can find a wide selection of quality hiking, camping, and outdoor activity products, as well as the booking counter for Kauai ATV tours.

In the courtyard near the Koloa History Center is the **James Hoyle Gallery** (808/742-1010). After years of maintaining a studio and gallery in Hanapepe, James Hoyle packed up and moved everything to Koloa in 2002, but he maintains his tradition of painting locally inspired subjects. Hoyle has been able to capture the spirit of Hawaii through fantastic color and movement. The sense that permeates all of Hoyle's work is that in Hawaii, humanity cannot conquer nature but must learn to live in harmony with the 'aina. Hoyle uses bright colors, strong brush strokes, and heavy gobs of pastels in a manner similar to masters like Van Gogh and Paul Gauguin. These fine works start from around $1,000. If you can't afford an original, perhaps a serigraph finished and embellished in vivid color by the artist might fit your pocketbook better.

Down Po'ipu Road beyond Fathom Five Divers is **Kebanu** (3440 Po'ipu Rd., 808/742-2727, 10 A.M.–7 P.M., until 6 P.M. Sun.) a gallery of modern art pieces and jewelry in wood, glass, stone, and pottery. Next door is **Pohaku T's** (3430 Po'ipu Rd., 808/742-7500, 10 A.M.–8:30 P.M., until 6 P.M. Sun.). More than a just a shop that sells T-shirts, Pohaku T's also assigns its prints to bring awareness to the area, enhance its cultural legacy, and help slow the development of the remainder of this coastline.

RECREATION
Snorkeling and Diving
Fathom Five Divers (3450 Po'ipu Rd., 808/742-6991 or 800/972-3078, www.fathomfive.com, 9 A.M.–6 P.M. daily), about 100 yards down from the Chevron station in Koloa, is a complete diving center offering lessons, certification, and rentals. Two-tank

boat dives for certified divers, including gear, are $100, shore dives $80. Introductory boat dives for the first-timer, including lesson and gear, are $140; a one-tank shore dive is $95. If the weather is right, either boat or shore dives at night are options. Certification courses take three to four days and run $395 with a small group or $495 for private instruction. Tank refills are also available. Boat dives go out of Kukui'ula Harbor near the Spouting Horn and shore dives at Koloa Landing. Fathom Five also does half-day snorkeling cruises and rents snorkel gear.

Snorkel Bob's (3236 Po'ipu Rd., 808/742-2206, http://snorkelbob.com, 8 A.M.–5 P.M. daily), farther along Po'ipu Road at the intersection of Waikomo Road, rents inexpensive snorkel gear that can be taken interisland. Snorkel Bob's has some of the best prices, equipment, and services on the island, including 24-hour a day rental return. Gear, which includes mask, snorkel tube, and fins, is rented for a 24-hour day or by the week. The snorkel set runs from $2.50 a day or $9 a week to $6.50 a day or $32 a week, depending on the quality. Prescription lenses, dry snorkels, rental boogie boards, flotation vests, and short wet suits are also available. This company also books various island activities, so you may get free or discounted equipment rental if you book here.

All-Terrain Vehicle Tours
Kauai ATV (5330 Koloa Rd., 808/742-2734 or 877/707-7088, www.kauaiatv.com), located in the Da Life Outdoor Gear shop next to the Chevron gas station in the center of town, runs four-wheel ATV tours through former cane land surrounding Koloa. These tours run several times a day on two different three- and four-hour routes, $99 and $145 per person. Riders must be 16 years old or older and no more than 350 pounds. For families with kids younger than 16, a ride on a 4WD passenger ATV will be the ticket. For safety reasons, no pregnant women or people with back injuries will be allowed to ride. Helmets, face shields, gloves, beverages, and instructions are

provided; long pants, a long-sleeve shirt, and closed-toe shoes are a must.

Fishing

For full- and half-day bass fishing excursions, mostly in the private reservoirs around Kalaheo and Koloa, but sometimes on the east side, contact **Cast & Catch** (808/332-9707). You'll take its 17-foot bass boat to one of Kaua'i's lovely freshwater reservoirs. All tackle, bait, and soft drinks are provided along with airport/hotel pick-up and delivery. Fares vary, but half-day trips run $150–300 for 1–3 persons, and full-day trips go for $250–350, three people maximum.

Also try **J.J.'s Big Bass Tours** (808/332-9219) with 1993 Big Bass Hawaii State Champion John Jardin. Tackle, license, refreshments, and hotel pick-up are included.

Tennis

Aside from its ball fields, Koloa Park has tennis courts that are open to the public, free, and lighted at night; they operate on a first-come, first-served basis.

FOOD

There are not many restaurants in town, but **❢ Pizzetta** (808/742-8881) is the best of the bunch and has established a fine reputation among locals. It's right in the center of town; its front tiled section with a counter window gives way to a wood-floor raised back portion and lanai. Pictures of Italian scenes line the walls, soft jazz fills the air, and a full-service bar mixes drinks—happy hour runs 3–6 P.M. Appetizers such as mozzarella sticks and stuffed mushrooms and a variety of salads start your meal. Pasta, calzone, and baked casserole dishes are tempting and reasonably priced for $8–16, but Pizzetta is best known for its pizza—handmade crust, homemade sauce—which can be ordered as a whole pie or by the slice until 6 P.M., eaten in or taken out. Standard or make-your-own pizzas run $12–22 or more depending on the number of toppings. Free delivery is available in the area.

From 11 A.M., lunch includes hot and cold sub sandwiches and panini.

An easygoing casual place that's a hit with the tourist crowd is **Tomkat's Grill** (808/724-8887). Enter via a hallway and proceed to the back, where seating is in two sections next to a small courtyard koi pond. The lunch menu is heavy on sandwiches and burgers, most under $8, and deep-fried *pu pu*. Other lunch items are a chef salad, half rotisserie chicken, and a teriyaki steak plate. The limited dinner specials, served after 5 P.M., include barbecued pork ribs, garlic seafood pasta, and fresh fish, most for under $20. A children's menu helps keep prices down. Order drinks from the bar or pick out a fresh pastry from the case. Takeout is available on all items.

Next door to the fish market is **Mi Casita** (808/742-2323, 5–9 P.M. Mon.–Sat.), the only place in town that serves a full assortment of Mexican dishes. Reasonably inexpensive for the large portions.

Adjacent to Sueoka's Store in downtown Koloa is a **plate-lunch window** that dishes out hearty, wholesome plate lunches and sandwiches 9 A.M.–3 P.M. Here it's difficult to spend more than $5 on any one item.

Lappert's Aloha Ice Cream (808/742-1272) along the boardwalk, dishes up creamy scoops of delicious Kaua'i-made ice cream. Connoisseurs of the dripping delight consider it among the best in the world. The ice-cream parlor doubles as an espresso bar, with pastries thrown in for good measure.

An alternative for fresh-brewed coffee is **Koloa Coffee Roasters,** tucked behind Kebanu Gallery and Pohaku T's shop, a few steps down Po'ipu Road.

Supermarkets

The newly remodeled **Big Save Supermarket** (7 A.M.–11 P.M. daily), located at the junction of Koloa and Waikomo roads, is a full-service grocery store with bakery and deli. **Sueoka's Store** (8 A.M.–9 P.M.), near the stream, is a family-owned, local grocery and produce market that's been around for decades. Both supermarkets carry everything you'll need for condo cooking.

MEAL MONEY-SAVERS

Only one thing is better than a great meal: a great meal at a reasonable price. The following are island institutions and favorites that will help you eat well and keep costs down.

KAUKAU WAGONS

These are lunch wagons, but instead of slick, stainless-steel jobs, most are old delivery trucks converted into portable kitchens. Some say they're remnants of World War II, when workers had to be fed on the job; others say that the meals they serve were inspired by the Japanese *bento,* a boxed lunch. These wagons park along beaches, in city parking lots, or on busy streets. Usually a line of local people will be placing their orders, especially at lunchtime – a tip-off that the wagons serve delicious, nutritious island dishes at reasonable prices. They might have a few tables, but basically they serve food to go. Kaukau wagons specialize in the "plate lunch."

PLATE LUNCH

One of the best island standards, these lunches give you a sampling of authentic island food that can include teriyaki chicken, mahimahi, *laulau,* and *lomi* salmon, among others. They're often served on paper or Styrofoam plates, are packed to go, and usually cost around $5. Standard with a plate lunch is "two-scoop rice" and a generous dollop of macaroni or other salad. Full meals, they're great for keeping food costs down and for instant picnics. Available everywhere, from *kaukau* wagons to restaurants.

BENTO

Bento are the Japanese rendition of the box lunch. Aesthetically arranged, they are full meals. They are often sold in supermar-kets and in some local eateries with takeout counters.

SAIMIN

Special "saimin shops" as well as restaurants serve this hearty, Japanese-inspired noodle soup. Saimin is a word unique to Hawaii. In Japan, these soups would be called *ramen* or *soba,* and it's as if the two were combined in "saimin." A large bowl of noodles in broth, topped with meat, chicken, fish, shrimp, or vegetables, costs only a few dollars and is big enough for an evening meal. The best place to eat saimin is in a local hole-in-the-wall shop run by a family.

EARLY BIRD SPECIALS

Even some of the island's best restaurants in the fanciest hotels offer early-bird specials – regular-menu dinners offered to diners who come in before the usual dinner hour, which is approximately 6 P.M. You pay as little as half the normal price and can dine in luxury on some of the best foods. The specials are often advertised in the free tourist books, which might also include coupons for two-for-one meals or limited dinners at much lower prices.

BUFFETS

Buffets are also quite common in Hawaii, and like lu'au are all-you-can-eat affairs. Offered at a variety of restaurants and hotels, they usually cost $12 and up, but will run $25-35 in the better hotels. The food ranges considerably from passable to quite good. At lunchtime, they're priced lower than at dinner, and breakfast buffets are cheaper yet. Buffets are always advertised in free tourist literature, which often include discount coupons.

Fish Market

At the upper end of town near the Big Save Supermarket is **Koloa Fish Market** (10 A.M.– 6 P.M. Mon.–Fri., until 5 P.M. Sat.) for the freshest whole fish and seafood in town, reasonably priced plate lunches, *pu pu,* and beer.

Farmers Market

Pick up fresh fruits and vegetables at the **Sunshine farmers market** held every Monday at noon at Koloa (Knudsen) Park. Depending on what's happening on the farms, you can get everything from coconuts to fresh-cut flowers while enjoying a truly local island experience.

SERVICES

The Koloa **post office** (5485 Koloa Rd.) is on Koloa Road across from the Big Save Supermarket. At the end of Koloa Road just beyond the post office is a branch of **First Hawaiian Bank** (3506 Waikomo Rd., 808/742-1642), the only bank in the Koloa–Po'ipu area. At the intersection of Koloa and Po'ipu Roads is a **Chevron gas station** (3480 Po'ipu Rd., 808/742-9350), the only one in town.

Koloa One Hour Photo (3450C Po'ipu Rd., 808/742-8918, 9 A.M.–5 P.M., 10 A.M.–2 P.M. Sun.), along Po'ipu Road near the Chevron gas station, offers camera needs, film, and print film processing.

The Kaua'i Medical Clinic's **Koloa Clinic** (808/742-1621 or 808/245-1831 after hours) offers medical services by appointment 8:30 A.M.–noon and 1:30–5 P.M. Mon.–Fri. and is located by the stream next to the Koloa Sugar Mill chimney. Located across from the clinic, the **Southshore Pharmacy** (5330 Koloa Rd., 808/742-7511, 9 A.M.–5 P.M. Mon.–Fri.) not only has a prescription service but also first-aid supplies and skin- and health-care products. The **Koloa Chiropractic Clinic** (3176 Po'ipu Rd., 808/742-9555) can also help with medical problems. (If these offices can't help, the Kauai Mortuary is right down the street.)

Po'ipu

Po'ipu Road continues south from Koloa for two miles until it reaches the coast. En route it passes a private cane road, and a bit farther it branches at a Y. Here, Lawa'i (Beach) Road turns right and hugs the coast past private homes, and a string of vacation rentals, terminating at the Spouting Horn and the entrance to the National Tropical Botanical Gardens. Po'ipu Road itself bends left past a string of condos and hotels, into what might be considered the town, except that nothing in particular makes it so. From Po'ipu Road, Kapili, Ho'owili, and Pe'e Roads lead to the beach. Ho'onani Road also runs along the water here, splitting from Lawa'i Road and crossing the Waikomo Stream just above Whaler's Cove. At the mouth of the stream you pass **Koloa Landing,** once the island's most important port. When whaling was king, dozens of ships anchored here to trade with the natives for provisions. Today nothing remains of the old wharf and storage buildings, but it is a favorite entry point for shore dives and a good place to watch for turtles in the morning and evening. Snorkeling and scuba diving are best to the sides of the bay, away from the sandy middle.

Po'ipu is the best established and most developed tourist area on Kaua'i, but it fields competition from developments in Kapa'a and Princeville. On the oceanfront in Po'ipu, luxury accommodations and fine restaurants front the beaches, the water beckons, and the surf is gentle most of the year. Behind this resort community on the east end are the low volcanic cones of Pu'u Hi, Pu'u Hunihuni, and Pu'u Wanawana, where the last volcanic eruptions occurred perhaps 15,000–20,000 years ago. A fourth such cone is now occupied by Po'ipu Crater Resort. To the west, beyond Prince Kuhio's birthplace, is the Spouting Horn, a plume of water that jets up through an opening in the volcanic rock shore with every incoming wave, and beyond that, the National Tropical Botanical Gardens. Whether you're exploring the sights, cultivating a tan on the beach, combing the shops for your gift list, or sampling island treats, Po'ipu will not fail to provide.

Hurricane 'Iniki pummeled Po'ipu like a boxer hitting a punching bag. In the aftermath, it took years for the devastated Po'ipu area to recover and rebuild. By the end of 1999, all hotel and condo properties were again up and running, except for the former Waiohai and Poipu Beach hotels. By 2003, the Waiohai had been torn down and the Marriott Waiohai Beach Club time-share property built in its place. Only slowly have other properties been developed here.

A paved **walking path** traces its way through the greenway amidst the gaggle of condos from Brennecke's Beach to the Hyatt property at the eastern end of Shipwreck Beach. This path is a convenient, safe, and quiet way to get between these two sections of Po'ipu, all while avoiding the traffic.

Although it continues to face some strident opposition by local activists and must meet strict county requirements, the largest new development planned in Po'ipu is for the Kukui'ula Bay area near Spouting Horn. Alexander and Baldwin plan a 200-room hotel fronting the lagoon basin, expansion of Kukui'ula Harbor facilities, greenways and bike paths, an 18-hole golf course, a shopping center, and over 3,000 condo units and residential lots that would stretch back to Po'ipu Road. To service this huge integrated development, a new road would have to be cut through former cane land to ease traffic on Lawa'i Road. While not directly fronting the water, this development will undoubtedly and dramatically change the face of Po'ipu, if and when it is completed.

SIGHTS
◖ The Great Po'ipu Beaches
Although given a lacing by Hurricane 'Iniki, **Po'ipu Beach County Park** has healed and is again Po'ipu's best-developed beach park,

ROBERT NILSEN

Po'ipu Beach

with its pavilion, picnic tables, showers, toilets, playground, walkways, and lifeguards on duty daily. There's plenty of parking along Ho'one Road or across the street. The swimming, snorkeling, and bodysurfing are great. Po'ipu Beach has something for just about everyone. A sheltered pool rimmed by lava boulders is gentle enough for any swimmer, and going just beyond it provides the more exciting wave action often used by local surfers. Follow the rocks out to Nukumoi Point, where there are a number of tidepools; snorkeling is best on the right side. Waves come in all sizes, and instructors use Po'ipu Beach for beginning surf lessons. The far eastern end of Po'ipu Beach is called **Brennecke Beach.** Popular with locals, it's one of the best spots on the island for boo-

gie boarding and bodysurfing. Following the shoreline around to the west is an additional crescent beach, one that fronts the Kiahuna Plantation Resort and Sheraton Kauai Resort. It slopes gently into the water and is sometimes the haunt of seals and turtles.

At the eastern end of the Hyatt an access road leads to **Shipwreck Beach;** at its parking lot is a pavilion with restrooms and showers. Shipwreck Beach is a half-mile strand of white sand on Keoneloa Bay. One of the only beneficiaries of Hurricanes 'Iwa and 'Iniki, the beach was broadened and widened with huge deposits of sand, making it bigger and better than ever. The swimming can be good, but, as always, use caution. The beach is perhaps best known for boogie boarding and bodysurfing, and these

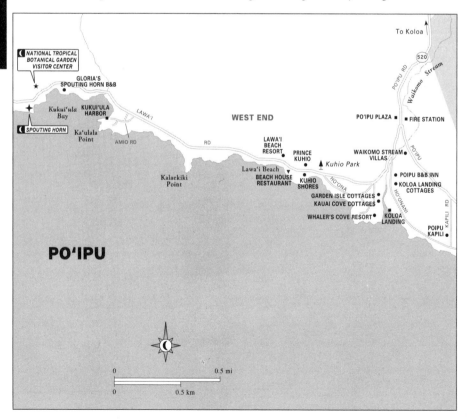

usually take place at the far eastern end near the sandstone bluff. It is below this bluff that a boat wreck lay for many years. Now only the heavy motor still lies here, exposed at times of heavy surf, the rest having been torn away by the last hurricane. Also near here, etched into the hardened sandstone and buried under beach sand most of the year, is one of the few petroglyph spots on the island. To see it, you have to be lucky enough to be there when the water pulls the sand away to expose these rock carvings. A pathway runs east from the beach along the bluff at the edge of the golf course, past several ancient historical sites, affording fantastic seascapes as you amble along.

Continue along Po'ipu Road—no longer paved—past the golf course and CJM Coun-try Stables. Take the right turn at the T intersection onto Maha'ulepu Road, another dirt road that runs down toward the water. Access to **Maha'ulepu Beach** is across private land. Be sure to note the time because this gate may be closed and locked 7 p.m.–7:30 a.m. The dirt access road leads down to a parking lot just behind the sand dunes; a rutted track to the left behind the dunes leads to two smaller parking spots. Maha'ulepu Beach is long. Its western extent is rather straight and exposed; near the stream at the west end is Makauwahi Sinkhole. At the eastern end it slips around into a nice protected cove, but there the beach is not as nice. Sand dunes back the beach through most of its length, and more are found inland and beyond the beach before the mountains

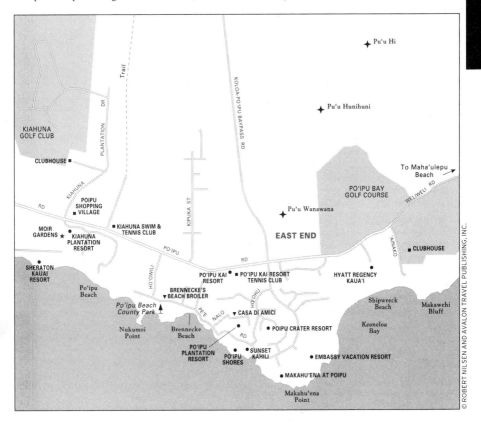

© ROBERT NILSEN AND AVALON TRAVEL PUBLISHING, INC.

begin. Numerous archaeological sites have been discovered in this general area, including remains of a *heiau,* and some charcoal deposits have been dated as some of the earliest man-made material on the island. There are even little-seen petroglyphs along the shore under sand that get exposed by strong wind and wave action only once every decade or so when the Kona storms are strong enough. Not many people frequent this beach—although George C. Scott came here to play Ernest Hemingway for the movie *Islands in the Stream*—but anglers come, and, when the waves are right, surfers. When the waves are not too big, swimming is good within the reef, which is also used by windsurfers and kiteboarders when the wind is sufficiently strong. No camping is allowed here and there are no facilities, but local people sometimes bivouac in the ironwoods at the east end. A trail along the lithified sandstone bluff runs past CJM Country Stables and the golf course to Shipwreck Beach, a distance of a mile or so. AOL founder Steve Case owns the Mahaʻulepu area, part of Grove Farm in Lihuʻe, where his father was the manager several decades ago. He has plans to develop this isolated beach area, but there is strong local sentiment to leave the land undeveloped. For more information on the preservation efforts for Mahaʻulepu, see www.malama-mahaulepu.org.

Just west of Kuhio Park, fronting Lawaʻi Beach Resort, is the narrow, roadside **Lawaʻi Beach,** also called Beach House Beach. Although the beach is not particularly good for swimming because of its rocky bottom and shoreline, these characteristics make it one of the best, and most family-safe, snorkeling spots in the area and a popular spot to put out the lounge chair and sunbathe. Enter at the sandy end near the Beach House Restaurant. Surfers and body boarders also come here for the breaks created by the reef. Back down the coast a few hundred yards, on the east side of Kuhio Park, is **Keiki Beach** (Baby Beach). Somewhat protected by the reef, with a narrow sand strip, this beach is secluded and used mostly for sunbathing.

Moir Gardens

Along Poʻipu Road, look for the driveway into the Kiahuna Plantation Resort on the right across from the Poʻipu Shopping Village. Wrapping around the resort reception area and restaurant is the site of this botanical garden. A second entrance is off Hoʻonani Road beyond the Sheraton property. These grounds, originally part of the old Koloa Sugar Company manager's estate, were a "cactus patch" started by Sandie Moir, wife of the manager, Hector Moir, back in 1938. Over the years, the gardens grew more and more lavish, with the inclusion of succulents, orchids, bromeliads, dry land trees, and several ponds, until they became a standard Poʻipu sight. Mrs. Moir was a horticulturist enamored of cacti. Whenever she went to the Mainland she collected these amazing plants, mainly from Texas and the Southwest, and transported them back to Hawaii to be planted in her cactus garden. However, before planting them she would invite a *ka-*

KOLOA HERITAGE TRAIL

As in other places in the islands, Koloa and Poʻipu have begun to pay more attention to the cultural and historical significance of their past and have made efforts to educate residents and visitors alike to the importance of the area. One of the results has been the establishment of the Koloa History Center in Koloa, which gives a brief historical sketch of the area. The Poʻipu resorts have also put effort into establishing cultural programs and hosting learning events. More recently, the *Koloa Heritage Trail* brochure has been created to direct you to 14 sites of significance in the Koloa/Poʻipu area, offering a map and description of each place of note, with numbered marker and description at each site. Pick up a brochure and follow along this 10-mile-long trail by car, bicycle, or on foot to learn more about this premier vacation area.

huna to bless the land and to pray for their acceptance. The cactus garden has flourished and by magic or mystery was the only thing in the entire area left relatively untouched when Hurricane 'Iniki swept away everything else in sight like a huge broom. The gardens are open free of charge to the public during daylight hours.

Kuhio Park

Turn onto Lawa'i Road to pass Kuhio Park, the birthplace of Prince Kuhio, Jonah Kalaniana'ole. Loved and respected, Prince Cupid—a nickname by which he was known—was Hawaii's delegate to Congress from the early 20th century until his death in 1922. In this capacity, he advocated for the rights of Hawaiians and fought for their respect. This "People's Prince" returned to the shores of his birth whenever his duties permitted. Containing a statue and monument, terraced lava walls, a *heiau,* palm trees, and the remains of a fishpond, this well-manicured acre faces the sea. Turtles often congregate off the rocks across the road.

Kukui'ula Bay

Farther west along Lawa'i Road and at the end of the short Amio Road, is Kukui'ula Bay. Before Hurricane 'Iwa and later 'Iniki pummeled this shoreline, the bay was an attractive beach park where many small boats anchored. The pier area has been put aright and is again functioning as before, and picnic tables, grills, and restrooms have been built. A handful of sailing, diving, and fishing companies leave from this harbor on their tours, shore fishermen come to try their luck, and scuba divers explore the coral reef offshore.

(Spouting Horn

In a moment, you arrive at the Spouting Horn. A large parking area has many stalls marked for tour buses; at the flea market here, you can pick up trinkets, jewelry, and souvenirs. Don't make the mistake of looking just at the Spouting Horn. Have "big eyes" and look around at the full sweep of this remarkable coastline.

ROBERT NILSEN

Spouting Horn

The Spouting Horn is a lava tube that extends into the sea, with its open mouth on the rocky shore. The inrushing wave action causes the spouting phenomenon through a hole in the cave roof, which can blow spumes up to 60 feet high, depending on surf conditions; it resembles the spouting of whales that winter along this coastline. They say it shot higher in the old days, but when the salt spray damaged the nearby cane fields, plantation owners supposedly had the opening made larger so the spray wouldn't carry as far. Photographers wishing to catch the Spouting Horn in action have an ally. Just before it shoots, a hole behind the spout makes a large belch—a second later, the spume flies. Be ready to click. For your safety, stay behind the guardrail.

(National Tropical Botanical Garden

The National Tropical Botanical Garden (NTBG) constitutes the only tropical plant research facility in the country. Its primary aims are to preserve, propagate, and dispense knowledge about tropical plants. This is

ROBERT NILSEN

on a tour at the National Tropical Botanical Garden

becoming increasingly important as large areas of the world's tropical forests are being destroyed, and Hawaiian native plants are now threatened or endangered at a rate far greater than anywhere else in the nation and most other places in the world. Chartered by Congress in 1964, this nonprofit botanical and horticultural research and educational organization is supported only by private contributions. The NTBG has three adjacent sections along the south shore of Kaua'i: the McBryde Gardens, the Allerton Gardens, and the recently restored and opened Allerton Estate and grounds. Aside from this location, the National Tropical Botanical Garden also maintains the Limahuli Gardens on the north coast of Kaua'i; the Kahanu Gardens at Hana, Maui, which contains Pi'ilanihale Heiau, the largest *heiau* in the islands; and The Kampong in Coconut Grove, Florida.

Currently, the 259-acre **McBryde Gardens'** living collection has more than 6,000 species of tropical plants, and many additional plants are added to the collection

each year. The staggering variety flourishing here ranges from common bamboo to romantic orchids. The gardens are separated into individual sections that include plants of nutritional and medicinal value, herbs and spices, and rare and endangered species in need of conservation; other groups include plants of special ethno-botanical interest, plants of unexploited potential, tropical fruits, and ornamentals.

Adjoining these gardens is 80-acre **Allerton Gardens,** started by John Allerton, a member of the Mainland cattle-raising family that founded the First National Bank of Chicago. This garden dates from the 1870s, when Queen Emma made the first plantings here at one of her summer vacation homes. In 1938, Robert Allerton bought this property, and for 20 years, he and adopted son John, helped by a host of gardeners, cleared the jungle and planted. John scoured the islands of the South Pacific to bring back their living treasures, and oftentimes, old *kama'aina* families would send cuttings of their rarest plants to be included in the collection. The Lawa'i River runs through the property, and pools, statuary, and garden "rooms" help set the mood. On the far side of the river is the restored Allerton Estate and its surrounding gardens.

These gardens are so enchanting that many visitors regard them as one of the real treats of their trip. The **visitors center** (4425 Lawa'i Rd., 808/742-2623, tours@ntbg.org, www.ntbg.org, 8:30 A.M.–5 P.M. daily), with its interpretive displays and small gift shop, is a restored plantation manager's house across from the Spouting Horn. Particularly nice are its selection of Ni'ihau shell lei, fine quilts, and books on Hawaii. This center opened in 1997, following the total destruction of the former visitors center by Hurricane 'Iniki. Feel free to take a self-guided walking tour of the demonstration gardens surrounding the center, which hold a variety of plants that might have been common around a plantation house during the sugar era. Trams run into the McBryde Gardens daily 9:30 A.M.–

2:30 P.M. every half hour for self-guided walking tours; no reservations, $15. Guided tours of the Allerton Gardens are given at 9 A.M., 10 A.M., 1 P.M., and 2 P.M. Mon.–Sat., and each is led by knowledgeable horticultural staff or a Na Lima Kokua (Helping Hands) volunteer. Reservations are a must and should be made four to five days in advance—longer during the Christmas and Thanksgiving seasons. The guided tours last about two and a half hours and cost $30—*kama'aina* rates are available. Wear good walking shoes, carry an umbrella if it looks like showers, and bring mosquito repellent! All tours leave from the visitors center. Annual membership is also an option, and this entitles you to many benefits not given casual visitors—write to the Donor Relations office at 3530 Papalina Rd., Kalaheo, HI 96741.

ENTERTAINMENT
Lounges and Music

If, after a sunset dinner and a lovely stroll along the beach, you find yourself with dancing feet or a desire to hear the strains of your favorite tunes, Po'ipu won't let you down. Several hotel restaurants and lounges in the area feature piano music or small combos, often with a Hawaiian flair.

The Point lounge (808/742-1661, 11 A.M.–midnight) at the Sheraton gives you a ringside seat for sunset and perhaps the best coastal view in Po'ipu. This lounge is open for drinks, cocktails, and *pu pu* and offers a free nightly hula show on the terrace at 5 P.M. Light meals of soups, salads, and sandwiches are served throughout the day. The Point follows sunset with the soft sounds of light contemporary music late into the evening, Thursday–Saturday.

For live jazz nightly from 8 P.M. try **Stevenson's Library** at the Hyatt. This is the poshest lounge on the island—resortwear requested—and it has a full range of excellent exotic drinks. With dark wood decor, a fancy bar, a saltwater aquarium, overstuffed chairs, pool and billiard tables, a grand piano, major world newspapers, and ornate

chess sets waiting for the first move, this is a wonderful spot for evening relaxation. Friday, Saturday, and Sunday evenings 6–9 P.M. are special sushi and martini nights. Be aware that smoking cigarettes and cigars in this lounge is OK.

Free Hawaiian music and hula are presented nightly starting around sundown at the Hyatt's **Seaview Terrace,** and this show is accompanied by a torch-lighting ceremony on Tuesday, Friday, and Saturday. Come for *pu pu* and cocktails and enjoy the captivating entertainment.

Keoki's, in the Po'ipu Shopping Village, gently sways with contemporary Hawaiian music Friday and Saturday evenings. Come for dinner or a quiet beer and *pu pu,* and let your cares drift away. The small dance floor is popular with those from the area.

Joe's on the Green at the Kiahuna Golf clubhouse accompanies its Wednesday and Thursday evening meals with live Hawaiian music.

The Po'ipu Shopping Village offers a free live **Polynesian shows** every Tuesday and Thursday at 5 P.M. in the center's outdoor courtyard.

Lu'au

Every Thursday and Sunday evening 6–8:30 P.M., the **Drums of Paradise Lu'au** (808/240-6456, adult $65, $50 for ages 13–20, while children 6–12 years old get in for half the adult price) is presented at the Ilima Garden at the Hyatt Regency. A full buffet dinner includes the usual complement of Hawaiian and Pacific foods, and the meal is followed by an enthusiastic and high-energy Polynesian show of music, hula, and a fire knife dance.

The Sheraton presents **Surf to Sunset Lu'au** (800/742-8200, $68 adults and $34 for children 6–12 years old) on Mondays and Fridays on the lawn only a few steps from the sand. Aside from the huge buffet and rousing Polynesian show, craftspeople display their wares and a short demonstration of tropical fashion is performed.

SHOPPING

Shopping in Po'ipu is varied and reasonably extensive for such a small area. The Po'ipu Shopping Village has the largest concentration of shops, but don't forget Po'ipu Plaza, the hotel arcades, and the Spouting Horn flea market.

Po'ipu Shopping Village

The Po'ipu Shopping Village offers unique one-stop shopping, and most shops are open 9 A.M.–9 P.M. daily. **Wyland Galleries** features some of the island's best painters and sculptors. **Hale Mana** handles Asian antiques, gifts, and imports. **The Black Pearl Collection** sells pearls and jewelry, and **Xan** does high-end designer jewelry. **Sand Kids** features distinctive children's wear, while half a dozen shops cater to adults. **Overboard** has casual to elegant alohawear, while two other shops carrying island clothing are **Crazy Shirts** and **Holualoa Surf Company. Bamboo Lace** offers dresses, blouses, hats, jewelry, and a smattering of alohawear. It's owned and operated by Nadine, who handpicks fashionable clothing from the continent. Shelves also hold bath and skin-care products, gift items, lingerie, fancy shoes, and straw hats. For general merchandise items, stop at the **Whalers General Store.** Parking can be a problem in the evening for dinner patrons because of limited space, so walk, go early, or take advantage of the free valet parking offered by several of the fancier restaurants.

Water Gear

Located right across from Brennecke Beach, **Nukumoi Surf Co.** (808/742-8019, 8:30 A.M.–7 P.M. daily) is the most convenient rental shop to the water. Not only does this shop arrange surf lessons, it rents surfboards and an assortment of other water and beach equipment. Boogie boards or snorkel gear go for $5 a day or $15 a week. Aside from its rentals, Nukumoi also is a full retail shop with an array of water equipment, sunglasses, and clothing for sale.

Additional water gear and other sports supplies and clothing can be found at **Seasport Divers** (808/742-9303) and Outfitters Kauai (808/742-9667), both located in the Poip'u Plaza center.

Photo Needs

Poipu One Hour Photo (808/742-9303), inside the Seasport Divers shop at the Po'ipu Plaza, does film developing.

SPORTS AND RECREATION

Golf

Designed by Robert Trent Jones Jr., the **Kiahuna Golf Club** (808/742-9595) is an 18-hole, par-70 course undulating over land just up the road from Po'ipu Shopping Village, that preserves several archaeological sites within its acreage. The course is open for play 7 A.M. until sunset; the pro shop hours are 6:30 A.M.–6:30 P.M., and a restaurant is available throughout the day. Greens fees run $50 for 9 holes and $90 for a full 18 holes; midday, twilight, hotel guest, resident, junior, and package rates are also available. Lessons can be arranged.

The Poipu Bay Golf Course (808/742-8711 or 800/858-6300), the site of the PGA Grand Slam of Golf since 1994, is a par-72 Scottish links-style course also designed by Robert Trent Jones Jr. and opened in 1991. With its fairways rolling along the oceanside cliffs with the mountains as backdrop, it's noted for stunning views and is described as the Pebble Beach of the Pacific. Seven of the 18 holes have water hazards, making for challenging play. For practice, try the driving range, putting greens, and practice bunker. The excellent pro shop is open 6:30 A.M.–6 P.M.; call for tee times or for use of the driving range. At the clubhouse, the Poipu Bay Grill and Bar serves breakfasts and light lunches until 2:30 P.M. and drinks until 5 P.M. Fees run $185, $120 after noon, and $65 for twilight; reduced fees for Hyatt Regency guests. Lessons, club rental, and the practice range are extra.

Tennis

Several hotels and condominiums in the Po'ipu area have tennis courts for their guests, but three are open to anyone. The largest is the **Kiahuna Swim and Tennis Club** (808/742-

ROBERT NILSEN

You, too, can pretend that you're Tiger Woods as you play a round of golf at Poipu Bay Golf Course.

9533, 8 A.M.–6 P.M. daily), just east of the Po'ipu Shopping Village and across the street from the Kiahuna Plantation Resort. Kiahuna has 10 plexipave courts, a pro shop, rental equipment, and swimming pool. Court fees are $10, ball machine rentals are $20 an hour, a basket of balls is $10, and rackets are $5 a session. Clinics are available for $10–12, and it's $50 for a one-hour private lesson. Call for court times and inquiries about clinics, round robins, and lessons.

The second well-equipped tennis facility is the **Po'ipu Kai Tennis Club** (808/742-8706, 7 A.M.–6 P.M. daily) with six Laykold hard courts and two synthetic grass courts. While it's $5 for resort guests, there is a $10 a day charge for others. Although it's more relaxed here than at the Kiahuna Tennis Club, proper attire is required, and you should leave the court ready for those who follow you. Round robins and clinics are held throughout the week for $10, and private lessons can be arranged for $40 an hour. Rackets and ball machines can be rented.

The Hyatt Regency **Tennis Garden** (808/249-6391, 8 A.M.–noon and 2–6 P.M.) has four hard courts. Court fees are $20 an hour, rackets can be borrowed, and a ball machine costs $15 an hour. Morning clinics are scheduled for $20 (minimum of three), and private lessons can be arranged for $75 an hour.

Biking, Kayaking, and Zipline

Outfitters Kauai (2827-A Po'ipu Rd., 808/742-9667 or 888/742-9887, www.outfitterskauai.com, 9 A.M.–5 P.M. daily), located in the Po'ipu Plaza, is an ecology-minded sports shop specializing in kayaking and biking tours and rentals that also sells sports clothing. These guys have lots of information and will do their best to match your interests with appropriate tours or rentals. Daily rental rates for bicycles are $20 for a cruiser or children's bike, $30 for a road bike, and $30–45 for a mountain bike. Multi-day discounts are available, and all bike rentals come with a helmet, lock, and map. Outfitters Kauai organizes a Bicycle Downhill bike ride that brings you up the Waimea Canyon so you can glide for 13 miles down to the coast for $90 adults, $70 kids. Rental kayaks at $40 a day for a tandem kayak and various

scuba divers

guided kayak tours are also available. Half-day guided kayak tour and waterfall hikes on the Hule'ia River in Lihu'e and Wailua River on the East side run $90–94 adult, $70–75 children. Full- and half-day hike and **zipline** tours run on the Hule'ia River, the full-day tour includes a kayak paddle up the river, for $94–145 adult and $75–105 for kids. A seven-hour South Shore Sea Kayak Tour that runs from Kukui'ula Harbor to Port Allen from mid-September through Mid-May only is $129 adults, $104 kids, and a full-day summertime-only Na Pali Coast Kayak Tour for $185, that runs the whole length of the coast from Ha'ena to Polihale, are other options for those in good physical condition. Some age restrictions apply. This company knows the water and knows how to treat its guests.

Scuba and Snorkeling
Seasport Divers (2827 Po'ipu Rd., 808/742-9303 or 800/685-5889, www.kauaiscuba diving.com), at Po'ipu Plaza, is a full-service snorkel/scuba/surf shop. Rentals include snorkel masks, fins, and snorkels at $8 per day, $25

per week, and surfboard rentals for $20 and up per day depending on quality. Two-tank introductory boat or shore dives run $140 and $130, and a one-tank shore dive is $105. Morning and afternoon boat dives for certified divers run $110 each with gear at $10–20, and dive sites will be determined by the weather and water conditions. On calm days only, a full-day three-tank dive goes to Lehua Rock and the channel between there and Ni'ihau for $260. A three-day certification course for small groups goes for $400. Seasport Divers is a reputable company that gets the thumbs-up from locals. It's also a sports boutique with boogie boards, surfboards, and all sorts of water equipment, and the shop also has a clothing section and a one-hour photo finisher.

You don't need all the scuba gear to enjoy the pretty fish on the reef. Numerous locations along the South Shore are just right for snorkeling. While you can easily put on your mask and fins and head to the water yourself, **Kauai Snorkel Tours** (808/742-7576 or 866/742-7283, www.kauaisnorkeltours.net) can take you and a small group to one of two great beaches in Po'ipu or Lawa'i and guide you for a fun-filled morning or afternoon of looking at the colorful down under. Running $57.60 per person, each 1.5-hour tour comes with snorkel and safety instructions and an underwater camera so you can take pictures home with you.

Specializing in boat-based snorkel tours, **Kauai Zodiac Tourz** (808/742-7422 or 888/998-6879, www.ztourz.com), launches its rigid-hull Zodiac raft from Kukui'ula Harbor for trips to Kipu Kai, Lawa'i Kai, or other appropriate spots along the South coast. The cost is $94 adult and $84 for children for a three-hour tour, and all needed gear and a snack are provided. On these tours, you not only get an up-close experience with fish, turtles, and other sea creatures, you also get an education about sea life and the marine environment.

Snuba
Snuba is more than snorkeling, less than scuba. You have a regulator, weight belt, mask, and

flippers, and you're tethered to scuba tanks that float above you on a sea-sled. Depth is limited to 20 feet, but the fun isn't limited at all. Snuba frees you from being encumbered by tanks and all the scuba apparatus. If you would like to start diving, this is a wonderful and easy way to get a feel for it. **Snuba Tours of Kauai** (808/823-8912, www.snubakauai.com) offers guided tours Mon.–Sat. off Lawaʻi Beach at the cost of $65 for 90 minutes with a small group.

Surfing

World surfing champion Margo Oberg or one the staff members of **Margo Oberg's Surfing School** (808/332-6100 or 808/652-9085, www.surfonkauai.com) will teach you how to mount a board and ride gracefully over the shimmering sea. Beginning classes of two hours of instruction and practice at Poʻipu Beach run $50 per person for small group lessons and $100 for a private lesson. Margo's been teaching since 1977 and she and her beach boys know how to teach their skills to you.

Garden Island Surf School (808/652-4841, www.gardenislandsurfschool.com), **Aloha Surf Lessons** (808/639-8614) with Chava Greenlee, and **Nukumoi Surf Co.** (808/742-8019, www.nukumoi.com) also offer lessons at Poʻipu Beach for roughly the same fees as Margo Oberg.

Sailing

While Captain Andy offers other trips along the Na Pali Coast, he and the crew of **Capt. Andy's Sailing Adventures** (808/335-6833 or 800/535-0830, www.sailing-hawaii.com) let the sails unfurl on their sleek motorized catamaran and cruise the South shore for a sunset sail every Sunday. This two-hour trip leaves from Kukuiʻula Harbor near Poʻipu and runs $59 per person, including cocktails, *pu pu,* and soft Hawaiian music. Whale-watching tours along the south coast are available in season. Kids always get discounts.

Horseback Riding

CJM Country Stables (808/742-6096, www.cjmstables.com) is the only outfit offering horseback rides in the Poʻipu area and all three of its rides are along or near the shore at Mahaʻulepu. The two-hour, easy beach ride leaves at 9:30 A.M. and 2 P.M. daily except Sunday and costs $90. Departing at 8:30 A.M. on Tuesday, Thursday, and Saturday, the beach breakfast ride takes you to a secluded beach girdled by high mountains where you relax while breakfast is prepared for you; it costs $105 and runs three hours. A longer beach, swim, and picnic ride can be arranged for groups of six or more for $115 per person. CJM is about 1.5 miles past the Hyatt Regency on the dusty and potholed section of Poʻipu Road.

The annual Koloa Plantation Day Rodeo, the only state-sanctioned rodeo on the island, is held at the stables and features bull riding, roping, and barrel racing.

Guided Hikes

Every other Monday at 9 A.M., the Hyatt Regency offers a free one-hour informational guided hike along the coastal bluffs and dunes toward Mahaʻulepu Beach. The Anara Spa, also at the Hyatt, sponsors a "sunrise walk" every morning at 7 A.M.

Spa

In its own facility at the Hyatt Regency is the distinctive green tile roof of the horseshoe-shaped **Anara Spa** (808/240-6440, www.anaraspa.com, 6 A.M.–8 P.M. daily). This spa offers total immersion into health and fitness, massages, body treatments, and general pampering of aching muscles and jangled nerves. The treatment rooms offer ancient Hawaiian and modern remedies for energy and rejuvenation. All rooms are indoor/outdoor, with mini-gardens and the serenade of falling waters to help relax and soothe. Various massages, facials, body treatments, and aromatherapies can be booked individually or as packages, and the salon offers hair, makeup, nail, and waxing services. The Anara Spa also offers a 25-meter lap pool, aerobics room, complete training equipment, fitness assessment, personal training, and a morning walk along the beach or sand bluffs near the golf course. After a serious workout, relax at the spa's poolside Kupono Cafe for a health-conscious, low-calorie meal.

ACCOMMODATIONS

Most of Po'ipu's available rooms are in medium- to high-priced condos; however, options include a multitude of vacation rental houses and cottages, several bed-and-breakfasts, and two first-class hotels. In the description below, the "east end" refers to properties including and east of Poipu Kapili, an area encompassing nearly all the larger establishments, and the "west end," west of Poipu Kapili, which has many of the bed-and-breakfasts and vacation rentals.

$250 and Up

Royal palms line the grand boulevard that ends at the elegant porte cochere where towering panes of glass open to a roiling sea frothing against periwinkle sky at the **(Hyatt Regency Kauai Resort and Spa** (1571 Po'ipu Rd., 808/742-1234 or 800/554-9288, www.kauai-hyatt.com). The Hyatt is a grand hotel in grand dimension that bespeaks the luxury of 1920s and 1930s Hawaii. This magnificent, 602-room hotel, deceptive in size, is architecturally designed so that its four floors rise no taller than the surrounding palms. Through the entry are the main reception and concierge desks, and to the sides in both directions are the numerous resort shops. To one side of the inner courtyard is Stevenson Library, one of the Hyatt's bars and some claim the best hotel lounge in the state. The main courtyard opens onto a terrace that overlooks the oceanside grounds of the hotel. Walking paths scented by tropical blooms lead through acres of pools, both fresh and saltwater, featuring slides, a rivulet flowing through a "gorge," and the watery massaging fingers of cascading waterfalls and bubbling whirlpools. Through the heart of the hotel, greenery and flowers, both wild and tamed, compose a living lei of floral beauty. Lustrous koa tables bear flowers ablaze with color. Artworks, tapa wall hangings, and birdcages filled with flitting plumage and trilling songs line the hallways, while the interplay of marble floors and rich carpets is counterpointed by weathered bronze.

Heavy mahogany doors open into large guest rooms, all done in soothing pastels with white on tan textured wallpaper. Each room features a full entertainment center with sitting area, private lanai with outdoor furniture, a mini-bar, double closets, and spacious bathrooms. Mahogany furniture, overstuffed chairs and footstools, and Chinese-style lamps ensure tasteful relaxation, and Hawaiian quilts cover the beds. Rates range from $455 for a garden view to $685 for a deluxe oceanfront room, $785 for a Regency Club room, and $1,300 to $4,800 for suites. In addition, a $15 per day resort fee is added to all bills.

The five restaurants at the Hyatt range from casual to elegant, and five lounges offer libations in poolside to formal settings; additionally, there is the Poipu Bay Grill and Bar next door at the golf course clubhouse. Myriad cultural activities are scheduled throughout the week, and of great interest is the nightly Hawaiian music program accompanied by a torchlighting ceremony and/or a *keiki* hula show. Drums of Paradise lu'au is held every Thursday and Sunday in the lower courtyard, and the on-property Anara Spa is perfect for those seeking a rejuvenating health retreat. For basic office services and Internet access, visit the hotel Business Center. Camp Hyatt keeps the kids busy while parents are off doing other things, and the hotel's tennis courts and adjacent golf links are for those who desire physical activity.

The **Sheraton Kauai Resort** (2440 Ho'onani Rd., 808/742-1661 or 800/782-9488, www.sheraton-kauai.com) reopened in 1997, the last of the major hotels on Kaua'i to do so after the devastating effects of Hurricane 'Iniki. Sheraton's two former properties were combined into a 413-room resort with ocean, beach, and garden wings, on 20 lovely acres. Casually elegant and elegantly modern, the Sheraton Kauai Resort is a tasteful, eminently comfortable accommodation, no taller than the coconut trees on the property, where

ROBERT NILSEN

Daily entertainment at the Sheraton Kauai Resort brings Hawaiian music and hula.

the tropics surround you and pretense is left at the door.

The porte cochere opens onto the open-air reception area. Check in and inquire about hotel events and cultural activities or book off-site activities at the concierge or activities desks. Notice the lovely mural of a Hawaiian family gracing the lobby. Around the court-yard beyond, look for the news library; re-tail shops for resortwear, sundries, fine art, and jewelry; a fitness center; beauty salon and massage center; and the hotel's main res-taurant and lounge. The Shells restaurant is known for its breakfasts and seafood buffet dinners, and for the perfect sunset spot, find a seat at The Point lounge. In a quiet corner at the back of the Shells, the Naniwa restaurant offers tastes of Japan, and at the other end of the large dining room is the newest addition, the Amore Ristorante Italiano. Lighter fare is served throughout the day at the Oasis Bar and Grill by the oceanside pool. The property holds two swimming pools, one in the garden, surrounded by waterfalls, and the other, just off the beach, boasting a hot tub and short

water slide. The beach activities center offers rental of water equipment, and the tennis courts are open to guests only 7 A.M.–10 P.M. Kids 5–12 years old can have great fun in su-pervised play through the Keiki Aloha Club. A complimentary on-demand shuttle operates 10 A.M.–10 P.M. within a three-mile radius.

Each spacious room is appointed with ame-nities for your comfort, including air-condi-tioning, entertainment center, refrigerator, personal safe, and private lanai. Room rates range from $335 for a garden view to $625 for an ocean luxury room; suites run $675–2,800. There is no charge for children under 17 stay-ing in the same room as parents and using only the beds in the room. Numerous packages are available. In addition to the room rate, there is a daily $15 per room resort activities fee. Guests at this resort can also use the facilities at the Princeville Hotel on the north shore and charge all expenses to their rooms.

East Shore Condos

Although the prices in Po'ipu can be a bit higher than elsewhere on Kaua'i, you get a lot for your money. More than a dozen well-appointed modern condos are lined up along the shore or just off it, with thousands of units available. Most are a variation on the same theme: comfortably furnished, fully equipped, with a tennis court here and there, nearly always a swimming pool, and maid service available. Most require a minimum stay of at least two nights, with discounts for longer visits. The following condos have been chosen to give you a general idea of what to expect. They are listed east to west.

Embassy Vacation Resort Poipu Point (1613 Peʻe Rd., 808/742-1888 or 800/845-7661, www.embassykauai.com) is a marriage of luxury condo and time-share units that sit on 23 manicured, oceanfront cliff acres. The Embassy is grand in scope but not pretentious. Upon arrival, you enter through a white porte cochere to the main lobby with its guest reception and concierge desk, which opens to the cascading pools and falls of the gardens below. The 10 neoclassic plantation-style buildings surround a central courtyard where you will discover, fronting a sandy beach, a large pool with one side tiled and the other sand-bottomed. At poolside is a hydrospa and, nearby, a complete fitness center. Mornings bring a complimentary healthy breakfast in an outdoor dining area near the pool. Here and there throughout the property you'll find little picnic nooks complete with tables and barbecue grills for your enjoyment. Notice a thick grove of ironwoods completely surrounded by a hedge; these protect the site of an ancient *heiau* that the resort is dedicated to preserving. Just below the pool area lies a stretch of dramatic coastline pounded by heavy wave action, frothing misty azure against the coalblack lava. These waters are too treacherous for recreational swimming, but a two-minute walk takes you to Shipwreck Beach. The one- and two-bedroom units, air-conditioned with ceiling fans throughout, feature full kitchens with marble-topped counters and all amenities and a dining/living room that opens to a wraparound lanai. Each unit has its own washer and dryer, along with steam iron and ironing board. Room charges range $384–538 for one-bedroom units and $425–641 for two-bedroom suites; package rates are available.

Makahuʻena at Poipu (1661 Peʻe Rd., 808/742-2482 or 800/367-5004, www.castleresorts.com/MKH) sits on Makahuʻena Point, with the crashing waves below. Managed by Castle Resorts, this complex offers one-, two-, and three-bedroom units with full kitchens, and a swimming pool and tennis courts are on the property for guests to use. Rates run $225–450 during regular season, $20–50 less during low season.

Poipu Crater Resort snuggles inside a small seaside caldera off Hoʻohu Rd. between Poʻipu and Shipwreck beaches. The Polynesian-inspired buildings are surrounded by greenery, and the property includes a swimming pool and tennis courts. Units here are available through Suite Paradise, Grantham, Poipu Connection, and R&R Realty (see *Vacation Rental Agencies*).

An older property with reasonable rates, **Sunset Kahili** (808/742-7434, www.sunsetkahili.com), sits high on the hill overlooking the east end of Poʻipu Beach. Call direct or go through R&R Realty (see below).

You can't get closer to the water than at the small oceanfront condo complex **Poipu Shores** (1775 Peʻe Rd., 808/742-7700 or 800/367-5004, www.castleresorts.com/psc), set along the rocky shoreline, surrounded by other small condos. All 24 units face the ocean, and the property offers a swimming pool and barbecue grills. The area's best beaches are only a short stroll away. Each unit has a complete kitchen, and all are clean, spacious, and airy. The one-bedroom units run $250–295, a standard two-bedroom is $325–375, a deluxe two-bedroom is $350–395, and a three-bedroom unit runs $395–450. There is a three-night minimum stay. Maid service is provided free every day. Poipu Shores is a Castle Resorts and Hotels property and one of the best for location and amenities along this section of the coast in Poʻipu.

With 110 acres, **Poʻipu Kai Resort** has the largest grounds in the area—one corner of which runs down to the ocean. Through this finely landscaped property, a walking path connects Brennecke Beach with Shipwreck Beach. Set among broad gardens, most units look out onto a swimming pool or the tennis courts. There are one-, two-, three-, and four-bedroom units, in numerous floor plans. Some are Hawaiian in theme; others are Spanish, with stucco and arched entryways; modern units show more glass and chrome; and a few may resemble your own Mainland abode. A handful of multi-bedroom homes are also available in the adjacent housing estate. Facilities on the grounds include tennis courts, six swimming pools, two outdoor hot tubs, numerous barbecue grills, and an activity center. Next to the resort office is the Poipu Beach Broiler, a casual restaurant and bar open for lunch and dinner. A complex structure of room rates exists, depending upon the season and length of stay, but generally the one-bedrooms run $133–370 during regular season, two-bedroom units $205–416, three-bedroom units $275–310, and four-bedrooms units $428. For larger groups, a number of five-bedroom units are also available. While a number of agencies handle rooms at the Po'ipu Kai, Suite Paradise does the most business and also manages units in half a dozen other condo properties in the Po'ipu area. For reservations, contact Suite Paradise (1941 Po'ipu Rd., Po'ipu-Koloa, HI 96756, 808/742-7400 or 800/367-8020, fax 808/742-9121, mail@suite-paradise.com, www.suite-paradise.com). ResortQuest Hawaii also manages numerous units at Po'ipu Kai that range $245–500 during regular season. For information on its units and rates, contact ResortQuest (1775 Po'ipu Rd., 808/742-7424 or 877/997-6667, fax 808/742-8798).

The **Kiahuna Plantation Resort** (2253 Po'ipu Rd., 808/742-6411 or 800/688-7444, fax 808/742-1698) is operated by Hawaii's own Outrigger Resorts; some units are managed by Castle Resorts and Hotels. Prior to opening to the public in 1972, these grounds were the estate and gardens of Mr. and Mrs. Hector Moir, a manager of the Koloa Sugar Company. Their private home, now serving as the reception center, is a breezy but stout lava-rock structure in the classic plantation style; their living room and adjoining rooms, appointed in lustrous koa, now house the dining room of the Plantation Garden Restaurant. In the yard is the Moir Gardens, a unique mix of cacti and tropical flowers and trees. The Kiahuna Plantation Resort has greatly expanded the original gardens; the property's 35 lovely acres fronting Po'ipu Beach are adorned with more than 3,000 varieties of tropical flowers, trees, and plants and a lovely lagoon. Except for the cactus patch, the resort property was heavily battered by the hurricane, but two dozen full-time gardeners restored everything to its former beauty. The resort has just over 300 units, divided into separate buildings. Contemporary in design, they are white inside and out with dark trim. Interior styling differs from one unit to another since each is individually owned, yet all are well appointed, as they must meet high standards. You enter the large one-bedroom units through louvered doors. Sliding doors at the far end allow breezes to filter through, assisted by ceiling fans in every room. The bedroom features a king- or queen-size bed, and across the hall, the bathroom has a shower and tub, dressing area, and handy hallway closets with complimentary safes. The comfy living room, separate dining area, and full modern kitchen are on the ocean side. Here you'll find all the amenities and comforts of home and, what's more, daily housekeeping service. Each unit has a covered lanai with table, chairs, and lounges overlooking the grounds. With the sea in the distance you'll feel like a transplanted flower in this magnificent garden, set amongst red ginger, yellow plumeria, and a painter's palette of greens. The two-bedroom units are bi-level and the size of most homes. All units are only a minute's walk from the beach, home to the Hawaiian monk seal March–July. Full beach service is provided, and the concierge desk can make arrangements for any activity on the island. Laundry facilities are on the premises. One-bedroom suites (maximum four guests) run $225–460, two-bedroom suites (for up to six) are $365–505. With several units located on the far end of the property, Castle

Resorts (808/742-2200 or 800/367-5004) has units that run $240–950 a night. Prices depend on the view; numerous packages are available. The Kiahuna Plantation Resort is a first-rate condominium, expertly managed, with a superb location.

⟨ **Poipu Kapili** (2221 Kapili Rd., 808/742-6449 or 800/443-7714, fax 808/742-9162, www.poipukapili.com) is a two- and three-story upscale condo complex with only 60 units on five acres. It has a touch of the Hawaiian plantation style, across the road from a rocky shoreline, beyond which waves continually break over the reef. All units have ocean views. The pool is in the center of the property, surrounded by flowering gardens and lawn. Free, lighted tennis courts are available, and rackets and balls are provided to guests. Each unit is huge, ranging from 1,200-foot one-bedroom suites to 2,600-foot two-bedroom penthouses. Bedrooms have ceiling fans and wicker furniture, kitchens are spacious and furnished with modern appliances, and the large living area opens onto a private lanai, many of which overlook the pool and garden, some of which look directly onto the ocean. Regular season rates range $220–240 for a one-bedroom unit to $290–500 for a two-bedroom; high season and holiday rates are higher, but monthly and weekly discounts are available, as are several packages. The condo also offers a convenient activities desk that will book any activity that strikes your fancy.

West End Condos
Waikomo Stream Villas (2721 Po'ipu Rd., 808/742-7220 or 800/325-5701) is the first condo complex you see as you approach the Po'ipu area. It's located just inland of Koloa Landing and backs up against the stream. Waikomo Stream Villas is managed by Grantham Resorts (see *Vacation Rental Agencies*).

On the far side of Koloa Landing is **Whaler's Cove** (2640 Pu'uholo Rd., 808/742-7571 or 800/225-2683, fax 808/742-1185, www.whalers-cove.com), a deluxe accommodation with only 38 units offering you an excellent sense of privacy and manageability. Set right on the point, the curved-front Whaler's Cove opens

to and embraces the sea, each unit offering an oceanfront view. All individually owned, most units are tastefully decorated in a contemporary island style. Here you'll find full kitchens and baths with all the amenities, daily housekeeping, laundry facilities, and a private swimming pool set above the rocky water's edge. One-bedroom units here run $369–499, and the large two-bedroom units are $507–656.

Farther down at Lawa'i Beach are the oceanfront **Kuhio Shores** (808/742-1391), the older and more spartan **Prince Kuhio** (808/742-1670), and newer and larger **Lawa'i Beach Resort** (808/240-5100, www.lawaibeach.org), a time-share property that rents out condo units from $249 a day when available.

East Shore Bed-and-Breakfasts and Vacation Rentals
Pua Hale (2381 Kipuka St., 808/742-1700 or 800/745-7414, www.kauai-puahale.com), is a lovely, deluxe 750-square-foot house where your privacy and serenity are assured. With a touch of Japan, Pua Hale features shoji screens, cool tile floors, a relaxing soaking tub, custom furniture and decorating, and a complete kitchen and laundry. This self-contained one-bedroom unit, only minutes from Po'ipu, is surrounded by a privacy fence and a manicured garden, so you can choose whether you want to socialize or simply enjoy the glorious quietude on your own. Rates are a reasonable $125 per night or $800 per week, with a $60 cleaning fee; four nights minimum. You'll be hard pressed to find better for the price.

Built in 1998 at the eastern end of Po'ipu is **Maluhia ma ka Honua.** With three bedrooms, four bathrooms, full kitchen, huge living/dining room, and wraparound lanai, this house is suited for families. It has all electric appliances in the kitchen and the amenities are modern throughout. Maluhia ma ka Honua makes you feel at home, and you can't help but relax and have a restful time. The rent rate is $2,100 per week, seven nights minimum, with a $225 cleaning fee. Contact Garden Island Rentals for reservations (see *Vacation Rental Agencies*).

Directly up from Brennecke Beach is **Plantation Cottage** (2254 Pane Rd.). Built in 1924 and restored in 1996, this two-bedroom, one-bath home evokes the sugar era with its spaciousness and front veranda. Sleeping up to five, this vacation rental rents for $195 a night or $975 a week. Contact Kauai Vacation Rentals (see *Vacation Rental Agencies*).

C Poipu Plantation Resort (1792 Pe'e Rd., 808/742-6757 or 800/634-0263, fax 808/742-8681, plantation@poipubeach.com, www.poipubeach.com) is a one-acre property that's just a few steps up the street from Brennecke Beach. Poipu Plantation has four comfy bed-and-breakfast rooms in its renovated 1938 plantation-era home, all with different configurations, but each has a private bath, TV, and air-conditioning. The front lanai serves as a common room and is where the fresh and filling homemade breakfast (menu changes daily) is served each morning for B&B guests. Rooms run $115–195 a night, three nights minimum, but are $10–15 cheaper per night for stays of seven nights or more. In three separate and more contemporary buildings tucked behind the front house are nine reasonably priced one- and two-bedroom light and breezy condo units, called "cottages," that have full kitchens, dining rooms, living rooms, a deck, and multiple amenities like rattan furniture, wood floors, and ceiling fans. The condo units range $120–150 a night, three nights minimum, somewhat less for stays of seven nights or more, and for the location are very reasonably priced. On site are a hot tub, a barbecue area, and coin laundry for guest use, and the office has beach gear to borrow. Staff members are more than willing to help you in planning activities and can make some reservations for you. In this quiet place with an easygoing feel, you wake to the sound of birds and fall asleep to the breeze in the flowering trees on the lawn.

West End Bed-and-Breakfasts and Vacation Rentals

Koloa Landing Cottages (2704 Ho'onani Rd., 808/742-1470 or 800/779-8773, www.koloa-landing.com) is directly across the street from the Koloa Landing cove. These colorfully painted basic units are some of Po'ipu's least-expensive accommodations, but because of their ambience, location, and price, they are in constant demand. The main house and two cottages, all two-bedroom, two-bath units, each sleep up to four people and have a full kitchen, lanai, and color television. Rates are $185 for the house and $150 for the cottages. Also on property is a one-bedroom unit for $125 and a cute and quirky studio for $105; both sleep two and are equipped with kitchens and color TVs. A one-time cleaning fee is added to the price of the room. Four nights minimum. Coin-laundry facilities are on the premises. The vegetation helps to keep the compound private and each unit secluded. In addition to these units, a small two-bedroom, one-bath house on a lazy residential street in Koloa rents for $150 a night and sleeps four. Reservations are suggested well ahead of time. Contact Ellie or Bret for information or to reserve.

Next door to Koloa Landing Cottages is **Poipu Bed and Breakfast Inn** (2720 Ho'onani Rd., 808/742-1146 or 800/808-2330, www.poipu-inn.com) a large and spacious renovated plantation house from the 1930s. Stained in tropical colors, this wooden house has all the comforts of home, plus antiques, art, and crafts from the island. If you have a childlike affection for carousel rides, you'll love this place because there are several carousel horses in the house. The bedrooms are on either side of the large, central sitting room. Each has a color TV, ceiling fan, and private bath. The sitting room has a TV, videotapes, books, and games. Smoking is not allowed inside the house; sit out on the large, comfortable lanai or walk in the garden. Daily room rates, including a continental breakfast, are $125–150. Rooms can be combined into two-bedroom, two-bath suites, and the entire house can be rented.

Garden Isle Cottages (2660 Pu'uholo Rd., 808/742-6717 or 800/742-6711, www.ocean-cottages.com) perches on the craggy rocks above Koloa Landing surrounded by lush foliage, offering privacy. The cottages are operated by artists Robert and Sharon Flynn, whose original works highlight each of the units. The cottages are two duplexes, each with upper and lower units. All the units have one bedroom and one bath and are self-contained and fully equipped; downstairs units have kitchens, upstairs units have kitchenettes. The price is $190 high season (mid-December to mid-April) and $170 low season, plus $10 for each person beyond two, and a $45 cleaning fee. Seven nights' deposit is required; weekly and monthly rates can be arranged.

Nearby along the same quiet residential road is **Kauai Cove Cottages** (2672 Puʻuholo Rd. 808/742-2562 or 800/642-9945, www.kauai cove.com). Set close to the road and lined up like row houses, they are not much to look at from the outside, but they are a wonderful surprise on the inside. Not overly large, but modern in style and well designed in light-colored hardwood and bamboo, each of the three studios is adorned in island tropical decor with island-inspired artwork on the walls. Tall cathedral ceilings make the rooms appear more spacious, and a kitchen is set up for full meal preparations. To give the sense of more space, all have an outdoor eating lanai. Each room comes with color TV and a CD player with a selection of contemporary Hawaiian music, and old-style hanging mosquito netting surrounds the queen bed. These are comfortable units that remind you in every way that you are on vacation in the tropics. Rates start at $95 a night for stays of three days or less. Nonsmoking only.

You will find no bedroom closer to the gentle surf than at **☒ Gloria's Spouting Horn Bed and Breakfast** (4464 Lawaʻi Beach Rd., tel./fax 808/742-6995, www.glo riasbedandbreakfast.com). Leveled by Hurricane ʻIniki, the one-time humble plantation house has come back as a perfectly designed and highly attractive B&B, with your comfort and privacy assured. Created by Bob and Gloria with the help of a California architect, the stout, hurricane-resistant, natural-wood post-and-beam structure supports a Polynesian longhouse-style roof. None of the three

guest rooms share a common wall, and the entire home is designed for maximum exposure to the outdoors. Wide bay windows with louvers underneath bring you as close as possible to the outdoors when opened simultaneously, and skylights let in the sun and stars. A nubby burgundy carpet (no shoes inside, please) massages your feet as you pad the hall to your cross-ventilated suite, which is further cooled by ceiling fans above four-poster beds in the bedroom and in your private bath. Every suite opens to a private lanai above an intimate seaside swimming pool where the rolling surf and dependable whoosh of the Spouting Horn serenade you throughout the evening. All baths are private, spacious, and offer a shower, commode, and *ofuro*-like soaking tub. Descend a central stairway to a small bar that holds port, brandy, and different liqueurs for your evening enjoyment. Breakfast is a combination of fresh fruits, fresh juices, piping hot coffee and tea, and perhaps a pizza pancake crunchy with macadamia nuts and smothered with homemade banana topping. Room rates are $350 per night, $325 for more than seven nights, $400 over Christmas, three nights minimum; no credit cards. Only a few steps from the Spouting Horn, at this absolutely excellent accommodation traffic disappears at night and the quiet settles in.

Vacation Rental Agencies

R&R Realty and Rentals (808/742-7555 or 800/367-8022, fax 808/742-1559, randr@r7r.com, www.r7r.com) arranges only condo rentals in Poʻipu. R&R has more than four dozen units in half a dozen properties, mostly in the low to midrange complexes. Studios start about $600 per week, one-, two-, and three-bedroom units run $800–1,700; monthly discounts are given, two weeks minimum during holidays.

Poipu Connection Realty (808/742-2233 or 800/742-2260, fax 808/742-7382, poipu@ha waiian.net, www.poipuconnection.com) handles private vacation condo rentals and homes exclusively along the Poʻipu coast. From the large complexes to a small six-plex, these units range from $75 a night for a studio to $275 a night for a deluxe oceanfront unit.

Garden Island Rentals (808/742-9537 or 800/247-5599, fax 808/742-9540, gir@kauai rentals.com, www.kauairentals.com) rents mostly high-end vacation homes and a few condo units, exclusively in the Po'ipu area. Nearly all are on or very close to the water. The condo units run $135–295 a night with a four-night minimum stay, and the homes range up to $10,000 a week with a seven-night minimum. Deposit and cleaning fees are required for all units.

Grantham Resorts (808/742-2000 or 800/742-1412, fax 808/742-9093, stay@grantham-resorts.com, www.grantham-resorts.com) is located in Koloa and manages both condo units and private homes, exclusively in Po'ipu. Most of its condo units are in the Waikomo Stream Villas and Nihi Kai Resort, but there are units in nine other complexes. The price range for these units is $99 a day for a one-bedroom garden-view unit in low season to $375 a day for a three-bedroom ocean front during high season; holiday rates are substantially higher, monthly rates are well discounted. Private home rentals run from a two-bedroom, two-bath bungalow for $200 a day to a four-bedroom, four-bath house with pool that sleeps eight for $1,140 a day. Well established and reputable, Grantham has been matching people with places since 1984.

Kauai Vacation Rentals (3-3311 Kuhio Hwy., Lihu'e, 808/245-8841 or 800/367-5025, aloha@kvrre.com, www.KauaiVacationRentals.com) handles mostly low to midrange condo and mid- to upper-end vacation rental homes in Po'ipu.

FOOD
Quick Eats

Brennecke's Beach Deli (808/742-1582) is just off Po'ipu Beach, below Brennecke's restaurant. The best deals are the takeout sandwiches, but it also has pastries, ice cream, and beer.

Puka Dog (808/742-6044), located in the back corner of the Poipu Shopping Village, sells Hawaiian-style meat and veggie hotdogs with homemade relishes that range from traditional to tropical, all on a fresh-baked bun. These are not your run-of-the-mill sausages, they are a simple taste of the island. Although just a tiny walk-up counter eatery, with a few tables to the side in a breezy setting, Puka Dog tantalizes the taste buds of Po'ipu visitors and residents alike for under $6 a dog.

American

Joe Batteiger is a football fanatic from Cleveland, Ohio, who spent many a fall afternoon in that city's "Dog Pound." After the game, Joe and his buddies wanted to wrap their meaty fists around huge sandwiches and wash them down with cold ones. No froufrou food for these bruisers. So Joe moved to Kaua'i and opened a restaurant, **[** **Joe's on the Green** (808/742-9696) at the Kiahuna Golf Club clubhouse. Breakfast is served 7–11:30 A.M. with discounted specials until 8:30 A.M. Breakfast here is eggs Benedict, biscuits and gravy, corned beef hash, and omelettes, as well as pancakes, bagels, and loco moco. Lunch (until 2:30 P.M.) brings a personalized house salad that you build yourself, beer-battered fish and chips, grilled plates, hot and cold sandwiches, and "a dog named Joe." Happy hour for drinks runs 3–6 P.M., and dinners, with the sweet sounds of Hawaiian music, are now served 5:30–8:30 P.M. Wednesday and Thursday. Joe's place is known mostly to local people who come time and again to get a fine meal at a reasonable price. Some swear it's the best breakfast in town. Expect breakfast and lunch prices in the $7–10 range, with dinner entrées starting at about $17.

Brennecke's Beach Broiler (808/742-7588), an open-air, second-story deck restaurant directly across from Po'ipu Beach County Park, offers a superb view. Seafood is the dinner specialty, but pasta and *kiawe*-broiled meat and chicken are also served; dinner prices range $18–25. Salads and sandwiches are served for lunch, and *pu pu* until closing. There is a children's menu for both lunch and dinner. Lunch is 11 A.M.–4 P.M., happy hour 3–5 P.M., dinner

4–10 P.M., with early dinner specials 4–6 P.M. Brennecke's is a fun, casual place with tasty food, a good choice for a family on vacation. As it's popular and not a big place, call for a reservation.

At the rear of Po'ipu Shopping Village is the casual, open-air **Tropical Burger** (808/742-1808, 6:30 A.M.–9:30 P.M.), with lots more on the menu than your usual two-fisters. The breakfast menu has eggs, omelettes, and griddle food; lunch starts at 11 A.M. with meat and meatless burgers, sandwiches, and salads. Although a rum-guava burger is the house special, dinner offers great variety. Entrées start at about $12. This is a comfortable, convenient, easy-on-the-pocketbook place for the family.

The main dining room at the Hyatt is the **Ilima Terrace** (808/240-6456), open daily for breakfast and lunch, and for dinner Monday and Sunday, with both specialty buffets and à la carte menus. Descend a formal staircase and step onto a slate floor covered with an emerald green carpet. Floor-to-ceiling beveled glass doors look out onto the lovely grounds, and seating is pleasant inside or out. Start your day with a choice of fresh chilled juices, hearty omelettes, or griddle items. If it's hard to choose, try the Ilima Breakfast Buffet, or sleep in Sunday for the hearty champagne brunch. Lunch is à la carte and brings starters like smoked chicken quesadillas, deli board items of soup, salad, and sandwiches, or more substantial dishes like seared 'ahi, prawn noodles, or your choice of pizza. Dinner is more of the same, with the addition of pasta, and a bit more expensive with main dishes up to $30.

The Sheraton also offers sumptuous food in a fine setting at what it calls its Galleria of Oceanfront Dining. Here, each of the hotel's three main restaurants occupies a different section of the main dining room. Set on a rocky point almost at water's edge, they face east and command a superb view of the white sand and rich blue water of the bay. **Shells** (808/742-1661, 5:30–9:30 P.M. nightly), the Sheraton's main restaurant, is a perfect place to start the day. Breakfast here has a well-deserved reputation and it includes traditional American and some international selections, off the menu or as a buffet. For an evening meal, items include any number of fresh fish, broiled or sautéed and covered in a black bean, green curry coconut, or ginger beurre blanc sauce. Other choices are roast prime rib, filet mignon, or roasted chicken breast glazed with honey-lime sauce. Entrées run $25–30.

Thai

An indoor/outdoor café, **Pattaya Asian Cafe** (808/742-8818, 11:30 A.M.–2:30 P.M. Mon.–Sat. for lunch and 5:30–9:30 P.M. daily for dinner) is located at the Po'ipu Shopping Village. This is a very tasteful, moderately priced restaurant appointed with a flagstone floor and Thai mahogany tables and chairs. The exotic menu starts with *mee grop,* a dish of crispy noodles, chicken, bean sprouts, and green onions, and includes a spicy lemongrass soup, a Thai ginger coconut soup with chicken or seafood, and fresh island papaya salad. More substantial meals include pad Thai and plenty of vegetarian selections. Mostly $9–18, all dishes can be ordered to the spice level you desire, and most come with your selection of tofu, beef, chicken, shrimp, or seafood. Pattaya Asian Cafe is a terrific and authentic restaurant with friendly service and good prices, and you know the food will be good because the owner uses herbs from his own garden.

Japanese

The traditional-style Japanese restaurant **Naniwa** (808/742-1661, 6–9:30 P.M. Tues.–Sat.) is located in the back corner of the main dining room at the Sheraton, overlooking the lawn and ocean. Sushi is a favorite here, as are the fish preparations, but you can also get traditional rice bowls. Entrées run $26–31, but the complete dinners, with rice, soup, and vegetables, are a bit more. A taste of traditional Japanese cuisine, Naniwa will not fail to please.

Italian and Mediterranean

Up Nalo Road behind the Nihi Kai condominiums is ◖ **Casa di Amici** (2301 Nalo

Rd., 808/742-1555, 6–8 P.M. daily), a fine Italian restaurant that's open for dinner only; reservations are recommended as seating fills up early. Casa di Amici offers a wide-ranging menu that includes a gnocchi quattro formaggio appetizer, Hawaiian purple potato salad, saffron-vanilla paella risotto, and various pasta dishes, or choose other entrées like fresh catch, black tiger prawns, pork loin saltimbocca, or porcini-crusted chicken. Most entrées fall into the $25–30 range; the "light" selection offers smaller portions and saves a bit on the bill. Save room for bananas Foster, a chocolate torte, or tiramisu for dessert. Soft piano music is offered as an accompaniment on Saturday evenings. All in all, Casa di Amici is an excellent place with a well-deserved reputation, and it has a relaxing atmosphere and tasty food at prices that are not too outrageous.

Casablanca (808/742-2929, 7:30 A.M.–10 P.M. Mon.–Sat., from 8:30 A.M. Sun.) is located at the Kiahuna Swim and Tennis Club in an open-air, white post-and-beam structure appropriate for its name. Offering a Mediterranean-inspired menu for all three meals of the day, Casablanca shines in the evening. Choose from such items as pasta puttanesca and anatra balsamico (crispy duck breast), or perhaps maiale con genipro (sautéed pork medallion) or pesca in pachetto (herbed white fish in parchment), both specialties of the house. Most non-pasta entrées run $18–32. If you're not hungry enough for a full meal, stop throughout the afternoon for tapas.

The newest of the three main restaurants at the Sheraton is **Amore Ristorante Italiano** (808/742-1661, nightly 6–9:30 P.M.). Choose either a romantic table inside or the less formal café seating. All the Italian favorites are on the menu, including calamari fritto appetizers, lobster-stuffed ravioli, pasta pesca fra diavolo, pasta primavera, scampi, and pollo al piccata. Most entrées are in the $18–28 range.

Hawaiian Regional

Keoki's Paradise (808/742-7534 11 A.M.–11 P.M.), at the Po'ipu Shopping Village, is an excellent choice for dinner or a night's entertainment. Enter past a small fountain into the longhouse-style interior with stone floor and thatched roof. Choose a seat at the long bar for a casual evening or at one of the tables overlooking the garden surrounding the restaurant. The varied menu lists savory items, including Thai shrimp stick appetizers, fresh catch prepared a variety of ways (including baked in an orange-ginger sauce, herb-sautéed, or seared), pesto macadamia shrimp, coconut-crusted chicken, or beef dishes like top sirloin and prime rib. Keoki's renowned dessert is its Hula Pie, a mound of ice cream filling an Oreo cookie crust, big enough for at least two. Simpler and cheaper, the Cafe Menu (available 11 A.M.–11:30 P.M. at the bar) includes *pu pu,* burgers, salads, sandwiches, and plate lunches. "Aloha Fridays" bring food and drink specials 4:30–7 P.M. A great selection of beer and mixed drinks adds to an enjoyable evening. Live entertainment is offered Fri.–Sat. by local bands specializing in contemporary Hawaiian music. Keoki's is a feel-good place that fills you up with large portions of tasty food.

At the Po'ipu Shopping Village, culinary magic is created nightly at **Roy's Poipu Bar and Grill** (808/742-5000, 5:30–9:30 P.M.). Here, in an open kitchen—one of Roy's trademarks—the chef de cuisine and a superbly trained staff create an array of marvelous dishes from the island's freshest meats, fish, poultry, fruits, and vegetables. The chef's "specials sheet" changes nightly, but a sampling of the delectable dishes that you may enjoy includes dim sum appetizers like crispy smoked duck gyoza and minted chicken and basil spring rolls. Healthy green salads and *imu*-baked pizzas are also available. A few entrées usually on the menu are lemongrass-crusted chicken, grilled shrimp, and pot roast trimmed with mashed potatoes and old-fashioned apple ginger pineapple sauce. The chef's special always has fresh fish and seafood, like basil-seared *ono* with Thai red curry and lobster sauce, macadamia nut-crusted whitefish with a lobster sauce, and sesame-seared *uku* with a shiitake cream sauce. Most entrées are in the under $30 range. Roy's offers a memorable dining experience. Reservations are recommended, as this is a popular place.

At the Kiahuna Plantation Resort, in what once was the plantation manager's home, overlooking the Moir Gardens under towering trees and surrounded by lush greenery, the casual yet dressy **Plantation Gardens Restaurant and Bar** (808/742-2121, nightly from 5:30 P.M.) serves up tempting fish and meat dishes, plus pasta and *kiawe* wood-fired grilled items, many of which you might have encountered during the old plantation days on the island. Start with one of several Asian-inspired appetizers and garden-fresh salads. More substantial are the full entrées, seafood laulau, Hawaiian Hotpot, Parker Ranch New York steak, crispy rotisserie chicken, or herb-crusted lamb chops. Most entrées run $18–25. The full bar (open at 4 P.M.) is always open for a complement to any meal, where *pu pu* and the full dinner menu are also available. Sit indoors in the main dining room, or on one of the verandas for refreshing evening breezes.

Fine Dining

Exquisite dining can be enjoyed at various restaurants, some overlooking Po'ipu's beaches—perfect for catching the setting sun—and others in elegant gardens bathed by tropical breezes. Prices are high, but you definitely get a full measure of what you pay for. Reservations are recommended at all these fine-dining establishments.

The **【 Beach House Restaurant** (808/742-1424, daily for dinner only 6–10 P.M., from 5:30 P.M. in winter) has a superb location at Lawa'i Beach. While the menu varies somewhat each night, expect a blending of East and West. Entrées, mostly in the $23–29 range, might be a hoisin-plum chicken breast, seared crab-stuffed pork medallions with Okinawan sweet potato mash and port demi sauce, Chinese-style roasted duck with lemon-orange Grand Marnier demi and seared miso shiitake risotto cake, and fire-roasted *ahi* with furikake mashed potatoes, cilantro black bean sauce, and beurre blanc. For the diehard dessert fans, don't miss the molten chocolate desire—it takes 20 minutes of

preparation, so let your waiter know ahead of time if you're indulging. Sunset at the Beach House couldn't be better, so call well ahead of time and reserve a window seat, or stop at the lounge, which opens at 5 P.M., and order an appetizer for the show. Without question, the Beach House is an outstanding restaurant for a romantic and sumptuous sunset dinner. The Beach House is operated by the owners of the first-rate SeaWatch and Plantation House restaurants on Maui.

Dondero's (808/240-6456, 6–10 P.M. Tues.–Sat.), featuring classic Northern Italian cuisine, is the Hyatt's signature restaurant. The continental room is classically formal, and the view through floor-to-ceiling windows, past the restaurant's terrace seating, is of manicured gardens. Dinner begins with antipasti, such as calamari fritti, and moves on to soups and salads. Linguine alla Bolognese and other traditional pastas, osso buco, pistachio-crusted rack of lamb, and many other fish and meat selections fill the menu and run up to around $42. Special selections are put on the menu weekly. Round out your meal with tiramisu or crème brûlée and coffee or cordials. In addition to dessert wines, Dondero's has table wine to complement any entrée. Reservations and resort attire are a must.

More casual, yet dignified in a tropical way, is the Hyatt's **【 Tidepool Restaurant** (808/240-6456, dinner only 5:30–10 P.M.), a mushroom cluster of thatched South Sea "huts" supported by huge beams forming an indoor/outdoor restaurant overlooking the tidepools. Low-lit and romantic, the Tidepool boasts fresh fish, sautéed, seared, grilled, or steamed, with a medley of sauces and toppings to choose from. The signature dish is macadamia nut-crusted mahimahi with a Kahlua, lime, and ginger butter sauce. This contemporary Hawaiian fusion cuisine also includes baked chicken, ribs, and vegetarian dishes. Entrées run $27–35. While the food is memorable, the setting adds to the experience.

Food Stores

Po'ipu is home to the generally well-stocked

Kukui'ula Store (2827 Po'ipu Rd., 808/742-1601, 8 A.M.–8:30 P.M. Mon.–Fri. and until 6:30 P.M. Sat.–Sun.), at Po'ipu Plaza, near the Y of Po'ipu and Lawa'i roads. Stocked with groceries, produce, bakery goods, sundries, and liquor, it's the only grocery store in Po'ipu. **Whaler's General Store** (808/742-9431, 7:30 A.M.–10 P.M. daily), at Po'ipu Shopping Village, is a well-stocked convenience store with a good selection of wines and liquors, souvenirs, and gifts. **Brennecke's Beach Deli** (808/742-1582), located below Brennecke's Beach Broiler restaurant across from Po'ipu Beach County Park, is a tiny place with a small selection of packaged snack foods, sandwiches, pastries, drinks, and beer to go.

If you're staying in a Po'ipu condo and are buying large quantities of food, you may save money and will definitely have a wider selection of choices by making the trip up the road to one of the larger markets in Koloa.

Farmers Markets

For fresh fruit and vegetables and ready-made gift baskets, try the open-air Po'ipu Southside Market stand at the corner of Po'ipu Road and the Koloa–Po'ipu Bypass. Local farmers also have a stand set up along Po'ipu Beach Road near the cane haul road between Koloa and the coast. One or both of these stands may not be open depending upon the supply of fruits and produce available.

INFORMATION

The **Po'ipu Beach Resort Association** (808/742-7444, http://poipu-beach.org) is an excellent nonprofit information and promotional organization that can help you plan your trip in the Po'ipu area, arrange for accommodations, and point you in the right direction for activities and recreation. It can provide brochures and tips on everything from dining to accommodations and transportation; ask for its 48-page planning brochure, also available on the Web.

Brennecke's Beach Center (808/742-7505) offers information and can set you up with any kind of activity on the island.

Located downstairs at the Po'ipu Kai Resort, **The Activity Hut** (808/742-6924, 8 A.M.–6 P.M. daily) can also arrange any sort of activity or tour anywhere around on island.

There are **no banks** in Po'ipu, but the two hotels will cash traveler's checks for their guests. The closest bank is in Koloa, as is the nearest post office and medical clinic.

SOUTH SHORE

Inland Towns

Like much of the island, the region west of Lihu'e and inland from Po'ipu was, until a couple of decades ago, filled with broad swaths of sugarcane and fields of pineapple—an old pineapple cannery, now put to other uses, still sits in the Lawa'i Valley along Koloa Road. Those crops are now gone, many replaced by coffee, macadamia nut trees, and others that are tinting the hillsides in new shades of green. In amongst these newcomers is a sprinkling of hobby ranches. Hit hard by the closing of the plantations, the towns of **Oma'o, Lawa'i,** and **Kalaheo** have hung on and are slowly expanding as outlying bedroom communities for Lihu'e and the Po'ipu tourist resort area. These towns snuggle up against the mountains below steep hillsides of trees, cut by the highway that runs west over the shoulder of the mountain from Lihu'e. For most, this area is just a pass-through to the warmer West End of the island or up to the higher elevations of Koke'e State Park. However, those wanting great views over the lowlands from the heights should take a drive up Pu'ulima Road, Kikala Road, Wawae Road, or Kua Road. Drive slowly and cautiously—these roads are very steep and run through residential areas.

In times past, *ali'i* from throughout the kingdom came to Lawa'i to visit an ancient fishpond in the caldera of an extinct volcano.

Legend says that this was the first attempt by Madame Pele to dig herself a fiery home. Today, several small reservoirs from the sugar era still dot these hills but are not easily seen unless you get off the highway and drive the back roads, where you might also find the occasional fruit and farm produce stand.

Throughout the state there are pockets of population groups with heavier concentrations than elsewhere; for Kalaheo, it's the Portuguese. Kalaheo seems to have fared better than Lawa'i or Oma'o. It has three gas stations, a liquor store, post office, medical clinic and pharmacy, a handful of restaurants, a minimart, and a new office/shopping plaza, all along Rt. 50, making it the first sizable town between Lihu'e and Hanapepe where you can pick up anything you may need before continuing west.

SIGHTS
◖ Kukui O Lono Park
Kukui O Lono Park (open 6:30 A.M.–6:30 P.M.) is a personal gift from Walter D. McBryde, the well-known plantation owner who donated the land to the people of Kaua'i in 1919. Accept it! It's off the beaten track but worth the trip. Turn left in Kalaheo at the Menehune Food Mart and go along Papalina Road for one mile until you come to the second Pu'u Road—the first turnoff to Pu'u Road skirts the hill below the park and circles back to the second Pu'u Road turnoff. A sharp right turn brings you through the large stone-and-metal gate. The park encompasses a public golf course and small Japanese-style garden. The entrance road leads through a tunnel of eucalyptus trees to a commemorative plaque to McBryde. A flock of green parrots that nest in the tall eucalyptus trees on the grounds can be heard in a symphony of sound in the early evening.

For the gardens and McBryde's memorial, go straight ahead to the parking lot; to get to the clubhouse, follow the road to your right for about a half mile. As the park is set on top of a hill, the sweeping views in all directions are striking. For the best view of the south coast, walk out to the pavilion but be watchful for golf carts. During the winter months, you may be able to spot whales spouting along the coast

golfing with the roosters at Kukuiolono Golf Course

ROBERT NILSEN

far below. Unfortunately, perfectly placed in the center of one of the nicest views is a microwave antenna and dish. Set amidst a grove of towering trees, the Japanese garden offers peace and tranquility. The whole scene is conducive to Zen-like meditation. Enjoy it. Just beyond the Japanese garden is a small collection of stones that were used by the Hawaiians for various purposes: for games, as a fish god, and for evaporating salt.

The **Kukuiolono Golf Course** clubhouse (808/332-9151) houses a pro shop and snack bar. A round of golf on the par-36 course is a very economical $8; carts and clubs are rented at a similarly reasonable rate. Having opened in 1929 for the workers of the McBryde sugar plantation, this is the second oldest golf course on the island.

SHOPPING
Lawaʻi

Next to the post office, at mile marker 10, is the **Menehune Food Mart** (808/332-8641, daily 5:30 A.M.–8 P.M.), a reasonably well-stocked way station. A short way down Koloa Road past the Hawaiian Trading Post is **Lawaʻi General Store** (3586 Koloa Rd., 808/332-7501), an older and more local shop that carries sundries and a few groceries.

At the intersection of Koloa Road and Kaumualiʻi Highway (Rts. 50 and 530) is the **Hawaiian Trading Post** gift shop (808/332-7404, 10 A.M.–5 P.M. Mon.–Saturday). Referred to by locals as "the tourist trap," the Hawaiian Trading Post sells a mind-boggling variety of handcrafted items as well as a large selection of souvenirs, treasures, and tourist junk. Other selections include T-shirts, right-price aloha shirts, jewelry, black pearls, postcards, and carvings, and an excellent display of Niʻihau shell lei that should be featured but are stuck away in the back. These Niʻihau shell lei, some for display only and some for sale, are perhaps the best collection of shell lei on the island—worth the stop by themselves. Priced from several hundred to several thousand dollars, many of these beauties take a couple of years to string. Occupying a portion of the

same building is **Lee Sands,** featuring goods made from eel skin and other exotic leathers. Around the side you can still stand on a surfboard and have your picture taken at the fake wave fashioned from plaster, while across the parking lot is a pleasant grove of coconut, breadfruit, orange African tulip, and purple Hong Kong orchid trees.

ACCOMMODATIONS
Lawaʻi Bed-and-Breakfasts

Perched on a steep hillside above a broad green horse pasture and facing the high mountains toward the center of the island, **C Marjorie's Kauai Inn** (808/332-8838 or 800/717-8838, marjorie@marjorieskauaiinn.com, www.marjorieskauaiinn.com), has an unbeatable location. You have your choice of three private rooms, two with showers and one with a tub, each with private mini-kitchen, flat screen TV, DVD and CD player, high-speed wireless Internet connection, phone, and its own entrance. Also included is access to a 10- by 50-foot lap pool and deck with hot tub on the hillside below, beach equipment and accessories, and a barbecue grill. Fresh fruit, juice, and scrumptious homemade banana bread await in your room when you arrive. Light, bright, and cheery with new furnishings and new paint in 2005, all rooms open onto a lanai that overlooks the valley. Very accommodating, the owners take the time to find out what you want to do and will gladly arrange activities for you. They encourage everyone to have wonderful adventures during their stay, and keep with the motto of the previous owner: "Do more than one fun thing a day." Marjorie's Kauai Inn is a real find: quiet, rural, relaxing, and smoke-free. Room rates are $130 for the Tradewind room, $140 for the Valley View room, and $160 for Sunset View room, which also has a private two-person hot tub, $15 for a third person.

Set amongst thick vegetation on a quiet cul-de-sac, with a fine view of the distant ocean, is **Victoria Place** (808/332-9300, fax 808/332-9465, edeev@aloha.net, www.hshawaii.com/kvp/victoria. Presided over by the gracious and warmhearted Edee Seymour, a transplant from the Mainland, this B&B is more like a home than a guesthouse. Edee fills you with a hearty breakfast and pastries, can clue you in on what to see and where to go, and always respects your privacy. The three rooms, one handicapped-accessible and another set up for a single traveler only, all have private bathrooms and run $70–90. These open onto the swimming pool at the front of the house. Down below, Victoria's Other Secret is a studio apartment with its own entrance, a king bed, private bath, and kitchen that goes for $125 a night—just right for honeymooners. For any of the rooms, add $10 per room for one-night stays. No credit cards accepted. Everyone shares the back lanai and can borrow books from Edee's huge collection.

Those looking for more independence should try the vacation rental **Hale Kua** (4896-E Kua Rd., 808/332-8570 or 800/440-4353, treefarm@halekua.com, www.halekua.com), set high up on the hill near horse pastures and overlooking Lawaʻi Valley and the distant ocean beyond. The five accommodations range from one-bedroom units for $105 to a cottage at $115 and three-bedroom house for $145.

Kalaheo

Behind the Kalaheo Steak House is the **Kalaheo Inn** (4444 Papalina Rd., 808/332-6023 or 888/332-6023, fax 808/742-6432, chet@aloha.net, www.kalaheoinn.com). This 15-unit inn has been totally remodeled into a bright and cheery place with lots of local character, a well-tended tropical garden, and plenty of on-site parking. These are basic apartment-like units, reasonably priced, and great for those who care more about what they eat and see than where they sleep. Some units have a separate living room/bedroom configuration; others are studios. Each has a kitchenette, queen or twin beds, ceiling fans, TV, and a bath with shower. The largest is a three-bedroom house with full kitchen and bathroom with tub. New tile and vinyl flooring take the place of carpet inside, and stone pavers line the veranda outside. A coin laundry is on-site for guest use. There are no phones in the rooms, but there is

one in the office for guest use. Rooms run $75 for studios, $85–95 for one bedroom, $115 for two bedrooms, and $155 for the three-bedroom quiet house in the back. Two nights minimum; discounts for extended stays.

You might drive past the **Bamboo Jungle House** (3829 Waha Road, 808/332-5515 or 888/332-5115, bamboojunglehouse@hawaii.rr.com, www.kauai-bedandbreakfast.com) without even knowing it. It's set inconspicuously in the neighborhood below Kukui O Lono Park, but once you pass through the front gate, a quiet and lush tropical world opens to you. Remodeled by its new owners, this B&B has three generous-size guests rooms with queen beds and private baths in one wing of a plantation-style house that are perfect for couples or single travelers. Light and breezy, each suite is painted white. The middle portion of the house contains the high-ceilinged dining room, where a full breakfast is served each morning, and the adjoining sitting room has books, games, and TV. Beyond the glass doors and windows of this room are the courtyard swimming pool and lava rock spa. If you want, a private massage can be arranged at the poolside gazebo. While the green foliage in the yard gives you the feeling of a tropical jungle, you do have distant views over the south coast and ocean from the front balcony. Aside from keeping the vegetation lush, the owners have made an effort to make this as environmentally "green" a place as possible, and they take the time to offer suggestions for your travel plans. The Waterfall and Jungle rooms run $110–120 with a three-night minimum, five nights during holidays, and the Bamboo Garden Suite is $130–140 with a five-night minimum. In addition, there is a $35–45 cleaning fee. This is a no smoking establishment.

FOOD

With Lawaʻi's economical restaurant closed, you now have to head to Kalaheo for a meal. Luckily, there are several good options.

Local Style

Another option is the blue-and-white **Camp**

House Grill (808/332-9755, 6:30 A.M.–9 P.M.) across from the Menehune Food Mart at the stoplight on the highway. The Camp House Grill specializes in burgers and Hawaiian-style barbecued chicken. Menu items are basic American standards with a Hawaiian twist and include the famous Camp House breakfasts, like a flour tortilla stuffed with scrambled eggs, sausage, and cheeses, topped with salsa and served with rice or Camp House hash browns; some early-bird specials go for as little as $2. Lunches and dinners start with salad, soup, and chili, but the restaurant is best known for its burgers and fries, all around $6.25. Evening brings barbecued pork ribs, fresh fish, and *huli* chicken, the best buy of the house. All the luscious homemade pies, like macadamia nut pie, pineapple cream cheese pie, and sour cream apple pie, are baked here in the kitchen, and you can have them by the slice or whole pie. Although not gourmet, nor as clean as it could be, the Camp House Grill offers honest and filling food at moderate prices.

Local people out for an evening meal at reasonable prices give the nod to **Kalaheo Steak House** (4444 Papalina Rd., 808/332-9780, daily 6–10 P.M.) where you can get a well-prepared and hearty portion of steak, seafood, pork, or poultry, and, reputedly, one of the best dinner salads on the island. While you wait for your main dish, try the steamer clams, brought to your table in a bucket, or the wonderful Portuguese bean soup. Most menu items range $17–27. Make a left at the signal along Rt. 50 in Kalaheo and look for a green building on the left with an awning. The interior, very much in steakhouse motif, is completely knotty pine—simple but tasteful, offering seating at a combination of black leatherette booths and tables with captain's chairs. A mural of tropical fish completes the decor. Local lore has it that when you leave the always-busy Kalaheo Steak House, the *doggie bag* contains more food than you're served at most restaurants.

Pizza

If you're interested in a pizza, stop in at **Brick Oven Pizza** (2-2555 Kaumuali'i Hwy.,

808/332-8561, 11 A.M.–10 P.M. Tues.–Sun.), on the mountain side just as you enter Kalaheo. Pizzas range from $10.45 for a 10-inch cheese pizza to $31.25 for a large 15-inch deluxe with all the toppings, on whole wheat or white crust with garlic butter glazing, baked on a hearth, with some corn meal in the crust to give it crispness. Many locals say it's the best pizza on the island. Brick Oven also prepares oven-baked sandwiches for around $7.50, pizza bread, and salads. Wine, beer, and soft drinks are available. If you're heading to Waimea or Polihale, call ahead to have a pizza ready for you to take out. While a bit on the pricey side, Brick Oven has a well-deservedly excellent reputation. It's been in business since 1977, so you know they're doing something right. While you're here, check out the license plate collection—there must be a couple hundred from most of the 50 states, and beyond—tacked up on the ceiling trusses. Most are fairly new, but there are a few from the mid-decades of the 1900s.

Café

For coffee in all its permutations, try the **Kalaheo Coffee Co. and Café** (808/332-5858, www.kalaheo.com, 6 A.M.–3:30 P.M. Mon.–Fri., 6:30 A.M.–3 P.M. Sat., 6:30 A.M.–2 P.M. Sunday), which relocated in 2005 to a new building across from Brick Oven Pizza. Aside from getting coffee by the cup, you can buy pound and half-pound packages of (mostly) Hawaiian coffee, whole bean or ground, blended or unblended, and even have it shipped. Breakfast items like omelettes, eggs, and pancakes are served until noon, and lunch runs 10:30 A.M.–closing for salads, deli sandwiches, and grill items you order at the counter. Pastries and baked goods are baked on-site. Wholesome, healthy, and filling, nearly everything on the menu is under $8.

Italian

Chefs Tony and Rosario serve a mix of traditional northern and southern Italian cuisine at **Pomodoro Ristorante Italiano** (808/332-5945, open 5:30–10 P.M. nightly except Sunday), located upstairs in the Rainbow Plaza on the left as you enter Kalaheo. The menu opens with classics like mozzarella, prosciutto, or calamari antipasti, a mixed green salad, and Caesar salad. Pasta is spaghetti with meatballs or Italian sausage, linguine shrimp marinara, fettuccine Alfredo, and an assortment of ravioli, cannelloni, manicotti, and lasagna in different sauces. Specialties are veal parmigiana or piccata, eggplant parmigiana, and chicken saltimbocca. Most entrées are under $20, so it's fairly easy on the pocketbook. The wine list, by the bottle or glass, includes wines from California and Italy. Top off your meal with an espresso and an Italian dessert made fresh daily. The dining room is intimate and island-flavored, and the waitstaff are professional. Locals give this small and out-of-the-way place accolades as one of the best Italian restaurants on the island. You'll be happy you came, and you'll leave well fed.

Groceries and Markets

At the signal along Rt. 50 in Kalaheo, the larger **Menehune Food Mart** stands catty-corner across the intersection from the smaller **Steve's Mini Mart.** Both supply sundries, light groceries, and liquor into the early evening.

A couple of hundred yards up the road toward the golf course from the highway intersection is the **Madieros Farm** store (4365 Papalina Rd., 808/332-8211, 8 A.M.–5 P.M. weekdays, until 3 P.M. Saturdays, closed Sundays), where you can pick up fresh eggs, meat, fish, and prepared Hawaiian foods. A great little place with lots to offer for those with a kitchen.

Every Tuesday at 3:30 P.M. a **farmers market** is held at the Kalaheo Neighborhood Center along the highway near the intersection for locally grown produce, fruits, and flowers. Check it out for good fresh food and a local experience.

SERVICES

The **post office** in Kalaheo is located behind Menehune Food Mart at the main intersection in town.

Next to the post office near the traffic light, the **Kalaheo Clinic** (4489 Papalina Rd., 808/332-8523) is open for checkups and minor emergencies 8 A.M.–8 P.M. Mon.–Fri. and 8 A.M.–noon Saturday.

For **Internet access,** head to Kalaheo Coffee Company; the fee is $5 minimum or $10 per hour.

WEST END

After Kalaheo, the highway dips south again and passes 'Ele'ele, the still-active Port Allen Harbor, and Hanapepe at the mouth of the Hanapepe River, whose basin has long been known as one of the best taro lands in the islands. You pass tiny "sugar towns" and hidden beaches until you enter Waimea, whose east flank was once dominated by a Russian fort, the last vestige of a dream of island dominance gone sour. Captain Cook landed at Waimea in the mid-afternoon of January 20, 1778; a small monument in the town center commemorates the great event. Secondary roads leading inland from Waimea and Kekaha farther west converge, then meander along Waimea Canyon, the Pacific's most superlative gorge. Kekaha, with its now-silenced sugar stacks, marks the end of civilization, and the hard road gives out

just past the Pacific Missile Range Facility. A cane road picks up and carries you to the wide, sun-drenched beach of Polihale, the end of the line, and the southernmost extremity of the Na Pali Coast.

This is the **Waimea District,** the broad and diverse west end of the island. Waimea means Red Water, and the area was so named for the distinctive color of the Waimea River, which bleeds from Mount Wai'ale'ale. It cuts through Waimea Canyon, depositing the rich red soil at its mouth.

The sometimes turbulent but forever enduring love affair between non-Polynesian travelers and the Hawaiian Islands began in west Kaua'i, when Captain Cook arrived off Waimea Bay and a longboat full of wide-eyed sailors made the beach. Immediately, journals were filled

ROBERT NILSEN

HIGHLIGHTS

◖ **Hanapepe Art Galleries:** Hanapepe has become the de facto art center on Kaua'i and has a concentration of artists and galleries as funky and casual as they are. A stop at the galleries should be a part of anyone's trip to the West End, particularly on Friday, when the galleries stay open late and the town sponsors Friday Art Night (page 114).

◖ **Polihale State Park Beach:** As one of the largest beaches on the island, this is an attraction for any beach bum. It's as remote as you can get on this island, a perfect spot to watch the sun set, and the exclamation point to the dramatic Na Pali Coast (page 130).

◖ **Waimea Canyon State Park Overlooks:** Driving up the mountain into the cool interior of the island means driving along the edge of the Waimea Canyon. Along the way are numerous overlooks, specifically located to get the best views into this awesome deep gash of a valley. Don't fail to stop (page 132).

◖ **Koke'e State Park Overlooks:** Looking down into Kalalau Valley and the deep blue ocean beyond is awe inspiring from these overlooks. Travel to the end of the road and peek over the edge into the valley far, far below (page 135).

◖ **Koke'e Natural History Museum:** Any trip to Koke'e State Park should include a stop here for an introduction to forest ecology, the rare plants and animals of the park, the geological growth of the island, and how strong weather has had a hand in shaping the island (page 137).

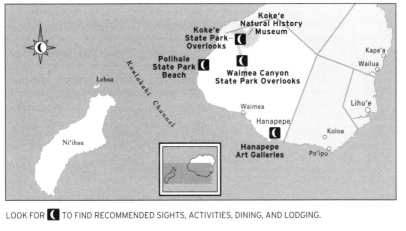

LOOK FOR ◖ TO FIND RECOMMENDED SIGHTS, ACTIVITIES, DINING, AND LODGING.

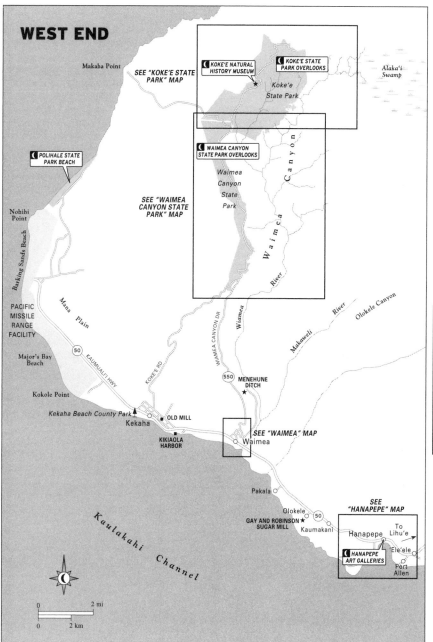

WEST END

Makaha Point

SEE "KOKE'E STATE PARK" MAP

🌙 **KOKE'E NATURAL HISTORY MUSEUM** ★

🌙 **KOKE'E STATE PARK OVERLOOKS**

Koke'e State Park

Alaka'i Swamp

🌙 **POLIHALE STATE PARK BEACH**

🌙 **WAIMEA CANYON STATE PARK OVERLOOKS**

Waimea Canyon State Park

SEE "WAIMEA CANYON STATE PARK" MAP

Waimea Canyon

Waimea River

Nohihi Point

Barking Sands Beach

PACIFIC MISSILE RANGE FACILITY

Mana Plain

Olokele Canyon

Makaweli River

50 KAUMUALI'I HWY

Major's Bay Beach

Kokole Point

KOKE'E RD

WAIMEA CANYON DR

Waimea

550

MENEHUNE DITCH ★

Kekaha Beach County Park 🔺

Kekaha ○

● **OLD MILL**

■ **KIKIAOLA HARBOR**

SEE "WAIMEA" MAP

○ Waimea

Pakala ○

SEE "HANAPEPE" MAP

Olokele ○

GAY AND ROBINSON SUGAR MILL ★

50

Kaumakani ○

Hanapepe

To Lihu'e

Ele'ele

🌙 **HANAPEPE ART GALLERIES**

Port Allen

Kaulakahi Channel

WEST END

© ROBERT NILSEN AND AVALON TRAVEL PUBLISHING, INC.

0 ___ 2 mi
0 ___ 2 km

with glowing descriptions of the loveliness of the newly found island and its people, and the liaison has continued unabated ever since.

PLANNING YOUR TIME

When planning your time for a trip to the West End of the island, you should consider a number of things. First, even though Kaua'i is a fairly small island, it's a fair distance there and back again and many of the worthy sites take some time to get to. There are relatively few accommodations on the West End, but it is possible to use Waimea as a home base because of its inn and cottages. Kekaha, farther to the west, also provides a number of vacation rentals. Take a full day for **Polihale Beach** if you want to lounge, walk the sand, or just read a book with your feet in the water. Better yet, go in the afternoon and stay through sunset, as there are few better and more isolated spots for this romantic activity. Don't miss a drive up the mountain to the state parks and their scenic **overlooks.** Even if you don't hike, make this trip a priority, as the natural environment of the upland forests is totally different than that along the coast. Definitely stop at the **Koke'e Natural History Museum** and spend an hour there learning about the area. If you do hike, try to spend a day or two along the trails. There is a full range of options, from a leisurely nature walk just right for children to strenuous full-day loops, with forest, canyon, swamp, and coastal scenery. Bring all your supplies, as you won't find anything there but a hot meal and a few snacks at the Koke'e Lodge restaurant.

With all its natural beauty, the West End is still intimately tied to agriculture, as it has been for decades. This is one of the two places in the state where the production of sugarcane is a profitable industry. A sugar mill tour would be a worthy side trip, as would a simple walk around Waimea or Hanapepe to catch a glimpse of an older Kaua'i. When in Hanapepe, either on the way to or on the way from a day at Polihale Beach or up the mountain, have a stroll through the **Hanapepe Art Galleries,** as this has the greatest concentration of such galleries on the island.

Hanapepe

As you roll along from Kalaheo to Hanapepe, you're surrounded by former sugarcane fields, now acres of coffee trees. In a moment, you come to **'Ele'ele** and **Port Allen,** separate communities on the east side of the Hanapepe River that are no more than outlying sections of Hanapepe. Predominantly residential, 'Ele'ele sits mostly on the bluff along the highway, where it curves around and turns down to Hanapepe. At the curve, turn off the highway and follow Waialo Road (Rt. 541) from 'Ele'ele Shopping Center down to the Port Allen commercial harbor, past a series of businesses and warehouse-type buildings, the new Port Allen Marine Center shops, and the small boat harbor. Numerous tour boat companies and fishing charters run out of Port Allen, and the Coast Guard keeps a few boats here as well. Kauai Electric has a power plant off to the side that generates about 85 percent of the island's electricity; the remainder is produced by four small hydroelectric plants at other locations on the island. After Hurricane 'Iniki, the powerline that cuts across the island from west to east and then over the mountain to Hanalei was erected, replacing the electrical lines that ran around the island along the highway. Although a shorter route to get electricity to its end users, the powerline is a transgression on the otherwise pristine landscape of Kaua'i.

Aside from the main highway, there is a second route from Kalaheo to Hanapepe. Just outside Kalaheo the road splits, and Highway 540 (Halewili Road) slopes down toward the ocean to the tiny town of Numila, where it turns and shoots across to meet the main highway at 'Ele'ele. **Numila** is a dusty former sugar town, rather disheveled and unkempt. Once a thriving, well-kept community, it now looks as if it's

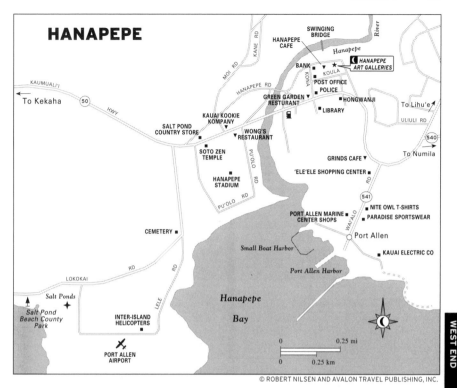

HANAPEPE

To Kekaha
To Lihu'e
To Numila

SWINGING BRIDGE
HANAPEPE CAFE
HANAPEPE ART GALLERIES
BANK
POST OFFICE
POLICE
GREEN GARDEN RESTURANT
HONGWANJI
LIBRARY
KAUAI KOOKIE KOMPANY
SALT POND COUNTRY STORE
WONG'S RESTAURANT
SOTO ZEN TEMPLE
HANAPEPE STADIUM
GRINDS CAFE
'ELE'ELE SHOPPING CENTER
NITE OWL T-SHIRTS
PARADISE SPORTSWEAR
PORT ALLEN MARINE CENTER SHOPS
Port Allen
KAUAI ELECTRIC CO
CEMETERY
Small Boat Harbor
Port Allen Harbor
Hanapepe Bay
Salt Ponds
Salt Pond Beach County Park
INTER-ISLAND HELICOPTERS
PORT ALLEN AIRPORT

KAUMUALI'I HWY
MOI RD
KANE RD
HANAPEPE RD
KOULA
KONA
ULIULI RD
Hanapepe River
PU'OLO RD
PU'OLO RD
WAIALO RD
LOKOKAI RD
RD
LELE RD

0   0.25 mi
0   0.25 km

WEST END

taking on the color of the ground on which it lies. Yet, it's still possible to see fine examples of plantation-era housing here and imagine what it was like during the good years. The McBryde sugar mill once kept this town vibrant, but now its mill and offices house the Kauai Coffee Company and its processing plant.

The town of **Hanapepe** lies at the Hanapepe River mouth. Hanapepe (Crushed Bay), billing itself as "Kaua'i's Biggest Little Town," has had a more glorious past than its present, although it has emerged as a center of the arts and has the greatest concentration of artists' studios on the island. Hawaiians cultivated taro in Hanapepe Valley, making this a significant settlement. Later, the Chinese and others came to grow rice. From the early 1900s until just after World War II, Hanapepe was a bustling town. With a growing population, Hanapepe became an economic center, one of the largest towns on the island, with its main street chockablock with shops and businesses, two movie theaters, and three skating rinks. During the 1940s, thousands of GIs were trained and billeted here before being shipped to the Pacific for overseas duty. Burns Field became the first commercial airstrip on the island, now used only by air tour companies, and Port Allen Harbor remains the island's second largest commercial port and one of the principal harbors for boat tours.

Hanapepe is divided into two sections. As you approach town from the east, look up to your right; if it's early winter, you'll see an entire hillside of bougainvilleas ablaze with a multicolored patchwork of blossoms. The newer section to town lies along Rt. 50; the other is Old Hanapepe, a "must-see" along Hanapepe Road; the Y intersections at both ends of town direct you by sign to the historic main street that parallels the highway. Along

Rt. 50 the police and fire departments, a public library, the Westside Pharmacy, the Hanapepe Hongwanji, a restaurant, and a Shell gas station appear in rapid succession before the bridge (1938). Beyond the bridge are more shops and restaurants, an ice cream shop, and Hanapepe stadium, often lit at night for ball games. Keep a lookout for the Soto Zen Temple Zenshuji on your left. It's quite large and interesting to people who haven't visited a temple before. At the western end of town is the famous Kauai Kookie Kompany. Heading out of town to the west and taking the first turn toward the ocean brings you to Burns Field and Salt Ponds State Park.

Old Hanapepe is a frozen-in-time still life of vintage false-front buildings housing art studios, a local dry goods store, two banks, an excellent restaurant, a swinging foot bridge, and a gift shop or two. Like the newer section of town, it lies on both sides of "the bridge," but most businesses on the west side of this one-lane bridge (built 1911) have closed their doors or moved away. For a greater understanding of the history of the town see www.kauai.net/hanapepe and, to help navigate its streets as you walk, locate a *Historic Hanapepe Walking Tour Map* at one of the businesses in town.

While there is some parking on Hanapepe Street, there are two small public parking lots, one directly in front of the swinging bridge and the other a few doors to the east. Alternately, you can park along Kona Street, behind the fire station near an in-town Hanapepe Park.

The road parallels and runs much closer to the coast after Hanapepe, bypassing a series of still-working "sugar towns" until you arrive in Waimea. **Kaumakani,** a small cluster of vernacular homes with a few dirt lanes where sugar plantation workers live, has a post office, minimart and bakery, and the Ni'ihau Helicopter office. Here, everything seems to be tinged with red. *Mauka* of the highway, surrounded by cane fields, is the refurbished, plantation-style United Methodist Church, established 1901, the oldest Methodist church on the island.

Less than a half mile west is **Olokele.** As counterpoint to the disheveled and dusty look of Kau-makani, Olokele is a one-street community of larger and better-kept houses, wide green lawns, and towering canopy-like monkeypod trees. Manifesting an air of an easier life from earlier decades, quaint lampposts line this road as it dips down to the still-active sugar mill. At night the town displays a genteel quality. This is where the plantation managers and mill higher-ups of days gone by lived. Take a drive down toward the mill and draw your own conclusions about those who made this town their own.

Next is **Pakala,** another dusty community where sugar plantation workers live, noted more for its surfing beach than anything else. At mile marker 21, a bunch of cars pulled off the road probably means the surf's up. Follow the pathway to try the waves yourself or just to watch the show. This beach is not a county park. Walk down past the bridge to a well-worn pathway leading through a field. In a few minutes is the beach, a 500-yard-long horseshoe of white sand. Off to the left is a rocky promontory popular with local anglers. The swimming is fair, and the reef provides good snorkeling, but the real reason to go is the surf. The beach is nicknamed "Infinity" because the waves last so long; they come rolling in in graceful arcs to spill upon the beach, then recede in a regular, hypnotic pattern, causing the next wave to break and roll perfectly.

SIGHTS
Hanapepe Valley Overlook
About halfway between Kalaheo and Hanapepe, along the inland side of the highway, an HVB Warrior points to an overlook. Stop. Hanapepe Valley Overlook is no farther away than your car door, served up as easily as a fast-food snack at a drive-through window. For no effort, you get a remarkable panorama of a classic Hawaiian valley, now somewhat overgrown, that slices into the lofty mountain interior. Small fields of taro are still planted at its lower end.

Kauai Coffee Company Visitor Center and Museum
Over 150 years ago, coffee was planted in this region of Kaua'i as the first coffee plantation in the Hawaiian Islands. After some years and little

success, coffee production was discontinued here but took hold on the Big Island, at Kona. Today, coffee is grown not only on the Big Island, but also on Maui, Moloka'i, O'ahu, and once again on Kaua'i, where it's relatively big business. The Kauai Coffee Company has a 3,400-acre plantation of drip-irrigated Hawaiian arabica coffee bean plants and produces roughly four million pounds of coffee a year. Harvest is done mechanically and takes place September through November, the busiest time of the year on the estate. This is the largest single coffee estate in Hawaii and captures about 60 percent of the Hawaiian coffee market. If you use Rt. 540, and particularly if you're a coffee connoisseur, stop at the Kauai Coffee Company Visitor Center and Museum (808/335-0813 or 800/545-8605, www.kauaicoffee.com, 9 A.M.–5 P.M. daily), just beyond Numila. Refurbished plantation build-

ings now hold the gift shop and museum. Stop in to peruse the historical artifacts and learn how coffee is handled at each stage from tree to cup; sample tastes are always available. Aside from the usual gift, clothing, and food items, you can purchase a bag or case of estate-grown ground or whole bean coffee in any of the numerous roasts. Mail orders are gladly welcome, and coffee club members can get regular shipments.

Swinging Bridge

Originally constructed to carry a water line across the river into town, this small, wood-plank, suspension foot bridge connects downtown Hanapepe to houses on the far side of the river. Although stable enough for foot traffic, it does bounce and sway somewhat, more so when two or more people are crossing at the same time. Crossing the bridge deposits you almost in someone's back yard, but you can turn left and walk the levee back to the old vehicular bridge and return into town along Hanapepe Road.

COFFEE PROCESSING

Coffee grows on short trees or bushes, and it can usually first be harvested about five years after planting. The fruits, which grow close to the tree's branches, are green when immature but turn bright red and are called "cherries" when they ripen in mid- to late fall. While much coffee is hand-picked – a labor-intensive process – the Kauai Coffee Company uses machines to pick the cherries by straddling the trees and shaking the cherries loose from the branches.

Once collected, the harvested cherries are trucked to the mill for wet processing. Here the ripe cherries are separated from the overripe and immature, and the skin and pulp removed to reveal the beans (usually two) inside. These beans are then washed and dried mechanically to a set moisture content, after which the parchment covering and silver-like skin is removed. Sorting is done by size, color, and density, and finally by hand if necessary to remove any stray unacceptable beans, then graded. After grading, samples from each batch are roasted and tasted as a final test, then bagged, inspected, and shipped.

Hanapepe's swinging bridge

ROBERT NILSEN

Salt Pond Beach County Park

On the western outskirts of town, a sign points *makai* (toward the sea) down Rt. 543. Follow the sign past a small veterans' cemetery, where an HVB Warrior points down Lele Road to Salt Pond Beach County Park, the best beach and windsurfing spot on this end of the island. This beach is at the west end of the Port Allen Airport (Burns Field) runway, once the major airport for the island but now only an airstrip with no facilities that helicopter and ultralight aircraft companies use. Local people from around Hanapepe enjoy this popular beach park. The swimming is excellent—a natural breakwater in front of the lifeguard stand makes a pool safe for tots—and snorkeling is fair out on the periphery of the bay. Even when the water is too rough at other south shore beaches, it is generally smoother here. Surfers enjoy the breaks here, and a constant gentle breeze makes the area popular with windsurfers. Bring a picnic lunch and make a day of it; on the weekends you might find a *kaukau* wagon parked here for light snacks. Amenities include several pavilions and picnic tables, toilets, and showers, and camping is allowed with a county permit.

Along the road to Salt Pond Beach, you pass the actual **salt ponds,** evaporative basins scraped out of the red earth that have been used for hundreds of years. The sea salt here is still harvested on a very small scale but isn't considered pure enough for commercial use. The local people know better; they harvest the salt in the spring and summer, and because of its so-called impurities (which actually add a special flavor), it is a sought-after commodity and an appreciated gift for family and friends. If you see salt in the basins, it belongs to someone. Please don't take any.

ENTERTAINMENT
Friday Art Night

Following in the footsteps of Lahaina, Maui, Hanapepe has established Friday Art Night, to celebrate its strong and growing connection with the Hawaiian art community. Of the galleries in town, most are one-artist shops. Every Friday evening 6–9 P.M., those along the old main drag keep their doors open, catering to art lovers and others looking to peruse or buy. Most artists are available at their galleries and proudly display their latest works. Some may even pull their easels out on the sidewalk and demonstrate there. Refreshments are often available, and musical performances are usually given near the entrance to the swinging bridge. As casual a place as this is, the scene sometimes carries a main street block party atmosphere.

◖ Hanapepe Art Galleries

Artists and their galleries come and go, but a few seem to stay for years. Listed below are some of the major players. All galleries are small.

As you enter town and make the bend in the road, the first building on the right houses **Kauai Fine Arts** (3905 Hanapepe Rd., 808/335-3778, www.brunias.com, open 9 A.M.–5 P.M. daily), which stocks prints, antique maps, some books, and various wooden art objects from around the world. A great place to get lost in the age of exploration or early 20th-century Hawaii.

Walking into **Giorgio's Gallery** (3871 Hanapepe Rd., 808/335-3940, www.giorgiosart.com) is like walking into a color palette. Filling the canvas with bold strokes and bright colors, local artist Giorgio paints only with a palette knife, doing most of his work outside. Sunflowers are a favorite, but you may see well-known spots around the island rendered in his work.

Combining a gallery and studio, **Banana Patch Studios** (3865 Hanapepe Rd., 808/335-5944, www.bananapatchstudio.com) lets you peruse the ceramic tiles and pottery displayed here and peek through the large windows of the studio as the artists work. Also displayed are oil paintings and prints of natural scenes of the island done by Joanna Carolan, the studio owner. Banana Patch Studios is located next to the swinging bridge, so stop by the gallery after you check out the river.

Across the street is the **Kama'aina Koa Gallery** (3848 Hanapepe Rd., 808/335-5483, closed Sunday), showing fine examples of wood carvings, furniture, and other wood pieces crafted with skill, experience, and a feeling of movement. Sharing the same storefront is **Uncle**

Eddie's Aloha Angels, which features these celestial beings in all their manifestations.

Stop in at the fine art studio of **Dawn Traina Gallery** (3840 Hanapepe Rd., 808/335-3993). Dawn, knowing she wanted to be an artist since childhood, pursued an education in art on both coasts. Working largely in oil and pencil, with acrylic and pastels on occasion, Dawn specializes in portraiture. She not only captures the feeling of what's current today, but somehow, since moving to Hawaii in 1979, has been able to tap into the lore of Hawaii and to visibly render the spirit of ancient chants, dances, legends, and the gentility of the plantation days.

Next door is the **Arius Hopman Studio Gallery** (3840C Hanapepe Rd., 808/335-0227, www.hopmanart.com) featuring mostly landscape watercolors and photography. Painted on location, each watercolor piece demonstrates a connectedness to the spot. Colors are vibrant, and there is feeling in every stroke. Commissions are accepted. Like the watercolors, his digital prints are evocative and render the living nature of the land.

SHOPPING

By and large, most shops in Hanapepe have moved out to the Port Allen turnoff, leaving the downtown area with art galleries, gift shops, and restaurants that cater to tourists.

At mile marker 16, in the shadow of McDonald's golden arches, is the **'Ele'ele Shopping Center,** with various eateries, a post office, First Hawaiian Bank branch, self-service laundry, Big Save Supermarket, and Ace Hardware.

The newest shopping Center here is **Port Allen Marine Center,** occupying two buildings along the road to the harbor. Among the shops here are Kauai Coffee Company, Kauai Chocolate Co., and a few clothing shops. In addition, Captain Andy's, Capt. Zodiac, Holo Holo Charters, and Blue Dolphin all have their tour offices here.

What began as a slap from Mother Nature turned an obscure tiny company, **Paradise Sportswear** (4350 Waialoa Rd., 808/335-5670 or 800/717-3478, www.dirtshirt.com, 9 A.M.– 5 P.M. daily) into one of the most famous in the state. After Hurricane 'Iniki ravaged Kaua'i in 1992, the staff returned to find the roof of the building completely torn off and the warehouse, containing shirts jobbed from other companies, inundated with red dirt that rendered the shirts unsellable—or maybe not! Amidst the devastation, the future seemed bleak, but as legend would have it, one person said, in effect, "Ah, these shirts actually look pretty cool." Perhaps spurred by desperation, the forlorn faces, after rolling their eyes heavenward, slowly reconsidered and began to smile. Voilà, the **Red Dirt Shirt** was born. Dedicated to the community, Paradise Sportswear is a true cottage industry, employing local families who pick up ordinary white shirts, take them home, and repeatedly dip them in vats of Kaua'i's famous red dirt. After they bring them back, other local people working on the premises apply original silk-screen designs. No two shirts—which range in color from deep copper to burnt orange—are the same. Tour the factory, in a large industrail building just up from Port Allen Harbor, daily 9 A.M.–noon and 1–4 P.M. to watch the silk-screening process, and make sure to stop in at the retail shop, where you can choose from numerous designs and styles, ranging from tiny tank tops for tots to XXXXXLs for walking Sherman tanks, and take advantage of discounts on factory seconds and discontinued designs. The largest Red Dirt T-shirt made, a special order 8XL, was for a Hawaiian sumo wrestler! Retail outlets featuring Red Dirt T-shirts are found on every island, with innumerable boutiques and shops carrying these very distinctive souvenirs. With new owners, the company has introduced a stonewashed Lava Blues line of dyed blue T-shirts with similar island-inspired designs.

In another section of the same warehouse is **Nite Owl T-shirts** (808/335-6119 or 888/430-9907, www.niteowlt-shirts.com, 9 A.M.–5 P.M. daily), which, in addition to the racks of shirts with its own intriguing designs, does printing for other retailers on the island. Stop here for a wide selection and good deals on pricing. Although Nite Owl doesn't have the name the Red Dirt Shirt company has, the quality and range of designs are equally good.

In town, only a few stores hang on. **Robert's** (3837 Hanapepe Rd., 808/335-5332) clothing and jewelry shop is a true survivor of decades past, and it's about the only standard retail business in town. Stop there to check out alohawear, shorts, slippers, and beachwear. Find it next to the swinging bridge.

The only retail operator on the west side of the bridge along Hanapepe Rd. is **Talk Story Bookstore** where you can pick up a used book to read at the beach. Along the highway, near the Y intersection at the western end of town, is the large **Mariko's** gift shop, which caters to tour buses.

RECREATION

Boating and scuba tour operators use Port Allen Harbor; those who fly the skies use Burns Field. Land tours of their sugar mill and plantation, as well as outlying ranch land, are offered by the Gay and Robinson company from their visitors center in Olokele.

Water Activities

Blue Dolphin Charters (808/335-5553 or 877/511-1311, www.kauaiboats.com) welcomes you aboard its 63-foot and 65-foot power catamarans on which you can sail, snorkel, scuba dive, use the water slide, photograph spinning dolphins, and watch the sun go down. All trips depart from Port Allen Harbor except for the Poʻipu Sunset cruise, which leaves from Kukuiʻula Harbor. Tours include a five- to six-hour Na Pali Coast snorkel and scuba run for $129 and a seven-hour Niʻihau snorkel and scuba trip for $169 that also takes in part of the Na Pali Coast. The additional fee for diving is $30. Blue Dolphin is one of only two companies that head to the north end of Niʻihau and Lehua Rock. A three-hour Na Pali sunset cruise costs $99, and the two-hour Poʻipu sunset tour is $64. All tours run daily—the sunset sail only during whale season—except for the Niʻihau trip, which goes on Tuesday and Friday.

Running under sail is possible with Captain Andy of **Capt. Andy's Sailing Adventures** (808/335-6833 or 800/535-0830, www.captandys.com). He lets the wind power his 55-foot catamaran as much as possible. Captain Andy and his crew will take you for a morning of sailing up the Na Pali Coast, snorkeling,

and beachcombing or an afternoon snorkel and dinner trip (summer only) for $129, or an afternoon snorkel and sunset cruise daily except Sunday also along the Na Pali Coast for $95. These tours leave from Port Allen and are always a good time. A two-hour sunset cruise for $59 leaves on Sunday only from Kukuiʻula Harbor near Poʻipu. Whale-watching tours along the south coast are available in season. Kids always get discounts.

Holo Holo Charters (808/335-0815 or 800/848-6130, www.holoholocharters.com) is another well-established and reputable company that also runs out of Port Allen Harbor. Its two cats, one motorized and one for sailing, offer various options, including a three-hour sunset cruise for $89, a full-day cruise to Niʻihau for snorkeling and sightseeing for $169, and morning and afternoon sailing snorkel trips up the Na Pali Coast for $119. Holo Holo Charters treats its guests right.

Also try **Catamaran Kahanu** (808/645-6176 or 888/213-7711, www.catamarankahanu.com). Operated by a family whose ancestors may have lived along the Na Pali Coast, this company offers an intimate experience on its powered catamaran on its morning Na Pali Coast tour for $115 or the afternoon sightseeing tour for $85. Check in is at the booth near the parking lot just up from the harbor.

Kauai Sea Tours (808/335-5309 or 800/733-7997, www.kauaiseatours.com) also offers similar power sailing catamaran tours at similar prices out of Port Allen, with the addition of rigid-hull raft tours.

The oldest and best known of the Hawaiian Zodiac companies is **Captain Zodiac** (808/335-2719, www.napali.com), operated by Capt. Andy's Sailing, with which it shares the same store space in the Port Allen Marine Center. From Port Allen Harbor, Captain Zodiac runs a 29-foot rigid-hull raft, making a five-hour snorkel trip and six-hour exploration trip up the Na Pali Coast in summer for $129–159. The longer trip makes a stop for hiking and a cultural lesson at the remote Nuʻalolo Beach. During the winter months, rates are reduced and two-hour whale-watching tours are added for $49.

Located in a shop at the entrance to the harbor, **Mana Divers** (808/335-0881 or 877/348-3669, www.manadivers.com) runs guided dive tours from it 32-foot catamaran. These tours run $105 with your own gear or $130 if they supply the gear. Various shore dives are also offered and first-time scuba divers are welcome. Certification courses are taught for those wishing to do more than a one-time dive.

Also operating out of Port Allen harbor, **Bubbles Below** (808/332-7333 or 866/524-6268, www.bubblesbelowkauai.com) also offers numerous boat and shore dives, including one to Lehua Island and Ni'ihau.

Sport Fishing Kauai (808/639-0013, www.fishing-kauai-hawaii.com) leaves from the Port Allen harbor for private or shared fishing trips on Bertram Sportfishers. Rates run from $95 per person on a shared boat for half a day to $1,075 for a 10-hour day charter boat trip to Ni'ihau waters.

Helicopter Tours

Using fast Hughes 500 four-seater machines with their doors off for an open-air experience, **Inter-Island Helicopters** (808/335-5009 or 800/656-5009, www.interislandhelicopters.com) flies the circle-island route but adds one tour with a waterfall picnic stop above Kilauea. The 60-minute tour runs $185 and the waterfall tour is $300. Its office is at the Burns Field airstrip.

Although based in Kaumakani, a few miles farther to the west, **Ni'ihau Helicopter** (808/335-3500 or 877/441-3500, www.niihau.us, 8 A.M.–2 P.M. Mon.–Sat.) also uses Burns Field. Set up to provide medical services for the residents of Ni'ihau, the twin-engine Agusta 109A helicopter is also employed for sightseeing tours and hunting trips when there is enough interest. Ni'ihau Helicopter runs completely different tours from all other helicopter companies on Kaua'i. Its four-hour tour leaves at 9 A.M. and flies you to Ni'ihau and back and gives you plenty of time on a Ni'ihau beach. Rates are $325 per person; tours can take up to seven individuals. This is virtually the only way to get to Ni'ihau unless you are an invited guest.

Ultralight Power Hang Gliding

Also flying out of Burns Field in a 70-horsepower ultralight power glider is **Birds in Paradise** (808/822-5309, www.birdsinparadise.com), which instructs you how to soar above the emerald green and azure blue of Kaua'i and have a truly unique experience in this "motorcycle with wings." Instructor Gerry Charlebois has thrilled over 10,000 brave and slightly wacky souls and advertises that it's "the most fun you can have with your clothes on." Safety features include a backup rocket parachute that will bring the entire craft safely to the ground, and a surprising structural strength certified twice as strong as a Cessna and capable of withstanding 6 Gs positive load and 3 Gs negative. This state-of-the-art tandem glider needs only about 100 feet for takeoff and landing. Gerry has mounted both a video and a still camera so you can write back home, "Look, Mom—no hands!"—and as she's always said, not much sense either. For those who enjoy pushing the envelope in a contraption soaring at 55 mph, prices run $115 for a 30-minute lesson, $190 for one hour. Advanced instructional flights run $270 for 90 minutes and $355 for two hours. For safety reasons, these flights are open to those over age 12 and less than 260 pounds; it's preferable to wear long pants, long-sleeve shirts, and closed-toe shoes or strapped sandals with socks.

Running a similar operation at similar prices from Burns Field is **Ultralight Adventures Kauai** (808/332-0790, www.kauaiultralight.com).

Skydiving

Want to do the jump without wings? Arrange to skydive with **Skydive Kauai** (808/335-5859, www.skydivekauai.com). After a 20-minute plane ride from Burns Field, you free fall to 4,500 feet where the chute opens and you begin your glide back to the airfield. This joy ride runs $229. You must be 18 years old and weigh less than 200 pounds.

Land Tours

Gay and Robinson, owners of the sugar mill in Olokele, offer two-hour bus and walking tours of the mill and surrounding fields as an overview of the sugar production process and everyday mill operation. Pants (or shorts) and closed-toe shoes must be worn, and it's a good idea to wear clothing that you wouldn't mind getting stained by the rich red dirt in the fields. Hard hats and goggles are provided for the part of the tour that goes through the mill. Perhaps the best time to visit is April–October, when the mill is active. These **sugar plantation tours** start at the visitors center and museum (808/335-2824, open 8 A.M.–4 P.M. Mon.–Fri., 11 A.M.–3 P.M. on Sat., www.gandrtours-kauai.com), near the mill office, where there are displays of artifacts relating to the sugar industry. Tours are offered at 8:45 A.M. and 12:45 P.M. Mon.–Fri., except holidays, and run $30 per person for adults with a 30 percent discount for children 8–15; call to make a reservation.

In addition to the sugar plantation tour, Gay and Robinson also offers a half-day ATV mountain tour on their property that starts at 7:45 A.M. and includes lunch and a swim in a mountain pool. A rough 13 miles, with plenty of elevation change, this outing is designed for intermediate and advanced riders who already know how to handle a powerful ATV. The ATV tour runs $139 and riders must be 16 years old or older, wear closed-toe shoes and long pants. Wear your swimsuit and bring a towel. All necessary gear is provided. Reservations are necessary.

FOOD
Coffee Shop and Desserts

Kauai Coffee Company (808/335-5333) in the Port Allen Marine Center is open 5:30 A.M.–3 P.M. and serves its own coffee, as well as panini, pastries, homemade gelato, and smoothies. For dessert, head a few doors down to **Kauai Chocolate Company** (808/335-0448) to sample their inventive chocolate concoctions, ice cream, and other homemade sweets. A stop at either, before or after a tour on the water, is a welcome respite.

The **Kauai Kookie Kompany** makes its well-loved cookies in Hanapepe but distributes them around the state. Stop by their factory outlet sales shop (1-3529 Kaumuali'i Hwy., 808/335-5003, www.kauaikookie.com, 8 A.M.–4 P.M. Mon.–Fri., 11 A.M.–4 P.M. Sat.–Sun.) for a taste of macada-

mia shortbread, Kona coffee, guava macadamia, or coconut krispies cookies, among others, and pick up a bag or two for the road or as a gift. The store is located at the back of a warehouse-type building across from Wong's Restaurant. Cookies and gift baskets, as well as its tropical salad dressings, are available by mail order.

Across the street from Wong's is [**Lappert's Ice Cream** (808/335-6121 or 800/356-4045), the original walk-up ice cream shop for this well-known and much-appreciated island-wide business, which now has outlets on O'ahu, Maui, and also in Princeville, Koloa, and Kapa'a on Kaua'i. Rich and creamy, Lappert's ice cream has about 16 percent butterfat in its regular flavors and some 8 percent in its fruit flavors. Once you taste, you'll know why it's an island favorite. Lappert's also bakes macadamia nut cookies and roasts its own coffee, and these plus T-shirts and mugs can be mail ordered to your door.

Local Style

In a separate building at the 'Ele'ele Shopping Center is **Grinds Cafe** (808/335-6027, 6:30 A.M.–9 P.M. daily), a local place serving mostly local foods at reasonable prices. Egg and grill items are served up for breakfast; for the rest of the day, sandwiches, burgers, and plate lunches are the norm. Any time of the day is coffee time here. Except for pizza, almost everything on the menu is less than $9.75. Eat in or pick up orders to go. Grinds gets a thumbs up from locals.

The **Green Garden Restaurant** (808/335-5422, 5–9 P.M. except Tuesday), an old standby along the highway between the fire station and the river in town, is marked by a tangle of vegetation that almost hides the building. Since 1948, this family-owned restaurant has offered tourist-quality food in large portions, with *aloha* service. The main dining room has a few plants, but the name is really held up by the green decor and overgrown exterior. Some time following the death of the family matriarch in 2002, the Green Garden decided to make changes to the restaurant. It now serves finer-quality dinner only and is a non-alcohol establishment. Entrées include broiled fresh catch, beef ribs, barbecue chicken, rack of lamb, and shrimp tempura. Dinners come with salad bar and homemade soup, with a choice of rice, fried rice, or French fries, and selections run mostly under $21. Save space for the famous and always delicious homemade pies.

For local food at moderate prices, try **Bobby's Restaurant** (3824 Hanapepe Rd.) offering plate lunches, or the **Da Imu Hut Cafe** (3771 Hanapepe Rd.) offering a full assortment of simple local grinds and refreshing drinks.

As you come into the old town from the east, the first store on your left—in an old house— is **Taro Ko,** a tiny mom-and-pop, house-front shop selling taro chips. It's nothing to look at on the outside, but the flavors of the chips draw people here. While mama is inside looking after the deep-fryers, papa might be out lounging under the tree.

Organic Vegetarian (Plus)

〖 **Hanapepe Cafe and Espresso Bar** (3830 Hanapepe Rd., 808/335-5011, open 11 A.M.– 3 P.M. Mon.–Thurs., 11 A.M.–2 P.M. Fri., and Fri. only for dinner 6–9 P.M.) is a fantastic eclectic restaurant for mind and body. It's the best restaurant in town—and for miles around. Housed in the old town drugstore (circa 1939), the original soda fountain counter is still used, tastefully modernized with a black-and-white

BRIEF SUGAR PRODUCTION OVERVIEW

The only operating sugar plantation on Kaua'i is the Gay and Robinson Company in Olokele. G&R has about 2,500 acres of planted sugar between Hanapepe and Waimea, with an additional 3,000 acres in Kekaha. Root stock, hand-cut into 18-inch sections from seed stocks, are laid into shallow rows, covered and irrigated. Drip irrigation is used to conserve water and allow for fertilizer and a maturing agent to be introduced easily. Cane grows for roughly two years before harvesting and can reach 30 feet in height. As it grows, its leaves shift hues of green, making a patchwork of different shades when seen from above. Just before harvesting, the leaves are burned off, allowing the tall stalks to be pushed into rows, scooped onto trucks, and hauled to the mill for processing.

At the mill, these cane stalks are loaded onto a conveyor and pressure washed before being chopped and pressed to release the juice. The juice is then heated, clarified of impurities and/or filtered, and sent to an evaporator to take out extra water. The thick "syrup" that results is sent to a centrifuge that separates the raw sugar crystals from the molasses. The raw sugar is then bagged and stored and eventually sent for refining, which is done at the C&H refinery in Crocket, California.

About 30 acres are harvested each day, just

unloading cut sugar cane at the Olokele Mill

about the production capacity of the mill. Each acre yields approximately 100 tons of sugarcane, which, when processed, makes 14 tons of raw sugar or about 25,000 pounds after refining, as well as over three tons of black strap molasses. In addition, the fibery residue of the cane stalk, called bagasse, is burned to fuel the mill boilers. To grow all this, plenty of water is needed – about a million gallons of water per ton of sugar – but Kaua'i's wet interior has never failed to produce this and plenty more for commercial and residential use. Processing runs for about nine months; repairs to the mill take place in winter.

checkerboard motif. All the food served is health-conscious vegetarian or seafood with an attempt at organic and locally grown whenever possible, but always fresh and definitely savory and satisfying. Lunch brings homemade soups, garden-fresh salads, sandwiches and garden burgers, and specialties like frittatas and lasagna, generally in the $6'10 range. The dinner menu is usually a half-and-half mix of vegetarian and seafood, sometimes with crepes or pasta specialties, and these often run $16–24. Although evening entrées can be somewhat limited, all meals are creative and you definitely get your money's worth. Dinner music is provided by solo slack-key performer Cindy Combs, who has been playing here for years and never fails to delight. If you are craving a snack, quiet cup of coffee, or a full meal, you can't beat the Hanapepe Cafe and Espresso Bar. As Hanapepe Cafe is open for dinner only during Friday Art Night, reservations are a must as everyone heads this way for the scrumptious food after a walk through the art galleries. Bring your own bottle if you care for a glass of wine with dinner.

Thai

Toi's Thai Kitchen (808/335-3111, 10:30 A.M.–2 P.M. and 5:30–9 P.M. Mon.–Sat.), family operated and one of the best Thai restaurants on Kaua'i, is in the back corner of the 'Ele'ele Shopping Center. Prepared by Mom and served by her lovely daughters, the menu starts with items like spicy sour soup with lemongrass and ginger, spring rolls, or deep-fried tofu. Entrées, generally under $10, include stir-fried eggplant and tofu in a spicy sauce with your choice of meat, savory satay, and yellow curry with your choice of meat. For most items, you have your choice of meat, poultry, fish, seafood, eggplant, or vegetarian, and, while food here has a zing, it can be adjusted to your preference in spiciness. One of the sweet Thai desserts comes with some meals, but if not, order one—it's a treat. Although some Thai decorations adorn the walls, it's not for the decor that you come, but for the tasty and reasonably priced food.

Chinese

Over the bridge and on your left is another island institution, **Wong's Chinese Restaurant** (1-3540 Kaumuali'i Hwy., 808/335-5066), open daily except Monday for breakfast, lunch, and dinner. Wong's is one giant dining room reminiscent of a small-town banquet hall that caters to local bowling leagues and wedding receptions. It's a favorite of the tour buses and can be crowded. The service is friendly, the portions large, and the food, while not memorable, is very reasonably priced; you won't complain, but you won't be impressed, either. Wong's specialties are Chinese and Japanese dishes, most $8–10. If that isn't enough, **Omoide's Deli and Bakery** occupies a second section of the same building, where you can pick up a sandwich or pizza, birthday cake, or slice of its island-famous homemade *liliko'i* (passion fruit) chiffon pie.

Groceries

The only large food store in the area is the Big Save Supermarket (open 6:30 A.M.–10 P.M. Mon.–Sat., until 9 P.M. Sunday) located in the 'Ele'ele Shopping Center. At the western end of town near the Y intersection is **Salt Ponds Country Store** for sundries, and across from the swinging bridge parking lot is **Aloha Spirits** for liquor and snacks.

Farmers Market

On Thursday 3:30–5:30 P.M. a Sunshine **farmers market** is held at Hanapepe Town Park behind the fire station. Stop by for the freshest in local organic produce.

SERVICES

A **post office** is located in the 'Ele'ele Shopping Center, along with the **self-service laundry,** which is open 24 hours a day but has no change machine or soap dispenser.

A short way down toward the harbor is the 'Ele'ele branch of the Kauai Medical Clinic (4382 Waialo Rd., 808/335-0499).

Waimea

Like the Hanapepe Valley back down the coast, the area near the mouth of the Waimea River was historically a large settlement area, and the river valley was used for taro production, some of which carries on today. Kaumuali'i, the last great king of Kaua'i, maintained a household here, so Waimea for a time was a seat of power. For decades, Waimea was one of the principal towns and ports on the island, but following the creation of Nawiliwili and Port Allen harbors, the increasing importance of Lihu'e as the seat of government, and the shifting of population to the eastern end of the island, Waimea slowly

began to lose its vibrancy, taking a big hit when the sugar mill closed in 1969.

The town of Waimea has several sights of interest—pick up a copy of the *Historic Waimea Town* brochure to help you navigate. You can walk to see its old buildings, churches, the Captain Cook landing site, the sugar mill ruins, mill camp housing, and a royal coconut grove; a Russian fort lies across the river on the far bank. Waimea also has two fine accommodations, a brewpub, some reasonably good restaurants, and limited shopping. In addition, you'll find two supermarkets, two gas stations (last chance

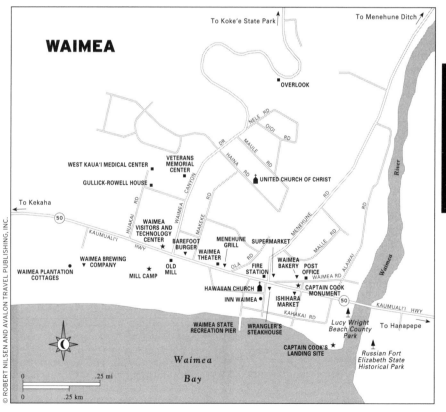

for gas), several boat tour companies, a self-service laundry, library, two banks, a sporting goods store, and a pharmacy. As Waimea is the gateway to the Waimea Canyon and Koke'e State Parks, one of the two roads up the mountain starts here in town. This is Waimea Canyon Drive (Rt. 550).

SIGHTS
Russian Fort Elizabeth State Historical Park

The remains of a Russian fort still guard the eastern entrance to Waimea town. Just east of the river, turn left into the parking lot at the sign for the park. The fort, roughly shaped like an eight-pointed star, dates from 1817, when a German doctor, Georg Anton Schaeffer, built it in the name of Czar Nicholas of Russia, naming it after the potentate's daughter. Schaeffer, a self-styled adventurer and agent for the Russian-American Company, saw great potential in the domination of Hawaii and built two other forts on Kaua'i, one on the bluff at Princeville, which overlooks Hanalei Bay, and the other down along the beachfront on the bay. Owing to political maneuverings with other European nations, Czar Nicholas never warmed to Schaeffer's enterprises and withdrew official support. For a time, Kaua'i's King Kaumuali'i flew the Russian flag, perhaps in a subtle attempt to play one foreign power against another. Soon, Schaeffer was unceremoniously kicked off Kaua'i, sent to Honolulu, and then forced to leave the islands altogether. The fort fell into disrepair and was virtually dismantled in 1864, when 38 guns of various sizes were removed. The stout walls, once 30 feet thick, are now mere rubble, humbled by encircling, nondescript underbrush. However, from points near its periphery you'll still get a reasonable view of Waimea Bay. Pick up a brochure at the entrance (if available) and walk the path inside and around the fortification. With money and effort from the state, this park could be a useful educational center and scenic location, rather than the overgrown neglected spot that it is.

Waimea Shoreline

Just after you cross the Waimea River, signs point to **Lucy Wright Beach County Park,** a five-acre park popular with the local folk. There's a picnic area, restrooms, showers, a playground, and tent camping with a county permit. The park is situated along the mouth of the river, which makes the water a bit murky. The swimming is fair if the water is clear, and the surfing is decent around the river mouth. The Kilohana Canoe Club launches here to practice on the bay if water conditions are good, or on the river if not. A few hundred feet to the west of this park is the **Waimea State Recreation Pier,** open for picnicking and good for open-ocean pole fishing and crabbing. Reach it by walking along the beach or down a back street behind the Waimea Library. The beach at both of these parks is not really recommended for swimming and is often full of driftwood. This narrow salt and pepper beach continues down past the Waimea Plantation Cottages property to Kikiaola Harbor.

Captain Cook Monuments

Captain Cook's achievements were surely deserving of more than the uninspiring commemorative markers around Waimea. Whether you revere him as a great explorer or denigrate him as an opportunistic despoiler, his accomplishments in mapping the great Pacific were unparalleled and changed the course of history. In his memory, **Captain Cook's Landing** displays a very modest marker attached to a boulder on the beach at Lucy Wright Beach Park, commemorating his "discovery" of the Sandwich Islands at 3:30 P.M. on September 20, 1778. A second landing marker and **Captain Cook's Monument** statue stand on the median strip Hofgaard Park in downtown Waimea.

Menehune Ditch

If you're fascinated by Kaua'i's half-legendary little people, you might want to take a look at what's left of the **Menehune Ditch** (Kiki a Ola), a stone wall encasing an aqueduct curiously built in a fashion unused by and apparently un-

a statue of Captain Cook in Waimea

of a time when Waimea was a much more thriving community and more of the river valley was farmed in taro and rice.

Historic Buildings

As a testament to its former importance, Waimea has numerous well-maintained old structures. Standing across from the Captain Cook Monument in Hofgaard Park in the middle of town is the 1929 First Hawaiian Bank Building. Around the corner is the older Electric Power Co. building (1907). Across from the fire station is the Hawaiian Church, built in 1865 and renovated in 1995—there's been a congregation since 1820. Across the street in two directions are the Fah Inn (1890), now a store for antiques and collectibles, and the old Ako Store (1909), now Wrangler's Steakhouse. The Yamase and Masuda buildings, one block up on either side of the intersection, date from 1919. The 1938 art deco Waimea Theater, renovated in 1999, is a few steps up the road and once again open for movies. Established in 1859, the Waimea United Church of Christ building is the oldest church extant in town. The oldest extant building in town, placed on the National Register of Historic Places in 1978, is the New England–style, quarried limestone Gullick-Rowell House (1829), set on a shaded, overgrown lot at the entrance to the hospital. This house was continually occupied until 2004 and is slated to become a museum at some point in the future.

From 1884 to 1969, Waimea was the home of a thriving small sugar mill and center for a plantation community. While the mill structure is in a state of disrepair, a number of the workers' houses survive, and the back lanes of this "camp" give evidence of what life in the former plantation was like. A guided **mill camp walking tour** starts at the small Faye Museum in the administration building of Waimea Plantation Cottages, in the coconut grove at the west end of town. Led by volunteers, this strolling tour focuses on the laborers' homes and gardens and the social role of such camp communities in past plantation life on the island. Tours are offered at 9 A.M. on Tuesday

known to the Polynesian settlers of Hawaii, in which mating stones are cut to match. The road now covers much of the ditch, which was cut into the riverside cliff face. The oral tradition states that this dressed stone ditch was built by order of Ola, high chief of Waimea, and that he paid his little workers in 'opae, a tiny shrimp that was their staple. On payday, they supposedly sent up such a great cheer that they were heard on O'ahu. Said to have once stretched 25 miles up the valley, the site is greatly reduced today as many of the distinctively handhewn boulders have been removed for use in buildings around the island, especially in the Waimea United Church of Christ building above the school grounds. Some steadfastly maintain that the Menehune never existed, but legends abound and works attributed to them are seen here and there around the island. To reach the ditch, follow Menehune Road in from the fire station. Similar to that in Hanapepe, a pedestrian footbridge crosses the river near the remnants of the ditch, used mostly in times of high water when it's impossible to drive a vehicle through the ford. It perhaps is a remnant

KING KAUMUALI'I AND CONTROL OF KAUA'I

Hawaii was in its great state of flux at the beginning of the 1800s. The missionaries were coming, along with adventurers and schemers from throughout Europe. One of the latter was Georg Schaeffer, a Prussian in the service of Czar Nicholas of Russia. He convinced King Kaumuali'i of Kaua'i to build a Russian fort in Waimea in 1817, which Kaumuali'i saw as a means to discourage other Europeans from overrunning his lands. A loose alliance was made between Kaumuali'i and Schaeffer. The adventurer eventually lost the czar's support, and Kaumuali'i ran him off the island, but the remains of Fort Elizabeth still stand.

King Kaumuali'i had been able, by his use of diplomacy, guile, and the large distances separating his island from the others, to remain independent even as the great King Kamehameha was conquering the other islands and uniting them under his rule. Finally, however, after all the other islands had been subjugated and Kaumuali'i had shrewdly joined Kamehameha through negotiations instead of warfare, Kaumuali'i retained control of Kaua'i – Kamehameha made him governor of the island. After Kamehameha died, his successor, Kamehameha II, forced Kaumuali'i to go to O'ahu, where arrangements were made for him to marry Queen Ka'ahumanu, the greatest surviving *ali'i* of the land. Kaumuali'i never returned to his native island.

and Saturday when guides are available and last about 90 minutes. The cost is $10 adult, with reduced rates for seniors and children. All proceeds go to help preserve the historic structures and support community events. Reservations are a must, as groups are kept to 12 or less; call 808/335-2824.

Waimea Visitor and Technology Center

For a brief look at the history of Waimea and the surrounding region, stop at the Waimea Visitor and Technology Center (808/338-1332, 9:30 A.M.–4 P.M. Mon., Wed., and Fri., noon–8 P.M. Tues. and Thurs.) on the west end of town where Waimea Canyon Drive meets the highway. Audiovisual displays and a few historical artifacts help illustrate the area's sugar past and technological present, and there often is an additional special exhibit. On Monday at 9:30 A.M., the center hosts a free historical walking tour around town; reservations required. Free Internet access is also available.

ENTERTAINMENT

Most of the entertainment in town is self-directed, unless you count the ball games that take place at the ball field across from the Waimea Plantation Cottages or court games at the high school. The only bar is at the Waimea Brewing Company, currently the only brewpub on the island. Basically, the only evening entertainment to step out for is a movie at the theater. The remodeled **Waimea Theater** (808/338-0282) runs first-run movies at 7:30 P.M. Wednesday–Sunday; adult admission is $6. Occasionally, concerts and other live performances are scheduled at the theater in place of movies. Call for details.

SHOPPING

The **West Kaua'i Craft Fair** (9 A.M.–4 P.M. Fri.–Sun.) is a small affair that sprouts its tents in front of the old mill building at the junction of Waimea Canyon Drive. Stop by to see what local arts and crafts you might like to take home as gifts. Food is available, as is Hawaiian music and a Sunday afternoon hula show.

For a variety of food and skin care products made from *liliko'i* (passion fruit), visit **Auntie Lilikoi** passion fruit products store (9633 Kaumuali'i Hwy., 808/338-1296), located near the intersection of the highway and Waimea Canyon Drive on the west end of town.

The small but tasteful **Liko Kaua'i Surf Shop** (9875 Waimea Road, 808/338-0333), across from the Captain Cook Monument, is open daily 8 A.M.–5 P.M. and sells beach and casual clothing, surfboards, kiteboarding gear, and sunglasses. Here too is the check-in office for Liko Kauai Cruises.

Several **antique shops** line the main drag just west of the fire station.

RECREATION

Liko Kauai Cruises (808/338-0333 or 888/732-5456, www.liko-kauai.com) operated by Debra Hookano, wife of Captain Liko, is located across from the Captain Cook monument in the center of town. Captain Liko runs his 49-foot power catamaran out of the tiny Kikiaola Harbor just up the road. This is the closest departure point for trips to the Na Pali Coast, so it gives you the shortest "commute." Born and raised on Kaua'i, Captain Liko worked for 10 years as a supervising lifeguard on the west end, and no one knows these waters better than he. After you board, Captain Liko begins telling Hawaiian tales, especially about Ni'ihau, the island of his ancestors. Captain Liko not only offers spectacular sights but also a chance to snorkel and swim if the weather is cooperating; he brings along snacks and drinks for the ride. If you are lucky, dolphins will play alongside the boat as you cruise, or you may see whales frolicking during the winter months. If sea conditions are right, the boat may go all the way to Ke'e Beach on the north shore. On the way back, since the boat is completely outfitted for fishing charters, some lucky person gets to reel in whatever bites. Morning cruises with check-in at 8 A.M. run about four hours long, $110 for adults and $75 for children 4–12 years. During the summer months, an afternoon cruise may be added, and, weather permitting, sunset cruises may also be run.

Napali Explorer (808/338-9999 or 877/355-9909, www.napali-explorer.com) has an office in Waimea near the 76 gas station but runs its boats from the Kikiaola Harbor. This company runs 48- and 26-foot, rigid-bottom inflatable rafts up the Na Pali Coast year-round. The five-hour snorkel adventure, which stops at Nu'alolo Kai on the Na Pali Coast, runs $125.

The 3.5-hour scenic afternoon tour and the whale-watching expeditions (in season) go for $79. Discounts for kids.

NaPali Riders (808/742-6331, www.napaliriders) offers about the same trip up the Na Pali Coast at roughly the same pricing.

ACCOMMODATIONS
$100-150

Right in town and up from Wrangler's Restaurant is **[** **Inn Waimea** (4469 Halepule Rd., 808/338-0031, fax 808/338-1814, www.innwaimea.com) a remodeled two-story plantation-era home called Halepule from the 1930s. A few steps from the business section of town and the beach, Inn Waimea is a convenient, quiet, and comfortable home away from home. Lovingly restored, modernized, and spacious, this comfy and attractive house offers one single room and three two-room suites that have private bathrooms, cable TV, phones, coffee maker, ceiling fans, and a small refrigerator. The downstairs room and suite have king beds; upstairs are queen-size beds. The living room on the lower level is a common area/sitting room. A bowl of fresh fruit is placed here for guests to have when they desire. Rates run $100 a night for the Taro room and $120 for the Bamboo, Hibiscus, and Banana suites, with reduced rates for multiple-night stays; $10 extra for each additional guest. Three homes also managed by the Inn are for rent, two overlooking the canyon and one situated across from Halepule in town. The in-town house is a remodeled plantation-era building and the other two are modern constructions, one with contemporary and some intriguingly quirky features. Rates for the houses are $100–150 a night with three nights minimum.

$150-250

Aside from a few private rental homes and the Inn, **[** **ResortQuest Waimea Plantation Cottages** (9400 Kaumuali'i Hwy. #367, 808/338-1625 or 866/774-2924, fax 808/338-2338, www.waimea-plantation.com) is one of the few places to stay along the south shore west of Kalaheo—and what a place it is. Owned by the Kikiaola Land Company, Ltd., and managed by ResortQuest Hawaii, this oceanfront property is set in a grove of more than 750 coconut palms and a few huge banyan trees at the west end of Waimea. Not victimized by big bucks or modern resort development, workers' and supervisors' cottages and the manager's house from the former Waimea sugar plantation have been renovated and preserved, and the grounds maintained in an old-style way. You are treated to a touch of the past. While some modern amenities such as color cable TVs and telephones have been added for comfort and convenience, an effort has been made to keep each unit as much in its original state (1920s–1930s era) as possible; period furniture and other furnishings add to the feel of that bygone era. Most buildings have bare wood floors and painted wood walls. Nearly all have ceiling fans and lanai. Housekeeping and linen service are included every three days. Complimentary washers and dryers are available on the premises. A swimming pool in the 1930s style has been constructed on the lawn, and there's croquet, horseshoes, and volleyball, along with a restaurant and brewpub, and on-site massage and day spa. In accordance with this philosophy of preservation, some longtime employees of the plantation (no longer a functioning entity) are still offered low- or no-rent cottages in the mill camp next door rather than being turned out to make way for development of the land. On check-in at the administration building, have a look at the small **Faye Museum,** which presents artifacts and photographs of the early days of sugar in West Kaua'i and of the Faye family.

Presently, there are 61 units, including 11 cottages moved from the Kekaha Plantation and others from the former town of Mana to the west. Regular season rates for the cottages run $160 for a studio, $235–310 for a one-bedroom, $300–375 for a two-bedroom, $355–415 for a three-bedroom, and $465 for a four-bedroom; weekly discounts, specials, *kama'aina,* and value season rates are available. The two-story, five-bedroom, four-bath Manager's House is available for $730 a night.

The average length of stay is 7–10 days, with a 35 percent return rate; make your reservations several months in advance. Low-key and unpretentious, this institution aims to please and offers an opportunity for seclusion and serenity. What could be better than to relax and read a favorite book on your breezy lanai, watch the sunset through the coconut grove, or take a moonlight stroll along the gently lapping shore? In addition, a three-bedroom harbor house just up the road in Kekaha for $394 and a six-bedroom house on Hanalei Bay for $788 are also operated by Waimea Plantation Cottages. Make reservations with Waimea Plantation cottages directly or through ResortQuest Hawaii (866/774-2924, info@resortquesthawaii.com, www.resortquesthawaii.com).

FOOD
Local Style
Waimea has limited restaurants, but it does present good choices. On the inexpensive end, the town has the **Barefoot Burger** (9643 Kaumuali'i Hwy., 808/338-2082) at the west end of town, and the **Menehune Grill** (9691 Kaumuali'i Hwy., 808/338-1502) next to the theater and closer in. With seating inside and out, Barefoot Burger is open daily until 6 P.M. for inexpensive and plentiful burgers, sandwiches, ice cream, smoothies, and coffee. Menehune Grill, open until 8 P.M. for lunch and dinner, serves burgers, fish and chips, and plate lunches. Both are clean and spartan, with most food under $8. A delight for everyone, **Jo-Jo's Shave Ice,** which advertises 60 flavors, also do business along the highway.

For a simple, quick meal, try **Pacific Pizza and Deli** (808/338-1020, 11 A.M.–9 P.M. Mon.–Sat.) for pizza, calzones, wraps, deli sandwiches, drinks, and ice cream. Along with the ordinary pizzas, you have your choice of Thai, Filipino, Portuguese, and Mexican, each with the flavors of the country. Pizzas run $8–21, wraps and sandwiches around $6. Refreshing drinks include Tropical Smoothies with pineapple, mango, or papaya, home-brewed iced tea, and coffee drinks from espresso to latte. Pacific Pizza shares the Wrangler's Restaurant building and is connected by double screen doors to the restaurant.

It's easy to imagine a grizzled *paniolo* contentedly dangling his spurs over the banister of the distinctive veranda at **Wrangler's Restaurant** (9852 Kaumuali'i Hwy., 808/338-1218, for lunch 11 A.M.–4 P.M. Mon.–Fri. and for dinner 4–9 P.M. Mon.–Sat.) in downtown Waimea. The interior is a large open-beamed room with hardwood floors, cooled by ceiling fans. You can dine inside at a private booth or table, or alfresco on the big veranda out front or in the red blaze—a ginger garden out back. A full-service bar is stocked with a complete assortment of liquors, wines, and beers to complement all meals. The lunch menu has burgers, sandwiches, and meat plates, mostly under $10, but you could also try the "Kau Kau" tin lunch, a meal of teriyaki beef, vegetable tempura, and *kim chee* that's served in a old-style plantation worker's lunch tin. As you might expect, the Wrangler dinner menu is heavy on the red meats, with some poultry, seafood, and vegetarian selections. The house specialty is a sizzling 16-ounce New York steak served with sautéed mushrooms and baked potato. Entrées, $17–28, come with soup and a salad bar (the only one in town). Wrangler's is excellent and friendly. While you're there, take a few minutes and have a look at the gift shop and small *paniolo* museum.

Hawaiian Regional

The 🍺 **Waimea Brewing Company** (808/338-9733, 11 A.M.–11 P.M. daily, food served until 9 P.M.) is on the property of Waimea Plantation Cottages. The breezy plantation-style building has large open windows, high ceilings, and ceiling fans. The hand-crafted beers, ranging from Wai'ale'ale golden ale, the brewery's principal beer, to hoppy Captain Cook's Original IPA and rich Pakala porter, are brewed in a room seen through the glass window behind the bar. These beers can only be bought here. Stop for a repast and cool yourself down with one of these sudsy drinks. If you have trouble deciding which beer will fit your palate best, try the sampler first. From the kitchen come a variety

of appetizers, including "searing hot" chicken wings, ale-steamed shrimp, and taro leaf goat cheese dip. Salads and sandwiches are favorites and run less than $11. Dinner entrées, such as ale-battered fish and chips, honey mango-glazed ribs, kalua pork, and Hawaiian chicken, range $14–25, and every evening there are specials. Save room for dessert. Sit inside so you can see the bar and brewing room or outside on the veranda under the stars—either way it's a very pleasant, relaxing experience. Reservations are not always necessary but may be a good idea on the weekend, when there might be live music. Anything on the menu can be ordered to go.

Coffee Shop and Bakery

A fine place for organic coffee, pastries, and light breakfast meals is **Waimea Bakery and Deli** (808/338-1950, 7 A.M.–2 P.M. daily except Tues.) across from the Captain Cook Monument. Many come for the espresso, but you can also get fountain drinks, juices, smoothies, and plate lunches for under $7. Good eats and good prices, and one of the few such spots in town open for breakfast.

Groceries

Along the main road, facing Captain Cook's statue, is **Ishihara Market** (6 A.M.–8:30 P.M. on weekdays and from 7 A.M. on weekends), where you'll find all the necessities, plus prepared hot meals and a fine deli. Across the street is a well-stocked **Big Save Supermarket** (6 A.M.–10 P.M., until 9 P.M. on Sun.). Its deli lunch counter, believe it or not, features terrific local dishes at very reasonable prices. For liquor of all sorts and a few eats, try **Da Booze Shop.**

SERVICES

The **post office** is located on Waimea Road, one short block in from the highway near the intersection with Alawai Road.

Located across from the theater, the **public library** (808/338-6848) is open various hours during weekdays, but always in the afternoon.

A couple of blocks up Waimea Canyon Drive from the highway is **West Kaua'i Medical Center** hospital (4643 Waimea Canyon Dr., 808/338-9431) and its clinic (808/338-8311). It's the only hospital on the west end of the island and offers 24-hour emergency services.

To the End of the Road

KEKAHA

Back on Highway 50 going west, you enter Kekaha, passing the former plantation workers' homes trimmed in neat green lawns and shaded from the baking sun by palm and mango trees. Japanese gardens peek from behind fences. Kekaha was a planned plantation town, a model community by some regards, that was built and maintained by sugar and thrived for a century. The highway skirts town, running right along the water, while the main street, Kekaha Road, veers off near Kikiaola Harbor and runs into town past the old sugar mill, the old plantation offices, and several abandoned commercial buildings to the shopping plaza at Alae Road. Koke'e Road (Route 552), the western road leading to Waimea Canyon and Koke'e State Parks, branches off here and runs inland, up the mountain. At the first major cane road intersection on the road out of town toward the mountain, a traffic light was hung in 1957—the island's first. The dearth of traffic now makes you wonder why it's still functioning.

Until 1996, cane trucks, like worker bees returning to the hive, carried their burdens into the ever-hungry jaws of the **Kekaha Sugar Mill,** whose smokestack owns the skyline but belches black soot no more, and the sweet smell of molasses no longer lingers in the air. Even with the closing of the mill, the town remains well-trimmed and ostensibly prosperous, perhaps because of the work available at the seed corn companies up the road (you may also see sunflowers and tobacco) and at Barking Sands, the Pacific Missile Range Facility farther on.

At the east end of Kekaha, **Kikiaola Harbor** serves the needs of area residents with a boat launch and is where a few water tour companies launch their boats. There are a few picnic tables and restrooms here, but no camping is allowed. Route 50, Kaumuali'i Highway, proceeds west along the coast. When still in town, you pass **Faye Park.** and **Kekaha Neighborhood Center,** site of the Saturday 9 A.M. **farmers market,** with its pavilion, tables, toilets, and grills. At the western end of town is **Kekaha Beach County Park,** where you will find a lifeguard tower, pavilions, picnic tables, and barbecue grills. Then the golden sands of the beach park stretch for miles, widening as you head west, with pulloffs and shade-tree clusters now and again. The sun always shines, so pick your spot anywhere along the beach. The area is good for swimming and snorkeling during calm weather, and fair for surfing, although the reef can be quite shallow in spots. The beach across the road from St. Theresa's Catholic church is perhaps the best for little kids. Since there's no tourist development in the area, it's generally empty.

Shopping

The only shopping and food in town is at the Waimea Canyon Plaza, at the intersection of Kekaha and Alae roads. **Forever Kauai** (808/337-2888) and **Waimea Canyon General Store** (808/337-9569) are side-by-side shops for postcards, cheap jewelry, outlet alohawear, and souvenirs. Forever Kauai carries some of the best Ni'ihau shells on the island at better prices than larger and more conveniently located outlets.

Accommodations

There are no hotels or condominiums in Kekaha, only a handful of vacation rentals. **Kekaha Vacation Rentals** (808/335-9565 or 800/677-5959) offers six rental units ranging from a one-bedroom suite to a three-bedroom house. Directly across the highway from the ocean, all units are comfortably furnished, supply all linens and towels, and have complete kitchens, TV, and washing machines. Bicycles and boogie boards are available for guests to use. These units range $85–150 a night, with an additional $75 cleaning fee; four nights minimum. They're often booked by return guests; inquire well in advance.

Try also **Kekaha Sunset Beach Vacation Rental** (808/337-1054, kekahasunset@yahoo .com), which offers a three-bedroom house across the highway from the beach. With full kitchen, laundry facilities, TV, and phone, the house sleeps up to seven and goes for $150 a night or $1,000 a week; four nights minimum, $85 cleaning fee. A one-bedroom studio in the back, with kitchenette, is just right for a couple. It rents for $85 a night or $500 a week.

Food
Along Kekaha Road, look for **Thrifty Mini Mart** (808/337-1057) open throughout the day for snack foods, drinks, and some prepared foods. All other shops are at the Waimea Canyon Plaza, where Koke'e Road heads inland. At this small mall are the **Menehune Food Mart**

(808/337-1335), your last chance for snacks and sundries; **Obsessions Cafe** (808/337-2224, 6:30 A.M.–3 P.M. daily, 6–8:30 P.M. Fri.–Sat.) which serves burgers, *bento,* sandwiches, and plate lunches for lunch and steak for dinner.

PACIFIC MISSILE RANGE FACILITY
The sea sparkles, and the land flattens wide and long, with green cane billowing all around. Dry gulches and red buttes form an impromptu inland wall. Six miles down the road you come to the gates of the Pacific Missile Range Facility (PMRF) (www.pmrf.navy.mil), also known as **Barking Sands.** Here howl the dogs of war, leashed but on guard. Run by the Navy but used by all sectors of the U.S. military, allied foreign military units, and select civilian and educational agencies, PMRF is a training ground for air, surface, underwater, and coastal maneuvers, target practice, electronic warfare and communication, and tracking. In essence, it's a training facility for sea warfare. As one of its brochures states, "PMRF is the world's largest instrumented, multidimensional testing and training range." Its range covers 42,000 square miles to the west and south with the addition of 1,000 square miles underwater. The

MANA PLAIN

Unlike the rest of the island, which is volcanic in nature, the Mana Plain is sedimentary, perhaps a combination of dirt swept down from the hills and sand pushed up from the sea. It stretches from the Waimea River to the Na Pali cliffs at Polihale, about 16 miles along its coastal periphery. Prior to the 1900s, the Mana Plain was marshy with numerous ponds and inland waterways – a great wildlife area for birds – and it was possible to boat from the former town of Mana on its west end to Waimea. The old town of Mana, which no longer exists, was a thriving sugar community in the middle of the 19th century but shrank to nothing with the decline of the sugar industry. The early Hawaiians lived along the coast and

near the cliff, and when immigrants moved into the area, rice was cultivated. In the early 20th century, the wetlands were drained to create productive sugarcane land, and much is still used as such today.

Recently, some of this land has been turned over to other uses. One huge strip along the coast, the Pacific Missile Range Facility at Barking Sands, has been in military hands since World War II, and large acreage is planted in seed corn by Mainland companies. The Barking Sands airfield was originally built in 1928 by the Kekaha sugar plantation and later used for both Hawaiian Airlines interisland flights and Pan Am transpacific flights between the U.S. West Coast and Asia.

main 2,000-acre facility along the coast boasts a 6,000-foot runway; an associated base, where training exercises are held, lies a short way up the Na Pali Coast on the end of Makaha Ridge. Built originally by NASA in 1960 to track the Mercury spacecraft, it's a state-of-the-art facility that is integral to maintaining the U.S. military's combat readiness.

In late 1996, NASA announced that one of the most advanced studies of the earth's atmosphere was to be conducted at the Pacific Missile Range Facility. That research featured "Pathfinder," an experimental remote-controlled light aircraft that was fueled entirely by solar power. This slow-speed "flying wing" was powered by six electric motors and reached a height of over 80,000 feet. It was followed by other high-altitude versions, including the Centurion, and in August 2001 the 14-propeller Hellios reached a height of 96,000 feet. NASA officials chose Kaua'i because its weather provides 360 clear days per year, offering perfect flying in virtually unobstructed air space. The program brought a substantial amount of money into the local economy and provided hands-on experience for some lucky students at Kaua'i's community college.

PMRF is home to over 100 military personnel and their families, and nearly 10 times that number of civilian workers are employed on the base. Most of its facilities are open only to these personnel. Some of the base used to be open to the public for swimming, camping, and fishing, but non-employee civilian access to the base was closed after September 11, 2001, and now only a small section of the coastline is open on a very limited basis for fishing and beach access during daylight hours for Kaua'i residents who pass a background check. Please call 808/335-4229 for information on current access status and offshore boating.

Barking Sands has the largest sand dunes on Kaua'i, due to the ocean's shallowness between the two islands. Supposedly, if you slide down the dunes, made from a mixture of sand and ground coral, the friction will cause a sound like a barking dog, an effect that's most evi-

STARGAZING

The **Kauai Educational Association for Science and Astronomy**, a.k.a. **KEASA** (808/332-7827, www.keasa.org.), welcomes islanders and visitors of all ages to peer through its 14-inch computerized telescope every month on the Saturday nearest the new moon at the ball field at the Kaumakani School in Kaumakani, near mile marker 18. Viewings may also be held at the Waimea Plantation Cottages on Fridays, but this has been an on-again, off-again happening. These viewings were once held at the KEASA observatory on the Pacific Missile Range Facility until it was closed to the general public in 2002. The skies on the west end of the island have near perfect conditions for sea-level stargazing, as it's usually clear and reasonably free of light pollution. The Saturday viewing starts around sunset, after the KEASA general meeting. For further information and current meeting dates and times, call 808/245-8250.

dent during the heat of the day when the sand is totally dry.

On occasion, missile launches can be seen at the base. During these training operations, access to the base is further restricted and the Navy blocks boat traffic past the facility. However, these launches can be seen from Polihale State Park and from the highway. Although a completely different sort of explosive activity altogether, a Fourth of July fireworks show is usually staged at the base, and this too can be seen from the highway, the park, as well as from Kekaha.

(POLIHALE STATE PARK BEACH

Route 50 curves to the right after you pass the missile range. After about 200 yards, take the dirt road to the left past fields of cane and corn to Polihale State Park (it may not be signed). You go in by four miles of dirt cane road that doesn't seem to get much attention. The earth is a definite buff color here, unlike the deep red that predominates throughout the rest of the island. You can day-trip to soak up the sights, and you'll find pavilions, showers, toilets, and grills. This area is hot and dry, so bring plenty to drink. Both RV and tent camping are allowed with a state park permit. The camping area is on the top of the dune on the left before you get to the day-use pavilions at the far north end. There are generally no hassles, but the rangers do come around, and you should have a permit with you—it's a long way back to Lihu'e to get one.

From the parking area, walk over the tall dunes and down to the beach. The broad powdery white sand beach stretches for nearly three miles, pushing up against the Na Pali cliffs to the north and skirting a hill on the military base to the south. However, this beach actually continues around the bend, running uninterrupted (although it narrows substantially in spots) all the way to Kekaha, a distance of about 15 miles, basically edging the Mana Plain. It is the longest beach by far in the state. The swimming can be dangerous, as currents are strong, but the hiking is grand. With a small reef offshore, the most protected spot is known as Queen's Pond; it's at the southern end of Polihale Beach. Turn left at the big tree where the road splits into a Y. You'll have your best chance to swim in summer. When the sea is not too rough, experienced surfers come to ride the waves.

Some locals come here to drive on the sand. If you choose to do so, be very cautious because vehicles can and do get stuck very easily. There is no tow service (or gas station) anywhere nearby—you would have to get very expensive assistance from Waimea—but if you do dare to drive on the sand, follow the tracks left by others and let some air out of your tires to help float your vehicle over the dry sand above the high water line.

Literally at the end of the road, this beach takes you away from the crowds, but you'll hardly ever be all by yourself. Here the cliffs come down to the sea, brawny and rugged

WEST END

ROBERT NILSEN

Polihale sunset

with the Na Pali Coast beginning around the far bend. Where the cliffs meet the sea is the ruin of **Polihale Heiau.** This is a powerful spot, where the souls of the dead made their leap from land into infinity. Their goal was the land of the dead, a mythical submerged mountain a few miles off the coast. The priests of this temple chanted special prayers to speed them on their way, as the waters of life flowed from a sacred spring in the mountainside. Even if you are not pulled here because of the mystical, this is a marvelous place for a picnic and beach walk. As it rains so little here and distant clouds do not often hamper the view, sunsets are super, and seeing the green flash is a definite possibility. With no lights or air pollution to speak of, stargazing at Polihale can be exceptional.

Mountain Parks

WAIMEA CANYON STATE PARK

The "Grand Canyon of the Pacific" is an unforgettable part of any trip to Kaua'i, and you shouldn't miss it for any reason. Waimea Canyon Drive begins in Waimea, heading inland past sugarcane fields for seven miles, where it joins Koke'e Road coming up from Kekaha. This serpentine route runs along a good but narrow road to Kaua'i's cool interior, with plenty of fascinating vistas and turnouts along the way. Going up, the passenger gets the better view. Behind you, the coastal towns fade into the pale blue sea, while the cultivated fields are a study of green on green. Waimea Canyon Drive is narrower, windier, and steeper in parts than the more gradually graded and better paved Koke'e Road, a gentle roller coaster of a road. Either route is worthwhile, and you can catch both by going in on one leg and coming out on the other. Less than a mile before these two roads meet, you enter Waimea Canyon State Park, a ridgetop park of more than 1,800 acres that flanks the road to Koke'e and overlooks the canyon and ridges beyond, most of which lie within the boundaries of Pu'u Ka Pele and Na Pali Kona Forest Reserves.

Ever climbing, you feel as though you're entering a mountain fortress. The canyon yawns, devouring clouds washed down by drafts of sunlight. The colors are diffuse, a blended strata of gray, royal purple, vibrant red, russet, jet black, and bubble-gum pink. You reach the thrilling spine, where the trees on the red bare earth are gnarled and twisted. The road becomes a roller coaster whipping you past raw beauty, immense and powerful. Drink deeply, contemplate, and move on into the clouds at the 2,000-foot level, where the trees get larger again. This mountain fastness took the full brunt of Hurricane 'Iniki. Along the highway—and farther into this arboreal wilderness—you will see evidence of 'Iniki's fury in the form of skeletal dead trees. Luckily, Mother Nature is able to regenerate herself quickly, so much of the destruction has disappeared behind new growth.

(Overlooks

As you climb, every lookout demands a photo. At **Waimea Canyon Overlook** (3,400 feet) you have the most expansive view of the canyon and across to valleys that slice down from the lofty peak. From here it's obvious why this canyon was given its nickname. Keep a watch out for soaring birds, mountain goats, and low-flying helicopters. The colors are quite amazing here, and the best time for photos is either early morning or late afternoon when shadows play across these mottled and deeply etched walls.

From **Pu'u Ka Pele Overlook,** Waipo'o Falls is seen tumbling forcefully off the hanging valley up the canyon. This overlook may be inaccessible and unsigned because it has undergone revegetation work to help stem erosion. A small rest area with a few picnic tables lies across the road. **Pu'u Hinahina**

BICYCLE DOWNHILL

A miniature version of the great Haleakala downhill bike ride is offered on Kaua'i. This 11-mile ride starts in the cool mountain air on the rim of Waimea Canyon at about 3,400 feet elevation. From this starting point, the route skirts the rim and then heads down the roller coaster foothills to the coast at Kekaha. All tours are done in groups, and each member is given a helmet and jacket to wear. The cruiser bikes are cushy, with big easy-chair seats, raised handlebars, and extra strong brakes. A sag wagon follows for those who need a rest and to alert traffic that comes from behind. Snacks are provided. Closed-toe shoes are a necessity, and long pants may be recommended. Don't forget to bring sunglasses and sunscreen. Both sunrise and sunset rides are offered. Count on 4.5-5 hours for the entire trip, although actual bike time is about one hour. If this sounds like a trip for you, contact **Outfitters Kauai** (808/742-9667, www.outfitterskauai.com).

Overlook (3,500 feet) provides the best views down the canyon toward the ocean. Walk up a short trail behind the restrooms and you may have a good view of Ni'ihau adrift in the ocean to the west, if not obscured by clouds. A little farther along is a NASA space flight tracking station, and at the same turnoff the gravel Halemanu Road leads into the Halemanu Valley. Beyond this point is Koke'e State Park, and from here on you start to see more forest birds—and encounter worse road conditions.

Trails

One of the best trails off Koke'e Road is the Kukui Trail. The well-marked trailhead is between mile markers 8 and 9. As there is not much parking here, pull all the way off the roadway. The trail starts with the **Iliau Nature Loop,** an easy, 15-minute, self-guided trail at about 3,000 feet in elevation. Notice the pygmy palm-like lobelia among the many varieties of plants and flowers. Some signage helps explain the various plants. The *iliau,* after which the trail is named, is a relative of the silversword that grows high on Haleakala on Maui and the greensword that grows on the Big Island. This rare plant grows only on the dry western mountain slopes of Kaua'i, and it seems that the greatest concentration is here. After years of growth, a tall spire shoots up in late spring bedecked with a profusion of small blossoms, only to die. Don't keep your nose to the ground here, however, because you can sometimes see white-tailed tropicbirds flying gracefully over the canyon or the brown-and-white *pueo* (Hawaiian owl) searching for its next meal.

From the nature trail loop you can look down into the canyon far below. Realize that the river at the bottom is the destination of the Kukui Trail. A hike on this trail is no Sunday stroll. Start the **Kukui Trail** near the shelter with picnic tables. It descends 2,000 feet through a series of switchbacks and steep grades in only two and a half miles, and as you might imagine there are grand views of the canyon vistas along the way. The trail starts off fairly shady but opens up to bare earth in its middle section before heading back into tall bush and trees toward the bottom. The trail ends on the floor of the canyon at Wiliwili Campsite. Turn around here if you think that the hike so far has been enough for you. Give the trail at least 1.5 hours, more going up. From here the hale and hardy can head up the Waimea River for a half mile, either to the dam or on the opposite side of the river to Kaluahaulu Camp and the beginning of the **Koai'e Canyon Trail.** This three-mile trail takes you up the south side of Koai'e Canyon, where there are plenty of pools and two additional campsites. This trail *should not* be attempted during rainy weather because of flash flooding. You can also branch south from the Kukui Trail and link up with the **Waimea Canyon Trail,** which takes you eight miles, mostly via an old 4WD track, to the town of Waimea. Because it crosses a game management area, you must have a special permit

WEST END

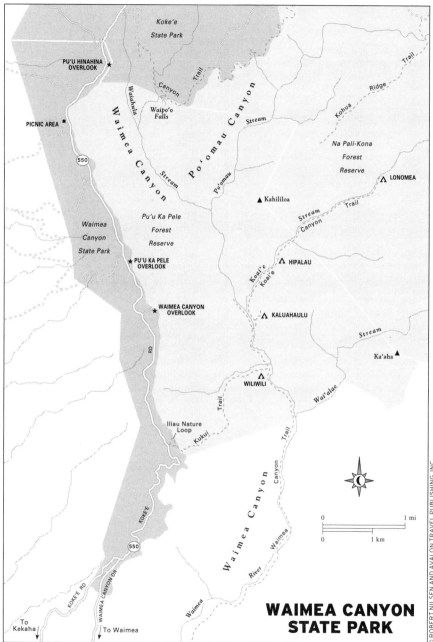

Koke'e
State Park

PU'U HINAHINA
OVERLOOK

Canyon   Trail

Waiahula

Waipo'o
Falls

PICNIC AREA

550

Po'omau Canyon

Po'omau   Stream

W a i m e a   C a n y o n

Stream

Stream

Po'omau

Kohua   Ridge

Trail

Na Pali-Kona
Forest
Reserve

▲ Kahililoa

LONOMEA

Waimea
Canyon
State Park

Pu'u Ka Pele
Forest
Reserve

Stream

Canyon   Trail

PU'U KA PELE
OVERLOOK

WAIMEA CANYON
OVERLOOK

Koai'e

Koai'e

▲ HIPALAU

▲ KALUAHAULU

Stream

Ka'aha ▲

RD

▲
WILIWILI

Wai'alae

Iliau Nature
Loop

Trail

Kukui

Canyon   Trail

W a i m e a   C a n y o n

Waimea

KOKE'E

River

550

Waimea

KOKE'E RD

WAIMEA CANYON DR

To
Kekaha

To Waimea

0   1 mi

0   1 km

© ROBERT NILSEN AND AVALON TRAVEL PUBLISHING, INC.

WAIMEA CANYON
STATE PARK

ROBERT NILSEN

Waimea Canyon

(available at the trailhead). There is no camping south of Waiʻalae Stream, the southern boundary of the forest reserve. The Waimea Canyon Trail is sometimes used by mountain bikers.

KOKEʻE STATE PARK

After passing Puʻu Hinahina Overlook, you enter Kokeʻe State Park and soon reach park headquarters, the lodge, and museum. At the museum, helpful staff can provide a map of walking trails in the park and plenty of information about the region's flora and fauna. Kokeʻe ranges 3,200–4,200 feet in elevation and is a huge 4,345 acres in area. Although its forest is mixed, koa and ʻohiʻa predominate. Temperatures here are several degrees cooler than along the coast and can be positively chilly at night, so bring a sweater or jacket. In January, the average daytime temperature is 45°F and in July it's 68°F. The average rainfall is 70 inches a year, with most of that coming from October to May. Wild boar hunting and trout fishing are permitted within the park in prescribed areas at certain times of the year, but check with the Department of Land and Natural Resources on the third floor of the state office building in Lihuʻe about licenses, limits, season, etc., *before* coming up the mountain. Trout fishing permits are also issued at the park headquarters during fishing season only. To see wildlife anywhere in the park, it's best to look early in the morning or late in the afternoon when animals come out to feed. The native forest birds attract many visitors to the park, and you don't always have to hike off the main roads to see them. You might see the reddish ʻapapane and ʻiʻiwi, the green-yellow ʻamakihi and ʻanianiau, and the brownish ʻelepaio. Of the nonnative birds, you probably will catch sight of the red-crested cardinal, the shama—a black bird with chestnut-colored breast and white on the tail—and, of course, the feral roosters.

◖ Overlooks
Two spectacular lookouts await you farther up the road. At **Kalalau Overlook** (4,120 feet), mile marker 18, walk a minute and pray that

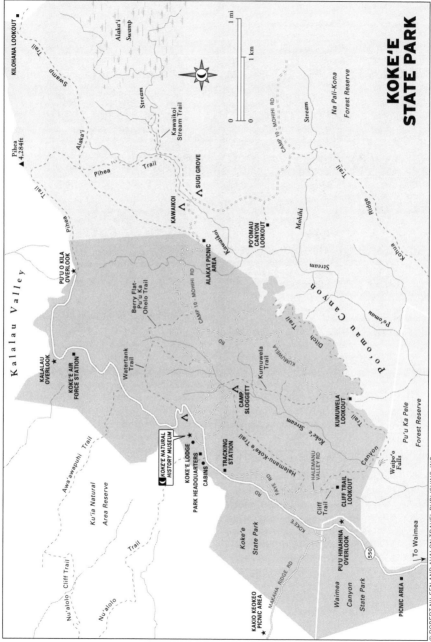

KOKE'E STATE PARK

KILOHANA LOOKOUT

Alaka'i Swamp

Swamp Trail

1 mi

1 km

Alaka'i Stream

Kawaikoi Stream Trail

0

0

CAMP 10-MOHIHI RD

Stream

Na Pali-Kona Forest Reserve

Pihea ▲ 4,284ft

Alaka'i

Pihea Trail

Pihea Trail

SUGI GROVE

KAWAIKOI

PO'OMAU CANYON LOOKOUT

Mohihi

Ridge

Kohua

Kalalau Valley

PU'U O KILA OVERLOOK ★

Berry Flat-Pu'u Ka Ohelo Trail

ALAKA'I PICNIC AREA

Kawaikoi Stream

CAMP 10-MOHIHI RD

Stream

Po'omau

Po'omau Canyon

KALALAU OVERLOOK ★

KOKE'E AIR FORCE STATION

Watertank Trail

RD

Kumuwela Trail

KUMUWELA

Ditch Trail

CAMP SLOGGETT

Kumuwela Trail

KUMUWELA LOOKOUT

Pu'u Ka Pele Forest Reserve

Awa'awapuhi Trail

Ku'ia Natural Area Reserve

KOKE'E NATURAL HISTORY MUSEUM ★

KOKE'E LODGE

PARK HEADQUARTERS

CABINS

TRACKING STATION

Halemanu-Koke'e Trail

Koke'e Stream

HALEMANU VALLEY RD

Canyon

Waipo'o Falls

CLIFF TRAIL LOOKOUT

Cliff Trail

Nu'alolo Cliff Trail

Trail

FAYE RD

Koke'e State Park

KOKE'E RD

MAKAHA RIDGE RD

PU'U HINAHINA OVERLOOK ★

550

To Waimea

Nu'alolo Trail

KAKIO KEOKEO PICNIC AREA ★

Waimea Canyon State Park

PICNIC AREA

the clouds are cooperative, allowing lasers of sunlight to illuminate the humpbacked, green-cloaked mountains, silent and tortured, plummeting straight down to the roiling sea far, far below. There is a picnic area here with toilets. **Pu'u O Kila Overlook** (4,176 feet), another mile farther, is the end of the road. From here you not only get a wonderful view into the Kalalau Valley—the widest and largest valley along the Na Pali Coast—but also up across the Alaka'i Swamp to Mount Wai'ale'ale if the clouds permit. The Pihea Trail starts here and teeters on the rim of the Kalalau Valley, partially over an abandoned road, then turns south into the Alaka'i Swamp.

There is another fine viewpoint in this high mountain region that is not along Rt. 550, but a wonderful spot nonetheless. A short distance up from Pu'u Hinahina Lookout, take the only paved road leading off to the left as you go up the mountain. There is no sign at the intersection, but this is Makaha Ridge Road. This narrow road—drive defensively and watch for oncoming traffic—leads steeply down the ridge, passing **Kakio Keokeo Picnic Area** and continuing about four miles to a PMRF tracking station—no entry. Cut through dense forest, the road affords no sweeping views. Almost to the end of the road, a secondary dirt road—for 4WD only—turns off to the left and runs for a little over one mile to the **Pine Forest Drive Picnic Area,** a great spot for a picnic and romantic sunsets.

C Koke'e Natural History Museum

This museum (808/335-9975, www.kokee.org, 9 A.M.–4 P.M. daily, 10 A.M.–2 P.M. on holidays, $1 suggested donation) is located to the side of a meadow just beyond the 15 mile marker. Be sure to stop. It's a good place to get detailed hiking maps of the park and the surrounding national forest lands and additional information about the mountain environment of Kaua'i. Inside are informative displays of native birds, descriptions of plants and animals found in the park, Hawaiian culture, an exhibit on weather with a focus on Hurricane 'Iniki and its aftermath, books on Kaua'i and Hawaii, local Kaua'i crafts, and a relief map of the island. The nonprofit museum (offering 50 years of excellent service to visitors as of 2003) sponsors periodic work crews to help remove alien plants and maintain native species, conducts an annual environmental fair, and holds the annual Emmalani Festival. By reservation, the museum offers easy to moderate, free, guided "Wonder Walks" appropriate for kids and adults on Sundays during summer months.

Trails

Maps of Koke'e's trails are available at the Koke'e Natural History Museum. Two of the best are Hawaii Nature Guide's *Kokee's Trails* map and the more detailed and broader scope *Northwestern Kaua'i Recreational Map* by Earthwalk Press. Also helpful for the casual hiker, but less precise and less expensive, are *Trails of Koke'e* and *Koke'e Trails,* both put out by the state. The list of trails below is not meant to be comprehensive; these are only several of the many trails in the area. The trail entries are not detailed accounts but general descriptions to characterize the trails. Please check at the Koke'e museum for up-to-the-minute trail information and use one of the popular trail books listed in the *Suggested Reading* section at the back of this book for more in-depth details of each trail.

Koke'e has about 45 miles of trails. Many start along Koke'e Drive or the dirt roads that lead off from it; most are marked and well maintained. Generally speaking, these trails are of four kinds: Na Pali Coast overlook trails; Alaka'i Swamp trails; forest trails; and canyon overlook trails. These trails are for hiking only. Bikes, horses, and motorcycles should be used on the park and forest reserve dirt roads only.

The first trails you encounter heading up from the coast are off Halemanu Road. **Cliff Trail** is only a few hundred yards long and leads to a spectacular overview of the canyon. Look for feral goats on the canyon ledges.

Canyon Trail continues off Cliff Trail for 1.5 miles. It's a strenuous trail that dips down to the upper section of Waipo'o Falls before climbing up and along the edge of the canyon, then on to the end of Kumuwela Road at Kumuwela Lookout; it takes no more than three hours round-trip. Waipo'o Falls, in two sections and cascades, is the highest on the island at about 800 vertical feet.

To make an easy circle, hike Halemanu Road to its end. There, cross the wooded valley by the short **Faye Trail** to reach an undrivable section of Faye Road, which leads left and back up to the highway not too far from the Halemanu Road turnoff. Going right at Faye Road will deposit you on the highway just below the state park cabins.

Perhaps the easiest trail to access is the **Nature Trail** that starts near the Koke'e museum and parallels the meadow. Requiring less than half an hour to the end and back, this trail is a favorite for small children and a good introduction to the forest plants.

A rewarding but strenuous hiking loop, at nearly eight miles, is a combination of three shorter trails, the Kumuwela, Canyon, and Halemanu–Koke'e trails. Park at the Halemanu–Koke'e trailhead off the gravel Waineke Road. There walk around and down to the end of the adjacent road to the Kumuwela Trailhead. Follow the **Kumuwela Trail** for about one mile in and out of several small valleys and then a long climb up to Kumuwela Road. Follow this downhill to its end at Kumuwela Viewpoint, for an expansive and rewarding view down the canyon, and the eastern end of the Canyon Trail. About three miles long, the **Canyon Trail** starts by heading into the forest but eventually runs out along the edge of the canyon with magnificent view down the Waimea canyon and up to Mount Wai'ale'ale. The trail continues down to Waipo'o Falls and eventually back up to Halemanu Road. As an alternate route, turn off of Canyon Trail and take **Black Pipe Trail** around the hill and up to a secondary road, which then goes downhill to Halemanu Road. Walk up

Waipo'o Falls

ROBERT NILSEN

Halemanu Road to the community of cabins and the Halemanu–Koke'e Trailhead, from where you can continue back to your starting point. **Halemanu-Koke'e Trail** is a reasonably flat trail that runs through the forest, in large part along a ridge. It travels just more than a mile and offers some views of the adjacent valleys. With plenty of native plants and trees, it's a favorite area for indigenous birds. This hike is just as easily started at Halemanu Road, following the Canyon, Kumuwela, and Halemanu–Koke'e trails in a counterclockwise direction. Either way, count on at least four hours, more for soaking in the sights and taking pictures.

At pole no. 320 near park headquarters, you find the beginning of Camp 10–Mohihi Road. For this road, 4WDs are recommended, but it might be crossed with a two-wheel-drive car *only* in dry weather. It leads to a number of trails, mostly heading into the forest; others run out along ridges for canyon views, while still others head into the Alaka'i Swamp. **Pu'u Ka Ohelo Berry Flat Trail,** an easy two-mile loop, gives you an up-close look at a vibrant upland forest. Under the green canopy watch for specimens such as *sugi* pine and California redwoods—both planted in the 1930s by CCC workers—Australian eucalyptus, and native koa and 'ohi'a, as well as ferns, ginger, and strawberry guava. Locals come here to harvest the methley plums, for which the area is famous. There is a midsummer season and limits for picking these plums, so check with the park headquarters first. Start at the Pu'u Ka Ohelo trailhead near a small community of cabins that's about a quarter mile up a secondary road off Camp 10–Mohihi Road and hike clockwise, as the hike from the Berry Flat trailhead back along Camp 10–Mohihi Road is somewhat downhill.

Less than half a mile beyond Berry Flat trailhead is the trailhead to the **Ditch Trail,** which gives views into Po'omau Canyon. Although it's less than four miles there and back, give it plenty of time. A short way farther is the Alaka'i Picnic Area and the start of the Alaka'i Trail, beyond which is **Sugi Grove,** where camping is limited to three days. This is the trailhead to the **Kawaikoi Stream Trail,** a 3.5-mile round-trip, moderate forest trail known for its scenic beauty. It follows the south side of the stream, crosses over, and loops back on the north side. Avoid this trail if the stream is high. About halfway up this trail, you can cross the stream to connect with the Pihea Trail.

The **Alaka'i Swamp Trail** is otherworldly and magical, crossing one of the most unusual pieces of real estate in the world. It begins off Camp 10–Mohihi Road near the state park-forest reserve boundary. The nearby **Alaka'i Picnic Area** offers views into Po'omau Canyon. The trail heads into the swamp for 3.5 miles. Once you had to slog through the bogs, but now much of the way is over a raised walkway—easier for you and more protection for the fragile environment. Still, it's a rainy area, so be prepared to get wet and muddy. If you smell anise along the way, that's the *mokihana* berry, used with *maile* for fashioning wedding lei. This trail, great for the

unique vegetation, is also very good for birding. The trail ends at the Kilohana Lookout, where there's an expansive vista of Wainiha and Hanalei Valleys on a very rare clear day; otherwise you'll be enveloped by thick clouds. This trail is a real gamble for views. An alternate route to the Alaka'i Swamp, providing easier access, starts by taking **Pihea Trail** from the end of the paved road up top near the Pu'u O Kila Overlook. This is a good general-interest trail because it gives you wonderful views into Kalalau Valley. Don't forget to turn around, however, for the views over the inner valleys and up to Mount Wai'ale'ale are superb. About one mile along, the trail turns south and descends into the forest where the Alaka'i Swamp Trail, which comes in from the right, bisects it. This trail is also good for birding, and, aside from the native birds, you might run into *moa,* wild jungle fowl. Continuing straight through this trail intersection, the Pihea Trail eventually dips down to Kawaikoi Stream and ends at Kawaikoi Campsite, from where you can return via Camp 10–Mohihi Road for an amazing loop of the area. Count on a long day to do the loop, or be dropped off at Pu'u O Kila Overlook and picked up at Kawaikoi campsite, a distance of about four miles.

One of the most rewarding trails for the time and effort is **Awa'awapuhi Trail.** The trailhead is after park headquarters, just past mile marker 17, beyond the crest of the hill. It's three miles long and takes you out onto a thin finger of *pali,* with the sea and an emerald valley 2,500 feet below. The sun dapples the upland forest, which still bears the scars of Hurricane 'Iniki. Everywhere flowers and fiddlehead ferns delight the eyes, while wild thimbleberries and passion fruit delight the taste buds. The trail is well marked and steady down. Connecting with the Awa'awapuhi at the three-mile marker is the **Nu'alolo Cliff Trail,** which connects with the Nu'alolo Trail and has an open shelter about halfway along. The **Nu'alolo Trail** starts near park headquarters and is the easiest trail to the *pali* with an overview of Nu'alolo Valley.

It's 3.4 miles to the Nuʻalolo Cliff Trail junction and 3.8 miles to the vista point at the Nuʻalolo Trail terminus. In comparison, this trail is more open to the sun, hence hotter, than the more shaded and tree-covered Awaʻawapuhi Trail. Either the Awaʻawapuhi or Nuʻalolo ridge trail can be done separately, without using the Nuʻalolo Cliff Trail, but all three together make a nice loop. Remember that the trail going in is downhill and coming out is uphill—a more than 1,500-foot elevation gain. Pace yourself, as it is strenuous. It's over 10 miles, so give it a full day for sightseeing and a picnic, although it can be done in a strong half day. It's recommended that this loop be done clockwise, going in on the Nuʻalolo Trail and coming out on the Awaʻawapuhi Trail. It's perhaps safer to leave your car at the museum parking lot rather than at the Awaʻawapuhi trailhead, and, anyway, the walk down the road from the Awaʻawapuhi trailhead back to the museum is easier at the end of a long day than hiking up the road back to your car.

Accommodations and Food

◖ Kokeʻe Lodge (P.O. Box 367, Waimea, HI 96796, 808/335-6061, 8 A.M.–4 P.M. daily) provides a dozen self-contained cabins, furnished with stoves, refrigerators, hot showers, cooking and eating utensils, and bedding; wood is available for woodstoves. The cabins cost $59 or $70 per night (five-night maximum; two-night minimum if one of the nights is Friday or Saturday) and vary from one large room for up to three people to two-bedroom units that sleep seven. There's no luxury here, just simple cabins, but the location and forest environment are hard to beat. The cabins are tough to get on weekends and holidays, in the Aug.–Sept. trout-fishing season, and during the wild plum harvest in June and July. For reservations, write well in advance (six months perhaps) and include an SASE, the number of people, and dates requested. Full payment is required within two weeks of making reservations, with a refund possible (less a $15 service fee)

if reservations are canceled at least one week before arrival. Check-in is 2 P.M., checkout is 11 A.M. The lodge office is in the gift shop at the restaurant.

The Kokeʻe Lodge **restaurant and gift shop** are open 9 A.M.–3 P.M. daily. The restaurant serves a full breakfast 9–11 A.M. and lunch 11 A.M.–3 P.M. The cool weather calls especially for hot soup and a sandwich, a slice of homemade pie (best know are its chiffon-like *likoʻi* pie and roasted coconut and chocolate cream pie), a steaming pot of coffee, or a cup of hot chocolate with a mountain of whipped cream. Prices for food and drink are on the high side, but, after all, everything has to be trucked up the mountain. The next nearest restaurant is 15 miles down the road at either Waimea or Kekaha. Also in the lodge is a gift shop that sells postcards, books, maps, T-shirts, snacks, sundries, and souvenirs; outside are a few picnic tables and a public telephone.

Tent camping is allowed with a permit at Kokeʻe State Park at a developed campground a few hundred yards across the meadow from the museum. Camping permits are issued for $5 per campsite at the state parks office in Lihuʻe. Picnic tables and toilets are provided. In addition, two forest reserve campgrounds along Camp 10–Mohihi Road and four primitive campgrounds in Waimea and Koaiʻe Canyons are open to campers with a free permit from the State Division of Forestry and Wildlife, which occupies the same office in Lihuʻe as the state parks office.

The YWCA maintains **Camp Sloggett** (808/245-5959, www.campingkauai.com) within Kokeʻe State Park for group and individual hostelling and tent camping. Tent campers use raised platforms. Hostel guests use the bunkhouse on a first-come, first-served basis, unless a group of 20 or more has arranged to use the entire camp. The bunkhouse has single or bunk-style beds, and everyone has access to hot showers and a kitchen. Hostel guests must provide their own bedding and towels. Space can be arranged through the resident caretaker, who also has information about hiking. Rates are $10 for tent campers, $20 for hostel campers. To reach the camp, take the first right turn, Waineke Road, after passing the Koke'e Lodge, and follow the dirt road to a clearing and camp entrance. While this road may be somewhat rugged, it is open year-round and can be traversed by two-wheel-drive rental cars.

Ni'ihau

The only thing forbidding about Ni'ihau is its nickname, "The Forbidden Island." Ironically, it's one of the last real havens of peace, tranquility, and tradition left on the face of the earth. This privately owned island, operating as one large cattle and sheep ranch (more so in past decades than today), is staffed by the last remaining pure Hawaiians in the state. To go there, you must have a personal invitation by the owners or one of the residents. Some people find this situation strange, but expecting to have free access to the island is akin to walking up to an Iowa farmhouse unannounced and expecting to be invited in to dinner. The islanders are free to come and go as they wish and are given the security of knowing that the last real Hawaiian place is not going to be engulfed by the modern world. Ni'ihau is a reservation, but a *free-will* reservation—something you'll admire if you've ever felt that the world was too much with you.

The 17-mile **Kaulakahi Channel** separates Ni'ihau from the western tip of Kaua'i. The island's maximum dimensions are 18 miles long by six miles wide, with a total area of 70 square miles. Low at both ends, a higher tableland makes up most of the middle of the island. The highest point on the island, Pani'au (1,281 feet), lies on the east-central coast. The whole of Ni'ihau is the western crescent remains of an ancient and much larger island, most of which broke away along the eastern cliff line and sank beneath the water. There are no port facilities on the island, but the occasional boats put in at Ki'i and Lehua Landings, both on the northern tip. Since Ni'ihau is so low and lies in the rainshadow of Kaua'i, it receives only 30 inches of precipitation per year, making it rather arid. Oddly enough, low-lying basins, eroded from the single shield volcano that made the island, act as a catchment system. In them is the state's largest naturally occurring lake, 182-acre Halulu Lake, and the larger, 841-acre, intermittent Halali'i Lake. Two uninhabited islets join Ni'ihau as part of Kaua'i County: Lehua, just off the northern tip and exceptional for scuba diving, and Ka'ula, a few miles off the southern tip; each barely covers one-half square mile.

HISTORY

After the goddess Papa returned from Tahiti and discovered that her husband, Wakea, was playing around, she left him. The great Wakea did some squirming, and after these island-parents reconciled, Papa became pregnant and gave birth to Kaua'i. According to the creation chants found in the *Kumulipo,* Ni'ihau popped out as the afterbirth, along with Lehua and Ka'ula, the last of the low reef islands.

Ni'ihau was never a very populous island because of the relatively poor soil, so the islanders had to rely on trade with nearby Kaua'i for many necessities, including poi. Luckily, the fishing grounds off the island's coastal waters are the richest in the area, and Ni'ihauans could always trade fish. The islanders became famous for Ni'ihau mats, a good trade item, made from *makaloa,* a sedge plant that's plentiful on the island. Craftsmen also fashioned *ipu pawehe,* a geometrically designed gourd highly prized in the old days. When Captain Cook arrived and wished to provision his ships, he remarked that the Ni'ihau natives were much more eager to trade than those on Kaua'i, and he secured potatoes and yams that seemed to be in abundant supply. Today, aside from raising some livestock and making charcoal (both are becoming less viable), Ni'ihau residents gather honey and still produce excellent-quality (and very expensive) shell lei, as their forebears have done for generations.

Kamehameha IV Sells

Along with Kaua'i, Ni'ihau became part of the kingdom under Kamehameha. It passed down to his successors, and in 1864, Kamehameha IV sold it to the Sinclair family for $10,000. Originally, the king didn't want to sell this island and offered them another property, a swampy beach area, but much closer to the center of island power. That property was Waikiki. The Sinclairs turned the king down. Apparently, Ni'ihau was in great form after a fine spring and looked like a much better deal. This Scottish family, which came to Hawaii via New Zealand, has been the sole proprietor of the 46,000-acre island ever since, although they now live on Kaua'i. Through marriage, the Robinson family now owns Ni'ihau, as well as vast tracts of land on west Kaua'i. They began

a sheep and cattle ranch, hiring the island's natives as workers. No one can say exactly why, but it's evident that this family felt a great sense of responsibility and purpose. Tradition passed down over the years dictated that islanders could live on Ni'ihau as long as they pleased, but that visitors were not welcome without a personal invitation. With the native Hawaiian population so devastated, the Robinsons felt that these proud people should have at least one place to call theirs and theirs alone. To keep the race pure, male visitors to the island were generally asked to leave by sundown.

Ni'ihau Invaded

During World War II, Ni'ihau was the only island of Hawaii to be occupied by the Japanese. A Zero pilot developed engine trouble after striking Pearl Harbor and had to ditch on Ni'ihau. At first the islanders took him prisoner, but he somehow managed to escape and commandeer the machine guns from his plane. He terrorized the island, and the residents headed for the hills. One old woman who refused to leave was like a Hawaiian Barbara Fritchie. She told the Japanese prisoner to shoot her if he wished, but to please stop making a nuisance of himself—it wasn't nice! He would have saved himself a lot of trouble if he had only listened. Fed up with hiding, one huge *kanaka,* Benehakaka Kanahele, decided to approach the pilot with *aloha.* He was convinced the intruder would see the error of his ways. This latter-day samurai shot Kanahele for his trouble. Ben persisted and was shot again. An expression of pain, disgust, and disbelief at the stranger's poor manners spread across Ben's face, but still he tried pleading with the prisoner, who shot him a third time. Ben had had enough, and he grabbed the astonished pilot and flung him headlong against a wall, cracking his skull and killing him instantly. This incident gave rise to a wartime maxim—"Don't shoot a Hawaiian three times or you'll make him mad"—and a song titled, "You Can't Conquer Ni'ihau, Nohow." Kanahele lived out his life on Ni'ihau and died in the 1960s.

NI'IHAU SHELLWORK

The finest shellwork made in Hawaii comes from Ni'ihau, in a tradition passed down over the generations. The shells themselves – tiny and very rare *kahelelani, laiki, momi,* and *kamoa* among them – are abundant in the deep waters off the windward coast. Sometimes, the tides and winds are just right and they are deposited on Ni'ihau's beaches, mostly from October to March, particularly after storms that disturb the reef and wash them onto the beach. When that does happen, island women and children, and now more and more men, stop everything and head for the shore to painstakingly collect them.

The shells are sorted according to size and color, and only the finest are kept: 80 percent are discarded. The most prized are so tiny that a dozen fit on a thumbnail. Colors are white, yellow, blue, red, and the very rare gold. The best shells are free from chips or cracks. After being sorted, the shells are drilled. Various pieces of jewelry are fashioned, but the traditional pieces are necklaces and lei. The lei are often done in a pattern imitating flower lei of the other islands, as few natural flowers grow on Ni'ihau. These works can be short,

single-strand chokers or heavy multi-strand pieces. The rice motif is always popular; these are usually multi-stranded with the main shells clipped on the ends with various colored shells strung on as highlights.

A necklace takes long hours to create, with every shell connected by intricate and minute knots. Usually the women of Ni'ihau do this work. Clasps are made from a type of cowry shell found only on Ni'ihau. No two necklaces are exactly alike. They sell by the inch, and the pure white and golden ones are very expensive – most are handed down as priceless heirlooms. Although Ni'ihau shellwork is available in fine stores all over the state, Kaua'i, perhaps because it's closest or because family members live there, seems to get the largest selection. For an introduction, have a look at the collection at the Hawaiian Trading Company in Lawa'i. If you're after a once-in-a-lifetime purchase, consider Ni'ihau shellwork.

The most comprehensive book covering this artistic subject is *Ni'ihau Shell Leis*, by Linda Paik Moriarty, published by the University of Hawai'i Press.

Life Today

The only reliable connection that the islanders have with the outside world is a World War II landing craft, which they use to bring in supplies from Kaua'i, and a new Agusta helicopter used for medical emergencies, supplies, and aerial tours. Homing pigeons were used to send messages, but they have been replaced by two-way radios. There's no communal electricity on the island, but people do have generators to power refrigerators, TVs, and computers. Radios are very popular, and most people get around either on horseback or in ranch pickup trucks. The population numbers around 160 people, 95 percent of whom are Hawaiian; the other 5 percent are Japanese. The main community is Pu'uwai, about midway down the west coast. There is one elementary school, in which English is

spoken, but most people speak Hawaiian at home. The children go off to Kaua'i for high school, but after they get a taste of what the "world at large" has to offer, a surprisingly large number return to Ni'ihau.

After Hurricane 'Iwa battered the island and Hurricane 'Iniki followed suit in 1992, the state was very eager to offer aid. The people of Ni'ihau thanked them for their concern but told them not to bother—they would take care of things themselves. Ni'ihau was the only island to reject statehood in the plebiscite of 1959. In November 1988, when a group of environmentally conscious Kaua'ians took a boat to Ni'ihau to try to clear some of the beaches of floating sea junk that had washed up on shore, the Ni'ihauans felt that the island was being trespassed upon. They didn't want such help in any case, and a few shots were fired, a warning to back off. Still unsettled, the controversy focuses on the question of who owns the beach—all beaches in Hawaii are open to all, yet the whole island of Ni'ihau is privately owned. Occasionally, boaters still try to land on the island, and some have their craft confiscated.

Today, some people accuse the Robinson family of being greedy barons of a medieval fiefdom, holding the Ni'ihauans as virtual slaves. This idea is utter nonsense. Besides the fact that the islanders have an open door, the Robinsons would make immeasurably more money selling the island off to resort developers than running it as a livestock ranch and hunting ground. As if the spirit of old Hawaii was trying to send a sign, it's interesting that Ni'ihau's official lei is fashioned from the *pupu,* a shell found only on the island's beaches, and the island's official color is white, the universal symbol of purity.

Tours

Ni'ihau Safaris (P.O. Box 690370, Makaweli, HI 96769, 808/335-3500 or 877/441-3500, fax 808/338-1463, www.niihau.us) offers two different types of tours to the island, one a helicopter tour and the other a hunting tour. Aside from being invited to the island, these are the only ways to set foot on Ni'ihau. Although it has no fixed schedule, **Ni'ihau Helicopters** flies charter tours on its twin-engine Agusta 109A when there are enough people to make a go of it. This three- to four-hour tour is not a sightseeing flight per se but takes you to the island and lets you enjoy the beach for a couple of hours to play in the water and walk on the sand. Total flight time is about one hour. Don't expect to meet any island residents, however, as they usually set you down away from where the people live. Rates are $325 per person with lunch included. Alternately, a **hunting expedition** can be arranged for wild pigs and feral sheep. Eland, Oryx, and Barbary sheep have also been introduced. The hunting rules for the island are strict but fair for a free chase hunt. Rates are $1,650 a day per hunter, with a maximum of four hunters, and this fee includes the helicopter flight to and ground transportation on Ni'ihau, guide, lunch, up to one animal each, and care and packing of all shot animals.

EAST SHORE

The roughly 10-mile stretch of East Coast Kaua'i, from the Wailua River north, is an ancient place of habitation. The Kaua'ian royalty lived at the mouth of the Wailua River, a place well supplied by waters from Mount Wai'ale'ale. The broad coastal plains, fertile river bottoms, and abundant ocean shore provided all that was needed to sustain them and the commoners who also called this coast their home. The importance of this area is obvious by the numerous *heiau* and other ancient stone remains, as well as the plethora of stories and legends of this region. It was here that canoes headed when coming from the other islands and from here that the great seafarers left on long voyages to the islands of the South Pacific.

More recently, this coastal region made great agricultural land and the rolling hills were covered in acre upon acre of pineapple and sugarcane fields through the mid-1900s. Because of the plantations, this is where the people lived, and the plantation towns that spouted then still survive. After the closing of the pineapple cannery and the demise of sugar, the coastal economy stagnated, only to be revived slowly by the growth of tourism. The once fabulous and emblematic Coco Palms Resort, built at the mouth of the Wailua River in amongst coconut trees and fishponds, was for many guests and residents alike the epitome of early Hawaiian resort style. It drew the famous and ordinary to its doors and set the standard for hospitality for many decades. Money followed, spurring more growth in tourism. Like the rest of the island, the Coconut Coast took a walloping

ROBERT NILSEN

HIGHLIGHTS

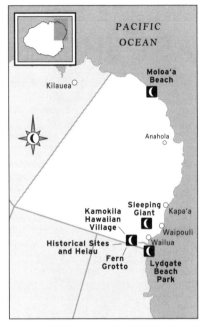

◖ Fern Grotto: A tourist attraction for years, and one perhaps symbolic of the East Shore, the Fern Grotto is a large but shallow depression in the cliff of the riverbank that's festooned with ferns and fronted by a thick canopy of trees. While it was better known in days past when Elvis sang the Hawaiian wedding song, the Fern Grotto still comes to mind when one thinks of weddings in a lush tropical Hawaiian setting (page 151).

◖ Kamokila Hawaiian Village: Just downriver from the Fern Grotto is this re-creation of an ancient Hawaiian village. As no such village exists today, Kamokila is a place where you can get some insight into what Hawaiian structures looked like, what plants were farmed to sustain the family and provide medicines, and a bit about the cultural makeup of the Hawaiian community (page 152).

◖ Historical Sites and Heiau: The Wailua River valley is dotted with ancient Hawaiian sites. These stone remains run from the mouth of the Wailua River all the way up to the top of the mountain. Most are near major roadways, can easily be accessed by car, and provide a good opportunity to learn more about the old Hawaiian culture and its ways (page 153).

◖ Lydgate Beach Park: This is the best beach park along this coast, offering decent swimming with a separate sheltered kiddie swim area, some snorkeling, picnic tables, shelters, and two wonderfully awesome play structures for children. It's perhaps the best spot in town for a day at the beach (page 155).

◖ Sleeping Giant: Otherwise known as Nounou Ridge, this recumbent hill backs the coastal area of Wailua and Kapa'a. The best viewpoint of this sleepy fellow is from along the highway just south of Kapa'a town center, but it is reasonably easy to trudge up to its chest and chin via several hiking trails (page 169).

◖ Moloa'a Beach: Of the beaches north of Kapa'a, before you enter the region of the North Shore, this is the loveliest. Somewhat secluded and with a small community of its own, this semicircular beach and the sheltered bay provide a perfect spot to spend the day, swim in the lazy surf, wade in the freshwater stream, look for turtles, or just sleep on the soft sand while waiting for sundown (page 182).

LOOK FOR ◖ TO FIND RECOMMENDED SIGHTS, ACTIVITIES, DINING, AND LODGING.

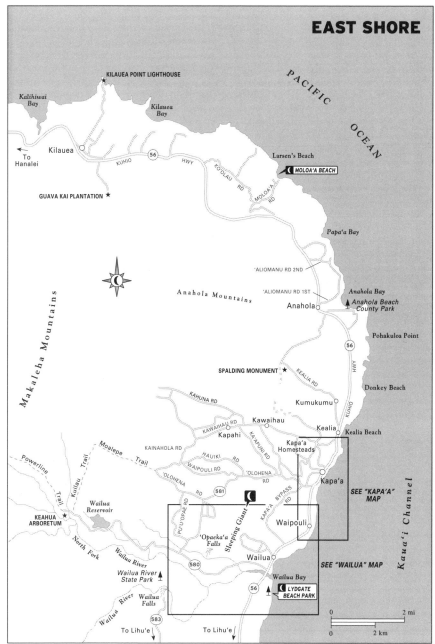

EAST SHORE

KILAUEA POINT LIGHTHOUSE

Kalihiwai Bay

Kilauea Bay

PACIFIC OCEAN

← To Hanalei

Kilauea

KUHIO HWY

56

KO'OLAU RD

MOLOA'A RD

Larsen's Beach

MOLOA'A BEACH

GUAVA KAI PLANTATION

Papa'a Bay

'ALIOMANU RD 2ND

Anahola Mountains

'ALIOMANU RD 1ST

Anahola Bay

Anahola

Anahola Beach County Park

Makaleha Mountains

Pohakuloa Point

56

KUHIO

SPALDING MONUMENT

KEALIA RD

Donkey Beach

KAHUNA RD

Kumukumu

Kealia

KAWAIHAU RD

Kawaihau

Kealia Beach

Kapahi

KAINAHOLA RD

KA'APUNI RD

Kapa'a Homesteads

Moalepe Trail

HAUIKI RD

WAIPOULI RD

'OLOHENA RD

Kapa'a

Powerline Trail

OLOHENA RD

'OLOHENA RD

581

KAPA'A BYPASS RD

SEE "KAPA'A" MAP

Kuilau Trail

PU'U'OPAE RD

Sleeping Giant

Waipouli

Kaua'i Channel

KEAHUA ARBORETUM

Wailua Reservoir

'Opaeka'a Falls

Wailua

SEE "WAILUA" MAP

North Fork

Wailua River

580

Wailua

Wailua Bay

LYDGATE BEACH PARK

Wailua River State Park

Wailua Falls

56

Wailua River

583

To Lihu'e

To Lihu'e

0   2 mi

0   2 km

EAST SHORE

© ROBERT NILSEN AND AVALON TRAVEL PUBLISHING, INC.

when Hurricanes 'Iwa and 'Iniki roared ashore in 1982 and 1992 and, like a punch-drunk boxer, reeled for years. Following the footsteps of the newer tourist developments in Po'ipu and Princeville, this coast has once again begun to blossom as a tourist area.

Aside from the numerous historical sites, the area has a bounty of natural features. The Wailua River valley is a sight in itself and along its banks is the Fern Grotto, a natural amphitheater. North of the river is the infamous Sleeping Giant, a short ridge of hills that overlooks the coast. Farther up is the Keahua Arboretum, a place of quiet and retreat, and the hills and mountains offer many trails to hike, bike, and ride a horse. While other areas of the island offer better swimming beaches and scuba locations, the miles of continuous sand beach here are great for a leisurely stroll and watching the sunrise, while the reef creates a number of good surf spots. Heading north, coastal beaches give way to low cliffs with smaller secluded beaches scattered here and there and only a few communities that have managed to hang on after the demise of sugar. This coast offers much for the visitor. It has the largest and most varied restaurants and shops, a good range of affordable accommodations, plenty of natural and man-made sites, and many options for activities.

PLANNING YOUR TIME

Kaua'i's east coast can easily occupy several days of your trip—if you are the outdoorsy, athletic type. If not, you might just hit the high points on your way to or from the better-known north shore spots or the more popular south shore. For anyone, however, a stop at the **historical sites** and remains of the area are well worth the time as they reveal tidbits of the ancient Hawaiian culture. Three *heiau* near the Wailua River mouth and one farther north along the bay, plus one more up overlooking the river from a high bluff, with the addition of a very sacred royal birthing site, can all be seen in a matter of a few hours. All are close to the highway or otherwise easily

accessible. To add to your knowledge of the Hawaiian culture, visit the riverside **Kamokila Hawaiian Village,** and while exploring the river, don't fail to visit **Fern Grotto** on a Wailua River motored-barge cruise for its lush and fabled setting. For the more adventurous, a leisurely kayak trip up the river with a side trip to a secluded waterfall may be preferable and one of the highlights of the area. Count on a long half day or more for the kayak trip.

Except for Koke'e State Park, this area has more hiking trails than other areas of the island, all easily accessible and many that can also be used by bikes and horses. These trails require anywhere from one hour to a full day, so you can pick just what fits into your time schedule. While those that traverse the **Sleeping Giant,** the ridge of hills just inland from Wailua and Kapa'a, give you a wonderful up-close view of the coastal areas, the more challenging trails near the Keahua Arboretum offer more sweeping vistas of the coast and

This stream below Mount Wai'ale'ale crater walls is at the end of one of East Kaua'i's hiking trails.

a more intimate experience with the island's central mountains. Definitely spend a few hours driving inland, either up to Keahua Arboretum or through the byways behind the Sleeping Giant to get a feel for this rural upland region.

Located right at the Wailua River mouth, **Lydgate Beach Park** is by far the best beach in the area and can satisfy most people's requirements for a place to swim, snorkel, and sunbathe. It's close to town, so you can be there in no time. Other beaches up the coast, like **Moloa'a Beach,** are more secluded, quieter, and worth a half day for rest and relaxation.

The east shore is not the tourist destination that either the Po'ipu or Princeville areas are, although this is changing somewhat now with new development along the coast. Generally, this makes the area less expensive, less exclusive, and more "common." Don't dismiss this coastal region as just a strip to get through, however; be sure to stop a while, explore, learn, and get in touch with both the ancient and modern facets of Kaua'i that this region offers.

Wailua

The east coast of Kaua'i has been called the Coconut Coast, and it's obvious why when you pass through. Even with the extensive development in the area, numerous stands of coconut trees can be seen from the Wailua Municipal Golf Course all the way through Kapa'a. The greatest concentration of these stately nut trees, and a fine representation of the area, is at the Coco Palms near the mouth of the Wailua River. It is here that the coconut grove takes on a magical feel and captivates all who see it.

Wailua (Two Waters) is heralded by the swaying fronds of extra-tall royal palms; whenever you see these, like the *kahili* of old, you know you're entering a special place, a place of royalty. The Hawaiian *ali'i* knew a choice piece of real estate when they saw one, and they cultivated this prime area at the mouth of the Wailua River as their own and referred to it as Wailua Nui Ho'ano (Great Sacred Wailua). This was an important gathering place, a spiritual center for the islands. Through the centuries many *heiau* were built in the area, some where unfortunates were slaughtered to appease the gods, and others where the weak and vanquished could find succor and sanctuary. The road leading inland along the Wailua River was called the King's Highway. Commoners were allowed to travel along this road and to approach the royal settlement by invitation only. The most exalted of the island's *ali'i* traced their proud lineage to Puna, a Tahitian priest who, according to the oral tradition, arrived in the earliest migrations and settled here.

Even before the Polynesians came, the area was purportedly settled by the semi-mythical Mu. This lost tribe may have been composed of early Polynesians who were isolated for such a long time that they developed different physical characteristics from their original ancestral stock. Or perhaps they were a unique people altogether, whom history never recorded. But like another island group, the Menehune, they were said to be dwarfish creatures who shunned outsiders. Unlike the industrious Menehune, who helped the Polynesians, the Mu were fierce and brutal savages whose misanthropic characteristics confined them to solitary caves in the deep interior along the Wailua River, where they led unsuspecting victims to their deaths.

The mountains behind Wailua form a natural sculpture of a giant in repose, aptly called the **Sleeping Giant.** You have to stretch your imagination just a little to see him (his outline is clearer from farther up in Waipouli), and although not entirely a bore, like most

EAST SHORE

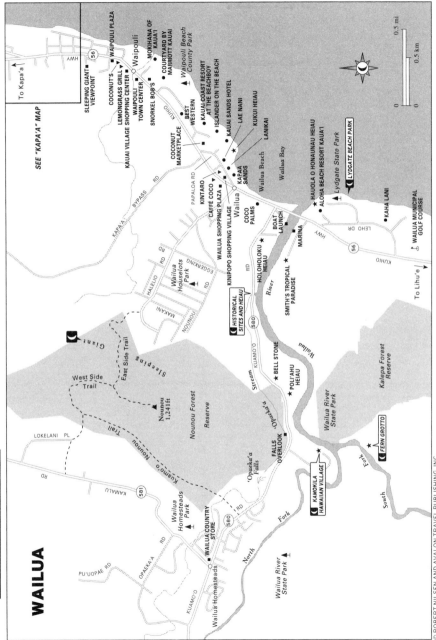

WAILUA

EAST SHORE

SEE "KAPA'A" MAP

To Kapa'a

SLEEPING GIANT VIEWPOINT
COCONUT'S
LEMONGRASS GRILL
KAUAI VILLAGE SHOPPING CENTER
WAIPOULI TOWN CENTER
SNORKEL BOB'S
WAIPOULI PLAZA
Waipouli
MOKIHANA OF KAUA'I
COURTYARD BY MARRIOTT KAUAI
Waipouli Beach County Park
BEST WESTERN
KAUAI COAST RESORT AT THE BEACHBOY
ISLANDER ON THE BEACH
KAUAI SANDS HOTEL
LAE NANI
KUKUI HEIAU
LANIKAI
COCONUT MARKETPLACE
KINTARO
CAFFÉ COCO
KAPA'A SANDS
WAILUA SHOPPING PLAZA
Wailua
COCO PALMS
KINIPOPO SHOPPING VILLAGE
HISTORICAL SITES AND HEIAU
HOLOHOLOKU HEIAU
BOAT LAUNCH
MARINA
SMITH'S TROPICAL PARADISE
HAUOLA O HONAUNAU HEIAU
ALOHA BEACH RESORT KAUA'I
Lydgate State Park
LYDGATE BEACH PARK
KAHA LANI
WAILUA MUNICIPAL GOLF COURSE
Wailua Beach
Wailua Bay
LEHO DR
To Lihu'e

Wailua Houselots Park
EGGERKING RD
HALELIO RD
MAKANI RD
NONOU RD
KAPA'A BYPASS
PAPALOA RD

Sleeping Giant
East Side Trail
West Side Trail
Nounou 1,241ft
Nounou Forest Reserve
LOKELANI PL
Kuamo'o Nounou Trail
RD
'Opaeka'a Stream
BELL STONE
POLI'AHU HEIAU
'Opaeka'a
FALLS OVERLOOK
'Opaeka'a Falls
KAMOKILA HAWAIIAN VILLAGE
KUAMO'O RD
Wailua Homesteads Park
WAILUA COUNTRY STORE
PU'UOPAE RD
OPAEKA'A RD
KAMALU RD
Wailua River State Park
North Fork
South Fork
FERN GROTTO
Wailua River State Park
Kalepa Forest Reserve
Wailua River

KAUMO'O RD
KUHIO
PAPALOA RD
KUAMO'O RD

giants, he's better left asleep. This giant and his green cover are part of the Nounou Forest Reserve.

Inland of Wailua (and also Kapa'a farther up the coast) is an upland district, not terribly high in elevation but located behind Nounou Ridge (Sleeping Giant) and definitely separated from the coast. This is former cane land that has been transformed into hobby farms, pastureland, and small agricultural plots. Numerous roads cut through this pastoral region, creating rural residential areas set amongst the rolling hills, with views of the nearby steep mountain slopes. Here it's easy to spot roosters picking for food along the roadway and cattle egrets standing tall and white in a horse pasture. For a glimpse of what this area is like, take Kuamo'o Road (Rt. 580) up from the coast and turn onto Kamalu Road (Rt. 581), following it around the mountain back to Kapa'a. Alternately, use either end of 'Opaeka'a Road to get to Pu'u'opae Road and follow this to Olohena Road. There turn uphill and follow it around as it slides down toward the sea via Waipouli Road, or a little farther to the north, Kainahola and Kawaihau Roads.

Wailua today has a population of more than 2,000, but you'd never know that driving past it, as most houses are away from the water, below Nounou Ridge; an additional 5,000 lie scattered on the upland hills of Wailua and Kapa'a homesteads. Though it's an older resort area, Wailua is not at all overdeveloped, yet new construction is happening here after years of neglect. The natural charm is as vibrant as ever. Depending on conditions, the beaches can be excellent, and hotels, shops, restaurants, and nightlife are close at hand. With development increasing both to the north and south, perhaps now, as in days of old, the beauty of Wailua will beckon once again.

SIGHTS
Wailua River State Park

To the traveling public, Wailua is famous primarily for two attractions: one natural, Fern Grotto, the other man-made, Smith's Tropical Paradise. People flock to these, as they are indeed beautiful spots, but there also exist many other spots of historical and cultural significance. Most of these lie within the boundary of Wailua River State Park, which runs from the mouth of the Wailua River up the narrow valley, along its south fork to Wailua Falls and its north fork almost to Wailua Reservoir and Keahua Arboretum. Within the arms of this 1,093-acre park are several other waterfalls (including 'Opaeka'a Falls), half a dozen *heiau,* sacred birthing stones, and vantages for meditative views of the river below. The Wailua Beach section with Kukui Heiau fronts the bay. The Wailua River State Park is not a park with one entrance and where you can see all the sites in neat order. Each of its attractions is widely disbursed and has its own location and access. These are listed separately below. There is no entrance fee.

⬛ Fern Grotto

Nature's attraction is the Wailua River itself, Hawaii's only navigable stream, which meanders inland toward its headwaters at the foot of forbidding Mount Wai'ale'ale. Along this route is the Fern Grotto, a tourist institution of legend, hype, and beauty rolled into one. A local company runs sightseeing trips to the grotto on large motorized barges. As you head the two miles upriver, the crew tells legends of the area and serenades visitors with Hawaiian songs. A hula demonstration is given, and visitors are encouraged to get up and swing along. The grotto itself is a huge rock amphitheater, whose ever-misty walls create the perfect conditions for ferns to grow. And grow they do, wildly and with abandon, filling the cavern with their deep musty smell and penetrating green beauty. Partially denuded of its lush green coat and overhead tree canopy by Hurricane 'Iniki in 1992, and suffering a lack of water seepage from a reservoir above after the closure of the sugar plantation, the grotto has partially filled back in but has not become the beauty it once was. Although the grotto is smaller than one might imagine, the resonating acoustics are wonderful from inside. Here in the natural cathedral, musicians break into the "Hawaiian Wedding Song"; over the years a steady stream of brides and grooms have come to exchange vows. The Fern Grotto trip is an amusement ride, and, aside from paddling yourself upriver in a kayak, it's the only way to get there. It's enjoyable and memorable, but you have to stay in the right frame of mind; otherwise, it's too easy to put down. Because of its deteriorating condition, improvements have been made, including improved water supply up top, planting of new ferns, trimming trees, removal of invasive plant species, and new walkways and guardrails. These improvements should, over time, bring the grotto back to the beauty that it once was. (See *Wailua River Cruises* for particulars on transportation.)

Smith's Tropical Paradise

Along the Wailua River is this 30-acre botanical and cultural garden. A large entranceway welcomes you and proclaims it a "tropical paradise." Inside, many plants are labeled; most are ordinary island foliage, but others are rare and exotic even for the Garden Island. The entire area is sheltered and well watered, and it's easy to imagine how idyllic life could have been for the ancient Hawaiian royalty who once inhabited this fertile and lush river bottom. The two main buildings are a lu'au house and a lagoon theater used in the evenings for an international musical show and lu'au. The "villages"—Philippine- and Polynesian-inspired settlements—are merely plywood facsimiles. However, the grounds themselves are beautifully kept and very impressive. Peacocks and chickens pecking beneath the trees are natural groundskeepers, preventing insects and weeds from overpowering the gardens. This garden provides an excellent opportunity to familiarize yourself with Kaua'i's plants, flowers, fruits, and trees. You are welcome to walk where you will, but signs guide you along a recommended one-mile route. Scheduled mini-trams carry tourists around the grounds for an additional fee. Entrance fees are $5.25 adults, $2.50 children 2–11. Smith's Tropical Paradise (808/821-

6895) is open 8:30 A.M.–4:30 P.M., after which the gardens are readied for the evening lu'au and musical entertainment. To get to the gardens, follow the road past the Wailua Marina on the south side of the river.

◖ Kamokila Hawaiian Village

At a bend in the Wailua River on the way to the Fern Grotto sits Kaua'i's only re-created folk village. Kamokila (Stronghold) has been cut from the jungle on the site of an *ali'i* village, the first of seven ancient villages in this valley; the villages farther up were for commoners. The prominent ridge across the river indicates the boundary past which an ordinary man could not tread for fear of his losing his life.

The old village sat on terraces on the hillside above the river, and fields were cultivated where the village now lies. Kamokila has been resurrected to give visitors a glimpse of what island life was like for the ancient Hawaiians. Opened in 1981, it was destroyed almost immediately by Hurricane 'Iwa in 1982 and badly knocked around again by Hurricane 'Iniki in 1992. Here you find examples of buildings, agricultural plots, fruit trees and medicinal plants, and perhaps demonstrations of ancient crafts and activities of everyday life. A *hale noa* (chief's sleeping quarters), *hale koa* (warrior's house), *pahoku hanau* (birthing house), *hale ali'i 'akoakoa* (assembly hall), *hale lapa'au* (herbal medicine office), and *lana nu'u mamao* (oracle tower) have been erected to give a sense of what ancient Hawaiian buildings were like. The *imu* pit for cooking is functional, and an athletic ground hosts games at festival times. There are also tikis (spirit containers) and *'aumakua* (ancestral spirit icons) set up at propitious spots around the village.

Use the informational sheet for a self-guided tour around the property and an explanation of the importance of each site. Ask the staff about the methods of creating handicrafts and tools, the uses of both the ordinary and medicinal plants, and how the village operated on a daily basis. You may drive down to the village by following a steep one-lane track that skirts the ridge—the turnoff is just above the 'Opaeka'a Falls overlook on Rt. 580. A trip to Kamokila Hawaiian Village (808/823-0559, Mon.–Sat. 9 A.M.–5 P.M., $5 adults, $3 for children under 12) is well worth the time and effort and will certainly add to your knowledge of the roots of Hawaiian life. Combining this tour with a kayak trip up the river costs $30. As the closest entry point onto the river for Fern Grotto, the secret falls, and swimming spots along the riverbank, entry here knocks off several miles of paddling.

◖ Historical Sites and Heiau

The King's Highway (Rt. 580), running inland from Wailua, and Rt. 56, the main drag, has a number of roadside attractions and historical sites dating from the precontact period. Most are just a short stroll from your car and well worth the effort.

Along Rt. 56, a tall stand of palms on the south side of the Wailua River is part of Wailua River State Park and marks the spot of **Hauola O Honaunau** (Pu'uhonua O Hauola), a temple of refuge that welcomed offending *kapu*-breakers of all social classes. Here miscreants could atone for their transgressions and have their spiritual slates wiped clean by temple priests, enabling them to return to society without paying with their lives. Both the refuge and **Hikina A Ka La Heiau,** a site of rituals and prayers to the rising sun, are marked by a low encircling wall. The area, where the Wailua River meets the sea, is extremely picturesque. Perhaps it's knowledge about the temple of refuge that creates the atmosphere, but here, as at all of these merciful temple sites, the atmosphere is calm and uplifting, as if some spiritual residue has permeated the centuries. At the river mouth and shallowly incised into the river rock are a handful of Kaua'i's few **petroglyphs**—human and geometric figures. These can usually be seen at low tide when not covered by sand. Over the road and on a low bluff near the entrance to the marina are the tumbled walls of **Malae Heiau.** Of unknown origin (some attribute its construction to Menehune) and use, this *heiau* has recently been partially cleared and is said to be the largest on the island.

ROBERT NILSEN

Poli'ahu Heiau

EAST SHORE

On the low point that forms the northern extent of Wailua Bay, now on Lae Nani condominium property, is **Kukui Heiau.** As this whole region was once populated by royalty and was a point of arrival and departure between the islands, and perhaps also for travelers from islands of the South Pacific, Kukui Heiau was used as a fire beacon site to direct canoes to a proper landing. It was perhaps 500 years old and once about 230 feet long by 70 feet wide; only a fragment of its former stone structure is evident today, affirming the skill of its builders and the importance of the site.

As Rt. 580 starts to meander inland, you pass the state park boat launch area. Almost immediately on your left look for **Holoholoku Heiau,** where the unfortunate ones who didn't make it to the temple of refuge were sacrificed to the never-satisfied gods. This temple is one of Kaua'i's most ancient; the altar itself is the large slab of rock near the front. As if to represent the universality of the life-death cycle, **Pohaku Ho'o Hanau,** the royal birthing stones, are within an infant's cry away. Royal mothers came here to deliver the future kings and queens of the island. The stones somehow look comfortable to lean against, and perhaps their solidity reinforced the courage of the mother. Behind the *heiau,* a silver guardrail leads up the hill to a small, neatly tended Japanese cemetery. The traditional tombstones chronicling the lives and deaths of those buried here have turned green with lichen against the pale blue sky.

Back on Rt. 580, you start to wend your way uphill. You can see how eroded and lush Kaua'i is from this upland perch. Notice, too, the dark green freshwater as it becomes engulfed by the royal blue of the ocean in the distance. As you climb, look for a pull-off on the right side and an HVB Warrior pointing to **'Opaeka'a Falls.** Stop here for pictures and carefully cross the road to another overlook; below is the Wailua River and the Kamokila Hawaiian Village. Take a look around to see how undeveloped Kaua'i is. From here you can get a sense of why this section of coast was a favorite spot for the ancient Hawaiian *ali'i* and how bountiful this region must have been.

Across the road and down a bit from the 'Opaeka'a turnoff is **Poli'ahu Heiau,** a one-acre site supposedly built by the Menehune and used by King Kaumuali'i, Kaua'i's last king. This is one of seven *heiau* known to have been constructed along the Wailua River from the river mouth to the mountaintop. While its use is not definitely known and all the structures inside are long since gone, it is assumed by the size to have been a *luakini heiau,* one that required a powerful leader and great manpower to build and one that may have been used for human sacrifice. Nothing is left but a rectangular wall enclosure with an enlargement at one corner that has once again been filled with rock to create a fairly level platform. Do not walk on the stones, as it's believed that the spirits of the ancestors are contained in the rocks.

Some distance down the hill beyond the end of a dirt track, past two prominent boulders, is a **bell stone.** Bell stones were historically pounded when a royal *wahine* gave birth, and their unique sound could be heard for miles. From the boulders at the end of the road, there is a great view over the river and down to the coast.

Kaua'i's Hindu Temple

Just over four miles up from the ocean, on the south side of Rt. 580, is Kaua'i's Hindu Temple and monastery (www.himalayanacadamy.com). Visitation is free and open every day of the year 9 A.M.–noon to the Kadaval Hindu Temple building and 6 A.M.–6 P.M. for the Ganesha Shrine and Bangalore Gallery. Special tour days (usually once a week) are also offered for a more extensive tour of the grounds and the new ornate temple structure of typical South Indian architectural design being built on the grounds. When completed, it will be one of the largest granite Hindu temples outside of India. Modest (no shorts, T-shirts, short skirts, revealing blouses, or swimwear) and appropriate dress, please, for all those who visit.

BEACHES AND PARKS
◖ Lydgate Beach Park

Lydgate Beach Park is a gem. It's on the south side of the Wailua River, behind the Aloha Beach Resort Kaua'i complex. A large lava rock barrier makes for great swimming and snorkeling even in high surf. The pool is completely protected and perfect for tots, but stay off the slippery rock barrier. Overseeing the whole beach is a lifeguard. This beach is never overcrowded, and you can find more seclusion by walking along the coast away from the built-up area toward the golf course. If you head to the river, the brackish water is refreshing, but stay away from the point where it meets the ocean; the collision creates tricky, wicked currents. One of the best on the island, Lydgate Beach Park also provides sheltered picnic tables under a cool canopy provided by a thick stand of ironwoods, plus grills, restrooms, and showers, but no camping. Here at the park is **Kamalani Playground,** a wonderful kids' play structure created for the community with community input. This is a child's dream come true: slides, swings, steps, tubes, passageways, and differ-

ent-level platforms. A short way back down the coast and fronting the golf course is a secluded and newly created section of Lydgate Beach Park. Drive to it by following the paved road at the northern end of the course until it branches toward the sea. In this second section, you'll discover tree-covered dunes, walkways and bike paths, more restrooms and covered picnic areas, and a second wonderful children's play structure that spans the access to the beach.

Wailua Beach

Wailua Beach, fronting the Coco Palms, is part of the Kaumuali'i section of Wailua River State Park. It can be treacherous and should only be entered on calm days when lifeguards are in attendance. It's a favorite for people who want to sunbathe, play in the water near shore, or stroll along the sand. Surfers come for the breaks on the northern edge of the bay, and body boarders can sometimes be seen near the river mouth. Park under the trees at either end.

Waipouli Beach County Park

Waipouli Beach County Park fronts the cluster

Lydgate Beach Park

of hotels near the Coconut Marketplace. Largely an undeveloped grassy area, the narrow beach is really not recommended for swimming because of the near shore reef, but it is fine for sunbathing and collecting driftwood.

A half-mile-long **beach walk,** partly over hotel sidewalks with the rest across the grassy sand of the county park, starts at the Kauai Sands Hotel on the south end and runs past the Courtyard by Marriott on the north end.

ENTERTAINMENT

The **Courtyard by Marriott** has a free torch-lighting ceremony in the central courtyard every evening at 6:30 P.M.; this is followed in the later half of the week by local musicians playing island music for a few hours.

The Kuhio Lounge at the Aloha Beach Resort Kaua'i comes alive on Saturday nights with music and dancing, so polish your shoes and practice your steps.

The Coconut Marketplace hosts a free **Polynesian Hula Show** Wednesday at 5 P.M. The young local dancers and musicians put as much effort into their routines as if this were the big time.

The Coconut Marketplace also has something to offer moviegoers: the two-screen **Coconut Marketplace Cinemas** (808/821-2324). Adult entrance is $7, seniors $6.50, and children $4.

A good watering hole for the younger crowd, where you can find cool drinks, good conversation, and lively music nightly, is **Tradewinds – A South Seas Bar** (808/822-1621, 10 A.M.– 2 A.M.) at the Coconut Marketplace courtyard. On some nights with live bands or DJs there's a cover charge, otherwise no-cover karaoke is what's happening.

Lu'au

Three lu'au are performed along this coast. Tihati's **Hiva Pacefika** (808/823-0311) at the Courtyard by Marriott holds its lu'au every evening except Monday in the *lu'au halau* under a canopy of coconut trees starting at 5:30 P.M. The buffet table is loaded with luscious island food, and there is an open bar throughout the

evening. Legends of the island are performed in music and dance—no extravaganza, just fine sights and sounds. The enthusiastic entertainment is a combination of dignified and refined *kahiko* (ancient hula) and more colorful and energetic *awana* (modern hula), performed by an accomplished troupe of both men and women. Adult tickets are $62, $40 for children 13–18, and $30 for those 3–12.

Kaua'i's Best Lu'au (808/635-7670) is performed at Aloha Beach Resort by Na Punua O Kaua'i hula school every Tuesday at 6 P.M. Advertised as a "traditional lu'au," the show includes music, dance, and legends of Hawaii, Samoa, and Tahiti. Prices run $65 adults, $62 seniors, $40 for teens, $30 for kids 6–12.

When asked about recommendations for a lu'au on Kaua'i, nearly everyone suggests the **Smith Family Garden Lu'au** (808/821-6895). As with most such lu'au, this one starts with an *imu* ceremony, followed by drinks and a full buffet meal. While the food is not necessarily better than anywhere else, the entertainment is different and separate from the meal. Not the typical Polynesian revue, here the spectacle includes Hawaiian music, a fiery volcanic eruption, and dances from all the major ethnic groups that have made Hawaii their home. This event is held on Monday, Wednesday, and Friday starting at 5 P.M. on the banks of the Wailua River within the Smith's Tropical Paradise gardens. Tickets are $56 for adults, $28.50 for children 7–13, and $18.75 for ages 3–6; for the show only with no buffet and entrance at 7:30 P.M., tickets run $15 adult and $7.50 children. Locals often rate this the best musical review on the island.

SHOPPING
Kinipopo Shopping Village

This diminutive mall, on the seaside of Kuhio Hwy. just beyond the end of Wailua Beach, offers most of Wailua's one-stop shopping. Aside from Korean, Chinese, and Mexican restaurants, you can find a handful of unique small shops, including **Style World** for an assortment of aloha shirts and casual dresses, **Kinipopo Fine Art** for a take-home treasure,

Goldsmith's Kauai for wearable jewels, and for a permanent memento, see what **Garden Isle Tattoo** has to offer. If you are an aficionado of old Hawaii, drop in to the **Tin Can Mailman** (808/822-3009, 11 A.M.–7 P.M. weekdays, noon–4 P.M. Sat.), the most unusual shop in this plaza. The Tin Can Mailman definitely has a heart for out-of-print books on Hawaii and Polynesia, battered travel guides filled with memories, antique maps, vintage menus, early botanical prints, rare missionary items, other collectibles, and even new Hawaiiana books. The shop is small, cramped, and bursting with ancient voices still quietly singing their songs.

To the side in an adjacent building is **Kauai Water Ski and Surf Co.** (808/822-3574, open daily 9 A.M.–7 P.M.), a complete sales and rental water-sports shop. Bathing suits, bikinis, sun visors, men's shorts, surfboards, boogie boards, wet suits, fins, masks, snorkels, underwater watches, and even a few day packs line the shelves of this small but jam-packed shop. Water-skiing can be arranged and kayak tours booked.

Unique Boutique

Across the highway from Kinipopo Shopping Village, in the Wailua Shopping Plaza, are several more eateries and a kayak rental shop. Set back in the trees in a separate building to the rear of this center, Caffé Coco serves scrumptious wholesome lunches and dinners. Next to it is **Bambulei** (808/823-8641, 10 A.M.–5 P.M.), an intriguing little shop that, along with a variety of antiques and collectibles, carries some women's clothing and men's aloha shirts. Although there is an eclectic mix, much is Asian or Asian-inspired, and there's a heavy predominance of Hawaiiana from the middle decades of the 1900s. This is worth the stop if a step back in time is of interest to you.

Coconut Marketplace

Prices at this cluster of more than 60 shops, restaurants, and galleries are kept down because of the natural competition of so many businesses, each of which tries to specialize, which usually means good choices for what strikes your

fancy. Any of the jewelry shops have enough stock on hand to drop even Mr. T to his knees. With so many apparel and footwear shops, the job of finding just the right aloha shirt, casual dress, sports clothing, or sandal shouldn't be a problem. Most shops are open 9 A.M.–8 P.M., Sunday 10 A.M.–6 P.M., but if you don't want to shop, just come for the free hula show on Wednesday at 5 P.M.

Ship Store Gallery (808/822-7758) sets sail for adventure with nautical artwork of tall-masted ships and contemporary Japanese art in a gallery filled with cannons, pistols, and swords. This is an amazingly full place that will get the mariner in everyone away from the dock. In addition to the plentiful artwork are fine antiques and collectibles. Showing works by artists that have become synonymous with Hawaii, **Kahn Galleries** (808/822-3636) has captivating paintings that might be just what you're looking for as a memento of your trip to the island. Other shops include **Island Surf Shop,** where you can purchase a boogie board, travel bag, *pareu,* beach hat, and T-shirts; **Sole Mates,** for those slippers and hats that you forgot to bring with you; **Products of Hawaii, Too** selling crafts and gifts; and **Jungle Rain** for casual clothing and gifts. For sundries and snacks, head for **Whaler's General Store.**

Wailua Country Store

At the intersection of Rt. 580 and Rt. 581 to the back of the Sleeping Giant, this small country shop (808/821-0808) has basic grocery supplies and snacks, good for those in a vacation rental home in this area or as a last stop for those heading up to Keahua Arboretum or the Powerline Trail.

RECREATION
Golf

Wailua Municipal Golf Course (808/241-6666) skirts the coast, fronting a secluded beach. Opened in 1920 but rebuilt several times, it is the oldest golf course on Kaua'i and the first built on an outer island. Because of its idyllic setting, it's perhaps the most beautiful public links in Hawaii, and it frequently

ROBERT NILSEN

Wailua Municipal Golf Course is considered one of the best public golf courses in the States.

gets cited as one of the finest municipal courses in the country. On occasion, tournaments are held here. As it's a municipal course with very reasonable fees, it usually is very busy on weekends and holidays. Go during the week. Even if you're not an avid golfer, you can take a lovely stroll beside the fairways as they stretch out along the coastline. The greens fees for nonresidents are a reasonable $32 weekdays, $44 weekends; carts are $16, and club rental is $15. The driving range is open until 10 P.M. For the convenience of golfers, the 19th Hole snack shop and bar at the clubhouse is open daily.

Wailua River Cruises

You too can be one of the many cruising up the Wailua River on a large, canopied, motorized barge. Anyone can fully enjoy this trip, most popular with middle-aged and older tourists, if they let the beauty of the spot surround them. The Fern Grotto, where the boat docks, is a natural amphitheater festooned with hanging ferns—one of the most tourist-visited spots in Hawaii. In operation since 1947, **Smith's Motor Boat Service** (808/821-6892)

is an extended family operation where family members serve in every capacity. During the 20-minute ride upriver on their green boats you're entertained with music and a recounting of legends, and at the Fern Grotto a small but well-done medley of island songs is performed. Daily cruises (90 minutes round-trip) depart every half hour from Wailua Marina 9–11:30 A.M. and 12:30–3 P.M.; on Monday, Wednesday, and Friday there's an additional 3:30 P.M. cruise. Adults cost $20, children (2–12) $10; discounts for seniors and *kama'aina* are available.

Kayaking

Kayaking in Wailua means kayaking up the gentle and slow-moving Wailua River. A well-traveled route is to head to Fern Grotto or perhaps a bit beyond to a river's edge swimming hole. It is not possible to paddle all the way up to Wailua Falls. Do not use the boat dock at Fern Grotto, as they are maintained only for the river barges. Although it has caused some bank degradation, the only way to disembark there is to tie your kayak to a bush on the bank

EAST SHORE

next to the dock and walk along the water to the paved walkway. A second route, now preferred by most, is to head to what is known as "Secret Falls" (or Misty Falls). Going upriver, turn right into the north fork of the river just past Kamokila Hawaiian Village. A short way up—stay to your left—look for the trailhead and tie your kayak up along the bank. From here it's about an hour's walk to the falls. Roughly, follow the south bank until you get to a water gauging station. Just beyond it, cross the stream that comes in from your left. Walk up this stream, cross the right branch, and recross the main stream for a short distance to the falls.

Whether going upstream or down on the Wailua River, stay hard to the north bank, as there is frequent barge traffic and a periodic motorboat pulling water-skiers.

Rates for kayak rentals generally run $25–30 for a single and $50 for a tandem. If needed, car carriers can also be rented. All places require that you return kayaks by 5 P.M. Kayak launching and retrieval should be done at the state park unit launch site, the third driveway on the left off Rt. 580 up from Kuhio Highway. Aside from the companies listed below, **Kamokila Hawaiian Village** also rents kayaks for $30, which includes entrance to the village. If you rent there, you don't have to paddle so far up the river and have more time for exploring.

To rent kayaks for a river adventures—be sure to ask for a river map—check with one of the following companies. **Wailua Kayak and Canoe** (808/821-1188) is next to the Smith Motorboat Company booth on Wailua Road, which is the first left turn off Kuamo'o Road (Rt. 580) after turning inland off of Kuhio Highway (Rt. 56). As this is the closest place to the river, it's easy to carry the kayak to the launch site. Make your arrangements at the Smith booth or at the reservation office just up the road next to Mema's restaurant. Wailua Kayak runs morning tours for $90 (with lunch) and an afternoon tour for $55 but also rents kayaks by the hour. Located in the Kinipopo Shopping Village, **Kauai Water Ski, Surf, and**

Kayak Co. (808/822-3575, www.kauaiwaterskisurfandkayak.com, daily 9 A.M.–7 P.M.) also offers two guided kayak trips a day as they have done for years. Other shops that have rental kayaks and/or run kayak tours are **Kayak Wailua** (808/822-3388, www.kayakwailua.com, $46), near the Shell gas station in the Kinipopo Shopping Village; **Duke's Kayak Adventures** (808/821-9097, $62–89), with shuttles from the Activity Warehouse at 4-788 Kuhio Hwy.; **Wailua River Kayak Adventures** (808/822-5795, $85), behind Lemongrass Restaurant, and **Paradise Outdoor Adventures** (808/822-1112, kayakers.com, $88–138), farther up in Kapa'a. Two other outfits that run guided tours on the Wailua River but have offices elsewhere are **Ali'i Kayaks** (808/241-7700 or 877/246-2544, www.aliikayaks.com) at Kalapaki Beach in Lihu'e and **Outfitters Kauai** (808/742-9667 or 888/742-9887, www.outfitterskauai.com) in Po'ipu.

Waterskiing

Ever thought of waterskiing in Paradise? Skimming the smooth waters of Wailua River is the only possibility on Kaua'i, and **Kauai Waterski, Surf, and Kayak Co.** (808/822-3574, www.kauaiwaterskisurfandkayak.com) at the Kinipopo Shopping Village has business to itself. The shop offers one pull for $30, a half hour of skiing for $55, and one hour for $100. Prices include boat, gas, driver, and all equipment.

East Kaua'i Hiking Trails

All these trails are in the mountains above Wailua. One trail system crisscrosses Nounou Ridge, otherwise known as the Sleeping Giant, while other individual trails are farther inland near Keahua Arboretum.

Nounou Mountain Trail, East Side, begins off Haleilio Road, which runs inland at the Kinipopo Shopping Village. Follow Haleilio Road for 1.2 miles until it begins to curve to the left. Near pole no. 38, park at the small trailhead parking lot. The trailhead leads to a series of switchbacks that scale the mountain for 1.75 miles. The trail climbs steadily through native and introduced forest and past one large volcanic outcrop. Near the top, it meets the west side trail coming in from the right, and shortly beyond that is a flat, grassy area with a picnic table, shelter, and bench. This is the "chest" of the giant. Stop here a while and take in the views down to Wailua and the coast or up toward the middle of the island. From the picnic area you can proceed along the spine of the mountain, the "throat," to the giant's "face." Although the going gets a little tougher and the mountain drops off quickly on both sides, the trail is passable and you may have it to yourself. From the face, you're rewarded with a superb 360-degree view but may not be able to see down the slope due to the thick brush cover.

A parking area and right of way for **Nounou Mountain Trail, West Side** is found at the end of Lokelani Street, off Rt. 581, north of Rt. 580. Alternately, a trail right of way leads directly up to this point from Rt. 581, but there is not much parking along the road. Follow the right of way until it joins the trail at the top end of the pasture. This trail leads you through a forest of introduced trees planted in the 1930s that includes Norfolk Pine, strawberry guava, and a forest of *hala* trees near the top. About a quarter mile from the start, a fork in the trail locates the junction of the **Kaumo'o Nounou Trail,** which traverses the west side of the mountain, through a bamboo forest and over 'Opaeka'a Stream, from its trailhead on Rt. 580 across from Melia Street. The West Trail joins the East Trail at the 1.5-mile marker and proceeds to the picnic table and shelter. This trail is slightly shorter and more forested than that on the ocean side. Bring water for both, as there is none on the way.

Follow Rt. 580 until you come to the University of Hawaii Agriculture Experimental Station. Keep going past the Wailua Reservoir until the pavement ends and then follow the dirt road for almost a mile to **Keahua Arboretum.** A developed picnic and freshwater swimming area is at the ford at Keahua Stream, about seven miles in from the highway. Two short trails run downstream on either side of the stream here, and another

enjoying a pool at the entrance to the Keahua Arboretum

leads into the marshy area beyond the hill. It would be helpful to have trees in the arboretum named, but it isn't so. The southern end of the **Powerline Trail** starts at the arboretum. Cross the stream and walk up the steep road on the far side. At the crest of the road, a 4WD track heads uphill to the right. This is the start, and from here it's a long half day's hike over the mountain to the trailhead on the Hanalei side, about 13 miles away. While there is some shade near the beginning, the majority of the trail is exposed to the sun virtually all day. If you're without a car at the north trailhead or someone to pick you up on that side, hike up to the top and return back down this side. Of the two halves of the trail, this south side is the shortest and steepest, but the prettiest, and from the top you have relatively close views up to the top of Mount Wai'ale'ale, the sheer mountainsides that swoop down from it, and numerous distant waterfalls. This trail, often used by mountain bikers and also by hunters during hunting season, takes you through the heart of the mountains that make up the eastern half of the island. On occasion a 4WD vehicle will attempt this trail, but several sections are virtually impassable due to erosion. Dirt bikers also like to use this trail, particularly on the weekend, so for the most peace and quiet it's perhaps best to walk this trail during the week.

If you follow the gravel road that runs across the stream at the arboretum and up over the short hill beyond, you will continue on into the center of the island. Beyond the arboretum, the road is fairly level with a gentle incline but it may be muddy and rutted during the rains. Although there are several jeep trails that run off either side of this main track, follow the main road for about four miles to a locked gate at its end. This is the spot where scenes of the entrance gate in the movie *Jurassic Park* were filmed. Walk around the gate and continue up the road for about 45 minutes to a gauging station and dammed section of the river and appreciate just how close you are to the center of the island. From here you can look up at the semicircular crater

wall and, if it's been raining, see dozens (or more) of wispy-thin waterfalls slithering down the incredibly steep crater sides. An additional 1.5-hour hike through the forest will bring you to the base of a waterfall and pool below Mount Wai'ale'ale.

The **Kuilau Trail** begins about 200 yards before the entrance to the arboretum, on the right. This gradual trail follows a muddy old roadway for a mile or so to a flat spot with a picnic area and shelter. Here are some magnificent views of the mountains, some of the best anywhere. You can look directly out at Mount Wai'ale'ale and what's known as the Wai'ale'ale crater or farther afield to Kilohana and the Ha'upu Ridge, or follow the power line as it marches up and over the pass. Like the arboretum below, this is a good area to listen to the birds. Continue on this trail, circling around the hill, and you'll eventually come to a small footbridge. At the bridge, about two miles from the trailhead, the Kuilau Trail meets the Moalepe Trail. After crossing the bridge, the trail climbs through a dense tunnel of trees to a small open flat spot and then turns to the east. The **Moalepe Trail** starts at the end of Olohena Road. From here a dirt track runs for some distance inland to a turnaround, but it may not be passable as it's extremely rutted and often slick in rainy weather. This route, a popular horseback-riding trail, gains the heights and offers some excellent panoramas before joining the Kuilau Trail at the footbridge, almost three miles from Olohena Road. Both these trails bring you to mid-elevation mountain slopes.

Horseback Riding

Kahana II Trail Rides (808/821-1516 or 800/320-9981, www.kahanaiitrailrides.com) has its office at the Kinipopo Shopping Center, but runs horseback rides up the Kuilau and Moalepe trails into the interior of the island, where you have views of mountain waterfalls as well as the distant coast. Two-hour rides run $85 while the three- to four-hour rides are $125. These are great for first-time and beginning riders; kids age 14 and up are welcome.

ACCOMMODATIONS
$100-150

Part of the Hawaiian-owned Sand and Seaside Hotels chain, **C Kauai Sands Hotel** (420 Papaloa Rd., 808/822-4951 or 800/560-5553, fax 808/822-0978, www.kauaisandshotel.com), located to the side of Coconut Marketplace, is a better-than-average economical hotel with a convenient location, spacious grounds, accommodating staff, a large relaxing lobby, a budget restaurant, two pools, beach access, and self-service laundry facilities. As with all four Sand and Seaside Hotels, this one is reminiscent of earlier days of Hawaiian tourism, a place that would seem familiar to someone who had visited Hawaii in the 1960s or 1970s. All rooms have one king-size or two double beds, a small refrigerator, air-conditioning, ceiling fans, a TV, telephone, and lanai. What the hotel lacks in luster it makes up for in price. Daily rates are $124 for a standard room, $140 for a superior pool room, $150 for the deluxe room, and $160 for a room with kitchenette. Room and car packages are offered for about $30 more. Numerous discounts are offered, including AARP, AAA, military, and Internet booking.

$150-200

Best Western has taken a former condo complex of 10 two-story buildings and turned the units into the comfortable **Best Western Plantation Hale Suites** (484 Kuhio Hwy., 808/822-4941 or 800/775-4253, fax 808/822-5599, www.plantation-hale.com). Plantation Hale is across the street from Waipouli Beach Park just north of the Coconut Marketplace. While not an oceanfront property, the water is only a short stroll away. Accommodations are all one-bedroom, spacious, and eminently comfortable apartment suites with full kitchens, bath, and living area, each with color cable TV and daily maid service. An open-air hallway runs the length of each unit. There are three swimming pools on the property, two spas, a putting green, barbecue areas, and laundry facilities, and the front has an activities desk. While the road side has a border of trees and bushes, it's a bit close to the highway and

some back units may get traffic noise. Rates are $165–185 for a basic suite, $175–195 for garden view, and $185–205 for scenic view rooms. Numerous discounts are offered. The Plantation Hale is a decent value all around.

Between the water and the Coconut Marketplace sits the **ResortQuest Islander on the Beach** (440 Aleka Place, 808/822-7417 or 877/997-6667, fax 808/822-1947), an easy eight-structure complex, newly remodeled in 2005. All rooms come with air-conditioning, wet bars, refrigerators, coffeemakers, color TVs, room safes, and lanai. Comfortable and up-to-date but not overly large, each room is decorated with island flavor and features travertine floors and granite countertops in the bathroom. Set right on the beach, this 198-room property has a newly landscaped courtyard with pool with jet spa, pool bar, and barbecue/picnic area, in addition to an activity desk and guest laundry. Only a few steps away are the myriad shops and eateries of the Coconut Marketplace. Slightly higher during the holiday season, room rates run $156 for garden view to $218 for oceanfront, with suites at $325.

Above $250

The 216-room **Aloha Beach Resort Kaua'i** (3-5920 Kuhio Hwy., 808/823-6000 or 888/823-5111, www.abrkauai.com) has a lovely setting at the mouth of the Wailua River just above Lydgate Beach Park. Incorporated into the architecture is a series of cascading pools and a koi pond that boils with frenzied color at feeding time. The main lobby is a huge affair with swooping beams in longhouse style, and the wings of rooms run toward the ocean from there. The feeling you get here is spaciousness and welcome, and this is where many of the Hawaiian cultural and art activities are held throughout the day. The hotel facilities include two swimming pools and a whirlpool spa, a small fitness room, one tennis court for guests only, volleyball and shuffleboard courts, coin-operated laundry, and a picnic area. For food, there's The Palms Restaurant with its attached Kuhio Lounge, and Kahanu poolside

COCO PALMS

The Coco Palms was a classic Hawaiian hotel, one of the first tourist destinations built on the island, but it took a terrible beating during Hurricane 'Iniki. The Polynesian-inspired buildings are interspersed through a monumental coconut grove planted by a German immigrant in the early 1800s. His aspiration was to start a copra plantation, and although it failed, his plantings matured into one of the largest stands of coconut trees in the islands.

When Hollywood needed "paradise" it came here. The Coco Palms served as movie backdrop for Elvis in *Blue Hawaii* and for Rita Hayworth in the movie *Sadie Thompson*, bringing the hotel (and the island) notoriety. The chapel built for *Sadie Thompson* was left standing, and more than 2,000 marriages were performed there over the years. Some scenes from the movie *South Pacific* were filmed at the Coco Palms, and after Tattoo informed Mr. Roarke of the arrival of "da plane, Boss" in the popular TV series *Fantasy Island*, it was into the hotel coconut grove that he drove his jeep.

Nightly, the hostelry's famous torch-lighting ceremony took place under the palm canopy, which encircles a royal lagoon once used to fatten succulent fish for the exclusive use of the *ali'i*. Everyone, hotel guest or not, was welcome at the ceremony. Some dismissed the ceremony as "fake traditional," but it was the *best* "fake traditional" on the island – both dramatic and fun. This ceremony was started by the now-deceased Grace Guslander – a legend in her own right – a congenial hostess and old-time hotelier famous for her cocktail parties.

The Coco Palms was a peaceful garden brought to its knees by the hurricane. It was and still is a landmark. The greenery has rebounded, of course, but one wonders how much of the "feel" of the grounds will be saved when the property is finally redeveloped into hotel rooms and time-share condominiums (planned opening of 2007).

---

bar and grill. The hotel rooms are large, and many have ocean views; sliding glass doors let in the breeze, but the rooms don't have balconies. The overall color scheme includes muted greens and peach. While the bathrooms are not large, they are tastefully done; one wing has showers and the other has bathtubs. Each room contains a small refrigerator, TV, room safe, and iron and ironing board—all the amenities needed. Room rates run $219–259 and $279–299 for suites; no charge for children 19 and under using existing bedding. Thirteen spacious two-room cabanas with kitchenettes are separate from the main facility and have unobstructed views of the beach park; they run $359 a night. Room and car and romance packages, as well as other discounts, are available so ask. This is a fine, quiet place, where you receive a lot for your money.

Amidst a huge grove of swaying coconut palms, a natural buffer offering peace and tranquility, with wings encircling a central courtyard, sits the sand-colored **C Courtyard by Marriott Kauai at Waipouli Beach** (4-484 Kuhio Hwy., 808/822-3455 or 800/760-8555, fax 808/822-0035). The palm grove once belonged to the family of the famous swimmer and actor Buster Crabbe, of *Buck Rogers* fame. He and his twin brother, Bud, were born and raised right here, and Buster learned to swim along this very coast. Built in 1978 and well used, this 311-room hotel was completely refurbished inside and out in 2005. The transformation starts at the port cochere, which opens to the large, bright, and expanded lobby. The hotel boasts sizable guest rooms with a warm Hawaiian feel of tropical hardwoods and prints, large-screen TV, Internet access, and private lanai, and bathrooms with all new quality fixtures. Also completely revamped are the indoor/outdoor Voyager Grille restaurants and Cook's Landing lounge, with new touches to the swimming pool, poolside spa, tennis courts, fitness center, and business center. At

6:30 P.M., a torch-lighting ceremony marks the beginning of the evening and is followed Wednesday–Saturday 7–9 P.M. by live Hawaiian music. Room rates run $229–299 for standard, pool view, and oceanview rooms, $329–449 for oceanfront rooms, and $899 for suites.

Condos

The luxury **Kaha Lani** (4460 Nehe Rd., 808/882-9331, fax 808/822-2828), occupying a wooded strip between the Wailua golf course and Lydgate Beach Park, is a quiet place with a broad oceanfront lawn, large swimming pool, and tennis courts. These spacious units have living rooms that face the ocean across the lanai, fully equipped kitchens, and separate bedrooms. Each unit is equipped with ceiling fan, color cable TV, and room safe, and a laundry facility is on property. One-bedroom units run $255–315, two-bedroom units $270–400, and three-bedroom units $375–450, somewhat less during value season.

A moderately priced condominium on Wailua Bay is the **Kapaa Sands** (380 Papaloa Rd., 808/822-4901 or 800/222-4901, fax 808/822-1556, www.kapaasands.com), with pool, laundry facilities, and maid service. The oldest condo on the island—open since 1968—the 24-unit Kapaa Sands is kept clean and up to date and has been completely refurbished since Hurricane 'Iniki. It is on old Japanese grounds that once housed a Shinto shrine. The Japanese motif is still reflected in the roofline of the units and the *torii* design above each door number. The well-landscaped grounds are rather compact but manage to include a swimming pool and a narrow grass lawn that fronts a thin sand beach. Each unit has a full kitchen, ceiling fans in all rooms, telephone, TV, VCR, and a lanai. Two-bedroom units occupy two levels, with the bedrooms upstairs. Room rates are $110 and $128 for oceanview and oceanfront studios, and $147 and $168 for two-bedroom oceanview and two-bedroom oceanfront units. Monthly rates are available; the minimum stay is three days except during winter, when it is seven days. Book well in advance as these units fill up with returning guests.

The two classiest places along the north edge of Wailua Bay are Lae Nani and Lanikai. Managed by Outrigger Resorts, ◖ **Lae Nani** (410 Papaloa Rd., 808/822-4938 or 800/688-7444, fax 808/822-1022, is a peach of a place. The rich decor varies by unit, but all have full kitchens, lanai, ceiling fans, TVs, and one and a half baths; most have ocean views. All are immaculately clean. There is a laundry room, daily maid service, one tennis court for guests only, a swimming pool, and poolside barbecue grill. The small Kukui Heiau is on the property beachside, adjacent to a rock-enclosed swimming area that's perfect for kids and others unsure of the waves and tides. One-bedroom units for up to four people are $240–295, and the two-bedroom units are $240–355, maximum six; value season rates are somewhat less. A two-night minimum stay is enforced. Some units here are managed by Castle Resorts (800/367-5004). There is public shoreline access at the edge of this property.

Also three stories tall with many of the same amenities, the **Lanikai** (390 Papaloa Rd., 808/822-7700 or 800/367-5004, fax 808/822-7456) sits next door to the Lae Nani. Here there are one- and two-bedroom units with kitchens that rent for $285–385 a day, $10–20 cheaper during low season. Ask about discounts. Most of the units at Lae Nani are managed by Castle Resorts.

The **Kauai Coast Resort at the Beachboy** (520 Aleka Loop, 808/822-3441 or 877/977-4355, fax 808/822-0843, www.kauaicoast-resort.com) is an attractive oceanfront condominium complex with just more than 100 one- and two-bedroom units with full kitchen and laundry facilities, air-conditioning, daily maid service, and other amenities that make for a comfortable vacation. The comfortable island-inspired property has a heated pool, children's pool, poolside bar, tennis courts, activity desk, fitness room, and on-site day spa. The Hukilau Lanai (operated by Gaylord's) serves food just off the lobby in the restaurant that overlooks the garden. Although primarily a time-share property, rooms are rented to others when available. Studio/garden view rooms run $195,

one-bedrooms $255–295, and two-bedroom units $330–375 a night.

Vacation Rental Agencies

Kauai Vacation Rentals (3-3311 Kuhio Hwy., Lihu'e, 808/245-8841 or 800/367-5025, fax 808/246-1161, aloha@kvrre.com, www.Kauai VacationRentals.com) handles condos and vacation rental homes throughout the island, but in Wailua it is nearly all condo units.

In addition to its B&B rooms, Rosewood Bed and Breakfast (see below) rents about 18 oceanfront condos, beach and upland homes, and cottages along this stretch of the coast. These range $75–300 a night, with a three-night minimum.

Bed-and-Breakfasts

In the uplands behind the Sleeping Giant is **Rosewood Bed and Breakfast** (872 Kamalu Rd., 808/822-5216, fax 808/822-5478, www.rosewoodkauai.com). Creamy yellow with white trim and set behind a neat picket fence, Rosewood is a finely kept plantation-style house with a smaller Victorian house, thatched house, and bunkhouse on the property. Least expensive, at $45–55, are the three cozy Bunkhouse rooms, which share a bathroom, but each has a refrigerator, microwave, and sink. One has a twin bunk bed; the second, a queen bed in a loft; and the third, a king bed in a loft with a queen futon. The Thatched Cottage, one large room with kitchenette and an outdoor shower, runs $115, and the second-story main house Traditional room with a private bath goes for $85. With two floors, two bedrooms, a full kitchen, and porch, the Victorian Cottage runs $135. It looks like a miniature of the main house. Breakfast is included for guests of the main house room, and on the first and last days of your stay for those in the Victorian Cottage and Thatched Cottage. No credit cards. Three-night minimum stay.

Up the hill in the last residential neighborhood before the arboretum sits the **Hale Lani Bed and Breakfast** (283 'Aina Lani Pl., 808/823-6434 or 877/423-6434, www.hale-lani.com). This B&B offers four room options for guests who desire to get away from the "strip" along the coast. Each room has its own entrance and private bath, three have a kitchen or kitchenette (although breakfast is served each morning for all guests), and all are designed with tropical appointments. Rates run $105–150 per night, with a three-night minimum.

FOOD
American

Directly across the street in the Wailua Shopping Plaza is **Wailua Family Restaurant** (808/882-3325). Open from early morning, this place becomes a fairyland of lights in the evening. A full menu is served all day, but many come for the very reasonably priced lunch and dinner buffets and salad bar.

Open for breakfast and dinner, **Aldon's Restaurant** (808/822-4221) at the Kauai Sands Hotel serves American standard food at very reasonable prices.

As the main dining room at the Aloha Beach Resort Kaua'i, **The Palms Restaurant** is open for breakfast and dinner. Sit inside or out on the lanai under tiki torches, where you can look out over the garden to the moon reflected off the water and hear soft evening sounds filter out through the huge open doors. While it serves an à la carte menu in the evening, it's perhaps best known for its reasonably priced morning buffets. Evening entrées include an 'ahi poke appetizer, seafood linguine with wine sauce, citrus shoyu chicken, and prime beef rib. Adjacent to the dining room is the **Kuhio Lounge.** Quiet most evenings, it does have music and dancing on Saturdays. For salads, sides, sandwiches, burgers, and cocktails during the day, try the afternoon-only **Kahanu Bar and Grill** at the oceanview pool.

Korean

Stark white with a few ethnic decorations, the **Korean Bar-B-Q Restaurant** (808/823-6744, daily 10:30 A.M.–9 P.M., Tues. from 4:30 P.M.) is located in the Kinipopo Shopping Village. While some items are authentic Korean, there is a mix of Hawaiian and American in the menu.

Single plates like kalbi (short ribs) and chap-chae (stir-fry clear noodles) mostly run $7–8, and the combo plates cost just a bit more. Plate dishes come with two-scoop rice and four vegetables, otherwise order à la carte for a few dollars less. Takeout is available.

Japanese

The Japanese legend of Kintaro, a pint-size boy born to an old couple from inside a peach pit, is slightly less miraculous than the excellent and authentic Japanese restaurant named for him, owned and operated by a Korean gentleman, Don Kim. **Restaurant Kintaro** (808/822-3341, 5:30–9:30 P.M. daily except Sun.) is open for dinner only next to the Kinipopo Shopping Village. While the exterior has been tastefully remodeled, inside it still transforms into the simple and subtle beauty of Japan. The true spirit of Japanese cooking is presented, with the food as pleasing to the eye as to the palate. For its variety, innovation, and quality, the sushi bar alone is worth stopping in for. The dinners are expertly and authentically prepared, equaling those served in fine restaurants in Japan. If you have never sampled Japanese food before, Restaurant Kintaro is Kaua'i's best place to start. Those who *are* accustomed to the cuisine can choose from favorites like tempura, sukiyaki, a variety of soba, and the old standby teriyaki. Most dinners run $14–20. Reservations are often necessary.

Thai

Located across the highway from Kintaro, **Mema Thai Chinese Cuisine** (4-369 Kuhio Hwy., 808/823-0899, 11 A.M.–2 P.M. Mon.–Fri. and 5–9:30 P.M. nightly) is a casual, family-operated restaurant with a touch of class. The ornate chairs and tables set the theme, while walls and cabinets are well appointed with decorations. Waiters, dressed in silky Thai clothing, carry their trays past a profusion of potted plants and flowers. The menu starts with shrimp rolls and continues through nearly 50 appetizers, curries, soups, noodle and rice dishes, and vegetable, chicken, and seafood items. Appetizers run $7–11, and most main entrées and soups range $9–18. Entrées include

HAWAIIAN FOOD

Hawaiian cuisine, the oldest in the islands, consists of wholesome, well-prepared, and delicious foods. All you have to do on arrival is notice the size of some of the local boys (and women) to know immediately that food to them is indeed a happy and serious business. An oft-heard island joke is that "local men don't eat until they're full; they eat until they're tired." Many Hawaiian dishes have become standard fare at a variety of restaurants, eaten at one time or another by anyone who spends time in the islands, but the best still is served at local-style restaurants. Hawaiian food in general is called *kaukau*, cooked food is *kapahaki*, and something broiled is called *ko'ala*. Any of these prefixes on a menu will let you know that Hawaiian food is served. Usually inexpensive, it will definitely fill you and keep you going.

broccoli with oyster sauce, seafood red curry cooked in coconut milk with basil and bamboo shoots, pad Thai, and black bean sauce stir-fry. Most entrées can be prepared vegetarian, and spiciness can be adjusted. Mema Thai offers complete wine, beer, cocktail, and dessert menus. If you are looking for a restaurant with excellent exotic food where you can enjoy a pleasant evening for a reasonable price, Mema Thai should be at the top of your list. It's a winner.

Hawaiian Regional

Behind the Wailua Shopping Plaza in a converted plantation house, almost hidden under tall trees and behind a prolific bougainvillea, is **C Caffé Coco** (4-369 Kuhio Hwy., 808/822-7990, 11 A.M.–5 P.M. Tues.–Fri., 5–9 P.M. daily except Mon.). Using local produce, fresh fish, and pork, the tiny kitchen puts nutritious food on your plate, a mix of European, Asian, Mexican, and American cuisine. Try Arista pork, pasta bella, cajun *'ahi*, or *ahi* charmoula with curried vegetable samosa, rice, salad, raiita, and chutney. Full-platter dinners run $16–21. Lighter fare includes soup, focaccia, and green salad; an **'ahi** nori wrap; barbecue pork sandwich; and seafood gumbo. Aside from the daily menu, numerous specials are posted. After dinner, pick one of the many tempting, homemade desserts from the deli case or order coffee from the espresso bar. This is island-casual cuisine at its best—tasty, wholesome, and healthy. Order at the counter and take a seat out back in the garden under the vine-covered canopy, amongst orchids, bananas, and lime trees. To add to the ambience, live music is performed every evening. As seating is outside, if the mosquitoes get too bothersome, feel free to use the organic "jungle juice" kept at the counter.

The **Hukilau Lanai** (808/822-0600, Tues.–Sun. 5–9 P.M.) commands space overlooking the central courtyard at the Kauai Coast Resort at the Beachboy. Open-air seating is inside under gently cooling ceiling fans or out on the covered lanai, and the low light makes for a romantic setting. Before you head in for dinner, have a drink at the bar or spend a few minutes listening to the music in the lobby lounge right at the entrance to the restaurant. While fish has the main spotlight on this menu, many meat dishes are also listed. One of the favorites is the Hukilau mixed grill, a mixture of grilled seafood and shrimp skewered on sugarcane. Start your meal with a sweet potato ravioli or shrimp bisque and move on to skewered mango chicken or rib eye steak, but save room for one of the tempt-ing desserts—goat cheese tart with mango or Big Island chocolate mousse cake, perhaps. Most entrées are in the $20–35 range, but a six-course food and wine pairing menu runs $40 and is available 5–6 P.M.only.

Coconut Marketplace Restaurants

Surrounded by hotels and condos, the **Coconut Marketplace** has more than a dozen eateries, the majority being simple food stands. Among the many, check out **Eggbert's** (808/822-3787, 7 A.M.–3 P.M. and 5–9 P.M.), a family-style restaurant that's popular for breakfast and serves mostly light fare. **Aloha Kauai Pizza** (808/822-4511, 11 A.M.–9 P.M.) serves some of the best pizza on the island and is a hit with locals. A short menu of other Italian food that includes lasagna and meatball sand-wiches is also available; many items are made from family recipes. For wraps, organic salads, grill plates, and Asian-inspired dishes, head to **Barefoot Cafe. Harley's Ribs and Chicken** says it all with its name. To satisfy your sweet tooth, step up to **Zack's** ice cream and frozen yogurt counter stall.

Near the front corner of Coconut Market Place is the open, breezy, and casual **Kauai Hula Girl Bar and Grill** (808/822-4422), open daily for lunch and dinner. Lunch includes items like salads, sandwiches, and an *imu* pork wrap. Entrées, more expensive in the $19–27 range, are various pasta dishes, fish, baked scampi, rack of lamb, and huli huli chicken. Music accompanies dinner every night.

Kapa'a

Kapa'a means "to hold," as in "to hold a canoe on course." In the old days, when the canoes set sail to O'ahu, they'd always stop first at Kapa'a to get their bearings, then make a beeline directly across the channel to O'ahu. Yachts still do the same today. It was probably a series of fishing villages in days past, but from 1913 to 1960 there was a huge pineapple cannery in Kapa'a, and much of the east shore bristled with these sweet golden fruits. More recently, sugarcane was raised, but that too is gone.

Old Town Kapa'a is where Rt. 56 and Rt. 581 meet. The heart of Kapa'a itself is a workers' settlement, a blue-collar community with modest homes, utilitarian shops, several churches, some down-home eateries, and modest accommodations. Only in the past few years has there been a move to yuppify shops and restaurants. Yet, the Kapa'a area is one of some contrasts. At the south end along the main drag is **Waipouli** (Dark Water), actually a separate community just north of Coconut Marketplace, though you'd never know it. Clustered here are newish condos, several full-service shopping malls, a multitude of restaurants, and some nightlife—sort of a live-in resort atmosphere. Inland from the center of Kapa'a are newer, rural bedroom communities that string along the roads that track in toward the mountains. The population is nearly 8,000, and at least half again that number live in the upland communities, so about the same number of people live here as in the greater Lihu'e area, but the vibe in Kapa'a is definitely more local. What distinguishes Kapa'a is its unpretentiousness. This is "everyday paradise," where the visitor is made to feel welcome and stands in line with everyone else at the supermarket. Generally, the weather is cooperative, beaches are fair, and the pace is unhurried. Kapa'a isn't the choicest vacation spot on the island, but you can have a great time here and save money.

A **guided walking tour** of Kapa'a, complete with snippets of history, culture, and legends, is offered by the Kaua'i Historical Society. These tours run about 90 minutes and take in sites in town and along the beach. Tours are run Tuesday, Thursday, and Saturday at 10 A.M. by appointment only for $15 adults and $5 children under age 12. Reservations are necessary; call 808/245-3373, and two adults minimum are required for tours.

To ease traffic through the heart of this community, the **Kapa'a Bypass Road** skirts around from Wailua to the north edge of Kapa'a. It runs through the agricultural fields behind town and is open 5:30 A.M.–9 P.M. daily. From where this bypass meets Olohena Road near the New Kapa'a Park, jog toward the ocean and turn onto Lehua Street to miss the downtown intersection.

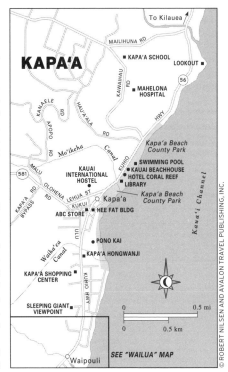

While in Kapa'a, spend your time checking out the shops, scanning the color-mottled mountains of the interior, and combing the beaches, especially those to the north. A few minutes up the coast, you're in wide-open spaces. Small oceanside communities pop up, their residents split between beach-house vacationers and settled *kama'aina*. The only town of size is Anahola.

SIGHTS
❰ Sleeping Giant

There are few sights per se, although near the middle of this strip, at Kipuni Place, is the **Sleeping Giant Viewpoint** pulloff. From this angle you get a good look at the mountain, and, using your imagination, you can distinctly see a recumbent figure with head, neck, and chest. Trails up both the front and back of this hill bring you to a picnic spot on the chest, from where a narrow trail leads over the throat to the chin and forehead.

Beach Park

Central Kapa'a's beach begins near Waika'ea Canal, and **Kapa'a Beach County Park** runs north from there for almost a mile until it ends near a community swimming pool and the Kapa'a Library. A number of small roads lead to the beach from the highway. Kapa'a Beach County Park has just over 15 acres, with a pavilion, picnic tables, showers, toilets, and grills at its southern end. At Waika'ea Canal near the Pono Kai Resort, a footbridge connects both sides of the canal, where locals often come to fish. A boat ramp backs into the canal here, and there is a deep enough channel through the reef for boats to get in and out. Just south of there is a stretch known as "baby beach," a protected spot inside a close-in reef that parallels the shore that is just right for toddlers and kids. At the park's north end, a second footbridge crosses Mohikeha Canal to the Hotel Coral Reef property. This beach is pretty enough to look at, but it is not a typical resort beach. The feeling here is that this area belongs to the locals, although no undue hassles have been reported.

A new paved **bike and pedestrian pathway** has been created along the old, oceanside cane

ROBERT NILSEN

EAST SHORE

Sleeping Giant in repose over Kapa'a

haul road that leads north from the park in Kapa'a to just past Donkey Beach, a distance of about four miles.

ENTERTAINMENT

The night scene in Kapa'a is less than extensive. For a cool island drink, canned music, and a local crowd try **Pau Hana Bar and Grill** (808/821-2900) at the Kauai Village shopping center. The **Lizard Lounge Bar and Grill** (808/821-2205, daily until 1:30 A.M.) at the Waipouli Center is another local bar that serves grill food until 1 A.M. and is more like a sports bar with its big-screen TV, pool tables, and dart boards.

Under the whale tower toward the back of the Kauai Village center is **Kaua'i Children's Discovery Museum** (808/823-8222, Tues.–Sat. 9 A.M.–5 P.M., Mon. during school breaks, $4 for children, $5 for adults, www.kcdm.org), a hands-on adventure gallery where young kids can learn about science, nature, technology, and culture, particularly as it pertains to Hawaii and Polynesia. While exhibits and activities vary, kids might explore an underwater coral reef, learn to navigate an outrigger canoe by the stars, ride a flight simulator into space, try virtual reality games, or create arts and crafts. This community-based, volunteer-staffed organization is set up to involve children in their surroundings. On your way out, stop by the gift shop and look over the selection of science toys, educational games, and gifts. This is a great place for young children to explore and learn.

SHOPPING

Kapa'a teems with shopping opportunities. Lining Kuhio Highway are several large and small shopping plazas along with the central downtown shops. All your needs are met by a variety of shops tucked away here and there. Like dealing with the sun in Hawaii, enjoy yourself but don't overdo it.

Kauai Village

Built around a plantation-era main street theme, this modern, large, and very diverse

ALOHAWEAR

A grand conspiracy in Kaua'i adhered to by everyone – tourist, traveler, and resident – is to "hang loose" and dress casually. Best of all, alohawear is just about all you'll need for comfort and virtually every occasion. The classic mu'umu'u for women is large and billowy, and aloha shirts for men are made to be worn outside the pants. The best of both are made of cool cotton or silk and often designed in bright-colored floral patterns or island scenes. Rayon is a natural fiber that isn't too bad, but polyester is hot, sticky, and not authentic. Not all mu'umu'u are of the "tent persuasion." *Holomu* are mu'umu'u fitted at the waist with a flowing skirt to the ankles. They are not only elegant but perfect for "stepping out."

shopping center, one of the newest and best that Kaua'i has to offer, is at 4-831 Kuhio Highway, a short way up the coast from the Coconut Marketplace on the mountain side of the road. Its three anchor stores are **Safeway** supermarket (8 A.M.–8 P.M. Mon.–Fri. and 9 A.M.–6 P.M. Sat. and Sun.), **Longs Drugs** (8 A.M.–9 P.M. Mon.–Sat. and until 6 P.M. Sun.), a complete variety store with photo equipment and a pharmacy, and an **ABC** store (7 A.M.–10:30 P.M.) for everything from suntan lotion to beach mats. Food options here include **Papaya's,** the island's best natural health-food store and café; **La Playita Azul,** for healthy Mexican with a touch of the islands; and **Ba Le** Vietnamese restaurant. Other stores include **Pai Moana Pearls,** for the increasingly popular Tahitian black pearls; **Wyland Galleries,** resplendent with some of the finest artworks in Hawaii and offering art lovers a chance to just look or select a favorite to take home as a tangible memory of their island vacation; and **Life's Treasures,** for paintings, crystals, jewelry, candles, and other eclectic gifts. **Kaua'i Children's Discovery Museum** is located at the back of the center under the Whale Tower.

Small Shopping Malls

A handful of small and mid-size shopping centers line the highway as you go north. These are listed below from south to north with a few of their shops. In the **Waipouli Town Center** you'll find Foodland, a Blockbuster Video for home/condo entertainment, and the Lounge Lizard bar. Beyond Kauai Village, **Waipouli Plaza** has Waipouli Variety, with clothing, gifts, and a great fishing/hunting section; The King and I Thai restaurant; and a seashell merchant selling retail and wholesale. Nearby and across the highway from a Shell gas station, the **Waipouli Complex** is the home of the Aloha Diner for local Hawaiian food and Popo's Cookies. Marked by another Shell gas station and a Burger King is the bite-size and functional **Kapa'a Shopping Center.** Here, you'll find a well-stocked Big Save food store, an Ace Hardware store, Sukhothai Restaurant, a post office, and self-service laundry.

Boutiques and Galleries

In a small shop on the corner of the highway and Kamoa Road across from Kauai Village Shopping Center is **Marta's Boat** (808/822-3926, open 10:30 A.M.–6 P.M. Mon.–Sat.) This is primarily a children's boutique, but the overflowing shelves also hold handmade quilts by local ladies, T-shirts, shorts, casual wear, elegant evening wear, and beautiful lingerie. A rack of games and educational items offers help in keeping the little ones happy on a return plane voyage or during an evening in the condo.

Up the road next to the Lemongrass Grill is **Jungle Girl** (4-855 Kuhio Hwy., 808/823-9351, 9 A.M.–9 P.M.), a boutique of "funk and flash" that carries the odd and exotic island-inspired clothing and a dizzying variety of imports from Indonesia. This is an all-around fun shop for ladies looking for something out of the ordinary. Guys may find it fun, too.

Right in the center of Kapa'a, in the old Kawamura Store building (built 1949 and rebuilt 1993), is **Hula Girl** (4-1340 Kuhio Hwy., 808/822-1950), for fine fashions, vintage alohawear, Hawaiian craft items, tropi-

cal Christmas ornaments, and much more. If you're looking for quality with island flavor, try here.

Only a few steps away is **Jim Saylor Jewelry** (808/822-3591), for hand-crafted jewelry and gemstones. Close by is **Grande's Gems and Gallery** (808/822-2345), a local jewelry chain.

As shiny and glittering as the sunbeams pouring through the windows, **Kela's Glass Gallery** (4-1354 Kuhio Hwy., 808/822-4527, 10 A.M.–7 P.M. weekdays, until 6 P.M. Sat., noon–5 P.M. Sun.), in the Hee Fat Marketplace building, is a showcase for more than 140 contemporary artists working in glass. The gallery features everything from classic vases to free-form sculptures ranging in price from affordable to not affordable. Kela's also sells and ships wooden flowers and other hand-carved and hand-painted items from Indonesia.

At the intersection across from the ABC Store, **Aloha Images** gallery (4504 Kukui St., 808/821-1382) displays an incredibly wide variety and large number of paintings at affordable prices. There's bound to be something you'd love to take home.

Featuring art by husband and wife team John and Hayley Davison, the **Davison Arts** gallery (4-1322 Kuhio Hwy., 808/821-8022, 9 A.M.–noon Mon., 9 A.M.–5 P.M. Tues.–Fri., 10 A.M.–2 P.M. Sat., www.davisonarts.com) displays paintings, sculpture, wooden furniture, glass, woven rugs, and other fine art pieces. On occasion, special exhibitions of island artists are mounted.

Earth Beads (1392A Kukui St., 808/822-0766, 9:30 A.M.–5 P.M. daily except Sunday) specializes in beads and imported items from India, Africa, and South America. Shimmering in the tiny shop are earrings, belts, incidental bags, and sterling silver jewelry from Thailand, as well as locally made designs. Primitive basketry, incense, perfumed oils, T-shirts, "jungle" umbrellas, and very unusual greeting cards complete the stock of this great little shop.

Walk into the **Island Hemp and Cotton Company** (4-1373 Kuhio Hwy., 808/821-0225, daily 10 A.M.–6 P.M.) and suddenly you're in

EAST SHORE

Asia. Stride across the reed mat floor while the soulful eyes of a Buddha sitting serenely atop a glass counter follow you in. Across from the ABC store in downtown Kapa'a, the shop is owned and operated by Nancee McTernan, a long-distance traveler and "old Asia hand" who has personally chosen every item in the store. Some special items include Buddha sculptures from Borneo, baskets from Bali, carved bone necklaces from New Zealand, local puka shell jewelry, and antique wood carvings from all parts of Indonesia. Men's and women's clothing, all made from organic cotton, hemp, linen, and other natural fibers, includes everything from casual shirts to elegant dresses, hats to backpacks. If you are after a truly distinctive gift, one-of-a-kind clothing, or an original artifact, visit this shop.

For a perfectly natural gift, slip down **Orchid Alley** (808/822-0486) for a beautiful potted plant. Send one home as a reminder of your tropical vacation—they ship. Back down the main drag next to Pono Market is **Flowers and Joys** (808/822-1569) for some of the best (although not the cheapest) lei on the island.

Kauai Products Fair (9 A.M.–5 P.M. Wed.–Mon.) is a small complex of arts and crafts shops up at the north end of town that put their wares out under tents. Stop by to peruse the locally made goods and perhaps you'll find something to take home.

The **M. Miura Store** (4-1419 Kuhio Hwy., 808/822-4401, 9 A.M.–5 P.M. Mon.–Sat.), a clothing and accessory store on the mountain side of the highway, is where local people shop for alohawear, T-shirts, sunglasses, sandals, caps, men's and women's shorts, and a good selection of bikinis.

Photo Needs

Try **Longs Drug** (808/821-0081) at Kauai Village for all your photo finishing needs.

RECREATION
Water Sports

Snorkel Bob's (808/823-9433, 8 A.M.–5 P.M., www.snorkelbob.com), just beyond the Coconut Marketplace in Waipouli, offers some of the best deals for snorkel rental in Hawaii (and free snorkeling maps and advice). Gear, which includes mask, snorkel tube, and fins, is rented for a 24-hour day or by the week. The basic set is $2.50 a day or $9 per week. Upgrades in quality run $22 and $34 a week, and for the ultimate optical correction mask the rate is $44 a week. For a "dry" tube add $2 a day. Bob's also rents boogie boards. If you'll be island-hopping, Snorkel Bob's allows you to take the gear with you and drop it off at a Snorkel Bob's location on the next island. Bob also books various island activities, so you may get free rental on some equipment if you book here.

Dive Kauai (1038 Kuhio Hwy., 808/822-0452 or 800/828-3483, www.divekauai.com) is a full-service scuba and snorkel shop. Dive Kauai offers sales and rental of all equipment and carries some water-sport clothing and accessories. Scuba gear packages run $40–50; introductory dives are $98 for a one-tank boat or shore dive or $125 for two tanks. For certified divers, most other dives run $80–100. A variety of certification courses are offered, but a basic four- to five-day course runs about $425. All boat trips leave from the Port Allen Harbor at Hanapepe and dives go only to South Shore sites.

Another well-respected dive company, **Seasport Divers** (4-976 Kuhio Hwy., 808/823-9222, www.kauaiscubadiving.com) has a gear and apparel shop in Kapa'a and also arranges a variety of dives that leave from Kukui'ula Harbor in Po'ipu, near its other shop.

Other companies that offer competitive pricing and similar tours are **Sacred Seas Scuba** (808/635-7327 or 877/441-3483, www.sacredseascuba.com), **Wet n' Wonderful** (808/822-0211, www.wet-n-wonderful.com), and **Scuba Diving Adventures** (808/822-7333, www.sunrisescuba.com)

Bicycling

One of the best bike shops on the island for sales, repair, and rental is **Kauai Cycle and Tour** (1379 Kuhio Hwy., 808/821-2115, 9 A.M.–6 P.M. Mon.–Fri., 9 A.M.–4 P.M. Sat.)

Beach cruisers rent for $15 for 24 hours, front-suspension mountain bikes or road bikes run $20 a day or $95 per seven-day week, and full-suspension mountain bikes are $35 a day and $150 a week. Each rental includes a helmet, lock, and water bottle. A car rack is available for $5. Stop in for great advice on where to ride for your type of bike and level of experience. Kauai Cycle runs a limited number of guided mountain bike tours starting at $65, Saturdays at 4 P.M. and Sundays at 9 A.M.

Horseback Riding

Esprit de Corps Riding Academy (808/822-4688, www.kauaihorses.com) offers four basic rides, plus specialty rides on request, and riding lessons. These rides, which go into the mountains from upper Kapa'a, tend to be long, so they are better suited to experienced riders. The three-hour Fast Half ride with trotting and cantering runs $148; the Wow!!! ride runs $215 for five hours, snack included; and the All Day Adventure ride allows time for a deli lunch and dip in a mountain pool for $345. If you desire a shorter ride and love to take pictures on the trail, try the two- to three-hour A Taste of Kauai ride for $112. Riders must be age 10 or older for the trail rides, and no more than five riders are allowed per group.

Van Tour

For movie buffs, **Hawaii Movie Tours** (4-885 Kuhio Hwy., 808/822-1192 or 800/628-8432, www.hawaiimovietour.com) has escorted luxury van tours that stop at many of the sites on the island used by Hollywood to make its feature films. On the way, you'll get regaled with stories of these movies and their actors, see scenes from the movies on the comfy van's TV monitor, sing along with songs from the movies, and be provided with lunch. The five-hour coastal tour costs $101 adult, $82 for kids 11 and under; a six- to seven-hour inland 4WD tour (except weekends) takes you to other movie locations back in lush valleys and on private land that are hard to get to otherwise for $113 for adults or $103 for children. All tours start in Kapa'a at the tour of-

fice behind Lemongrass Grill; hotel pickup is available.

ACCOMMODATIONS
Under $50

Kauai International Hostel (4532 Lehua St., 808/823-6142, www.kauaihostel.net) welcomes international guests with a friendly multilingual staff. Rates are $20 for a dorm bunk (no reservations, private female dorm available) and $50 for one of the five private rooms with double bed (reservations accepted); $10 key deposit. Reduced rates for those with hostel cards. Although the hostel is open 24 hours, quiet time is at 11 P.M.; checkout is by 10 A.M. Occasionally, staff members or guests organize an impromptu barbecue (everyone contributes to cover the cost), and the hostel runs van tours (tip the driver), mostly hikes to waterfalls, canyons, and pristine beaches,

---

MOVIES MADE ON KAUA'I

For decades, filmmakers have been drawn to Kaua'i. About five dozen feature films or parts of films have been made on the island. While Kaua'i is varied in its topography and climate, most filmmakers use the lush vegetation, waterfalls, beaches, sheer cliffs, and tropical scenery as backdrops. Everyone seems to know that Kaua'i was used in *South Pacific* with Mitzi Gaynor in 1958 and in *Blue Hawaii* with Elvis in 1961, but others include scenes from *White Heat* (1934), *Raiders of the Lost Ark* and *The Thorn Birds* (1983), *King Kong* (1976), *Outbreak* (1995), *Jurassic Park* (1993), *Islands in the Stream* (1977), *Hook* (1991), and *Dragonfly* (2002).

To fill in the details and the trivia, pick up a copy of *The Kaua'i Movie Book* by Chris Cook, published in 1996 by Mutual Publishing of Honolulu. Alternately, have a look at the Kaua'i Film Commission's website (www.filmkauai.com) for a complete list of movies made on the Garden Island and additional information and trivia about movie-making on Kaua'i.

---

when there is enough interest and the van is running. Airport pick-up and delivery run $10 each way. Facilities include a large communal kitchen, an indoor lounge with comfortable couches and cable TV, a covered outdoor lanai with a pocket billiard table, and coin washers and dryers. Store your valuables in the office safe. Dorm rooms, each with a sink and private bath, contain either four or six bunks. The private rooms are small but sufficient, and they share a bath. With room for 42, the hostel is reasonably clean and well managed. While it has an official seven-night maximum stay, there have been some long-term residents. This is a good place to meet young people from all over the world.

Just past the park in Kapaʻa, across the street from Kojima's grocery is **Kauai BeachHouse** (4-1552 Kuhio Hwy., 808/822-3424, www.kauai-blue-lagoon.com). A real beach house converted into a hostel-like accommodation, it offers women's and coed dorms and a couple of private rooms. Most rooms look out across a grassy lawn to the still water "lagoon" inside the reef. The table on the second-floor lanai is a gathering place, and a mini-kitchen to the side is for guest use. Also for guests are cable TV, a washing machine (line dry), free weights, and a few exercise machines. The roof can also be used for relaxation. Rooms contain double bed bunks, each with a privacy curtain; rates are $25 single, $35 double, or $55 for a private room. The baths are shared. No smoking. The place sits amongst a tangle of trees behind a garage that barely escaped the last hurricane; look for a blue wall and turn in there. The public bus stops out front. A funky place with easygoing island character, it's not for everyone but might be right for backpackers, bicycle riders, budget travelers, or anyone who cares more about what they eat than where they sleep.

$50-100

Women looking for an environment that is supportive of women travelers and seekers of self-enlightenment should try **Mahina's Women's Guest House** (808/823-9364, www.mahinas.com), a four-bedroom beach house near the center of Kapaʻa that's neat and tidy and well run. Each of the four rooms is different in size; three have queen beds and one has a double. Rates run from $65 single/$75 double to $95 single/$105 double. Weekly rates are available. Everyone shares the rest of the house, where you can make breakfast in the morning and share conversation in the evening with other guests. On occasion, workshops and events are held here to celebrate women. There is no smoking inside.

$100-150

Hotel Coral Reef (1516 Kuhio Hwy., 808/822-4481 or 800/843-4659, fax 808/822-7705, www.hotelcoralreef.com) is relatively inexpensive and definitely has character. Toward the north end of Kapaʻa between the main road and the beach, this 25-unit family-style hotel, one of the first built in the area, has a deluxe view of the ocean and a small grove of coconut trees on the lawn. Following a change of ownership, many improvements were made to the rooms and grounds, taking it from just serviceable to attractive island style. Not perfect yet, but much improved over its former days, Hotel Coral Reef is an economical alternative for a spot right on the water. The rates for the recently refurbished rooms are: garden view $99, oceanfront $149, and one-room suite $159, with a $25 charge for additional guests. The hotel offers room and car packages and *kamaʻaina* and senior citizen discounts. Rooms are all non-smoking and feature single and double beds, refrigerators, cable TV, and air-conditioning. Rooms downstairs have tile; upstairs, carpet. There is daily maid service, guest-use laundry, activity bookings, coffee and pastries in the lobby each morning, and a new swimming pool. The Hotel Coral Reef is very affordable for a family vacation.

Condos

Two moderate condos in Waipouli are **Mokihana of Kauai** (796 Kuhio Hwy.), and **Kauai Kailani** (856 Kuhio Hwy.). For information and reservations for both, call 808/822-

3971 or 360/676-1434 if more than 30 days in advance. These old-time establishments are primarily time-share properties but do vacation rentals when space permits. On the south side of the canal, the Mokihana has all studios with two double beds and kitchenettes for $65 a day. Kauai Kailani, on the north side of the canal, has two-bedroom units with full kitchens for $65–75. Not luxury by any means, these properties are good value for the money, and you're right on the water near restaurants and shopping.

The largest property on the Coconut Coast, the **Pono Kai** (4-1250 Kuhio Hwy., www.ponokai-resort.com) is a 241-unit property on 12 acres, just to the north of the Waika'ea Canal. While principally a time-share, it has a good number of vacation rental units. Built in 1975 but kept up to date, the property's units are individually owned and decorated; one-bedrooms are $190–240, two-bedrooms $250–280. All have full kitchens, cable TV, and lanai; many have a/c, and each building has laundry facilities. On the property you'll find a swimming pool, jet spa, sauna, shuffleboard lanes, lighted tennis courts for guests only, a small Japanese garden, and numerous barbecue areas. Various craft and cultural activities are offered throughout the week, and the activities desk can arrange excursions for you. For reservations, call Bluegreen Vacation Rentals (800/456-0009). Marc Resorts (808/823-8427 or 800/535-0085) manages many units in this complex and maintains front desk staffing 8 A.M.–5 P.M. daily.

Bed-and-Breakfasts

Inland high above Kapa'a on a working tropical flower farm in an area called Kawaihau is **Kakalina's Bed and Breakfast** (6781 Kawaihau Rd., 808/822-2328 or 800/662-4330, fax 808/823-6833, www.kakalina.com). Decorated with tropical motifs, Kakalina's has a two-bedroom, two-bath unit with full kitchen, dining, and living area on the ground floor of the main building that runs $155–175 (or $90 for half the unit), and a separate house with upstairs and downstairs units. The downstairs studio has a full kitchen, while the upstairs one-bedroom unit with kitchenette has the best views. These run $85–90 a day including a simple fruit, juice, pastry, and coffee breakfast. In addition, a one-bedroom house down the road has a complete kitchen and rents for $75 a day, no breakfast included. Two nights minimum.

Not far away is **Alohilani Bed and Breakfast** (1470 Wana'ao Rd., 808/823-0128 or 800/533-9316, www.hawaiilink.net/~alohila). Alohilani has three suites that run $99–119 a night, with queen beds, private baths, ceiling fans, refrigerator and microwave, and a guest cottage for $119 that has an efficiency kitchen. The hot tub pool is shared, and a continental breakfast is served.

Vacation Rental Agencies

Garden Island Properties (4-928 Kuhio Hwy., 808/822-4871 or 800/801-0378, fax 808/822-7984, sue@kauaiproperties.com, www.kauaiproperties.com), focuses its efforts on the east side of the island. It manages more than two dozen vacation rentals and numerous condo units mostly on the Coconut Coast but also has several along the North Shore as far as Ha'ena and a few in Lihu'e, everything from a $130 per night casual oceanside "hut" to a sumptuous four-bedroom house that sleeps 12 for over $2,000 a week. There is a one-week minimum on most of these units.

FOOD

From the Waipouli Town Center to the north edge of Kapa'a, there are dozens of places to eat. The vast majority are either inexpensive diners or mid-priced restaurants, but there are the ubiquitous fast-food chains, several bakeries, fruit stands, markets, and grocery stores.

Local Style

In the Waipouli Complex, a tiny mall at 971 Kuhio Hwy., is the **Aloha Diner** (808/822-3851, 11:30 A.M.–3 P.M. and 5:30–9 P.M. daily except Sunday). Serving Hawaiian food, it offers à la carte selections like *kalua* pig, chicken lu'au, *lomi* salmon, rice and poi, *haupia*, and *kulolo.* Dinner specials run $6–8, with full dinners around $10. Takeout is available. There is no atmosphere, the service is slow but friendly, and most people eating here are residents who know where to come for filling food.

Soda Fountain Grill

Marilyn Monroe, skirt tossed by the Kaua'i breeze, and the big bow tie and bigger smile of owner and chief soda jerk Kriss Erickson welcome you to **Beezers** (1389 Kuhio Hwy., 808/822-4411, 11 A.M.–10 P.M.) a vintage 1950s soda fountain, at the main intersection in downtown Kapa'a. Kriss, a bartender for two decades, researched the soda-fountain idea for years before opening Beezers—and actually got his best idea after visiting Disneyland. He scoured Hawaii and then finally the Mainland before finding a real soda fountain. The floor of red, black, and white tiles leads to low stools facing a counter made from glass brick and featuring a light show inside that matches the tunes coming from a real jukebox in the corner. Let your eyes play over the splendid 16-foot mahogany back bar, cabinet, and mirror as you sip your soda, slurp your shake, or savor your sandwich. Besides standard cones, Beezers serves such scrumptious dishes as an old-fashioned banana split and a Mustang Sally—a rich chocolate brownie with two scoops of creamy vanilla, hot fudge, whipped cream, and nuts. Handmade malts, shakes, and flavored Cokes can be created, or choose a soda, brownie wedge, homemade pie, sandwich, or sloppy Joe. Beezers is the kind of place where, if you're not smiling going in, you're definitely smiling coming out.

American

When you don't want to fool around deciding where to get a good meal for breakfast or lunch, head for the north end of Kapa'a and the local favorite, **Kountry Kitchen** (1485 Kuhio Hwy., 808/822-3511, 6 A.M.–1:30 P.M.), where the country decor sets the theme. The wooden bench booths are usually packed with regulars and there's often a line for breakfast, where full American standard meals like hefty omelettes, pancakes, French toast, and corned beef hash and eggs are on the menu, mostly for under $9. Lunches of salads, sandwiches, and specialty plates cost about the same. The food is tasty, the service prompt and friendly, and the portions large. True to its advertising, you'll find "no fancy napkins, just good home cooking."

The **Ono Family Restaurant** (4-1292 Kuhio Hwy., 808/822-1710, daily 7 A.M.–2 P.M.), next to the Pono Kai Resort, is cozy and functional, with nice touches like carpeted floors, ceiling fans, and front lanai seating. An established business, the restaurant gives friendly service, pays attention to detail, and always serves large portions. Creative breakfasts include eggs Canterbury, with turkey, tomatoes, jack cheese, mushrooms, and hollandaise sauce over poached eggs on an English muffin; a tropical stack of pancakes with bananas, macadamia nuts, and coconut; and a variety of omelettes. For lunch, you can't go wrong with a sandwich or burger, meat loaf and mashed potatoes, or teriyaki chicken from the broiler. The daily fish special is always terrific, and everything is reasonably priced, with virtually everything under $10. The Ono Family Restaurant is a local favorite.

Look for yellow and white umbrellas shading a few picnic tables across from the field at the town park that mark **Bubba's** (4-1384 Kuhio Hwy., 808/823-0069, daily 10:30 A.M.–8 P.M.), an old-fashioned burger joint. The mainstay here is the assortment of beef burgers: the Bubba, Double Bubba, Big Bubba, and Slopper, all under $6.95. Other menu items include a teriyaki burger, chicken burger, fish and chips, corn dog, and chicken Caesar salad, all for under $7. Burgers come on a toasted bun with mustard, ketchup-based relish, and diced onions. Anything else you want on it— cheese, teriyaki, lettuce, or tomatoes—you pay for. Hey, they've been doing things this way since 1936—it's worked for them. Bubba's is a throwback to the days when a diner owner was also the short-order cook and all the burgers were handmade. Yet, Bubba's has kept up. Try the free Internet access or buy a Bubba shirt or hat to take with you. Rock and roll, grease, and Elvis lives, man! Enjoy!

The Olympic Cafe (4-1354 Kuhio Hwy., 808/822-5825), a fixture in downtown Kapa'a for more than half a century, torn up by Hurricane 'Iniki, relocated and morphed into a breakfast place, now is located in the upstairs of the Hee Fat building and serves breakfast, lunch, and dinner. The street side of the restaurant is an open-air affair with awnings, so you can sit out of the veranda overlooking the street activity or inside under ceiling fans. Breakfasts are mostly scrambles, omelettes, and the like; lunch is wraps and sandwiches, while dinners are most filling with fish, pasta, and Mexican dishes, as well as burgers. A full bar provides all libations, and there may be live music in the evening.

With views from its second-story location (parking below) and overlooking the reef at the north end of town, **Scotty's** (4-1546 Kuhio Hwy. 808/823-8480, 11 A.M.–9 P.M. except Sun.) has an excellent spot to offer its mostly smoked-meat barbecue menu. Here you get the most tender pieces, as Scotty smokes his meats for at least 15 hours. A casual, breezy place, Scotty's entices guests up to eat with heady smells wafting from the kitchen. While grilled sandwiches and burgers are available for lunch, try the heartier St. Loius Style ribs, smoked half chicken, or smoked brisket for dinner. All meals except the combinations are under $11, and they all come with one of Scotty's sauces, cole slaw, bread, and another side.

Since 1973, the **Bull Shed** (4-796 Kuhio Hwy., 808/822-3791) has been serving happy customers on the Coconut Coast from its dining room overlooking the water at the Mokihana of Kauai condo in Waipouli. Heavy on the meats, the menu includes rack of lamb and prime rib, both favorites. The Bull Shed also serves plenty of fish and seafood. When available, Alaskan king crab and rock lobster tail go for whatever the market will bear. Entrées are under $24, and all dinners include a salad bar. Not as polished as other high-end establishments, the Bull Shed just gives you great food at reasonable prices with friendly service in a pleasing location. You can't go wrong here.

Organic Take-Out

Papaya's (808/823-0190, 9 A.M.–8 P.M. daily except Sunday), a natural-food café and market below the Whale Tower at Kauai Village, is not only the largest but also the best natural-food store on the island. While it once did full breakfast and lunches, it now has a salad/hot food/soup bar that runs $6.49 a pound, a good price for the quality and quantity of food served. Outdoor tables are available, or sit on the grass in the courtyard. If you are into healthy organic food, there is no place better than Papaya's!

The **C Mermaid Cafe** (4-1384 Kuhio Hwy., 808/821-2026, daily 11 A.M.–9 P.M.) is an unpretentious walk-up window restaurant with outside seating that does tacos, two-fisted wraps, and plate lunches with flavorful sauces for the healthy, organic, veggie, bean sprout, brown rice, tofu-eating crowd. Most dishes are $8.95. This is one of the best bargains in town.

Hawaiian Regional

An easygoing place, with a sophisticated atmosphere, reasonable prices, and tasty food is **C Coconuts** (4-919 Kuhio Hwy., 808/823-8777, 4–10 P.M. Mon.–Sat.) You will pass through the front bar on the way to the dining room, which is softly lit to set the mood, or to patio seating. Furniture is made from tropical woods, panels of reed grass cover the ceiling, while murals and paintings of tropical scenes adorn the walls. Seafood is the specialty at Coconuts, but meats are also served. Start with fried calamari, crab-stuffed mushrooms, or a salad before moving on to the main dish. Entrées can be from the sea, like grilled and teriyaki-dipped salmon, seafood paella, or tempura *'ono,* or meats like beef tenderloin, veal scaloppine, or cured pork chops, most under $26. Although the food is flavorful, the chef does not overindulge the spices. Save space for flan, crème brûlée, or chocolate hazelnut mousse cake to round out your dining experience.

While the **Lemongrass Grill Seafood and Sushi Bar** (4-885 Kuhio Hwy., 808/821-2888, 5–9 P.M.) has the appearance of a thoroughly Thai restaurant, it mixes Thai dishes with borrowings from other cultures and adds to this mix the wonderful seafood from Hawaiian waters. Some menu items are lemongrass seafood stew, fresh catch on Thai spiced eggplant, braised short ribs with Korean accompaniments, and *huli huli* chicken breast. A variety of sushi is always available. Artistically presented, entrées run $16–24, and sushi is generally in the $3.50–7.50 range. Full bar. The Lemongrass Grill is popular, so call for reservations.

Vegan

If you want to try wholesome, flavorful, and well-presented vegan food, head to the 🅒 **Blossoming Lotus** restaurant (4504 Kukui St., 808/822-7678, 11 A.M.–3 P.M., 5:30–9:30 P.M.) on the ground floor of the Dragon Building at the traffic light in Kapa'a. Blossoming Lotus calls its food "vegan world fusion cuisine," and incorporates Indian, Mexican, and "living" (uncooked) foods. Lunch brings innovative wraps, salads, and sandwiches. Dinner might be Padma's living pad Thai, super Shakti's spanakopita, or Senorita Bombia's enchilada casserole, all in the $14–19 range. This is more than just a good karma-hippie restaurant, here the food is done with love, attention, and respect, and it has become a certified green restaurant for its sustainable business practices. To accompany dinner, there's live music on most nights. Just up the road on the opposite side, at the restaurant's former site, is its sister shop, the **Lotus Root** (4-1384 Kuhio Hwy., 808/823-6658, 7 A.M.–6 P.M.), which offers vegan pastries, ice cream, juices, and smoothies, all made without refined sugar or dairy products. Give them both a try for giving us healthy food choices.

Thai and Vietnamese

The Waipouli Plaza has one of the best moderately priced restaurants on the island, **The King and I** (808/822-1642, daily 4:30–9 P.M.). This Thai restaurant serves wonderful food that will make your taste buds stand up and be counted. Most dinners, which include many vegetarian specials, are $8–12.

Serving the same basic type of food, with the addition of Chinese and Vietnamese dishes, at roughly the same prices is **Sukhothai Restaurant** (808/821-1224, 10:30 A.M.–9:30 P.M. Mon.–Fri., from 11:30 A.M. on Sat. and Sun.) in the Kapa'a Shopping Center up the road.

Also in the Kauai Village shopping center is **Ba Le** (808/823-6060, 10 A.M.–9 P.M. daily) a Vietnamese restaurant that has built a loyal clientele. Short on ambience, Ba Le has a long menu of economically priced foods. *Pho,* a traditional, beef broth soup is a mainstay here, but stir-fry noodles, fried rice, seafood dishes, and a variety of rice and curry dishes round out the menu, nearly all under $10. Eat in or take out.

Mexican

Norberto's El Cafe (4-1373 Kuhio Hwy., 808/822-3362, 5–9 P.M. Mon.–Sat.), near the intersection of Kukui St. and Rt. 56 in downtown Kapa'a, is a family-run Mexican restaurant that's has been doing business for well over two decades. What's it doing in a small town on a Pacific Island, you ask? Gringo, don't look a gift burro in the mouth! Norberto's serves nutritious, delicious, wholesome food and caters to vegetarians—all dishes are prepared without lard or animal fats. The smell of food wafting out of the front door around dinnertime is its best advertisement. This is some of the best Mexican food on the island. Most full-course meals of burritos, enchiladas, and tostadas are under $18; children's plates and à la carte dishes are also available. The best deals are the chef's specials of burrito el café, rellenos tampico, fajitas, and enchiladas grande. Dinners are served with soup, beans, and rice; chips and salsa are complimentary. There's beer on tap or, if you really want to head south of the border, try a pitcher of margaritas. If you have room after stuffing yourself like a chimichanga, try a delicious chocolate-cream pie or homemade rum cake. The café is extremely popular with local folks and tables don't stay empty.

Italian

Having experienced great success in Koloa, **Pizzetta** (4-1387 Kuhio Hwy., 808/823-8882) opened a branch restaurant in Kapa'a and now serves its same fine menu of pizza and Italian foods to east shore residents and guests, but this one also does breakfast. This casual restaurant has French doors that open onto the sidewalk, soothing music in the background, and happy hour at the bar 3–5 P.M. Breakfast is pastries, eggs, and griddle items. Lunch is mostly pasta, pizza, and panini. Dinner entrées get more varied and extravagant but are still mostly under $16, with pizzas running $11–23. Free delivery in the area after 5 P.M. for orders over $20.

Wasabi's (4-1388 Kuhio Hwy., 808/822-2700) sushi restaurant goes the Japanese route for lunch Monday–Friday and dinner nightly until 10 P.M. Its main focus is affordable sushi rolls, but the lengthy menu also has tempura, fish, and other dinners, mostly in the $15–17 range.

La Playita Azul (808/821-2323, for lunch 11:30 A.M.–2 P.M. Tues.–Fri., 5:30–9 P.M. for dinner daily), at the Kauai Village shopping center, is an eat-in or takeout place that serves fresh Mexican fare. Look for the red chili peppers on the curtains in the windows. On the menu are the usual salads, tacos, burritos, tostadas, and enchiladas, and every evening there are specials. This place offers healthy, wholesome food at decent prices; most items are under $15. Give it a try.

Markets

For a full-service supermarket, try **Safeway** (8 A.M.–8 P.M. Mon.–Fri. and 9 A.M.–6 P.M. Sat. and Sun.) at Kauai Village, **Big Save** (7 A.M.–11 P.M.) at the Kapa'a Shopping Center, or **Foodland** (5 A.M.–11 P.M.) at the Waipouli Town Center. Older (since 1946) and more local is **Kojima's** (from 7 A.M. daily, until 8 P.M. weekdays, 6 P.M. Sat., and

1 P.M. Sun.). This well-stocked grocery store on the mountain side of the road beyond the Aloha Lumber yard at the north end of town carries produce, meat, liquor, beer, and picnic supplies—all you might need for your vacation.

Along the main highway, the local family-run **Pono Market** (4-1300 Kuhio Hwy., 7 A.M.–6 P.M. Mon.–Fri., until 5 P.M. Sat.) is stuffed to the gills with mini-mart items, along with takeout sushi, *bento,* and deli sandwiches.

Papaya's (808/823-0190, daily except Sun. 9 A.M.–8 P.M.), at the Kauai Village, is the best natural-food market on the island. Coolers and shelves hold items like wild tropical guava juice, organic sprouted hot dog buns, and mainstays like organic fruits and vegetables, yogurt, whole-grain bread, and bulk foods. If you buy fruit from the produce section, the staff will cut it up for you so you can eat it out front. There is also a good selection of organic teas, flavored coffees, and premium microbrewery beers, along with racks of fine wines. Spices, oils, vinegars, organic salad dressings, homeopathic medicines, cruelty-free cosmetics, vitamins, minerals, and an assortment of biodegradable cleaning products are also well represented. If you're looking for something to eat right now, have a look at the salad/hot food/soup bar for the daily selections.

Farmers Market

There's a county-sponsored **Sunshine Farmers Market** every Wednesday at 3 P.M. at the Kapa'a New Town Park, near the armory behind town. This is a lively, local event with great options for vegetables, fruit, and flowers. Stop and pick up food for your evening meal or try coconut milk right out of the shell.

Coffee Estate

Unlike the Big Island, which has hundreds of small coffee farms producing its Kona coffee, Kaua'i has one large coffee estate. Still, there are a few small-time coffee growers on the island, and **Blair Estate** (6200B Kawaihau Rd., 808/822-4495 or 800/750-5662,

ROBERT NILSEN

shoppers at Kapaʻa's Sunshine Farmers Market

www.blairestatecoffee.com) is one. Located up above Kapaʻa in Kapahi, Blair Estate not only grows, roasts, and sells its own and others' coffee beans, it offers free informational tours of its small farm and its organic agricultural practices. Call to make sure someone's home before you head up.

SERVICES

A number of services are centrally located in or around the Kapaʻa Shopping Center, just south of the center of Kapaʻa. At the shopping center you'll find the full-service Kapaʻa branch **post office** and the **Kapaʻa clinic** (4-1105 Kuhio Hwy., 808/822-3431) of the Kauaʻi Medical Clinic. A few buildings up on the same side of the street is the **Shoreview Pharmacy** (4-1177 Kuhio Hwy., 808/822-1447, Mon.–Fri. 8:30 A.M.–6 P.M., Sat. 8:30 A.M.–noon).

Just north of the pharmacy, across the street from the Kapaʻa Hongwanji, is **Business Support Services** (4-1191 Kuhio Hwy., 808/822-5504, 8 A.M.–6 P.M. Mon.–Sat., 10 A.M.–4 P.M. Sun.), which can take care of all your shipping and packing needs. Also available are fax, photocopy, and DSL Internet services, and you can rent time on a typewriter or computer. Internet use runs $2.50 for 15 minutes, so you can check your email here.

In the Kapaʻa Shopping Center is the **Kapaʻa Laundry Center** (daily 6:30 A.M.–9:30 P.M.) with self-service machines that run $2 a load and boxed soap machines. Pricey, but the best in the area. For dry cleaning services, head to the **Pono Cleaners** (808/822-6994) on the main street next to Pono Market.

Just north of the Kapaʻa Beach County Park is the town **library.**

Heading North

Route 56 north from Kapa'a is a visual treat. At first, the coastline glides along in an ever-changing panorama. Shortly, the road moves inland through former cane fields, then passes a large dairy farm before moving into orchard and pasture land. While there are a few new residential developments in the works, overall development is sparse until you get to Kilauea in the Hanalei District. To your left are the dominant **Anahola Mountains,** jagged, pointed, and intriguing. Until recently, you could crane your neck and see Hole-in-the-Mountain, a natural arrangement of boulders that formed a round *puka* (legend says it was formed by an angry giant who hurled his spear with such force that he made the hole), but time and storms have taken their toll, and the old hole has collapsed. More recently, a second hole has begun to open up just below the ridge; this is best seen from the highway beyond Anahola.

SIGHTS
Kealia
Just north of Kapa'a the road rises slightly around a point. On this point is a somewhat trashy **scenic lookout** from where you have decent views up and down the coast. As soon as you cross Kapa'a Stream you're in what's left of the village of Kealia; its school, store, and post office are now closed, but the rodeo corral still gets occasional use. The wide, white strand of **Kealia Beach** curves along the coast for a half mile. Once just an out-of-the-way spot along the road, it now has restrooms and a lifeguard tower. During calm weather the swimming, bodysurfing, and boogie boarding are good—particularly near the jetty at the north end—or you may find a few local anglers. The beach is at its busiest and the waves most challenging during winter swells, but anytime of the year can be crowded when the surf is right.

Inland, Kealia Road takes you up over patched asphalt, past the community of Kumukumu, and through former sugarcane fields to the deteriorating Spalding Monument. While

surfing at Kealia Beach

the monument itself is not worth the drive up, from this upcountry vantage point, now cowboy country and an area of hobby farm development, you can glimpse both the ocean and Anahola Mountains, the shoreline from Lihue to Kapa'a, and perhaps see horseback riders and dirt bikers on the open grassland on the weekends.

Donkey Beach
Continue along Rt. 56 heading north past mile marker 11 to a shoreline access parking lot. Follow the trail for 10 minutes through the lots of the new Kealia Kai subdivision until you come to a surfing beach that the locals call Donkey Beach. A tall stand of ironwoods shadows its south end. Unfortunately, the undertow is severe, especially during rough weather, and only experienced surfers challenge the waves here. You can sunbathe and take dips, but remain in the shallows close to shore. This area is very secluded, and some come here to spend

time au naturel, but the new housing development above the beach will certainly make this area accessible and more frequented in coming years. Bicycle riders on the newly paved bike trail, the old shoreline cane road from Kapa'a to Anahola, skirt this beach on their way north.

Anahola

The first village you come to is Anahola. While the old village is down along the bay, the commercial part of town and newer homes in the Hawaiian Homelands tract have been built up along the highway. As you approach Anahola, you may see signs on the highway advertising **lei for sale.** Families here make a few extra dollars by selling these beautiful and fragrant symbols of *aloha*. Although prices vary, expect to pay up to $5 for a *ti*-leaf lei or $5–10 for a flower lei. Stop and pick one up for your sweetie; many last for several days if refrigerated.

Just before mile marker 14 you hit "town" and find a **Handi Pantry** (808/822-5818, 6 A.M.–9:30 P.M.) selling groceries, souvenirs, vegetables, and liquor, as well as the Anahola post office and **Duane's Ono Char Burger,** a well-known local eatery. Anahola Road off Rt. 56 just before Handi Pantry leads to Anahola Beach, a long strand of white sand. Just a minute north of Handi Pantry, look to your right for 'Aliomanu Road (first) and follow it for a few minutes to the mouth of the Anahola River as it spills into the bay. Along the curve of the bay north of the river mouth is the narrower and less-frequented section of Anahola Beach. Beyond the point along 'Aliomanu Road (first) is the more secluded 'Aliomanu Beach.

'Aliomanu Road used to run from the highway down to and along the coast before turning inland again to the highway. During one of the last hurricanes, the bridge over a small stream at the north end of 'Aliomanu Beach was washed out and hasn't been replaced. The result is that each section of 'Aliomanu Road is a cul-de-sac. 'Aliomanu Road (second) is the north section of this road, and there is access to 'Aliomanu Beach from that end as well.

Anahola Beach County Park

Stretching from the river mouth along the south curve of the bay, this park has a developed picnic area, grills, showers, restrooms, and numerous camping spots—county permit required. Tall ironwood trees provide a natural canopy along the narrow strip of sand that slides gently into the water. The swimming is safe in the protected cove and in the freshwater river, good for a refreshing dip. As you walk north the waves and rips get tougher. It's not advisable to enter the deep water, although some experienced board riders do challenge the waves here, as the Hawaiians did long ago, in an area called Kanahawale, which means Easily Broken. However, the reef comes close to shore at this end, and wherever you can find a sheltered pocket it's good for snorkeling. Local anglers love this spot for near-shore fishing, and families come to have a weekend sunset dinner and evening bonfire on the beach. The entire area is popular with local people and at times begins to look like a tent city of semi-permanent campers and squatters. Although the county works to maintain the park, these long-term residents tend to make the area messy at times. If you camp, don't leave your stuff unattended for too long.

On the north side of the stream, the mostly narrow 'Aliomanu Beach runs for a good distance past private homes and vacation rentals and is sometimes used by locals for beach bonfires. Access this shoreline via Aliomanu Road (first). A short ways up the coast near Papa'a Bay is a small and secluded cove with beach access and a parking area off Kalakea View Drive, which can be reached via either Aliomanu Road (second) or Papa'a Road.

◖ Moloa'a Beach

The turnoff to Moloa'a (Matted Roots) Bay is between mile markers 16 and 17 near the dairy farm. Turn down the rough Ko'olau Road, follow it to Moloa'a Road, and take this narrow but paved road to the end. Look for the brilliant poinsettias blooming in early winter along Ko'olau Road—they are the island's clue that Christmas and the New Year are near. Moloa'a Bay has a magnificent but rarely visited beach. The road leading down is a luscious little thoroughfare, cutting over domed hillocks in a series of curves. The jungle canopy is thick and then opens into a series of glens and pastures. Off to the sides, homes perch on stilts made from telephone poles. A short drive takes you to road's end and a small cluster of dwellings near where the stream empties into the bay. There is limited space to park your vehicle here, but find a spot where signs indicate it's OK and follow the right-of-way signs to the beach. The beach is lovely, bright, and wide, forming a crescent moon. To the north the beach ends in a grassy hillock; south, it's confined by a rocky headland where the swimming is best. As at all east and north shore beaches, swimming is advised only during calm weather. Snorkeling is good, but you'll have to swim the channel out to the base of the *pali,* which is inadvisable if the waves are rough. Although a few homes are around, Moloa'a is a place of peaceful solitude. Sunsets are light shows of changing color, and you'll probably be a solitary spectator.

Larsen's Beach

From Moloa'a Bay, return to Ko'olau Road (the old coast road) and follow it north as it twists into and then out of the valley. As it comes up on the heights near an old cemetery, turn seaward and follow a narrow gravel road for half a mile to a small parking lot at the crest of the cliff. From here, a path leads down to Larsen's Beach, named after L. David Larsen, a manager of the Kilauea sugar plantation. He built a home for his family nearby. Not particularly good for swimming because of the rocky bottom and close-in reef, this beach is a place where locals come to harvest a type of seaweed or do throw-net fishing. The narrow sand shore may be good for sunbathing, however, and, except on weekends, you'll probably have the place to yourself.

ACCOMMODATIONS

Several rental properties line 'Aliomanu Road. **Mahina Kai** (808/822-9451 or 800/337-1134,

www.mahinakai.com) is a Japanese-style house with a cobalt blue tile roof that's backed into a hillside and has views of the ocean. An indoor koi pond in the atrium, open spaces, Oriental furnishings and artwork, and paper *shoji* screens help create the atmosphere. The finely landscaped yard is tended with care, and there is even a small *heiau* on the property. Down below the house, set in a walled garden amidst thick vegetation, is the very private free-form swimming pool. Each of the three rooms in the house has its own bathroom and lanai; two have adjoining sitting rooms. These rooms share a kitchenette. Up a set of steps above the main house is the "tea house," the B&B's largest room and the one with the best views. The detached Bamboo Cottage sits close to the pool and has its own small kitchen and sitting room. Rooms run $175–325 a night with a three-night minimum. Mahina Kai is gay friendly.

Moloa'a Kai on Moloa'a Bay gives you all the amenities of a two-bedroom, two-bath house right on the beach. This three-floor house, with parking on the ground level below the living quarters, can sleep up to seven and rents for $1,185–1,385 a week. Daily rental—five-night minimum—is also an option for $185–235 a night. Contact Hawaii Beachfront Vacation Homes (46-535 Haiku Plantation Place, Kane'ohe, HI 96744, 808/247-3637, fax 808/235-2644, www.hibeach.com, hibeach@lava.net).

Jade Lily Pad is tucked away a short distance up Moloa'a Stream and reachable via a dirt driveway by 4WD vehicles. Wood floors and a cathedral ceiling make this cottage seem larger than it is. Its two bedrooms are good for a family, and the full kitchen makes it easy and convenient to prepare meals and save a few bucks. The Jade Lily Pad rents for $250 a night, with a three-night minimum. Contact Rosewood Vacation Rentals (808/822-5216, fax 808/822-5478, www.rosewoodkauai.com) for additional information and reservations.

Several other vacation rentals in the Anahola area can be arranged through **Garden Island Properties** (4-928 Kuhio Hwy., 808/822-4871

EAST SHORE

or 800/801-0378, fax 808/822-7984, sue@kau-aiproperties.com, www.kauaiproperties.com) in Kapaʻa.

FOOD

Duane's Ono Char Burger (808/822-9181, Mon.–Sat. 10 A.M.–6 P.M., Sun. 11 A.M.–6 P.M.) is known far and wide. It's a clean, friendly roadside stand—next to Handi Pantry at the turnoff for Anahola Road—where you can get burgers, fish and chips, sides, and drinks. Some of the double-fisted burgers include the Ono; an Old Fashioned, with cheddar, onions, and sprouts on a Kaiser roll; the Local Boy, made with teriyaki, cheddar cheese, and pineapple; a Local Girl, made with teriyaki and Swiss cheese; and even a meatless Boca Burger. The burgers are oversize and heavy with cheese and trimmings, and most everything is under $7. For an extra treat, try a delicious marionberry shake. Umbrella tables are to the side, but hold your appetite for a few minutes and make it a picnic at the nearby beach.

Across the road from Duane's and up a bit closer to the ʻAliomanu Rd. (first) turnoff, look for the Anahola Baptist Church and a small lane leading to the **Polynesian Hide-a-Way,** a local Hawaiian restaurant, open daily 10 A.M.–5 P.M. The Hide-a-Way is a hut in a grove of trees for eat-in or takeout that offers plate lunches such as *huli huli* chicken, *laulau, kalua* pig, and fish and chips. Polynesian Hide-a-way is down-home, clean, friendly, inexpensive, delicious, and filled with the *aloha* spirit. You can't go wrong.

Up the road at the turnoff for Moloaʻa Beach is **Moloaʻa Sunrise Fruit Stand** (808/822-1441). Great for a rest stop as you cruise the highway, here you not only have a choice of fresh fruit and produce, but also sandwiches, espresso, and smoothies.

NORTH SHORE

The north shore is a soulful song of wonder, a contented chant of dream-reality, where all the notes of the Garden Island harmonize gloriously. The refrain is a tinkling melody, rising, falling, and finally reaching a booming climax deep in the emerald green of Na Pali. In so many ways this region is a haven: tiny towns and villages that refused to crumble when sugar pulled out; a patchwork quilt of diminutive *kuleana* of native Hawaiians running deep into luxuriant valleys, where ageless stone walls encircle fields of taro; a winter sanctuary for migrating birds and gritty native species desperately holding on to life; a refuge for myriad visitors—the adventuring, vacationing, life-tossed, or work-weary who come to its shores seeking a setting to find peace of body and soul.

The north shore is only 30 miles long, but, oh, what miles! Along its undulating mountains, one-lane roads, and luminescent bays are landlocked caves still umbilically tied to the sea; historical sites, the remnants of peace or domination once so important and now reduced by time; and living movie sets, some occupied by villas of stars or dignitaries. Enduring, too, is the history of old Hawaii in this fabled homeland of the Menehune, overrun by the Polynesians who set up their elaborate kingdoms built on strict social order. The usurpers' *heiau* remain, and from one came the hula, swaying, stirring, and spreading throughout the island kingdoms.

Starting in **Kilauea,** an old plantation town, you can marvel at the coastline from bold promontories pummeled by the sea and

ROBERT NILSEN

HIGHLIGHTS

◖ Kilauea Point National Wildlife Refuge: This is one of the best places on the island to see huge frigate birds, dressy red-footed boobies, swift tropic birds, the indigenous Hawaiian *nene*, as well as other sea birds, monk seals, and whales during their summer migration to the islands. On this promontory stands the sturdy Kilauea Lighthouse, a site in and of itself and historically one of the most important lighthouses in the islands. From its yard are expansive views of the North Shore coastline (page 190).

◖ Hanalei Valley: A heavily farmed wildlife preserve, the lower valley is a patchwork quilt of shades of green taro fields best seen from the scenic overlook on the bluff at Princeville (page 207).

◖ Wai'oli Mission House Museum: This is a superb example of an early missionary home; a tour lends insight into the lives of those who came to preach and teach (page 208).

◖ Hanalei Bay: One of the most perfect bays in the Hawaiian Island chain, its beach sweeps in a thin crescent for two miles. The bay and its periphery teemed with life and provided sustenance to sustain the early Hawaiians, and today many others have found refuge in its mothering arms (page 210).

◖ Limahuli Botanical Garden: Part of the National Tropical Botanical Garden, Limahuli makes a wonderful stop for a short walk through native and introduced plants. Here too are refurbished, terraced taro fields once used by Hawaiians of old (page 220).

◖ Ke'e Beach: Literally the end of the road, this is a good spot to swim and snorkel safely within the reef, cast your eyes down the immensely awesome Na Pali Coast, begin a hike to Kalalau Valley, pay tribute to those who gave the gift of hula, or simply to watch a brilliant sunset (page 221).

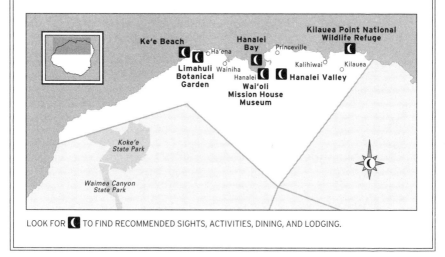

LOOK FOR ◖ TO FIND RECOMMENDED SIGHTS, ACTIVITIES, DINING, AND LODGING.

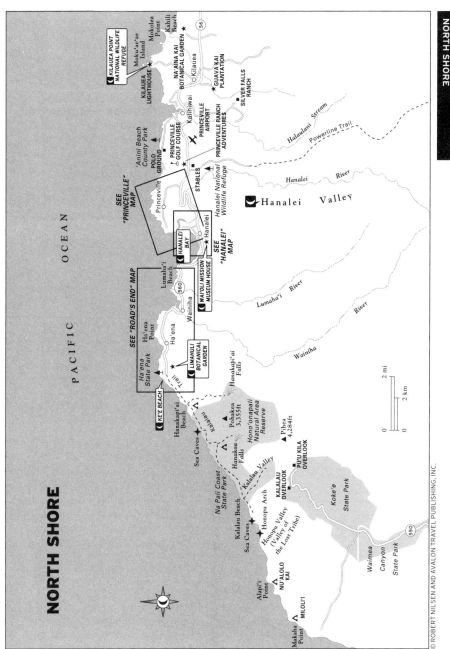

NORTH SHORE

PACIFIC

OCEAN

KILAUEA POINT NATIONAL WILDLIFE REFUGE

Moku'ae'ae Island

Mokolea Point

Kahili Beach

KILAUEA LIGHTHOUSE

NA'AINA KAI BOTANICAL GARDEN

Kīlauea

GUAVA KAI PLANTATION

SILVER FALLS RANCH

SEE "PRINCEVILLE" MAP

'Anini Beach County Park

PRINCEVILLE GOLF COURSE

POLO GROUND

Kalihiwai

Princeville

PRINCEVILLE AIRPORT

PRINCEVILLE RANCH ADVENTURES

STABLES

Halaulani Stream

Powerline Trail

Hanalei River

Hanalei National Wildlife Refuge

Hanalei Valley

HANALEI BAY

Hanalei

SEE "HANALEI" MAP

Lumaha'i Beach

WAI'OLI MISSION MUSEUM HOUSE

Wainiha

Lumaha'i River

SEE "ROAD'S END" MAP

Ha'ena Point

Ha'ena

Wainiha River

Ha'ena State Park

LIMAHULI BOTANICAL GARDEN

KE'E BEACH

Trail

Hanakapi'ai Beach

Hanakapi'ai Falls

Na Pali Coast State Park

Sea Caves

Kalalau Trail

Pohakea 3,355ft

Hono'onapali Natural Area Reserve

Pihea 4,284ft

Hanakoa Falls

PU'U KILA OVERLOOK

Kalalau Valley

KALALAU OVERLOOK

Koke'e State Park

Kalalau Beach

Honopu Arch

Sea Caves

Honopu Valley (Valley of the Lost Tribe)

NU'ALOLO KAI

MILOLI'I

Alapi'i Point

Makaha Point

Waimea Canyon State Park

550

2 mi

2 km

0

0

© ROBERT NILSEN AND AVALON TRAVEL PUBLISHING, INC.

observe seabirds at the wildlife sanctuary. Then there are the north shore beaches—fans of white sand, some easily visited as official parks, others hidden, the domains of simplicity and free spirits. **Princeville** follows, a convenient but incongruous planned community, vibrant with its own shopping mall and flexing condo muscles. Over the rise is **Hanalei,** a tiny town even more poetic than its lovely name. A yachties' anchorage with good food, Hanalei is spirited, slow, a bay of beauty and enchantment. Movie cameras once rolled at neighboring **Lumaha'i Beach,** and an entire generation shared the dream of paradise when they saw this spot in *South Pacific.* Next in rapid succession are **Wainiha** and **Ha'ena,** with their few amenities, a little of the world's most relaxed lifestyle. The road ends at **Ke'e Beach,** where adventure begins with the start of the **Na Pali Coast Trail.** The north shore remains for most visitors the perfect setting for seeking and maybe actually finding peace, solitude, the dream, yourself.

PLANNING YOUR TIME

Many of those who know the island head straight up the road to the North Shore and stay there through their vacation. For others, the trip up should definitely be on your itinerary. One day on the North Shore is good, but for fuller exposure to its many grand sights, count on a couple of days.

Everyone traveling north should stop in Kilauea to see the **Kilauea Point National Wildlife Refuge** and Kilauea Lighthouse. Take a short stroll to this promontory for an up-close look at the many seabirds that claim this coastal point as their home. Either with naked eye or with the aid of binoculars, you can easily spot frigate birds with their eight-foot wingspan, the sleek tropic birds with their forked tails, red-footed boobies, and, during the right time of year, albatross nesting on the hillside and whales swimming in the blue waters below. The sturdy lighthouse stands on this tall promontory just begging to be photographed. It's easy to see why this spot was chosen and why it remains an integral beacon

site. While in Kilauea, add a couple of hours to your trip if you desire to tour the private Na 'Aina Kai Botanical Gardens, a private reserve of hardwood trees, landscaped lawns, flowering bushes, fruit trees, enchanting life-size statues, and seascapes.

The lower **Hanalei Valley** is another wildlife refuge, where coots, gallinule, stilts, and ducks reign supreme. This wonderful valley snakes down from the tall mountain center of the island only a few miles inland and is best seen from the valley overlook along the highway just past Princeville. Golf enthusiasts should turn in to the Princeville Resort for a morning or afternoon go at one of the two challenging resorts courses here. Even those not staying at Princeville should take an hour to drive through the resort and peer down onto **Hanalei Bay** from Pu'u Poa Bluff.

Slowly continue down the road to the town of Hanalei and let the slower pace of life of the North Shore envelop you. Be sure to stop in Hanalei for food, as there is precious little beyond. Head to the pier or beach to take in the beauty of this protected spot, a perfect place to swim, surf, or sunbathe. From Hanalei, kayak tours head out for a morning or afternoon adventure along the coast or up the lazy Hanalei River. For the physically fit, full-day summertime trips traverse the entire length of the coast as far as Polihale Beach. Continue by car or bike to snorkel at Tunnels Beach or swim within the protected reef at **Ke'e Beach,** the end of the road. Ke'e Beach is the start of the famous Kalalau Trail, and while you can spend a half day hiking into Hanakapi'ai Valley, or another three hours up the side valley to Hanakapi'ai Waterfall and back, it will take five days to hike into Kalalau Valley, spending time there to appreciate its magic, and hiking out again. For those with less time or no hiking permit, satisfy yourself with the awe-inspiring views along the coast and sunset from shore.

While at the end of the road, take an hour or so to explore the paths of **Limahuli Gardens.** Located in the last valley before the end of the road, this garden is part of the National Tropical Botanical Gardens and is a good introduction to native and introduced tropical plants. Either on your way through or on your return from the end of the road, stop at **Wai'oli Mission House Museum** for a tour of this missionary home and a glimpse into the lives of these early settlers. It will take a couple of hours.

A couple of days should do it for seeing this coast unless you intend to do several of the many outdoor adventures offered from Hanalei. If you stay, the North Shore has one developed tourist resort, the Princeville Resort, where a luxury hotel, upscale condos, golf course, tennis courts, high-end restaurants, and other fine amenities prevail; this could be your base for exploring the North Shore. Otherwise, Kilauea, Hanalei, and Ha'ena all have accommodations that also include the moderate and economical. While Princeville has a handful of upscale restaurants, much more variety is available in Hanalei.

Kilauea

There's no saying *exactly* where it begins, but Kilauea is generally considered the gateway to the north shore. The village proper was built on sugar, but that foundation melted away in the early 1970s. Now the town holds on as a way station to some of the most intriguing scenery along this fabulous coast. Notice the bright, cheery, well-kept homes as you pass through this community. The homeowners may be short on cash but are nonetheless long on pride and surround their dwellings with lovingly tended flower gardens. The bungalows—pictures of homey contentment—are ablaze with color. Like other areas of the island, Kilauea is experiencing some new residential and business development, creating more vibrancy than the sleepy town has known for a few decades.

To get into town, look for mile marker 23 and a Shell gas station on your right, along with the Menehune Food Mart, a small store selling sundries and general groceries. This is where you turn onto Kolo Road, following the signs to Kilauea Lighthouse and the national wildlife refuge. The promontory that the lighthouse occupies, Kilauea Point, is the northernmost point of the main Hawaiian Islands. A second way into Kilauea is by turning off the highway just before mile marker 23 at Hookui Road. Go one block and turn left onto Kolo Street. Pass St. Sylvester's Church and proceed over a bridge, past the Kilauea School, and on into town. Kilauea's first commercial area is at the corner of Kolo Street and Kilauea Road near the gas station. Down Kilauea Road at Keneke Street are the Kong Lung Co. and other concerns, the real business hub of town. Behind this group of businesses is a small community park. One block away on Oka Street are two medical clinics and a pharmacy.

SIGHTS
Kilauea Churches
Where Kolo Road intersects Kilauea Road sits **Christ Memorial Episcopal Church** on the right. Hawaii seems to sprout as many churches as bamboo shoots, but this one is special. The shrubbery and flowers immediately catch your eye; their vibrant colors are matched by the stained-glass windows, imported from England. The present church was built in 1941 from cut lava stone. Inside is a hand-hewn altar, and surrounding the church a cemetery holds several tombstones of long-departed parishioners. Go in, have a look, and perhaps meditate for a moment. Before turning on Kilauea Road, have a look at **St. Sylvester's Catholic Church.** This house of worship is octagonal, with a roof resembling a Chinese hat. Inside are murals painted by the modernist Jean Charlot, a famous island artist. The church, built by Friar John Macdonald, was an attempt to reintroduce art as one of the bulwarks of Catholicism.

Guava Kai Plantation

Just before you arrive at the turnoff to Kilauea, turn inland on Kuawa Road and follow the signs to the 480-acre Guava Kai Plantation, the largest guava-producing and -processing venture in the nation. Proceed along the access road lined with ferns, banana trees, ironwoods, and flowering bushes, and stop in at the visitor center/snack shop (808/828-6121, daily 9 A.M.–5 P.M.), where you can learn about guava processing; taste guava juice, jams, and jellies; and purchase a guava product, T-shirt, or sundry item. The free self-guided tour is actually just a view of the beginning stages of fruit processing (unloading and washing), as you are not allowed into the factory itself to see the sorting, pulping, squeezing, and packaging. Come early—much of the work in this outdoor receiving area starts before 6 A.M. You're invited to pick a handful of guava fruit from the orchard at no charge as a take-away treat—staff members will point you to an area where the fruit is ripe. Don't hurry away, however; treat yourself to a stroll through the small botanical garden. Follow a well-trodden path through a covered archway where tropical plants grow, and cross a tiny stream to find many of Hawaii's flowers and plants. The path winds along for just five minutes and leads to a pond surrounded by taro, bird of paradise, hibiscus, torch ginger, ferns, and various palms. Before leaving, stop at the snack shop for guava juice, a juice float or slush, ice cream cone, or bowl of saimin.

Botanical Gardens

Just east of Kilauea at the end of Wailapa Road, **Na 'Aina Kai Botanical Gardens** (808/828-0525, www.naainakai.com, 8 A.M.–noon Mon. and Fri., 8 A.M.–5 P.M. Tues.–Thurs.) is a botanical garden of grand proportions. Its 240 acres include well over 100 acres of a tropical hardwood plantation with nearly two dozen types of trees, such as teak, mahogany, zebra wood, rosewood, and cocobolo, and another large tract of tropical fruit trees. In the heart of the property several theme gardens specialize in various types of plants, and throughout the gardens some 60 life-like bronze sculptures add a playful touch. After years of loving preparation, this property has opened to the public for guided tours by reservation only; call weekdays 8 A.M.–8 P.M. Five different tours are given on Tuesday, Wednesday, and Thursday at 9 A.M. and 1 P.M. only and involve some walking and/or a covered tram ride. They range from a 90-minute stroll for $25 to a five-hour walk and ride through all the sections of the property for $70. Adults and children 13 and above, please. Although pricey, the gardens are quite a treat. Even if you don't care to have a tour, stop by the visitor's center/gift shop at the garden entrance to peruse the plants, books, and gift items on display.

〔 Kilauea Point National Wildlife Refuge

Head down Kilauea Road (sometimes referred to as Lighthouse Road) past Kong Lung Co., following it as it makes a hard swing to the left, then winds around, ending at Kilauea Point National Wildlife Refuge (http://paci-

Kilauea Lighthouse

ROBERT NILSEN

ficislands.fws.gov/wnwr/kkilaueanwr.html) and **Kilauea Lighthouse,** a designated national historical landmark. This facility, built in 1913, was at one time manned by the Coast Guard but is now under the jurisdiction of the Department of the Interior's Fish and Wildlife Service. Stately and solid, the lighthouse stands about 50 feet tall, the base more than 200 feet above the sea. Boasting the largest "clamshell lens" in the world, it was capable of sending a beam 20 miles out to sea. The clamshell lens was discontinued in 1976, when a small, high-intensity beacon was activated as the reference point for mariners.

The refuge, which encompasses the high cliffs from Kilauea Point past Crater Hill to Mokolea Point (one-half of an ancient and eroded crater rim), is alive with permanent and migrating seabirds. Keep your eyes peeled for the great frigate bird, kiting on its nearly eight-foot wingspan, and the red-footed booby, a white bird with black wingtips darting here and there, always wearing red dancing shoes. The *nene,* wedgetail shearwaters, and red- and white-tailed tropicbirds are also common here. The wildlife refuge is attempting to relocate albatross from the Midway Islands, where they have virtually taken over the island. More than 40 have been successfully relocated, and you can watch them floundering around on nearby Albatross Hill. At certain times of the year, Hawaiian monk seals and green sea turtles can be seen along the shore and around Moku'ae'ae Island just off Kilauea Point. Dolphins are also spotted offshore during spring and summer, and whales play in these waters, part of the Hawaiian Islands Humpback Whale National Marine Sanctuary, during winter and spring.

A leisurely walk takes you out onto this amazingly narrow peninsula to the lighthouse and visitor center (808/828-0168). Don't keep your eyes only in the air, however. Look for the coastal *naupaka* plants, which surround the parking lot and line the walk to the lighthouse. Common along the seashore and able to grow even in arid regions, these plants have bunches of bright green, moisture-retaining, leathery leaves; at their centers are white half-flowers the size of a fingernail and small white seeds. Information at the visitors center gives you a fast lesson in birdlife, plantlife, and a pictorial history of the lighthouse—worth reading. Also available is a good selection of books on Hawaiian flora, fauna, history, and hiking, as well as maps of the islands. There are usually informative docents in the yard, and the center

WHALE-WATCHING ON KAUA'I

If you're in Hawaii from late November to early May, you have an excellent chance of spotting a humpback whale. March is perhaps the best month. You can often see a whale from a vantage point on land, but this is nowhere near as thrilling as seeing them close-up from a boat. Either way, binoculars are a must. Telephoto and zoom lenses are also useful, and you might even get a nifty photo in the bargain. But don't waste your film unless you have a fairly high-powered zoom: fixed-lens cameras give pictures with a lot of ocean and a tiny black speck. If you're lucky enough to see a whale breach (jump clear of the water), keep watching – they often repeat this a number of times. If a whale dives and lifts its fluke high in the air, expect it to be down for at least 15 minutes and not come up in the same spot. Other times they'll dive shallowly, then bob up and down quite often. During the season, many boats run whale-watching tours. From shore, a favorite place to look for whales is the Kilauea Point National Wildlife Refuge. The waters off this point are part of the Hawaiian Islands Humpback Whale National Marine Sanctuary. But whales can be seen from just about anywhere along the coast, including the Kalalau Trail on the north shore, and Kukui O Lono Park at Kalaheo and Po'ipu Beach on the south shore.

often sets up binoculars on tripods trained on particular birds or nesting sites on the nearby cliffs.

From Crater Hill, 568 feet straight up from the water, the wide Pacific stretches virtually unobstructed until it hits the Aleutian Islands of Alaska. A result of one of the last spates of volcanic activity on the island (perhaps some 12,000 years ago), this sea cliff is like a giant stack of pancakes, layered and jagged, with the edges eaten by age and covered with a green syrup of lichen and mosses. The cliff is undercut, giving the sensation of floating in midair. Profuse purple and yellow flowers spread all along the edge. Like Kilauea Point to the west and Mokolea Point to the east, these cliffs serve as a giant rookery for seabirds. The military found it a perfect spot, too, and erected a radar station here during World War II; the abandoned structures remain.

This lighthouse and sanctuary are open daily 10 A.M.–4 P.M., except federal holidays. The entrance fee is $3 adults, free for children under 16; the cost of an annual refuge permit is $10. Golden Eagle, Golden Access, and Golden Age Passes, and a Federal Duck Stamp are honored for free entrance.

BEACHES
Kahili Beach

Kilauea Bay offers great fishing, unofficial camping, and beautiful scenery. Between mile markers 21 and 22, turn seaward on Wailapa Road and proceed for the better part of a mile. Follow the dirt road that veers off to the left and downhill to Kahili Beach, also known as **Quarry Beach,** on Kilauea Bay. This very pretty bay has headlands on each end, and the beach is split in the middle by a tongue of rock. Characteristic of Kaua'i, Kilauea Stream runs into the bay, and in this case meets the water on the west end of the beach, having first backed up against the sand bar to form a rather large pond. Swimming is good in the placid water of the stream, and some bring kayaks for a paddle around the pond. During calm periods, swimming is possible in the bay, but when the waves are up, local residents come to surf or use boogie boards. Plenty of places along the streambank or on the beach are good for pic-

Kalihiwai Beach

ROBERT NILSEN

nicking and camping. It's especially popular on weekends when families come to play. At other times, the beach may be empty. Many local anglers come here to catch a transparent fish called *'o'io,* which they often use for bait. It's too bony to fry, but they have figured out an ingenious way to get the meat. They cut off the tail and roll a soda pop bottle over it, squeezing the meat out through the cut. They then mix it with water, hot pepper, and bread crumbs to make delicious fish balls. This beach can also be reached from Kilauea town. Proceed past Kong Lung Co. and take the second dirt road to the right; it angles through what used to be cane fields. Follow this rutted road a mile and a half down to the now-abandoned Kahili Quarry at the end of the road, from where you must wade across the stream to the beach.

Kauapea Beach

Kauapea Beach, more commonly called **Secret Beach,** deserves its name. After passing through Kilauea, look for Banana Joe's tropical fruit stand on the left; just past it is Kalihiwai Road. Make a right there and then take the very first dirt road on the right—through the cut in the roadbank—and down to a parking area. Follow the trail along the horse pasture barbed-wire fence and then steeply down the slippery ravine before emerging at the beach in less than 15 minutes. Even some local residents ruefully admit that the secret is out. However, if you venture to this beach, be conscious that there are private homes nearby and that it's a place locals come to enjoy themselves away from the crowds of tourists. If you expect Secret Beach to be small, you're in for a shock. This white-sand strand is huge and backed by steep cliff walls. Reasonably calm during summer months, waves thunder in and crash on the beach during winter. Dolphins seem to like this area as well—please give these intelligent animals plenty of space—and whales can be seen offshore during the winter months. Secret Beach is a de facto nude beach and is accepted as such by most local residents. Beyond the far end of the beach you can see

Kilauea Lighthouse, proud and dominant and dazzling white in the sun. Along the beach a fine stand of trees provides shade perfect for pitching a tent, but be aware that police sometimes patrol here and issue tickets for camping without a permit. Nonetheless, some people make this beach home for a few weeks or months at a time—unofficially, of course. For drinking water, head along the beach and keep your eyes peeled for a freshwater spring coming out of the mountain. What more can you ask for?

Kalihiwai Beach

Kalihiwai Beach is at the end of Kalihiwai Road. If you go over the Kalihiwai River, you've gone too far—even though another section of the Kalihiwai Road also leads from there down to the coast. This road was once part of the coastal road, but the devastating tsunami of 1946 took out the lower bridge, and the road is now divided by the river. As on many such rivers in Kaua'i, a ferry was used here to ease early transportation difficulties. Less than half a mile down the first Kalihiwai Road you come to an off-the-track, white-sand beach lined with ironwoods. The swimming, bodysurfing, and boogie boarding are outstanding here, given the right conditions. The river behind the ironwoods forms a freshwater pool. There are no amenities here whatsoever. People sometimes camp among the ironwoods. The second Kalihiwai Road—take the right fork in the road—leads you to the west side of the river, where locals come to fish. Some people put kayaks in the river here for a short paddle upriver, followed by a 10-minute hike through this lush valley to get to the waterfall that can be seen from the highway bridge. A hundred yards or so before the bridge on the highway, a tall thin waterfall slices through a tight ravine right at the road's edge, almost out of view of traffic. This spot is directly on the busy highway, so look quickly as you drive past. You zip by in the blink of an eye.

'Anini Beach County Park

Follow the second Kalihiwai Road to the Y

and take the left fork—'Anini Road—and follow it to the remarkable 'Anini Beach County Park. This area was known as one of the best fishing grounds on the island and was reserved for the exclusive use of the *ali'i*. 'Anini was traditionally called Wanini, but time and sea air weathered a latter-day sign until the W rusted off completely. Newcomers to the area mistakenly called it 'Anini, and the name stuck. The reef here, at two miles, is the longest exposed reef off Kaua'i; consequently, the snorkeling is first-rate. It's amazing to snorkel out to the reef in no more than four feet of water and then to peer over the edge into waters that seem bottomless. Stay away from the boat landing and the route that boats take to cross the reef. Windsurfers also love this area, and their bright sails can be seen year-round. Those in the know say this is the best spot on Kaua'i for beginning windsurfers, as the trade winds generally blow gently and steadily toward the shore, the water is shallow, and the beach protected. Beginning lessons are often given here. Longer than the reef, the beach is fine sand, and swimming is excellent. Follow the road to the end, where a shallow, brackish lagoon and a large sandbar make the area good for wading. This park has full amenities—toilets, picnic tables, grills, and a pavilion. Camping by county permit is allowed in designated areas toward the western end of the park; the day-use picnic spot is at the other end of the park. There are private homes and vacation rentals at both ends of this beach, so be considerate when coming and going.

A **polo ground** is across the road from the beach park's camping area. On Sundays from May to August, matches are held here beginning at 3 P.M. and lasting until about 5 P.M. Admission is $10 adults, $5 children 12–17. The exciting matches are both fun and stylish. The local horsemen are excellent players who team with their trusty mounts to perform amazing athletic maneuvers. Bring your own snacks and drink and make an afternoon out of the game. Call the Kauai Polo Club (808/826-4472, www.kauaipoloclub.org) for information.

SHOPPING

In Kilauea across from the Shell station look for **Shared Blessing Thrift Shop** (2–5 P.M. Tues. and Thurs. and 9:30 A.M.–12:30 P.M. Wed. and Sat.) in a vintage plantation building, a good place to pick up secondhand treasures or curios from Kaua'i.

An institution in this area is **Kong Lung Co.** (808/828-1822, open daily 10 A.M.– 6 P.M.) along Kilauea Road at the intersection of Keneke Street, which has been serving the needs of the north shore plantation towns for more than a century. But don't expect bulk rice and pipe fittings. Rather, this is a collection of fine fashions and jewelry, bath products, antiques, art and crafts, and home accessories, much of which has a distinctive Asian flavor. It bills itself as an "exotic gift emporium," and you'll agree. Sharing the Kong Lung Co. space are **Banana Patch Studio** for gifts and **Cake** for women's fashions and accessories.

Lining the courtyard next to Kong Lung Co. are several other shops of interest. Follow your nose to **Island Soap and Candle Works** (808/828-1955, www.kauaisoap.com, 9 A.M.– 9 P.M.), where the owners, a husband and wife team, along with their assistants, hand-pour the soap, perfuming the raw bars with coconut, plumeria, ginger, and other tropical scents. They also produce scented coconut oils, lotions, and bath gels capturing the floral essence of the islands, and a wide variety of scented candles. Business has been good, and the company has a second shop in Koloa on the south shore, with others on O'ahu and Maui. Island Soap products are available at boutiques throughout Hawaii and can also be purchased online. Next to Island Soap is **Coconut Style** (808/828-6899), which sells bright and bold hand-painted shirts and sarongs from designs by the owner. A few steps away you'll find exquisite fine art and jewelry at the **Lotus Gallery.** This store, along with its sister shop at the Beach House restaurant in Po'ipu, also sells expensive and finely crafted silk clothing and carpets, many from Asia or designed with Asian themes.

The visitors center **gift shop** at the Kilauea Lighthouse stocks many books relating to

Kauaʻiʻs natural environment, postcards, and gift items that make fine souvenirs of your trip to the refuge.

RECREATION

Sea Breeze from **Anini Fishing Charters** (808/828-1285, kauaifishing@hawaiian.net) with skipper Bob Kutkowski, specializes in sport and bottom fishing and tours up the Na Pali Coast. He and Robert McReynolds of **North Shore Charters** (808/828-1379) both leave from ʻAnini Beach and fish the waters of the north coast. Going with either of these guys is perhaps the best introduction to sportfishing in Kauaʻi.

Anini Beach Windsurfing (808/826-9463) is a one-man operation. The owner will load his truck with windsurfing gear and come to you. Well known on the north shore, Keith will tailor your windsurfing lesson to fit your ability. Rentals for all levels available.

Windsurf Kauai (808/828-6838), owned by Celeste Harvel, specializes in beginner lessons. Three-hour group lessons (six people maximum) are $75 with equipment. Those who already know how can rent sailboards here as well.

On a 400-acre property, two miles into the mountains above the highway, is **Silver Falls Ranch** (808/828-6718, www.silverfallsranch.com), a professional equine organization that treats its horses well, like it does its guests. Three horseback options are offered: a 1.5-hour Hawaiian Discovery Ride at $80 that takes you into the hills below Mount Namahana and two- and three-hour Silver Falls Rides for $100 and $120 that include a stop for lunch and a swim at the pool below a cascade falls. Private rides can be arranged. This is fun for every level of rider, and the rides surround you with wonderful scenery between Kalihiwai and Kamoʻokoa Ridges.

ACCOMMODATIONS
Vacation Rentals

Strung along ʻAnini Beach Road, only steps from the beach, are a series of vacation rentals from small older beach houses to new and modern mansions; several representative properties are listed below.

ʻAnini Beach Hale (808/828-6808 or 877/262-6688, www.yourbeach.com) is a modern two-bedroom, two-bath house, with full kitchen, laundry facilities, and entertainment center. It sleeps four adults and two children. The rates is $1,400 a week, plus tax and a cleaning fee, one week minimum.

For the large family, the 2,000-square-foot **Anini Hale** (808/826-6167, fax 808/826-6067, www.aninihale.com) will fit the bill for up to eight people with its three bedrooms, two baths, complete kitchen, laundry room, large living and dining rooms, and wraparound lanai. The house goes for $1,500 a week for two people, plus $125 for each additional person, tax, and cleaning fee. A smaller one-bedroom cottage in the back, with queen bed and with full amenities, rents for $125 a night or $750 a week for a couple.

Just right for a couple is **Anini Beach Hideaway** (808/828-1051, www.aninibeachhideaway.com), which goes for $875 per week. This breezy cottage with deck is set behind the main house on the property and has one bedroom and a full kitchen.

Hawaii Beachfront Vacation Homes (808/247-3537, www.ihbeach.com) has two well-kept properties at ʻAnini Beach. The smaller and older **Kuʻu Home Oʻwanini** has three bedrooms and three baths and runs $140–170 a night with a five-night minimum. The newer 3,000-square foot **Menehune Hale** has four bedrooms and four baths and can sleep up to a dozen people. It rents for $625 a night with a five-night minimum.

Vacation Rental Agencies

Anini Aloha Properties (808/828-0067 or 800/246-5382, www.aninialoha.com) arranges rentals for numerous upper-end properties along ʻAnini Road, on the cliff overlooking the beach, in Kilauea, and on Kalihiwai Bay.

Handling many vacation rentals from Anahola to Haʻena is **Hanalei North Shore Properties** (808/826-9622 or 800/488-3336, www.rentalsonkauai.com).

Covering pretty much the same ground and offering upscale vacation rentals is **Kauai Vacation Rentals** (808/245-8841 or 800/367-5025, www.kauaivacationrentals.com), which handles many midrange homes in the Anahola to 'Anini Beach area.

Bali Hai Realty (808/826-8000 or 866/400-7368, www.balihai.com), can set you up with an upper-end vacation home in Kilauea, Kalihiwai, or 'Anini.

FOOD
Quick Eats
Look for the kiosk marking **Mango Mama's Cafe** (808/828-1020, 7 A.M.–6 P.M. Mon.–Sat.) at the Hookui Road turnoff along Rt. 56, just as you approach Kilauea from the south. You can't miss it; it's shocking pink with black and white zebra stripes! Mango Mama's is ripe with papayas, bananas, macadamia nuts, fresh juices, smoothies, coffee, honey, and healthful sandwiches, and an assortment of baked goods. Aside from the food, Mango Mama can send you on your way with plenty of information on north shore activities as well.

After visiting all the sights, you need a rest. The perfect stop is just west of town at **Banana Joe's** (808/828-1092, 9 A.M.–6 P.M., until 5 P.M. Sun.) fruit stand, *mauka* of the highway (toward the mountains). Run by Joe Halasey, his wife, and friends, this little yellow stand offers fresh fruit, smoothies and other drinks, baked goods with fruit, and locally produced honey. They have more kinds of fruit than you've ever heard of—try something new. After Banana Joe's and Mango Mama's, what's next in the related-to-a-tropical-fruit department? Sister Soursop and Brother Breadfruit?

Bakery and Pizza
Just behind Kong Lung Co. is **Kilauea Bakery and Pau Hana Pizza** (808/828-2020, 6:30 A.M.–9 P.M. daily, pizza from 11 A.M.). Using all natural ingredients, Kilauea Bakery supplies some of the best restaurants along the north shore. The extensive selection of baked goods is tempting, the breadsticks famous,

and occasionally something a bit offbeat, like pumpkin coconut muffins, is for sale. As with the other shops in this little complex, Kilauea Bakery succeeds in offering something special. The pizzas are made with garlic-infused olive oil, whole-milk mozzarella, and homemade sauce. All are gourmet, topped with sautéed mushrooms, feta cheese, grated Parmesan, homemade pesto, sun-dried tomatoes, locally grown peppers, or the like, priced from $8.65 for a small cheese pizza to $30.25 for a 16-inch large with six toppings. Some are sold by the slice, and specialty pizzas are also available. Enjoy your treat inside, or sit outside under a shade umbrella. Coffee, made by the cup, is served at the espresso bar. Before leaving, have a look at the bulletin board on the wall for alternative healing practitioners, naturopathic doctors, massage therapists, and local jacks and jills of all trades.

Hawaiian Regional
Next door to Kong Lung Co. is **Lighthouse Bistro** (808/828-0480, noon–2 P.M. daily except Sun., nightly 5:30–9 P.M.), the town's fine dining restaurant. Lunch choices include a fish taco, fish burrito, Caesar wrap, burgers, and salads, all in the $7–11 range. Dinners are pricier at $18–27, and entrées include broiled, blackened, or ginger-crusted fresh-catch fish, panko- and coconut-crusted shrimp, baked stuffed pork loin, sautéed chicken breast, and an all-you-can-eat pasta bar. Not overly formal, the bistro does have a full selection of wines to accompany each meal.

Markets
A few steps away is the Kilauea Theater, and beyond that **Kilauea Farmers Market** (808/828-1512, 8 A.M.–8 P.M. daily, until 8:30 P.M. on Fri. and Sat.), a deli/grocery store/lunch counter. The deli carries food items and beverages and makes filling homemade soups, garden salads, and sandwiches. Much of the limited selection of produce is organic, and the market has packaged natural foods and a gourmet section with imported cheeses, fine food items, wines, and microbrews.

At the restored Kilauea Plantation office building, now the Kilauea Plantation Center, is the **Healthy Hut Natural Foods Store** (808/828-6626, 8:30 A.M.–9 P.M.), a tiny shop with plenty of packaged goods and some fresh fruit and veggies tucked into its shelves.

Fish Market

Around back you'll find the **Kilauea Fish Market** (808/828-6244, 11 A.M.–7 P.M. Mon.–Sat.), where you not only can find fresh fish but also fish preparations, party platters, and plate lunches to go.

Farmers Markets

Two farmers markets are held each week in Kilauea. The county-sponsored Sunshine farmers market is Thursday at 4:30 P.M. at the Kilauea Neighborhood Center in the middle of town, and the private Saturday market is held at the Christ Memorial Church 9–11 A.M. Each has the usual collection of organic food and flower stands, but some say the Saturday market is bigger and better.

SERVICES

For medical emergencies while on the north shore, stop in at **Hale Le'a Family Medicine Clinic** (808/828-2885) on Oka Street. Next door is the **North Shore Pharmacy** (808/828-1844), and a few steps away the **North Shore Clinic** (808/828-1418).

The new Kilauea **post office** is located behind the Kilauea Plantation Center on Keneke Road.

Princeville

Princeville is 9,000 acres of planned luxury overlooking Hanalei Bay. This bluff-top plateau was considered by the ancient Hawaiians a place of mana and appropriately was the site of various *heiau*. This highland was also a great source of *hala* leaves because a forest of pandanus grew here, and these leaves were important for many uses to the ancient Hawaiians. When Europeans first surveyed the island, they knew this point could have strategic importance. In the early 1800s, the Russian Fur Trading Company built Fort Alexander on this headland, one of three forts it constructed on Kaua'i to establish and maintain influence over the independent Kaua'ian King Kaumuali'i. This fort served the company only for a few short months before the newcomers were forced to leave the island. It, and a fort erected in Hanalei below, fell into disrepair, and the stones were carted away for other purposes. All that remains are outlines of walls on the grassy lawn to the front of the Princeville Hotel, a great place to watch the sunset. Only the stone walls at Fort Elizabeth in Waimea on the south coast of the island remain to hint at the scope of these Russian fortifications.

In the 1800s, the surrounding countryside was a huge sugar and coffee plantation—one of Kaua'i's oldest, established in 1853 by Scotsman R. C. Wyllie. After an official royal vacation to the ranch by Kamehameha IV and Queen Emma in 1860, the name was changed to Princeville in honor of the royal son, Prince Albert. The young heir unfortunately died within two years, and his heartbroken father soon followed. In 1865, Wyllie also died, and the plantation was sold. While coffee never really did well here, sugar continued to be raised and milled in Hanalei. The operation turned to cattle ranching around 1900, and this lasted until 1969 when the land changed hands again. That year, Consolidated Gas and Oil of Honolulu took these acres and began developing them into a prime vacation community designed to keep the humdrum world far away. Bought by the Princeville Development Corporation, a subsidiary of Quitex Australia, the hotel went through a major renovation and other development began. Then in 1990, the Princeville resort was taken over by the Japanese consortium of Suntory, Mitsui, and Nippon Shinpan. Unfortunately, Hurricane 'Iniki

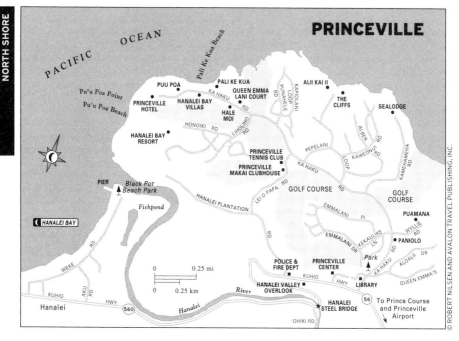

© ROBERT NILSEN AND AVALON TRAVEL PUBLISHING, INC.

struck in 1992, necessitating major repairs to the hotel, condos, homes, and other facilities. The Princeville community now provides everything: accommodations, shopping, dining, a community park, the island's newest public library, golf and tennis facilities, a gas station, banks, and even a fire and police force. Several dozen first-rate condo complexes are scattered around the property, many hundred private luxury homes cluster around the golf links, and the superb multitiered Princeville Hotel perches on the hill over the bay. The guests expect to stay put, except for an occasional day trip. Management and clientele are in league to provide and receive satisfaction. And without even trying, it's just about guaranteed. The community maintains a website at www.princeville.com.

BEACHES

Set on a high headland, Princeville is not known for its beaches. Yet, there are a few fairly isolated sandy spots tucked into the cliff face

that are used for sunning and more often as entry points for surfers. The largest and most easily accessed is **Pu'u Poa Beach,** the beach directly below the Princeville Hotel. Stretching toward the mouth of the Hanalei River, the white sandy bottom here is enclosed by a narrow reef and is decent for swimming and snorkeling when the surf is not high. If you're not coming from the hotel pool area, try the beach access steps that lead down from the guard house at the hotel entrance. There is a small public parking lot here. **Pali Ke Kua Beach** is reached by a steep and sometimes slippery public access path that runs between the Princeville Hotel parking lot and the Puu Poa condo complex. This beach is actually split into two pocket-like sections, separated by a rocky outcrop. To get to the other end of this beach, use the cement path that leads down from Pali Ke Kua condominium. A sign here may say that the beach is for guests only, but all beaches in Hawaii are open to everyone.

Other paths down the cliff lead to the rocky

shoreline and not to sandy beaches. One of these paths leads to **Queen's Bath,** basically a large crescent tidepool gouged out of the lava shelf at water's edge. Where Punahele Road and Kapiʻolani Loop meet, a sign indicates the parking lot and another points the way to the trail. Head down the slippery trail for about 10 minutes, following a small stream that tumbles into a crevasse in the lava shelf at the bottom, then follow the shoreline around to the left another 10–15 minutes or so, to this pool where you can swim right at the edge of the ocean. On calm days you can almost lie with your toes in the pool and hands in the sea; on days of heavy surf, waves crash against the pool's outer edge in white thunder. This trail was closed by the county in spring of 2002 to assess its safety following several injuries but has been reopened following some improvements.

ENTERTAINMENT

There is little in the way of evening entertainment in Princeville; however, the following are definitely worth checking out.

The **Happy Talk Lounge,** with an outrigger canoe suspended from its ceiling, mixes its fantastic views of Hanalei Bay with exotic drinks, wine by the glass, and frothy beers for a night of relaxation and entertainment. A limited menu is served through happy hour and into the evening. The bar swings with live entertainment 6:30–9:30 P.M. Monday–Saturday—everything from contemporary music to Hawaiian ballads performed by slack-key artists. A very special performance that shouldn't be missed is the free jazz jam every Sunday 3–7 P.M. Local musical talent is fantastic, but to make things even better, top-name musicians who happen to be on the island are frequently invited to join in. If you love jazz, you can't find a more stunning venue than the Happy Talk.

The **Living Room,** in the main lobby of the Princeville Hotel, is a dignified venue of couches and stuffed chairs for a variety of island-theme entertainment that's open to everyone. Besides that, there are spectacular views from the glass wall that overlooks Hanalei Bay. Music is performed 7–11 P.M. nightly. Preceding that, from 6:30 P.M. on Tuesday, Thursday, and Sunday, there is a special Hawaiian ceremony of chanting and hula. In keeping with the grand setting, a formal afternoon tea (reservations required) is served 3–5 P.M., *pu pu* and desserts are available 3:30–10 P.M., the sushi bar opens 5:30–9:30 P.M., and cocktails can be ordered until midnight. This is the center of convivial evening activity at the hotel.

Don't forget **The Landing Pad** (808/826-9561, from 8 P.M. Wed.–Sun.) upstairs at the Princeville Airport, with different styles of music (live or DJ) and dance each evening. This friendly neighborhood-style pub serves bar food along with its drinks.

Luʻau

Paʻina ʻO Hanalei beachside luʻau (808/826-2788), performed Monday and Thursday at 6 P.M. near the swimming pool at the Princeville Hotel, is the only luʻau in this resort community. An entertaining tourist-oriented affair, the food is great and the island music and dance performances are rousing. Adult tickets are $69, seniors $58, and children 6–12 $35.

SHOPPING

Aside from the shops at the hotels, the shopping in Princeville is clustered in the **Princeville Shopping Center,** with most shops open daily 8 A.M.–6 P.M. Since Princeville is a self-contained community, many of these are practical shops: bank, hardware store, gas station, real estate offices, post office, and restaurants. **Foodland** (808/826-9880, 6 A.M.–11 P.M.) is important because it offers the cheapest groceries on the north shore and has a large bakery and deli section. Some of the shops here include **Lappert's Ice Cream** (808/826-7393), for a quick pick-me-up and **J Ms Jewels** (808/826-6920), for a quick pick-*her*-up. **Magic Dragon Toy and Art Supply** (808/826-9144) has one-of-a-kind items to fascinate the kids and keep them occupied, while mama shops at **Last Mango in Paradise** (808/826-0077) for island-style clothing. Or everyone can head to **SanDudes Kauai** (808/826-7300), a clothing boutique for men and women with sandals, sun hats, waterproof watches, perfume, ladies' dresses, jewelry, T-shirts, and beach bags.

RECREATION

Those addicted to striking hard, dimpled white balls or fuzzy soft yellow ones have come to the right spot. In Princeville, golf and tennis are the royal couple. However, they are not the only sporting options available. Horseback riding and hiking are becoming popular, and for those less inclined to the physical, a helicopter ride is better suited. To help keep yourself in condition or to ease your tired muscles after a hard day of exercise, pay a visit to the health spa.

Golf

The **Princeville Makai Golf Course** (808/826-5070), offers 27 holes of magnificent golf designed by Robert Trent Jones Jr. in 1971. This course, rated one of the top 25 golf courses in America for 2004-2005 by *Golf Magazine,* has hosted the 26th annual World Cup in 1978, the LPGA Women's Kemper Open 1986–1989, and the 1990 first Itoman LPGA World Match Play Championship. Radiating from the central clubhouse are three nine-hole, par-36 courses you can use in any combination. They include the Woods, Lake, and Ocean courses—the names highlighting the special focus of each. The cliff-top Ocean 7 is a challenging hole (you must shoot over a deep ravine), and the Lake 9 sets two lakes in your way, but the most difficult hole is Woods 6, which features a long dogleg into the trade winds. The pro shop will set you up with a tee time, and the snack shop offers reasonably priced sandwiches, burgers, and drinks. Greens fees are $125 ($110 for resort guests), with many discounts and packages available.

Opened in 1987, the 18-hole **Prince Course** (808/826-5070), on the bluff above 'Anini Beach, also welcomes the public. It's off Hwy. 56 about one mile east of the Princeville Resort entrance and has its own clubhouse. For this course, accuracy and control are much more important than power and distance. Many expert golfers judge the Prince extremely difficult. With a course rating of 75.3 and slope of 145, it's one of the most challenging in Hawaii and is continually rated one of the top courses in the country. In 2004, *Golf Digest* rated the Prince Course #1 in Hawaii. Greens fees are $175 ($150 for resort guests). Fitting into its natural environment, thick tropical woods, deep ravines, and streams are among the obstacles. The driving range is open during daylight hours. The clubhouse has an extensive pro shop and houses the Princeville Health Club and Spa and, on the lower level, the Princeville Restaurant and Bar.

Health Club and Spa

The **Princeville Health Club and Spa** (808/826-5030, 6:30 A.M.–8 P.M. Mon.–Fri., 8 A.M.–8 P.M. Sat., and 8 A.M.–6 P.M. Sun.) at the Prince Course clubhouse, keeps you healthy with a full schedule of fitness classes, free weights, a complete set of conditioning machines, a lap pool, hot tub, steam room, sauna, massage by appointment, and skin and body treatments. Nutrition programs can be set up with the staff, who also have information about running courses. One such **jogging path** runs between this clubhouse and the Princeville main entrance gate—about one mile. To enhance these offerings spectacular views out the plate glass windows look toward waterfall-draped mountains and over the rolling fairways to the Pacific Ocean. There's nothing like fabulous surroundings to add incentive to your aerobic exercise. The daily admission fee for use of the facilities is $20; weekly and monthly rates are also available.

Tennis

You can charge the net on six professional plexipave tennis courts at the **Princeville Tennis Club** (808/826-1236, 8:30 A.M.–6 P.M. daily) just down the rise from the Makai Golf Course clubhouse. The club offers a pro shop, private lessons by appointment, and racket and ball machine rental. Court fees for a 90-minute reserved time are $18 ($12 for Princeville guests); weekly, monthly, quarterly, and annual memberships also available.

The **Hanalei Bay Resort Tennis Club** (808/826-6522, 8 A.M.–noon and 3–6 P.M. Mon.–Sat., 2–6 P.M. Sun.) has eight courts open to the public; court fee is $6 per person. Men's and women's clinics and round robins are scheduled, and equipment is rented. Call to reserve court time. Several condos in Princeville also have tennis courts for guests only.

Princeville Ranch Activities

Princeville Ranch Stables (808/826-6777, www.princevilleranch.com), a half mile east of Princeville Shopping Center and on the uphill side of the highway, is open Monday–Saturday. You can rent a mount here for group rides that take you throughout the ranch's fascinating countryside. Prices are $65, $110, and $120 for the scenic ocean bluff ride, waterfall picnic ride, and participatory "cattle drive ride." Private rides can also be arranged. Riders must be at least eight years old and weigh no more than 230 pounds; all riders must wear closed-toe shoes, and long pants are preferable.

Princeville Ranch Adventures (808/826-7669, www.adventureskauai.com) offers day hikes, kayaking, and zipline tours on Princeville Ranch property. The hiking office is located across the highway from the stable office. Hikes include a waterfall hiking excursion for $79, a combination hike and kayak trip for $94, and an eight-section zipline experience ending in a jungle pool swim for $115. All tours run about four hours; drinking water, picnic lunch, and all equipment are provided. No hikes on Sunday.

Hiking Trail

The only public hiking trail of length in the Princeville area is the 13-mile-long **Powerline Trail,** which runs across the hump of the island to the Keahua Arboretum above Wailua. Longer, more gradual, and overall less spectacular than the south side, this route gives you plenty of mountain views with only a peek here and there into the Hanalei Valley. Hot and dry, there is virtually no shade, yet the trail passes two small bogs on the way. Near the pass, masterful views take in the Hanalei region and the core of the island's central mass, plus you have a view of both the north and south shores. Unless you have a car waiting at the arboretum, just hike up as far as you like—or the weather permits—and return to the north trailhead. About two hours from the trailhead, the pass is a good place to turn around. To reach the north-end trailhead, turn at the Princeville Stables. Continue uphill about two miles until the pavement gives out. Proceed a bit farther until you reach an area to park near a green water tank. This trail is sometimes used by mountain bikers. As there are sections that are virtually impassable, 4WD vehicles are not recommended.

Helicopter Tours

The only helicopter company currently operating at the Princeville Airport is **Heli USA** (808/826-6591 or 866/936-1234, www.heliusahawaii.com). Flying A-Star machines, the company offers five different 35-, 45- and 60-minute flights for $109–199, one of which is a sunset flight.

ACCOMMODATIONS

All hotel rooms and virtually all condos in Princeville fall into the luxury category. The best deals naturally occur off-season (fall), especially if you plan on staying a week or more. Oddly enough, a project like Princeville should make booking one of its many condos an easy matter, but it's sadly lacking on this point. Lack of a centralized organization handling reservations causes the confusion. Each condo building can have half a dozen booking agents, all with different phone numbers and differing rates. The units are privately owned, and the owners simply choose one agency or another. If you're going through a travel agent at home, be aware of these discrepancies and insist on the least-expensive rates. A situation that reduces the number of units available is that many of the condos are moving to exclusively timeshare programs, while others still offer rental units along with the time-share units, so check out the possibilities.

Above $250

The ◖ **Princeville Hotel** (5520 Ka Haku Rd., 808/826-9644 or 800/325-3589, fax 808/826-1166, www.starwood.com/princeville), is a dramatic architectural opus, built in four cascading tiers on the extreme point of this rugged peninsula. From its perch, all but 16 of the 252 rooms offer breathtaking views of the frothing azure of Hanalei Bay as it stretches toward the emerald green of Mount Makana (Bali Hai) down the coast. The other rooms offer panoramic views of Pu'u Poa Marsh, a wildlife wetlands that offers sanctuary to exotic birdlife. This is one of Kaua'i's most opulent hotels, and the only hotel on the north shore. The main lobby offers elegance on a grand scale, with gold-capped Egyptianesque columns, teardrop chandeliers, and a central reflecting pool set in a floor of swirled black and white marble that's studded with Louis XIV chairs and plush couches. Here you'll find the concierge and activities desks. Opposite the front desk is the Living Room, a dignified area serving as library, cocktail lounge, and music room. Choose a plush chair just before sunset and sip a cocktail as the sun streaks the sky with lasers of light dancing across the endless blue of the wide Pacific. There is entertainment every night: Hawaiian and contemporary music, and weekly sonorous Hawaiian chanting with hula. In addition, an artisans' program with demonstrations of Hawaiian arts and crafts is held daily in the lobby. This lobby level has a small mini-mall with a cluster of shops, and the grand staircase at the far end leads one floor down to the hotel's two fine dining restaurants.

The hotel entrance is on level nine. Taking elevators and walkways to level one deposits you at the swimming pool and poolside Beach Restaurant and Bar, next to which the twice-weekly lu'au is performed. A few steps away is the beach and its activity center. The white-sand beach fronting the hotel is perfect for swimming, and the reef below, alive with tropical fish, is excellent for snorkeling. At dusk, descend to the pool area and immerse yourself in one of the hot tubs to watch the sun melt into the Pacific as you melt into the foaming bubbles. Summer and winter Keiki Aloha children's programs will look after kids with entertaining excursions and arts and crafts. A free drop-off and pick-up shuttle service is offered anywhere in the Princeville resort area, including the Prince Golf Course clubhouse and the airport. Request a shuttle ride from the bell desk—be sure to ask for the telephone number to call for a return ride. No matter how formal the surroundings may seem, the staff infuse this property with the casual and genuine spirit of Hawaiian *aloha*.

All rooms feature bathrooms with double vanities, terry robes, slippers, and deep immersion tubs, some of which are mini-spas. Bathroom windows are of liquid crystal that can be controlled to change from opaque for privacy to clear so you can enjoy the view while you soak. These finely decorated rooms in beige or green also feature king beds, remote-control color TVs, safes, ironing boards, and 24-hour room service; suites have an extra large and plush sitting area. All rooms feature in-room aromatherapy, where a distinctive smell of the island will lightly permeate the room and its memory will travel with you when your stay is done. A mountain/garden view room runs $465, partial oceanview and oceanview rooms $595–695, and junior suites are $820; other suites run $2,000–5,000. There is a $75 extra person charge, with a maximum of four to a room. Children under 18 room free in existing beds. Numerous packages are available.

Managed by ResortQuest Hawaii, the ◖ **Hanalei Bay Resort** (5380 Honoiki Rd., 808/826-6522 or 877/997-6667, fax 808/826-6680, www.hanaleibayresort.com) is a condo resort with some private units. You enter through a spacious open foyer paved with flagstone and face the front desk. To the side is the Happy Talk lounge, done in longhouse style with a palm-frond roof, koa long bar, and magnificent matching koa canoe. From the bar, you have a spectacular panorama of distant Bali Hai dappled by passing clouds and Hanalei Bay, a sheet of foam-fringed azure. Evening brings live music, with everything from jazz to a local slack-key combo. Just as good for views of the bay and the waterfalls on the mountains is the Bali Hai Restaurant. Stepping down the hillside from the front is the resort's free-form pool, complete with one sand edge, a 15-foot waterfall, and whirlpool grotto—all surrounded by landscaping inspired by the area's natural beauty. The cobalt blue tile of the second pool matches the color of the bay beyond. For a swim in the bay, take the beach path down the hill to the water. The resort's 16 buildings are situated along walking paths, and all units have a stupendous view. There is no driving on the property, so you must leave your car in the parking lot at the front and you and your luggage will be shuttled to your unit. The resort has amenities including TV, phone, and air-conditioning, full kitchens in the suites (only refrigerators in the few hotel rooms), and laundry facilities. Daily cultural activities are scheduled. Sign up for these at the concierge desk, where other island activities can also be booked. The eight tennis courts here are open to all, and the pro shop arranges clinics and round robins. Single hotel rooms, studios with kitchenettes, and one-bedroom suites with mountain or ocean view are available; rates start at $185 for a room, run $215–240 for the studios, and $350–390 per night for the suites. A made-to-order breakfast and two afternoon cocktails daily are complimentary with each suite.

Condos

There are nearly two dozen condominium properties in Princeville. Most of the high-end condos are far into the development near the Princeville Hotel or strung along the cliff edge overlooking the pounding surf. They are out to please and don't skimp on the luxuries. About a third are managed strictly as time-share properties, and several others have blocks of units that are also managed that way. Even in this luxury development there are a few median-range complexes. Although low-end properties and subsidized housing were supposed to be incorporated into this development, it seems all of those have been shifted

down the road. What follows is a sampling of what's available.

Marc Resorts Hawaii (5300 Ka Haku Rd., 808/826-9066 or 800/535-0085, www.marc-resorts.com) manages units in three properties closest to the Princeville Hotel. Sleek and modernistic, with its curved exterior and step-terrace construction, **Puu Poa** is perhaps the most luxurious. It has spacious two-bedroom, two-bath units with complete kitchens that run $500 for up to six people, and guest-use tennis courts and a swimming pool. Next along the cliff is **Pali Ke Kua,** which boasts one of the best restaurants on the north coast. This property is a mix of one- and two-bedroom, garden view, oceanview, and oceanfront units, priced $270–450. Comfortable and well furnished, each unit has cable TV, washer and dryer, and a full kitchen—just right for families. Swim in the pool topside or walk the path down to the gazebo and secluded beach to sunbathe. Across the road, overlooking the golf course, are the more economical **Hale Moi** cottages—four-plexes with pleasing mountain views. Suites and one-bedroom units here are $220–250; all have kitchens. All Marc Resort guests check in at the Pali Ke Kua office. There is a two-night minimum for each of these properties.

Set high on the bluff overlooking the Pacific Ocean is **The Cliffs at Princeville** (808/826-6219 or 800/367-8024). These one-bedroom condo units have two full-size baths, a fully equipped kitchen, and a large living room. Two large lanai, one at each end of the unit, offer both ocean and mountain views. Although all units are individually owned, furnishings are basically of a contemporary style. Some third-floor units have a loft, and the living-room ceiling slants up to the second floor. While this is largely a time-share property, units are rented when available. One-bedroom units are $200–225, with lofts $230–250; there's a two-night minimum. The property also has a pool with spa, putting green, volleyball court, four tennis courts free to guests, a breezy recreation room with TV and reading material, and a laundry room. The activity desk will gladly arrange tours for you, offer suggestions for day trips, or rent you a bicycle. Like The Cliffs, the **Alii Kai** is also poised on the edge of the cliff. Its units are generally a bit more affordable. For units in either complex, contact Oceanfront Realty (808/826-6585 or 800/222-5541, www.oceanfrontrealty.com) about rooms.

The older and weathered gray Cape Cod–style **Sealodge** condos have one of the best locations for views along this coast, but the units are smaller. All individually owned, these units all have full amenities, and most have washers and dryers. Although rates vary a little, expect to pay about $145 for a one-bedroom or $165 for a two-bedroom unit with a $60–80 cleaning charge; there may be a three-night minimum stay, and discounted weekly rates are available. Most of the units here are managed by Jack Waring, 800/446-4384; Herb Hubbard, 800/585-6101; and Carol Goodwin, 650/573-0636.

The **Paniolo, Paliuli, Mauna Kai,** and **Puamana** are lower-end complexes for this development, where you would expect a better deal. None is along the cliff edge nor has particularly good ocean views, but each has a landscaped courtyard. Of these, you might have larger rooms at the Puamana. Check for room availability with the vacation rental agencies below.

Vacation Rentals

Handling vacation rentals principally in Princeville is **Re/Max,** at the Princeville Shopping Center, 808/826-9675 or 877/838-8149, www.real-estate-kauai.com). Most of these properties are high-end condos and homes that rent for $800–2,700 a week.

Also dealing exclusively with high-end condo and home properties in Princeville is **Pacific Paradise Properties** (808/826-6530 or 800/800-3637, www.princeville-vacations.com).

Hanalei North Shore Properties (808/826-9622 or 800/488-3336, www.rentalsonkauai.com) handles over 50 economy to high-end vacation rental homes and condos in Princeville and along the north shore from its office at the Princeville Shopping Center. This

company can find the right place for you as it has done for many years.

Also try **Hanalei Vacations** (808/826-7288 or 800/487-9833, www.hanalei-vacations.com), which manages a full range of condos in Princeville and homes and cottages in Hanalei and Ha'ena.

FOOD
American

For light meals, try the Princeville Hotel's casual, pavilion-type **The Beach Restaurant and Bar** (11 A.M.–5:30 P.M.), where you can order snacks, salads, or sandwiches, or swim up to the pool's water bar until sunset for a mid-lap mai tai. Try the crispy taco salad with black beans and vegetables, spicy buffalo wings, Black Angus burger, or fresh island fish sandwich, all priced $7.95–14.95. A children's menu helps keep prices down for the little ones. On Monday and Thursday from 6 P.M., the courtyard and accompanying stage area are transformed into the Pa'ina 'O Hanalei lu'au and Polynesian show.

The **Princeville Restaurant and Bar** (808/826-5050) serves breakfast 8–11 A.M., lunch 11 A.M.–3 P.M., and cocktails 11 A.M.–6 P.M. at the Prince Golf Course clubhouse. The breakfast menu includes the usuals, like eggs, waffles, omelettes, and fruit plates. Salads, sandwiches (with names like Birdie, Double Eagle, and Bogey), and a limited number of entrées are served for lunch. In addition, the Monday night Japanese sushi bar, the only evening meal served here, is as popular as ever. This is a perfect spot in well-appointed surroundings for a day on the links.

Fine Dining

Fine dining in Princeville means eating at the resort restaurants. The **◖ Bali Hai Restaurant** (808/826-6522) at the Hanalei Bay Resort enjoys an excellent reputation not only for its food but also for its superb atmosphere and prize-winning view of the sunset through the wraparound windows of this bi-level and informal yet elegant restaurant. It's appropriately named; you look out between tall coconut trees, across the spectacular view of Hanalei Bay, and down the coast toward Bali Hai (Mount Makana), the sentinel of the north coast. Reminiscent of a Polynesian longhouse, with a vaulted thatched roof, it's open daily for breakfast, lunch, and dinner. The Bali Hai chefs grow their own herbs on the premises and insist on fresh local vegetables, meat, and fish prepared in a mixture of continental and Pacific Rim cuisine. Start your day with chilled fresh fruit, muffins or bread from the hotel bakery, or a light continental breakfast, or go local with a taro patch breakfast of two fried eggs, Portuguese sausage, poi pancakes, and taro hash browns. Lunchtime brings soups and salads, sandwiches, and an assortment of fish and pasta entrées. For dinner, you can start with appetizers like blackened 'ahi or Bali Hai crab cakes. Entrée specialties include fresh island fish prepared with a variety of tempting sauces such as papaya ginger beurre blanc or green coconut milk with sweet chili and peanut sate sauce. Standard but wonderful offerings are pesto linguine with grilled breast of chicken, sautéed tiger shrimp and scallops, and steak Olowalu, all in the $21–33 range. For lighter fare, try the resort's breezy Happy Talk lounge, which serves pu pu 2:30–9 P.M.

The Princeville Hotel is home to three restaurants. The **Cafe Hanalei** (6:30 A.M.–2:30 P.M., 5:30–9:30 P.M.) offers indoor or outdoor seating in a casual setting for all three meals a day. It's continental with a heavy dose of Oriental. Breakfast at Cafe Hanalei is either continental for $18.50 or full buffet for $25.95; à la carte and Japanese breakfasts are also available. The continental breakfast is much more than you might expect, and the full breakfast buffet is complete with an omelette station and an array of savory breakfast meats. On Sunday, breakfast stops early and gives way to Sunday brunch 10 A.M.–2 P.M. for $42 or $46 with champagne. Lunch may be a reasonably priced Japanese noodle salad with fish cake, Thai coconut curry with chicken and vegetables, Caesar salad, or any of a number of gourmet sandwiches, wraps, or seafood dishes. Dinner entrées include Hawaiian salt–rubbed

steak, Kaua'i coffee rack of lamb, lemon-crusted *ahi,* Thai-style salmon roll, or stuffed mochiko chicken, mostly in the $24–34 range. Finish with desserts like *liliko'i* (passion fruit) cheesecake, crème brûlée, or chocolate torte with minted truffle cream, all delicious and prepared daily. On Friday evening, a full seafood buffet is offered for $50. The food at Cafe Hanalei is a delight.

Also down a flight of steps from the main lobby, **(La Cascata** (6–9:30 P.M.) offers tremendous views of the island's inland waterfalls and the setting sun. Open nightly for dinner only, this is the hotel's most formal and upscale restaurant, the finest on the north shore and one of the premier dining experiences on the island. Designed after a famous restaurant in Positano, Italy, it features elegant decor, including hand-painted terra cotta floors, columns and arches, inspiring trompe l'oeil scenery murals, and formally set tables. After antipasti and insalata, the Italian menu features such items as fish, shrimp, scallops, and clams over linguine pasta, pan-roasted duck breast, herb-roasted breast of chicken, penne pomodoro, and fennel coriander roasted rack of lamb. Special attention is paid to the sauces, and a fine glass or bottle of wine from the well-stocked cellar can be chosen to accompany any entrée. Meals are perfectly finished with desserts like classic tiramisu, mango cheesecake, and macadamia nut pie, or with a cup of espresso or cappuccino, or a glass of fine port. A dinner for two with wine can easily run $150.

Sabella's at Princeville (808/826-6225, 5:30–10:30 P.M. Tues.–Sun.), on the grounds of the Pali Ke Kua condo complex, is a casual fine dining restaurant where the chef offers a fine selection of Italian dishes with heavy emphasis on seafood. Sabella's has four generations of restaurateurs serving the best of seafood to back its reputation, and it gets good reviews from guests and residents alike. While the menu changes periodically, you might expect to find starters like calamari fritti, pan-seared scallops, *ahi* tartare, and cherry wood–smoked mussels; salads include a Kaua'i goat cheese, tomato, and Maui onion creation and a shrimp and artichoke salad. Entrées might be prawns piccata, chicken or eggplant parmesan, apple brandy lobster, crab- and bacon-stuffed *ono,* and herb-crusted rack of lamb. A variety of pasta dishes are also fine choices. Most entrées run $24–32, with pastas at $17–24. Your sweet tooth will be happy, too, as the dessert menu has great depth. Sabella's also has a full-service bar stocked with fine wine, a good selection of beer, and house specialty tropical drinks. Reservations are suggested as this bi-level restaurant is small and the tables tend to fill up quickly. Even though the restaurant has no stunning scenic views, the setting can be romantic and live music adds to the charm.

Princeville Shopping Center

At the Princeville Shopping Center you'll find two restaurants that serve American standard food, with, as usual, a Hawaiian twist. **CJ's Steak and Seafood** (808/826-6211, 11:30 A.M.–2 P.M. Mon.–Fri., 6–9:30 P.M. nightly) has a very loyal clientele that comes not only for prime rib and juicy corn-fed Angus beef but for the fresh fish as well. With an open-beamed ceiling, a choice of booth or table inside or on the lanai, and a few saddles and barrels placed here and there for effect, you might call CJ's "casual country." The lunch menu has salads and *pu pu* such as "loaded fries," which are covered with bacon, cheese, and sour cream, and Caesar salad. Burgers and sandwiches go from a simple burger to a barbecue prime rib sandwich. Dinner is delicious, with the fresh catch broiled, sautéed, baked, or Cajun, shrimp Hanalei, juicy prime rib, barbecued baby-back pork ribs, and teriyaki chicken breast. Most entrées run $20–27, and an assortment of combination dinners are priced $28 and up. A senior and children's menu relieves the bottom-line total. Chuck's has a full-service bar separate from the dining area that's open until

10:30 P.M. CJ's is a good choice for a family-style restaurant offering hearty portions, but it's not inexpensive.

Also at the Princeville Shopping Center, you can get a reasonably inexpensive brew and burger, or something more sophisticated like garlic shrimp, rib eye steak, fish salad, and crab legs, at the **Paradise Bar and Grill** (808/826-1775). Having the same menu for lunch and dinner means that an evening meal here is quite affordable. This is a friendly and easygoing place that locals frequent and send guests to.

Need something fast or on the go? Head to the bakery and deli section of **Foodland** where you can fill up a picnic basket with tasty savory and sweet treats.

SERVICES

Mail Service Center (808/826-7331, Mon.–Fri. 9 A.M.–5:30 P.M.) off the courtyard near the back of the Princeville Shopping Center has postal, shipping, and packaging supplies. It also offers business services, copy machines, and Internet access at $3 for 15 minutes.

The pleasing **Princeville Library** is located in a separate building at the Princeville Shopping Center entrance (open 10 A.M.–5 P.M. Tues. and Thurs.–Sat., 1–8 P.M. Wed.; closed Sun. and Mon.. Its elegant design with arched ceiling and chandelier fits well in this resort community.

Both **Bank of Hawaii** and **First Hawaiian Bank** have branch offices with ATM machines at the Princeville Shopping Center.

The last **gas station** on the north shore is Princeville Chevron, open 6 A.M.–10 P.M. Mon.–Sat., until 9 P.M. Sun.. If your gauge is low, make sure to fill up if you're driving either direction along the coast.

Avis (808/826-9773) maintains a small rental car booth at the Princeville Airport that's open 7:30 A.M.–4 P.M. daily.

Hanalei

If Puff the Magic Dragon had resided in the sunshine of Hanalei instead of the mists of Hanalee, Little Jackie Paper would still be hangin' around. You know you're entering a magic land the minute you drop down from the heights and cross the Hanalei River. The narrow, one-lane bridge is like a gateway to the enchanted coast, forcing you to slow down and take stock of where you are.

Hanalei (Crescent Bay) compacts a lot into a little space. You're in and out of the town in two blinks, but you'll find plenty of shops, some terrific restaurants, the beach, ocean activities, and historical sites. You also get two superlatives for the price of one: the epitome of a laid-back north shore village and a truly magnificent bay. In fact, if one were forced to choose the most beautiful bay in all of Hawaii, Hanalei would definitely be among the finalists.

Mile markers on Hwy. 56 going west are renumbered from one at Princeville. It is 10 miles from there to the end of the road at Ke'e Beach. On occasion, during periods of heavy rain when water threatens to swallow the bridge, it will be closed to traffic and the road blocked by gates. That means no cars in or out until the water recedes!

SIGHTS
◖ Hanalei Valley

The sights around Hanalei are exactly that—beautiful sweeping vistas of Hanalei Valley and the sea, especially at sunset. People come just for the light show and are never disappointed. When you proceed past the Princeville turnoff, keep your eyes peeled for the Hanalei Valley **scenic overlook.** Don't miss it! Drifting into the distance is the pastel living impressionism of Hanalei Valley, most dramatic in late afternoon, when soft shadows from deeply slanting sun rays create depth in this quilt of fields. Down the center, the liquid silver Hanalei River flows until it meets the sea, where the valley broadens into a wide

flat fan. Along its banks, impossible shades of green vibrate as the valley steps back for almost nine miles, all cradled in the protective arms of 3,500-foot *pali*. Controlled by rains, waterfalls either tumble over the *pali* like lace curtains billowing in a gentle wind or with the blasting power of a fire hose. Local wisdom says, "When you can count 17 waterfalls, it's time to get out of Hanalei." The valley has always been one of the most accommodating places to live in all of Hawaii, and its abundance was ever blessed by the old gods. Madame Pele even sent a thunderbolt to split a boulder so that the Hawaiians could run an irrigation ditch through its center to their fields.

Unlike the Princeville bluff, Hanalei was an area for the common man. In the old days, Hanalei produced taro, and deep in the valley the outlines of the ancient fields can still be discerned. The bay produced great quantities of fish, and others were raised in ponds, one of which still remains between the town and a twist in the river. Then the white people came and planted coffee that failed and sugarcane that petered out and finally raised cattle that over-grazed the land. During these times, Hanalei had to *import* poi from the Kalalau Valley to the west. From the early days, Hanalei Bay was a commercial harbor for trading and whaling. From here, produce of all sorts was sent near and far. Even oranges from Na Pali farms were shipped from here around the time of the California gold rush. Later, when Chinese plantation laborers moved in, the valley was terraced again, but this time the wet fields were given to rice. This crop proved profitable for many years and was still grown as late as the 1930s. Then, amazingly, the valley began to slowly revert back to taro patches.

In 1972, 917 acres of the Hanalei Valley were designated **Hanalei National Wildlife Refuge;** the endangered native water birds Hawaiian coot, black-necked stilt, *koloa* duck, and gallinule, as well as several migrant species, loved it and reclaimed their ancient nesting grounds. Today, the large, green, heart-shaped leaves of taro carpet the valley, and the abundant crop supplies about half of Hawaii's poi. You can go into Hanalei Valley; however, you're not permitted in the designated wildlife areas except to fish or hike along the river. Never disturb any nesting birds. Look below to where the one-lane bridge crosses the river. Just there, 'Ohiki Road branches inland. Drive along it slowly to view the simple and quiet homesteads, the historic Haraguchi Rice Mill, nesting birds, wildflowers, and terraced fields of this enchanted land.

In addition, and more recently, the **Hanalei River** itself has been designated an American heritage river, one of only 14 in the nation, and the only one whose total length is so designated. Federal money will help protect its unique character and enhance its preservation.

📘 Wai'oli Mission House Museum

As you leave town, look to your left to see the deep green clapboard and shingle **Wai'oli Hui'ia Church.** If you're in Hanalei on Sunday, do yourself a favor and go to the 10 A.M. service; you will be uplifted by a choir of rich voices singing enchanting hymns in Hawaiian. Justice is done to the word *wai'oli,* which means "joyful water." Although the congregation was established in 1834, the church was built in 1912 on land given to the congregation by the governor of Kaua'i. American Gothic in style, it looks as if it could have been plunked down here from some sleepy New England community—except, perhaps, for the steeple's typically Hawaiian double pitch hip roof. Inside, pay attention to the stained glass windows that mimic the rich colors of the surrounding sea, land, and sky, and appreciate the delicate but sturdy open-beam supports upholding the roof. This church was part of a mission station that also included a home for the preacher, a school for Hawaiian boys, and accommodations for the teacher.

Set behind the church, the **Wai'oli Mission**

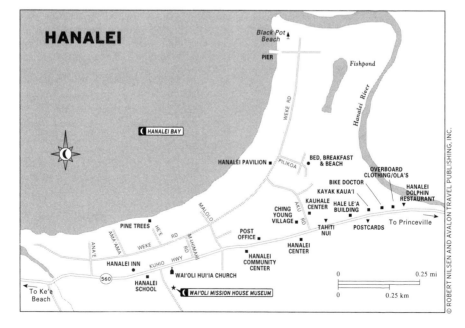

HANALEI

© ROBERT NILSEN AND AVALON TRAVEL PUBLISHING, INC.

House was the teacher's house. You know you're in for a treat as soon as you pull into the parking lot, which is completely surrounded by trees, creeping vines, ferns, and even papaya. Head through the gate and over the lush lawn to see the jagged mountains framing a classical American homestead; the acreage was also a self-sufficient farm where the resident teacher and family raised chickens and cattle. Most mission homes are New England–style, and inside this one is, too. But outside, it seems somehow different. It was built in 1836 by Rev. William P. Alexander, who arrived with his wife, Mary Ann, two years previously by double-hulled canoe from Waimea. The home's second occupants moved in in 1837, and in 1846, Abner and Lucy Wilcox arrived and took up residence. They lived here until 1865, the year they both passed away on a trip to New England. This home became synonymous with the Wilcox family. Indeed, it was owned and occupied by the family until very recently. It was George, the son of Abner and Lucy, who founded Grove Farm on the south side in Lihu'e. His niece, Mabel, created the nonprofit organization that operates both the Wai'oli Mission House and the Grove Farm Homestead.

You enter the parlor, where Lucy Wilcox taught native girls who'd never seen a needle and thread to sew. In the background, an old clock ticks. Paintings of the Wilcoxes line the walls, and Abner's books line the shelves. Abner, in addition to being a missionary, was a doctor, teacher, public official, and veterinarian. His preserved letters show that he was a very serious man, not given to humor. He and Lucy didn't want to come to Wai'oli at first, but they learned to love the place. He worried about his sons and about being poor. He even wrote letters to the king urging that Hawaiian be retained as the first language, with English as the second.

During the time that this was a mission household, eight boys were raised here—four born in the main bedroom. Behind it is a nursery, the only room that has had a major change; a closet was built and an indoor bath-

Wai'oli Hui'ia Church

ROBERT NILSEN

room installed there in 1921. Upstairs is a guest bedroom the Wilcoxes dubbed the "room of the traveling prophet" because it was invariably occupied by visiting missionaries. It was also used by Abner Wilcox as a study, and the books in the room are the original primers printed on O'ahu.

The house has been added to several times and is surprisingly spacious. Around the home are artifacts, dishes, knickknacks, and a butter churn from the 1800s. Lucy Wilcox churned butter, which she shipped to Honolulu in buckets and which brought in some good money. The furniture is mostly donated period pieces; only a few were actually used by the Wilcoxes. From an upstairs window, the view has remained unchanged from the last century: Hanalei Bay, beautifully serene and timeless, with the dripping rampart of green mountains behind. The Wai'oli Mission House (808/245-3202) is open 9 A.M.–3 P.M. Tuesday, Thursday, and Saturday for guided tours, and admission is free! At the end of the tour, there is a container for donations; please be generous.

(Hanalei Bay

Since the days of the migrating Polynesians, Hanalei Bay has been known as one of the Pacific's most perfect anchorages. Used as one of Kaua'i's three main ports until very recently, it's still an occasional port of call for world-class yachts. They start arriving in mid-May, making the most of the easy entrance and sandy bottom, and stay throughout the summer. They leave by October, when even this inviting bay becomes rough, with occasional 30-foot waves. The Hanalei Pier was constructed in 1912 to transport rice from this fertile valley but was discontinued as a commercial port of call with the decline of that commodity. It has, however, continued to serve boaters and is still a favorite of fishermen. When you drive to the bay, the section under the trees between the pier and the river is called **Black Pot.** It received this name during an earlier time, when the people of Hanalei would greet the yachties with island *aloha,* which, of course, included food. A fire was always going with a large black pot hanging over it, into which everyone contributed and then shared in the meal. Across the road and upriver a few hundred yards is **Hanalei Canoe Club.** This small local club has produced a number of winning canoe teams in statewide competitions, oftentimes going up against much larger clubs.

The sweeping crescent bay is gorgeous—nearly two miles of narrow beach that sweeps out gently to a sandy bottom. The Hanalei River and three smaller streams empty into it, and all around it's protected by embracing mountains. A long pier slices into it, and two reefs front the bay: Queen to the left and King to the right. The bay provides excellent sailing, surfing, and swimming—mostly in the summer when the water can be as smooth as a lake. The swimming is good near the river and at the west end, but rip currents can appear anywhere, even around the pier area, so be careful. The best surf rolls in at the outside reef below Pu'u Poa Point on the east side of the bay, but it's definitely recommended only for expert surfers who often come to catch the bigger waves of winter. Beginners should try the middle of the bay during summer, when the surf is smaller and gentler.

ROBERT NILSEN

Hanalei Pier

The county maintains three parks on the bay: **Black Pot,** at the Hanalei River mouth, **Hanalei Pavilion,** in the middle of the bay, and **Pine Trees,** farther on. All three have picnic areas, grills, restrooms, and showers, although these amenities are sometimes vandalized and unusable, and Hanalei Pavilion and Pine Trees have lifeguards. You'll find beach access and parking for Pine Trees at the end of He'e, Ama'ama, and Ana'e roads, and more parking for beach access down the way at Waipa. Camping is permitted at Black Pot only on Friday, Saturday, and holidays. A small *kaukau* wagon selling plate lunches is often near the river here; local fishermen launch their boats in the bay and are often amenable to selling their catch.

ENTERTAINMENT AND EVENTS

Hanalei is a quiet town, but there are a few options for at least some entertainment.

The **Hanalei Gourmet** restaurant offers lighthearted live music periodically throughout the week, and every night there is live music at **Sushi Blues,** upstairs in the Ching Young Village.

Tahiti Nui often has someone playing on Friday and Saturday evenings from about 8 P.M. You've got to stop at the Tahiti Nui, if just to look around and have a cool drink. Opened years ago by Louise Marston, a real Tahitian (although her name doesn't sound like it), the bar is dedicated to creating a friendly family atmosphere, and it succeeds admirably. The bar, open from noon to midnight, is the center of action; happy hour is 4– 6 P.M. daily. Old-timers drop in to "talk story," and someone is always willing to sing and play a Hawaiian tune. The mai tais are fabulous. If it's too busy inside, sit out on the porch, kick back, and sip away.

Each Friday at 4 P.M. and Sunday at 3 P.M., Doug and Sandy McMaster perform slack-key guitar music at the Hanalei Community Center—turn in by the soccer field before Wai'oli Church. With a different theme each afternoon, these concerts are a tribute to this purely Hawaiian musical form and to the old-time masters. A real down-home, local affair, these events are enjoyed by all. Tickets run $10 adults and $8 for seniors and kids. Call 808/826-1469 for reservations, which are highly recommended.

If in Hanalei in autumn (dates vary by year), make time to participate in the **Kaua'i Taro Festival,** an annual series of events held to promote and educate about the taro plant, one of the most useful and mythical of the traditional Hawaiian foods. Some activities include trips to taro fields, a cooking competition with taro as the centerpiece, and a daylong festivity of entertainment, crafts, and food.

SHOPPING

The first building as you enter town has several shops and art galleries. **Ola's** (808/826-6937, 10 A.M.–9 P.M.) is an "American" craft store with an eclectic assortment of items from many of the 50 states, like glass work from Oregon, ceramics from California, wood products from Hawaii, and jewelry from New York. Other items are greeting cards, hairbrushes, wooden boxes, leather purses, and pottery. Here as well are **Overboard Clothing** (808/826-8999), which stocks casual island wear for men and women, and **Black Pearl** (808/826-9992), selling jewelry made from those dark orbs from Tahiti.

In Hale Le'a, the next streetfront building down, **Kai Kane** (808/826-5594), a.k.a. The Water Man, not only catches your eye but also helps keep the sun out of it with a display of hats for both men and women. It also sells a large selection of alohawear and casual beachwear. Glass cases hold watches and sunglasses, while two outrigger canoes hang overhead and paddles line the walls. Although Kai Kane is primarily a clothing shop, it does double duty as a surf shop filled with surfboards and a wide selection of wet suits, leashes, and shorts.

At the corner of Aku Road in a small Kauhale Center shops is **Royal Hawaiian Hammocks** (808/826-0377), selling that perfect item of comfortable relaxation in its many manifestations, and the **Bikini Room** (808/826-9711), where ladies might find that just-right swimsuit in a Brazilian or European cut.

Ching Young Village Shopping Center

The Ching Young Village Shopping Center in the center of town includes a small shopping center plus nearby freestanding buildings. At **Hanalei Video and Music** (808/826-9633) you can pick up some entertainment for the evening, a favorite Hawaiian CD, or perhaps an ukulele to strum. **Pedal and Paddle** (808/826-9069) has rental sports equipment and clothing. Among the clothing shops, **Hanalei Surf Company Back Door** (808/826-1900) handles casual clothing and alohawear as well as a variety of beach and surf gear, while at **Coconut Kids and Gifts** you can pick up something for the wee ones. **Bali Hai Photo** is the shop for film and developing. For a unique collection of gifts, crafts, clothing, and imports, stop at the eclectic, upscale shop **On the Road to Hanalei,** which fronts the highway across the road from the old Hanalei school. Next door is **Evolve Love,** something like a co-op of area artists, where you'll find musings in paint, fine woodwork, artistic jewelry, and exquisite hand-painted silk cloth. Occupying the same shop and selling art and crafts items done mostly on the island is **Artists Gallery of Kaua'i.**

Hanalei Center

The Hanalei Center, located *mauka* of the highway across the street from Ching Young Village, has an excellent assortment of shops and boutiques. The original portion of this center is in the converted school building, but another section is in a newer multistory structure to the west. Between them sit several smaller freestanding buildings. Some of the many shops are **Rainbow Ducks** (808/826-4741), specializing in children's wear and toys; **Hula Beach** (808/826-4741), carrying tropical fashions for grownups; and **Sand People** (é826-1008), which offers casual island clothing for men and women, gifts, and jewelry. **Yellowfish Trading Company** (808/826-1227, open until 8 p.m.,

7 p.m. Sun.), a fascinating store neatly stuffed from floor to ceiling with Hawaiiana, antiques, collectibles, hula-doll lamps, classic Hawaiian aloha shirts, costume and silver jewelry, floral day bags, candles, swords, antique hats, Matson Steamship Line posters, and koa carvings and incidentals is a veritable feast for the eyes for those interested in Hawaiiana. The old Hanalei School section of the center houses several additional shops, such as the **Hanalei Surf Company** (808/826-9000) with boards, water gear, and clothing; and **Tropical Tantrum** (808/826-6944), a small Hawaii chain that designs its own fabrics, which are then turned into original clothing in Indonesia. At Tropical Tantrum, women can rage in the most vibrant colors of purple, blue, red, green, and yellow, transforming themselves into walking rainforests. Next door is **Kahn Galleries** (808/826-6677), specializing in original artworks and limited edition prints created by some of the finest artists Hawaii has to offer.

RECREATION

Hanalei is alive with outdoor activities. The following is merely a quick list of what's available.

Until August 1998 motorized boats could use Hanalei Bay for commercial purposes, many starting right from the river mouth. After that date, by governor's decree, only nonmotorized uses of the bay were allowed, to the consternation of many in the business sector. However, the reduced activity in the bay has made it a much quieter place, less busy, and more enjoyable for the nonmotorized recreational users. In 2001, following legal battles, three companies which were legally permitted to operate before the governor's edict were again allowed to operate from the bay. The small number of operators and their environmental stance has kept the bay and waters in healthy and pristine condition.

Kayaking

The company to see for a kayaking adventure up the Hanalei River or, during summer, along the Na Pali Coast, is **Kayak Kaua'i** (808/826-

9844 or 800/437-3507, www.kayakkauai.com). Leaving twice a day, river trips run $60 adults, $45 kids. The daylong Na Pali Coast trip is for those in very good physical condition only and runs $185 per person. Kayak Kaua'i has a storefront along the highway where they do sales and rentals. Rental rates for a single river kayak are $28 per day and $52 for a double; multiday and weekly rates are also available. Lessons, guide service, shuttle support, and storage can be arranged. Other water equipment—snorkel gear, surfboards, boogie boards—is also rented, as are camping gear and beach cruiser bikes. Beach cruiser bikes are $15; backpacks go for $8 a day, two-person tents $8, sleeping bags $6, pads $4, and camp stoves $6. If you want to buy, Kayak Kaua'i is one of the few places on the island that sells good quality camping and backpacking equipment. It also has hiking food, utensils, and insect repellant for those planning to hike the Kalalau Trail.

A second company that does guided Na Pali coastal kayak tours is **NaPali Kayak** (808/826-6900 or 866/977-6900, www.napalikayak.com). Operating April through November, this all-day adventure runs the entire length of the coast with lunch and snorkel stops for $175 per person. The water portion of your trip ends at Polihale Beach, from where you are escorted by van back around to Hanalei.

Doing guided trips into the bay and up the river is **Kayak Hanalei** (808/826-1881, www.kayakhanalei.com). Trips run 3–5 hours, including lunch, and cost roughly $60–75 per person.

Sailing

One of the few companies allowed to use motorized craft in Hanalei Bay is **Na Pali Catamarans** (808/826-6853 or 866/255-6853, www.napalicatamaran.com). Your trip starts from shore near the mouth of the Hanalei River, where you are ferried out to a waiting power catamaran by an outrigger canoe. Once on board, you cruise the Na Pali Coast from the east, with less time spent traveling to and from than the tours that leave from Port Allen on the South Coast. At 32 feet long, with a capacity of 15 passengers, this boat offers a more intimate ride yet allows easier access to some coastal sites. Four-hour morning and afternoon snorkeling tours during the calmer summer months runs $135, while a shorter three-hour whale-watching tour during the winter months—weather permitting—runs $100. Lunch and drinks are included.

For a larger catamaran, the only sailing cat out of Hanalei, try **Captain Sundown** (808/826-5585, www.captainsundown.com). Captain Sundown has a morning snorkel and sail tour for $150 adults and $125 children, and a late afternoon sightseeing sail and sunset tour for $120 adults and $99 kids.

Biking

John Sargent's **Bike Doctor** (808/826-7799, 9 A.M.–5 P.M. Tues.–Thurs., until 3 P.M. Fri., 10 A.M.–4 P.M. Sat.) does bike repair and is stocked with everything for the casual and serious cyclist. John is intimately familiar with roads and trails all over the island, has information on group rides and races, and is happy to give advice on touring. The Bike Doctor is the only shop in town that rents high-quality mountain bikes for the serious off-road rider, and these babies run $25 a day or $100 a week.

Rentals

The **Hanalei Surf Company** (808/826-9000) in the Hanalei Center is a water-sports shop that rents and sells snorkeling equipment, boogie boards, surfboards, and other water equipment. Rental rates for surfboards run $15 per day or $65 a week, boogie boards are $5 or $7 with fins, and snorkel equipment goes from $5 a day to $20 a week; three- and five-day rates are also available on all rentals. Hanalei Surf Co. has a "rent to buy" option on its snorkel equipment—ask. The store is also stocked with a good selection of shirts, shorts, thongs, bathing suits, incidental bags, sunglasses, sunblock, and dresses.

Pedal 'n Paddle (808/826-9069, 9 A.M.–6 P.M.) in the Ching Young Village rents snorkel gear, boogie boards, kayaks, bikes, and some camping gear. Prices are: snorkel gear $5 a day or $20 per week; boogie boards $5/$20; single kayaks $15 a day, double kayaks $35 a day, cruiser bikes $10/$40; ordinary mountain bikes $20/$80, two-person dome tents $15/$35; backpacks $5/$20; light sleeping bags $3/$10; and sleeping pads $3/$10. A rental day begins the hour you rent and ends at 5 P.M. the following day. Pedal 'n Paddle does not sell bikes or kayaks but has snorkel and camping gear, camp food, hats, sandals, and much more for sale. This store has all you need for a day on the water as well as a week on the trail.

Right across the street is **Activity Wholesalers** (808/826-9983), with competitive rental rates for beach and water gear, as well as cruiser bikes.

ACCOMMODATIONS

There are no hotels in Hanalei, only a handful of bed-and-breakfasts, one small motel-like inn, and plenty of vacation rental homes. Many of the rental homes, which range from economy to sumptuous, sit right on the beach, while others are scattered around town. Wherever you stay, however, you're never far from the beach and always surrounded by exquisite scenery.

$100-150

The moderately priced **Hanalei Inn** (5-5468 Kuhio Hwy., 808/826-9333, www.hanaleiinn .com), is on the west side of town across from the school. It's tucked in among flowering bushes and trees, so it's not real obvious from the road. With only five studio apartments, it's a quiet place. Each unit has a living/bedroom area with queen-size bed, an efficiency kitchen sufficient to make light meals (one unit has no kitchen), a full bath, and a coin-operated washer and dryer to the rear of the overgrown pavilion. Room rates are $99 for the rooms with kitchens and $89 for the unit with no kitchen. In addition, a house by Pine Trees has rooms that run $189 for a large bedroom and loft, five-night minimum; $149 for a one-bedroom apartment, three-night minimum; and a single room with bath for $109. Not

exceptional in any way, nor with any particular character, it still offers some of the least expensive beds in town.

Bed-and-Breakfast

Bed, Breakfast, and Beach (P.O. Box 748, Hanalei, HI 96714, 808/826-6111, www.best-ofhawaii.com/hanalei), owned by Carolyn Barnes, is a neo-classic trilevel plantation-style home in a quiet residential area only a minute's walk from the beach. It gives you a strong feeling that you are part of the community. Upstairs offers a wide, covered lanai, perfect for catching the breeze or listening to the soft patter of a morning shower while eating breakfast. On the upper levels you'll find plenty of windows from which to enjoy a postcard view of the surrounding mountains. The common area, a casual lounging parlor, is cool and inviting with smooth parquet floors, an open-beamed ceiling, and knotty-pine paneling. The decor throughout is a mixture of classic Hawaiian and tasteful New England antique. Nooks and crannies are filled with objets d'art and plenty of reading material. From the common area, a staircase ascends to the Bali Hai Suite, a 700-square-foot unit that occupies the entire top floor; three-night minimum. Off the central area are the Pualani Suite and Country Cedar Room—smaller, but alive, like a living floral arrangement with pastel blooms from ceiling to bedspread; two-night minimum. Bed, Breakfast, and Beach is an excellent choice of accommodation for relaxation, a feeling of hominess, and extremely good value. Rates are $90–145; no credit cards please. If you're looking for a bit more privacy, ask about **Tutu's Cottage,** a small two-bedroom, one bath plantation-style house just a bit closer to downtown Hanalei. This cottage is rented by the week, $1,000 for a couple, plus $100 each for a third or fourth person; one-week minimum. The cottage has all amenities, such as ceiling fans, TV, and telephone, and it has a full kitchen, so you have the freedom to fix your own meals.

Vacation Rental Agencies

Na Pali Properties, Inc. (808/826-7272 or

800/715-7273, www.napaliprop.com), with an office at the Ching Young Village, has everything from $500-a-week cottages to an $8,750-a-week luxury mansion on the beach.

Hanalei North Shore Properties (808/826-9622 or 800/488-3336, www.rentals-onkauai.com) in the Princeville Shopping Center handles dozens of vacation rentals in Hanalei as well as along the entire north shore from Anahola to Haʻena.

Kauai Vacation Rentals (3-3311 Kuhio Hwy., 808/245-8841 or 800/367-5025, fax 808/246-1161, www.KauaiVacationRentals.com) also has numerous rentals mostly in the medium to expensive range all the way to the end of the road.

Handling upper-end vacation homes along the entire north shore is **Bali Hai Realty** (808/826-8000 or 866/400-7368, www.balihai.com).

FOOD

Hanalei has many eating institutions, ranging from simple *kaukau* wagons to excellent gourmet restaurants. The food is great at any time of day, but those in the know time their evening meal to coincide with sunset. They watch the free show and then go for a great dinner.

Coffee Shop and Shave Ice

In a freestanding building in the Hanalei Center, follow the aroma of fresh-brewed coffee to **Java Kai** (808/826-6717, 6:30 A.M.–6 P.M.), where you can revitalize with a cup of espresso, cappuccino, latte, café au lait, or an old-fashioned hot chocolate. If you're in the mood for something else, try a flavored Italian soda or smoothie while you use the Internet access. Java Kai serves a limited breakfast and lunch menu that includes waffles, sandwiches, and quiche; you can eat inside or out on the lanai. Smaller items—all made on the premises—include muffins and cheesecake, or you might like to bring home a pound of bulk coffee. Occupying a window in the same building is **Shave Ice Paradise** (11:30 A.M.–5:30 P.M.). Choose from a multitude of flavors of traditional shave ice, including coconut and papaya, with fruit

cocktail and adzuki beans thrown in for good measure. There's ice cream and a signature drink called a Summer Breeze, somewhat like an Orange Julius with a special twist. Servers scoop the ice cream and make the shave ice as if they were doing it for family and friends. Your only problem is trying to lick faster than these hefty babies can melt.

Local Style

Hanalei Mixed Plate (808/826-7888), in a freestanding building in the Ching Young Village, serves up plate lunches of rice with one, two, or three entrées ($6.95–8.95) that might include shoyu ginger chicken, *kalua* pork and cabbage, and vegetable stir-fry. Hearty sandwiches of sautéed mahimahi, marinated and grilled teriyaki chicken, and the like are also on the menu, as are salads, flame-broiled beef, buffalo, garden, or tempeh burgers and fries, and hot dogs. Hanalei Mixed Plate is basically a walk-up counter with outdoor bar stool seating where prices are reasonable, servings generous, and the music free.

In the Hale Leʻa building next to Kai Kane, **Tropical Taco** (808/827-8226, 11 A.M.–5 P.M. Mon.–Sat.) serves up fish and vegetarian tacos, tostadas, burritos, and other quick Mexican fare for under $8 in a clean and cheery sit-down place. Having served his tasty treats from a taco truck for years, the owner knows how to please his customers.

Healthy Take-Out

Papaya's (808/828-0089, 9 A.M.–8 P.M. Mon.–Sat., 9 P.M.–3 P.M. Sun.), along the highway at the Hanalei Center, carries healthy and organic produce and fruits, bulk and packaged natural foods, a refrigerator section, supplements and vitamins, and a salad bar/hot bar where the prepared foods to go run $6.49 a pound. Always nutritious, this is some of the best ready-to-eat food in town.

American

Cubbyhole small, one of the few early-morning places in town is **Hanalei Wake-Up Cafe** (808/826-5551, 6–11 A.M.) at the Kauhale

Center at the corner of Aku Road. The cheery help, the smell of freshly brewed coffee, and the good home cookin' should help start your day off on the right foot. With plastic chairs and pictures on the walls, there is nothing high-class here, just good food.

Bubba Burger (808/826-7839, 10:30 A.M.–8 P.M.) is still doing what it's always done: serving up double-fisted burgers, individually made, at great prices. It's mostly a window restaurant, but there is seating on the lanai, with a few tables inside. Bubba's burgers range in price $3–6.50, with other offerings on the menu like a chicken sandwich or taro burger, and a Hubba Bubba—rice, a burger patty, and hot dog smothered with chili. Bubba's burgers come with mustard, relish, and onions; anything else you want on it is extra. Try side orders like chili fries or Caesar salad, all light on the wallet but not so light on the waistline.

Zelo's (808/826-9700, 11 A.M.–10 P.M. daily with happy hour 3:30–5:30 P.M.), established in Princeville but moved to Hanalei in late 1995 after the hurricane, has been serving generous island fare at its corner location since then. The interior of this indoor/outdoor restaurant is distinctive, with a long bamboo bar covered with a corrugated roof supported by old beams and tree trunks, *lau hala* matting on the walls, and ceiling fans rotating above. The lunch menu offers salads and sandwiches, including a Philadelphia steak sandwich and turkey and cheese, plus a full range of burgers with all the fixings—including teriyaki, pesto, and a Cajun fish burger. Dinner brings a menu of items like Zelo's famous beer-battered fish and chips, baby back ribs, crab-stuffed *ahi,* and seafood artichoke fettuccini. The pasta, meat, and fish dishes run mostly in the $15–25 range. For those who don't want a full meal, the *pu pu* are large and almost a meal in themselves. The atmosphere is pleasant, the staff friendly, the food flavorful, and sometimes there's music on weekends.

The **Hanalei Gourmet** (808/826-2524, 8 A.M.–10:30 P.M.) open for deli items, lunch, and dinner in the old schoolhouse at the Hanalei Center, is a born-again, one-stop, nouveau cuisine deli, semi-gourmet food vendor, and good-time bar for tropical drinks and imported beers. To top it off, it's friendly, the food is exceptionally good, the prices are right, and there's even live entertainment some nights of the week. In the right-hand door and fronting the kitchen is the deli, with cases filled with lunchmeats, cheeses, salads, and smoked fish, while the main door leads to the dining area and bar. From the deli, you can also order a picnic lunch to go, side salads, plenty of baked goods, and even a fine bottle of wine. In the restaurant, ceiling fans keep you cool, while blackboards, once used to announce hideous homework assignments, now herald the daily specials. Behind the bar, windows through which kids once stared amid daydreams of summer now open to frame green-silhouetted mountains. Original wood floors, white walls bearing local artworks and hanging plants, two big-screen TVs for sports enthusiasts, and a wide veranda with a few tables for dining alfresco complete the restaurant. Lunch sandwiches, $7–10, are huge wedges. Dinners are served 5:30–9:30 P.M. and feature specialty pastas, fresh fish, ginger chicken, and other meat and poultry dishes; entrées run $16–26. The Hanalei Gourmet is the perfect spot for a meal or a social drink.

Pizza

In the Ching Young Village is **Pizza Hanalei** (808/826-9494, 11 A.M.–9 P.M.). Made with thin, white, or whole-wheat crust, these pizzas run $11.95 for plain cheese to $37.95 for the Lizzy Special. Other made-to-order pizzas are priced by the ingredients, and all take some time to prepare and bake. Cheese and pepperoni pizza by the slice are available 11 A.M.–4 P.M. Fresh green salads and garlic bread are also on the menu. Pizza Hanalei has garnered a good reputation.

Hawaiian Regional

Directly behind Hanalei Mixed Plate is the open-air ◖ **Polynesia Café** (808/826-1999), which advertises "gourmet food on paper plates" and is open for three meals a day.

This restaurant indeed puts out some savory treats, like macadamia nut- and herb-crusted *ahi,* Shanghai tofu, and chicken taco salad, mostly in the affordable $10–15 range, with sandwiches, Mexican items, and desserts less. Order at the counter and have your food at the picnic tables in the courtyard. Well prepared and tasty, the food here is less expensive than at a more sophisticated sit-down, indoor eatery. Save room for coffee, ice cream, or dessert—all pastries, breads, and other sweets are made on-site—and you can bring your own bottle of wine to complement your meal as the Polynesia Café doesn't serve alcoholic beverages.

At the first building on the right as you enter town, flanking the Hanalei River, look for a hanging dolphin sign marking the **Hanalei Dolphin Restaurant** (808/826-6113, 11 A.M.–10 P.M.). The interior is casual, with an open-beamed ceiling, corrugated roof, shutters that hinge open to the garden, trophy fish, hanging glass floats, and ships' lanterns. Alternately, sit outside under the umbrellas along the bank of the river. Lunch is mostly salads, sandwiches, and sides. Dinner appetizers include ceviche and stuffed mushrooms. Seafood, mainly from the owners' fish market around back, includes fresh catch, teriyaki shrimp, and calamari, mostly in the $20–28 range. Fish, the specialty, is your best option, charbroiled or blackened, but Hawaiian chicken, New York steak, and other items are also on the menu for $16–32. All entrées are served with family-style salads, pasta, steak fries, or rice, and hot homemade bread. There's a full bar for tropical cocktails. First come, first served; no reservations are taken. Open since 1977, the Dolphin serves consistently good but not memorable food.

A great place to write home from is the covered veranda of the 100-year-old plantation home that was once the Hanalei Museum. The owners of **Postcards Café** (808/826-1191, 6–9 P.M.), a gourmet natural food restaurant, have refurbished the building to a condition as close to the original as possible, and today it is listed on the National Register of Historic Places. Dinner is served daily and seating is inside or out on the front and side porches. Tables are covered with old postcards under glass, and the restaurant is always full. Postcards is an upbeat, health-conscious vegetarian restaurant that prides itself on using organic ingredients and making every dish and sauce from scratch. While the menu changes periodically, vegetables, pasta, and seafood are the mainstays—no red meat or poultry is served. Dishes are simple but hearty, and while not inexpensive (mostly $16–22), the quality is excellent. Save room for dessert; they're all made here in the kitchen. Postcards is wheelchair-friendly, and smokers are completely prohibited from lighting up—even outside. Reservations recommended. Postcards is an excellent choice.

Bamboo Bamboo (808/826-1177), in the Hanalei Center, is a casually refined restaurant with seating inside and out on the lanai. Offering lunch and dinner daily, this open-air restaurant has a full bar and periodic weekend music. Crispy Thai spring rolls and fried calamari with papaya cocktail sauce appear as appetizers, and light dinners include fish and chips and Hanalei taro burgers. More substantial entrées, $18–25, include seafood pasta, potato-crusted mahimahi, and rack of lamb in port wine sauce. For something quicker and easier, try fresh-baked pizza on Friday, Saturday, and Sunday evenings. Bamboo Bamboo gets high marks from nearly everyone in the know. It serves flavorful, well-presented food in pleasing surroundings for a relaxing, memorable evening. Call for reservations.

Japanese

Upstairs in Ching Young Village, serving sushi, sashimi, rice rolls, and other Asian-inspired dishes, is ◖ **Sushi Blues** (808/826-9701, 6–10 P.M. nightly). Special rolls and sushi run $4–15, while entrées, mostly under $25, include such fine offerings as linguine and scallops, hibachi shrimp scampi, and grilled kiwi teriyaki chicken. Beverages include a full selection of beers, sake, wine, martinis, and tropical drinks, and there's live music nightly. Sit at the sushi bar and watch the magic being done on inspired imaginative rolls or at one of the window tables overlooking main street Hanalei. Sushi Blues has a lively atmosphere and is perhaps the most happening place in town.

For a fresh and healthful glass of refreshment, stop at the nearby **Hanalei Juice Bar** (808/826-6990, 9 A.M.–7 P.M.), also at the Ching Young Village.

Brazilian

Brazilian food in Hanalei? Well, yes! Head for the rear of the Hanalei Center to **Neide's** (808/826-1851, 11:30 A.M.–2 P.M., 5–9 P.M.) for Brazilian and Mexican food. You can order such favorites as *muqueca,* a dish of fresh fish with coconut sauce, shrimp, and cilantro; *ensopado,* baked chicken and vegetables; or *bife acebolado,* an onion-smothered beef steak. A handful of Mexican standbys round out the reasonably priced menu.

Supermarket

The **Big Save Supermarket** (808/826-6652, 7 A.M.–9 P.M. daily) at the Ching Young Center is the only large grocery store in town and from here to the end of the road. A full-service shop, Big Save has all you need for a quick picnic or a week at the condo, as well as sundries and other supplies.

Fish Market

The **Hanalei Dolphin Fish Market,** around back behind the Hanalei Dolphin restaurant, is open 10 A.M.–8 P.M. daily, selling fresh, locally caught fish, some ready-to-cook prepared items, sauces, and dressings. It can—with a day's notice—create a luscious sashimi and sushi platter.

Farmers Markets

Every Tuesday 2–4 P.M., pick up some farm-fresh fruit and vegetables from the Hawaiian Farmers of Hanalei farmers market, a half mile west of town, in Waipa, on the road to Ha'ena. Look for the sign *mauka* along the road.

The Hanalei Neighborhood Center and ballpark, across the road and up from the post office is the location of the private farmers market held Saturday 9:30–11:30 A.M. Come early as this is not a big event and the organic produce tends to go fast. Some craft and art items may also be for sale here.

INFORMATION AND SERVICES

Kauai Adventure Activities (808/826-9998 or 877/266-8400), located along the highway in Hanalei next to Big Save, is the best place in town to stop for activity information and bookings for anywhere on the island. This is a full-service company that can put you not only on the water in a boat or kayak, but also on the back of a horse, up in a helicopter, at a lu'au, or into north shore accommodations. Kauai Adventure Activities offers the highest quality service, so your experience is a rewarding one.

ROAD ETIQUETTE

The narrow north shore highway beyond Hanalei, with its many one-lane bridges, requires that you drive with a certain degree of caution and road etiquette. First of all, slow down and enjoy the scenery. This road is full of curves, so drive defensively. If you need to stop, pull all the way off the roadway so other cars can get by safely.

White lines on the road and yield signs will alert you to where you must stop at one-lane bridges to let traffic from the other direction pass. There is not always a good line of sight at these bridges, so be cautious. If two cars approach a bridge at the same time, let the other car go first. If you are in a line of cars that is crossing the bridge when others are waiting to cross from the other direction, and if you are in the first half dozen of this line of cars, cross. Otherwise, stop and let the oncoming traffic cross before you proceed across the bridge. Above all, always be polite, smile, and give the other cars that wait the *shaka* sign.

The **post office** in Hanalei is just west of Ching Young Village.

For **Internet service** in Hanalei, see **Bali Hai Photo** (808/826-9181) in the Ching Young Center or **Java Kai** (808/826-6717) across the street in the Hanalei Center.

North Shore Cab (808/826-4118) and **Taxi Hanalei** (808/639-1188) both do pickup and delivery service on the north shore. The ordinary fare from Hanalei to Prince-ville runs about $12, to the end of the road at Ke'e Beach is $15, and to the Lihu'e Airport about $62. **Kauai North Shore Limousine** (808/828-6189) offers luxury limo service with its stretch limos or Lincoln Towncars. You must pre-arrange this luxury service, and the driver will be waiting, resplendent in his casual chauffeur's uniform. Full day tours also available. Fares must be negotiated; two-hour minimum.

Road's End

Past Hanalei you have six miles of pure magic until the road ends at Ke'e Beach. To thrill you further and make your ride even more enjoyable, you'll find historical sites; natural wonders; an oceanside resort; the *heiau* where hula was born, overlooking a lovely beach; and the trailhead to Kaua'i's premier hike, the Kalalau Trail. The Hanalei Valley is the largest along this coast; nearly as large but more serpentine is the Wainiha Valley. Between these lie the deep and green Wai'oli, Waipa, and Lumaha'i Valleys. At mile marker 7 is the tiny village of Wainiha (Angry Water), and beyond that the small community of **Ha'ena** (Red Hot), not a town per se, more a state of mind. The Wainiha Valley is said to have been inhabited long ago by the race of dwarfish Mu people. While many legends revolve around these mythical pre-Hawaiians, an official census from the late 1700s mentions 65 Mu living in Wainiha Valley. As you drive along, you cross one-lane bridges, travel through tunnels of trees, and pass little beaches and bays, one after another, invariably with small streams flowing into

Limahuli Botanical Garden

ROBERT NILSEN

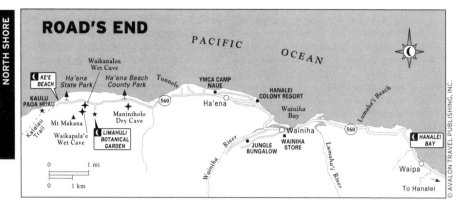

ROAD'S END

them. Try not to get jaded peering at "just another gorgeous north shore beach."

◖ LIMAHULI BOTANICAL GARDEN

Limahuli Botanical Garden (808/826-1053, 9:30 A.M.–4 P.M. Tues.–Fri. and Sun.), in the last valley before the beginning of the Kalalau Trail, is a half mile past mile marker 9. Presided over by the towering Mount Makana, this garden is part of the National Tropical Botanical Garden, a showcase of tropical plants both ancient and modern. The 14 original acres of the garden were donated by Juliet Rice Wichman in 1976, later expanded to 17 acres, and an additional 985-acre preserve in the valley above was donated by her grandson, Chipper Wichman, the garden's director, in 1994. There are both self-guided ($10) and guided ($15) walking tours of the gardens; guided tours are 10 A.M. and 2 P.M. only—by reservation. Wear good shoes; umbrellas are provided. Tours start at the visitors center, which has a fine collection of books on Hawaiian flora and other subjects. As you walk through this enchanted area you pass taro patches growing behind stone terraces believed to be at least 900 years old, plants introduced to Hawaii by the early Polynesians, living specimens of endangered native Hawaiian species, and post-contact tropicals; your guide treats you to legends of the valley (or you can read them in your brochure) as

you follow the three-quarter-mile loop trail. Only this part of the garden is open to the public; the vast interior of the preserve is accessible only to biologists and botanists doing research. For those who love the living beauty of plants and flowers, a trip to Limahuli Botanical Garden is well worth the effort.

Just beyond the botanical garden driveway, the road dips and crosses a small stream. On the mountain side of the road is a small shallow pool known as the "cool pond," where some come for a refreshing freshwater dip after their saltwater bath in the ocean.

BEACHES
Lumaha'i Beach

Lumaha'i Beach is a femme fatale, lovely to look at but treacherous. This hauntingly beautiful beach (whose name translates as Twist of Fingers) is what dreams are made of: white sand curving perfectly at the bottom of a dark lava cliff with tropical jungle in the background. The riptides here are fierce even with the reef, and the water should never be entered except in very calm conditions during the summer. Look for a vista point after mile marker 5, just beyond the west end of Hanalei Bay. Cars invariably park here. It's a sharp curve, so make sure to pull completely off the road or the police may ticket you. An extensive grove of hala trees appears just as you set off down a steep and often muddy footpath leading down to the east end of the beach. Several more overlooks

HAWAIIAN MONK SEAL SAFETY TIPS

Hawaiian monk seals that frequent the beaches of Kaua'i are relatively few in number, so any sighting causes great excitement among residents and visitors alike. These creatures are fun to watch, but they are an endangered species and therefore are in need of great protection. Please do your part to insure that they are not disturbed.

Stay well back from any monk seal basking on a beach or on rocks. If signs or other markers have been placed around an animal, do not go beyond. When you happen upon a seal in an unmarked area, you are asked to stay at least 100 feet away and remain on the inland side; don't walk between the seal and the water. If both mother and pup are together on the beach, be especially careful and maintain your distance, as mother seals are very protective

and might become agitated or aggressive if their comfort space is challenged. Keep an eye on your kids so that they don't approach or disturb any animal, and teach them the respect that these seals deserve.

Remain quiet. Seals come out of the water to rest and sleep. Don't feed them food or throw anything at them. Feel free to take non-flash pictures, but do so from an appropriate distance.

If and when you witness any harassment of Hawaiian monk seals, please call the Kaua'i police department (808/241-6711), the state monk seal hotline (808/983-5715), or the NOAA marine mammal hotline (888/256-9840). There are stiff penalties for disturbing or harassing Hawaiian monk seals, with fines of $25,000 or more and up to five years in prison.

are just a ways beyond that let you peer down onto the beach from above. The best, easiest, and safest place to park is among the ironwood trees at the west end of the beach near the bridge that crosses the Lumaha'i River; an emergency phone is across the road from this parking area. From here you can walk to the east end if you want seclusion.

Makua Beach

About six-tenths of a mile past the YMCA camp, a short dead-end road turns off the highway and a trail through the trees leads to Makua Beach, commonly known as **Tunnels.** It's superb for snorkeling and scuba diving, perhaps the best on the island, with a host of underwater caves off to the left as you face the sea. Look for the small fish inside the reef; for the bigger fish (experienced snorkelers and divers only) you must go into the sea caves or over the edge of the awesome drop-off. Both surfing and windsurfing are great, and so is the swimming if the sea is calm. Watch out for boats that come inside the reef. Off to the right and down a bit is a nude beach. There are no facilities here and parking is very limited along the roadway, but

it's less than half a mile east down the beach from Ha'ena Beach Park.

Ha'ena Beach County Park

Ha'ena Beach County Park, just a mile before road's end, is a large, flat, fieldlike area, where you stake out your own camping site. For your convenience, the county provides tables, a pavilion, grills, showers, and camping (permit required). The sand on this long crescent beach is rather coarse, and the swimming is good only when the sea is gentle, but in summertime a reef offshore is great for snorkeling. The cold stream running through the park is always good for a dip. Across the road is the broad and low **Maniniholo dry cave.** Notice the gorgeous grotto of trees, and the jungle wild with vines. You walk in and it feels airy, like it would be nice living quarters, but it has never been suggested that the cave was used for permanent habitation. Luckily, even with all the visitors going in and out, it hasn't been trashed.

(Ke'e Beach

Up the road, just after entering **Ha'ena State Park,** an HVB Warrior points the way to the

ROBERT NILSEN

Kaulu O Laka Heiau

first of the **wet caves. Waikanaloa** is directly to the side of the road. Farther up the road and 150 yards up the side of a hill is **Waikapala'e.** There is no indication of its location except for a small pulloff along the road for parking. The wide openings of these two wet caves are almost like gaping frogs' mouths, and the water is liquid crystal. Amazingly, while Maniniholo dry cave is down by the road, Waikapala'e wet cave, subject to the tides, is inland and uphill! Look around for *ti* leaves and a few scraggly guavas. Straight up, different lava that has flowed over the eons has created a stacked pancake effect. Waikapala'e is sometimes referred to as the "Blue Room," as it is said to take on an otherworldly blue hue from the back wall looking out toward the opening. If azure could bleed, it might be this color. The 66-acre Ha'ena State Park encompasses not only these caves but also Ke'e Beach and the trailhead for the Kalalau Trail.

The road ends at **Ke'e Beach,** a popular spot with restrooms and showers. Here is the beginning of the Kalalau Trail. Although there are many parking spaces, the lot begins to fill early, particularly on warm, dry days. As always, the swimming is good only in the summertime, but snorkeling inside the wide reef is great most of the year. Around the point to the right you

might find the beach less crowded, and it was up in the trees here that Taylor Camp, the most well known of the north coast hippie communities of the 1960s, was located. Sometimes seals haul themselves out of the water to bask in the sand on the beach here. Give them plenty of space and just let them be. If conditions are right and the tide is out, you can walk left along the shore to get a dazzling view of the Na Pali cliffs. Don't attempt this when the sea is rough! This path takes you past a hidden beach home, once used as the setting for the famous love rendezvous in the miniseries *The Thorn Birds.* Past the home, another path takes you up the hill to the ancient sites of **Kaulu Paoa Heiau** and **Kaulu O Laka Heiau,** birthplace of the hula, where the goddess Laka bestowed to the Hawaiians this wonderful expression of dance and story. Please enter respectfully and don't disturb the site. The views from the *heiau* are remarkable and worth the short climb, especially during winter, when the sun drops close to the cliffs and backlights Lehua Island, then sinks into its molten reflection. In the past, after novitiates had graduated from the hula *heiau,* they had to jump into the sea below, swimming around to Ke'e Beach as a sign of dedication. Tourists aren't required to perform this act.

ACCOMMODATIONS

Aside from the few places listed below, rental homes—and there are dozens along this coast—can be arranged through any of the vacation rental agencies listed above in the Hanalei and Princeville sections, or check Kauai Vacations (808/826-8968, www .kauaiavacation.com) for additional accommodation listings.

Above $250

In Ha'ena, look for signs to the five-acre, 48-unit **(Hanalei Colony Resort** (808/826-6235 or 800/628-3004, fax 808/826-9893, www.hcr.com)—literally the last resort and the only resort on the beach along the north coast. You can rent very comfortable, spacious, two-bedroom condos here, each with a living room, full kitchen, shower/tub, and lanai in board-and-batten buildings that blend into the surroundings. Now past 30 years old, this property was extensively renovated in 2005. While not luxurious, the oceanfront units have some of the most spectacular views anywhere along this coast, and the other units bring in lush tropical garden views. All in all it's a superb location and fine property. The resort has a small swimming pool and hot tub tucked away in a corner, barbecue grills, coin-operated washers and dryers, and twice-weekly maid service. There are no TVs or phones in any rooms; you get the peace and quiet for no extra charge. The beach in front of the resort is great for a stroll at sunset, but be very careful swimming during winter months or periods of high surf. Based on occupancy of up to four people, units range from $210 for a garden view to $335 for a premium oceanfront, $10–40 more during the high season of summer and the Christmas/ New Year holiday, with the seventh night free for a weeklong stay. There is a five-night minimum during high season. Car-rental packages are available if arranged before arriving on Kaua'i. On property is the **Hanalei Day Spa** (826-6621) for rejuvenating physical conditioning, massages, body wraps, and more, while the **Na Pali Art Gallery and Coffee**

FIRE SHOWER

After Hanalei Bay, the most notable feature along the north coast is the towering spire of Mount Makana. Rising directly above Ke'e Beach at the end of the road, Mount Makana is popularly known as Bali Hai – made famous in the movie *South Pacific*. This peak was one of the two spots on the island – the other being the ridge end above Nu'alolo Beach just down the coast to the west – where, for special occasions, fire throwers would toss burning branches of *papala* or *hau* trees off the cliff at night in a Fourth of July-style spectacular similar to the old firefalls at Yosemite National Park. Updrafts of wind would carry these burning pieces of wood out to sea in a shower of red sparks. Crowds would gather along the shore and in canoes on the water to watch, and those whose firebrands went the farthest would be accorded great acclaim.

shop serves up morning libations and pastries and sells hand made crafts and artwork.

Vacation Rentals

If you're looking for a really quiet, secluded place to stay, you'll find it at the **(Jungle Bungalow** and **Jungle Cabana** (P.O. Box 521 Hanalei, HI 96714, 808/826-5141 or 888/886-4969, www.junglebungalow.com, www.jungle-cabana.com) on the island in the Wainiha River. Surrounded by thick tropical greenery and the sound of the rushing river, the Jungle Bungalow is a two-story cottage that offers a real tropical hideaway. Downstairs is a complete kitchen and living room; upstairs is the master bedroom and toilet. Outside, the lanai fronts a large private lawn, and around the side, surrounded by greenery for your privacy, is a clawfoot tub and shower. The bungalow goes for $145 for a couple, $10 each additional person up to three, and a one-time $90 cleaning fee; four nights minimum. A few yards up the driveway is the Jungle Cabana, a smaller single-level unit that sleeps two in a queen bed with a similar bathing setup outside. It holds a living/sleeping area, kitchen, and toilet; the cabana goes for $120 a night with a four-night minimum and a $60 cleaning fee; weekly rates are available. Both units are basic, simple, and comfortable and envelop you with the sounds of the forest. No TV, no phone, no smoking—just the sounds of nature and the quiet of a peaceful tropical valley.

Nearby, the **Wainiha River Estate** (808/826-6411) offers three self-contained homes that can be rented separately or together for a group of up to 20. With a five-night minimum and a cleaning fee, these homes run $175–225 a night.

Offering a few options in Ha'ena on a daily, weekly, or monthly basis is **Aunties Holiday Rentals** (808/826-5566).

Camping

Just past Hanalei Colony Resort, between mile markers 7 and 8 on the highway, look toward the ocean for the entrance to **YMCA Camp Naue.** Here, several buildings are filled with bunks with a separate toilet area and cooking facilities. The camp caters to large groups but is open to single travelers on a first-come, first-served basis for the staggering sum of $12 per night. The cost for tent camping is $10 per person. The bunkhouses lie under beachside trees, and campers stay in the yard. All guests must provide their own sleeping bags or bed-

ding. Hot showers are available to all, but the cooking facilities are only for groups. On the property is a pavilion with grills, but you must provide your own wood or bring a camp stove. As with most YMCAs, there are many rules to be followed. You can get full information from YMCA headquarters in Lihu'e or by writing YMCA of Kaua'i, P.O. Box 1786, Lihu'e, HI 96766, 808/246-9090, or 808/826-6419 in Ha'ena.

FOOD

There are no options for a sit-down dinner on the North Coast west of Hanalei, yet a couple of shops do offer snacks and drinks and minimal supplies for the road.

Over a small white bridge in the village of Wainiha is the tiny **Wainiha Store** (808/826-6251, 9:30 A.M.–7 P.M.) where you can pick up drinks and sundries. People from around the area come to the store to post flyers if they have rooms to rent.

Last in line is **Na Pali Art Gallery and Coffee House** (808/826-1844, 7 A.M.–5 P.M.). Located on the grounds of the Hanalei Colony Resort, this small shop offers coffee, chai, sodas, smoothies, pastries, bagels, and sandwiches, not only to resort guests but also to early risers heading up the coast to the beach or the trail.

Na Pali Coast

The Na Pali Coast, from Ke'e Beach on the north shore to Polihale Beach on the west end, is less than 15 miles long, but they are miles so beautiful you must speak in superlatives to describe it. Here the seacliffs rise sharply out of the water to nearly 4,000 feet in height. Of the numerous valleys, the largest and most majestic is Kalalau Valley, the site of ancient habitation, archaeological remains, and many myths and legends. Deep cuts in this rock face have created numerous narrower chasms, including several hanging valleys, and these hold evidence of other inhabited sites. Rain is

abundant along this coast, and streams course through each lush valley, creating many refreshing waterfalls; Hawaiians used the waterfalls that fall directly into the sea like faucets, to fill freshwater containers. While all sorts of huge trees (native and introduced), bushes, flowers, and vines fill the large Kalalau Valley and other valley floors, many of the steep valley walls are covered in ferns. A handful of sea caves, one with a collapsed ceiling, puncture this rampart at water level, and several beaches dot the coast. Fishing is good, particularly inside the fringe reefs at Ke'e, Nu'alolo Kai, and

ROBERT NILSEN

Na Pali Coast cliffs viewed from the ocean

Miloli'i. The Na Pali Coast is home to a large community of spinner dolphins that often play in the wake of passing boats, and gracefully slow green sea turtles are spotted periodically. During winter months, whales migrate from the cold waters of the north Pacific to bask in the warmer Hawaiian waters to birth, nurse, and raise their young.

Accessibility

No roads enter the Na Pali Coast area, so there is no option that way. However, it is not inaccessible. It can be approached by land, air, and water. **Sea kayaks** can be rented for a trip down the coast—during calm summer weather only. Nonmotorized and quiet, this is undoubtedly as close an experience to early Hawaiian outrigger canoe travel along the coast as most can get these days. **Boat tours** from the west end and south shore regularly make trips to this section of the island for a close-up look at the cliffs and valleys from the water—a truly awe-inspiring sight. **Helicopters** fly overhead, offering riders an unparalleled view of the entire coastline and

dipping into valleys along the way, bringing you nose to nose with these green chasms. Even though there are flight restrictions, helicopter tours along this coast, as in other areas of the island, are not without critics, as they intrude on the serenity of an otherwise solitary and tranquil place. The Na Pali can also be seen by looking down from the Kalalau Valley **overlooks** and from several trails that traverse the razor ridges above the coast's deep valleys. Perhaps the best way to get up close and personal with the Na Pali Coast is to **hike** in on the Kalalau Trail, which starts at road's end at Ke'e Beach.

Na Pali Coast State Park

The Kalalau Valley and the trail leading to it, plus strips at Nu'alolo Kai and Miloli'i, are all part of the sprawling 6,175-acre Na Pali Coast State Park. The remainder of the coastline, cliffs, and valleys are either state forests or natural area reserves. A ranger at Kalalau Valley oversees the park. For those hiking in, the trailhead has a box where you sign in. Day-use permits are required beyond

Hanakapi'ai (two miles in); camping permits are required to stay overnight at Hanakapi'ai, Hanakoa, or Kalalau. You can camp for up to five nights, but no two consecutive nights are allowed at either Hanakapi'ai or Hanakoa. You need a good waterproof tent, sleeping bag, mosquito repellent, first-aid kit, biodegradable soap, food, and toiletries. There are many streams along the trail, but the water can be biologically contaminated and cause horrible stomach distress. Boil it or use purification tablets, or treat it with a filter. Little firewood is available, and you can't cut trees, so take a stove. Don't litter; carry out what you carry in.

Because of heavy use and environmental concerns, the Kalalau Trail and/or Hanakoa campsite have been closed from time to time during the past decade for repair and rejuvenation. Check with the DLNR State Parks office (808/274-3444) for the current status on use and accessibility.

The Nu'alolo Kai and Miloli'i sections can only be reached by boat or kayak. While Nu'alolo Kai is reserved for day use only (commercial boat tours stop here during the summer months), primitive campsites are available at Miloli'i for a maximum of three nights for those who desire real isolation.

The Kalalau Trail

Originally carved out by Hawaiians who needed an overland route between the Kalalau Valley and Ha'ena, the Kalalau Trail not only leads you physically along the Na Pali Coast, but also back in time to classic romantic Hawaii. You leave the 21st century farther and farther behind with every step and reenter a time and place where you can come face to face with your nature self.

Getting to the trailhead is simple: follow Rt. 56 until it ends and then hike. This hike is *the* premier hike on Kaua'i and perhaps in the entire state. The Kalalau is a destination in and of itself, and those who have walked these phenomenal 11 miles never forget it. The trail leads down the Na Pali Coast—as close as you can get to the Hawaiian paradise of old. The trail is well marked by countless centuries of use, so you won't get lost, but it's rutted, root strewn, and muddy. Remnants of mileage posts are all along the way. Streams become torrents during rains but recede quickly—just wait it out. Mountain climbing is dangerous because of the crumbly soil, and the swimming along the coast is unpredictable, with many riptides. Summers, when the wave action returns sand to the beach, are usually fine, but stay out of the water September–April. At Hanakapi'ai, a grim reminder lists the names and ages of those who have lost their lives at this beach. Pay heed! Also, in keeping with the tradition of "Garden of Eden," many people go au naturel at Kalalau Beach. Private parts unaccustomed to sunshine can make you wish you hadn't, so cover up with either sunblock or clothing.

Many people hike in as far as **Hanakapi'ai.** This is a fairly strenuous two-mile hike, the first mile uphill to about 800 feet, the last down, ending at the beach. Camp at spots on the far side of the stream up from the beach. You can also camp in the caves at the beach,

ROBERT NILSEN

Hanakapi'ai Falls

but only during the summer and at low tide. If you hike in and out, leave yourself three hours. From the west side of the stream, the unmaintained **Hanakapi'ai Trail** leads two miles inland up the valley to the splendid **Hanakapi'ai Falls,** taking you past some magnificent mango trees and crumbling stone-walled enclosures of ancient taro patches. This trail crosses and recrosses the stream several times and is often overgrown. If the stream looks high and is running swiftly, turn back; the trail up ahead is narrow and dangerous during periods of high water. If it's low, keep going—the 300-foot falls and surrounding amphitheater are magnificent. You can swim in the pools away from the falls, but not directly under—rocks and trees can come over at any time. As a side trip from Hanakapi'ai camp, this trail should take about 2–3 hours round-trip, perhaps 5–6 hours from Ke'e Beach.

Hanakapi'ai to **Hanakoa** is 4.5 miles of serious hiking as the trail climbs steadily, not returning to sea level until reaching Kalalau Beach nine miles away. Switchbacks take you 600 feet out of Hanakapi'ai Valley. Although heavily traversed, the trail can be very bad in spots. Before arriving at Hanakoa, you must go through **Ho'olulu** and **Waiahuakua** hanging valleys. Both are lush with native flora and are parts of Hono'onapali Nature Area Preserve. Shortly, Hanakoa comes into view. Its many wide terraces are still intact from when it was a major food-growing area. Coffee plants gone wild can still be seen. Hanakoa is rainy, but the rain is intermittent, and the sun always follows. The swimming is fine in the many stream pools. A 0.3-mile hike up the east fork of the stream, just after the six-mile marker, takes you past more terraces good for camping before coming to **Hanakoa Falls.** The terraces are wonderful, but the trail is subject to erosion and treacherous, with many steep sections.

Hanakoa to **Kalalau Beach** is less than five miles but takes about three tough hours. Start early in the morning; it's hot, and although you're only traveling five miles, it gets noticeably drier and more open as you approach Kalalau. The views along the way are ample reward.

KOOLAU THE LEPER

During the 1870s and 1880s, leprosy raged throughout the kingdom, and strong measures were taken. Those believed to be afflicted were wrenched from their families and sent to the hideous colony of Kalaupapa on Moloka'i. One famous Kaua'ian leper, Kaluaikoolau (Koolau), born in 1862 in Kekaha, refused to be brought in and took his family to live in the mountain fortress of the Kalalau Valley. With brilliance, cunning, and fierce determination, he fought the authorities for years and killed all those sent to take him in. Eluding all attempts at capture, he became a symbol of resistance and died a free man. His story became legendary in Hawaii, and he was made famous on a broader scale by Jack London in his short story "Koolau, The Leper." A detailed and more realistic account of the last years of Kaluaikoolau's life was recounted by his wife in 1906 and a recent translation (2001) of it has been published by the University of Hawaii Press as "The True Story of Kaluaikoolau: As Told by his Wife, Piilani."

The power and spirit of the incomparable 'aina predominate. Around the seven-mile marker you enter land that until the late 1970s was part of the Makaweli cattle ranch. The vegetation turns from lush foliage to lantana and sisal, a sign of the aridness of the land. After crossing Pohakuao Valley, you climb the *pali;* on the other side is Kalalau. The lovely valley, two miles wide and three deep, beckons with its glimmering freshwater pools. It's a beauty among beauties and was cultivated until the 1920s. Many terraces and house sites remain. Plenty of guava, mango, and Java plum trees can be found. You can camp only in the trees fronting the beach or in the caves west of the waterfall. You are not allowed to camp along the stream, at its mouth, or in the valley. The waterfall has a freshwater pool, where feral goats come in the morning and evening to water.

A *heiau* is atop the little hillock on the west side of the stream. Follow the trail here up-valley for two miles to **Big Pool,** making one stream crossing on the way. Big Pool is really two pools connected by a natural water slide. Riding it is great for the spirit but tough on your butt. Enjoy! Along the way you pass Smoke Rock, where *pakalolo* growers at one time came to smoke and talk story.

Honopu, Nu'alolo Kai, Miloli'i

Less than a half mile to the west of Kalalau Valley is **Honopu Valley.** This valley is known as the "Valley of the Lost Tribe," as legend tells of a race of small people inhabiting it in great isolation. These Mu were also said to have lived in the Wainiha Valley to the east. The two-part beach at Honopu is unique in that it's split by a huge rock arch; it has been the setting of at least two movie sequences.

Beyond Awa'awapuhi Valley is **Nu'alolo Kai,** an area of beach and dunes backed up tight against the cliff. Nu'alolo Kai was inhabited by a small community of Hawaiians until 1919, and remains of their habitation still exist in stone enclosures, walls, and *heiau* platforms. Fishing was good within the protected reef, and taro was raised in the adjoining Nu'alolo 'Aina Valley. Between these two areas, however, is a sheer cliff, so a rope ladder was hung from a ledge above, from where a trail led around the point to the fields. Because of the reef, there was good anchorage here at Nu'alolo Kai, and it was often used as a rest stop by canoes going between Hanalei and Waimea.

About a mile to the west is **Miloli'i,** also an ancient inhabited site. Here the valley is more easily accessible, and small amounts of taro were cultivated to sustain a small population. There is anchorage on the beach for boats, a primitive camping area with restrooms and a shelter, and down the beach a *heiau* site. Notice that Miloli'i is much drier than the rest of the Na Pali Coast—the heavy rains that pelt Kalalau Valley peter out before they make it this far, and Miloli'i gets only about 20 inches a year.

BACKGROUND

The Land

GEOGRAPHY

Kaua'i, 100 miles northwest of O'ahu, is the northernmost and westernmost of Hawaii's six major islands and the fourth largest. It is approximately 33 miles long and 25 miles wide at its farthest points, with an area of 552 square miles and 90 miles of coastline. Kaua'i is the most regularly shaped of all the major islands—more or less round, like a partially deflated beach ball. The puckered skin around the coast forms bays, beaches, and inlets, while the center is a no-man's-land of mountains, canyon, valleys, and swamp. The island was built by one huge volcano that became extinct about five million years ago. Specula-tion holds that Ni'ihau, a separate and smaller shield volcano 20 miles off the west coast, may have been connected to Kaua'i at one time. The volcanic "hot spot" under Kaua'i was sealed by the weight of the island; as Kaua'i drifted northward the hot spot burst through again and again, building the string of islands from O'ahu to Hawai'i.

A simplified but chronologically accurate account of Kaua'i's emergence is found in a version of the Pele myth retold in the *Kumulipo*. It depicts the fire goddess as a young, beautiful woman who visits Kaua'i during a hula festival and becomes enraptured with Lohiau, a handsome and mighty chief. She wants him

ROBERT NILSEN

KAUA'I'S RED DIRT

Although several of the Hawaiian Islands sport red earth, Kaua'i has what seems to be an inordinate amount of especially red dirt, and the color of this dirt is due to its high mineral bauxite content. As the oldest of the major islands, Kaua'i has been exposed to the elements for the longest time, allowing the hard volcanic rock to break down into fine red particles. Seeing opportunity where others see trouble, at least one entrepreneur decided to make use of this ubiquitous island commodity and dye clothing in it. These are the increasingly popular Red Dirt Shirts of Kaua'i. But what dyes also stains, and your light-colored clothing might be affected. If you venture off the beaches and away from paved roads and walkways, you will undoubtedly encounter red dirt at some time during your stay. Be aware, treat it with respect, and know that at least your shoes may take on a slightly reddish tinge.

now enter this mist-shrouded world aboard helicopters that fly through countless rainbows and hover above a thousand waterfalls. The top of the island is buffeted by strong winds that, with the cool temperatures, keep the plants that grow here close to the ground.

Draining Wai'ale'ale is **Alaka'i Swamp,** a dripping sponge of earth covering about 30 square miles of a near trackless bog. This patch of mire contains flora and fauna found nowhere else on earth. For example, 'ohi'a trees, mighty giants of upland forests, grow here as natural bonsai that could pass as potted plants. Bordering the Alaka'i Swamp on the west is **Waimea Canyon,** where eons of whipping winds, pelting rain, and the incessant grinding of streams and rivulets have chiseled the red bedrock to depths of 3,000 feet and expanses two miles wide. Up and over the canyon wall from there is the **Na Pali Coast,** an incredibly scalloped, undulating vastness of valleys and *pali* forming a bulwark 4,000 feet high.

Other mountains and outcroppings around the island have formed curious natural formations. The **Ha'upu Ridge,** a diminutive range barely 2,000 feet tall south of Lihu'e, forms a profile of Queen Victoria. Above Wailua, the **Nounou Ridge** gives the impression of a man in repose and has been dubbed the Sleeping Giant. Another small range in the northeast, the **Anahola Mountains,** had until recently an odd series of boulders that formed "Hole in the Mountain," mythologically created when a giant hurled his spear through sheer rock. Erosion has collapsed this formation, but another hole is forming, as if to continue the legend.

as a husband and determines to dig a fire-pit home where they can reside in contented bliss. Unfortunately, her unrelenting and unforgiving sea-goddess sister pursues her, forcing Pele to abandon Kaua'i and Lohiau. Thus, she wandered and sparked volcanic eruptions on O'ahu, Maui, and finally atop Kilauea Crater on Hawai'i, where she now resides.

Phenomenal Features of Kaua'i

Located almost smack-dab in the middle of the island are **Mount Kawaikini** (5,243 feet) and adjacent **Mount Wai'ale'ale** (5,148 feet), the highest points on Kaua'i. These two high points are thought to be the western rim of the island's collapsed main volcanic crater. Mount Wai'ale'ale is an unsurpassed "rain magnet," drawing an estimated 450 inches (37.5 feet) of precipitation per year and earning itself the dubious distinction of being "the wettest spot on earth." Don't be intimidated—this rain is amazingly localized, with only 20 inches per year falling just 20 miles away. Visitors can

Channels, Lakes, and Rivers

Kaua'i is separated from O'ahu by the **Kaua'i Channel.** Reaching an incredible depth of 10,900 feet and a width of 72 miles, it is by far the state's deepest and widest channel. On the far side, Kaua'i and Ni'ihau lie some 17 miles apart across the 3,570-foot-deep **Kaulakahi Channel.** Inland, human-made **Waita Reservoir** north of Koloa is the largest body of fresh water in Hawaii, covering 424 acres with a three-mile shoreline. The

ROBERT NILSEN

Waipo'o Falls tumbles into Waimea Canyon.

Waimea River, running through the floor of the canyon, is the island's longest at just under 20 miles, while the **Hanalei River** moves the greatest amount of water, emptying 140 million gallons per day into Hanalei Bay. But the **Wailua River** has the distinction of being the state's only truly navigable waterway, although passage by boat is restricted to a scant three miles upstream. **Hule'ia River** at Lihu'e is used by kayaks and motorized outrigger canoes for a couple of miles but is not deep enough for boat traffic. The flatlands around Kekaha were at one time Hawaii's largest body of inland water. The ponds that were there were brackish and drained last century to create cane fields.

Island Builders

The Hawaiians worshipped Madame Pele, the fire goddess whose name translates equally well as "Volcano," "Fire Pit," or "Eruption of Lava." When she was angry, she complained by spitting fire, which cooled and formed land. Volcanologists say that the islands are huge mounds of cooled basaltic lava surrounded by billions of polyp skeletons that have formed coral reefs.

Kaua'i, like all the Hawaiian Islands, is in essence a shield volcano that erupted rather gently, creating an elongated dome much like a turtle shell. Once above sea level, its tremendous weight sealed the fissure below. Eventually the giant tube that carried lava to the surface sank in on itself and formed a caldera. Wind and water took over and relentlessly sculpted the raw lava into deep crevices and cuts that became valleys, as evidenced by Waimea, the "Grand Canyon of the Pacific," and adjacent Hanapepe Valley on the south shore, and Hanalei and Wainiha Valleys on the north shore.

Lava

Lava flows in two distinct types, for which the Hawaiian names have become universal geological terms: **'a'a** and **pahoehoe.** They're easily distinguishable in appearance, but chemically they're the same. 'A'a is extremely rough and spiny and will quickly tear up your shoes if you do much hiking over it. Also, if you have the misfortune to fall down, you'll immediately know why they call it 'a'a. Pahoehoe, a billowy, rope-like lava resembling burned pancake batter, can mold into fantastic shapes. Kaua'i has had no recent lava flows. Major rejuvenated-stage activity stopped some 1.5 million years ago, and the youngest cinder cones, at some 15,000–20,000 years old, appear to be Pu'u Hunihuni, on the south shore, and Pu'u Kilauea, next to the Kilauea Lighthouse on the north shore.

Being the oldest of the main islands, Kaua'i has had great time to weather and the lava here has mostly been broken down into cinder and dirt, the fertile earth of Kaua'i. While much is gray, there are large patches of red volcanic dirt, for which the island is so well known, and this is due to the high iron oxide content. At various spots around the island, you can see pancake-like layers of lava and a few hard lava dikes that still hold the crumbling hands of wind and rain at bay.

Tsunami

Tsunami is the Japanese word for "tidal wave."

It ranks up there with the worst of them in sparking horror in human beings. But if you were to count up all the people in Hawaii who have been swept away by tidal waves in the last 50 years, the toll wouldn't come close to those killed on bicycles in only a few Mainland cities in just five years. A Hawaiian tsunami is actually a seismic sea wave that has been generated by an earthquake that could easily have originated thousands of miles away in South America or Alaska. Some waves have been clocked at speeds up to 500 mph. The safest place during a tsunami, besides high ground well away from beach areas, is out on the open ocean where even an enormous wave is perceived only as a large swell. A tidal wave is only dangerous when it is opposed by land. The worst tsunami to strike Hawaii in modern times occurred on April 1, 1946. Maui's Hana Coast bore the brunt with a tragic loss of many lives as entire villages were swept away. The same tsunami also struck Halawa Valley on the eastern end of Moloka'i, and the Waipi'o Valley on the Big Island, also with devastating results. Kaua'i was affected relatively little by that event, but the small north shore Kaua'i communities of Ha'ena, Wainiha, and Kalihiwai were devastated in 1957 by water from a tsunami generated in the Aleutian Islands of Alaska.

Earthquakes

These rumblings are also a concern in Hawaii and offer a double threat because they can generate tsunami. If you ever feel a tremor and are close to a beach, get as far away as fast as possible. Kaua'i very rarely experiences earthquakes but, like the other islands, has an elaborate warning system against natural disasters. You will notice loudspeakers high atop poles along many beaches and coastal areas; these warn of tsunami, hurricanes, and earthquakes. The loudspeakers are tested at 11 A.M. on the first working day of each month. All island telephone books contain a civil defense warning and procedures section with which you should acquaint yourself—note the maps showing which areas traditionally have been inundated by tsu-

nami, and what procedures to follow in case an emergency occurs.

CLIMATE

Kaua'i's climate will make you happy. Along the coastline the average temperature is 80°F in spring and summer and about 75° during the remainder of the year. The warmest areas are along the south coast from Lihu'e westward, where the mercury can hit the 90s in midsummer. Nighttime temperatures usually drop 10–15° and may drop into the upper 50s in winter, even along the coast. To escape the heat any time of year, head for Koke'e, in the mountains, where the weather is always moderate with temperatures about 10° lower than along the coast and may be downright chilly in winter.

Precipitation

Although Mount Wai'ale'ale is "the wettest spot on earth," in the areas most frequented by visitors, rain is not a problem. The driest section of Kaua'i is the arid Mana Plain near Polihale Beach in the west. From there across the south shore to the Po'ipu Beach resort area, rainfalls run from five inches per year up to 20 inches, with greater amounts falling on the inland towns. Lihu'e receives about 30 inches. As you head north to Kapa'a and then swing around the coast past Kilauea toward Hanalei, rainfall becomes more frequent but is still a tolerable 45 inches per year. Farther down the coast it may reach 75 inches a year. Cloudbursts in winter are frequent but usually short-lived. Overall, there is less rain during summer months.

"So Good" Weather

The ancient Hawaiians had words to describe climatic specifics such as rain, wind, fog, and even snow, but they didn't have a general word for "weather." The reason is that the weather is just about the same throughout the year and depends more on where you are on any given island than on what season it is. The Hawaiians did distinguish between *kau* (the drier and warmer summer months of May–October with reliable trade winds from the northeast) and

GREEN FLASH

Nearly everyone who has visited a tropical island has heard of the "green flash" – but few have seen it. Some consider the green flash a fable, a made-up story by those more intent on fantasy than reality – but the green flash is real! This phenomenon doesn't just happen on tropical islands; it can happen anywhere around the midriff of the earth where an unobstructed view of the horizon is present, but the clear atmosphere of a tropical island environment does seem to add to its frequency.

The green flash is a momentary burst of luminescent green color that happens on the horizon the instant the sun sets into the sea. If you've seen the green flash you definitely know; there is no mistaking it. If you think you saw something that might have been green but you just weren't sure, you probably didn't see it. Try again another day.

The green flash requires a day where the atmosphere is very clear and unobstructed by clouds, haze, or air pollutants. Follow the sun as it sinks into the sea. Be careful not to look directly at the sun until it's just about out of sight. If the conditions are right, a green color will linger at the spot that the sun sets for a fraction of a second before it too is gone. This "flash" is not like the flash of a camera, but more a change of color from yellow to green – an intense green – that is instantaneous and momentary.

However romantic and magical, this phenomenon does have a scientific explanation. It seems that the green color is produced as a refraction of the sun's rays by the thick atmosphere at the extreme low angle of the horizon. This bending of the sun's light results in the green spectrum of light being the last seen before the light disappears.

Seeing the green flash is an experience. Keep looking, for no matter how many times you've seen it, each time is still full of wonder and joy.

---

ho'oilo (the cooler and wetter winter months of November–April with more erratic winds), but this distinction included social, religious, and even navigational factors, far beyond a mere distinction of weather variations.

The Trade Winds
Temperatures in the 50th state are both constant and moderate because of the trade winds, a breeze from the northeast that blows at about 5–15 miles per hour. These breezes are so prevailing that the northeast sides of the islands are always referred to as **windward,** regardless of where the wind happens to blow on any given day. You can count on the trades to be blowing an average of 300 days per year, hardly missing a day during summer, and occurring half the time in winter. While usually calm in the morning, they pick up during the heat of the afternoon, then weaken at night. Just when you need a cooling breeze, there they are, and when the temperature drops at night, it's as if someone turned down a giant fan.

The trade winds are also a factor in keeping down the humidity. They will suddenly disappear, however, usually in winter, and might not resume for a few weeks. The tropic of Cancer runs through the center of Hawaii, yet the latitude's famed oppressively hot and muggy weather is joyfully absent in the islands. Honolulu, on the same latitude as sweaty Hong Kong and Havana, has an acceptable 65–75 percent daily humidity factor.

Kona Winds
"Kona" means "leeward" in Hawaiian, and when the trades stop blowing, these southerly winds often take over. To anyone from Hawaii, "kona wind" is a euphemism for bad weather, for it brings in hot, sticky air. Luckily, kona winds are most common October–April, when they appear roughly half the time. The temperatures drop slightly during the winter so these hot winds are tolerable, and even useful for moderating the thermometer. In the

summer they are awful, but luckily—again—they hardly ever blow during this season.

A "kona storm" is another matter. These subtropical low-pressure storms develop west of the Hawaiian Islands, and as they move east they draw winds up from the south. Usual only in winter, they can cause considerable damage to crops and real estate. There is no real pattern to kona storms—some years they come every few weeks while in other years they don't appear at all.

Severe Weather

With all this talk of ideal weather it might seem as if there isn't any bad. Read on. When a storm does hit an island, conditions can be bleak and miserable. The worst storms occur in the fall and winter and often have the warped sense of humor to drop their heaviest rainfalls on areas that are normally quite dry. It's not unusual for a storm to dump more than three inches of rain an hour; this can go as high as 10 inches, making Hawaiian rainfalls some of the heaviest on earth.

Hawaii has also been hit with some walloping hurricanes in the last few decades. There haven't been many, but they've been destructive. The vast majority of hurricanes originate far to the southeast off the Pacific coasts of Mexico and Latin America; some, particularly later in the season, start in the midst of the Pacific Ocean near the equator south of Hawaii. Hurricane season is generally considered June–November. Most hurricanes pass harmlessly south of Hawaii, but some, swept along by kona winds, strike the islands. The most recent and destructive was Hurricane ʻIniki, which battered the islands in 1992, killing eight people and causing nearly $2 billion in damage. It had its greatest effect on Niʻihau, the Poʻipu Beach area of Kauaʻi, and the leeward coast of Oʻahu.

Hurricanes ʻIwa and ʻIniki

The Garden Island is much more than just another pretty face—the island and its people have integrity. Thanksgiving was not a very nice time on Kauaʻi back in November 1982. Along with the stuffing and cranberries came an unwelcome guest that showed

destruction by Hurricane ʻIniki

J. D. BISIGNANI

HURRICANE FACTS

A **tropical depression** is a low-pressure system or cyclone with winds below 39 mph. A **tropical storm** is a cyclone with winds 39-73 mph. A **hurricane** is a cyclone with winds over 74 mph. These winds are often accompanied by torrential rains, destructive waves, high water, and storm surges.

The National Weather Service issues a **Hurricane Watch** if hurricane conditions are expected in the area within 36 hours. A **Hurricane Warning** is issued when a hurricane is expected to strike within 24 hours. The state of Hawaii has an elaborate warning system against natural disasters. You will notice loudspeakers high atop poles along many beaches and coastal areas; these warn of tsunami, hurricanes, and earthquakes. These sirens are tested briefly at the beginning of each month. As the figures below attest, property damage has been great but the loss of life has, thankfully, been minimal.

MAJOR HURRICANES SINCE 1950

Name	Date	Islands Affected	Damages
Hiki	Aug. 1950	Kaua'i	1 death
Nina	Dec. 1957	Kaua'i	–
Dot	Aug. 1959	Kaua'i	$5.5 million
Fico	July 1978	Big Island	–
'Iwa	Nov. 1982	Kaua'i, O'ahu	1 death; $234 million
Estelle	July 1986	Maui, Big Island	$2 million
'Iniki	Sept. 1992	Kaua'i, O'ahu	8 deaths; $1.9 billion

no *aloha,* Hurricane 'Iwa. What made this rude 80-mph party crasher so unforgettable was that she was only the fourth such storm to come ashore on Hawaii since records have been kept—the first since the late 1950s. All told, 'Iwa caused $200 million worth of damage. A few beaches were washed away, perhaps forever, and great destruction was suffered by beach homes and resorts, especially around Po'ipu. One life was lost. The people of Kaua'i rolled up their sleeves and set about rebuilding. In short order, the island recovered, and most residents thought, "that was that."

Unfortunately, on Friday, September 11, 1992, **Hurricane 'Iniki** with unimaginable ferocity ripped ashore with top wind speeds of 175 mph and slapped Kaua'i around like a moll in a Bogart movie. The name 'Iniki has two meanings in Hawaiian: "piercing winds"

and "pangs of love," both devastatingly painful in their own way. The hurricane virtually flattened or tore to shreds everything in its path. There was hardly a structure on the entire island that wasn't damaged to some extent. Proud yachts were thrown like toy boats into a jangled heap; cars were buried whole in the red earth; a full third of Kaua'i's 20,000 homes were broken into splinters; and 4,200 hotel rooms became a tangled heap of steel and jagged glass. No one was immune from the savage typhoon. Renowned director Steven Spielberg and his cast were on the island filming scenes for the blockbuster *Jurassic Park.* They, along with other guests, bellmen, maids, groundskeepers, and cooks, rode out the storm huddled in the ballroom of the Westin Kaua'i Lagoons, now the Kaua'i Marriott. In the aftermath, the Kaua'i mayor and her staff worked day and night from her office in Lihu'e, which had no roof, to help with the recovery. Insurance companies were stressed to the breaking point; some were very slow to pay, and a few literally went broke trying to pay all of the claims brought against them.

By the grace of God, and because of a very competent warning system, no more than eight lives were lost, and fewer than 100 people had to be admitted to the hospital due to injury. Psychologically, however, many people who lost everything were scarred; special counseling services were set up to offer techniques to deal with the stress and sense of loss.

Undaunted and with a pride and a will that far surpassed the fury of the storm, Kaua'i's inhabitants rebuilt, while nature took care of the rest. Some philosophical souls hold that Kaua'i wasn't hurt at all, that only a bunch of buildings were destroyed. They contend that in her millions of years of existence, Kaua'i has been through many storms, and Hurricane 'Iniki was merely a "$1.5 billion pruning… for free." Trees were twisted from the ground and bushes were flattened, but Kaua'i is strong and fertile and the damage was only temporary. Now, 'Iniki is mostly a memory; Kaua'i has emerged a touch more self-assured and as beautiful as ever.

Flora and Fauna

The Mystery of Migration

Anyone who loves a mystery will be intrigued by the speculation about how plants and animals first came to Hawaii. Most people's idea of an island paradise includes swaying palms, dense mysterious jungles ablaze with wildflowers, and luscious fruits just waiting to be plucked. In fact, for millions of years the Hawaiian chain consisted of raw and barren islands where no plants grew and no birds sang. Why? Because they are geological orphans that spontaneously popped up in the middle of the Pacific Ocean. The islands, more than 2,000 miles from any continental landfall, were therefore isolated from the normal ecological spread of plants and animals. Even the most tenacious travelers of the flora and fauna kingdoms would be sorely tried in crossing the mighty Pacific. Those that made it by pure chance found a totally foreign ecosystem. They had to adapt or perish. The survivors evolved quickly, and many plants and birds became so specialized that they were limited not only to specific islands in the chain but to habitats that frequently encompassed a single isolated valley. It was as if after traveling so far and finding a niche, they never budged again. Luckily, the soil of Hawaii was virgin and rich, the competition

from other plants or animals was nonexistent, and the climate was sufficiently varied and nearly perfect for most growing things.

The evolution of plants and animals on the isolated islands was astonishingly rapid. A tremendous change in environment, coupled with a limited gene pool, accelerated natural selection. For example, many plants lost their protective thorns and spines because there were no grazing animals or birds to destroy them. Before settlement, Hawaii had no fruits, vegetables, coconut palms, edible land animals, conifers, mangroves, or banyans. The early Polynesians brought 27 varieties of plants that they needed for food and other purposes. About 90 percent of plants on the Hawaiian Islands today were introduced after Captain Cook first set foot here. Tropical flowers, wild and vibrant as we know them today, were relatively few. In a land where thousands of orchids now brighten every corner, there were only three native varieties, the least in any of the 50 states. Today, the indigenous plants and animals have the highest rate of extinction anywhere on earth. By the beginning of this century, native plants growing below 1,500 feet in elevation were almost completely extinct or totally replaced by introduced species. The land and its living things have been

KAUA'I'S BOTANICAL GARDENS

For those interested in the flora of Kaua'i, beyond what can be seen out of the car window, a visit to the following will be both educational and inspiring.

National Tropical Botanical Garden in Po'ipu is the only research facility for tropical plants in the country and the premier botanical garden on Kaua'i. Guided tours of the Allerton Garden lasting about 2.5 hours are given daily except Sunday for $30 a person. Self-guided tours of the McBryde Garden run $15. The visitor center/museum/gift shop (808/742-2623, www.ntbg.org, 8:30 A.M.-5 P.M. daily) is open for walk-in visitors. You can take a short self-guided walk around the visitor center garden, but to go into the main gardens you need advance reservations. Pricey but exceptional.

Limahuli Botanical Garden (808/826-1053, 9:30 A.M.-4 P.M. Tues.-Fri. and Sun.) on Kaua'i's extreme north shore showcases tropical plants both ancient and modern. It's part of the National Tropical Botanical Gardens, and there are both self-guided and guided walking tours, $10 and $15, respectively. As you walk this 0.75-mile loop trail, you'll pass patches of taro plants introduced to Hawaii by early Polynesians, living specimens of endangered native species, and post-contact tropicals, all while enjoying listening to the legends of the valley.

Moir Gardens is at the Kiahuna Plantation Resort in Po'ipu. Over a 27-year period during the mid-1900s, five acres of this former plantation site were cultivated with about 2,500 plants from Africa, the Americas, the Pacific, and India, including cactus and orchid sections. Open daily during daylight hours for self-guided walks, no admission fee.

Smith's Tropical Paradise (808/821-6892, 8:30 A.M.-4 P.M. daily, $5.25 adults, $2.50 children), a finely manicured and well-kept private botanical and cultural garden with a bountiful, beautiful collection of ordinary and exotic plants, is on 30 riverfront acres adjacent to the Wailua Marina. Have a look here before heading upcountry.

The private 240-acre **Na 'Aina Kai Botanical Gardens** (808/828-0525; www.naainakai.com) near Kilauea has numerous individual gardens of various themes, a large tropical hardwood plantation, and bronze sculptures set throughout. Guided tours are given Tuesday, Wednesday, and Thursday only and range from a 90-minute stroll for $25 to a five-hour walk and ride for $70.

greatly transformed by humans and their agriculture. This inexorable process began when Hawaii was the domain of its original Polynesian settlers, then greatly accelerated when the land was inundated by Western peoples.

The indigenous plants and birds of Kaua'i have suffered the same fate as those of the other Hawaiian Islands; they're among the most endangered species on earth and disappearing at an alarming rate. There are some sanctuaries on Kaua'i where native species still live, but they must be vigorously protected. Do your bit to save them; enjoy but do not disturb.

FLORA
Introduced Plants

Hawaii's indigenous and endemic plants, flowers, and trees are both fascinating and beautiful, but unfortunately, like everything else that was native, they are quickly disappearing. The majority of flora considered exotic by visitors was introduced either by the original Polynesians or by later white settlers. The Polynesians who colonized Hawaii brought foodstuffs including coconuts, bananas, taro, breadfruit, sweet potatoes, yams, and sugarcane. They also carried along gourds to use as containers, 'awa to make a basic intoxicant, and the *ti* plant to use for offerings or to string into hula skirts. Non-Hawaiian settlers over the years have brought mangos, papayas, passion fruit, pineapples, and the other tropical fruits and vegetables associated with the islands. Also, most of the flowers, including protea, plumeria, anthuriums, orchids,

PAKALOLO GROWING

In the 1960s and 1970s, mostly *haole* hippies from the Mainland began growing marijuana *(pakalolo)*, usually in the more remote sections of the islands, such as the North Shore of Kaua'i, Puna on Hawai'i, and around Hana on Maui. They discovered what legitimate planters had known for centuries: plant a broomstick in Hawaii, treat it right, and it'll grow. *Pakalolo*, after all, is only a weed, and it grows in Hawaii like wildfire. The locals quickly got into the act when they realized that they, too, could grow a "money tree." As a matter of fact, they began resenting the *haole* usurpers, and a quiet and sometimes dangerous feud has been going on ever since. Much has been made of the viciousness of the backcountry "growers" of Hawaii, as in other areas of the States. There are tales of booby traps and armed patrols guarding plants in the hills, but mostly it's a cat-and-mouse game between the authorities and the growers. Marijuana is one of the crops with the largest monetary turnover in the islands, and as such is now considered a major source of agricultural revenue, albeit illicit and underground.

If you as a tourist are tramping about in the forest and happen upon someone's "patch," don't touch anything. Just back off and you'll be okay.

heliconia, ginger, and most hibiscus, have come from every continent on earth. Tropical America, Asia, Java, India, and China have contributed their most beautiful and delicate blooms. Hawaii is blessed with national and state parks, gardens, undisturbed rainforests, private reserves, and commercial nurseries that offer an exhaustive botanical survey of the island. The following is a sampling of the common native and introduced flora that add dazzling color and exotic tastes to the landscape.

Native Trees

Koa and 'ohi'a are two indigenous trees still seen on Kaua'i. The **koa,** a form of acacia, is Hawaii's finest native tree. It can grow to over 70 feet high and has a strong, straight trunk that can measure more than 10 feet in circumference. Koa is a quickly growing legume that fixes nitrogen in the soil. It is believed that the tree originated in Africa, where conditions were very damp. It then migrated to Australia, where it was very dry, which caused the elimination of leaves, so all that was left were bare stems that could survive in the desert climate. When koa came to the Pacific islands, instead of reverting to the true leaf, it just broadened its leaf stem into sickle-shaped, leaf-like foliage that produces an inconspicuous, pale yellow flower. When the tree is young or damaged it reverts to the original feathery, fern-like leaf that evolved in Africa millions of years ago. Koa does best in well-drained soil in deep forest areas, but scruffy specimens will grow in poorer soil. The Hawaiians used koa as the main log for their dugout canoes, and elaborate ceremonies were performed when a log was cut and dragged to a canoe shed. Koa wood was also preferred for paddles, spears, even surfboards. Today it is still considered an excellent furniture wood; although fine specimens can be found in the reserve of Hawaii Volcanoes National Park on the Big Island, loggers elsewhere are harvesting the last of the big trees.

The **'ohi'a** is a survivor and therefore the most abundant of all the native Hawaiian trees. Coming in a variety of shapes and sizes, it grows as miniature trees in wet bogs or as 100-foot giants on cool, dark slopes at higher elevations. This tree is often the first life in new lava flows. The 'ohi'a produces a tuft-like flower—usually red, but occasionally orange, yellow, or white, the last being very rare and elusive—that resembles a natural pompon. The flower was considered sacred to Pele; it was said that she would cause a rainstorm if people picked 'ohi'a blossoms without the proper prayers. The flowers were fashioned into lei that resembled feather boas. The strong, hard wood was used to make canoes, poi bowls, and especially temple images. 'Ohi'a logs were also used as railroad ties and shipped to the Main-

KUKUI

Reaching heights of 80 feet, the *kukui* (candlenut) was a veritable department store to the Hawaiians, who made use of almost every part of this utilitarian giant. Its nuts, bark, and flowers were ground into potions and salves to be taken as a general tonic, applied to ulcers and cuts as an effective antibiotic, or administered internally as a cure for constipation or asthma attacks. The bark was mixed with water and the resulting juice was used as a dye in tattooing, tapa-cloth making, and canoe painting, and as a preservative for fishnets. The oily nuts were burned in stone holders as a light source, and they were ground and eaten as a condiment called 'inamona. Polished nuts took on a beautiful sheen and were strung as lei. Lastly, the wood itself was hollowed into canoes and used as fishnet floats.

land from Pahoa on the Big Island. It's believed that the golden spike linking rail lines between the U.S. East and West Coasts was driven into a Puna 'ohi'a log when the two railroads came together in Ogden, Utah.

Tropical Rainforests

When it comes to pure and diverse natural beauty, the United States is one of the finest pieces of real estate on earth. As if purple mountains' majesty and fruited plains weren't enough, it even received a tiny, living emerald of tropical rainforest. A tropical rainforest is where the earth takes a breath and exhales pure sweet oxygen through its vibrant green canopy. Located in the territories of Puerto Rico and the Virgin Islands, and in the state of Hawaii, these forests represent only one-half of one percent of the world's total, and they must be preserved. The U.S. Congress passed two bills in 1986 designed to protect the unique biological diversity of its tropical areas, but their destruction has continued unabated. The lowland rainforests of Hawaii, populated mostly by native 'ohi'a, are being razed. Land-

owners slash, burn, and bulldoze them to create more land for cattle and agriculture, and, most distressingly, for wood chips to generate electricity! Introduced wild boar gouge the forest floor, exposing sensitive roots and leaving tiny fetid ponds where mosquito larvae thrive. Feral goats roam the forests like hoofed locusts and strip all vegetation within reach. Rainforests on the higher and steeper slopes of mountains have a better chance as they are harder for humans to reach. One unusual feature of Hawaii's rainforests is that they are "upside down." Most plant and animal species live on the forest floor, rather than in the canopy as in other forests.

Almost half of the birds classified in the United States as endangered live in Hawaii, and almost all of these make their homes in the rainforests. We can only lament the passing of the rainforests that have already fallen to ignorance, but if this ill-fated destruction continues on a global level, we will be lamenting our own passing. We must nurture the rainforests that remain, and with simple enlightenment, let them be.

BIRDS IN KAUA'I

Kaua'i exceeds its reputation as the Garden Island. It has had a much longer time for soil building and rooting of a wide variety of plantlife, so it's lusher than the other islands. Kaua'i lies on a main bird migratory route, and some of its land has been set aside for the benefit of these birds. Aside from the wildlife refuges, impenetrable inland regions surrounding Mount Wai'ale'ale and dominated by the Alaka'i Swamp have provided a natural sanctuary for Kaua'i's own birds. Because of this, Kaua'i is home to the largest number of indigenous birds extant in Hawaii, though even here they are tragically endangered.

One of the great tragedies of natural history is the continuing demise of Hawaiian birdlife. Perhaps only 15 original species of birds remain of the more than 70 native families that thrived before the coming of humans. Since the arrival of Captain Cook in 1778, 23 species have become extinct, with 31 more in danger.

ROOSTER ALERT

An ever-present entity on Kaua'i, and to a lesser extent on the other islands, is the feral rooster. Early Polynesians brought chickens with them on their journeys from the South Pacific. Later, Europeans and others brought different varieties of fowl, and the Filipinos brought their fighting cocks. Over the years these animals mingled, mixing breeds. Many were kept in people's backyards for their meat, eggs, or ability to slit the throats of other birds during cockfights. As in any rural place, these animals would herald the dawn by crowing.

Hurricane 'Iniki changed this bucolic setting in a dramatic way. In its fury, it set many of these previously caged animals free to wander where they might – and they did with abandon. In essence, they've become the island animal kingdom's homeless. Today they seem to be everywhere, and more than that, make a racket at all times of the day. It was impossible to round up all these fugitive birds, so now they roam. To make matters worse, many of the cane fields they used to hunt in search of food are gone, given over to other crops or let grow fallow. They look for food where they still can find it, often near residential areas. Many island residents now consider these birds a nuisance, and some hope the state will open a hunting season on them to help control their increasingly obnoxious population. In the meantime, if you hit one on the road, probably few will care.

And what's not known is how many species were wiped out before white explorers arrived. Experts believe that the Hawaiians annihilated about 40 species, including seven species of geese, a rare one-legged owl, ibis, lovebirds, sea eagles, and honeycreepers—all gone before Captain Cook arrived. Hawaii's endangered birds account for 40 percent of the birds officially listed as endangered or threatened by the U.S. Fish and Wildlife Service. In the last 200 years, more than four times as many birds have become extinct in Hawaii as in all of North America. These figures unfortunately suggest that a full 40 percent of Hawaii's endemic birds no longer exist. Almost all of O'ahu's native birds are gone, and few indigenous Hawaiian birds can be found on any island below the 3,000-foot level.

Native birds have been reduced in number because of multiple factors. The original Polynesians helped wipe out many species. They altered large areas for farming and used fire to destroy patches of pristine forests. Also, bird feathers were highly prized for making lei, for featherwork in capes and helmets, and for the large *kahili* fans that indicated rank among the *ali'i*. Introduced exotic birds and the new diseases they carried are another major reason for reduction of native bird numbers, along with predation by the rat—especially upon ground-nesting birds. Bird malaria and bird pox were also devastating to the native species. Mosquitoes, unknown in Hawaii until a ship named the *Wellington* introduced them at Lahaina in 1826 through larvae carried in its water barrels, infected most native birds, causing a rapid reduction in birdlife. Feral pigs rooting deep in the rainforests knock over ferns and small trees, creating fetid pools in which mosquito larvae thrive. However, the most damaging factor by far is the assault upon native forests by agriculture and land developers. The vast majority of Hawaiian birds evolved into specialists. They lived in only one small area and ate a very limited number of plants or insects, which once removed or altered soon killed the birds.

You'll spot birds all over Kaua'i, from the coastal areas to the high mountain slopes. Some are found on other islands as well, but the indigenous ones listed below are found only or mainly on Kaua'i. Every bird listed is either threatened or endangered.

Indigenous Forest Birds

Kaua'i's upland forests are still home to many Hawaiian birds; they're dwindling but holding on. You may be lucky enough to spot some of the following. The **Hawaiian owl** *(pueo),* one of the friendliest *'aumakua* in ancient Hawaii, hunts by both day and night. It was an especially benign and helpful guardian. Old Hawaiian stories abound where a *pueo* came to the aid of warriors in distress. The warriors would head for a tree in which a *pueo* had alighted; once there, they were safe from their pursuers, under the protection of "the wings of an owl." There are many introduced barn owls in Hawaii, easily distinguished from *pueo* by their distinctive heart-shaped faces. The *pueo* is about 15 inches tall with a mixture of brown and white feathers. The eyes are large, round, and yellow, and the legs are heavily feathered, unlike a barn owl. *Pueo* chicks are a distinct yellow color.

The **'elepaio** is an indigenous bird found around Koke'e and so named because its song sounds like its name. A small brown bird with white rump feathers, it's very friendly.

Found above 2,000 feet, feeding on a variety of insects and flowers, is the **'i'iwi,** a bright red bird with a salmon-colored hooked bill. While most often sounding like a squeaking hinge, it can also produce a melodious song.

'Anianiau is a four-inch, yellow-green bird found around Koke'e. Its pending demise is due to a lack of fear of humans. The **nukupu'u,** extinct on the other islands except for a few on Maui, is found in Kaua'i's upper forests and bordering the Alaka'i Swamp. It's a five-inch bird with a drab green back and a bright yellow chest.

Birds of the Alaka'i Swamp

The following scarce birds are some of the last indigenous Hawaiian birds, saved only by the inhospitality of the Alaka'i Swamp. All are endangered species and under no circumstances should they be disturbed. The last survivors include: the **'o'u,** a chubby seven-inch bird with a green body, yellow head, and lovely whistle ranging over half an octave; the relatively common **Hawaiian creeper,** a hand-sized bird with a light green back and white belly, which travels in pairs and searches bark for insects;

and the **puaiohi,** a dark brown, white-bellied, seven-inch bird so rare that its nesting habits are largely unknown. As with some other lucky Hawaiian birds, *puaiohi* chicks have been bred in captivity and released into the wild and seem to be adapting well. The **'O'o'a'a,** although its name may resemble the sounds you make getting into a steaming hot tub, is an eight-inch black bird that played a special role in Hawaiian history. Its blazing yellow leg feathers were used to fashion the spectacular capes and helmets of the ali'i. Even before white explorers came, this bird was ruthlessly pursued by specially trained hunters who captured it and plucked its feathers. The **'akialoa** is a seven-inch, greenish-yellow bird with a long, slender, curved bill.

Sea Birds and Shore Birds

Among the millions of birds that visit Kaua'i yearly, some of the most outstanding are its marine and water birds. Many beautiful individuals are seen at Kilauea Point National Wildlife Refuge, where they often nest in the trees, on the cliff face, or on Moku'ae'ae Islet. The **Laysan albatross** *(moli)* is a far-ranging Pacific flier whose seven-foot wingspan carries it in effortless flight. This bird has little fear of humans and while on the ground is easily approachable. It also nests along Barking Sands at Polihale.

The **wedge-tailed shearwater** *('ua'u kani)* is known as the "moaning bird" because of its doleful sounds. These birds have no fear of predators and often fall prey to feral dogs and cats. Also seen making spectacular dives for squid off Kilauea Point is the **red-footed booby,** a fluffy white bird with a blue bill and a three-foot wingspan. Kiting from the same cliffs is the **white-tailed tropicbird,** snow-white elegance with a three-foot wingspan and a long, wispy, kite-like tail.

One of the most amazing species is the **great frigate bird,** an awesome specimen with nearly an eight-foot wingspan. Predominantly black, with a long forked tail, the males have a red throat pouch that they inflate like a balloon to attract females during mating season. These

ROBERT NILSEN

Hawaiian gallinule

giants, the kings of the rookery, often steal food from lesser birds. They populate Kilauea Point and are also seen along Kalalau Trail and even at Po'ipu Beach, but they breed and nest on several of the Northwestern Islands as well as in other places of the world.

Many of Kaua'i's water birds are most easily found in the marshes and ponds of Hanalei National Wildlife Refuge, though they have also been spotted on some of the island's reservoirs, especially Alakoko Fishpond in the Hule'ia National Wildlife Refuge and its vicinity. The **Hawaiian stilt** *(ae'o)* is an 18-inch-tall wading bird with pink, stick-like legs. The **Hawaiian coot** *('alae ke'oke'o)* is a gray-black, duck-like bird with a white belly and face. The **Hawaiian gallinule** *('alae 'ula),* an endemic Hawaiian bird often found in Hanalei's taro patches, has a duck-like body with a red face tipped in yellow. It uses its huge chicken-like feet to hop across floating vegetation. The **Hawaiian duck** *(koloa maoli)* looks like a mallard and, because of interbreeding with common ducks, is becoming rarer as a distinct species.

Introduced Common Birds

Kaua'i is rich in all manner of birds, from migratory marine birds to upland forest dwellers. Many live in areas you can visit; others you can see by taking a short stroll and remaining observant. Some, of course, are rare and very difficult to spot. Some of the most easily spotted island birds frequent almost all areas from Kekaha around to Kalalau and the upland regions of Koke'e, including the blazing red northern cardinal; the comedic, brash common mynah; the operatic Western meadowlark, introduced in 1930 and found in Hawaii only on Kaua'i; the ubiquitous Japanese white-eye; sudden fluttering flocks of house finches; that Arctic traveler the golden plover, found along mudflats everywhere; and the cattle egret, a white, 20-inch-tall heron found anywhere from the backs of cattle to the lids of garbage cans. Egrets were introduced from Florida in 1960 to control cattle pests; they have so proliferated they are now considered a pest by some.

MAMMALS

Hawaii had only two indigenous mammals, the monk seal (found mostly in the Northwest-

NATIONAL WILDLIFE REFUGES ON KAUA'I

For information on Kaua'i's refuges, write to P.O. Box 87, Kilauea, HI 96754, or call 808/828-1413.

KILAUEA POINT NWR

Kilauea Point lies one mile north of Kilauea on a paved road; the headquarters and parking area are on Kilauea Point. This refuge protects red-footed boobies, shearwaters, great frigate birds, brown boobies, red-tailed and white-tailed tropicbirds, and Laysan albatross, as well as green sea turtles, humpback whales, and dolphins. It covers 31 acres of cliffs and headlands with native coastal plants. Open 10 A.M.–4 P.M. Mon.-Fri.; admission is $3 for those over age 16.

HANALEI NWR

This refuge is on the north coast of Kaua'i outside Hanalei. You can observe wildlife from 'Ohiki Road, which begins at the west end of the Hanalei River bridge, or from the highway overlook in Princeville. Hanalei NWR protects *koloa* (Hawaiian duck), Hawaiian coot, Hawaiian gallinule, and Hawaiian stilt. It covers 917 acres of river bottomland, taro farms, and wooded slopes in the Hanalei River Valley. This refuge was established in 1972.

HULE'IA NWR

At Hule'ia, viewing is best from the Alakoko Fishpond overlook along Hulemalu Road west of Lihu'e. The refuge protects *koloa* (Hawaiian duck), Hawaiian coot, Hawaiian gallinule, and Hawaiian stilt on 238 acres of seasonally flooded river bottomland and wooded slopes of the Hule'ia River Valley. Hule'ia was established in 1973. No general admittance.

---

ern Islands) and the hoary bat (found primarily on the Big Island); both are threatened and endangered. The remainder of Kaua'i's mammals are transplants. But like anything else, including people, that has been in the islands long enough, they take on characteristics that make them "local." There are no native amphibians, reptiles, ants, termites, or cockroaches. All are imported.

The **Hawaiian monk seal** or *'ilio holu i ka uaua* is a solitary creature, usually seen only when it hauls itself up on a sandy beach or lava shelf to sun itself, sleep, or birth a pup. Baby pups are dark black in color, about three feet long, and weigh up to 30 pounds. They change colors as they age to a dark brown or gray on top and lighter brown to beige below. Females are somewhat larger than males, weigh up to 600 pounds, and can be eight feet long. While there may be several dozen that make the waters around Kaua'i their home, most of the 1,500 or so thought to exist live near the uninhabited islands to the northwest.

The **Hawaiian hoary bat** *('ope'ape'a)* is a cousin of the Mainland bats, a strong flier that made it to Hawaii eons ago and developed its own species. Its tail has a whitish coloration, hence the name. Small populations of the bat are found on Maui and Kaua'i, but most are on the Big Island. The hoary bat has a 13-inch wingspan and, unlike other bats, is a solitary creature, roosting in trees. It gives birth to twins in early summer and can often be spotted darting over a number of bays just around sundown.

Hawaiian Whales and Dolphins

Perhaps it's their tremendous size and graceful power, coupled with a dancer's delicacy of movement, that render whales so aesthetically and emotionally captivating. In fact, many people claim that they even feel a spirit-bond to these obviously intelligent mammals that at one time shared dry land with us and then re-evolved into creatures of the great seas. Experts often remark that whales exhibit behavior akin to the highest social virtues. For example, whales rely much more on learned behavior than on instinct, the sign of a highly evolved intelligence. Gentle mothers and protective "escort" males join to teach the young to survive. They display loyalty and bravery in times of distress, as well as innate gentleness and curiosity. Their songs, especially those of the humpbacks, fascinate scientists and are considered a unique form of communication in the animal kingdom.

Humpback whales migrate to Hawaii every year from November to May. Here, they winter, mate, give birth, and nurture their young until returning to food-rich northern waters in the spring. It's hoped that the human race can peacefully share the oceans with these magnificent giants forever. Then, perhaps, we will have taken the first step in saving ourselves.

The role of whales and dolphins in Hawaiian culture seems quite limited. Unlike fish, which were intimately known and individually named, only two generic names apply to whales: *kohola* (whale) and *palaoa* (sperm whale). Dolphins were all lumped together under one name, *nai'a;* Hawaiians were known to harvest dolphins on occasion by herding them onto a beach. Whale jewelry was worn by the *ali'i.* The most coveted ornament came from a sperm whale's tooth, called a *lei niho palaoa,* which was carved into one large curved pendant. Sperm whales have upward of 50 teeth, ranging in size from four to 12 inches and weighing up to two pounds. One whale could provide numerous pendants. The most famous whale in Hawaiian waters is the humpback, but others often sighted include the sperm, killer, false killer, pilot, Cuvier's, Blainsville, and pygmy killer. There are technically no porpoises, but dolphins include the common, bottlenose, spinner, white-sided, broad- and slender-beaked, and rough-toothed. The mahimahi, a favorite eating fish found on many menus, is commonly referred to as dolphin fish but is unrelated and is a true fish, not a cetacean.

History

Kaua'i is the first of the Hawaiian Islands in many ways. Besides being the oldest main island geologically, some believed that Kaua'i was the first island to be populated by Polynesian explorers. Theoretically, this colony was well established as early as A.D. 200, which predates the populating of the other islands. Even Madame Pele chose Kaua'i as her first home and was content here until her sister drove her away. Her fires went out when she moved on, but she, like all visitors, never forgot Kaua'i.

THE ROAD FROM TAHITI
The Great Navigators
No one knows exactly when the first Polynesians arrived in Hawaii, but the great "deliberate migrations" from the southern islands seem to have taken place A.D. 500–800, though anthropologists keep pushing the date backward in time as new evidence becomes available. Even before that, however, it's reasonable to assume that the first people to set foot on Hawaii were probably fishermen, or perhaps defeated warriors whose canoes were blown hopelessly northward into unfamiliar waters. They arrived by a combination of extraordinary good luck and an uncanny ability to sail and navigate without instruments, using the sun by day and the moon and rising stars by night. They could feel the water and determine direction by swells, tides, and currents. The movements of fish and cloud formations were also utilized to give direction. Since their arrival was probably an accident, they were unprepared to settle on the fertile but barren lands, having no stock animals, plant cuttings, or women. Forced to return southward, undoubtedly many lost their lives at sea, but a few wild-eyed stragglers must have made it home to tell tales of a paradise to the north where land was plentiful and the sea bounteous. This is affirmed by ancient navigational chants from Tahiti, Moorea, and Bora Bora, which, passing from

father to son, revealed how to follow the stars to the "heavenly homeland in the north." Possibly a few migrations followed, but it's known that for centuries there was no real reason for a mass exodus, so the chants alone remained and eventually became shadowy legend.

Where They Came From

It's generally agreed that the first planned migrations were from the violent cannibal islands that Spanish explorers called the **Marquesas,** 11 islands in extreme eastern Polynesia. The islands themselves are harsh and inhospitable, breeding a toughness into these people that enabled them to withstand the hardships of long, unsure ocean voyages and years of resettle-

ment. Marquesans were a fiercely independent people whose chiefs could rise from the ranks because of bravery or intelligence. They must have also been a savage-looking lot. Both men and women tattooed themselves in complex blue patterns from head to foot. The warriors carried massive, intricately designed ironwood war clubs and wore carved whale teeth in slits in their earlobes that eventually stretched to the shoulders. They shaved the sides of their heads with sharks' teeth, tied their hair in two topknots that looked like horns, and rubbed their heavily muscled and tattooed bodies with scented coconut oils. They worshipped mummified ancestors while the bodies of warriors of defeated neighboring tribes were consumed.

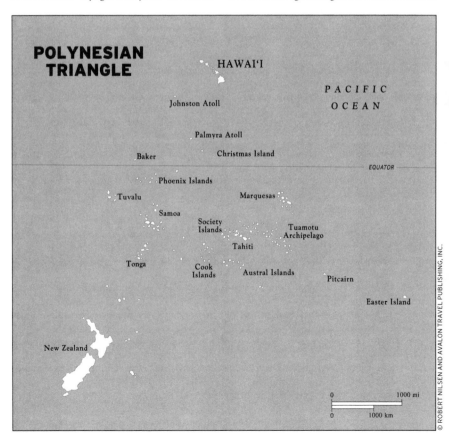

© ROBERT NILSEN AND AVALON TRAVEL PUBLISHING, INC.

THE *KUMULIPO*

The great genealogies, finally compiled in the late 1800s by order of King Kalakaua, were collectively known as the *Kumulipo, A Hawaiian Creation Chant*, basically a Polynesian account of Genesis. Other chants related to the beginning of this world, but the *Kumulipo* sums it all up and is generally considered the best. The chant relates that after the beginning of time, there is a period of darkness. The darkness, however, mysteriously brims with spontaneous life; during this period plants and animals are born, as well as Kumulipo, the man, and Po'ele, the woman. In the eighth chant, darkness gives way to light and the gods descend to earth. Wakea is "the sky father" and Papa is "the earth mother," whose union gives birth to the islands of Hawaii. First born is Hawai'i, followed by Maui, then Kaho'olawe. Apparently, Papa becomes bushed after three consecutive births and decides to vacation in Tahiti. While Papa is away recovering from postpartum depression and working on her tan, Wakea gets lonely and takes Ka'ula as his second wife; she bears him the island-child of Lana'i. Not fully cheered up, but getting the hang of it, Wakea takes a third wife, Hina, who promptly bears the island of Moloka'i. Meanwhile, Papa gets wind of these shenanigans, returns from Polynesia, and retaliates by taking up with

Lua, a young and virile god. She soon gives birth to the island of O'ahu. Papa and Wakea finally decide that they really are meant for each other and reconcile to conceive Kaua'i, Ni'ihau, Ka'ula, and Nihoa. These two progenitors are the source from which the *ali'i* ultimately traced their lineage, and from which they derived their god-ordained power to rule. Basically, there are two major genealogical families: the Nanaulu, who became the royal *ali'i* of O'ahu and Kaua'i, and the Ulu, who provided the royalty of Maui and Hawai'i.

One well-known translation of *The Kumulipo* was done in 1951 by Martha Beckwith; previously, one had been done by Queen Lili'uokalani. The best sources of information in English on Hawaiian myth and legend are Martha Beckwith's *Hawaiian Mythology* and the monumental three-volume opus *An Account of the Polynesian Race*, compiled by Abraham Fornander from 1878 to 1885. Fornander, after settling in Hawaii, married an *ali'i* from Moloka'i and had an illustrious career as a newspaperman, Maui circuit judge, and finally Supreme Court justice. For years Fornander sent scribes to every corner of the kingdom to listen to the elder *kupuna*. They returned with firsthand accounts, which he dutifully recorded.

They were masters at building great double-hulled canoes launched from huge canoe sheds. Two hulls were fastened together to form a catamaran, and a hut in the center provided shelter in bad weather. The average voyaging canoe was 60–80 feet long and could comfortably hold an extended family of about 30 people. These small family bands carried all the staples they would need in the new lands.

The New Lands

For five centuries the Marquesans settled and lived peacefully on the new land, as if Hawaii's *aloha* spirit overcame most of their fierceness. The tribes coexisted in relative harmony, especially since there was no competition for land.

Cannibalism died out. There was much coming and going between Hawaii and Polynesia as new people came to settle for hundreds of years. Then, it appears that in the 12th century a deliberate exodus of warlike Tahitians arrived and subjugated the settled islanders. They came to conquer. This incursion had a terrific significance on the Hawaiian religious and social system. Oral tradition relates that a Tahitian priest, Pa'ao, found the mana of the Hawaiian chiefs to be low, signifying that their gods were weak. Pa'ao built a *heiau* at Waha'ula on the Big Island, then introduced the warlike god Ku and the rigid *kapu* system through which the new rulers became dominant. Voyages between Tahiti and Hawaii continued for

THE STRIFES OF MAUI

Of all the heroes and mythological figures of Polynesia, Maui is the best known. His "strifes" are like the great Greek epics, and they made excellent tales of courage and action that elders loved to relate to youngsters around the evening fire. Maui was abandoned by his mother, Hina of Fire, when he was an infant. She wrapped him in her hair and cast him upon the sea, where she expected him to die. But he lived and returned home to become her favorite. She knew then that he was a born hero and had strength far beyond that of ordinary mortals. His first exploit was to lift the sky. In those days, the sky hung so low that humans had to crawl around on all fours. A seductive young woman approached Maui and asked him to use his great strength to lift the sky. In fine heroic fashion, the big boy agreed, if the beautiful woman would, euphemistically, "give him a drink from her gourd." He then obliged her by lifting the sky, and he might even have made the earth move for her once or twice.

The territory of humanity was small at that time. Maui decided that more land was needed, so he conspired to "fish up islands." He descended into the land of the dead and petitioned an ancestress to fashion him a hook from her jawbone. She obliged and created the mythical hook, *Manai ikalani*. Maui then secured a sacred *'alae* bird, which he intended to use for bait, and bid his brothers paddle him far out to sea. When he arrived at the deepest spot, he lowered *Manai ikalani*, baited with the sacred bird, and his sister, Hina of the Sea, placed it into the mouth of "Old One Tooth," who held the land fast to the bottom of the waters. Maui then exhorted his brothers to row but warned them not to look back. They strained at the oars with all their might and slowly a great landmass arose. One brother, overcome by curiosity, looked back, and, when he did so, the land shattered into all of the islands of Polynesia.

Maui still desired to serve humanity. People were without fire, the secret of which was held by the sacred *'alae* birds, who learned it from Maui's far-distant mother. Hina of Fire gave Maui her burning fingernails, but he oafishly kept dropping them into streams until all had fizzled out and he had totally irritated his generous progenitor. Hina pursued him, trying to burn him to a cinder; Maui chanted for rain to put out her scorching fires. When she saw that they were being quenched, she hid her fire in the barks of special trees and informed the mud hens where they could be found, but first made them promise never to tell humans. Maui knew of this and captured a mud hen, threatening to wring its scrawny, traitorous neck unless it gave up the secret. The bird tried trickery and told Maui first to rub together the stems of sugarcane, then banana, and even taro. None worked, and Maui's determined rubbing is why these plants have hollow roots today.

Finally, with Maui's hands tightening around the mud hen's gizzard, the bird confessed that fire could be found in the *hau* tree and also the sandalwood, which Maui named *'ili aha* (fire bark) in its honor. He then rubbed all the feathers off the mud hen's head for being so deceitful, which is why their crowns are featherless today.

Maui's greatest deed, however, was in snaring the sun and exacting a promise that it would go slower across the heavens. The people complained that there were not enough daylight hours to fish or farm. Maui's mother could not dry her tapa cloth because the sun rose and set so quickly. She asked her son to help. Maui went to his blind grandmother, who lived on the slopes of Haleakala and was responsible for cooking the sun's bananas, which he ate every day in passing. She told him to personally weave 16 strong ropes with nooses from his sister's hair. Some say these came from her head, but other versions insist that it was no doubt Hina's pubic hair that had the power to hold the sun god. Maui positioned himself with the rope, and as each of the 16 rays of the sun came across Haleakala, he snared them until the sun was defenseless and had to bargain for his life. Maui agreed to free him if he promised to go more slowly. From that time forward the sun moved more slowly, and Haleakala (House of the Sun) became his home.

about 100 years, and Tahitian customs, legends, and language became the Hawaiian way of life. Then suddenly, for no recorded or apparent reason, the voyages discontinued and Hawaii returned to total isolation.

The islands remained forgotten for almost 500 years until the indomitable English seaman Captain James Cook sighted Oʻahu on January 18, 1778, and stepped ashore at Waimea on Kauaʻi two days later. At that time Hawaii's isolation was so complete that even the Polynesians had forgotten about it. On an earlier voyage, Tupaia, a high priest from Raiatea, had accompanied Captain Cook as he sailed throughout Polynesia. Tupaia demonstrated his vast knowledge of existing archipelagos throughout the South Pacific by naming over 130 islands and drawing a map that included the Tonga group, the Cook Islands, the Marquesas, and even tiny Pitcairn, a rock in far eastern Polynesia where the mutinous crew of the *Bounty* found solace. In mentioning the Marquesas, Tupaia said, *"he maʻa te kaʻata,"* which means "food is man" or simply "cannibals." But remarkably absent from Tupaia's vast knowledge was the existence of Easter Island, New Zealand, and Hawaii.

The next waves of people to Hawaii would be white, and the Hawaiian world would be changed quickly and forever.

THE WORLD DISCOVERS HAWAII

The late 18th century was an extraordinary time in Hawaiian history. Monumental changes seemed to happen all at once. First, Captain James Cook, a Yorkshire farm boy fulfilling his destiny as the all-time greatest Pacific explorer, found Hawaii for the rest of the world. For better or worse, it could no longer be an isolated Polynesian homeland. For the first time in Hawaiian history, a charismatic leader, Kamehameha, emerged, and after a long civil war he united all the islands into one centralized kingdom. The death of Captain Cook in Hawaii marked the beginning of a long series of tragic misunderstandings between whites and natives. When Kamehameha died, the old

religious system of *kapu* came to an end, leaving the Hawaiians in a spiritual vortex. Many takers arrived to fill the void: missionaries after souls, whalers after their prey and a good time, traders and planters after profits and a home. The islands were opened and devoured like ripe fruit. Powerful nations, including Russia, Great Britain, France, and the United States, yearned to bring this strategic Pacific jewel under their own influence.

The 19th century brought the demise of the Hawaiian people as a dominant political force in their own land and with it the end of Hawaii as a sovereign monarchy. An almost bloodless yet bitter military coup followed by a brief Hawaiian Republic ended in annexation by the United States. As the United States became completely entrenched politically and militarily, a new social and economic order was founded on the plantation system. Amazingly rapid population growth occurred with the importation of plantation workers from Asia and Europe, which yielded a unique cosmopolitan blend of races like nowhere else on earth.

By the dawning of the 20th century, the face of old Hawaii had been altered forever; the "sacred homeland in the north" was hurled into the modern age. The attack on Pearl Harbor saw a tremendous loss of life and brought Hawaii closer to the United States by a baptism of blood. Finally, on August 21, 1959, after 59 years as a territory, Hawaii officially became the 50th state of the United States.

Captain Cook Sights Hawaii

In 1776 Captain James Cook set sail for the Pacific from Plymouth, England, on his third and final expedition into this still largely unexplored region of the world. On a fruitless quest for the fabled Northwest Passage across the North American continent, he sailed down the coast of Africa, rounded the Cape of Good Hope, crossed the Indian Ocean, and traveled past New Zealand, Tasmania, and the Friendly Islands (where the "friendly" natives hatched an unsuccessful plot to murder him). On January 18, 1778, Captain Cook's 100-foot flagship HMS *Resolution* and its 90-foot companion HMS *Discovery* sighted Oʻahu. Two days later, they sighted Kauaʻi and went ashore at the village of Waimea. Though anxious to get on with his mission, Cook decided to make a quick sortie to investigate this new land and reprovision his ships. He did, however, take time to remark in his diary about the close resemblance of these newfound people to others he had encountered as far south as New Zealand and marveled at their widespread habitation across the Pacific.

The first trade was some brass medals for a mackerel. Cook also stated that he had never before met natives so astonished by a ship, and that they had an amazing fascination with iron, which they called *koʻi,* Hawaiian for "adze." There is even some conjecture that a Spanish ship under one Captain Gaetano had landed in Hawaii as early as the 16th century, trading a few scraps of iron that the Hawaiians valued even more than Europeans valued gold. It was also noted that the Hawaiian women gave themselves freely to the sailors with the apparent good wishes of the island men. This was actually a ploy by the *kahuna* to test if the newcomers were gods or men—gods didn't need women. These sailors proved immediately mortal. Cook, who was also a physician, tried valiantly to keep the 66 men (out of 112) who had measurable cases of venereal disease away from the women. The task proved impossible as women literally swarmed the ships; when Cook returned less than a year later, it was logged that signs of VD were already apparent on some natives' faces.

Cook was impressed with the Hawaiians' swimming ability and with their well-bred manners. They had happy dispositions and sticky fingers, stealing any object made of metal, especially nails. The first item stolen was a butcher's cleaver. An unidentified native grabbed it, plunged overboard, swam to shore, and waved his booty in triumph. The Hawaiians didn't seem to care for beads and were not at all impressed with a mirror. Cook provisioned his ships by trading chisels for hogs, while common sailors gleefully traded nails for sex. Landing parties were sent inland to fill casks with fresh water. On one such excursion a Mr. Williamson, who was eventually drummed out of the Royal Navy for cowardice, unnecessarily shot and killed a native. After a brief stop on Niʻihau, the ships sailed away, but both groups were indelibly impressed with the memory of each other.

Cook Returns

Almost a year later, when winter weather forced Cook to return from the coast of Alaska, his discovery began to take on far-reaching significance. Cook had named Hawaii the Sandwich Islands, in honor of one of his patrons, John Montague, the Earl of Sandwich. On this return voyage, he spotted Maui on November 26, 1778. After eight weeks of seeking a suitable harbor, the ships bypassed it, but not before the coastline was duly drawn by Lieutenant William Bligh, one of Cook's finest and most trusted officers. (Bligh would find his own drama almost 10 years later as commander of the infamous HMS *Bounty.*) The *Discovery* and *Resolution* finally found safe anchorage at Kealakekua Bay on the Kona Coast of the Big Island. It is very lucky for history that on board was Mr. Anderson, ship's chronicler, who left a handwritten record of the strange and tragic events that followed. Even more important were the drawings of John Webber, ship's artist, who rendered invaluable impressions in superb drawings and etchings. Other noteworthy men aboard were George Vancouver, who would lead the first British return to Hawaii after Cook's death and introduce many fruits, vegetables, cattle, sheep, and goats; and James Burney, who would become a long-standing leading authority on the Pacific.

By all accounts Cook was a humane and just captain, greatly admired by his men. Unlike many other supremacists of that time, he was known to have a respectful attitude toward people he discovered, treating them as equals and recognizing the significance of their cultures. Not known as a violent man, he would use his superior weapons against natives only in an absolute case of self-defense. His hardened crew had been at sea facing untold hardship for almost three years; returning to Hawaii was truly like reentering paradise.

A strange series of coincidences sailed with Cook into Kealakekua Bay on January 16, 1779. It was *makahiki* time, a period of rejoicing and festivity dedicated to the fertility god of the earth, Lono. Normal *kapu* days were suspended and willing partners freely enjoyed each other sexually, along with dancing, feasting, and the islands' version of Olympic games. It was long held in Hawaiian legend that the great god Lono would return to earth. Lono's image was a small wooden figure perched on a tall, mast-like crossbeam; hanging from the crossbeam were long, white sheets of tapa. Who else could Cook be but Lono, and what else could his ships with their masts and white sails be but his sacred floating *heiau*? This explained the Hawaiians' previous fascination with his ships, but to add to the remarkable coincidence, Kealakekua Harbor happened to be considered Lono's private sacred harbor. Natives from throughout the land prostrated themselves and paid homage to the returning god. Cook was taken ashore and brought to Lono's sacred temple, where he was afforded the highest respect. The ships badly needed fresh supplies so the Hawaiians readily gave all they had, stretching their own provisions to the limit. To the sailors' delight, this included full measures of the *aloha* spirit.

The Fatal Misunderstandings

After an uproarious welcome and generous hospitality for over a month, it became obvious that the newcomers were beginning to overstay their welcome. During the interim a seaman named William Watman died, convincing the Hawaiians that the *haole* were indeed mortals, not gods. Watman was buried at Hikiau Heiau, where a plaque commemorates the event to this day. Incidents of petty theft began to increase dramatically. The lesser chiefs indicated it was time to leave by "rubbing the Englishmen's bellies." Inadvertently many *kapu* were broken by the Englishmen, and once-friendly relations became strained. Finally, the ships sailed away on February 4, 1779.

After plying terrible seas for only a week, *Resolution's* foremast was badly damaged. Cook sailed back into Kealakekua Bay, dragging the mast ashore on February 13. The natives, now totally hostile, hurled rocks at the sailors. Orders were given to load muskets with ball; firearms had previously been loaded only with shot and a light charge. Confrontations increased when some Hawaiians stole a small boat and Cook's men set after them, capturing the fleeing canoe, which held an *ali'i* named Palea. The English treated him roughly; to the Hawaiians' horror, they even smacked him on the head with a paddle. The Hawaiians then furiously attacked the marines, who abandoned the small boat.

Cook Goes Down

Next the Hawaiians stole a small cutter from the *Discovery* that had been moored to a buoy and partially sunk to protect it from the sun. For the first time, Captain Cook became furious. He ordered Captain Clerk of the *Discovery* to sail to the southeast end of the bay and stop any canoe trying to leave Kealakekua. Cook then made a fatal error in judgment. He decided to take nine armed marines ashore in an attempt to convince the venerable King Kalani'opu'u to accompany him back aboard ship, where he would hold him for ransom in exchange for the cutter. The old king agreed, but his wife prevailed upon him not to trust the *haole*. Kalani'opu'u sat down on the beach to think while the tension steadily grew.

Meanwhile, a group of marines fired upon a canoe trying to leave the bay, and a lesser chief, No'okemai, was killed. The crowd around Cook and his men reached an estimated 20,000, and warriors outraged by the killing of the chief armed themselves with clubs and protective straw-mat armor. One bold warrior advanced on Cook and struck him with a *pahoa* (dagger). In retaliation, Cook drew a tiny pistol lightly loaded with shot and fired at the warrior. His bullets spent themselves on the straw armor and fell harmlessly to the ground. The Hawaiians went wild. Lieutenant Molesworth Phillips, in charge of the nine marines, began a withering fire; Cook himself slew two natives.

Overpowered by sheer numbers, the marines headed for boats standing offshore, while Lieutenant Phillips lay wounded. It is believed that Captain Cook, the greatest seaman ever to enter the Pacific, stood helplessly in knee-deep water instead of making for the boats because he could not swim! Hopelessly surrounded, he was knocked on the head, then countless warriors passed a knife around and hacked and mutilated his lifeless body. A sad Lieutenant James King lamented in his diary, "Thus fell our great and excellent commander."

The Final Chapter

Captain Clerk, now in charge, settled his men and prevailed upon the Hawaiians to return Cook's body. On the morning of February 16 a ghastly piece of charred meat was brought aboard: the Hawaiians, according to their custom, had afforded Cook the highest honor by baking his body in an underground oven to remove the flesh from the bones. On February 17 a group of Hawaiians in a canoe taunted the marines by brandishing Cook's hat. The English, strained to the limit and thinking that Cook was being desecrated, finally broke. Foaming with blood lust, they leveled their cannons and muskets on shore and shot anything that moved. It is believed that Kamehameha the Great was wounded in this flurry, along with four *ali'i;* 25 *maka'ainana* (commoners) were killed. Finally, on February 21, 1779, the bones of Captain James Cook's hands, skull, arms, and legs were returned and tearfully buried at sea. A common seaman, one Mr. Zimmerman, summed up the feelings of all who sailed under Cook when he wrote, "… he was our leading star." The English sailed next morning after dropping off their Hawaiian girlfriends, who were still aboard.

THE UNIFICATION OF OLD HAWAII

Hawaii was already in a state of political turmoil and civil war when Cook arrived. In the

1780s, the islands were roughly divided into three kingdoms: venerable Kalani'opu'u ruled Hawaii and the Hana District of Maui; the wily and ruthless warrior-king Kahekili ruled Maui, Kaho'olawe, Lana'i, and later O'ahu; and Kaeo, Kahekili's brother, ruled Kaua'i. War ravaged the land until a remarkable chief, Kamehameha, rose and subjugated all the islands under one rule. Kamehameha initiated a dynasty that would last for about 100 years, until the independent monarchy of Hawaii forever ceased to be.

To add a zing to this brewing political stew, Westerners and their technology were beginning to come in ever-increasing numbers. In 1786, Captain Jean de François La Pérouse and his French exploration party landed in what's now La Pérouse Bay in South Maui, foreshadowing European attention to the islands. In 1786 two American captains, Portlock and Dixon, made landfall in Hawaii. Also, it was known that a fortune could be made in the fur trade between the Pacific Northwest and Canton, China; stopping in Hawaii could make the trip feasible. After this was reported, the fate of Hawaii was sealed.

Hawaii under Kamehameha was ready to enter its "golden age." The social order was medieval, with the *ali'i* as knights owing their military allegiance to the king, and the serf-like *maka'ainana* paying tribute and working the lands. The priesthood of *kahuna* filled the posts of advisors, sorcerers, navigators, doctors, and historians. This was Polynesian Hawaii at its apex. But like the uniquely Hawaiian silversword plant, the old culture blossomed, and as soon as it did, began to wither. Ever since, everything purely Hawaiian has been supplanted by the relentless foreign influences that began bearing down upon it.

Young Kamehameha

The greatest native son of Hawaii, Kamehameha was born under mysterious circumstances in the Kohala District on the Big Island, probably in 1753. He was royal-born to Keoua Kupuapaikalaninui, the chief of Kohala, and Kekuiapoiwa, a chieftess from Kona.

Accounts vary, but one claims that before his birth, a *kahuna* prophesied that this child would grow to be a "killer of chiefs." Because of this, the local chiefs conspired to murder the infant. When Kekuiapoiwa's time came, she secretly went to the royal birthing stones near Mo'okini Heiau and delivered Kamehameha. She entrusted her baby to a manservant and instructed him to hide the child. He headed for the rugged and remote coast around Kapa'au. Here Kamehameha was raised in the mountains, mostly by men. Always alone, he earned the nickname "The Lonely One."

Kamehameha was a man noticed by everyone; there was no doubt he was a force to be reckoned with. He had met Captain Cook when the *Discovery* unsuccessfully tried to land at Hana on Maui. While aboard, he made a lasting impression, distinguishing himself from the multitude of natives swarming the ships by his royal bearing. Lieutenant James King, in a diary entry, remarked that Kamehameha was a fierce-looking man, almost ugly, but that he was obviously intelligent, observant, and very good-natured. Kamehameha received his early military training from his uncle Kalani'opu'u, the great king of Hawai'i and Hana who fought fierce battles against Alapa'i, the usurper who stole his hereditary lands. After regaining Hawai'i, Kalani'opu'u returned to his Hana District and turned his attention to conquering all of Maui. During this period young Kamehameha distinguished himself as a ferocious warrior and earned the nickname of "The Hard-shelled Crab," even though old Kahekili, Maui's king, almost annihilated Kalani'opu'u's army at the sand hills of Wailuku.

When the old king neared death, he passed on the kingdom to his son Kiwala'o. He also, however, empowered Kamehameha as the keeper of the family war god Kuka'ilimoku: Ku of the Bloody Red Mouth, Ku the Destroyer. Oddly enough, Kamehameha had been born not 500 yards from Ku's great *heiau* at Kohala, and he had heard the chanting and observed the ceremonies dedicated to this fierce god from his first breath. Soon after Kalani'opu'u

died, Kamehameha found himself in a bitter war that he did not seek against his two cousins, Kiwala'o and his brother Keoua, with the island of Hawai'i at stake. The skirmishing lasted nine years, until Kamehameha's armies met the two brothers at Moku'ohai in an indecisive battle in which Kiwala'o was killed. The result was a shaky truce with Keoua, a much-embittered enemy. During this fighting, Kahekili of Maui conquered O'ahu, where he built a house of the skulls and bones of his adversaries as a reminder of his omnipotence. He also extended his will to Kaua'i by marrying his half-brother to a high-ranking chieftess of that island. A new factor would resolve this stalemate of power—the coming of the *haole*.

The Olowalu Massacre

In 1790 the American merchant ship *Ella Nora,* commanded by Yankee Captain Simon Metcalfe, was looking for a harbor after its long voyage from the Pacific Northwest. Following a day behind was the *Fair American,* a tiny ship sailed by Metcalfe's son Thomas and a crew of five. Simon Metcalfe, perhaps by necessity, was a stern and humorless man who would brook no interference. While his ship was anchored at Olowalu, a beach area about five miles east of Lahaina on Maui, some natives slipped close in their canoes and stole a small boat, killing a seaman in the process. Metcalfe decided to trick the Hawaiians by first negotiating a truce and then unleashing full fury upon them. Signaling he was willing to trade, he invited canoes of innocent natives to visit his ship. In the meantime, he ordered that all cannons and muskets be readied with scatter shot. When the canoes were within hailing distance, he ordered his crew to fire at will. Over 100 people were slain; the Hawaiians remembered this killing as "the day of spilled brains." Metcalfe then sailed away to Kealakekua Bay and in an unrelated incident managed to insult Kameiamoku, a ruling chief, who vowed to annihilate the next *haole* ship he saw.

Fate sent him the *Fair American* and young Thomas Metcalfe. The little ship was entirely overrun by superior forces. In the ensuing battle, the mate, Isaac Davis, so distinguished himself by open acts of bravery that his life alone was spared. Kameiamoku later turned over both Davis and the ship to Kamehameha. Meanwhile, while harbored at Kealakekua, the senior Metcalfe sent John Young to reconnoiter. Kamehameha, having learned of the capture of the *Fair American,* detained Young so he could not report, and Metcalfe, losing patience, marooned his own man and sailed off to China. (Metcalfe never learned of the fate of his son Thomas and was later killed with another ship while trading with Native Americans along the Pacific coast of the Mainland.) Kamehameha quickly realized the significance of his two captives and the *Fair American* with its brace of small cannons. He appropriated the ship and made Davis and Young trusted advisors, eventually raising them to the rank of chief. They would all play a significant role in the unification of Hawaii.

Kamehameha the Great

Later in 1790, supported by the savvy of Davis and Young and the cannons from the *Fair American* (which he mounted on carts), Kamehameha invaded Maui, using Hana as his power base. The island's defenders under Kalanikupule, son of Kahekili, who was lingering on O'ahu, were totally demoralized, then driven back into the deathtrap of the 'Iao Valley of Maui. There, Kamehameha's forces annihilated them. No mercy was expected and none given, although mostly commoners were slain, with no significant *ali'i* falling to the victors. So many were killed in this sheer-walled, inescapable valley that the battle was called *ka pani wai,* which means "the damming of the waters"—literally with dead bodies.

While Kamehameha was fighting on Maui, his old nemesis Keoua was busy running amok back on Hawai'i, again pillaging Kamehameha's lands. The great warrior returned home flushed with victory, but in two battles he could not subdue Keoua. Finally, Kamehameha had a prophetic dream in which he was told that Ku would lead him to vic-

tory over all the lands of Hawaii if he would build a *heiau* to the war god at Kawaihae. Even before the temple was finished, old Kahekili attempted to invade Waipi'o, Kamehameha's stronghold. But Kamehameha summoned Davis and Young and, with the *Fair American* and an enormous fleet of war canoes, defeated Kahekili at Waimanu. Kahekili had no choice but to accept the indomitable Kamehameha as the king of Maui, although Kahekili remained the administrative head until his death in 1794.

Now only Keoua remained in the way, and he would be defeated not by war but by the great mana of Ku. While Keoua's armies were crossing the desert on the southern slopes of Kilauea, the fire goddess Pele trumpeted her disapproval and sent a huge cloud of poisonous gas and mud-ash into the air. It descended upon and instantly killed the middle legions of Keoua's armies and their families. The footprints of this ill-fated army remain to this day outlined in the mud-ash as clearly as if they were deliberately encased in wet cement. Keoua's intuition told him that the victorious mana of the gods had swung to Kamehameha and that his own fate was sealed. Kamehameha sent word that he wanted Keoua to meet with him at Ku's newly dedicated temple in Kawaihae. Both knew that Keoua must die. Riding proudly in his canoe, the old nemesis came gloriously outfitted in the red-and-gold feathered cape and helmet signifying his exalted rank. When he stepped ashore he was felled by Kamehameha's warriors. His body was ceremoniously laid upon the altar along with 11 others who were slaughtered and dedicated to Ku, of the Maggot-Dripping Mouth.

Increasing Contact

By the time Kamehameha had won the Big Island, Hawaii was becoming a regular stopover for numerous ships seeking the lucrative sandalwood trade with China. In February 1791, Captain George Vancouver, still seeking the Northwest Passage, returned to Kealakekua, where he was greeted by a throng of 30,000.

The captain at once recognized Kamehameha, who was wearing a Chinese dressing gown that he had received in tribute from another chief who in turn had received it from the hands of Cook himself. The diary of a crewmember, Thomas Manby, relates that Kamehameha, missing his front teeth, was more fierce-looking than ever as he approached the ship in an elegant double-hulled canoe propelled by 46 rowers. The king invited all to a great feast prepared for them on the beach. Kamehameha's appetite matched his tremendous size. It was noted that he ate two sizable fish, a king-sized bowl of poi, a small pig, and an entire baked dog. Kamehameha personally entertained the English by putting on a mock battle in which he deftly avoided spears by rolling, tumbling, and catching them in midair, all the while hurling his own spear a great distance. The English reciprocated by firing cannon bursts into the air, creating an impromptu fireworks display. Kamehameha requested from Vancouver a full table setting, with which he was provided, but his request for firearms was prudently denied.

Captain Vancouver became a trusted advisor of Kamehameha and told him about the white people's form of worship. He even interceded for Kamehameha with his headstrong queen, Ka'ahumanu, and coaxed her from her hiding place under a rock when she sought refuge at Pu'uhonua O Honaunau. The captain gave gifts of beef cattle, fowl, and breeding stock of sheep and goats. The ship's naturalist, Archibald Menzies, was the first *haole* to climb Mauna Kea; he also introduced a large assortment of fruits and vegetables. The Hawaiians were cheerful and outgoing, and they showed remorse when they indicated that the remainder of Cook's bones had been buried at a temple close to Kealakekua. John Young, by this time firmly entrenched in Hawaiian society, made no request to sail away with Vancouver. During the next two decades of Kamehameha's rule, the French, Russians, English, and Americans discovered the great whaling waters off Hawaii. Their increasing visits shook and finally tumbled the ancient religion and social order of *kapu*.

Finishing Touches

After Keoua was laid to rest, it was only a matter of time until Kamehameha consolidated his power over all of Hawaii. In 1794 the old warrior Kahekili of Maui died and gave O'ahu to his son, Kalanikupule, while Kaua'i and Ni'ihau went to his brother Kaeo. In wars between the two, Kalanikupule was victorious, though he did not possess the grit of his father nor the great mana of Kamehameha. He had previously murdered a Captain Brown, who had anchored in Honolulu, and seized his ship, the *Jackall*. With the aid of this ship, Kalanikupule now determined to attack Kamehameha. However, while en route the sailors regained control of their ship and cruised to the Big Island to inform and join with Kamehameha. An army of 16,000 was raised and sailed for Maui, where they met only token resistance, destroyed Lahaina, pillaged the countryside, and subjugated Moloka'i in one bloody battle.

The war canoes sailed next for O'ahu and the final showdown. The great army landed at Waikiki, and though defenders fought bravely, giving up O'ahu by the inch, they were steadily driven into the surrounding mountains. The beleaguered army made its last stand at Nu'uanu Pali, a great precipice in the mountains behind present-day Honolulu. Kamehameha's warriors mercilessly drove the enemy into the great abyss. Kalanikupule, who hid in the mountains, was captured after a few months and sacrificed to Ku, the Snatcher of Lands, thereby ending the struggle for power.

Kamehameha put down a revolt on Hawai'i in 1796. The king of Kaua'i, Kaumuali'i, accepting the inevitable, recognized Kamehameha as supreme ruler without suffering the ravages of a needless war. Kamehameha, for the first time in Hawaiian history, was the undisputed ruler of all the islands of "the heavenly homeland in the north."

Kamehameha's Rule

Kamehameha was as gentle in victory as he was ferocious in battle. Under his rule, which lasted until his death on May 8, 1819, Hawaii enjoyed a peace unlike any the warring islands had ever known. The king moved his royal court to Lahaina, where in 1803 he built the Brick Palace, the first permanent building of Hawaii. The benevolent tyrant also enacted the "Law of the Splintered Paddle." This law, which protected the weak from the exploitation of the strong, had its origins in an incident of many years before. A brave defender of a small overwhelmed village had broken a paddle over Kamehameha's head and taught the chief—literally in one stroke—about the nobility of the commoner.

However, just as Old Hawaii reached its golden age, its demise was at hand. The relentless waves of *haole* both innocently and determinedly battered the old ways into the ground. With the foreign ships came prosperity and fanciful new goods after which the *ali'i* lusted. The *maka'ainana* were worked mercilessly to provide sandalwood for the China trade. This was the first "boom" economy to hit the islands, but it set the standard of exploitation that would follow. Kamehameha built an observation tower in Lahaina to watch for ships, many of which were his own, returning laden with riches from the world at large.

In the last years of his life Kamehameha returned to his beloved Kona Coast, where he enjoyed the excellent fishing renowned to this day. He had taken Hawaii from the darkness of warfare into the light of peace. He died true to the religious and moral *kapu* of his youth, the only ones he had ever known, and with him died a unique way of life. Two loyal retainers buried his bones after the baked flesh had been ceremoniously stripped away. A secret burial cave was chosen so that no one could desecrate the remains of the great chief, thereby absorbing his mana. The tomb's whereabouts remain unknown, and disturbing the dead remains one of the strictest *kapu* to this day. The Lonely One's kingdom would pass to his son, Liholiho, but true power would be in the hands of his beloved but feisty wife Ka'ahumanu. As Kamehameha's spirit drifted from this earth, two forces sailing around Cape Horn would forever change Hawaii: the missionaries and the whalers.

MISSIONARIES AND WHALERS

The year 1819 was of the utmost significance in Hawaiian history. It marked the death of Kamehameha, the overthrow of the ancient *kapu* system, the arrival of the first "whaler" in Lahaina, and the departure of Calvinist missionaries from New England determined to convert the heathen islands. Great changes began to rattle the old order to its foundations. With the *kapu* system and all of the ancient gods abandoned (except for the fire goddess Pele of Kilauea), a great void permeated the souls of the Hawaiians. In the coming decades Hawaii, also coveted by Russia, France, and England, was finally consumed by America. The islands had the first American school, printing press, and newspaper *(The Polynesian)* west of the Mississippi. Lahaina, in its heyday, became the world's greatest whaling port, accommodating over 500 ships of all types during its peak years.

The Royal Family

Maui's Hana District provided Hawaii with one of its greatest queens, Ka'ahumanu, born in 1768 in a cave within walking distance of Hana Harbor. At the age of 17 she became the third of Kamehameha's 21 wives and eventually the love of his life. At first she proved totally independent and unmanageable and was known to openly defy her king by taking numerous lovers. Kamehameha placed a *kapu* on her body and even had her attended by horribly deformed hunchbacks in an effort to curb her carnal appetites, but she continued to flout his authority. Young Ka'ahumanu had no love for her great, lumbering, unattractive husband, but in time (even Captain Vancouver was pressed into service as a marriage counselor) she learned to love him dearly. She in turn became his favorite wife, although she remained childless throughout her life. Kamehameha's first wife was the supremely royal Keopuolani, who so outranked him that the king himself had to approach her naked and crawling on his belly. Keopuolani produced the royal children Liholiho and Kauikeaouli, who became King

Kamehameha II and III, respectively. Just before Kamehameha I died in 1819 he appointed Liholiho his successor, but he also had the wisdom to make Ka'ahumanu the *kuhina nui,* or queen regent. Initially, Liholiho was weak and became a drunkard. Later he became a good ruler, but he was always supported by his royal mother Keopuolani and by the ever-formidable Ka'ahumanu.

Kapu Is Pau

Ka'ahumanu was greatly loved and respected by the people. On public occasions, she donned Kamehameha's royal cloak and spear and, so attired and infused with the king's mana, she demonstrated that she was the real leader of Hawaii. For six months after Kamehameha's death, Ka'ahumanu counseled Liholiho on what he must do. The wise *kuhina nui* knew that the old ways were *pau* (finished) and that Hawaii could not hope to function in a rapidly changing world under the *kapu* system. In November 1819, Ka'ahumanu and Keopuolani prevailed upon Liholiho to break two of the oldest and most sacred *kapu* by eating with women and by allowing women to eat previously forbidden foods such as bananas and certain fish. Heavily fortified with strong drink and attended by other high-ranking chiefs and a handful of foreigners, Ka'ahumanu and Liholiho ate together in public. This feast became known as 'Ai Noa (Free Eating). As the first morsels passed Ka'ahumanu's lips, the ancient gods of Hawaii tumbled. Throughout the land, revered *heiau* were burned and abandoned and the idols knocked to the ground. Now the people had nothing but their weakened inner selves to rely on. Nothing and no one could answer their prayers; their spiritual lives were empty and in shambles.

Missionaries

Into this spiritual vortex sailed the brig *Thaddeus* on April 4, 1820. It had set sail from Boston on October 23, 1819, lured to the Big Island by Henry Opukaha'ia, a local boy born at Napo'opo'o in 1792. Coming ashore at Kailua/Kona, the Reverends Bingham and Thurston were granted a one-year trial missionary period by King Liholiho. They established themselves on the Big Island and O'ahu and from there began the transformation of Hawaii. The missionaries were people of God, but also practical-minded Yankees. They brought education, enterprise, and, most importantly (unlike the transient seafarers), a commitment to stay and build. By 1824, the new faith had such a foothold that Chieftess Keopuolani climbed to the firepit atop Kilauea and defied Pele. This was even more striking than the previous breaking of the food *kapu* because the strength of Pele could actually be seen. Keopuolani ate forbidden *'ohelo* berries and cried out, "Jehovah is my God." Over the next decades the governing of Hawaii slipped away from the Big Island and moved to the new port cities of Lahaina on Maui and, later, Honolulu on O'ahu.

Rapid Conversions

The year 1824 also marked the death of Keopuolani, who was given a Christian burial. She had set the standard by accepting Christianity, and a number of the *ali'i* had followed the queen's lead. Liholiho had sailed off to England, where he and his wife contracted measles and died. Their bodies were returned by the British in 1825 on the HMS *Blonde,* captained by Lord Byron, cousin of *the* Lord Byron. During these years, Ka'ahumanu allied herself with Reverend Richards, pastor of the first mission in the islands, and together they wrote Hawaii's first code of laws based upon the Ten Commandments. Foremost was the condemnation of murder, theft, brawling, and the desecration of the Sabbath by work or play. The early missionaries had the best of intentions, but like all zealots they were blinded by the singlemindedness that was also their greatest ally. They weren't surgically selective in their destruction of native beliefs. *Anything* native was felt to be inferior, and they set about wiping out all traces of the old ways. In their rampage they reduced the Hawaiian culture to ashes, plucking self-will and determination from the hearts of a once-proud people. More so than the whalers, they terminated the Hawaiian way of life.

The Early Seamen

A good portion of the common seamen of the early 19th century came from the dregs of the Western world. Many a whoremongering drunkard had awoken from a stupor and found himself on the pitching deck of a ship, discovering to his dismay that he had been "pressed into naval service." For the most part these sailors were a filthy, uneducated, lawless rabble. Their present situation was dim, their future hopeless, and they would live to be 30 if they were lucky and didn't die from scurvy or a thousand other miserable fates. They snatched brief pleasure in every port and jumped ship at every opportunity, especially in an easy berth like Lahaina. They displayed the worst elements of Western culture—which the Hawaiians naively mimicked. In exchange for *aloha* they gave drunkenness, sloth, and insidious death by disease. By the 1850s the population of native Hawaiians tumbled from the estimated 300,000 reported by Captain Cook in 1778 to barely 60,000. Common conditions such as colds, flu, venereal disease, and sometimes smallpox and cholera devastated the Hawaiians, who had no natural immunities to these foreign ailments. By the time the missionaries arrived, *hapa haole* children were common in Lahaina streets.

The earliest merchant ships to the islands were owned or skippered by lawless opportunists who had come seeking sandalwood after first filling their holds with furs from the Pacific Northwest. Aided by *ali'i* hungry for manufactured goods and Western finery, they raped Hawaiian forests of this fragrant wood so coveted in China. Next, droves of sailors came in search of whales. The whalers, decent men at home, left their morals back in the Atlantic and lived by the slogan "no conscience east of the Cape." The delights of Hawaii were just too tempting for most.

Two Worlds Tragically Collide

The 1820s were a time of confusion and soul-searching for the Hawaiians. When Kamehameha II died the kingdom passed to Kauikeaouli (Kamehameha III), who made his lifelong residence in Lahaina. The young king was only nine years old when the title passed to him, but his power was secure because Ka'ahumanu was still a vibrant *kuhina nui.* The young prince, more so than any other, was raised in the cultural confusion of the times. His childhood was spent during the very cusp of the change from old ways to new, and he was often pulled in two directions by vastly differing beliefs. Since he was royal born, he was bound by age-old Hawaiian tradition to mate and produce an heir with the highest-ranking *ali'i* in the kingdom. This mate happened to be his younger sister, Princess Nahi'ena'ena. To the old Hawaiian advisors, this arrangement was perfectly acceptable and encouraged. To the increasingly influential missionaries, incest was an unimaginable abomination in the eyes of God. The problem was compounded by the fact that Kamehameha III and Nahi'ena'ena were drawn to each other and were deeply in love. The young king could not stand the mental pressure imposed by conflicting worlds. He became a teenage alcoholic too royal to be restrained by anyone in the kingdom, and his bouts of drunkenness and womanizing were both legendary and scandalous.

Meanwhile, Nahi'ena'ena was even more pressured because she was a favorite of the missionaries, baptized into the church at age 12. She too vacillated between the old and the new. At times she was a pious Christian; at others she drank all night and took numerous lovers. As the prince and princess grew into their late teens, they became even more attached to each other and hardly made an attempt to keep their relationship from the missionaries. Whenever possible, they lived together in a grass house built for the princess by her father.

In 1832, the great Ka'ahumanu died, leaving the king on his own. In 1833, at the age of 18, Kamehameha III announced that the "regency" was over and that all the lands in Hawaii were his personally, and that he alone was the ultimate law. Almost immediately, however, he decreed that his half-sister Kinaʻu would be "premier," signifying that he would leave the actual running of the kingdom in her hands. Kamehameha III fell into total drunken confusion, until one night he attempted suicide. After this episode he seemed to straighten up a bit and mostly kept a low profile. In 1836, Princess Nahiʻenaʻena was convinced by the missionaries to take a husband. She married Leleiohoku, a chief from the Big Island, but continued to sleep with her brother. It is uncertain who fathered the child, but Nahiʻenaʻena gave birth to a baby boy in September 1836. The young prince survived for only a few hours, and Nahiʻenaʻena never recovered. She died in December 1836 and was laid to rest in the mausoleum next to her mother, Keopuolani, on the royal island in Mokuhinia Pond (in Lahaina). After the death of his sister, Kamehameha III became a sober and righteous ruler. Often seen paying his respects at the royal mausoleum, he ruled longer than any other king, until his death in 1854.

The Missionaries Prevail

In 1823, the first mission was established in Lahaina, Maui, under the pastorship of Reverend Richards and his wife. Within a few years, many of the notable *aliʻi* had been, at least in appearance, converted to Christianity. By 1828 the cornerstones for Waineʻe Church, the first stone church on the island, were laid just behind the palace of Kamehameha III. The struggle between missionaries and whalers centered on public drunkenness and the servicing of sailors by native women. The normally God-fearing whalers had signed on for perilous duty that lasted up to three years, and when they anchored in Lahaina they demanded their pleasure. The missionaries were instrumental in placing a curfew on sailors and prohibiting native women from boarding ships, which had become customary. These measures certainly did not stop the liaisons between sailor and *wahine,* but they did impose a modicum of social sanction and tolled the end of the wide-open days. The sailors were outraged; in 1825 the crew from the *Daniel* attacked the home of

Early missionaries often built homes in Hawaiʻi that reflected the style of their former New England homes.

the meddler, Reverend Richards. A year later a similar incident occurred. In 1827, confined and lonely sailors from the whaler *John Palmer* fired their cannons at Reverend Richards' newly built home.

Slowly the tensions eased, and by 1836 many sailors were regulars at the Seamen's Chapel adjacent to the Baldwin home. Unfortunately, even the missionaries couldn't stop the pesky mosquito from entering the islands through the port of Lahaina. The mosquitoes arrived from Mexico in 1826 aboard the merchant ship *Wellington.* They were inadvertently carried as larvae in the water barrels and democratically pestered everyone in the islands from that day forward, regardless of race, religion, or creed.

Foreign Influence

By the 1840s Honolulu was becoming the center of commerce in the islands; when Kamehameha III moved the royal court there from Lahaina, the ascendant fate of the new capital was guaranteed. In 1843, Lord Paulet, commander of the warship *Carysfort,* forced Kamehameha III to sign a treaty ceding Hawaii to the British. London, however, repudiated this act, and Hawaii's independence was restored within a few months when Queen Victoria sent Admiral Thomas as her personal agent of good intentions. The king memorialized the turn of events by a speech in which he uttered the phrase, *"Ua mau ke e'a o ka 'aina i ka pono"* ("The life of the land is preserved in righteousness"), now Hawaii's motto. The French used similar bullying tactics to force an unfavorable treaty on the Hawaiians in 1839; as part of these heavy-handed negotiations they exacted a payment of $20,000 and the right of Catholics to enjoy religious freedom in the islands. In 1842, the United States recognized and guaranteed Hawaii's independence without a formal treaty, and by 1860 over 80 percent of the islands' trade was with the United States.

The Great Mahele

In 1840, Kamehameha III ended his autocratic rule and instituted a constitutional monarchy. This brought about the Hawaiian Bill of Rights, but the most far-reaching change was the transition to private ownership of land. Formerly, all land belonged to the ruling chief, who gave wedge-shaped parcels called *ahupua'a* to lesser chiefs to be worked for him. The commoners did all the real labor, their produce heavily taxed by the *ali'i.* The fortunes of war, the death of a chief, or the mere whim of a superior could force a commoner off the land. The Hawaiians, however, could not think in terms of "owning" land. No one could *possess* land; one could only *use* land, and its ownership was a strange foreign concept. (As a result, naive Hawaiians gave up their lands for a song to unscrupulous traders, which remains an integral, unrectified problem to this day.) In 1847 Kamehameha III and his advisors separated the lands of Hawaii into three groupings: crown land (belonging to the king), government land (belonging to the chiefs), and people's land (the largest parcels). In 1848, 245 *ali'i* entered their land claims in the *Mahele Book,* assuring them ownership. In 1850 the commoners were given title in fee simple to the lands they cultivated and lived on as tenants, not including house lots in towns. Commoners without land could buy small *kuleana* (farms) from the government at 50 cents per acre. In 1850, foreigners were also allowed to purchase land in fee simple, and the ownership of Hawaii from that day forward slipped steadily from the hands of its indigenous people.

KING SUGAR

It's hard to say just where the sugar industry began in Hawaii. The Koloa Sugar Plantation on the southern coast of Kaua'i successfully refined sugar in 1835. Others tried, and one success was at Hana, Maui, in 1849. A whaler named George Wilfong hauled four blubber pots ashore and set them up on a rocky hill in the middle of 60 acres he had planted in sugar. A team of oxen turned "crushing rollers" and the cane juice flowed down an open trough into the pots, under which an attending native kept a roaring fire burning. Wilfong's methods of refining were crude, but the resulting high-quality sugar turned a neat profit in Lahaina.

ROBERT NILSEN

Of the dozens of sugar mills that once dotted the Hawaiian Islands, most are now only empty shells like this mill in Kekaha, or are gone completely.

The main problem was labor. The Hawaiians, who made excellent whalers, were basically indentured workers. They became extremely disillusioned with their contracts, which could last up to 10 years. Most of their wages were eaten up by manufactured commodities sold at the company store, and it didn't take long for them to realize that they were little more than slaves. At every opportunity they either left the area or just refused to work.

Imported Labor

The **Masters and Servants Act of 1850,** which allowed importation of laborers under the contract system, ostensibly guaranteed an endless supply of cheap labor for the plantations. Chinese laborers were imported but were too enterprising to remain in the fields for a meager $3 per month. They left as soon as opportunity permitted and went into business as small merchants and retailers. In the meantime, Wilfong had sold out, releasing most of the Hawaiians previously held under contract, and his plantation fell into disuse. In 1860,

two Danish brothers, August and Oscar Unna, bought land at Hana to raise sugar. They solved the labor problem by importing Japanese laborers, who were extremely hardworking and easily managed. The workday lasted 10 hours, six days a week, for a salary of $20 per month plus housing and medical care. Plantation life was very structured, with stringent rules governing even bedtimes and lights out. A worker was fined for being late or for smoking on the job. The workers couldn't function under these circumstances, and improvements in benefits and housing were slowly gained.

Sugar Grows

The demand for "Sandwich Island Sugar" grew as California was populated during the gold rush and increased dramatically when the American Civil War demanded a constant supply. The only sugar plantations on the Mainland were small plots confined to the Confederate states, whose products would hardly be bought by the Union and whose fields, later in the war, were destroyed. By the 1870s it was clear to the planters, still mainly New Englanders, that the United States was their market; they tried often to gain closer ties and favorable tariffs. The Americans also planted rumors that the British were interested in annexing Hawaii; this put pressure on the U.S. Congress to pass the long-desired **Reciprocity Act,** which would exempt sugar from import duty. It finally passed in 1875, in exchange for U.S. long-range rights to the strategic naval port of Pearl Harbor, among other concessions. These agreements gave increased political power to a small group of American planters in Hawaii whose outlooks were similar to those of the post–Civil War South, where a few powerful whites were the virtual masters of a multitude of dark-skinned laborers. Sugar was now big business, and the Hana District alone exported almost 3,000 tons per year. All of Hawaii would have to reckon with the "sugar barons."

Changing Society

The sugar plantation system changed life in Hawaii physically, spiritually, politically, and economically. Now boatloads of workers came not only from Japan, but from Portugal, Germany, and even Russia. The white-skinned workers were most often the field foremen *(luna)*. With the immigrants came new religions, new animals and plants, unique cuisines, and a plantation language known as pidgin or, better yet, *da'kine.* Many Asians and, to a lesser extent, the other groups, including the white plantation owners, intermarried with Hawaiians. A new class of people properly termed "cosmopolitan" but more familiarly and aptly known as "locals" was emerging. These were the people of multiple-race backgrounds who couldn't exactly say *what* they were but it was clear to all just *who* they were. The plantation owners became the new "chiefs" of Hawaii who could carve up the land and dispense favors. The Hawaiian monarchy was soon eliminated.

A KINGDOM PASSES
The Beginning of the End

Like the Hawaiian people themselves, the Kamehameha dynasty in the mid-1800s was dying

from within. King Kamehameha IV (Alexander Liholiho) ruled 1854–63; his only child died in 1862. He was succeeded by his older brother Kamehameha V (Lot Kamehameha), who ruled until 1872. With his passing, the Kamehameha line ended. William Lunalilo, elected king in 1873 by popular vote, was of royal, but not Kamehameha, lineage. He died after only a year in office and, being a bachelor, left no heirs. He was succeeded by David Kalakaua, known far and wide as the "Merrie Monarch," who made a world tour and was well received wherever he went. He built 'Iolani Palace in Honolulu and was personally in favor of closer ties with the United States, helping push through the Reciprocity Act. Kalakaua died in 1891 and was replaced by his sister Lydia Lili'uokalani, last of the Hawaiian monarchs.

The Revolution

When Lili'uokalani took office in 1891, the native population was at a low of 40,000, and she felt that the United States had too much influence over her homeland. She was known to personally favor the English over the Americans. She attempted to replace the liberal constitution of 1887 (adopted by her pro-American brother) with an autocratic mandate in which she would have had much more political and economic control of the islands. When the McKinley Tariff of 1890 brought a decline in sugar profits, she made no attempt to improve the situation. Thus, the planters saw her as a political obstacle to their economic growth; most of Hawaii's American planters and merchants were in favor of a rebellion. She would have to go! A central spokesperson and firebrand was Lorrin Thurston, a Honolulu publisher who, with a central core of about 30 men, challenged the Hawaiian monarchy. Although Lili'uokalani rallied some support and had a small military potential in her personal guard, the coup was ridiculously easy—it took only one casualty. Captain John Good shot a Hawaiian policeman in the arm and that did it. Naturally, the conspirators could not have succeeded without some solid assurances from a secret contingent in the U.S. Congress as well as outgoing President Benjamin Harrison, who favored Hawaii's annexation. Marines from the *Boston* went ashore to "protect American lives," and on January 17, 1893, the Hawaiian monarchy came to an end.

The provisional government was headed by Sanford B. Dole, who became president of the Hawaiian Republic. Lili'uokalani surrendered not to the conspirators but to U.S. Ambassador John Stevens. She believed that the U.S. government, which had assured her of Hawaiian independence, would be outraged by the overthrow and would come to her aid. Incoming president Grover Cleveland *was* outraged, and Hawaii wasn't immediately annexed as expected. When queried about what she would do with the conspirators if she were reinstated, Lili'uokalani said that they would be hanged as traitors. The racist press of the times, which portrayed the Hawaiians as half-civilized, bloodthirsty heathens, publicized this widely. Since the conspirators were the leading citizens of the land, the queen's words proved untimely. In January 1895 a small, ill-fated counterrevolution headed by Lili'uokalani failed, and she was placed under house arrest in 'Iolani Palace. Officials of the republic insisted that she use her married name (Mrs. John Dominis) to sign the documents forcing her to abdicate her throne. She was also forced to swear allegiance to the new republic. Lili'uokalani went on to write *Hawaii's Story* and the lyric ballad "Aloha O'e." She never forgave the conspirators and remained "queen" to the Hawaiians until her death in 1917.

Annexation

The overwhelming majority of Hawaiians opposed annexation and desired to restore the monarchy. But they were prevented from voting by the new republic because they couldn't meet the imposed property and income qualifications—a transparent ruse by the planters to control the majority. Most *haole* were racist and believed that the "common people" could not be entrusted with the vote because they were childish and incapable of ruling themselves. The fact that the Hawaiians had existed quite well for 1,000 years before white people even reached Hawaii was never considered. The Philippine theater of the Spanish-American War also prompted annexation. One of the strongest proponents was Alfred Mahon, a brilliant naval strategist who, with support from Theodore Roosevelt, argued that the U.S. military must have Hawaii in order to be a viable force in the Pacific. In addition, Japan, victorious in its recent war with China, protested the American intention to annex, and in so doing prompted even moderates to support annexation for fear that the Japanese themselves coveted the prize. On July 7, 1898, President McKinley signed the annexation agreement, and this "tropical fruit" was finally put into America's basket.

MODERN TIMES

Hawaii entered the 20th century totally transformed from what it had been. The old Hawaiian language, religion, culture, and leadership were all but gone; Western dress, values, education, and recreation were the norm. Native Hawaiians were now unseen citizens who lived in dwindling numbers in remote areas. The plantations, new centers of social order, had a strong Asian flavor; more than 75 percent of their workforce was Asian. There was a small white middle class, an all-powerful white elite, and a single political party ruled by that elite. Education, however, was always highly prized, and by the turn of the 20th century all racial groups were encouraged to attend school. By 1900, almost 90 percent of Hawaiians were literate (far above the national norm), and schooling was mandatory for all children ages six to 15. Intermarriage was accepted, and there was a mixing of the races like nowhere else on earth.

The military became increasingly important to Hawaii. It brought in money and jobs, dominating the island economy. The Japanese attack on Pearl Harbor, which began U.S. involvement in World War II, bound Hawaii to America forever. Once the islands had been baptized by blood, the average Mainlander felt that Hawaii was American soil. A movement among Hawaiians to become part of the Union began to grow. They wanted a real voice in Washington, not merely a voteless delegate as provided under their territory status. Hawaii became the 50th state in 1959, and the jumbo-jet revolution of the 1960s made it easily accessible to growing numbers of tourists from all over the world.

Pearl Harbor Attack

On the morning of December 7, 1941, the Japanese carrier *Akagi,* flying the battle flag of the famed Admiral Togo of the Russo-Japanese War, received and broadcast over its PA system island music from Honolulu station KGMB. Deep in the bowels of the ship a radioman listened for a much different message, coming thousands of miles from the Japanese mainland. When the ironically poetic message "east wind rain" was received, the attack was launched. At the end of the day, 2,325 U.S. servicemen and 57 civilians were dead, 188 planes were destroyed, 18 major warships were sunk or heavily damaged, and the United States was in the war. Japanese casualties were ludicrously light. The ignited conflict would rage for four years until Japan, through the bombings at Nagasaki and Hiroshima, was vaporized into total submission. By the end of hostilities, Hawaii would never again be considered separate from America.

Statehood

A number of economic and political reasons explain why the ruling elite of Hawaii desired statehood, but put simply, the vast majority of people who lived there, especially after World War II, considered themselves Americans. The first serious mention of making "The Sandwich Islands" a state was in the 1850s under President Franklin Pierce, but it wasn't taken seriously until the monarchy was overthrown in the 1890s. For the next 50 years, statehood proposals were made repeatedly to Congress, but there was stiff opposition, especially from the southern states. With Hawaii a territory, an import quota system beneficial to Mainland producers could be enacted on produce, especially sugar. Also, there was prejudice against creating a state in a place where the majority of the populace was not white.

During World War II, Hawaii was placed under martial law, but no serious attempt to intern the Japanese population was made, as in California. There were simply too many Japanese, and many went on to gain the respect of the American people by their outstanding fighting record during the war. Hawaii's own 100th Battalion became the famous 442nd Regimental Combat Team, which gained notoriety by saving the Lost Texas Battalion during the Battle of the Bulge and went on to be *the* most decorated battalion in all of World War II. When these GIs returned home, no one was going to tell them that they were not loyal Americans. Many of these AJAs (Americans of Japanese Ancestry) took advantage of the GI Bill and received higher educations. They were from the common people, not the elite, and they rallied grassroots support for statehood. When the vote finally occurred, approximately 132,900 voted in favor of statehood, with only 7,800 votes against. Congress passed the Hawaii State Bill on March 12, 1959, and on August 21, 1959, President Eisenhower announced that Hawaii was officially the 50th state.

Government and Economy

The difference between the government of the state of Hawaii and those of other states is that it's "streamlined," and in theory more efficient. There are only two levels of government: the state and the county. With no town or city governments to deal with, considerable bureaucracy is eliminated. Hawaii, in anticipation of becoming a state, drafted a constitution in 1950 and was ready to go when statehood came. Politics and government are taken seriously in the Aloha State, which consistently turns in the best national voting record per capita. For example, in the first state elections, 173,000 of 180,000 registered voters voted—a whopping 94 percent of the electorate. In the election to ratify statehood, hardly a ballot went uncast, with 95 percent of the voters opting for statehood. The bill carried in every island of Hawaii except Ni'ihau, where most of the people (total population 250 or so) were then and are now of relatively pure Hawaiian blood. When Hawaii became a state, Honolulu became its capital. Since statehood, the legislative and executive branches of state government have been dominated by the Democratic party. Breaking a 40-year Democratic hold on power and becoming the first woman to hold the position, former Maui Mayor and Republican Linda Lingle was elected governor of Hawaii in 2002. Hawaii is represented in the U.S Congress by two senators, currently Daniel K. Inouye (D) and Daniel K. Akaka (D), and two representatives, currently Neil Abercrombie (D) and Ed Case (D).

National and state flags often fly together in Hawai'i.

ROBERT NILSEN

Kaua'i County

Kaua'i County is composed of the inhabited islands of Kaua'i and Ni'ihau and the uninhabited islands of Ka'ula and Lehua. Lihu'e is the county seat. It's represented by two state senators elected from the 6th District—a split district including north Kaua'i and portions of the South, Upcountry, and Hana regions of Maui—and the 7th District, which includes all of southern Kaua'i and Ni'ihau.

Kaua'i has three state representatives—from the 12th District, which is again a split district with north Kaua'i and eastern Maui; the 13th District around Lihu'e; and the 14th District, which includes all of southwestern Kaua'i and Ni'ihau. The current mayor of Kaua'i is Bryan Baptiste, a Republican who was elected to his first term of office in 2002. For Internet information on the government of Kaua'i County see www.kauai.gov.

ECONOMY

Hawaii's mid-Pacific location makes it perfect for two prime sources of income: tourism and the military. Tourists come in anticipation of endless golden days on soothing beaches, while the military is provided with the strategic position of an unsinkable battleship. Each economic sector nets Hawaii more than $4 billion annually, money that should keep flowing smoothly and even increase in the foreseeable future. These revenues remain mostly aloof from the normal ups and downs of the Mainland U.S. economy. Also contributing to the state revenue are, in descending proportions, manufacturing, construction, and agriculture (mainly sugar and pineapples). As long as the sun shines and the balance of global power requires a military presence, the economic stability of Hawaii is guaranteed.

Tourism

Kaua'i is the fourth most-visited island after O'ahu, Maui, and the Big Island. Regaining momentum after Hurricane 'Iniki and then again following an immediate and precipitous nose-dive in tourist arrivals as a result of the September 11, 2001, terrorist attacks on the Mainland, it is once again attracting just over one million visitors annually, accounting for about 15 percent of the state's total. On any given day, on average, there will be about 19,000 visitors on the island. Approximately 8,100 accommodation units are available, averaging a 74 percent occupancy rate. At one time, Kaua'i was the most difficult island on which to build a resort because of a strong grassroots anti-development faction. This trend has been changing due to the recession that hit everyone after Hurricane 'Iwa and then 'Iniki scared off many tourists. Island residents realized how much their livelihood was tied to tourism, and an ad campaign depicting tourists as visitors (rather than unwelcome invaders) has helped in their acceptance. Also, the resorts being built on Kaua'i are first-rate, and the developers are savvy enough to create "destination areas" instead of more high-rise boxes of rooms. That doesn't mean that development on Kaua'i is easy. There are many strict regulations to meet, and there is still a vocal opposition to unplanned development.

It was some time after tourism became a major economic factor in the state that tourists started finding their way in sizable numbers from the beach at Waikiki to the Neighbor Islands. On Kaua'i, these first souls came to the Kalapaki Beach area of Lihu'e, where the island's first major hotel was built, and to the

Much of the taro grown in Hawai'i is grown in the Hanalei Valley.

Coconut Coast. Later, Po'ipu became the island's first major resort development. With its balmy weather and white sand beaches, how could it go wrong? Later Princeville was developed, shifting tourism and money to the north shore; it is now Kaua'i's second major resort area. Following years of neglect, the East Shore is once again attracting tourist and development dollars and is beginning to shine its once tarnished image. Still underdeveloped is the dry, hot west end, yet it too has great historical and cultural importance and natural beauty that tempt mostly day-trippers from the other areas of the island.

Agriculture

Agriculture still accounts for a hefty portion of Kaua'i's income. While sugar, for decades the backbone of the island's economy, has taken a downward dip, it's still grown commercially on the island, although fewer acres are in production and only one mill still processes cane. Kaua'i produces about 12 percent of the state's diversified agricultural crop, with a strong yield in papayas. In 1982, California banned the importation of Kaua'i's papayas because they were sprayed with EDB, a fumigant used to control fruit flies. The chemical is no longer used, and the papaya market has rebounded. Hanalei Valley and many other smaller areas produce over four million pounds of taro annually, which is quickly turned into poi, and the county produces two million pounds of guavas, as well as pineapples, beef, and pork for its own use.

A growing aquaculture industry produces prawns, and a tropical flower sector is now emerging. In the mid-1980s, nearly 4,000 acres stretching from 'Ele'ele to Koloa, on what was McBryde sugar land, was planted in coffee and a few other crops like tea and macadamia nuts. This was, reputedly, the largest economic rediversification project in the state. Since then, coffee on Kaua'i has turned into a thriving industry and now produces more beans than any other island, about 50 percent of the state total. Kaua'i coffee, known to be milder than Kona coffee, has become a major player in the state. While stores around the state are retailing this hearty brew, by far the majority is sent to the Mainland and Japan. On the south shore, some

corn is raised, and seed production facilities west of Kekaha grow seed corn to be shipped all over the world.

Military

The military influence on Kaua'i is small but vital. With about 125 military personnel and nearly 1,000 civilian contract workers, the only sizable military facility on the island is **Pacific Missile Range Facility** at Barking Sands on the far west end of the island, which supports the testing of missiles, underwater warfare, and communications. In addition, an associated tracking facility sits on Makaha Ridge overlooking the south end of the Na Pali Coast. Operated by the Navy, this facility is available to all branches of the U.S. military, the Department of Defense, NASA, the Department of Energy, and select foreign military units.

Land Ownership

Of Kaua'i County's total usable land area of approximately 399,000 acres, about 45,700 is the privately owned island of Ni'ihau. On Kaua'i about 200,000 acres are set aside as conservation lands, 140,000 as agricultural

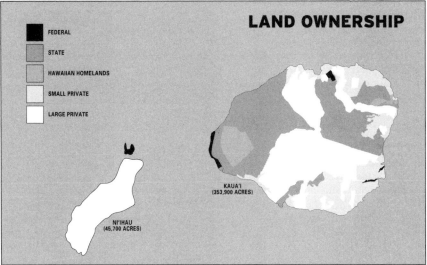

LAND OWNERSHIP

FEDERAL

STATE

HAWAIIAN HOMELANDS

SMALL PRIVATE

LARGE PRIVATE

KAUA'I
(353,900 ACRES)

NI'IHAU
(45,700 ACRES)

lands, and 14,000 as urban lands. The federal government owns just over 3,000 acres, the state has approximately 150,000 acres, of which 20,000 are Hawaiian Homelands, and the county controls 600 acres, largely in parks. About 196,000 acres are privately owned, or 49 percent of the island. Of this, almost three-quarters is controlled by only half a dozen or so large landholders, mainly Robinson family, Amfac, Alexander & Baldwin, Grove Farm, Kamehameha Schools, Knudsen Estate, and Princeville Development Corporation. As everywhere in Hawaii, no one owns the beaches, and public access to them is guaranteed.

The People

Nowhere else on earth can you find such a kaleidoscopic mixture of people as in Hawaii. Every major race is accounted for, and over 50 ethnic groups are represented throughout the islands, making Hawaii the most racially integrated state in the country. Its population of 1.2 million includes some 80,000 permanently stationed military personnel and their dependents, and it's the only state where whites are not a majority. About 56 percent of Hawaiian residents were born there, 26 percent were born in the Mainland United States, and 18 percent are foreign-born.

The population has grown steadily in recent times but has fluctuated wildly in the past. In 1876, it reached its lowest ebb, with only 55,000 permanent residents. This was the era of large sugar plantations; their constant demand for labor was the primary cause for importing various peoples from around the world and led to Hawaii's racial mix. World War II saw the population swell from 400,000 to 900,000. These 500,000 military personnel left at war's end, but many returned to settle after getting a taste of island living.

Kaua'i Population Figures

The density of Kaua'i is about 110 people per square mile. Kaua'i County's 62,000 people, including about 160 on Ni'ihau, account for only five percent of the state's total population, making it the least populous county. Also, about 325 military personnel and their dependents live on the island. The largest town is Kapa'a with 7,600 people, followed by Lihu'e with 5,200. The island's population is distributed as follows: 18,500 along the east coast, 12,000 in Lihu'e and suburban areas, 5,400 in the Po'ipu/Koloa area, 16,000 along the south coast, and 6,400 along the north shore.

Ethnically, there is no clear majority on Kaua'i. The people of Kaua'i include: 36 percent Asian, 29 percent Caucasian, 24 percent mixed, 9 percent Hawaiian, and 2 percent other.

THE HAWAIIANS

The study of the native Hawaiians is ultimately a study in tragedy because it ends in their demise as a viable people. When Captain Cook first sighted Hawaii in 1778, there were an estimated 300,000 natives living in perfect harmony with their ecological surroundings; within 100 years a scant 50,000 demoralized and dejected Hawaiians existed almost as wards of the state. Today, although more than 240,000 people claim varying degrees of Hawaiian blood, experts say that fewer than 1,000 are pure Hawaiian, and this might be stretching it.

It's easy to see why people of Hawaiian lineage could be bitter over what they have lost, being strangers in their own land now, much like Native Americans. The overwhelming majority of "Hawaiians" are of mixed heritage, and the wisest take the best from all worlds. From the Hawaiian side comes simplicity, love of the land, and acceptance of people. It is the Hawaiian legacy of *aloha* that remains immortal and adds that special elusive quality that *is* Hawaii.

MU AND MENEHUNE

Hawaiian legends give accounts of dwarf-like aborigines on Kaua'i called the Mu and the Menehune. These two hirsute tribes were said to have lived on the island before and after the arrival of the Polynesians. The Mu were fond of jokes and games, while the Menehune were dedicated workers, stonemasons par excellence, who could build monumental structures in just one night. Many stoneworks that can still be seen around the island are attributed to these hardworking nocturnal people.

Anthropological theory supports the legends that say some non-Polynesian peoples actually did exist on Kaua'i. According to oral history, their chief felt that too much interplay and intermarriage was occurring with the Polynesians. He wished his race to remain pure, so he ordered them to leave on a "triple-decker floating island," and they haven't been seen since. If you ask a Kaua'ian whether he or she believes in the Menehune, the answer is likely to be, "Of course not! But, they're there anyway." Speculation holds that they may have been an entirely different race of people, or perhaps the remaining tribes of the first Polynesians. It's possible that they were cut off from the original culture for so long they developed their own separate culture, and the food supply became so diminished their stature became reduced in comparison to other Polynesians.

Polynesian Roots

The Polynesians' original stock is muddled and remains an anthropological mystery, but it's believed that they were nomadic wanderers who migrated from both the Indian subcontinent and Southeast Asia through Indonesia, where they learned to sail and navigate on protected waterways. As they migrated they honed their sailing skills until they could take on the Pacific, and as they moved, they absorbed people from other cultures and races until they had coalesced into what we now know as Polynesians.

Abraham Fornander, still considered a major authority on the subject, wrote in his 1885 *Account of the Polynesian Race* that he believed the Polynesians started as a white (Aryan) race that was heavily influenced by contact with the Cushite, Chaldeo-Arabian civilization. He estimated their arrival in Hawaii at A.D. 600, based on Hawaiian genealogical chants. Modern science seems to bear this date out, although it remains skeptical about his other surmises. According to others, the intrepid Polynesians who actually settled Hawaii are believed to have come from the Marquesas Islands, 1,000 miles southeast of Hawaii. The Marquesans were cannibals and known for their tenacity and strength, attributes that would serve them well. Tahitians and other islanders arrived several hundred years later, creating a mix even in Polynesian blood.

The Caste System

Hawaiian society was divided into rankings by a strict caste system determined by birth and from which there was no chance of escaping. The highest rank was the *ali'i*—the chiefs and royalty. The impeccable genealogies of the *ali'i* were traced back to the gods themselves, and the chants *(mo'o ali'i)* were memorized and sung by professionals (called *ku'auhau*) who were themselves *ali'i*. Rank passed from both father and mother, and custom dictated that the first mating of an *ali'i* be with a person of equal status.

A *kahuna* was a highly skilled person whose advice was sought before any major project was undertaken, such as building a house, hollowing a canoe log, or even offering a prayer. The *mo'o kahuna* were the priests of Ku and Lono, and they were in charge of praying and following rituals. They were very powerful *ali'i* and kept strict secrets and laws concerning their various functions.

Besides this priesthood of *kahuna,* there were other *kahuna* who were not *ali'i* but commoners. The two most important were the healers *(kahuna lapa'au)* and the black magicians *(kahuna 'ana'ana),* who could pray a person to death. The *kahuna lapa'au* had a marvelous

TRADITIONAL FOODS

In old Hawaii, although the sea meant life, and indeed a great variety of fish and other seafood was eaten, many more people were involved in cultivating beautifully tended garden plots of taro, sugarcane, breadfruit, and various sweet potatoes (*'uala*) than with fishing. They husbanded pigs – a favorite for the *imu* oven – and barkless dogs (*'ilio*), and they prized *moa* (chicken) for their feathers and meat but found eating the eggs repulsive. Their only farming implement was the *'o'o*, a sharpened hardwood digging stick.

The Hawaiians were the best farmers of Polynesia, and the first thing they planted was taro, a tuberous root created by the gods at the same time humans were created. This main staple of the old Hawaiians was pounded into poi. Every lu'au will have poi, a glutinous purple paste. It comes in liquid consistencies referred to as one-, two-, or three-finger poi. The fewer fingers you need to eat it, the thicker it is. Poi is one of the most nutritious carbohydrates known, but people unaccustomed to it find it bland and tasteless. Some of the best, fermented for a day or so, has an acidic bite. Poi is made to be eaten *with* something, but locals who love it pop it in their mouths and smack their lips. Those unaccustomed to it will suffer constipation if they eat too much. While poi grew out of favor during the middle of the 20th century, it is once again becoming popular, and several sizable factories are now producing poi for sale. One of the state's largest poi producing areas is the Hanalei Valley on the North Shore of Kaua'i. You can find plastic containers of this food refrigerated in many supermarkets and local food stores. In addition, deep-fried slices of taro root, plain or spiced, are now packaged and sold like potato chips.

A favorite dessert is *haupia*, a custard made from coconut that is found at most social gatherings. Like a tiny meal in a pouch, *laulau* is a package of meat, fish, and veggies wrapped in *ti* leaves and baked or steamed. *Poke* is a seafood salad made with a variety of seafood, seaweed, and onions that's frequently found on traditional island menus and more and more in fish markets or deli sections of supermarkets. Hawaii even has a festival dedicated to the innovative creation of this dish. One of its ingredients is *limu*, a generic term for edible seaweed that has been gathered as a garnish since precontact times. Many people still gather *limu* from the shoreline and eat it as a salad, or mix with ground *kukui* nuts and salt as a relish. There's no other seaweed except *limu* in Hawaii. Because of this, the heavy, fishy-ocean smell that people associate with the sea but that is actually seaweed is absent in Hawaii.

A favorite Hawaiian snack is *'opihi*, small shellfish (limpet) that cling to rocks. *'Opihi* are cut from the shell and eaten raw by all peoples of Hawaii. Those who gather them always leave some on the rocks for the future. *'A'ama* are the ubiquitous little black crabs that you'll spot on rocks and around pier areas. They're everywhere. For fun, local fishermen try to catch them with poles, but the more efficient way is to throw a fish head into a plastic bucket and wait for the crabs to crawl in and trap themselves. The *'a'ama* are about as big as two fingers and make delicious eating. A traditional liquor made from *ti* root is *'okolehao*. It literally means "iron bottom," reminiscent of the iron blubber pots used to ferment it.

pharmacopoeia of herbs and spices that could cure over 250 diseases common to the Hawaiians. The *kahuna 'ana'ana* could be hired to cast a love spell over a person or cause his or her untimely death. They seldom had to send out a reminder for payment!

The common people were called the *maka'ainana,* "the people of land"—farmers, artisans, and fishermen. The land they lived on was owned by the *ali'i* but they were not bound to it. If the local *ali'i* was cruel or unfair, the *maka'ainana* had the right to leave and reside on another's lands. The *maka'ainana* mostly loved their local *ali'i,* much as a child loves a parent, and the feeling was reciprocal. *Maka'ainana* who lived close to the *ali'i* and could be counted on as warriors in times of trouble were called *kanaka no lua kaua,* "men for the heat of battle." They were treated with greater favor than those who lived in the back-country, *kanaka no hi'i kua,* whose lesser standing opened them up to discrimination and cruelty. All *maka'ainana* formed extended families called *'ohana* who usually lived on the same section of land, called *ahupua'a.* Those farmers who lived inland would barter their produce with the fishermen who lived on the shore, and thus all shared equally in the bounty of land and sea.

A special group called *kauwa* was a landless, untouchable caste confined to living on reservations. Their origins were obviously Polynesian, but they appeared to be descendants of castaways who had survived and become perhaps the aboriginals of Hawaii before the main migrations. It was *kapu* for anyone to go onto *kauwa* lands, and doing so meant instant death. If a human sacrifice was needed, the *kahuna* would simply summon a *kauwa,* who had no recourse but to mutely comply. To this day, to call someone *kauwa,* which now supposedly means only servant, is still considered a fight-provoking insult.

Kapu and Day-to-Day Life

Occasionally there were horrible wars, but mostly the people lived quiet and ordered lives based on a strict caste society and the *kapu* system. Famine was known only on a regional level, and the population was kept in check by birth control, crude abortions, and the repulsive practice of infanticide, especially of baby girls. The Hawaiians were absolutely loving and nurturing parents under most circumstances and would even take in a *hanai* (adopted child or oldster), a lovely practice that lingers to this day.

A strict division of labor existed among men and women. Men were the only ones permitted to have anything to do with taro: this food-stuff was so sacred that there were a greater number of *kapu* concerning taro than concerning people. Men pounded poi and served it to the women. Men also were the fishermen and the builders of houses, canoes, irrigation ditches, and walls. Women tended to gardens and shoreline fishing and were responsible for making tapa cloth. The entire family lived in the common house, called the *hale noa.*

Certain things were *kapu* between the sexes. Primarily, women could not enter the *mua* (men's eating house), nor could they eat with men. Certain foods such as pork, coconut, red fish, and bananas were forbidden to women, and it was *kapu* for a man to have intercourse before going fishing, engaging in battle, or attending a religious ceremony. Young boys lived with the women until they underwent a circumcision rite called *pule ipu.* After this was performed, males were required to keep the *kapu* of men. A true Hawaiian settlement required a minimum of five huts: the men's eating hut, women's menstruation hut, women's eating hut, communal sleeping hut, and prayer hut. Without these five separate structures, Hawaiian "society" could not happen, since the *i'a kapu* (forbidden eating between men and women) could not be observed.

Ali'i could also declare a *kapu* and often did so. Certain lands or fishing areas were temporarily made *kapu* so that they could revitalize. Even today, it is *kapu* for anyone to remove all the *'opihi* (a type of limpet) from a rock. The great King Kamehameha I even placed a *kapu* on the body of his notoriously unfaithful child bride, Ka'ahumanu. It didn't work! The greatest *kapu (kapu moe)* was afforded to the highest ranking *ali'i:* everyone coming into their presence had to prostrate themselves. Lesser ranking *ali'i* were afforded the *kapu noho:* lessers had to sit or kneel in their presence. Commoners could not let their shadows fall upon an *ali'i,* nor enter an *ali'i*'s house except through a special door. Breaking a *kapu* meant immediate death.

The Causes of Decline

Less than 100 years after Captain Cook's arrival, King Kalakaua found himself with only 48,000 Hawaiian subjects. Wherever the king went, he would beseech his people, *"ho'oulu lahui"*—increase the race—but it was already too late. It was as if nature herself had turned her back on these once-proud people. Many of their marriages were barren, and in 1874, when only 1,400 children were born, a full 75 percent died in infancy. The Hawaiians could do nothing but watch as their race faded from existence.

The ecological system of Hawaii has always been exceptionally fragile and this included its people. When the first whites arrived they found a great people who were large, strong, and virile. But when it came to fighting off the most minor diseases, the Hawaiians proved as delicate as hothouse flowers. To exacerbate the situation, the Hawaiians were totally uninhibited toward sexual intercourse between willing partners, and they engaged in it openly and with abandon. Unfortunately, the sailors who arrived were full of syphilis and gonorrhea. The Hawaiian women brought these diseases home, and, given the nature of Hawaiian society at the time, they spread like wildfire. By the time the missionaries came in 1820 and helped to halt the unbridled fornication, they estimated the native population at only 140,000—less than half of what it had been only 40 years after initial contact. In the next 50 years measles, mumps, influenza, and tuberculosis further ravaged the people. Furthermore, Hawaiian men were excellent sailors, and it's estimated that during the whaling years at least 25 percent of all able-bodied Hawaiian men sailed away, never to return.

But the coup de grâce that really ended the Hawaiian race, as such, was that all racial newcomers to the islands were attracted to the Hawaiians and the Hawaiians were attracted to them. With so many interracial marriages, the Hawaiians literally bred themselves out of existence. By 1910, there were still twice as many full-blooded Hawaiians as mixed-bloods, but by 1940 mixed-blooded Hawaiians were the fastest-growing group, and full-blooded fastest declining.

Hawaiians Today

Many of the Hawaiians who moved to the cities became more and more disenfranchised. Their folk society stressed openness and a giving nature but downplayed the individual and the ownership of private property. These cultural traits made them easy targets for users and schemers until they finally became either apathetic or angry. Most surveys reveal that although Hawaiians number only 13 percent of the population, they account for almost 50 percent of the financially destitute families and also about half of all arrests and illegitimate births. Ni'ihau, a privately owned island, is home to about 160 pure-blooded Hawaiians, representing the largest concentration of them, per capita, in the islands. The Robinson family, which owns the island, restricts visitors to invited guests only.

The second-largest concentration is on Moloka'i, where 2,700 Hawaiians, living mostly on 40-acre *kuleana* of Hawaiian Homelands, make up 40 percent of that island's population. The majority of mixed-blooded Hawaiians, 240,000 or so, live on O'ahu, where they are particularly strong in the hotel and entertainment fields. People of Hawaiian extraction are still a delight to meet, and anyone so lucky as to be befriended by one long regards this friendship as the highlight of his or her travels. The Hawaiians have always given their *aloha* freely to all the peoples of the world, and it is we who must acknowledge this precious gift.

PACIFIC RIM (A.K.A. "HAWAII REGIONAL") CUISINE

Hawaii is a gastronome's Shangri-La, a sumptuous smorgasbord in every sense of the word. The varied ethnic groups that have come to Hawaii in the last 200 years have each brought their own special enthusiasms and cultures – and, lucky for all, they didn't forget their cookpots, hearty appetites, and exotic taste buds.

The Polynesians who first arrived found a fertile but empty land. Immediately they set about growing taro, coconuts, and bananas, and raising chickens, pigs, fish, and dogs, though the latter was reserved for nobility. Harvests were often bountiful, and the islanders thanked the gods with the traditional feast called the lu'au. Most food was baked in an underground oven (imu). Participants were encouraged to feast while relaxing on straw mats and enjoying the hula and various entertainments. The lu'au is as popular as ever, a treat that's guaranteed to delight anyone with a sense of eating adventure.

The missionaries and sailors came next, and their ships' holds carried barrels of ingredients for puddings, pies, dumplings, gravies, and roasts – the sustaining "American foods" of New England farms. The mid-1800s saw the arrival of boatloads of Chinese and Japanese peasants, who wasted no time making rice instead of bread the staple of the islands. The Chinese added their exotic spices, creating complex Sichuan dishes as well as workers' basics like chop suey. The Japanese introduced shoyu (soy sauce), sashimi, boxed lunches (bento), delicate tempura, and rich, filling noodle soups. The Portuguese brought their luscious Mediterranean dishes of tomatoes and peppers and plump spicy sausages, nutritious bean soups, and mouthwatering sweet treats like malasadas (holeless donuts) and pao dolce (sweet bread). Koreans carried crocks of zesty kimchi and quickly fired up barbecue pits for pulgogi, marinated beef cooked over a fire. Filipinos served up their delicious adobo stews – fish, meat, or chicken in a rich sauce of vinegar and garlic.

Recently, Thai and Vietnamese restaurants have been offering their irresistible dishes next door to restaurants presenting fiery burritos from Mexico or elegant Marsala cream sauces from France. The ocean breezes of Hawaii not only cool the skin but waft with them some of the most delectable aromas on earth, to make the taste buds tingle and the spirit soar.

THE CHINESE

Next to Yankees from New England, the Chinese are the oldest migrant group in Hawaii, and their influence has far outshone their meager numbers. They brought to Hawaii, along with their individuality, Confucianism, Taoism, and Buddhism, although many have long since become Christians. The Chinese population, at 56,000, makes up only 5 percent of the state's total, and the majority of them reside on O'ahu. As an ethnic group they account for the least amount of crime, the highest per capita income, and a disproportionate number of professionals.

The First Chinese

No one knows his name, but an unknown Chinese immigrant is credited with being the first person in Hawaii to refine sugar. This Asian wanderer tried his hand at crude refining on Lana'i in 1802. Fifty years later, the sugar plantations desperately needed workers, and the first Chinese brought to Hawaii under the newly passed Masters and Servants Act were 195 coolies from Xiamen who arrived in 1852. These conscripts contracted for three to five years and were given $3 per month plus room and board. They worked 12 hours a day, six days a week, and even in 1852 their wages were the pits. The Chinese almost always left the plantations the minute their contracts expired. They went into business for themselves and promptly monopolized the restaurant and small-shop trades.

The Chinese Niche

Although many people in Hawaii considered

Why then was "tourist food" in Hawaii so woeful for so long? Of course, there have always been a handful of fine restaurants, but for the most part food served to visitors lacked soul, with even the fine hotels opting to offer second-rate renditions of food more appropriate to large Mainland cities. Surrounded by some of the most fertile and pristine waters in the Pacific, you could hardly find a restaurant offering fresh fish, and it was an ill-conceived boast that even the fruits and vegetables lying limp on your table were "imported." Beginning with a handful of extremely creative and visionary chefs in the early 1980s who took the chance of perhaps offending the perceived simple palates of visitors, a delightfully delicious new cuisine was born. Based upon the finest traditions of continental cuisine, including, to a high degree, its sauces, pastas, and presentations, the culinary magic of Pacific Rim foods boldly combines the pungent spices, oils, and unique ingredients of Asia, the fantastic fresh vegetables, fruits, and fish of Hawaii, and, at times, the earthy cooking methods of the American Southwest. The result is a cuisine of fantastic tastes, subtle yet robust, and satiating but health-conscious – the perfect marriage of fresh foods prepared in a fresh way. Now restaurants on every island proudly advertise "Pacific Rim," "Hawaiian Regional," "fusion," or some other such name as a proud sign of this trend. As always, some are better than others, but the general result is that the "tourist food" has been vastly improved, and everyone benefits. Many of these exemplary chefs left lucrative and prestigious positions at Hawaii's five-diamond hotels and opened signature restaurants of their own, making this fine food much more available and affordable. In 1998, a new and younger group called Hawaiian Island Chefs came together to further enhance the offering of innovative foods made with island-grown produce and the bounty of the sea. In addition, this group has as one of its goals to influence culinary programs in the state to help carry on this fine tradition. With the incredible mix of peoples and cultures in Hawaii, the possibilities are endless, and this new group of chefs intends to shepherd the experience along, while promoting local farming enterprises and more nutritious food for everyone in the process.

all Chinese ethnically the same, they were quite different. The majority came from Guangdong Province in southern China. They were two distinct ethnic groups: the Punti made up 75 percent of the immigrants, and the Hakka made up the remainder. In China, they remained separate from each other, never mixing; in Hawaii, they mixed out of necessity. For one thing, hardly any Chinese women came over at first, and the ones who followed were at a premium and gladly accepted as wives, regardless of ethnic background. The Chinese were also one of the first groups who willingly intermarried with the Hawaiians, from whom they gained a reputation for being exceptionally caring spouses.

The Chinese accepted the social order and kept a low profile. For example, during the turbulent labor movements of the 1930s and 1940s in Hawaii, the Chinese community produced not one labor leader, radical intellectual, or left-wing politician. When Hawaii became a state, one of the two senators elected was Hiram Fong, a racially mixed Chinese. Since statehood, the Chinese community has carried on business as usual as they continue to rise both economically and socially.

THE JAPANESE

Most scholars believe that (inevitably) a few Japanese castaways floated to Hawaii long before Captain Cook arrived and might have introduced the iron with which the islanders seemed to be familiar before the white explorers arrived. The first official arrivals from Japan were ambassadors sent by the Japanese shogun to negotiate in Washington; they stopped en route at Honolulu in March 1860. But it was as plantation workers that the Japanese were brought en masse to the islands. A small group arrived in 1868, and mass migration started in 1885.

In 1886, because of famine, the Japanese government allowed farmers mainly from southern Honshu, Kyushu, and Okinawa to emigrate. Among these were members of Japan's little-talked-about untouchable caste, called *eta* or *burakumin* in Japan and *chorinbo* in Hawaii. They gratefully seized this opportunity to better their lot, an impossibility in Japan. The first Japanese migrants were almost all men. Between 1897 and 1908, migration was steady, with about 70 percent of the immigrants being male. Afterward, migration slowed because of a "gentlemen's agreement," a euphemism for racism against the "yellow peril." By 1900 there were over 60,000 Japanese in the islands, constituting the largest ethnic group.

AJAs – Americans of Japanese Ancestry

Parents of most Japanese children born before World War II were *issei* (first generation), who considered themselves apart from other Americans and clung to the notion of "we Japanese." Their children, the *nisei,* or second generation, were a different matter altogether. In one generation they had become Americans, and they put into practice the high Japanese virtues of obligation, duty, and loyalty to the homeland; that homeland was now unquestionably the United States. After Pearl Harbor was bombed, the FBI kept close tabs on the Japanese community, and the menace of the "enemy within" prompted the decision to place Hawaii under martial law for the duration of the war. It has since been noted that not a single charge of espionage or sabotage was ever reported against the Japanese community in Hawaii during the war.

AJAs as GIs

Although Japanese had formed a battalion during World War I, they were insulted at being considered unacceptable American soldiers in World War II. Some Japanese-Americans volunteered to serve in labor battalions, and because of their flawless work and loyalty, it was decided to put out a call for a few hundred volunteers to form a combat unit. Over 10,000 signed up! AJAs formed two distinguished units in World War II: the 100th Infantry Battalion and later the 442nd Regimental Combat Team. They landed in Italy at Salerno, and even fought from Guadalcanal to Okinawa. They distinguished themselves by becoming the most decorated unit in American military history.

The AJAs Return

Many returning AJAs took advantage of the GI Bill and received college educations. The "Big Five" corporations for the first time accepted former AJA officers as executives, and the old order was changed. Many Japanese became involved with Hawaiian politics, and the first elected to Congress was Daniel Inouye, who had lost an arm fighting in World War II. Hawaii's past governor, George Ariyoshi, elected in 1974, was the country's first Japanese-American to reach such a high office. Most Japanese, even as they climb the economic ladder, tend to remain Democrats.

Today, one out of every two political offices in Hawaii is held by a Japanese-American. In one of those weird quirks of fate, it is now the Hawaiian Japanese who are accused by other ethnic groups of engaging in unfair political practices—nepotism and reverse discrimination. Many of these accusations against AJAs are undoubtedly motivated by jealousy, but the AJAs' record in social fairness issues is not without blemish; true to their custom of family loyalty, many do stick together.

There are now 290,000 people in Hawaii of Japanese ancestry (another 100,000 of mixed Japanese blood), nearly one-quarter of the state's population. They are the least likely of any ethnic group in Hawaii to marry outside of their group—especially the men—and they enjoy a higher-than-average standard of living.

CAUCASIANS

White people have a distinction separating them from all other ethnic groups in Hawaii: they are lumped together as one. You can be anything from a Protestant Norwegian dockworker to a Greek Orthodox shipping tycoon, but if your skin is white, in Hawaii you're a *haole*. What's more, you can have arrived at Waikiki from Missoula, Montana, in the last 24 hours, or your *kama'aina* family can go back five generations, but again, if you're white, you're a *haole*.

The word *haole* has a floating connotation that depends upon the spirit in which it's used. It can mean everything from a derisive "honky" or "cracker" to nothing more than "white person." The exact Hawaiian meaning is clouded, but some say it meant "a man of no background," because white men couldn't chant a genealogical *koihonua* telling the Hawaiians who they were. The word eventually evolved to mean "foreign white man" and, today, simply "white person."

White History

Next to Hawaiians themselves, white people have the oldest stake in Hawaii. They've been there as settlers in earnest since the missionaries of the 1820s and were established long before any other migrant group. From last century until statehood, old *haole* families owned and controlled mostly everything, and although they were generally benevolent, philanthropic, and paternalistic, they were also racist. They were established *kama'aina* families, many of whom made up the boards of the Big Five corporations or owned huge plantations and formed a social circle that was closed to the outside. Many managed to find mates from among close family acquaintances.

Their paternalism, which they accepted with grave responsibility, at first only extended to the Hawaiians, who saw them as replacing their own *ali'i*. Asians were considered primarily instruments of production. These supremacist attitudes tended to drag on in Hawaii until quite recent times and are today responsible for the sometimes sour relations between white and nonwhite people in the islands. Today, all white people are resented to a certain degree because of these past acts, even though they personally were in no way involved.

White Plantation Workers

In the 1880s, the white landowners looked around and felt surrounded and outnumbered by Asians, so they tried to import white people for plantation work. None of their schemes seemed to work out. Europeans were accustomed to a much higher wage scale and better living conditions than were provided on the plantations. Although only workers and not considered the equals of the ruling elite, they still were expected to act like a special class. They were treated preferentially, which meant higher wages for the same jobs performed by Asians. Some of the imported workers included: 600 Scandinavians in 1881; 1,400 Germans 1881–85; 400 Poles in 1897–98; and 2,400 Russians 1909–12. Many proved troublesome, like the Poles and Russians who staged strikes after only months on the job. Many quickly moved to the Mainland. A contingency of Scots, who first came as muleskinners, did become successful plantation managers and supervisors. The Germans and Scandinavians were well received and climbed the social ladder rapidly, becoming professionals and skilled workers.

The Depression years, not as bad economically in Hawaii as in the continental United States, brought many Mainland whites seeking opportunity, mostly from the South and the West. These new people were even more racist toward brown-skinned people and Asians than the *kama'aina haole,* and they made matters worse. They also competed more intensely for jobs. The racial tension generated during this period came to a head in 1932 with the infamous Massie Rape Case, in which five local men were accused on circumstantial evidence of raping the wife of a naval officer—considered one of the greatest miscarriages of justice in American history.

The Portuguese

The last time anyone looked, Portugal was still

attached to the European continent, but for some anomalous reason the Portuguese weren't considered *haole* in Hawaii for the longest time. About 12,000 arrived between 1878 and 1887 and another 6,000 came between 1906 and 1913. Accompanied during this period by 8,000 Spanish, they were considered one and the same. Most of the Portuguese were illiterate peasants from Madeira and the Azores, and the Spanish hailed from Andalusia. They were very well received, and because they were white but not *haole,* they made a perfect "buffer" ethnic group. Committed to staying in Hawaii, they rose to be skilled workers—the *luna* class on the plantations. However, they de-emphasized education and became very racist toward Asians, regarding them as a threat to their job security.

By 1920, the 27,000 Portuguese made up 11 percent of the population. After that, they tended to blend with the other ethnic groups and weren't counted separately. Portuguese men tended to marry within their ethnic group, but a good portion of Portuguese women married other white men and became closer to the *haole* group, while another large portion chose Hawaiian mates and drew further away. Although they didn't originate pidgin English (see "Language" below), the unique melodious quality of their native tongue did give pidgin that certain lilt it has today. Also, the ukulele was closely patterned after the *cavaquinho,* a Portuguese stringed folk instrument.

The White Population

Today Caucasians make up the largest racial group in the islands at about 25 percent of the population. With mixed white blood, that number jumps to nearly 40 percent. They are spread evenly throughout Kaua'i, O'ahu, Maui, and the Big Island, with much smaller percentages on Moloka'i and Lana'i. On Kaua'i, there are heavy concentrations in Lihu'e, Po'ipu, and Wailua. The white population is the fastest growing in the islands because most people resettling in Hawaii are white Americans predominantly from the West Coast.

FILIPINOS

The Filipinos who came to Hawaii brought high hopes of amassing personal fortunes and returning home as rich heroes; for most, it was a dream that never came true. Filipinos had been American nationals ever since the Spanish-American War of 1898 and as such weren't subject to immigration laws that curtailed the importation of other Asian workers at the turn of this century. The first to arrive were 15 families in 1906, but a large number came in 1924 as strikebreakers. The majority were illiterate peasants called Ilocanos from the northern Philippines; about 10 percent were Visayans from the central cities. The Visayans were not as hardworking or thrifty but were much more sophisticated. From the first, Filipinos were looked down upon by all the other immigrant groups and were considered particularly uncouth by the Japanese. The value they placed on education was the least of any group, and even by 1930 only about half could speak rudimentary English, the majority remaining illiterate. They were billeted in the worst housing, performed the most menial jobs, and were the last hired and first fired.

One big difference between Filipinos and other groups was that the men brought no Filipino women to marry, so they clung to the idea of returning home. In 1930 there were 30,000 men and only 360 women. This hopeless situation led to a great deal of prostitution and homosexuality; many of these terribly lonely bachelors would feast and drink on weekends and engage in the gruesome but exciting pastime of cockfighting on Sunday. When some did manage to find wives, their mates were inevitably part Hawaiian. Filipino workers continued to be imported, although sporadically, until 1946, so even today there are a few old Filipino bachelors who never managed to get home, and Sunday cockfights remain a way of life.

The Filipinos constitute 14 percent of Hawaii's population, some 170,000 individuals, with almost 75 percent living on O'ahu. Some 275,000 are of mixed Filipino blood. Many visitors to Hawaii mistake Filipinos for Hawaiians because of their dark skin, and this is a minor irritant to both groups. Some streetwise Filipinos even claim to be Hawaiians, because being Hawaiian is "in" and goes over well with the tourists, especially the young women tourists. For the most part, these people are hardworking, dependable laborers who do tough work for little recognition. They remain low on the social totem pole and have not yet organized politically to stand up for their rights.

OTHER GROUPS

About 10 percent of Hawaii's population is a conglomerate of other ethnic groups. Of these, one of the largest and fastest growing is Korean, with 25,000 people. About 8,000 Koreans came to Hawaii from 1903 until 1905, when their government halted emigration. During the same period about 6,000 Puerto Ricans arrived, and today about 30,000 consider themselves a Puerto Rican mix. There were also two attempts made in the 1800s to import other Polynesians to strengthen the dying Hawaiian race, but they were failures. In 1869 only 126 central Polynesian natives could be lured to Hawaii, and from 1878 to 1885 2,500 Gilbert Islanders arrived. Both groups became immediately disenchanted with Hawaii. They pined for their own islands and departed for home as soon as possible.

Today, however, 16,000 Samoans have settled in Hawaii, and with more on the way they are one of the fastest-growing minorities in the state. For unknown reasons, Samoans and native Hawaiians get along extremely poorly and have the worst racial tensions and animosity of any groups. The Samoans ostensibly should represent the archetypal Polynesians that the Hawaiians are seeking, but it doesn't work that way. Samoans are criticized by Hawaiians for their hot tempers, lingering feuds, and petty jealousies. They're clannish and are often the butt of "dumb" jokes. This racism seems especially ridiculous, but that's the way it is.

Just to add a bit more spice to the stew, there are about 22,000 African Americans, 3,500 Native Americans, 4,000 Tongans, 7,000 other Pacific Islanders, and 8,000 Vietnamese refugees living on the islands.

Culture

RELIGION

The Lord saw fit to keep His island paradise secret from humans for a few million years, but once we finally arrived we were awfully thankful. Hawaii sometimes seems like a floating tabernacle; everywhere you look there's a church, temple, shrine, or *heiau*. The islands are either a very holy place, or there's a powerful lot of sinning going on that would require so many houses of prayer. Actually, it's just America's "right to worship" concept fully employed in microcosm. All the peoples who came to Hawaii brought their own forms of devotion. The Polynesian Hawaiians praised the primordial creators, Wakea and Papa, from whom their pantheon of animistically inspired gods sprang. To a modern world these old gods would never do. Unfortunately for the old gods, there were too many of them, and belief in them was looked upon as superstition, the folly of semi-civilized pagans. So the famous missionaries of the 1820s brought Congregational Christianity and the "true path" to heaven.

Inconveniently, the Catholics, Mormons, Reformed Mormons, Adventists, Episcopalians, Unitarians, Christian Scientists, Lutherans, Baptists, Jehovah's Witnesses, Salvation Army, and every other major and minor denomination of Christianity that followed in their wake brought their own brands of enlightenment and never quite agreed with each other. Chinese and Japanese immigrants established the major sects of Buddhism, Confucianism, Taoism, and Shintoism. Allah is praised, the Torah is chanted in Jewish synagogues and nirvana is available at a variety of Hindu temples. If the spirit moves you, a Hare Krishna devotee will be glad to point you in the right direction and give you a free flower for only a dollar or two. If the world is still too much with you, you might find peace at a Church of Scientology, or meditate at a Kundalini yoga institute, or perhaps find relief at a local assembly of Baha'i. Anyway, rejoice, because in Hawaii you'll not only find paradise, you might even find salvation.

Hawaiian Beliefs

The Polynesian Hawaiians worshipped nature. They saw its forces manifested in a multiplicity of forms to which they ascribed godlike powers, and they based daily life on this animistic philosophy. Hand-picked and specially trained storytellers chanted the exploits of the gods. These ancient tales, kept alive in a special oral tradition called *mo'olelo,* were recited only by day. Entranced listeners encircled the chanter; in respect for the gods and in fear of their wrath, they were forbidden to move once the tale was begun. This was serious business, during which a person's life could be at stake. It was not like the telling of *ka'ao,* which were simple fictions, tall tales, and yarns of ancient heroes related for amusement and to pass the long nights. Any object, animate or inanimate, could be a god. All could be infused with mana, especially a dead body or respected ancestor.

'Ohana had personal family gods called *'aumakua* on whom they called in times of danger or strife. There were children of gods called

HAWAIIAN FOLK MEDICINE AND COMMON CURATIVE PLANTS

Hawaiian folk medicine is well developed, and its cures for common ailments have been used effectively for centuries. Hawaiian *kahuna* were highly regarded for their medicinal skills, and Hawaiians were by far some of the healthiest people in the world until the coming of the Europeans. Many folk remedies and cures are used to this day and, what's more, they work. Many of the common plants and fruits that you'll encounter provide some of the best remedies. When roots and seeds and special exotic plants are used, the preparation of the medicine is as painstaking as in a modern pharmacy. These prescriptions are exact and take an expert to prepare. They should never be prepared or administered by an amateur.

Arrowroot, for diarrhea, is a powerful narcotic used in rituals and medicines. Kava *(Piper methysticum),* also called *'awa,* is chewed and the juice is spat into a container for fermenting. Used as a medicine for urinary tract infections, rheumatism, and asthma, it also induces sleep and cures headaches. A poultice for wounds is made from the skins of ripe bananas. Peelings have a powerful antibiotic quality and contain vitamins A, B, and C, phosphorous, calcium, and iron. The nectar from the plant was fed to babies as a vitamin juice. Breadfruit sap is used for healing cuts and as a moisturizing lotion. Coconut is used to make moisturizing oil, and the juice was chewed, spat into the hand, and used as a shampoo. Guava is a source of vitamins A, B, and C. Hibiscus has been used as a laxative. *Kukui* nut oil makes a gargle for sore throats and a laxative, plus the flowers are used to cure diarrhea. *Noni,* an unappetizing, hand-grenade-shaped fruit that you wouldn't want to eat unless you had to, reduces tumors, diabetes, and high blood pressure, and the juice is good for diarrhea. Sugarcane sweetens many concoctions, and the juice of toasted cane was a tonic for sick babies. Sweet potato is used as a tonic during pregnancy and juiced as a gargle for phlegm. Tamarind is a natural laxative and contains the most acid and sugar of any fruit on earth. Taro has been used for lung infections and thrush and as suppositories. Yams are good for coughs, vomiting, constipation, and appendicitis.

kupua who were thought to live among humans and were distinguished either for their beauty and strength or for their ugliness and terror. It was told that processions of dead *ali'i,* called "Marchers of the Night," wandered through the land of the living, and unless you were properly protected it could mean death if they looked upon you. There were simple ghosts known as *akua lapu* who merely frightened people. Forests, waterfalls, trees, springs, and a thousand forms of nature were the manifestations of *akua li'i,* "little spirits" who could be invoked at any time for help or protection. It made no difference who or what you were in old Hawaii; the gods were ever-present and took a direct and active role in your life.

Behind all of these beliefs was an innate sense of natural balance and order. It could be interpreted as positive-negative, yin-yang, plus-minus, life-death, light-dark, whatever, but the main idea was that everything had its opposite. The time of darkness when only the gods lived was *po.* When the great gods descended to the earth and created light, this was *ao,* and humanity was born. All of these *mo'olelo* are part of the *Kumulipo,* the great chant that records the Hawaiian version of creation. From the time the gods descended and touched the earth at Ku Moku on Lana'i, the genealogies were kept. Unlike the Bible, these included the noble families of female as well as male *ali'i.*

Heiau and Idols

A *heiau* is a Hawaiian temple. The basic *heiau* was a masterfully built and fitted rectangular stone wall that varied in size from about as big as a basketball court to as big as a football field. Once the restraining outer walls were built, the interior was backfilled with smaller stones and the top dressing was expertly laid and then rolled, perhaps with a log, to form a pavement-like surface. All that remains of Hawaii's many *heiau* are the stone platforms or walls. The buildings upon them, made from perishable wood, leaves, and grass, have long since disappeared.

Some *heiau* were dreaded temples where human sacrifices were made. Tradition says that this barbaric custom began at Waha'ula Heiau, on the Big Island, in the 12th century and was introduced by a ferocious Tahitian priest named Pa'ao. Other *heiau,* such as Pu'uhonua o Honaunau, also on the Big Island, were temples of refuge where the weak, widowed, orphaned, and vanquished could find safety and sanctuary.

The Hawaiian people worshipped gods who took the form of idols fashioned from wood, feathers, or stone. The eyes were made from shells, and until these were inlaid, the idol was dormant. The hair used was often human hair, and the arms and legs were usually flexed. The mouth was either gaping or formed a wide figure-eight lying on its side, and more likely than not was lined with glistening dog teeth. Small figures made of woven basketry were expertly covered with feathers. Red and yellow feathers were favorites taken from specific birds by men whose only work was to roam the forests in search of them.

Missionaries

In Hawaii, when you say "missionaries," it's taken for granted you're referring to the small and determined band of Congregationalists who arrived aboard the brig *Thaddeus* in 1820, and the follow-up groups, called "companies" or "packets," that reinforced them. They were sent from Boston by the American Board of Commissioners for Foreign Missions (ABCFM), which learned of the supposed sad and godless plight of the Hawaiian people through returning sailors and especially through the few Hawaiians who had come to America to study.

The person most instrumental in bringing the missionaries to Hawaii was a young man named Opukaha'ia. He was an orphan befriended by a ship's captain and taken to New England, where he studied theology. Obsessed with the desire to return home and save his people from certain damnation, Opukaha'ia wrote accounts of life in Hawaii that were published and widely read. These accounts were directly responsible for the formation of the Pioneer Company to the Sandwich Islands

Missions in 1819. Unfortunately, Opukaha'ia died in New England from typhus the year before they left.

The first missionaries had the straightforward task of bringing the Hawaiians out of paganism and into Christianity and civilization. They met with terrible hostility—not from the natives, but from the sea captains and traders who were very happy with the open debauchery and wanton whoremongering that was status quo in the Hawaii of 1820. Many direct confrontations between these two factions even included the cannonading of missionaries' homes by American sea captains who were denied the customary visits of island women, thanks to meddlesome "do-gooders." The most memorable of these incidents involved "Mad Jack" Percival, the captain of the USS *Dolphin,* who bombed a church in Lahaina to show his rancor. The truth of the situation was much closer to the sentiments of James Jarves, who wrote, "The missionary was a far more useful and agreeable man than his Catholicism would indicate; and the trader was not so bad a man as the missionary would make him out to be." The missionaries' primary aim might have been conversion, but the most fortuitous by-product was education, which raised the consciousness of every Hawaiian, regardless of religious affiliation. In 40 short years, Hawaii was considered a civilized nation well on its way into the modern world, and the American Board of Missions officially ended its support in 1863.

Non-Christians

By the beginning of the 20th century, both Shintoism and Buddhism, brought by the Japanese and Chinese, were firmly established in Hawaii. The first official Buddhist temple was Hongpa Hongwanji, established on O'ahu in 1889. All the denominations of Buddhism account for 17 percent of the islands' religious total, and there are about 50,000 Shintoists. The Hindu religion has perhaps 2,000 adherents, and the Hindu Temple on Kaua'i is strong and vigorous with one of the largest stone temple structures outside of India. About the same number of Jewish people live throughout Hawaii with only one synagogue, Temple Emanu-El, on O'ahu. The largest number of people in Hawaii (300,000) remain unaffiliated, and about 10,000 people are in new religious movements and lesser-known faiths such as Baha'i and Unitarianism.

LANGUAGE

Hawaii is part of America and people speak English there, but that's not the whole story. If you turn on the TV to catch the evening news, you'll hear "Walter Cronkite" English, unless, of course, you happen to tune in to a Japanese-language broadcast designed for tourists from that country. You can easily pick up a Chinese-language newspaper or groove to the music on a Filipino radio station, but let's not confuse the issue. All your needs and requests at airports, car-rental agencies, restaurants, hotels, or wherever you happen to travel will be completely understood, as well as answered, in English. However, when you happen to overhear islanders speaking, what they're saying will sound somewhat familiar but you won't be able to pick up all the words, and the beat and melody of the language will be noticeably different.

Hawaii—like New England, the Deep South, and the Midwest—has its own unmistakable linguistic regionalism. All the ethnic peoples who make up Hawaii have enriched the English spoken there with words, expressions, and subtle shades of meaning commonly used and understood throughout the islands. The greatest influence on English has come from the Hawaiian language itself, and words such as aloha, hula, lu'au, and *lei* are familiarly used and understood by most Americans.

Other migrant peoples, especially the Chinese, Japanese, and Portuguese, influenced the local dialect to such an extent that the simplified plantation lingo they spoke has become known as "pidgin." A fun and enriching part of the "island experience" is picking up a few words of Hawaiian and pidgin. English is the official language of the state, business, education, and perhaps even the mind, but pidgin

CHANTS

Until the 1820s, when New England missionaries began a phonetic rendering of the Hawaiian language, the past was kept vividly alive only by the sonorous voices of special *kahuna* who chanted the sacred *mele*. The chants were beautiful, flowing word pictures that captured the essence of every aspect of life. These *mele* praised the land *(mele 'aina)*, royalty *(mele ali'i)*, and life's tender aspects *(mele aloha)*. Chants were dedicated to friendship, hardship, and favorite children. Entire villages sometimes joined together to compose a *mele* – every word was chosen carefully, and the wise old *kupuna* would decide if the words were lucky or unlucky. Some *mele* were bawdy or funny on the surface but contained secret meanings, often bitingly sarcastic, that ridiculed an inept or cruel leader. But the most important chants took the listeners back into the dim past, even before people lived in Hawaii. From these genealogies *(koihonua)*, the *ali'i* derived the right to rule, since these chants went back to the gods Wakea and Papa, from whom the *ali'i* were directly descended.

Today, the art of chanting continues in a manner that is, perhaps, less strict but still serious and is generally used for cultural events, meetings, and ceremonies where the importance is beyond question. Often the *kahuna* dresses in traditional Hawaiian garb and his resonant voice still casts a spell upon listeners like similar voices have done for generations. Chants also appear on some modern Hawaiian music CDs, so this ancient form is getting a wider hearing.

is the language of the people, the emotions, and life, while Hawaiian (also an official language of the state, but used "only as provided by law") remains the language of the heart and the soul.

Note: Many Hawaiian words are commonly used in English, appear in English dictionaries, and therefore would ordinarily be subject to the rules of English grammar. The Hawaiian language, however, does not pluralize nouns by adding an "s"; the singular and plural are differentiated in context. For purposes of this book, and to highlight the Hawaiian culture, the Hawaiian style of pluralization will be followed for common Hawaiian words. The following are some examples of plural Hawaiian nouns treated this way in this book: *haole* (not *haoles*), *kahuna*, lei, lu'au, and *nene*.

Pidgin

The dictionary definition of pidgin is: a simplified language with a rudimentary grammar used as a means of communication between people speaking different languages. Hawaiian pidgin is a little more complicated than that. It had its roots during the plantation days of the 19th century when white owners and *luna* (foremen) had to communicate with recently arrived Chinese, Japanese, and Portuguese laborers. It was designed as a simple language of the here and now, primarily concerned with the necessary functions of working, eating, and sleeping. It has an economical noun-verb-object structure (although not necessarily in that order).

Hawaiian words make up most of pidgin's non-English vocabulary. It includes a good smattering of Chinese, Japanese, and Samoan; the distinctive rising inflection is provided by the melodious Mediterranean lilt of the Portuguese. Pidgin is not a stagnant language. It's kept alive by hip new words introduced by cool people, or especially by slang words introduced by teenagers. It's a colorful English, like "jive" or "ghettoese" spoken by American blacks, and is as regionally unique as the speech of Cajuns in Louisiana's bayous. *Maka'ainana* of all socio-ethnic backgrounds can at least understand pidgin. Most islanders are proud of it, while some consider it a low-class jargon. The Hawaiian House of Representatives has given pidgin an official sanction, and most people

NOTE ON HAWAIIAN DIACRITICS

Aside from the five vowels and seven consonants, written Hawaiian uses two diacritical marks to distinguish spoken sounds. These are the 'okina, or glottal stop, written as a reverse apostrophe (') before a vowel; and the macron kahako, a short line written over a vowel indicating that the vowel is stressed. For technical reasons, the kahako is not used in this book. The 'okina is used in Hawaiian place names, names of historical persons, and ordinary Hawaiian words, where appropriate. It is not used in business names if the business itself does not use this symbol. The name Hawai'i, written with an 'okina refers to the island of Hawai'i, the Big Island; without the 'okina, it refers to the state. The word Hawaiian, written without the glottal stop, refers to both the Polynesian inhabitants of the islands before Western contact and to those people of all races who currently reside in the state.

feel that it adds a real local style and should be preserved.

Pidgin is first learned at school where all students, regardless of background, are exposed to it. The pidgin spoken by young people today is "fo' real" different from that of their parents. It's no longer only plantation talk but has moved to the streets and picked up some sophistication. At one time there was an academic movement to exterminate it, but that idea died away with the same thinking that insisted on making left-handed people write with their right hands. It is strange, however, that pidgin has become the unofficial language of Hawaii's grassroots movement, when it actually began as a white owners' language used to supplant Hawaiian and all the languages brought to the islands.

Although hip young haole use pidgin all the time, it has gained the connotation of being the language of the nonwhite locals and is part of the "us against them" way of thinking. All local people, haole or not, do consider pidgin their own island language and don't really like it when it's used by malihini (newcomers). If you're in the islands long enough, you don't have to bother learning pidgin; it'll learn you. There's a book sold all over the islands called Pidgin to da Max, written by (you guessed it) a haole—a Nebraskan named Doug Simonson. You might not be able to understand what's being said by locals speaking pidgin (that's usually the idea), but you should be able to feel what's being meant.

Hawaiian

The Hawaiian language sways like a palm tree in a gentle wind. Its words are as melodious as a love song. Linguists say that you can learn a lot about people through their language; when you hear Hawaiian you think of gentleness and love, and it's hard to imagine the ferocious side so evident in Hawaii's past. With its many Polynesian root words easily traced to Indonesian and Malay, Hawaiian is obviously from this same stock. The Hawaiian spoken today is very different from old Hawaiian. Its greatest metamorphosis occurred when the missionaries began to write it down in the 1820s, but in the last couple of decades there has been a movement to reestablish the Hawaiian language. Not only are courses in it offered at the University of Hawaii, but there is a successful elementary immersion school program in the state, some books are being printed in it, and more and more musicians are performing it. Many scholars have put forth translations of Hawaiian, but there are endless, volatile disagreements in the academic sector about the real meanings of Hawaiian words. Hawaiian is no longer spoken as a language except on Ni'ihau, and the closest tourists will come to it are in place-names, street names, and words that have become part of common usage, such as "aloha" and "mahalo." A few old Hawaiians still speak it at home, and sermons are delivered in Hawaiian at some local churches. Kawaiaha'o Church in downtown Honolulu is the most famous of these.

Thanks to the missionaries, the Hawaiian language is rendered phonetically using only

12 letters. They are the five vowels, a-e-i-o-u, sounded as they are in Italian, and seven consonants, h-k-l-m-n-p-w, sounded exactly as they are in English. Sometimes "w" is pronounced as "v," but this occurs only in the middle of a word and always follows a vowel. A consonant is always followed by a vowel, forming two-letter syllables, but vowels are often found in pairs or even triplets. A slight oddity about Hawaiian is the glottal stop, called *'okina.* This is an abrupt break in sound in the middle of a word, such as "oh-oh" in English, and is denoted with a reverse apostrophe. A good example is *ali'i,* or, even better, the O'ahu town of Ha'iku, which actually means Abrupt Break.

Pronunciation Key

For those unfamiliar with the sounds of Italian or other Romance languages, the vowels are sounded as follows:

A—in stressed syllables, pronounced as in "ah" (that feels good!). For example, Haleakala is pronounced "hah-lay-AH-kah-lah.

E—short "e" is "eh," as in "pen" or "dent" (thus *hele* is "HEH-leh"). Long "e" sounds like "ay" as in "sway" or "day." For example, the Hawaiian goose *(nene)* is a "nay-nay," not a "knee-knee."

I—pronounced "ee" as in "see" or "we" (thus *pali* is pronounced "PAH-lee").

O—pronounced as in "no" or "oh," such as "KOH-uh" (koa) or "OH-noh" (ono).

U—pronounced "oo" as in "do" or "stew"; for example, "KAH-poo" *(kapu)* or "POO-nah" (Puna).

Diphthongs

There are also eight vowel pairs known as "diphthongs" (ae-ai-ao-au-ei-eu-oi-ou). These are the sounds made by gliding from one vowel to another within a syllable. The stress is placed on the first vowel. In English, examples would be soil and euphoria. Common examples in Hawaiian are lei and *heiau.*

Stress

The best way to learn which syllables are stressed in Hawaiian is by listening closely. It becomes obvious after a while. There are also some vowel sounds that are held longer than others; these can occur at the beginning of a word, such as the first "a" in *"aina,"* or in the middle of a word, like the first "a" in "lanai." Again, it's a matter of tuning your ear and paying attention.

When written, these stressed vowels, called *kahako,* occur with a macron, or short line, over them. Stressed vowels with marks are not written as such in this book. No one is going to give you a hard time if you mispronounce a word. It's good, however, to pay close attention to the pronunciation of street and place-names because many Hawaiian words sound alike and a misplaced vowel here or there could be the difference between getting where you want to go and getting lost.

ARTS OF OLD HAWAII

Since everything in old Hawaii had to be fashioned by hand, almost every object was either a genuine work of art or the product of a highly refined craft. With the "civilizing" of the natives, most of the old ways disappeared, including the old arts and crafts. Most authentic Hawaiian art by master craftsmen exists only in museums, but with the resurgence of Hawaiian roots, many old arts are being revitalized, and their legacy lives on in a few artists who have become proficient in them.

Magnificent Canoes

The most respected artisans in old Hawaii were the canoe makers. With little more than a stone adze and a pump drill, they built canoes that could carry 200 people and last for generations—sleek, well proportioned, and infinitely seaworthy. The main hull was usually a gigantic koa log, and the gunwale planks were minutely drilled and sewn to the sides with sennit rope. Apprenticeships lasted for years, and a young man knew that he had graduated when one day he was nonchalantly asked to sit down and eat with the master builders. Small family-sized canoes with outriggers were used for fishing and perhaps carried spear racks; large oceangoing double-hulled canoes were used for migration and warfare. On these, the giant logs had been adzed to about two inches thick. A mainsail woven from pandanus was mounted on a central platform, and the boat was steered by two long paddles. The hull was dyed with plant juices and charcoal, and the entire village helped launch the canoe in a ceremony called "drinking the sea."

Carving

Wood was a primary material used by Hawaiian craftsmen. They almost exclusively used koa because of its density, strength, and natural luster. It was turned into canoes, woodware, calabashes, and furniture used by the *ali'i.* Temple idols were also a major product of woodcarving. Many varieties of stone artifacts were turned out, including poi pounders, mirrors, fish sinkers, and small idols.

Weaving

Hawaiians became the best basket makers and mat weavers in all of Polynesia. *Ulana* (woven mats) were made from *lau hala* (pandanus) leaves. Once split, the spine was removed and the leaves stored in large rolls. When needed, they were soaked, pounded, and then fashioned into various floor coverings and sleeping mats. Intricate geometric patterns were woven in, and the edges were rolled and well fashioned. Coconut palms were not used to make mats in old Hawaii, but a wide variety of basketry was made from the aerial root *'ie'ie.* The shapes varied according to use. Some baskets were tall and narrow, some were cones, others were flat like trays, while many were woven around gourds and calabashes.

Featherwork

This highly refined art was found only on the islands of Tahiti, New Zealand, and Hawaii, while the fashioning of feather helmets and idols was unique to Hawaii. Favorite colors were red and yellow, which came only in a very limited supply from a small number of birds such as the *'o'o, 'i'iwi, mamo,* and *'apapane.* Professional bird hunters in old Hawaii paid their taxes to *ali'i* in prized feathers. The feathers were fastened to a woven net of *olona* cord and made into helmets, idols, and beautiful flowing capes and cloaks. These resplendent garments were made and worn only by men, especially during battle, when a fine cloak became a great trophy of war. Featherwork was also employed in the making of *kahili* and lei, which were highly prized by the noble *ali'i* women.

Lei-Making

Any flower or blossom can be strung into a lei, but the most common are carnations or the lovely smelling plumeria. Lei, like babies, are all beautiful, but special lei are highly prized by those who know what to look for. Of the different stringing styles, the most common is *kui*—stringing the flower through the middle or side. Most "airport-quality" lei are of this type. The *humuhumu* style, reserved for making flat lei, is made by sewing flowers and ferns to a *ti,* banana, or sometimes *hala* leaf. A *humuhumu* lei makes an excellent hatband. *Wili* is the winding together of greenery, ferns, and flowers into short, bouquet-type lengths. The most traditional form is *hili,* which requires no stringing at all but involves braiding fragrant ferns and leaves such as *maile.* If flowers are in-

GICLÉE

Many galleries now offer unbelievable prints produced by a rather expensive computer-based method called *giclée.* A picture of the original is made into a transparency that is scanned to match subtle strokes and color variations perfectly, and then airbrushed at four million droplets per second (each one-fourth the diameter of a human hair) onto paper or canvas, creating a cyberspace copy of near-perfect similarity to the original.

To add more personality to these prints and to make them "one of a kind," artists will sometimes touch them up with additional paint so they are not exact replicas of other prints.

terwoven, the *hili* becomes the *haku* style, the most difficult and most beautiful type of lei.

Every major island is symbolized by its own lei made from a distinctive flower, shell, or fern. Each island has its own official color as well, though it doesn't necessarily correspond to the color of the island's lei. Kaua'i, oldest of the main islands, is represented by the *mokihana lei* and the regal color purple. The *mokihana* tree produces a small cube-like fruit that smells like anise. Green when strung into Kaua'i's lei, they then turn a dark brown and keep their scent for months.

Tapa Cloth

Tapa, cloth made from tree bark, was common throughout Polynesia and was a woman's art. A few trees such as the *wauke* and *mamaki* produced the best cloth, but a variety of other types of bark could be utilized. First the raw bark was pounded into a felt-like pulp and beaten together to form strips (the beaters had

---

KAUA'I HISTORICAL SOCIETY AND MUSEUMS

Kaua'i Historical Society (P.O. Box 1778, Lihu'e, HI 96766, 808/245-3373, www.kauai-historicalsociety.org) was established in 1914. The society remains Kaua'i's only general historical archive, preserving printed and audio material, photographs, maps, and a variety of other objects. Members work toward the preservation of historical and cultural sites, offer educational programs, and organize periodic tours. Located in the historic county building in Lihu'e, the archives are free and open to the public for research weekdays by appointment.

Kaua'i Museum (4428 Rice St., Lihu'e, 808/245-6931, www.kauaimuseum.org, 9 A.M.-4 P.M. Mon.-Fri. and 10 A.M.-4 P.M. Sat., with free admission for the whole family on the first Saturday of each month. The story of Kaua'i and Ni'ihau is told through art and ethnic exhibits. This should be one of your first stops on the island. Hawaiiana books, maps, and prints are available at the museum shop.

Grove Farm Homestead (P.O. Box 1631, Lihu'e, HI 96766, 808/245-3202) is open by reservation for guided tours at 10 A.M. and 1 P.M. Monday, Wednesday, and Thursday. Donations requested are adults $5 and children 2-12 $2. This is the homestead of early sugar planter George N. Wilcox, with a plantation owner's house, workers' cottages, outbuildings, and garden. Definitely worth a visit.

Koke'e Natural History Museum (808/335-9975, www.kokee.org, 9 A.M.-4 P.M. daily, 10 A.M.-2 P.M. on holidays, $1 suggested donation). Exhibits interpret the geology and unique plants and animals of Kaua'i's mountain wilderness. Great to visit while at Waimea Canyon and Koke'e State Park.

Wai'oli Mission House (808/245-3202, 9 A.M.-3 P.M. Tues., Thurs., and Sat.) is run by the same group that oversees Grove Farm Homestead in Lihu'e. No reservations are needed. Entrance by donation.

The **Kaua'i Children's Discovery Museum** (808/823-8222, 9 A.M.-5 P.M. Tues.-Sat., $4 for children, $5 for adults, www.kcdm.org) under the Whale Tower at the Kauai Village Shopping Center in Kapa'a, is a hands-on museum dedicated to science, culture, and the arts as it relates to Hawaii, its past, and its environment.

The **Faye Museum** (9 A.M.-9 P.M. daily) at the Waimea Plantation Cottages is a small museum presenting photographs and artifacts of the sugar plantation years of west Kaua'i.

For a short historical perspective on coffee, a few artifacts, and the story on coffee production and processing on Kaua'i, stop in at the **Kauai Coffee Company Museum** (808/335-0813 or 800/545-8605, www.kauaicoffee-.com, 9 A.M.-5 P.M. daily) in Numila.

Many old artifacts, pictures, and paraphernalia regarding sugar and the sugar era on Kaua'i have been drawn together and exhibited in the Gay and Robinson Sugar Company's visitors center shop (808/335-2824, 8 A.M.-4 P.M. Mon.-Fri., 11 A.M.-3 P.M. on Saturday).

distinctive patterns that helped to make the cloth supple). They were decorated by stamping (a form of block printing) and dyed with natural colors from plants and sea animals in shades of gray, purple, pink, and red. They were even painted with natural brushes made from pandanus fruit, with an overall gray color made from charcoal. The tapa cloth was sewn together to make bed coverings, and fragrant flowers and herbs were either sewn or pounded in to produce a permanent fragrance. Tapa cloth is still available today, but the Hawaiian methods have been lost; most cloth comes from other areas of Polynesia.

ARTS TO BUY

Referring to Hawaii as "paradise" is about as hackneyed as you can get, but when you specify "artists' paradise" it's the absolute truth. Something about the place evokes art (or at least personal expression) from most people. The islands are like a magnet: They not only draw artists to them, but they draw art *from* the artists.

The inspiration comes from the astounding natural surroundings. The land is so beautiful yet so raw; the ocean's power and rhythm are primal and ever-present; the riotous colors of flowers and fruit leap from the deep-green jungle background. Crystal water beads and pale mists turn the mountains into mystic temples, while rainbows ride the crests of waves. The stunning variety of faces begging to be rendered suggests that all the world sent delegations to the islands. And in most cases it did! Inspiration is everywhere, as is art, good and bad.

Sometimes the artwork is overpowering in itself and in its sheer volume. Though geared to the tourist market of cheap souvenirs, there is hardly a shop in Hawaii that doesn't sell some item that falls into the general category of "art." You can find everything from carved monkey-face coconut shells to true masterpieces.

ARTS AND CULTURE ORGANIZATIONS

State Foundation on Culture and the Arts (250 South Hotel St., Honolulu 808/586-0300, www.state.hi.us/sfca) was begun by the State Legislature in 1965 to preserve and promote Hawaii's diverse cultural, artistic, and historical heritage. It manages grants, maintains programs in folk arts and art in public places, and supports an events calendar.

Garden Island Art Council (P.O. Box 827, Lihu'e, HI 96766, 808/245-2733, www.gardenislandarts.org) promotes arts, art education, and cultural events around the island.

For more than two decades, the **Kauai Community Players** troupe (P.O. Box 343, Lihu'e, HI 96766, 808/245-7700, www.kauaicommunityplayers.org), has been entertaining audiences year-round with adult and children's theater.

The **Kaua'i Society of Artists** (P.O. Box 3344, Lihu'e, HI 96766, www.kauaisocietyofartists.org) holds public exhibitions at least three times a year. The Kaua'i Society of Artists periodically prints *Guide to Kaua'i Artists*, a magazine-size brochure on Kaua'i resident artists including brief descriptions of their work, studio addresses, contact information, and where their work can be found.

Hawaii Children's Theater (808/246-8985) presents various live performances during the year.

College, community, and state events, as well as concerts, film, theater, and pageants are performed year-round at the **Kaua'i Community College Performing Arts Center** (808/245-8270, www.kauai.hawaii.edu/pac) on the college campus in Puhi.

A full slate of world-renowned music and vocal groups comes to Kaua'i each year through the **Kaua'i Concert Association** (808/245-7464, www.kauai-concert.org). All performances are held at the Performing Arts Center on the Kaua'i Community College campus, and tickets usually range $20-30.

Alohawear

Wild Hawaiian shirts or bright mu'umu'u, especially when worn on the Mainland, have the magical effect of making the wearer feel like they're in Hawaii, while at the same time eliciting spontaneous smiles from passers-by. Maybe it's the colors, or perhaps it's just the vibe that signifies party time or "hang loose," but nothing says Hawaii like alohawear. More than a dozen fabric houses in Hawaii turn out distinctive patterns, and many dozens of factories create their own personalized designs. These factories often have attached retail outlets, but in any case you can find hundreds of shops selling alohawear. Aloha shirts were the brilliant idea of a Chinese merchant in Honolulu, who used to hand-tailor them and then sell them to the tourists who arrived by ship in the glory days before World War II. They were an instant success. Mu'umu'u or "Mother Hubbards" were the idea of missionaries, who were appalled by Hawaiian women running about au naturel and insisted on covering their new Christian converts from head to foot. Now the roles are reversed, and it's Mainlanders who come to Hawaii and immediately strip down to as little clothing as possible.

At one time alohawear was exclusively made of cotton or from man-made, natural fiber—based rayon, and these materials are still the best for any tropical clothing. Beware, however: polyester has slowly crept into the market! No material could possibly be worse for the island climate, so when buying your alohawear make sure to check the label for material content. On the bright side, silk also is used and makes a good material but is a bit heavy for some. Mu'umu'u now come in various styles and can be worn for the entire spectrum of social occasions in Hawaii. Aloha shirts are basically cut the same as always, but the patterns have undergone changes; apart from the original flowers and ferns, modern shirts might depict an island scene in the manner of a silk-screen painting. A basic good-quality mu'umu'u or aloha shirt is guaranteed to be worth its price in good times and happy smiles. The connoisseur might want to purchase *The Hawaiian Shirt, Its Art and History,* by R. Thomas Steele. It's illustrated with more than 150 shirts that are now considered works of art by collectors the world over.

Scrimshaw

The art of etching and carving on bone and ivory has become an island tradition handed down from the times of the great whaling ships. Examples of this Danish sailors' art date all the way back to the 15th century, but, like jazz, it was really popularized and raised to an art form by Americans—whalers on decade-long voyages from "back east" plying vast oceans in search of great whales. Frederick Merek, who sailed aboard the whaling ship *Susan,* was the best of the breed; however, most sailors only carved on the teeth of great whales to pass the time and have something to trade for whiskey, women, and song in remote ports of call. When sailors, most of whom were illiterate, sent scrimshaw back to family and friends, it was considered more like a postcard than artwork. After the late 1800s, scrimshaw faded from popular view and became a lost art form until it was revived, mostly in Lahaina, during the 1960s. Today, scrimshaw can be found throughout Hawaii, but the center remains the old whaling capital of Lahaina, Maui.

Scrimshaw is used in everything from belt buckles to delicate earrings and even coffee-table centerpieces. Prices go from a few dollars up to thousands, and works can be found in limited quantities in some galleries and fine art shops around the island.

Woodwork

While the carving and fashioning of old traditional items has by and large disappeared, lathe-turning of wooden bowls and the creation of wooden furniture from native woods is alive and strong. Old Hawaiians used koa almost exclusively because of its density, strength, and natural luster, but koa is becoming increasingly scarce. Costly *milo* and monkeypod, as well as a host of other native woods, are also excellent for turnings and household items and have largely replaced koa. These modern wooden objects are available at numerous shops and galleries. Countless inexpensive carved items are sold at variety stores, such as tikis, hula dancers, or salad servers, but most of these are imported from Asia or the Philippines.

Weaving

The tradition of weaving has survived in Hawaii but is not strong. Older experienced weavers are dying and few younger ones are showing interest in continuing the craft. The time-tested material of *lau hala* is still the best, although much is now made from coconut fronds. *Lau hala* is traditional Hawaiian weaving from the leaves *(lau)* of the pandanus *(hala)* tree. These leaves vary greatly in length, with the largest over six feet, and they have a thorny spine that must be removed before they can be worked. The color ranges from light tan to dark brown. The leaves are cut into strips one-eighth- to one-inch wide and are then employed in weaving. Any variety of items can be made or at least covered in *lau hala*. It makes great purses, mats, baskets, and table mats. You can still purchase items from bags to a woven hat, and all share the desirable qualities of strength, lightness, and ventilation.

Woven into a hat, it's absolutely superb but should not be confused with a palm-frond hat. A *lau hala* hat is amazingly supple and even when squashed will pop back into shape. A good one is expensive and with proper care will last for years. All *lau hala* should be given a light application of mineral oil on a monthly basis, especially if it's exposed to the sun. For flat items, iron over a damp cloth and keep purses and baskets stuffed with paper when not in use. Palm fronds are also widely used in weaving. They, too, are a great natural raw material, but not as good as *lau hala*. Almost any woven item, such as a beach bag woven from palm, makes a good authentic yet inexpensive gift or souvenir.

Quilts

Along with the gospel and the will to educate, the early missionaries brought skills and machines to sew. Aside from wanting to cover the naked bodies of their new converts, many taught the Hawaiians how to quilt together small pieces of material into designs for the bed. Quilting styles and patterns varied over the years and generally shifted from designs familiar to New Englanders to those more pleasing to Hawaiian eyes, and a number of standard patterns include leaves, fruits, and flowers of the islands. Most Hawaiian-design quilts seen for sale in the islands today are made in the Philippines under the direction of Hawaiian designers. Because of labor costs, they are far less expensive than any quilt actually made in Hawaii.

Paintings

One thing is for sure: Like the rest of the Hawaiian Islands, Kaua'i draws painters. Multitudes of painters. Captivated by the island's beauty, color, natural features, and living things, these artists interpret what they see and sense in a dizzying display from realism to expressionism. From immense *pali* cliffs to the tiniest flower petals, and humble workers' homes to the faces of the island people, they are all portrayed. Color, movement, and feeling are captured, and the essence of Kaua'i is the result. Galleries and shops around the island display local artists' work, but there is a concentration of galleries in the small South Shore town of Hanapepe. Well-known artists charge a handsome fee for their work, but you can find some exceptional work for affordable prices hidden here and there.

Gift Items

Jewelry is always an appreciated gift, especially if it's distinctive, and Hawaii has some of the most original. The sea provides the basic raw materials of pink, gold, and black coral that are as beautiful and fascinating as gemstones. Harvesting coral is very dangerous work. The Lahaina beds off Maui have one of the best black coral lodes in the islands, but unlike reef coral, these trees grow at depths bordering the outer limits of a scuba diver's

PERSONALIZED NOVEL

Perhaps the most one-of-a-kind gift you can take home from Kaua'i is a book called *Kauai Calling*. This little novel is written with you and your sweetie as the main characters and Kaua'i as the backdrop. Reading and rereading this romantic adventure where you play the main parts should be a kick for you and all your friends and family back home. Authors Ron Christmas and Amy King plug your names and some basic information about you into the text, and like magic (or should I say, like the work of the Menehune) you have your book delivered to your hotel the next morning, complete, printed, and bound. If it would intrigue you to star in this adventure, contact the authors at Paradise Works, Inc. (5443 Makaloa St., Kapa'a808/821-2067, www.ParadiseWorks-Inc.com).

capabilities. Only the best can dive 180 feet after the black coral, and about one diver per year dies in pursuit of it. Conservationists have placed great pressure on the harvesters of these deep corals, and the state of Hawaii has placed strict limits and guidelines on the firms and divers involved.

Puka (shells with little naturally occurring holes) and *'opihi* shells are also made into jewelry. Many times these items are very inexpensive, yet they are authentic and are great purchases for the price.

Hawaii also produces some unique food items appreciated by most people. Bags of rich, gourmet-quality coffee are great gifts. Guava, pineapple, passion fruit, and mango are often gift-boxed into assortments of jams, jellies, and spicy chutneys. And for that special person in your life, you can bring home island fragrances in bars of soap and bottles of perfumes and colognes in the exotic odors of gardenia, plumeria, and even ginger. All of these items are reasonably priced, lightweight, and easy to carry.

HULA

The hula is more than an ethnic dance; it is the soul of Hawaii expressed in motion. It began as a form of worship during religious ceremonies and was danced only by highly trained men. It gradually evolved into a form of entertainment, but in no regard was it sexual. The hula was the opera, theater, and lecture hall of the islands all rolled into one. It was history portrayed in the performing arts. In the beginning, an androgynous deity named Laka descended to earth and taught men how to dance the hula. In time, the male aspect of Laka departed for the heavens, but the female aspect remained. The female Laka set up her own special hula *heiau* at Ha'ena on the Na Pali Coast of Kaua'i, where it still exists. As time went on, women were allowed to learn the hula. Scholars surmise that men became too busy wresting a living from the land to maintain the art form.

Men did retain a type of hula for themselves called *lua*. This was a form of martial art employed in hand-to-hand combat that evolved into a ritualized warfare dance called *hula ku'i*. During the 19th century, the hula almost vanished because the missionaries considered it vile and heathen. King Kalakaua is generally regarded as saving it during the 1800s, when he formed his own troupe and encouraged the dancers to learn the old hula. Many of the original dances were forgotten, but some were retained and are performed to this day. Although professional dancers were highly trained, everyone took part in the hula. *Ali'i*, commoners, young, and old all danced.

Hula is art in swaying motion, and the true form is studied rigorously and taken very seriously. Today, hula *halau* (schools) are active on every island, teaching hula and keeping the old ways and culture alive. Ancient hula is called *hula kahiko*, and modern renditions are known as *hula auana*. Performers still spend years perfecting their techniques. They show off their accomplishments during the fierce competition of the Merrie Monarch Festival in Hilo every April. The winning *halau* is praised and recognized throughout the islands.

Hawaiian hula was never performed in grass

skirts; tapa or *ti*-leaf skirts were worn. Grass skirts came to Hawaii from the Gilbert Islands, and if you see grass and cellophane skirts in a "hula revue," it's not traditional. Almost every major resort offering entertainment or a lu'au also offers a revue. Most times, young island beauties accompanied by proficient local musicians put on a floor show for the tourists. It'll be fun, but it won't be traditional.

A hula dancer has to learn how to control every part of her/his body, including facial expressions, which help to set the mood. The hands are extremely important and provide instant background scenery. For example, if the hands are thrust outward in an aggressive manner, this can mean a battle; if they sway gently overhead, they refer to the gods or to creation; they can easily become rain, clouds, sun, sea, or moon. Watch the hands to get the gist of the story, though in the words of one wise guy, "You watch the parts you like, and I'll watch the parts I like!" The motion of swaying hips can denote a long walk, a canoe ride, or sexual intercourse. Foot motion can portray a battle, a walk, or any kind of conveyance. The overall effect is multidirectional synchronized movement. The correct chanting of the *mele* is an integral part of the performance. These story chants, accompanied by musical instruments, make the hula very much like opera; it is especially similar in the way the tale unfolds.

THAT GOOD OLD ISLAND MUSIC

The missionaries usually take a beating when it's recounted how much Hawaiian culture they destroyed while "civilizing" the natives. However, they seem to have done one thing right. They introduced the Hawaiians to the diatonic musical scale and immediately opened a door for latent and superbly harmonious talent. Before the missionaries, the Hawaiians knew little about melody. Though sonorous, their *mele* were repetitive chants in which the emphasis was placed on historical accuracy and not on "making music." The Hawaiians, in short, didn't *sing*. But within a few years of the missionaries' arrival, they were belting out good old Christian hymns, and one of their favorite pastimes became group and individual singing.

Early in the 1800s, Spanish *vaqueros* from California were imported to teach the Hawaiians how to be cowboys. With them came guitars and moody ballads. The Hawaiian *paniolo* (cowboys) quickly learned how to punch cows and croon away the long lonely nights on the range. Immigrants who came along a little later in the 19th century, especially from Portugal, helped create a Hawaiian-style music. Their biggest influence was a small, four-stringed instrument called a *braga* or *cavaquinho*. One owned by Augusto Dias was the prototype of a homegrown Hawaiian instrument that became known as the ukulele. "Jumping flea," the translation of ukulele, is an appropriate name devised by the Hawaiians when they saw how nimble the fingers were as they "jumped" over the strings.

King Kalakaua (The Merrie Monarch) and Queen Lili'uokalani were both patrons of the arts who furthered the Hawaiian musical identity at the turn of the 20th century. Kalakaua revived the hula and was also a gifted lyricist and balladeer. He wrote the words to "Hawai'i Pono'i," which became the anthem of the nation of Hawaii and later the state anthem. Lili'uokalani wrote the hauntingly beautiful "Aloha O'e," which is often pointed to as the "spirit of Hawaii" in music. Detractors say that its melody is extremely close to that of the old Christian hymn, "Rock Beside the Sea," but the lyrics are so beautiful and perfectly fitted that this doesn't matter.

Just prior to Kalakaua's reign, a Prussian bandmaster, Captain Henri Berger, was invited to head the fledgling Royal Hawaiian Band, which he turned into a very respectable orchestra lauded by many visitors to the islands. Berger was open-minded and learned to love Hawaiian music. He collaborated with Kalakaua and other island musicians to incorporate their music into a Western format. He headed the band for 43 years, until 1915, and was instrumental in making music a serious pursuit of talented Hawaiians.

HAWAIIAN LU'AU

The lu'au is an island institution. For a fixed price, you get to gorge yourself on a tremendous variety of island foods, sample a few island drinks, and have a night of entertainment as well. Generally, lu'au run from about 5 or 5:30 P.M. to 8:30 or 9 P.M. On your lu'au day, eat a light breakfast, skip lunch, and do belly-stretching exercises! Lu'au food is usually served buffet-style, although a few do it family-style. All lu'au have pretty much the same format, although the type of food and entertainment differ.

To have fun at a lu'au you have to get into the swing of things. Entertainment is provided by local performers in what is usually called a "Polynesian Revue." This includes the tourist's hula, the fast version with swaying hips and dramatic lighting, a few wandering troubadours singing Hawaiian standards, and someone swinging swords or flaming torches. Although individual lu'au vary, some also offer an *imu* ceremony where the pig is taken from the covered oven, traditional games, arts and crafts, or a *hukilau* (pulling in a fishnet) demonstration. All the Hawaiian standards like poi, *haupia* (coconut custard), *lomi lomi* salmon (a salad of salmon, tomatoes, and onions with garnish and seasonings), *laulau* (a package of meat, fish, and veggies wrapped in *ti* leaves), and *kalua* (*imu*-baked) pig are usually served. If these don't suit your appetite, various Asian dishes plus chicken, fish, and roast beef might do. If you leave a lu'au hungry, it's your own fault!

The lu'au master starts the *imu* every morning; stop by and watch if it's permitted. He lays the hot stones and banana stalks so well that the underground oven maintains a perfect 400° temperature. In one glance, the lu'au master can gauge the weight and fat content of a succulent porker and decide just how long it should be cooked. The water in the leaves covering the pig steams and roasts the meat so that it falls off the bone. Local wisdom has it that "The only thing you can't eat in the *imu* is the hot stones."

Lu'au generally cost $60-70 for adults and about half that for children, including entertainment. This is the tourist variety – a lot of fun, but definitely a show. The least expensive, most authentic, and best lu'au are often put on by local churches or community groups. If you ask locals which lu'au is the best, you won't get two to agree. It's literally a matter of taste.

Popular Hawaiian Music

Hawaiian music has a unique twang, a special feeling that says the same thing to everyone who hears it: "Relax, sit back in the moonlight, watch the swaying palms as the surf sings a lullaby." This special sound is epitomized by the bouncy ukulele, the falsettos of Hawaiian crooners, and the smooth ring of the "steel" or "Hawaiian" guitar. The steel guitar is a variation originated by Joseph Kekuku in the 1890s. Stories abound of how Kekuku devised this instrument; the most popular versions say that Joe dropped his comb or pocket knife on his guitar strings and liked what he heard. Driven by the faint rhythm of an inner sound, he went to the machine shop at the Kamehameha Schools and turned out a steel bar for sliding over the strings. To complete the sound he changed the catgut strings to steel and raised them so they wouldn't hit the frets. Voilà!—Hawaiian music as the world knows it today.

The first melodious strains of **slack-key guitar** *(ki ho'alu)* can be traced back to the time of Kamehameha III and the *vaqueros* from California. The Spanish had their way of tuning the guitar, and they played difficult and aggressive music that did not sit well with Hawaiians, who were much more gentle and casual in their manners.

Hawaiians soon became adept at making their own music. At first, one person played the melody, but it lacked fullness. There was no body to the sound. So, as one *paniolo* fooled with the melody, another soon learned to play bass, which added depth. But players were often alone, and by experimenting they learned that they could get the right hand going with the melody, and at the same time play the bass notes with the thumb to improve the sound. Singers also learned that they could "open tune" the guitar to match their rich voices.

Hawaiians believed knowledge was sacred, and what is sacred should be treated with utmost respect—which meant keeping it secret, except from sincere apprentices. Guitar playing became a personal art form whose secrets were closely guarded, handed down only to family members, and only to those who showed ability and determination. When old-time slack-key guitar players were done strumming, they loosened all the strings so no one could figure out how they had their guitars tuned. If they were playing, and some interested folks came by who weren't part of the family, the Hawaiians stopped what they were doing, put the guitars down, and put their feet across the strings to wait for the folks to go away. As time went on, more and more Hawaiians began to play slack-key, and a common repertoire emerged.

Accomplished musicians could easily figure out the simple songs, once they had figured out how the family had tuned the guitar. One of the most popular tunings was the "open G." Old Hawaiian folks called it the "taro patch tune." Different songs came out, and if you were in the family and were interested in the guitar, they took the time to sit down and teach you. The way they taught was straightforward—and a test of your sincerity at the same time. The old master would start to play. They just wanted you to listen and get a feel for the music—nothing more than that. You brought your guitar and *listened*. When you felt it, you played it, and the knowledge was transferred. Today, only a handful of slack-key guitar players know how to play the classic tunes classically. The best-known and perhaps greatest slack-key player was Gabby Pahinui, with the Sons of Hawaii. He has passed away, but he left many recordings behind. A slack-key master still singing

and playing is Raymond Kane. Not one of his students is from his own family, and most are *haole* musicians trying to preserve the classical method of playing.

Hawaiian music received its biggest boost from a remarkable radio program known as *Hawaii Calls.* This program sent out its music from the Banyan Court of Waikiki's Moana Hotel from 1935 until 1975. At its peak in the mid-1950s, it was syndicated on over 700 radio stations throughout the world. Ironically, Japanese pilots heading for Pearl Harbor tuned in island music as a signal beam. Some internationally famous classic tunes came out of the 1940s and 1950s. Jack Pitman composed "Beyond the Reef" in 1948; more than 300 artists have recorded it, and it has sold well over 12 million records. Other million-sellers include "Sweet Leilani," "Lovely Hula Hands," "The Crosseyed Mayor of Kaunakakai," and "The Hawaiian Wedding Song."

By the 1960s, Hawaiian music began to die. Just too corny and light for those turbulent years, it belonged to the older generation and the good times that followed World War II. One man was instrumental in keeping Hawaiian music alive during this period. Don Ho, with his "Tiny Bubbles," became the token Hawaiian musician of the 1960s and early 1970s. He's persevered long enough to become a legend in his own time, and his Polynesian Extravaganza at the Hilton Hawaiian Village packed visitors in until the early 1990s. He's now at the Waikiki Beachcomber and still doing a marvelous show. Of this type of entertainment, perhaps the most Hawaiian was Danny Kaleikini, the Ambassador of Aloha, who entertained his audience with dances, Hawaiian anecdotes, and tunes on the traditional Hawaiian nose flute.

The Beat Goes On

Beginning in the mid-1970s, islanders began to assert their cultural identity. One of the unifying factors was the coming of age of Hawaiian music. It graduated from the "little grass shack" novelty tune and began to include sophisticated jazz, rock, and contemporary rhythms. Accomplished musicians whose roots were in traditional island music began to highlight their tunes with this distinctive sound. The best embellish their arrangements with ukuleles, steel guitars, and traditional percussion and melodic instruments. Some excellent modern recording artists have become island institutions. The local people say that you know Hawaiian harmonies are good if they give you "chicken skin."

Each year special music awards, **Na Hoku Hanohano,** or Hoku for short, are given to distinguished island musicians. The following are some of the Hoku winners considered by their contemporaries to be among the best in Hawaii: Barney Isaacs and George Kuo, Na Leo Pilimihana, Robi Kahakalau, Kealii Reichel, Darren Benitez, Sonny Kamahele, Ledward Kaapana, Hapa, Israel Kamakawiwoʻole, Amy Hanaialiʻi, and Pure Heart. Though most do not perform on Kauaʻi, if they're playing on one of the other islands while you're in Hawaii, don't miss them. Some, unfortunately, are no longer among the living, but their recorded music can still be appreciated.

Past Hoku winners who have become renowned performers include Brothers Cazimero, who are blessed with beautiful harmonic voices; Krush, highly regarded for their contemporary sounds; The Peter Moon Band, fantastic performers with a strong traditional sound; Henry Kapono, formerly of Kapono and Cecilio; and the Beamer Brothers. Others include Loyal Garner, Del Beazley, Bryan Kessler & Me No Hoa Aloha, George Kahumoku Jr., Olomana, Genoa Keawe, and Irmagard Aluli.

Those with access to the Internet can check out the Hawaiian music scene at one of the following: Hawaiian Music Island (www.mele.com), Nahenahenet (www.nahenahe.net) and Hawaiian Music Guide (www.hawaii-music.com). While these are not the only Hawaiian music websites, they are a good place to start. For listening to Hawaiian music on the Web, try Kauaʻi Community Radio (http://kkcr.org) or Radio Breeze (www.breezeofhawaii.com).

FESTIVALS, HOLIDAYS, AND EVENTS

In addition to all the American national holidays, Hawaii celebrates its own festivals, pageants, ethnic fairs, and a multitude of specialized events. They occur throughout the year—some particular to only one island or locality; others, such as Aloha Festival and Lei Day, are celebrated on all the islands. At festival time, everyone is welcome. Many happenings are annual events, while others are one-time affairs. Check local newspapers and the free island magazines for exact dates. Island-specific information is also available on the Web at http://calendar.gohawaii.com/kauai, which can also be linked from the Kauaʻi Visitors Bureau (www.kauaivisitorsbureau.org) website. Useful information can also be found on the country Office of Economic Development's festivals website (www.kauaifestivals.com).

For additional events of all sorts throughout the state, visit the calendar of events listing on the HVB website (http://calendar.gohawaii.com) or visit the Hawaii State Foundation on Culture and the Arts calendar (www.state.hi.us/sfca), which features arts and cultural events, activities, and programs.

January

The annual Kokeʻe Natural History Museum (808/335-9975) **bird count** is held just at the new year. This event is for avid birders. Call for information.

February

The two-day **Waimea Town Celebration** is held at Waimea, the spot where Captain Cook first made contact. Food, entertainment, canoe races, a rodeo, and a partial marathon add to the fun. This annual event has been held for more than two decades.

March

The **Prince Kuhio Celebration of the Arts,** at Prince Kuhio Park in Poʻipu and in Lihuʻe, features cultural festivities from the era of Prince Kuhio along with cultural education, a luʻau, music, and dance. The Prince Kuhio festival has been held for more than 30 years.

April

Wesak, or **Buddha Day,** is on the Sunday closest to April 8 and celebrates the birthday of the Buddha. Ornate offerings of tropical flowers are placed at temple altars throughout Hawaii. Flower festivals, pageants, and dance programs take place at many island temples.

Enjoy the best the island has to offer at the **Annual School Art Festival,** at the Kaua'i Museum.

May

May 1, or May Day in some of the world, is **Lei Day** in Hawaii, where red is only one of the profusion of colors when everyone dons their flower garlands. Festivities abound throughout Hawaii. On Kaua'i, events take place at the Kaua'i Museum and the Kaua'i Community College.

The four-day **Prince Albert Music Festival** takes place at the Princeville Hotel on the north shore and features a combination of classical music, slack-key guitar, and hula demonstrations, plus fashions, food, and crafts.

Banana Poka Festival at the Koke'e Natural History Museum is an outdoor educational fair that also features foot and bike races.

June

King Kamehameha Day, June 11, is a state holiday honoring Kamehameha the Great with festivities on all islands. Check local papers for times and particulars. On Kaua'i, enjoy parades, *ho'olaule'a,* and arts and crafts.

July

Fourth of July offers parades and other events, including the island's best fireworks show at Vidinha Stadium in Lihu'e. Fireworks may also be shot off at the Pacific Missile Range Facility west of Kekaha.

The **Garden Island Championship Canoe Races** take place at different locations on the island in late July. This and other canoe events are sponsored by Garden Island Canoe Racing Association (P.O. Box 43, Lihu'e, HI 96766).

Koloa Plantation Days (www.koloaplantationdays.com) celebrates Hawaii's plantation life with a parade, crafts fair, music and dance entertainment, ethnic foods, rodeo, and sports competitions. Events take place in and around Koloa.

August

August 17 is **Admission Day,** a state holiday recognizing the day that Hawaii became a state.

At the **Kaua'i County Fair** in late August, gardeners, stockmen, and craftspeople of the Garden Island display their wares at Vidinha Stadium in Lihu'e. Look for pageantry, games and rides, great local foods, and terrific bargains. Admission is $3 adults and $2 for kids.

September

The **Mokihana Festival** (www.mokihana .kauai.net), a weeklong event with festivities at various locations along the south coast, is a grassroots festival featuring lei-making, hula, music composition and performance, along with folk-arts workshops and local entertainment.

Aloha Festival (www.alohafestivals.com) is a weeks-long series of events in the fall where everyone celebrates Hawaii's own intangible quality, *aloha.* There are parades, lu'au, historical pageants, balls, and various other entertainment. The spirit of *aloha* is infectious, and all are welcome to join in. Check local papers and tourist literature for happenings near you.

October

The annual two-day **Coconut Festival** held on the Coconut Coast at Kapa'a Beach Park includes food, games, crafts, and performances.

Eo E Emalani I Alaka'i is a festival that commemorates Queen Emma's journey to Koke'e and the Alaka'i Swamp. Activities include hula performances, chants, Hawaiian music, and craft demonstrations. Held at the Koke'e Natural History Museum at Koke'e State Park.

The **Kaua'i Taro Festival,** held annually in Hanalei and Princeville to educate about the economic and cultural aspects of this traditional Hawaiian food, includes farm visits, entertainment festivities, and cooking competitions.

November

November 11 is **Veterans Day.** All islands have parades. Get information through the local newspaper.

The **Hawaii International Film Festival** (808/528-3456 or 800/752-8193, www.hiff.org) brings new and engaging films mainly from Asia and the Pacific to various theaters on Kaua'i.

December

The **Christmas Craft Faire** is an annual event known for attracting the island's best in hand-crafted items and home-baked goodies. It takes place at the Kaua'i Museum, Lihu'e (808/245-6931).

On the Saturday before Christmas, Waimea hosts the **Waimea Lighted Christmas Parade,** featuring a parade through town, caroling, and plenty of food.

ESSENTIALS

Recreation

BEACHES

Kaua'i is the oldest of the main Hawaiian Islands and has had the longest time to create beaches. It's done a superb job. There are about 90 miles of coastline on the island and over half are sand beaches, each with a different quality and character. People come to the island for different reasons, but nearly everyone likes to spend some time at the beach. Many hotels and other accommodations are located on or near the island's finest beaches, but if you desire to explore the remainder of the island, the following are some recommendations to help you decide where to lay out your towel.

All beaches are open to the public. Most are accessed through beach parks, but some access is over private property. All hotels and condominiums must by law offer pathway access to beaches they front, and each has some parking set aside for public use.

For the record, there are no nude beaches on Kaua'i—or anywhere in the state, for that matter. Being nude on a beach is a punishable offense. That said, locals and visitors alike have found spots on various beaches or in secluded coves where they can strip down and spend the day au naturel.

Generally speaking, the beaches on the north and west have high surf conditions and

ROBERT NILSEN

strong ocean currents during winter months—use extreme caution—and those on the south and east experience some high surf during the summer months. Trade winds blow onshore most of the year for beaches in the eastern and northeastern areas of the island. North shore beaches are known for their reefs and good snorkeling, south shore beaches are general recreation beaches, and those on the west end are great sandy expanses.

There are lifeguard stations at Ha'ena, Hanalei Pine Trees, Hanalei Beach Park Pavilion, Kealia, Wailua, Lydgate, Po'ipu Beach Park, Salt Ponds, and Kekaha, and these are manned during their posted hours. At some beaches, flags warn you of ocean conditions. A yellow flag means use caution. A half-yellow, half-red sign signifies caution because of strong winds. A red flag indicates hazardous water conditions—beach closed, no swimming. In addition, yellow and black signs are sometimes posted at certain beaches to indicate other warnings: dangerous shore break, high surf spot, strong currents, presence of jellyfish, or beach closed. Take the signs and the water seriously. Every year, several dozen people lose their lives in Hawaiian waters, and often up to a dozen are lost on Kaua'i alone.

Direct ocean safety questions to the Ocean Safety Bureau of the Fire Department (808/241-6506). For general information, pick up a copy of the free brochure *Kaua'i Beach Safety Guide* when you arrive on the island.

Lihu'e

By far the best beach in the Lih'e area and the most convenient to town is **Kalapaki Beach.** Fronting the Marriott hotel on Nawiliwili Bay, this beach is gentle, just right for learning how to body surf, boogie boarding, swimming, or sand activities. The snorkeling is only fair, but the beach is generally decent for beginning surf lessons. Drawback: the beach sits next to the working Nawiliwili Harbor. Advantage: you can watch the colorful cruise ships enter and exit the bay against the backdrop of a sheer green mountainside.

South Shore

Po'ipu is the most developed tourist area on the island and **Po'ipu Beach**—accommodating, tame, relaxing, and convenient—lies at its center. You can swim, snorkel, and bodysurf here to your heart's content. It's a favorite place for surf lessons. The section in front of the Sheraton is picture perfect and sometimes the haunt of turtles or monk seals, which come to bask in the sand. You'll find a protected kiddie beach as well as tidepools at the Po'ipu Beach Park area. The eastern end of this beach is referred to as **Brennecke Beach.** It and **Shipwreck Beach,** farther beyond and fronting the Hyatt Regency, are the best in the area for boogie boarding. Beyond that is the lonely expanse of **Maha'ulepu Beach,** with its windswept dunes and silence. Long, narrow, and backed by tall, tree-covered dunes, this stretch of coast is more suited to sunbathing and playing in the sand than swimming, but the windsurfers and kite boarders find it almost perfect. Maha'ulepu coastal area is one of numerous ancient archaeological sites and the focus of a community effort to keep it natural and not let it be developed. Narrow and rocky, **Lawa'i Beach** is best for snorkeling.

West End

Polihale Beach is the end of the road. It's a long broad swath of light sand, backed by high dunes that abut the end of the Na Pali Coast cliffs. It is actually just the end of a longer beach that skirts the military's Pacific Missile Range Facility at Barking Sands (not open to the general public) and turns the corner to become the long and narrow Kekaha Beach, perhaps 15 miles in total. Polihale Beach is good for strolling, sunbathing, picnics, camping, building sand castles, views of Ni'ihau, and solitude, peace, and quiet. There is one small and fairly protected spot near its south end to swim inside a small reef, but the rest of the beach is generally too rough with strong currents and undertows to be safe for swimming. However, local surfers do come here when the waves are right—but they know the water well. Far removed from the rest of the island, many find it a perfect "getaway" beach, a romantic location, and definitely one of the best places to watch the sun set on Kaua'i.

If you don't want to tackle the rough dirt track that leads to Polihale, stop at **Kekaha Beach** for miles of excellent swimming, snorkeling, and surfing.

A very good family beach is **Salt Pond Beach.** The swimming and windsurfing are good inside the reef, and it's often calmer here than at other beaches. A large semi-shaded grassy area fronts the water with facilities for picnicking and camping.

East Shore

Lydgate Beach, with its sheltered children's pool and snorkel area bounded by large lava rocks, is a safe beach, and its picnic facilities and excellent children's play structures make it one of the most family-oriented beach parks on the island. And what's better, it's conveniently located to Wailua and Kapa'a. Across the river mouth is **Wailua Beach,** also fine but best during calm weather. Broad and open, it gets a fair amount of wave action.

North of there is **Kealia Beach.** When the winds are right, this is one of the best surfing beaches on the island; at other times, it's nearly empty. **Anahola Beach,** at the south end of Anahola Bay, has safe swimming in a protected cove, freshwater swimming in the stream that empties into the bay, picnicking, and camping. Snorkel a short distance up the shore to where the reef comes in close—an area where locals come for shore fishing. Still farther north are a number of small, secluded beaches tucked into small coves. The best of these is **Moloa'a Beach,** a picture-perfect half-moon swath of sand, just right for a leisurely and uncrowded day of relaxation.

North Shore

A local favorite, **Secret Beach** is all that its name implies. Located at the end of a tiny dirt road, the start of which eludes many people, and down a steep, often muddy bank, Secret Beach is surprisingly broad and open, and often empty. Summer here can be calm, but the waves during winter can be thunderous. Unseen from the highway, with no posted signs, Secret Beach backs up against a steep cliff, as if hidden from the world.

A bit farther on is **Kalihiwai Beach,** great for swimming, bodysurfing, and boogie boarding for most of the year. Located just around the point, **'Anini Beach** is a winner, and the park that fronts it has excellent camping. It's a fine place to snorkel, as it has the longest exposed reef in Kaua'i. Due to consistent breezes and the calm shallow water inside the reef, it's considered Kaua'i's best windsurfing location.

Hanalei Bay is a prime spot on the north coast, and one of the most romantic locations on the island. The beach at Hanalei Bay is an all-around good beach. Swim at the mouth of the Hanalei River or at various spots along this long, narrow crescent of sand. Experienced surfers ride the waves below the Princeville Hotel; snorkeling is good closer to the cliffs. The bay's gentle waves also make it fine for kayaking and outrigger canoe paddling. Just past the point west of Hanalei is **Lumaha'i Beach,** a beautiful curve of white sand backed by cliffs and thick jungle that was the silent star of the movie *South Pacific.* The inviting water here has a fierce riptide, so enter only when the water is calm.

Ha'ena Beach and nearby **Tunnels** are terrific swimming and snorkeling spots. Tunnels is usually given the nod for the best snorkeling on the island. **Ke'e Beach** marks the end of the road. It's a popular place with some amenities, fine swimming in summer, good snorkeling, unsurpassed views up the Na Pali Coast, and a romantic location for sunsets. Like at Po'ipu Beach on the south coast, turtles and monk seals sometimes haul themselves out of the water to rest and relax along the more secluded sections of this beach.

SURFING

Surfing has long been the premier water sport in Hawaii. Long before Westerners accidentally stumbled onto the islands, Hawaiians enjoyed *he'e nalu,* or "sliding the waves." The old Hawaiians named many favorite surfing sites,

WINDSURFING AND KITESURFING

Windsurfing, or sailboarding, has grown popular on Kaua'i as it has done in the rest of the country. The best spots for beginners are 'Anini Beach on the north coast, Po'ipu Beach on the south, and Kalapaki Beach in Lihu'e. More challenging is Salt Ponds Beach on the west end, and, for the advanced only, Ha'ena Beach on the north coast is preferred, or Tunnels just down the way. On the south shore, try Maha'ulepu Beach east of Po'ipu. Ask at water-sports shops for other local favorites that would match your ability.

The newest water sport to make a splash in the islands is **kitesurfing,** and this may be described as a cross between flying a kite and wakeboarding. A foil-sail kite, perhaps six meters or more in length is attached by long ropes to a grab bar clipped to a harness that's worn around the waist. Steering is done by pulling one end of the bar or other to raise or lower the kite, catching more or less wind. A wide ski is used, similar to a wakeboard ski, except that this one has a short rudder. Booties, a neoprene version of snowboard boots, keep you attached to the board. Some beginners content themselves with being dragged through the water as they learn to control the kite, while the proficient skim the water as fast and as freely as windsurfers. Those who really know how to use the wind to their advantage can get 20-30 feet of loft. Sound intriguing? Approach with caution and take lessons. Those who know the sport say that it's not for the timid, nor as easy as it might appear.

---

some still used today, and now there are over 1,700 named surfing spots throughout the islands. While there have been many well-known surfers through the years, the most famous is Duke Kahanamoku, a Hawaiian athlete and waterman of the early 1900s who brought the sport of surfing to the world.

Locals and now "surfies" from all over the world know where the best waves are and when they come. While Anahola Beach was a traditional surfing spot on Kaua'i for Hawaiians of yesterday, the north shore has the beaches of choice today. The east side of Hanalei Bay provides a good roll in winter for experts, as does Tunnels. Quarry Beach, near Kilauea, and Kealia Beach and Donkey Beach, both north of Kapa'a, are used mostly by locals. On the south coast, the surfers' favorite is the west end of Po'ipu Beach, or west of there, near Pakala. Both Lawa'i Beach and Salt Ponds Beach are used if conditions are right, and waves for all levels can be found along the lengthy Kekaha Beach on the west end. For beginners, Kalapaki and Po'ipu beaches are two of the best and often used for instruction.

Generally speaking, surf is high on the north shore in winter and flat in summer. On the south shore, it's the reverse, with better surf in summer. As onshore trade winds blow fairly constantly at east shore beaches, the surfing can be decent there at any time of year. Listen to local advice as to where and when to ride and why. Check with the shops that sell or rent surfing gear or those that give lessons. The sea is unforgiving—and particularly unpredictable in winter.

Boogie boarding is also a fun sport on smaller waves close to shore. Some well-known boogie board beaches are Brennecke Beach and Shipwreck Beach in Po'ipu, Kalihiwai Beach near Kilauea, and Black Pot Beach on Hanalei Bay.

SCUBA

With its rich sealife and varied underwater geological formations (ledges, pinnacles, caverns, and coral beds), Kaua'i is an excellent place to scuba dive. Kaua'i's underwater temperature hovers at 75–80°F year-round, and visibility is often good to 100 feet. There are several dozen frequented dive spots around the island. Most on the south and north shores are good for all levels of divers, while the few off the east and west coasts are generally for experienced divers.

The south shore dive sites are mostly between Po'ipu Beach and Spouting Horn, while the north shore dive sites lie between Hanalei and Ke'e Beach. By and large, boat dives go to the south shore in winter and the north shore in summer. The most preferred shore dive spot on Kaua'i is at Koloa Landing on the south shore. In addition, some dive tours go to Lehua Island off the north point of Ni'ihau. Not only is Lehua undisturbed, but there is very little run-off from the islands to cloud the water. Lehua reputedly has some of the best diving in the state with exceptionally clear water and deep drop-offs. Companies that offer dive tours vary their sites depending upon weather and water conditions and the skill level of the group.

Scuba divers can bring their own equipment or rent it on Kaua'i. If you bring your own, pack it well so it doesn't get damaged in transit. Rental gear runs $40–50 from most shops. To get just what you need at the right price,

be sure to call ahead and ask for particulars about what each company offers. Many shops also offer certification classes. There are many types of certification, but a four- to five-day open water certification usually runs about $350 for a group lesson and up to $500 for private lessons. If you want to get certified, bring your medical paperwork with you. If you are certified, bring your C-card and logbook. If you plan other island adventures, let at least 24 hours go by between your last dive and any significant altitude change, which on Kaua'i might be a helicopter ride or a drive up Waimea Canyon to Koke'e State Park (4,000 feet).

Various tour operators offer many different ent shore and boat tours. See the individual travel chapters for specifics. Be sure to check around for the one that suits you. Ask about cost, places and times of departure, boat size, number of passengers, dive sites, and the crew's experience. Basic tours and approximate prices are: introductory shore dive, $130; one-tank shore dive, $105; introductory boat dive, $140; two-tank boat dive, $110; and the ultimate three-tank dive to Lehua, $250.

SNORKELING

Those interested can buy or rent equipment in snorkel and dive shops and from some activity booths. Sporting goods stores and department stores like Kmart and Wal-Mart also have this equipment for sale; a basic set might run as little as $20. Sometimes condos and hotels offer snorkeling equipment free to their guests, but if you have to rent it, don't get it from a hotel or condo, where it's usually more expensive, often $5 an hour. Dive shops also rent gear (mask, snorkel, and fins), and prices depend upon the quality of the gear.

The following are examples of some of the best and safest snorkeling sites on Kaua'i. All of the beaches mentioned below are covered in greater detail in the travel chapters. **Ke'e Beach** at the end of the road at Ha'ena is tops (definitely stay inside the reef); **Tunnels** has a wonderful view of the mountains (*experienced snorkelers only* at the reef edge; beginners

CORAL

Whether you're an avid scuba diver or a novice snorkeler, you'll become aware of Kaua'i's underwater coral gardens and grottoes whenever you peer at the fantastic seascapes below the waves. Coral in Hawaii grows in many shapes, sizes, and colors, like it does elsewhere in the world. Although there is plenty of it, the coral in Hawaii doesn't do as well as in other more equatorial areas because the water is too wild and not quite as warm. Coral looks like a plant fashioned from colorful stone, but it's the skeleton of tiny animals, zoophytes, which need algae in order to live. Coral grows best in water that is quite still, where the days are sunny, and where the algae can thrive. Coral can be fragile. Please do your part to protect these underwater gardens by not stepping on it or breaking off pieces. Many of Hawaii's reefs have been dying in the last 20 years, and no one seems to know why. Pesticides used in agriculture have been pointed to as a possible cause, but no one has a definitive answer yet.

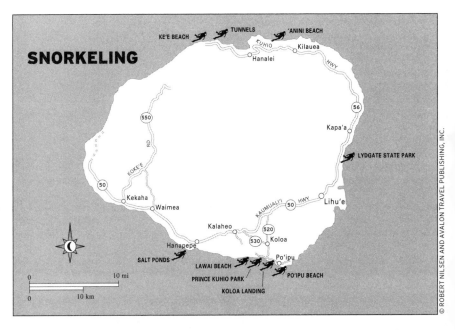

should stay on top of the reef); **'Anini Beach** is almost always gentle and day-outing-friendly, and terrific for windsurfing as well; **Lydgate State Park** is the safest for families and children; **Po'ipu Beach,** which is also safe for children, has the best entry to the right of the sand spit; **Koloa Landing,** an entry point for scuba shore dives, is a frequent haunt of sea turtles and eels; **Prince Kuhio Park** is best known for the turtles; and **Lawa'i Beach** along Lawa'i Road leading to the Spouting Horn has good coral and fish, and sometimes seals, and is most often used as a snuba site.

Before you put your mask on, however, ask at a snorkel shop about which locations are best for the season and water conditions. Inquire about types of fish and other sea creatures you might expect to see, water clarity, entry points, surf condition, water current, and parking.

KAYAKING

Kayaking has become very popular in Hawaii, and kayaking in Kaua'i is very good. In this island state, sea kayaking is the most predominant, but on Kaua'i, at least three rivers can be kayaked for a short distance as well. Wailua River runs up to Fern Grotto from the town of Wailua, Hule'ia River slides by the Alakoko Fishpond outside Lihu'e, and the Hanalei River skirts the Hanalei Wildlife Reserve on the north shore. Hawaii has no whitewater kayaking. The two stretches of ocean most commonly used by kayakers, and those used by tour operators, are the magnificent Na Pali Coast on the north shore and a section of the south shore west of Po'ipu. Because of water conditions, the south shore stretch is best in the winter. North shore water conditions are better in the summer; water is generally flattest then, so you'll be fighting the wind and waves less. The north coast sea current runs from east to west, so if you kayak along the Na Pali Coast, do it from Ha'ena to Polihale (as tour groups do), not the other way around. If you are out only for the day, make sure that you save enough strength for the return trip, or arrange to be picked up at the other end.

SEASICKNESS

Many people are affected by motion sickness, particularly on sailing vessels. If you tend to get queasy, try one of the following to prevent symptoms. Although there are others, oral medications widely available through pharmacies are Dramamine, Bonine, and Triptone. Dramamine and Bonine may cause drowsiness in some people; Triptone seems not to. Although these medications are usually taken just before boarding a ship, they might work better if a half dose is taken the night before and another half dose is taken the morning of your ride. In all cases, however, take medication as prescribed by the manufacturer.

An alternative to medication is Seabands, elastic bands worn around the wrists that put gentle pressure on the inside of the wrist by way of a small plastic button. They are available at pharmacies and at most scuba shops and can be reused until the elastic wears out. Follow directions for best results.

Without medication or pressure bands, you can still work to counter the effects of motion sickness. The night before, try not to eat too much, particularly greasy food, and don't drink alcohol to excess. If your stomach begins to feel upset, try a few soda crackers. If you begin to feel dizzy, focus on the horizon or a mountaintop – something stationary – and try to direct your thoughts to something other than your dizziness or queasiness. With children (and perhaps adults as well), talking about what animal figures they can see in the clouds or how many houses they can spot along the shoreline may be enough to distract them until they begin feeling better.

Be sure to check with the kayak shops to get the latest information about sea conditions, and consider taking one of their organized tours. Guided tours on the three rivers are also offered by many kayak companies around the island. See the individual travel chapters in the "Explore" section for details. Whether you paddle on the river or ocean, wear a swimsuit or shorts and T-shirt that you don't mind getting wet, and water shoes or sandals. Be sure to take a brimmed hat and sunglasses, put on sunscreen, take a towel and a dry change of clothes (a dry bag is usually provided on tours), and don't forget drinking water and snacks. A windbreaker is recommended for the open ocean.

Kayaks (the sit-upon kind) generally rent for about $25 single or $50 tandem for a day. Most shops want day-rental kayaks back by 5 P.M. Some shops rent carriers to haul the kayak. A few are located near a launch site, but many have shops away from the water so you will have to strap the kayak to a rack and drive to where you want to set in the water.

FISHING

Hawaii has some of the most exciting and productive "blue waters" in all the world. Here you can find a sportfishing fleet made up of skippers and crews who are experienced professional anglers. You can also fish from jetties, piers, rocks, and shore. If rod and reel don't strike your fancy, try the old-fashioned throw net, or take along a spear when you go snorkeling or scuba diving. There's nighttime torch fishing, which requires special skills and equipment, and freshwater fishing in public areas. Streams and irrigation ditches yield introduced trout, bass, and catfish. While you're at it, you might want to try crabbing or working low-tide areas after sundown hunting octopus, an island delicacy.

Deep-sea fishing is a thrill for many sportsmen. Most game-fishing boats work the waters on the calmer leeward side of the islands. Some skippers, carrying anglers who are accustomed to the sea, will also work the much rougher windward coast and island channels where the fish bite just as well. Trolling is the preferred method of deep-sea fishing; this is done usually in waters of 1,000–2,000 fathoms (a fathom is six feet). The skipper will either "area fish"—which means running in a crisscrossing pattern over a known productive area, or "ledge fish," which involves trolling over submerged ledges where game fish are known to feed. The most advanced marine technology, available on many boats, sends sonar beeps searching for fish. On deck, the crew and anglers scan the horizon in the age-old Hawaiian tradition, searching for clusters of seabirds feeding on bait fish pursued to the surface by the huge and aggressive game fish. "Still fishing" or "bottom fishing" with hand lines yields some tremendous fish.

Kaua'i has excellent fishing waters year-round. The most thrilling **game fish** is **marlin,** generically known as billfish or *a'u* to the locals. The king of them is the blue marlin, with record catches well over 1,000 pounds, and these are called "granders." There are also striped marlin and sailfish, which are often over 200 pounds. The best times for marlin are during spring, summer, and fall. The fishing tapers off in January but picks up again by late February. "Blues" can be caught year-round, but, oddly enough, when they stop biting it seems as though the striped marlin pick up. Second to the marlin is **tuna.** 'Ahi (yellowfin tuna) are caught in Hawaiian waters at depths of 100–1,000 fathoms. Large schools of 'ahi come to Kaua'i in the spring, and the fishing is fabulous, with 200-pounders possible and fish 25–100 pounds common. There are also *aku* (skipjack tuna) and the delicious *ono,* which averages 20–40 pounds. **Mahimahi,** with its high prominent forehead and long dorsal fin, is another strong, fighting, deep-water game fish abundant in Hawaii. These delicious fish can weigh up to 70 pounds and often appear on restaurant menus.

Shore fishing and bait casting yield *papio,* a jack tuna. *Akule,* a scad (locally called *halalu*), is a smallish, schooling fish that comes close to shore and is great to catch on light tackle. *Ulua* are shore fish found in tidepools. They're excellent eating, averaging 2–3 pounds, and are taken at night or with spears. 'O'io are bone-

fish that come close to shore to spawn. They're caught by bait-casting and bottom fishing with cut bait. They're bony, but they're a favorite for fish cakes and *poke. Awa* is a schooling fish that loves brackish water. It can get up to three feet long and is a good fighter; a favorite of throw netters, it's even raised commercially in fishponds. Besides these, there are plenty of goatfish, mullet, mackerel, snapper, sharks, and even salmon.

Some excellent fishing grounds are off Kaua'i, especially around Ni'ihau, and a few **charter boats** are for hire. Most are berthed at Nawiliwili Harbor, with a couple on the north coast, a few more running out of Port Allen, and at least one in Kekaha. Captains of these vessels invariably have been fishing these waters for years and know where to look for a catch. Rates vary, as do the length of outings (usually four, six, or eight hours) and number of passengers allowed on the boats. Fishing excursions run in the vicinity of $100 a half-day, $140 per three-quarter day, and $180 for a full-day shared charter—half again that much when the shared charters take only four passengers; and $500 half-day, $600 three-quarter day, and $700 full-day for an exclusive charter. A few companies run fishing trips to Ni'ihau for about $1,100 and overnight fishing for about the same fee, and you might find someone who does a two-day trip to Ni'ihau and Ka'ula for about $2,000.

Freshwater fishing on Kaua'i usually means going for trout, bass, and *tucanare,* although channel catfish, bluegill sunfish, tilapia, and carp are also present in some streams and reservoirs. Rainbow trout were introduced in 1920 and thrive in 13 miles of fishable streams, ditches, and one reservoir in the Koke'e Public Fishing Area. Large and small bass and the bass-like *tucanare* are also popular game fish on Kaua'i. They're hooked in reservoirs and in the Wailua River and its feeder streams.

No license is needed for recreational saltwater fishing. A license is needed for freshwater fishing only. A **Freshwater Game Fishing License** is good for one year, July 1–June 30.

KAUA'I GOLF COURSES

Course	Par	Yards	Fees	Cart	Clubs
Kaua'i Lagoons Golf Club 3351 Ho'olaule'a Way Lihu'e, HI 96766 808/241-6000 800/634-6400 www.kauailagoonsgolf.com	72	6,960 (Mokihana) 7,070 (Kiele)	$120 $170	incl.	$40
Kiahuna Golf Club 2545 Kiahuna Plantation Drive Po'ipu, HI 96756 808/742-9595 www.kiahunagolf.com	70	6,885	$50-90	incl.	$40
Kukuiolono Golf Course 854 Pu'u Road Kalaheo, HI 96741 808/332-9151	36	3,173	$8	$7	$7 $2
Poipu Bay Golf Course 2250 Ainako St. Koloa, HI 96756 808/742-8711 800/858-6300 www.poipubaygolf.com	72	7,108	$65-185	incl.	$40-60

Licenses cost $25 for nonresidents, $10 for 7-day tourist use, and $20 for 30-day tourist use; $5 for residents over age 15 and active duty military personnel, their spouses, and dependents over age 15; $3 for children ages 9–15; and free to senior citizens over age 65 and children under age 9 when accompanied by an adult with a license. You can pick up a license at the State Division of Aquatic Resources on each of the main islands or at most sporting goods stores. For free booklets and information, write Division of Aquatic Resources (1151 Punchbowl St., Room 330, Honolulu, HI 96813). On Kaua'i, write to the Division of Aquatic Resources (3060 'Eiwa St., Lihu'e, HI 96766, 808/274-3344) or stop by Room 306 of the state office building in Lihu'e. Be sure to ask for the *Hawaii Fishing Regulations* and *Freshwater Fishing in Hawaii* booklets. All game fish may be taken year-round, except trout. Trout, on Kaua'i only, may be taken for 16 days commencing on the first Saturday of August. Thereafter, for the remainder of August and September, trout can be taken only on Saturday, Sunday, and state holidays. Fishing is usually allowed in most State Forest Reserve Areas. Owners' permission must be obtained to fish on private property.

GOLF

Kaua'i offers varied and exciting golfing all around the island at eight golf courses. Kukuiolono Golf Course, a mountaintop course in Kalaheo, is never crowded and is worth visiting just for the scenery. Wailua Municipal Golf Course is a public course with reasonable greens fees and is considered excellent by visitors and residents—one of the best municipal courses in the country and the longest running on the island. Princeville boasts 45 magnificent holes sculpted above Hanalei Bay and the

Course	Par	Yards	Fees	Cart	Clubs
Princeville Makai Golf Course 4080 Lei O Papa Rd. Princeville, HI 96722 808/826-3580 800/826-1105 www.princeville.com	36 36 36	3,430 (Ocean) 3,445 (Woods) 3,456 (Lake)	$125	incl.	$45
Princeville Prince Golf Course 5-3900 Kuhio Hwy. Princeville, HI 96722 808/826-5000 800/826-1105 www.princeville.com	72	7,309	$175	incl.	$45
Puakea Golf Course 4150 Nuhou Street Lihu'e, HI 96766 808/245-8756 866/773-5554 www.puakeagolf.com	72	6,954	$65-125	incl.	$30
Wailua Municipal Golf Course 3-5350 Kuhio Hwy. Lihu'e, HI 96766 808/241-6666	72	6,981	$32-44	$15	$16

'Anini bluffs. Both the Princeville courses have been certified as Audubon Cooperative Sanctuaries for their work in preserving and maintaining an environment that sustains native birdlife. A favorite for years, Kaua'i Lagoons Golf Club in Lihu'e has the added interest of the more challenging Kiele Course. Also in Lihu'e is the up-and-coming Puakea Golf Course, the newest on the island. In Po'ipu, Kiahuna Golf Club and the newer Po'ipu Bay Golf Course are fabulous courses on the sunny south shore.

Often, if you are a guest of one of the hotels affiliated with a golf course, you are offered guest golfing rates at substantial savings. Most golf courses offer lessons. Many have driving ranges, some lighted. All have pro shops and clubhouses with a restaurant or snack shop. Greens fees listed in the chart are for non-Hawaii residents. All courses offer off-peak and other reduced rates. Be sure to ask about these rates as they often afford substantial savings.

For printed information on golf in Hawaii, pick up a free copy of the *Guide to Golf: Hawaiian Islands* or *Golf in Paradise* pamphlets or the newspaper-format *Hawai'i Golf News and Travel.*

HIKING

Hike with someone—share the experience. If possible, don't hike or camp alone, especially if you're a woman. Don't leave your valuables in your tent, and always carry your money, papers, and camera with you. At the least, let someone know where you are going and when you plan to be back; supply an itinerary and your expected route, then stick to it.

Stay on designated trails—this not only preserves Kaua'i's fragile environment, it also keeps you out of dangerous areas. Occasionally, trails will be closed for maintenance, so stay off those routes. Most trails are well maintained, but trailhead markers are often missing. Look for mileage markers along many park and forest reserve trails to gauge your progress. They are usually metal stakes set about a foot off the ground with numbers indicating the distance from a trailhead. The trails themselves

hiking on a trail toward the center of the island

can be muddy, which can make them treacherously slippery.

Buy and use trail maps and a hiking trail book and/or check general information and trail descriptions on the Division of Forestry and Wildlife's Na Ala Hele—Hawai'i Trail and Access System—website (www.hawaiitrails .com) before planning a hike.

Refer to the destination chapters for discussions of individual hiking trails.

Wear comfortable clothing. Shorts and a T-shirt will suffice on many trails, but long pants and long-sleeved shirts are better where it's rainy and overgrown. Bring a windbreaker or raingear—it can rain and blow at any time in Kaua'i—especially on trails in the Alaka'i Swamp area. Wear sturdy walking or hiking shoes that you don't mind getting wet and muddy—it's almost guaranteed on some trails. Some very wet spots and stream crossings may be better done in water shoes or *tabi.* Your clothes may become permanently stained with mud—a wonderful memento of your trip. Officials and others often ask hikers to pick clinging seeds off their clothes when coming out at the trailhead and to wash off boots so as not to transport seeds to nonnative areas.

Always bring food because you cannot, in most cases, forage from the land. Carry plenty of drinking water, at least two quarts per day. Heat can cause your body to lose water and salt. If you become woozy or weak, rest, take salt, and drink water as you need it. Remember, it takes much more water to restore a dehydrated person than to stay hydrated as you go; take small, frequent sips. No matter how clean it looks, water in most streams is biologically polluted and will give you bad stomach problems if you drink it without purifying it; boil it, filter it, or treat it with tablets. For your part, please don't use the streams as toilets.

Wear sunscreen, as the sun can be intense and UV rays penetrate the clouds. Bring and use mosquito repellent—even in paradise pesky bugs abound. Carry a dedicated trash bag and pack out all your garbage.

Many trails are used by hunters of wild boar, deer, or game birds. If you hike in hunting areas during hunting season, wear brightly colored or reflective clothing. Often, forest reserve trails have check-in stations at trailheads. Hikers and hunters must sign a logbook, especially if they intend to camp. The comments by previous hikers are worth reading for up-to-the-minute information on trail conditions.

Many roads leading to the trailheads are marked for 4WD vehicles only. Heed the warnings, especially during rainy weather, when roads are very slick and swollen streams can swallow your rental car. Remember that going in may be fine, but a sudden storm can leave you stranded. Be mindful of flash floods; small creeks can turn into raging torrents with upland rains.

Twilight is short in the islands, and night sets in rapidly. In June, sunrise is around 6 A.M. and sunset 7 P.M.; in December, these occur at 7 A.M. and 6 P.M. If you become lost, find an open spot and stay put; at night, stay as dry as you can. If you must continue, walk on ridges and avoid the gulches, which have more obstacles and make it harder for rescuers to spot you. Do not light a fire. Some forest areas are very dry, and fire could spread easily. Fog is only encountered at the 1,500- to 5,000-foot level, so be careful of disorientation, particularly in that height range.

Hawaii is made of crumbly volcanic rock, so never attempt to climb steep *pali*. You *cannot,* for example, go from Koke'e directly down to the valleys of the Na Pali Coast. Every now and again someone attempts it, falls, and is killed. The cliffs are impossibly steep and brittle, and your handholds and footholds will break from under you, so don't be foolish.

Generally, stay within your limits, be careful, and enjoy yourself.

Hiking Tour Groups

Aside from heading out onto the trail alone, you can walk with others on an organized group tour. The two groups listed below are well established and well respected, but each offers very different types of hikes.

Sierra Club announces group hikes in *The Garden Island* newspaper. You can also find the Kaua'i group outing schedule on the Internet at www.hi.sierraclub.org/kauai/kauai .html. Some hikes are along well-used trails, while others are to destinations seldom seen. Hikes are led by local volunteers, and a waiver must be signed to join. A minimal donation is requested.

The most education-oriented hikes on the island are done by **Kaua'i Nature Tours** (808/742-8305 or 888/233-8365, www.teok .com). Full-day hikes, all in the easy to moderate level, focus on the natural environment; hikers learn about Kaua'i's geology, natural history, and flora and fauna. Various hikes throughout the week go to Waimea Canyon, the Na Pali Coast, Maha'ulepu Beach and dune area, and other beach and mountain areas around the island. Hikes run in the $82–97 range, including lunch. If you want your day to be more than a physical adventure, these hikes may be for you.

BICYCLING

Riding a bike around Kaua'i is fairly easy, thanks to the lack of big hills—except for the road up to Koke'e State Park. Traffic is moderate, especially in the cool of early morning, when it's best for making some distance. Roads are generally good, but shoulders aren't wide and are sometimes nonexistent, particularly on the back roads. Peak season brings a dramatic increase in traffic and road congestion. Take care! Some wide shoulders and bike/pedestrian paths have been constructed, but these are found mostly near tourist resorts. Perhaps the best riding is by mountain bike on the roads that head into the interior. Wherever you ride, watch for rocks, sticks, wet surfaces, and crumbled asphalt; on gravel back roads, keep an eye out for bumps, ruts, and mud puddles.

Wear a helmet, bring sunglasses, use bike gloves, and wear appropriate bike shoes. If possible, have a bike pump, extra tube, and repair kit with you. Bring plenty of water and some snacks. Take a map, but get information from a bike shop about the kind of riding you want to do before you head out. Most are more than willing to offer advice.

If you're out for a joy ride, rent a cruiser and ride through the resort communities or along beach paths. For distance or training, there are no really good options. However, the main highway west of the Koloa/Po'ipu turnoff and north of Kapa'a, as well as the secondary roads up to Koke'e and around the back side of the Sleeping Giant, are perhaps the best. Mountain biking in Kaua'i is not for the uninitiated. Get some experience and get in shape before you ride here. For mountain biking and trail information on all the major islands, pick up a copy of *Mountain Biking the Hawaiian Islands, 2nd ed.* by John Alford, Ohana Publishing, Honolulu (877/682-7433, www.bikehawaii.com).

Mountain biking on most cane roads is not encouraged, as you would be riding through private property. Stay off of other private property and do not go beyond locked gates. Some roads that will lead you off the main highways are Rt. 583 to Wailua Falls (easy); the upland residential roads above Wailua and Kapa'a (easy-moderate); roads uphill between Lawa'i and Kalaheo (slow, steep, and tough); the coastal trail from Kapa'a Beach Park to Anahola, about six miles one-way (relatively easy); and Po'ipu Road past the Hyatt Regency Resort to Maha'ulepu Beach (dusty and slow but easy). Others to try are Kealia Road from Kealia up the mountain to the Spalding Monument and from there down to Anahola (moderate uphill and easy down); the back road past the end of Hauaala Road to the Spalding monument (moderate—you must walk the bike a short ways due to the deteriorating condition of the road); and Ko'olau Road near Moloa'a Beach (easy). The 4WD dirt tracks in Koke'e State Park and the adjacent forest reserves are easy to moderate for mountain bikers and give you a good workout. Some hiking trails on state forest reserve land are also open to mountain biking, including the 13-mile Powerline Trail over the mountain from Keahua Arboretum to Hanalei (strenuous), the Kuilau and Moalepe Trails, the Kuamo'o Trail on the Sleeping Giant, and the Waimea Canyon Trail on the west end. Biking is not allowed on any state park trail or forest reserve trail other than those listed above.

One commercial company does a bike tour on Kaua'i; this is a 13-mile downhill bike ride from the rim of Waimea Canyon at about 3,400 feet elevation to the coast at Kekaha. Please see the South Shore chapter in the "Explore" section of the book for details.

Getting your bike to Kaua'i from one of the neighbor islands is no problem. All of the interisland carriers will fly it for you for about $20 one-way on the same flight you take—just check it as baggage. Bikes must be packed in a box or hard case, supplied by the owner. Handlebars must be turned sideways and the pedals removed or turned in. Bikes go on a space-available basis—usually not a problem. In addition, a release of liability for damage must be signed before the airline will accept the bike. If you plan ahead, you can send your bike the previous day by air freight, but that is more expensive.

The ease of getting your bike to Hawaii from

the Mainland will depend upon which airline you take. Some accept bicycles as baggage traveling with you (approximate additional charge of $50) if the bikes are properly broken down and boxed in a bicycle box, while others will only take them as air freight, in which case the rates are exorbitant. Check with the airlines well before you plan to go to ascertain its particulars.

CAMPING

All campgrounds, except for the state parks along the Na Pali Coast and in the forest reserve campsites in Waimea Canyon, provide grills, pavilions (some with electricity), picnic tables, toilets, cold-water showers, and drinking water, but no individual electrical hookups for RVs. Unfortunately, at some parks, toilets and showers have been vandalized and no longer function, but this may vary according to park maintenance schedules. Camping fuel is not provided, so bring your own wood or charcoal for the grill. No one can camp "under the stars" at official campgrounds; you must

have a tent. Campsites are unattended, so be careful with your gear—especially electronic equipment and cameras—but your tent and sleeping bag will generally be okay. Always be prepared for wind and rain, especially along the north shore.

At times, police aggressively issue tickets and hefty fines for illegal camping, especially along north shore beaches. *Sometimes* they will merely issue a warning, but definitely do not count on it! Multiple offenders have been sentenced to jail time.

A permit is required for camping at all **county beach parks** with camping facilities: Ha'ena, Hanalei Black Pot, 'Anini, Anahola, Hanama'ulu, Salt Pond at Hanapepe, and Lucy Wright in Waimea. RV camping is permitted at only the Ha'ena and Hanama'ulu parks. Permits are good for up to seven days per campground. Camping is limited to 60 days total in any one-year period.

The permit-issuing office is the **Division of Parks and Recreation** (444 Rice St., Pi'ikoi Bldg., Suite 350, Lihu'e, HI 96766,

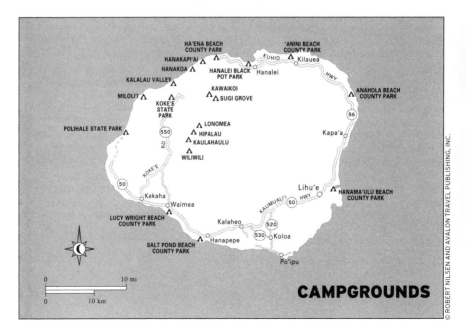

CAMPGROUNDS

© ROBERT NILSEN AND AVALON TRAVEL PUBLISHING, INC.

808/241-4463, Mon.–Fri. 8:15 A.M.–4 P.M.) An application must include the name, address, and telephone number of the principle adult, names and copies of official identification for all adults in the party, and the number of tents that will be used. The cost is $3 per person per day (except Hawaii residents); children under 18 are free if accompanied by parent or guardian. If you write in advance for information and reservations, the office will send you an application—or download it from the County website (www.kauai.gov), "Camping Information" link. Return it with the appropriate information, and your request will be logged in the reservations book. You'll also receive brochures and maps of the campgrounds. When you arrive, you must pick up and pay for your permit at the Parks and Recreation office. Be aware that each beach park is closed one day a week for maintenance, except for Hanalei Black Pot Park, which is only open Friday, Saturday, and holidays. When you make your application to camp, ask the parks office for its current closure schedule.

Camping is allowed at three **state parks** on Kaua'i: Koke'e, Na Pali Coast, and Polihale.

A camping permit is required. RV camping is permitted at Koke'e and Polihale only. Permits run $5 per campsite per night at Polihale and Koke'e and $10 per night for the Na Pali Coast sites. Camping is restricted to five consecutive nights within a 30-day period per campground, with one night allowed at Hanakapi'ai when going in along the Kalalau Trail and one night when coming out from the valley, and a three-night maximum at Miloli'i farther along the coast. On occasion, one or more of these coastal campsites will be closed, so check with the state office for up-to-date information. At Polihale, campsites are on top of the dunes that back the beach, and at Koke'e, the camping area is in the open meadow at the far end from the museum.

Permits are issued no more than one year in advance. An application for a permit should be made at the **Department of Land and Natural Resources** (DLNR) (Division of State Parks, 3060 'Eiwa St., Rm. 306, Lihu'e, HI 96766, 808/274-3444, www.hawaii. gov/dlnr/dsp, 8 A.M.–3:30 P.M. Mon.–Fri.). No permits will be issued without proper

camping at Polihale Beach State Park

HELICOPTER TOURS OVER KAUA'I

Flying in a chopper is a thrilling experience, and one of the highlights for many visitors to Kaua'i. A helicopter adventure is like flying in a light plane – with a twist. It can take you into all kinds of otherwise inaccessible little nooks and crannies, but the highlights are flying through the colorful gouge of the Waimea Canyon, along the giant sea cliffs of the Na Pali Coast, and into the Mount Wai'ale'ale crater – where it almost never stops raining and where you see dozens of waterfalls and even 360-degree rainbows floating in midair. Earphones cut the noise of the aircraft and play soul-stirring music as a background to the pilot's narration. Each pilot's stories are as different as the pilots themselves, so you take your chances in that regard, but all are skilled in bringing you up close to the island. All flights on Kaua'i run in a clockwise circle around the island along the same basic route. Longer flights linger at certain scenic spots and dart into more valleys, and a couple even make a stop for a picnic. One company does a flight to the beaches on Ni'ihau for $325. The basic one-hour around-the-island flight runs about $200 per person, a shorter 45-minute flight is around $150, and longer 75- to 90-minute flights run $250; most offer Internet discounts. Some provide complimentary videos of your flight or a professionally made "standard" flight, while others will sell you a video if you want one. Discounts from some of the companies are always featured in the ubiquitous free tourist brochures, and greater savings are occasionally offered through tourist activity and information centers, often as part of a time-share presentation deal.

Outdoor purists disparage this mode of transport, saying, "If you can't hike in, you shouldn't be there," but that's tunnel vision. To go deep into the mist-shrouded interior, especially through the Alaka'i Swamp, the average traveler "can't get there from here"; it's just too rugged and dangerous. The only reasonable way to see it is by helicopter and, except for the noise, choppers actually have less of an impact on the ecosystem than hikers do! A compromise – limiting numbers and times of flights – seems to be the best answer.

Everyone has an opinion as to which company offers the best ride, the best narration, and the best service. All the helicopter companies on Kaua'i are safe and reputable. Nearly all pilots have been trained by the military, and most fly five- or six-seat ASTAR machines with a few four-passenger Bell Jet Rangers and Hughes 500s still in use. Most have two-way microphones so you can communicate with the pilot. Each gives a pre-flight briefing to go over safety regulations and other details. Remember, however, that the seating arrangement in a helicopter is critical to safety. The pre-flight crew is expertly trained to arrange the chopper so that it is balanced, and with different people of various sizes flying every day, their job is very much like a chess game. This means that the seating goes strictly according to weight. If you are not assigned the seat of your choice, for safety's sake, please do not complain and definitely do not trade or move. Think instead that you are part of a team whose goal is not only enjoyment but also safety. It's very difficult not to have a fascinating flight, no matter where you sit.

Nearly everyone wants to take photographs of their helicopter tour. Who wouldn't? Here are a few things to consider. Most of the newer helicopters are air-conditioned, which means that the windows don't open, so you might experience glare or some distortion. If you need absolutely clear shots, choose a chopper where the windows open or one that flies with its doors off. Also, if you are the only one taking pictures on a tour and you're seated in the middle of the rear seat, you won't be happy. Choose a ride in a smaller rig where everyone gets a window seat.

Of the helicopter companies on Kaua'i, the majority operate from Lihu'e Airport, with two flying from Burns Field in Hanapepe and one flying from the Princeville Airport. Those companies without offices adjacent to the Lihu'e heliport shuttle guests to the tarmac in vans.

identification. You can also write well in advance for permits, which will be mailed to you, but you must include photocopies of identification for each camper over 18. Children under 18 will not be issued a permit, and they must be accompanied by an adult. Allow at least one month for the entire process, and no reservations are guaranteed without at least a seven-day notice. Include name, address, and telephone numbers of those in the group, number of campers (with ID photocopies), dates of use, and number of tents. Reservations can now be made online.

Run by a concessionaire, **Koke'e Lodge** (P.O. Box 819, Waimea, HI 96796, 808/335-6061, 9 A.M.–3:45 P.M. daily) also provides self-contained housekeeping cabins that run $59 or $70. They are furnished with stoves, refrigerators, hot showers, cooking and eating utensils, beds, and linens; wood is available for the fireplaces. The cabins vary from one large room that accommodates three to two-bedroom units that sleep seven. The cabins are tough to get on holidays, during trout-fishing season in August and September, and during the wild plum harvest in June and July.

Forest Reserve camping is allowed in specified sites only within the Na Pali Kona and Pu'u Ka Pele Forest Reserves, which encompass Waimea and adjacent canyons and the upper Koke'e region. Permits are required and issued free of charge. Apply at the state **Division of Forestry and Wildlife** (3060 'Eiwa St., Rm. 306, Lihu'e, HI 96766, 808/274-3433, 8 A.M.–3:30 P.M. Mon.–Fri.). Applications must include the names of all campers and the exact dates for which the campsite is requested. Be sure to pick up the very useful *Recreational Map of Western Kauai* when applying. The Kawaikoi and Sugi Grove campsites along Camp 10–Mohihi Road are accessible by 4WD vehicles. Camping at these camps is limited to three nights total within a 30-day period. The four campsites in Waimea and Koai'e Canyons are reachable by foot only, either from Kukui Trail off Koke'e Road or by hiking up the Waimea Canyon from the town of Waimea. Camping is limited to four nights total at these camps. Be sure to sign in and out at the trailheads.

Getting There

With the number of visitors each year approaching seven million—and another several hundred thousand just passing through—the state of Hawaii is one of the easiest places in the world to get to... by plane. About half a dozen large North American airlines (plus additional charter airlines) fly to and from the islands. About twice that number of foreign carriers, mostly from Asia and Oceania, also touch down here on a daily or weekly basis. Hawaii is a hotly contested air market. Competition among carriers can be fierce, and this makes for some sweet deals and a wide choice of fares for the money-wise traveler. It also makes for pricing chaos. Airlines usually adjust their flight schedules about every three months to account for seasonal differences in travel and route changes. Before planning a trip to and around the islands, be sure to contact the airlines directly, view the airlines' Internet sites, check well-established Internet travel sites, go through your travel agent for the most current information on routes and flying times, or seek out charter companies, as they offer attractive alternatives. Familiarize yourself with the alternatives at your disposal so that you can make an informed travel selection.

BY AIR

There are two categories of airlines that you can take to Hawaii: **domestic,** meaning American-owned, and **foreign**-owned. An American law, penned at the turn of the 20th century to protect American shipping, says that *only* an American carrier can transport

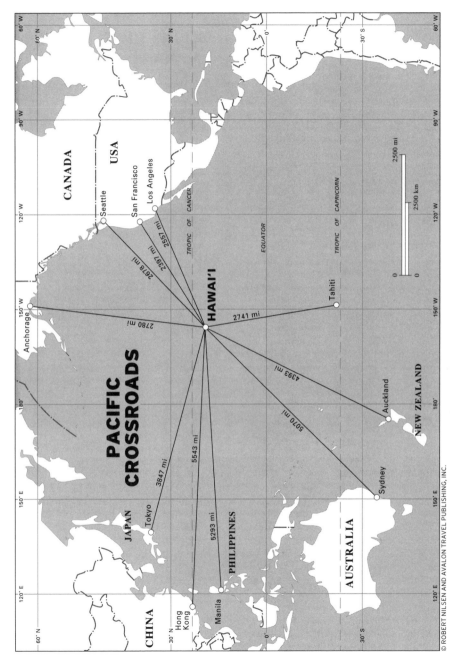

PACIFIC CROSSROADS

CANADA

USA

Seattle

San Francisco

Los Angeles

2557 mi

2597 mi

2678 mi

TROPIC OF CANCER

EQUATOR

TROPIC OF CAPRICORN

HAWAI'I

Tahiti

2741 mi

Anchorage

2780 mi

4393 mi

Auckland

NEW ZEALAND

5070 mi

3847 mi

5543 mi

Sydney

Tokyo

JAPAN

5293 mi

PHILIPPINES

AUSTRALIA

Manila

Hong Kong

CHINA

2500 mi

2500 km

you between two American cities. In the airline industry, this law is still very much in effect. It means, for example, that if you want a round-trip flight between San Francisco and Honolulu, you *must* fly on a domestic carrier. If, however, you are flying from San Francisco to Tokyo, you are at liberty to fly a foreign airline, and you may even have a stopover in Hawaii, but you must continue to Tokyo or some other foreign city before flying back to San Francisco on the foreign airline. Travel agents know this, but if you're planning your own trip, be aware of this fact.

If you fly to Hawaii from a foreign country, you are free to use either an American or foreign carrier.

Flights to Hawaii

Depending on where you are coming from, you may have to fly from your home to a "gateway city," from where flights go to Hawaii, either direct or nonstop. On direct flights you fly from point A to point B without changing planes; it doesn't mean that you don't land in between. Direct flights do land, usually once to board and deplane passengers, but you sit cozily on the plane along with your luggage, and off you go again. Nonstop is just that; you board, and when the doors open again you're at your destination. All flights from the West Coast gateway cities are nonstop, God willing—because there is only the Pacific in between!

Flights to Kaua'i

Until very recently, there were no nonstop flights to Kaua'i. All passengers had to go through Honolulu to get to Kaua'i. Since 1999, United Airlines has run daily fights from Los Angeles to Kaua'i and then added a flight from San Francisco. In 2002, American Airlines also added nonstop daily flights from Los Angeles to Lihu'e. All other major domestic and foreign carriers fly to Honolulu and have arrangements with either Hawaiian Airlines or Aloha Airlines for getting you to Kaua'i. If you fly from the Mainland with Hawaiian or Aloha, you have the added convenience of dealing with

---

FLIGHT TIMES TO HAWAII

Flights from West Coast California take about five hours, a bit longer from the Northwest or Pacific Canada; you gain two hours over Pacific Standard Time when you land in Hawaii (three hours during daylight saving time). From the East Coast it takes about 11 hours and you gain five hours over Eastern Standard Time. Flights from Japan take about seven hours, and there is a five-hour difference between the time zones. Travel time between Sydney, Australia, or Auckland, New Zealand, and Hawaii is about nine hours. Sydney and Auckland are ahead of Hawaii time by 20 and 22 hours, respectively.

---

just one airline to get you to Kaua'i. Several charter airlines also fly to Kaua'i nonstop from the Mainland.

Visas

Entering Hawaii is like entering anywhere else in the United States. Foreign nationals must have a current passport and most must have a proper visa, an ongoing or return air ticket, and sufficient funds for the proposed stay in Hawaii. A visa application can be made at any U.S. embassy or consular office outside the United States and must include a properly filled out application form, two photos 1.5 inches square, and a nonrefundable fee of $100. Canadians do not need a visa or passport but must have proper identification such as a passport, driver's license, or birth certificate. Visitors from 28 countries do not need a visa to enter the United States for 90 days or less. As this list is amended periodically, be sure to check in your country of origin to determine whether you need a visa for U.S. entry.

Agricultural Inspection

Remember that before you leave Hawaii for the Mainland, all of your bags are again subject to an agricultural inspection, a usually painless procedure taking only a minute or two. To facilitate your departure, leave all bags unlocked until after inspection. There are no restrictions on beach sand from below the high water line, coconuts, cooked foods, dried flower arrangements, fresh flower lei, pineapples, certified pest-free plants and cuttings, and seashells. However, papayas must be treated before departure. Some restricted items are berries, fresh gardenias, jade vines, live insects and snails, cotton, plants in soil, soil itself, and sugarcane. Raw sugarcane is okay, however, if it is cut between the nodes, has the outer covering peeled off, is split into fourths, and is commercially packaged. For any questions pertaining to plants that you want to take to the Mainland, call the U.S. Department of Agriculture, Plant Protection and Quarantine office in Kaua'i (808/245-2831).

Foreign countries may have different agricultural inspection requirements for flights from Hawaii (or other points in the United States) to those countries. Be sure to check with the proper foreign authorities for specifics.

Pets and Quarantine

Hawaii has a very rigid pet quarantine policy designed to keep rabies and other Mainland diseases from reaching the state. All domestic pets are subject to **120 days' quarantine** (a 30-day quarantine or a newer five-day-or-less quarantine is allowed by meeting certain pre-arrival and post-arrival requirements—inquire), and this includes substantial fees for boarding. Unless you are contemplating a move to Hawaii, it is not feasible to take pets. For complete information, contact the Department of Agriculture, Animal Quarantine Division, 99-951 Halawa Valley St., 'Aiea, HI 96701, 808/483-7171, www.hawaiiag.org/hdoa/ai_aqs_info.htm.

Kaua'i's Airports

Lihu'e Airport, less than two miles from downtown Lihu'e, receives all of Kaua'i's commercial flights. On arrival, you're immediately struck by the warm balmy temperature and gentle island breezes. No public transportation to or from the airport is available, so you must either rent a car or hire a taxi. The terminal, long and low, has arrival lounges at both ends and the departure lounge in the middle. The departure lounge holds a restaurant and cocktail lounge, snack shop, flower shop, gift shop, restrooms, public telephones, and ATM machines. The gift shop sells pre-inspected island fruit that's boxed and ready to transport. For your entertainment, Hawaiian music is performed several mornings each week in the main lobby 9–11:30 A.M., and historical and cultural displays are located here and there around the terminal. Baggage pick-up is at either end, Aloha and United to the left as you enter the terminal from the plane, and Hawaiian Airlines and others to the right—follow the signs. In each baggage claim area are restrooms, public telephones, and free tourist brochures. Outside the baggage claim areas are tourist information booths (usually staffed for incoming flights) with additional brochures and a courtesy phone for information.

Kaua'i's Lihu'e Airport is connected to Honolulu and Maui by direct nonstop interisland flight, and to Moloka'i, Lana'i, and the Big Island by connections in Honolulu or Maui. Average flying time from Kaua'i to Honolulu is 30 minutes, about 40 minutes to Maui, and a little less than two hours to the Big Island, depending upon stops. Outgoing and incoming flights are dispersed equally throughout the day.

The old terminal at the Lihu'e Airport, a few hundred yards down Ahukini Road, is now used by flightseeing airplane and interisland charter companies. Across the street is the heliport, used actively by more than half a dozen helicopter companies offering sightseeing tours of the island.

Burns Field (Port Allan Airport) in Hanapepe was the first commercial airstrip on the island, but it hasn't been used as such for years. There are no facilities there whatsoever, and the strip is used only by a handful of helicopter, ultralight, and skydiving companies.

Princeville Airport, along Rt. 56 just east

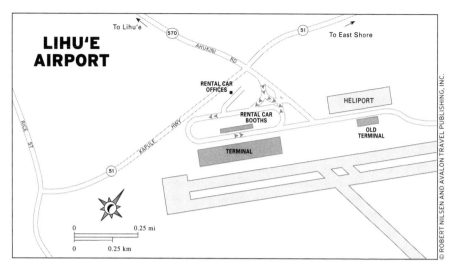

LIHU'E AIRPORT

To Lihu'e

570

AHUKINI RD

51

To East Shore

RENTAL CAR OFFICES

HELIPORT

RENTAL CAR BOOTHS

OLD TERMINAL

TERMINAL

RICE ST

KAPULE HWY

51

0   0.25 mi

0   0.25 km

© ROBERT NILSEN AND AVALON TRAVEL PUBLISHING, INC.

of Princeville, served commercial commuter air flights until the mid-1990s when those routes were discontinued. Since then, at least one small airline started regular commuter flights between Princeville and Honolulu, but shortly after it too shut down the service as uneconomical. The Princeville Airport is used by an occasional private plane that only needs a short runway but much more frequently by the HeliUSA helicopter company, and residents of the area often refer to it as the heliport. The terminal is a cute little building made inconspicuous by the immense beauty surrounding it. Here you'll find a toilet, telephone, an Avis car rental office, and an upstairs bar.

DOMESTIC CARRIERS

The following are the major domestic carriers to and from Hawaii. The planes used are primarily wide-body D10, L10, and 747s, with a smaller 737, 767, and the like flown now and again. A list of the "gateway cities" from which they fly direct and nonstop flights is given, but "connecting cities" are not. The majority of flights, by all carriers, land at Honolulu International Airport, with the remainder of flights going directly to Kaua'i. Only the established companies are listed. Entrepreneurial small air-

lines such as the now-defunct Mahalo Air pop up now and again and specialize in lower fares. There is a hectic frenzy to buy their tickets and business is great for a while, but then the established companies lower their fares and the gamblers fold. The Lihu'e Airport cannot at present land jumbo jets, so planes flown there are the smaller varieties.

Hawaiian Airlines

Hawaiian Airlines (800/882-8811 or 800/367-5320 Mainland and Canada, www.hawaiian air.com) operates daily direct flights from Los Angeles, San Francisco, Sacramento, and San Jose, California; Las Vegas; Phoenix; Seattle; and Portland to Honolulu, with flights also connecting Maui to Portland and Seattle. Scheduled flights to the South Pacific run on a less frequent basis between Honolulu and Pago Pago, Samoa; Papeete, Tahiti; and Sydney, Australia. Hawaiian Airlines offers special discount deals with Dollar rental cars and select major island hotels.

Aloha Airlines

Aloha Airlines (800/554-4833 or 800/367-5250 Mainland and Canada, www.alohaair-lines.com) flies daily between Honolulu and

Oakland and Orange County, California, and Las Vegas and Reno via Orange County. From Honolulu, there are connecting flights to all islands. Aloha also flies daily between Maui and Oakland, Sacramento, Orange County, and San Diego. There are also flights from Kona direct to Oakland and to Orange County with a continuation to Reno. Like Hawaiian Airlines, Aloha Airlines is always adjusting its West Coast operation, so changes will undoubtedly be in store in the future.

United Airlines

Since its first island flight in 1947, United (800/241-6522, www.united.com) has become top dog in flights to Hawaii. United's Mainland routes connect more than 100 cities to Hawaii. The main gateway cities of San Francisco and Los Angeles have direct daily flights to Honolulu, with additional flights from Denver on the weekends; flights from all other cities connect through these. United also offers direct flights to Maui, Kona, and Kaua'i from San Francisco and Los Angeles. Continuing through Honolulu, United flights go to Tokyo (Narita), where connections can be made for other Asian cities. United offers a number of packages, including flight and hotel on O'ahu, and flight, hotel, and car on the Neighbor Islands. United inter-lines with Aloha Airlines and deals with Hertz rental cars. United is the "big guy" and intends to stay that way—its packages are hard to beat.

American Airlines

American (800/433-7300, www.aa.com) offers daily flights to Honolulu from Los Angeles, San Francisco, Dallas/Fort Worth, and Chicago. It also flies daily from it main hubs to Maui, Kona, and Kaua'i. American does not fly to points in Asia or other Pacific destinations from Hawaii. American inter-lines with Hawaiian Airlines.

Continental Airlines

Continental (800/525-0280 or 800/231-0856, www.continental.com) flights from all Mainland cities to Honolulu connect via Los Angeles, Newark, and Houston. Also available are direct flights from Honolulu to Guam, from where flights run to numerous other Asian and Pacific cities and islands. Continental inter-lines with Hawaiian Airlines.

Northwest Airlines

Northwest (Call 800/225-2525, www.nwa .com) flies into Honolulu from Los Angeles, Seattle, Portland, San Francisco (via Seattle), and Minneapolis. There are onward nonstop flights to Narita and Osaka in Japan, from where all other Asian destinations are connected.

Delta Air Lines

In 1985, Delta (800/221-1212, www.delta .com) entered the Hawaiian market; when it bought out Western Airlines, its share became even bigger. Delta has nonstop flights to Honolulu from Atlanta, Los Angeles, Minneapolis, Portland, San Francisco, Salt Lake City, and Atlanta; nonstop flights to Maui from Los Angeles, Salt Lake City, and Houston; and a flight from Seattle to Kona.

FOREIGN CARRIERS

The following carriers operate throughout Asia and Oceania but have no U.S. flying rights. This means that in order for a U.S. citizen to vacation in Hawaii using one of these carriers, the flight must originate or terminate in a foreign city. You can have a stopover in Honolulu with a connecting flight to a Neighbor Island.

Air Canada

Nonstop Air Canada (888/247-2262, www .aircanada.ca) flights from Canada to Honolulu originate in Vancouver. In Hawaii, you can use either Hawaiian Airlines or Aloha Airlines to get to other island destinations.

Air New Zealand

Air New Zealand (800/262-1234, www .airnewzealand.com) flights link New Zealand, Australia, and numerous South Pacific islands via Auckland to Honolulu.

Japan Air Lines

The Japanese are the second-largest group, after Americans, to visit Hawaii. JAL (800/525-3663, www.jal.co.jp) flights to Honolulu originate in Tokyo (Narita), Nagoya, Osaka (Kansai), and Fukuoka. In addition, there are flights between Tokyo (Narita) and Kona on the Big Island. JAL flights continue beyond Hawaii to San Francisco and Los Angeles.

Qantas

Qantas (800/227-4500, www.qantas.com.au) daily flights connect Sydney and Melbourne, Australia, with Honolulu; all other flights feed through this hub.

China Airlines

Routes to Honolulu with China Airlines (800/227-5118, www.china-airlines.com) are only from Taipei and Tokyo. Connections are available in Taipei to most Asian capitals.

Korean Air

Korean Air (800/438-5000, www.koreanair .com) offers some of the least expensive flights to Asia. All flights are direct between Honolulu and Seoul, with connections there to many Asian cities.

Air Pacific

Air Pacific (808/227-4446, www.airpacific .com) offers once weekly nonstop flights between Nadi (Fiji) and Honolulu.

Polynesian Airlines

If flying to Samoa, use Polynesian Airlines (808/842-7659, www.polynesianairlines.com) for weekly flights directly from Honolulu to Apia.

Philippine Airlines

Three times weekly, Philippine Airlines (808/435-7725, www.philippineair.com) offers nonstop flights between Honolulu and Manila.

TRAVEL COMPANIES

Many tour companies advertise packages to Hawaii in large city newspapers every week. They offer very reasonable airfares, car rentals, and accommodations. Without trying, you can get round-trip airfare from the West Coast and a week in Hawaii for $600–700 using one of these companies, with prices invariably more expensive during summer. Some airlines offer great package deals that are hard to beat. United Vacations (800/377-1816, www.united-vacations.com) by United Airlines is one. The following companies also offer great deals. This list is by no means exhaustive.

Pleasant Hawaiian Holidays

A California-based company specializing in Hawaii, Pleasant Hawaiian Holidays (800/742-9244, www.pleasantholidays.com) makes arrangements for flights, accommodations, and transportation only. For flights, it primarily uses American Trans Air but also uses select commercial airlines and regularly scheduled flights. Aside from the air connection, Pleasant Hawaiian offers a choice of accommodation levels from budget to luxury, a fly/drive option if you have your own accommodation, and numerous perks, like a flower lei, first morning orientation, service desks at hotels, and coupons and gift certificates. Pleasant Hawaiian is easy to work with and stands behind its services. A deposit is required after booking, and there is a time frame for full payment that depends upon when you make your reservation. Fees are assessed for changing particulars after booking, so apprise yourself of all financial particulars. Most major travel agents work with Pleasant Hawaiian, but you can also contact the company directly.

SunTrips

This California-based tour company (800/786-8747, www.suntrips.com) runs flights to the four major islands of Hawaii from Oakland, Portland, Seattle, and Denver. It offers flight, accommodation, and/or car rental packages that match any for affordability. Most of its flights use Ryan International or North American airlines. Your price will depend upon your choice of accommodations and type of car. Using both charter and commercial air carriers, SunTrips does not offer assigned seating until you get to the airport. They recommend you get there two hours in advance, and they ain't kidding! This is the price you pay for getting such inexpensive air travel. SunTrips financial regulations are similar to those at Pleasant Hawaiian; be sure to inquire.

STA Travel

STA Travel (800/781-4040 or visit www.statravel.com) is a full-service travel agency specializing in student travel, regardless of age. Those under 26 do not have to be full-time students to get special fares. Through STA, bona fide students can get an International Student Identification Card (ISIC), which often gets you discount fares and fees, and anyone can get a Hosteling International card. Older independent travelers can avail themselves of services; although they are ineligible for student fares, STA works hard to get you discounted or budget rates. Many tickets issued by STA are flexible, allowing changes with no penalty, and are open-ended for travel up to one year. Aside from airfares, STA also books accommodations and packages. STA has some 300 offices around the world. STA also maintains Travel Help, a service available at all offices designed to solve all types of problems that may arise while traveling. STA is a well-established travel agency with an excellent and well-deserved reputation.

Getting Around

BY AIR

Getting to and from Kaua'i via the other islands is easy and convenient. The only effective way for most visitors to travel between the Hawaiian Islands is by air. Luckily, Hawaii has excellent air transportation that boasts one of the industry's safest flight records. All interisland flights have a no-smoking regulation. Items restricted on flights from the Mainland and from overseas are also restricted on flights within the state. Baggage allowances are the same as anywhere, except that due to space constraints, carry-on bags on the smaller prop planes may be limited in number and size, but this does not affect flights to and from Kaua'i. Hawaiian and Aloha airlines have competitive prices, with interisland flights starting at about $100 each way, with some savings for state residents. The only commercial airport on Kaua'i is at Lihu'e.

Note: Although every effort has been made for up-to-date accuracy, remember that schedules are constantly changing. The following should be used only as a point of reference. Please call the airlines listed below for their latest schedules.

Hawaiian Airlines

The majority of flights from Lihu'e on Hawaiian Airlines (808/245-4516 on Kaua'i, 800/882-8811 statewide, 800/367-5320 Mainland and Canada, www.hawaiianair.com) are to and from Honolulu, with more than a dozen and a half per day in each direction. Hawaiian Airlines flights to Lihu'e from Honolulu begin at 5:30 A.M., with flights thereafter about every hour until 7 P.M. Flights from Lihu'e to Honolulu begin at 6:35 A.M. and go all day until 8:30 P.M. About a dozen flights from Lihu'e connect in Honolulu for Kahului, Maui, starting around 7 A.M. and running until almost 5 P.M. Also running through Honolulu and spaced throughout the day are nearly two dozen flights a day from Lihu'e to Kona on the Big Island and over a dozen connections a day to Hilo on the opposite side of the Big Island. Hawaiian Airlines uses Island Air as a commuter link to the smaller island airports and partners with Alaska Airlines, American Airlines, Continental Airlines, and Northwest Airlines.

Aloha Airlines

Aloha Airlines (808/245-3691 on Kaua'i,

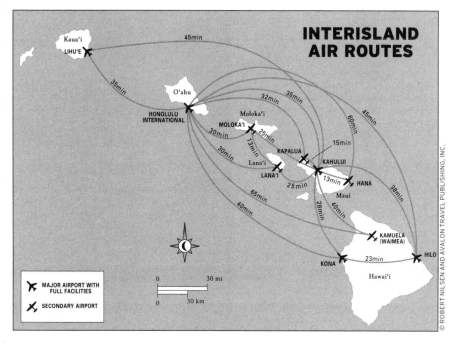

INTERISLAND AIR ROUTES

© ROBERT NILSEN AND AVALON TRAVEL PUBLISHING, INC.

800/367-5250 Mainland and Canada, www. alohaairlines.com), with its all-jet fleet of 737s, offers about the same number of flights to or-from Kaua'i as Hawaiian Airlines. It flies from Lihu'e to Honolulu about a dozen and a half times per day beginning at 6:50 A.M. with the last flight at about 6:30 P.M.; return flights from Honolulu start at 5:50 A.M., with the last at 5:25 P.M. Multiple flights throughout the day to/from Maui, all via Honolulu, begin at around 7 A.M. and run until after 5:30 P.M. About a dozen daily flights also connect through Honolulu to both Hilo and Kona on the Big Island. Aloha Airlines has no flights from Kaua'i to either Moloka'i or Lana'i. All passengers to those two islands need to use Island Air. Aloha Airlines uses Island Air as a commuter link to the smaller island airports and partners with United Airlines.

Charter Air Service

If you've got the bucks or just need to go when there's no regularly scheduled flight, try the following company for island-wide charter service: **Paragon Air** (866/946-4744, www.para-gon-air.com). Private charter service operates 24 hours a day. Sample fares for the rental of a private aircraft run about $675 from Kaua'i to Honolulu and $1450 from Kaua'i to Kona.

BY SEA

In 2001, following the terrorist attacks on the Mainland and a dramatic dip in numbers of travelers to the Hawaiian Islands, American Hawaii Cruises stopped all interisland cruise service within the Hawaiian Islands. This company had operated seven-day cruises to four of the islands for years.

In December 2001, Norwegian Cruise Lines (888/625-4292 or 800/327-7030, www .ncl.com), a subsidiary of Star Cruises PLC of Malaysia, began running a weekly seven-day round-trip cruise that went throughout the Hawaiian Islands with a leg down to Fanning Island and back. Now under the name NCL America, it offers a 10-day Hawaii and

SCENIC BUS AND VAN TOURS

On Kaua'i, many small tour companies run vans, but the two large companies also use buses. Though cheaper, tours on full-sized coaches are generally less personalized. Wherever a bus can go, so can your rental car, but on a tour you can relax and enjoy the scenery without worrying about driving. Also, tour drivers are very experienced with the area and know many stories and legends with which they annotate and enrich your trip. General-interest coach tours vary, but typical trips go to the Waimea Canyon and south coast sights, or combine these tours with a trip to the Wailua River and Fern Grotto. Each agency has its own routes and schedules, but all hit the major tourist sights. Rates some-times include entrance fees and lunch. A trip to the Waimea Canyon runs about $40, about the same for the Fern Grotto. Combining these two or going to the north shore runs about $60. Children's fares are about 25 percent less. Fares may vary according to the area of pick-up. Often a tour to the Fern Grotto is considered the highlight. Companies offering these sightseeing tours include **Polynesian Adventure Tours** (808/246-0122 or 800/622-3011, www.polyad.com); **Kauai Island Tours** (808/245-4777 or 800/733-4777); **Roberts Hawaii Tours** (800/831-5541, www.robertshawaii.com); and **Kauai Paradise Tours** (808/246-3999), which specializes in German narration.

Fanning Island trip on *Norwegian Wind*. In addition, *Pride of Aloha* and *Pride of America* (newly christened in June 2005) run seven-day round-trip cruises to the four main islands, making stops at Nawiliwili Harbor on Kaua'i, Honolulu on O'ahu, Kahului on Maui, and both Kona and Hilo on the Big Island. From summer 2006, *Pride of Hawaii* will be added to the fleet for these Hawaii-only routes. The itineraries of these ships differ somewhat, with some spending more time in port and others more time at sea. All the ships begin their journey at Honolulu; however, you may also start your trip on Maui for interisland routes. For specific information on routes, itineraries, and pricing, contact the company directly or work through a travel agent.

BY LAND

The most common way to get around Kaua'i is by rental car. The abundance of agencies keeps prices competitive. Kaua'i also has limited bus service; expensive taxis; reasonable bicycle, motorcycle and moped rentals; and the good old (legal) thumb. For bicycle, motorcycle, and moped rental companies, see the individual travel chapters in the "Explore" section.

Highway Overview

As Kaua'i is nearly round, there is one major highway that (nearly) circles the island. Starting in Lihu'e and running west, Hwy. 50, Kaumuali'i Highway, runs past Kekaha nearly to Polihale; running north, Hwy. 56, Kuhio Highway, goes as far as Ke'e Beach past Hanalei. From the far west end to the end of the road on the North Shore, it's about 70 miles and will take about two hours of driving at a comfortable speed. Only a few major roadways lead off of this highway. In and near Lihu'e, they are Rt. 570, Ahukini Road, which runs from the center of town to the airport; Rt. 51, Kapule Highway, leading from Hanama'ulu to Nawiliwili Harbor; Rt. 58, Nawiliwili Road, running from Kukui Grove Shopping Center also to Nawiliwili Harbor; and Rt. 583, Ma'alo Road, which goes to Wailua waterfall from Kapaia. North of Lihu'e, they are Rt. 580, Kuamo'o Road, running inland from Wailua to the Keahua Arboretum, and Rt. 581, Kamalu Road, which circles inland from Kapa'a around the backside of the "Sleeping Giant" to meet Rt. 580. Along the south shore, Rt. 520, Maluhia Road, leaves Rt. 50 at the Tunnel of Trees and runs down to Koloa and Po'ipu. Rt. 530, Koloa Road, connects Lawa'i and Koloa, and Rt. 540, Halewili Road, sweeps down through the coffee plantation, running from Kalaheo to 'Ele'ele. The longest and most significant highway running inland is Rt. 550, Waimea Canyon Drive, connecting Waimea to Koke'e State Park. A connector road, Rt. 552, Koke'e Road, runs uphill from Kekaha to meet Rt. 550.

Aside from these major roads, many smaller residential roads are found in the Kalaheo/Lawa'i/Omao area, in the uplands above Wailua and Kapa'a, and between Kilauea and Princeville.

Emergency Call Boxes

Spaced every few miles along the island's major highways are emergency call boxes connected directly to a police emergency response network. These telephones are to be used strictly for emergencies. They can be located by a yellow box on a tall pole topped by a small solar panel and blue light. They are located along Kuhio Highway, Rt. 56, and its extension, Rt. 560, which runs north from Lihu'e to the end of the road at Ke'e Beach on the north shore, and along Kaumuali'i Highway, Rt. 50, which runs west from Lihu'e past Kekaha on the west end. In addition, there are a few boxes along Koke'e Road, which goes up the mountain from Kekaha to Koke'e State Park.

Rental Cars

Rental car options in Hawaii are as numerous as anywhere in the states, from a subcompact to a full-size luxury land yacht. The most numerous seem to be midsize sedans, but convertibles and 4WD jeeps are very popular, and some vans and SUVs are also available. Nearly all have automatic transmissions and air-conditioning. Generally, you must be 21 years old—a few agencies will rent to 18-year-olds, while some require you to be 25 for certain vehicles. Those ages 21–24 will usually be charged an extra fee, which may be significant.

If you're traveling during the peak seasons of Christmas, Easter, or summer, absolutely reserve your car in advance. If you're going off-peak, you stand a very good chance of getting the car you want at a price you like once you land in the islands. You can get some sweet deals. To be on the safe side, and for your own peace of mind, it's generally best to book ahead.

All major car rental companies in Hawaii use flat rate pricing, which provides a fixed daily rate and unlimited mileage. Most car companies, local and national, offer special rates and deals, like AAA discounts. These deals are common, but don't expect rental companies to let you know about them. Make sure to inquire. The basic rates aren't your only charges, however. On top of the actual rental fee, you must pay an airport access fee, airport concession fee, state tax, and a road tax surcharge—in total, an additional 25–30 percent.

Most companies have child seats available for rent on a daily basis, $5 a day or $40–50 maximum, and can install right- or left-hand controls for handicapped drivers. Agencies generally require 48–72 hours advance notice to install hand controls.

Car Rental Agencies

The following major national firms maintain booths at the Lihu'e Airport. These companies have some reserved cars waiting at the airport, but shuttle most guests to the base yard to pick up their vehicles. Local companies offer airport pickup.

Dollar (808/245-3651 or 800/800-4000 worldwide, www.dollar.com) has an excellent reputation and very competitive prices. Dollar rents mostly Chrysler vehicles, as well as Jeeps and convertibles. Great weekly rates, and all major credit cards are accepted.

Alamo (808/246-0646 or 800/327-9633, www.goalamo.com) has good weekly rates and mostly GM cars.

National Car Rental (808/245-5636 or 800/227-7368 nationwide, www.nationalcar .com) features GM and Nissan cars and accepts all major credit cards.

Avis (808/245-3512 or 800/230-4898 nationwide, www.avis.com) features late-model GM cars as well as most imports and convertibles. Avis is the only company that main-

single-lane north shore coastal road bridge

tains a small booth at the Princeville Airport (808/826-9773).

Budget (808/245-9031 or 800/527-0700 worldwide, www.budget.com), offers competitive rates on a variety of late-model Ford and Lincoln-Mercury cars and specialty vehicles.

Hertz (808/245-3356 or 800/654-3011, www.hertz.com) is competitively priced with many fly/drive deals.

Thrifty (808/246-6252 or 800/847-4389 worldwide, www.thrifty.com) uses Chrysler vehicles.

Don't be misled by the name, because the locally owned franchise of **Rent-A-Wreck** (808/632-0741) at the Harbor Mall in Lihu'e can pick you up and put you into a quality used vehicle for $25/day and up. All vehicles are 1–5 years old and under warranty.

The Kaua'i Bus

One of the benefits to come out of the destruction caused by Hurricane 'Iniki was the establishment of limited public bus transportation. The 'Iniki Express, set up after the hurricane and free at one time, has morphed into the Kaua'i Bus, run by the Transportation Agency of the county Offices of Community Assistance (808/241-6410). Call 7 A.M.–5 P.M. Mon.–Sat. for a current route schedule, or check the county website (www.kauai.gov) for details—follow the prompts from the Home page. Operating times are 5:15 A.M.–7:15 P.M. Mon.–Fri., 7:15 A.M.–3:15 P.M. Sat. (no operation Sunday and holidays). The regular **fare** is $1.50 ($15 for a monthly pass) or $.75 for seniors, students, and people with disabilities if carrying identification. The bus will only pick-up and drop-off at designated bus stops and will not allow large bags or items—including oversize backpacks with metal frames and surfboards—but baby strollers are okay.

Each bus displays a route sign at the front and on its curb side. The Kaua'i Bus runs two main **routes** along the coast highway, north to Hanalei and west to Kekaha, with the addition of one circle route in Lihu'e and one route up to Kapahi above Kapa'a. Although buses have scheduled times, they do not run at regular intervals; there may be as little as a half hour or as much as two and a half hours between runs. Please check a current printed bus schedule. Route 100 runs from Kekaha to Lihu'e, and Route 200 makes the reverse run. One bus a day in each direction—early morning and late afternoon—dips down for a circle of Koloa and Po'ipu via Lawa'i before proceeding. Route 400 connects Hanalei to Lihu'e, and Route 500 does the reverse, while Route 600 runs from Lihu'e to Kapahi via Kapa'a and returns. The Lihu'e Extension, Route 700, 8 A.M.–3 P.M. only, starts at the Kukui Grove Shopping Center, runs down to Nawiliwili Harbor, and up Rice Street to the County Building. From there it goes along the highway to the Wilcox Memorial Hospital before returning to the center of town, Nawiliwili Harbor, and Kukui Grove Shopping Center. Saturday service is reduced by about half, with no service at all on Routes 600 and 700. One wonders just how long this bus system will maintain funding, as most of these buses seem to run nearly empty. If you do not have a rental car, it is possible to get around by bus, but it will not be convenient nor will it necessarily take you exactly where you want to go.

Travelers with Disabilities

The county Transportation Agency (808/241-6410) offers both public transportation with wheelchair-accessible buses and door-to-door "paratransit" services. Call for details and assistance.

The **Kauai Center for Independent Living** (808/245-4034), **Akita Enterprise** (808/245-5344), and **Polynesian Adventure Tours** (808/246-0122) all have lift-equipped vans that can be reserved and rented with about five days' notice. Each has different stipulations for

van use, so be sure to contact them directly with your needs.

Taxi

Taxis are all metered and charge a hefty price for their services; all have the same rates. While many are sedans, minivans are increasing in number. Airport taxis have a monopoly on pick-ups at the airport, although others can drop off there. Sample fares: $5–10 from Lihu'e to the airport; $35–40 from Lihu'e to Po'ipu; $15–20 from Lihu'e to Wailua; $20–25 from Lihu'e to Kapa'a; $60 from Lihu'e to Waimea; $72 from Lihu'e to Princeville; and $25 from Princeville to Ke'e Beach and the Kalalau trailhead. Reputable taxi companies include **Akiko's** (808/822-7588) in Kapa'a; **City Cab** (808/245-3227) and **Kauai Taxi** (808/246-9554) in Lihu'e; **Southshore Cab** (808/742-1525) in Poi'pu; and **North Shore Cab** (808/826-4118) and **Taxi Hanalei** (808/639-1188) in Hanalei.

For limousine service, try **Kauai Limo Corporation** (808/245-4855). On the north shore, call **Kauai North Shore Limousine** (808/826-6189).

Hitchhiking

Using your thumb to get around is legal on Kaua'i, but you must stay off the paved portion of the road. For short hops in and around the towns—like from Koloa to Po'ipu or from the airport to Lihu'e—thumbing may not be difficult. But getting out to the Kalalau Trail or to Polihale on the west end, when you're toting a backpack and appear to be going a longer distance, is tough. As on all the islands, your best chance of being picked up is by a visiting or local *haole*. Sometimes locals in pickup trucks will stop to give you a ride for short distances. Women *should not* hitch alone!

Tips for Travelers

TRAVELERS WITH DISABILITIES

A person with a disability can have a wonderful time in Hawaii; all that's needed is a little pre-planning. The following general advice should help your preparations.

Commission on Persons with Disabilities

This commission was designed with the express purpose of aiding handicapped people. It is a source of invaluable information and distributes self-help booklets, which are published jointly by the Disability and Communication Access Board and the Hawaii Centers for Independent Living. Any person with disabilities heading to Hawaii should write first or visit its offices on arrival. For the *Aloha Guide to Accessibility* (Part I is free; $3–5 charge for Parts II and III), write or visit Hawaii Centers for Independent Living (414 Kuwili St. #102, Honolulu, HI 96817, 808/522-5400). On Kaua'i, write Hawaii Centers for Independent Living (4340 Nawiliwili Rd., Lihu'e, HI 96766, 808/345-4034).

General Information

The key for a smooth trip is to make as many arrangements ahead of time as possible. Tell the transportation companies and hotels you'll be dealing with the nature of your disability in advance so they can make arrangements to accommodate you. Bring your medical records and notify medical establishments of your arrival if you'll be needing their services. Travel with a friend or make arrangements for an aide on arrival. Bring your own wheelchair if possible, and let airlines know if it is battery-powered; boarding some interisland carriers requires steps. They'll board you early on special lifts, but they must know that you're coming. Many hotels and restaurants accommodate persons with disabilities, but always call ahead just to make sure.

Kaua'i Services

At Lihu'e Airport, handicapped parking is available in the public parking lot across from the main terminal building. All rental car agencies can install hand controls on their cars if given enough notice—usually 48–72 hours. There are few sidewalks and fewer cut curbs on Kaua'i. Special **parking permits** are available from the Drivers Licensing office in Lihu'e at 444 Rice Street; your own state placard will be honored here. Medical equipment rentals are available from: **Gammie Homecare** (808/632-2333, www.gammie.com), **Home Infusion Associates** (808/245-3787), and **Kuhio Home Health** (808/822-0927). For medical support services, contact **Kauai Center for Independent Living** (808/245-4034).

TRAVELING WITH CHILDREN

No need to leave home without the baby—no matter how appealing a few weeks away from that little bundle of joy might seem. If you don't have room to take everything you will need for your child, you can find it in Kaua'i. A few companies, like **Baby Ready Rental** (808/823-8008 or 800/599-8008, www.readyrentals.com), specialize in the needs of little ones and rent everything from high chairs to strollers and play pens to cribs.

ALTERNATIVE WAYS TO THE ISLAND
Ecotours to Hawaii

Sierra Club Trips offers Hawaii trips for nature lovers interested in an outdoor experience. Various trips include birding on the Big Island, and kayak and camping trips on Kaua'i. All trips are led by experienced guides and are open to Sierra Club members only ($35 per year to join). For information contact the Sierra Club Outing Department (85 2nd St., 2nd Fl., San Francisco, CA 94105, 415/977-5522, www.sierraclub.org/outings).

DRIVING TIPS

Wear your seat belt – it's the law! Police keep an eye out for miscreants and often ticket those who do not use their restraints. Protect your small children as you would at home with car seats. Either bring one from home or rent one from a car rental company.

Mile markers are great for pinpointing sights and beaches. The lower number on these small signs is the highway number, so you can always make sure that you're on the right road.

Gas prices in Hawaii are consistently above the national average, sometimes as much as $.30-.40 a gallon. Prices may be a few cents more per gallon in communities that are more distant from the main population centers.

Many people on the roads in Hawaii are tourists and can be unsure about where they're going. Slow down, be aware, and drive defensively.

In Hawaii, drivers don't generally honk their horns except to say hello or signal an emergency. It's considered rude, and honking to hurry someone might earn you a knuckle sandwich. Hawaiian drivers reflect the climate: they're relaxed and polite. Often on smaller roads, they'll brake to let you turn left when they're coming at you. They may assume you'll do the same, so be ready, after a perfunctory turn signal from another driver, for him or her to turn across your lane. The more rural the area, the more apt this is to happen. Don't expect it in the large cities.

Respect Do Not Enter and Private Property signs – *Kapu* means the same thing. Stay off cane haul roads. These too are on private property.

Car rental agencies state that their cars are not to be driven off paved roads – read your policy. This seems absolutely ridiculous for 4WD vehicles, but true nonetheless. There should be some reasonable exceptions to this, such as the well-used dirt road to Polihale State Park, which is specifically open to traffic,

and some of the graded gravel roads in Koke'e State Park. Still, it's best to check with your rental car agency to verify its policy.

When a road is signed for 4WD only, assume that's the case for a good reason.

Speed limits change often along the highways of Kaua'i. Police routinely check the speed of traffic by use of radar equipment. Be aware of this so you don't go home with more than a suntan. Because the speed limit changes frequently and there are few long stretches of highway, cruise control is all but useless.

Believe it or not, Kaua'i is afflicted by a type of **rush hour traffic** on weekday mornings about 6 A.M.-8:30 A.M. and in the afternoons 3-5 P.M. Weekends, so far, have escaped this peril. This heavy traffic is due principally to workers commuting into Lihu'e from as far east as Kapa'a and west from the Koloa/Po'ipu turnoff. Three-lane sections of the highway are marked with bright orange plastic cones, with two lanes open to traffic going into Lihu'e in the morning and two lanes of traffic going out of town in the afternoon. Watch for "contra-flow" road signs indicating the sections of highway with this traffic pattern and the exact times of day that it is in force. Also, drive with caution when workers are out on the roadway setting these cones and doing road construction.

To ease some traffic congestion, two highway bypasses have been constructed on the island. The first is the Koloa-Po'ipu Bypass, which runs from just north of Koloa town to the eastern end of Po'ipu, rerouting some traffic from the very busy Po'ipu Beach Road. The second is the Kapa'a Bypass, which starts in Wailua near the Coconut Marketplace and runs through former cane fields to the far north end of Kapa'a, missing the concentrated commercial district between these two points. This road is open 5 A.M.-9 P.M. only.

TIME-SHARES

While time-share accommodations are a factor on all the major islands except Lana'i, Kaua'i has taken to the concept in a big way. Over 30 percent of the state's total time-share units (about 8 percent of the state's total accommodations units) are on the Garden Island. Whether condo apartments or hotel suites, these units are handled in various ways. Generally speaking, specific units are bought for a specified length of time during the year, usually in one-week increments, guaranteeing you vacation accommodations year after year – whether you use them or not. With some organizations, these units can be traded for rooms in other associated time-share complexes around the country (or world). If you do not use your time-share during your time slot, most overseeing companies can rent it for you for that time. With some time-share groups, no specific units are negotiated, but points are bought and these can be used to reserve space wherever the company has properties.

The price of purchasing a time-share unit varies based on its luxury and location, and there will be some additional annual fees involved for maintenance and administration. Units are sold directly through time-share companies, some real estate agents, and time-share resale offices. Time-share companies have requirements for sales that may include, among other things, ownership of a house, specific minimum income level, and U.S. citizenship.

One of the favorite means employed by time-share companies to get you to look at their properties is to offer greatly reduced activity prices – you'll see these activity booths all over the island – in exchange for your attendance at a seminar and sales session. If you don't mind the sales pitch and accompanying pressure to purchase, try one out. Others wouldn't waste their time with such dealings while on vacation, even if it meant reduced activity rates.

Educational Trips

Not a tour company per se, but an educational opportunity, **Elderhostel Hawaii** offers short-term programs on five of the Hawaiian Islands. Different programs focus on history, culture, cuisine, and the environment in association with one of the colleges or universities in the islands. Most programs use hotels for accommodations. For information, contact Elderhostel (11 Avenue de Lafayette, Boston, MA 02111-1746, 877/426-8056, www.elderhostel.org).

PREVENTING THEFT

From the minute you sit behind the wheel of your rental car you'll be warned not to leave valuables unattended and to lock your car up tighter than a drum. Signs warning about theft at most major tourist attractions help to fuel your paranoia. Many hotel and condo rooms offer safes, so you can lock your valuables away and relax while getting sunburned. The majority of theft in Hawaii is of the "sneak thief" variety. If you leave your hotel door unlocked, a camera sitting on the seat of your rental car, or valuables on your beach towel, you'll be inviting a very obliging thief to pad away with your stuff. You'll have to take precautions, but they won't be anything like those employed in rougher areas of the world—just normal American precautions. Hawaii's reputation is much worse than the reality. Besides, Hawaiians are still among the friendliest, most giving, and understanding people on earth.

If you must walk alone at night, stay on the main streets in well-lit areas. Always lock your hotel door and windows and place valuable jewelry in the hotel safe. When you leave your hotel for the beach, there is absolutely no reason to carry all your travelers checks, credit cards, or a big wad of money. Just take what you'll need for drinks and lunch. If you're uptight about leaving money in your beach bag, stick it in your bathing suit. American money is just as negotiable if it's damp. Don't leave your camera on the beach unattended. While sightseeing in your shiny new rental car, which immediately brands you as a tourist, again, don't take more than what you'll need for the day. Many people lock valuables away in the trunk, but remember that most good car thieves can "jimmy" it as quickly as you can open it with your key.

Campers face special problems because their entire scene is open to thievery. Most campgrounds don't have any security, but who, after all, wants to fence an old tent or a used sleeping bag? Many tents have zippers that can be secured with a small padlock. In the end, you must just take what precautions that you can and trust the goodness of others.

Health and Safety

In a survey published some years ago by *Science Digest,* Hawaii was cited as the healthiest state in the United States in which to live. Indeed, Hawaiian citizens live longer than those of anywhere else in America: men to 76 years and women to 82. Lifestyle, heredity, and diet help with these figures, but Hawaii is still an oasis in the middle of the ocean, and germs just have a tougher time getting there. There are no cases of malaria, cholera, or yellow fever. Because of a strict quarantine law, rabies is also nonexistent. On the other hand, tooth decay—perhaps because of the wide use of sugar and the enzymes present in certain tropical fruits—is 30 percent above the national average. Also obesity and related heart problems, as well as hard drug use—especially "ice"—is prevalent among native Hawaiians. With the perfect weather, a multitude of fresh-air activities, soothing negative ionization from the sea, and a generally relaxed and carefree lifestyle, everyone feels better there. Hawaii is just what the doctor ordered: a beautiful, natural health spa. That's one of its main drawing cards. The food and tap water are perfectly safe, and the air quality is some of the best in the country.

Handling the Sun

Don't become a victim of your own exuberance. People can't wait to strip down and lie on the sand like beached whales, but the tropical sun will burn you to a cinder if you're silly. The burning rays come through more easily in Hawaii because of the sun's angle, and you don't feel them as much because there's always a cool breeze. The worst part of the day is 10 A.M.–3 P.M. Kaua'i lies at 22 degrees north latitude, not even close to the equator, but it's still over 1,000 miles south of sunny southern California beaches. Force yourself to go slowly. Don't worry; you'll be able to flaunt your best souvenir, your golden Hawaiian tan, to your green-with-envy friends when you get home. It's better than showing them a boiled lobster body with peeling skin! There is, of course, no safe way to tan under the sun, but if you do want to get yours the old-fashioned way, ease into it. If your skin is snowflake white, 15 minutes per side on the first day is plenty. Increase by 15-minute intervals every day, which will allow you a full hour per side by the fourth day. Have faith; this is enough to give you a golden, uniform tan. If you lie out on the beach, are simply out in the sun during the day, if you're off hiking or kayaking, or have rented a convertible car (an unexpected culprit for sunburn), use sunblock lotion that has greater strength than you use at home—most people recommend SPF 25 or higher—and reapply every couple of hours. If you do burn, try taking aspirin as quickly as you can. No one knows exactly what it does, but it seems to provide some relief. Alternately, apply a cold compress or aloe juice, but be careful with aloe because it may stain clothing.

Whether out on the beach, hiking in the mountains, or just strolling around town, be very aware of dehydration. The sun (and wind) tend to sap your energy and your store of liquid. Bottled water in various sizes is readily available in all parts of Hawaii. Be sure to carry some with you or stop at a store or restaurant for a fill-'er-up.

Don't forget about your head and eyes. Use your sunglasses and wear a brimmed hat. Some people lay a towel over their neck and shoulders when hiking and others will stick a scarf under their hat and let it drape down over their shoulders to provide some protection.

Haole Rot

A peculiar condition caused by the sun is referred to locally as *haole* rot. It's called this because it supposedly affects only white people, but you'll notice some dark-skinned people with the same condition. Basically, the skin becomes mottled with white spots that refuse to tan. You get a blotchy effect, mostly on the shoulders and back. Dermatologists have a fancy name for it, and they'll give you a fancy prescription with a very fancy price tag to cure it. It's common knowledge throughout the islands that Selsun Blue shampoo has an ingredient that stops the white mottling effect. Just wash your hair with it and then make sure to rub the lather over the affected areas, and it should clear up.

Bugs

Everyone, in varying degrees, has an aversion to vermin and creepy crawlers. Hawaii isn't infested with a wide variety, but it does have its share. Mosquitoes were unknown in the islands until their larvae stowed away in the water barrels of the *Wellington* in 1826 and were introduced at Lahaina. They bred in the tropical climate and rapidly spread to all the islands. They are a particular nuisance in the rainforests. Be prepared; bring a natural repellent like citronella oil, available in most health stores on the islands, or a commercial product available in groceries and drugstores. Campers will be happy to have mosquito coils to burn at night as well.

Cockroaches are very democratic insects. They hassle all strata of society equally. They breed well in Hawaii, and most hotels are at war with them, trying desperately to keep them from being spotted by guests. One comforting thought is that in Hawaii they aren't a sign of filth or dirty housekeeping. They love the climate like everyone else, and it's a real problem keeping them under control.

WATER SAFETY

Hawaii has one very sad claim to fame: more people drown here than anywhere else in the world. Moreover, there are dozens of victims yearly with broken necks and backs or with injuries from scuba and snorkeling accidents. These statistics shouldn't keep you out of the sea, because it is indeed beautiful—and benevolent in most cases—and a major reason to go to Hawaii. But if you're foolish, the sea will bounce you like a basketball and suck you away for good. The best remedy is to avoid situations you can't handle. Don't let anyone dare you into a situation that makes you uncomfortable. "Macho men" who know nothing about the power of the sea will be tumbled like Cabbage Patch Kids dolls in short order. Ask lifeguards or beach attendants about conditions, and follow their advice. If local people refuse to go in, there's a good reason. Even experts get in trouble in Hawaiian waters. Some beaches are as gentle as a lamb; others, especially on the north coasts during the winter months, are frothing giants.

While beachcombing, or especially when walking out on rocks, never turn your back to the sea. Be aware of undertows (the waves drawing back into the sea). They can knock you off your feet. Study the sea for rocks, breakers, reefs, and riptides. Look for ocean currents, especially those within reefs that can cause riptides when the water washes out a channel. Observe the water well before you enter. Note where others are swimming or snorkeling and go there. When snorkeling, wear a T-Shirt. It may save your back from major sunburn. Don't swim alone if possible, and obey all warning signs. Come in *before* you get tired.

When the wind comes up, get out. Stay out of the water during periods of high surf. High surf often creates riptides that can pull you out to sea. Riptides are powerful currents,

Lifeguard stands are staffed at numerous beaches around the island.

ROBERT NILSEN

like rivers in the sea, which can drag you out. Mostly they peter out not too far from shore, and you can often see their choppy waters on the surface. If caught in a "rip," don't panic or fight to swim directly against it. You'll lose and only exhaust yourself. Swim diagonally across it, while going along with it, and try to stay parallel to the shore until you are out of the strong pull.

When bodysurfing, never ride straight in; come to shore at a 45-degree angle. Remember, waves come in sets. Little ones can be followed by giants, so watch the action awhile instead of plunging right in. Standard procedure is to duck under a breaking wave. You can survive even thunderous oceans using this technique. Don't try to swim through a heavy froth and never turn your back and let it smash you.

Stay off of coral. Standing on coral damages it, as does breaking it with your hands, and it might give you a nasty infection.

Leave the fish, turtles, and seals alone. Fish should never be encouraged to feed from humans. Green sea turtles and seals are endan-gered species and stiff fines can be levied on those who knowingly disturb them. Have a great time looking, but give them space.

Hawaiians want to entertain you, and they want you to be safe. The county has produced the *Kaua'i Beach Safety Guide,* a brochure with general water safety tips and specific cautions for most beaches on the island. Pick up a copy when you arrive and spend a few minutes looking over it. It's time well spent. Also, the county doesn't put up ocean conditions signs at beaches just to waste money. They're there for your safety. Pay heed. The last rule is, "If in doubt, stay out."

Yikes!

Sharks live in all the oceans of the world. Most mind their own business and stay away from shore. Hawaiian sharks are well fed—on fish—and don't usually bother with unsavory humans. If you encounter a shark, don't panic! Never thrash around because this will trigger their attack instinct. If they come close, scream loudly.

Portuguese man-of-wars put out long, floating tentacles that sting if they touch you. It seems that many floating jellyfish are blown into shore by winds on the eighth, ninth, and 10th days after the full moon. Don't wash the sting off with freshwater, as this will only aggravate it. Hot salt water will take away the sting, as will alcohol (either the drinking or rubbing kind), lemon juice, after-shave lotion, meat tenderizer, or MSG, which can be found in any supermarket or Chinese restaurant.

Coral can give you a nasty cut, and it's known for causing infections because it's a living organism. Wash the cut immediately and apply an antiseptic. Keep it clean and covered, and watch for infection.

Poisonous sea urchins, such as the lacquer-black *wana,* can be beautiful creatures. They are found in shallow tidepools and will hurt you if you step on them. Their spines will break off, enter your foot, and burn like blazes. There are cures. Vinegar and wine poured on the wound will stop the burning. If those are not available, the Hawaiian solution is urine.

It might seem ignominious to have someone pee on your foot, but it'll put the fire out. The spines will disintegrate in a few days, and there are generally no long-term effects.

Hawaiian reefs also have their share of moray eels. These creatures are ferocious in appearance but will never initiate an attack. You'd have to poke around in their holes while snorkeling or scuba diving to get them to attack. Sometimes, this is inadvertent on the diver's part, so be careful where you stick your hand while underwater.

Present in streams, ponds, and muddy soil, **Leptospirosis** is a *freshwater*-borne bacteria, deposited by the urine of infected animals. From two to 20 days after the bacteria enter the body, there is a *sudden* onset of fever accompanied by chills, sweats, headache, and sometimes vomiting and diarrhea. Preventive measures include staying out of freshwater sources where cattle and other animals wade and drink, not swimming in freshwater if you have an open cut, and not drinking stream water.

MEDICAL SERVICES
Hospitals
The island's principal medical facility is the full-service **Wilcox Memorial Hospital** (3420 Kuhio Hwy., Lihu'e, 808/245-1100 or 808/245-1010 for emergencies). A smaller facility is **West Kaua'i Medical Center** (4643 Waimea Canyon Dr., Waimea, 808/338-9431), which is also open 24 hours for medical emergencies and surgical needs.

Medical Clinics
Medical services are also available from **Kaua'i Medical Clinic** (3420 B Kuhio Hwy. in Lihu'e, 808/245-1500; after hours 808/245-1831), which is associated with Wilcox Memorial Hospital. The urgent-care walk-in clinic runs 9 A.M.–4 P.M. Mon.–Sat. and 10 A.M.–3 P.M. Sunday; the regular clinic runs 8 A.M.–5 P.M. weekdays and 8 A.M. to noon weekends. There are additional offices in 'Ele'ele, Kapa'a, Koloa, Kukui Grove Shopping Center, and Kilauea.

About half a dozen other clinics operate around the island. Specifics are found in the appropriate travel chapter in the "Explore" section.

Alternately, check out the **Natural Health and Pain Relief Clinic** (3095 Akahi, 808/245-2277) in Kapa'a.

Pharmacies
Longs Drugs in Lihu'e and Kapa'a have pharmacies. Independent pharmacies are located in Waimea, Kalaheo, Koloa, Lihu'e, Kapa'a, and Kilauea. Contact information is found in the appropriate travel chapter in the "Explore" section.

Alternative Health Care
Many people say they are drawn to the healing powers of Kaua'i. Like all the islands, Kaua'i does seem to have restorative energy. The ancient Hawaiians knew natural pharmacology and could cure many ailments and diseases, and their healing hands would poke and prod tired muscles with *lomi lomi* massage. Some non-Hawaiians who have come to live on the islands have tapped into this knowledge, and others have brought their own unique experiences that pertain to the healing arts. First, perhaps, were acupuncture and Oriental medicine brought by Asians who came to work the fields. Much later it was chiropractic care, western massage, bodywork, naturopathy, reflexology, and a whole host of modern paths. All sorts of alternative medicine—Hawaiian, Asian, and Western—are available on Kaua'i, but aside from those who practice massage (there is a list of several pages in the phone book), you'll have to do some research on your own to contact practitioners. To get you started, have a look at Yellow Pages listings or check out the following to see if it meets your needs: **Kauai Center for Holistic Medicine and Research** (4504 Kukui St., Kapa'a, 808/823-0994). Alternately, look at the information racks at the airport and public bulletin boards for advertisements and business cards.

Information and Services

MONEY
Currency
U.S. currency is among the drabbest in the world. It's all the same size, with little variation in color; those unfamiliar with it should spend some time getting acquainted so they don't make costly mistakes. U.S. coins in use are: one cent (penny), five cents (nickel), 10 cents (dime), 25 cents (quarter), 50 cents (half dollar), and $1; paper currency is $1, $2 (uncommon), $5, $10, $20, $50, and $100. Bills larger than $100 are not in common usage. Since 1996, new designs have been issued for the $100, $50, $20, $10, and $5 bills. Both the old and new bills are accepted as valid currency.

Banks
Full-service bank hours are generally 8:30 A.M.–4 P.M. Monday–Thursday and until 6 P.M. Friday. There are no weekend hours, and weekday hours will be a bit longer at counters in grocery stores and other outlets. All main towns on Kaua'i have one or more banks: Waimea, Hanapepe, Koloa, Lihu'e, Kapa'a, and Princeville. Virtually all branch banks have ATM machines for 24-hour service, and these can be found at some shopping centers and other venues around the island. ATMs work only when the Hawaiian bank you choose to use is on an affiliate network with your home bank. Of most value to travelers, banks sell and cash travelers checks, give cash advances on credit cards, and exchange and sell foreign currency (sometimes with a fee).

Travelers Checks
Travelers checks are accepted throughout Hawaii at hotels, restaurants, car rental agencies, and most stores and shops. However, to be readily acceptable they should be in U.S. currency. Some larger hotels that frequently have Japanese and Canadian guests will accept their currency. Banks accept foreign currency travelers checks, but it'll mean an extra trip and inconvenience. It's best to get most of your travelers checks in $20–100 denominations; anything larger will be harder to cash in smaller shops and boutiques, though not in hotels.

Credit Cards
More and more business is transacted in Hawaii using credit cards. Almost every form of accommodation, shop, restaurant, and amusement accepts them. For renting a car they're a must. With "credit card insurance" readily available, they're as safe as travelers checks and even more convenient. Write down the numbers of your cards in case they're stolen. Don't rely on them completely, because there are some establishments—many bed-and-breakfasts, for example—that won't accept them or perhaps won't accept the kind you carry.

Taxes
Hawaii does not have a state sales tax, but it does have a general excise tax that runs at four percent, and this will usually be added to most sales transactions. In addition, there is an accommodations tax of 7.25 percent, so approximately 11.4 percent will be added to your hotel bill when you check out.

COMMUNICATIONS AND MEDIA
Post Offices
Normal business hours are 8 A.M.–4:30 P.M. Monday–Friday, 9 A.M.–1 P.M. Saturday, although some branch offices now have slightly different hours, particularly on Saturday. The central post office on Kaua'i is at 4441 Rice St., Lihu'e. Main branches are located at Kapa'a, Koloa, Waimea, Princeville, and Hanalei, with nearly a dozen others scattered throughout the island. Larger hotels and condominiums also offer limited postal services.

Telephone
The telephone system on the main islands is

modern and comparable to any system on the Mainland. Any phone call to a number on that island is a **local call;** it's **long distance** when dialing to another island. As they do everywhere else in the United States, long-distance rates for land lines go down at 5 P.M. and again at 11 P.M. until 8 A.M. the next morning. Rates are cheapest from Friday at 5 P.M. until Monday at 8 A.M. Local calls from public telephones cost 50 cents. Public telephones are found at hotels, street booths, restaurants, most public buildings, and some beach parks. It is common to have a phone in most hotel rooms and condominiums, though a service charge is usually collected, even on local calls. Emergency calls are always free. You can "direct dial" from Hawaii to the Mainland and more than 160 foreign countries. Undersea cables and satellite communications ensure top-quality phone service. Toll-free calls are preceded by 800/, 888/, 877/, or 866/; there is no charge to the calling party. Many are listed in this book.

For directory assistance, dial: 411 (local), 555-1212 (interisland), area code/555-1212 (Mainland), or 800/555-1212 (toll-free). **The area code for all the islands of Hawaii is 808.**

Newspapers

There is one main island newspaper on Kaua'i, *The Garden Island* (www.kauaiworld.com). This paper is published daily and sells for 50 cents and $1.50 on Sunday. It can be picked up at numerous stands around the island.

Hawaii's two main English-language dailies are the *Honolulu Star Bulletin* (www.starbulletin.com) and the *Honolulu Advertiser* (www.honoluluadvertiser.com). These are also available at stands around the island for $0.75 daily or $2 on Sunday. *USA Today* and other papers with nationwide distribution, as well as some international newspapers, can be picked up at Borders Books in Lihu'e.

Kaua'i Radio Stations

The following stations are broadcast on Kaua'i. Some high-powered stations from O'ahu can be picked up on Kaua'i as well.

KONG 570 AM: news, talk, and sports

KUAI 720 AM: contemporary, sports, surf reports, requests, some Hawaiian oldies

KKCR 91.9 and 90.9 FM: nonprofit community radio station with various formats

KONG 93.5 FM: the "big gorilla" on the island—contemporary and requests

KSRF 95.9 FM: "Surf"; island sounds

KFMN 96.9 FM: adult contemporary

KITH 98.9 FM: island sounds

KTOH 99.9 FM: oldies from the 1950s to the 1990s

KSHK 103.3 FM: "Shaka"; classic rock and roll

Libraries

The Kaua'i central **library** is at 4344 Hardy St., Lihu'e, 808/241-3222. Branch libraries are located in Hanapepe, Kapa'a, Koloa, Princeville, and Waimea. Hours of operation vary for each library, so check with each branch for times and services. Library cards are available free for Hawaii state residents and military personnel stationed in Hawaii, $25 for nonresidents (valid for five years), and $10 for three months for visitors. Free Internet access is available to library cardholders only.

Bookstores

The only major bookstore on Kaua'i, located in the Kukui Grove Shopping Center in Lihu'e, is **Borders Books and Music** (808/246-0862, open every day at 9 A.M., it closes at 10 P.M. Mon.–Thurs., at 11 P.M. Fri.–Sat., and at 8 P.M. Sun.). This store is an excellent full-service bookshop, music center, and coffee bar. Along with the usual array of books, maps, and newspapers are the fullest Hawaiiana section and one of the most thorough Hawaiian music sections on the island.

Of the independent shops, that with the widest selection of Hawaiiana and Kaua'iana is the gift shop at the **Kaua'i Museum.** Others to check for books on these subjects are the **Koke'e Natural History Museum** in Koke'e State Park, the **National Tropical Botanical Garden Visitor Center** in Po'ipu, the **Lumaha'i Garden Visitor Center** west of Ha'ena, and the **Kilauea Lighthouse Visitor**

Center in Kilauea. Numerous gift shops throughout the island and hotel sundries shops also carry books on Hawaiian subjects.

Books on health, cooking, natural foods, and other related subjects can be found at **Papaya's Natural Food and Cafe** in Kapaʻa and Hanalei.

For books on diving, snorkeling, reef fish, and marine topics, check dive shops and water sport activity shops. Some outdoor adventure shops carry books on camping, hiking, and natural history.

Internet Access

Most hotels offer reasonably priced Internet access to their guests through a business center. Some other accommodations also make access available, but not all do. You may have to look elsewhere. If you have a Hawaii state library card, you can use dedicated library computers free. The Waimea Visitor and Technology Center also offers free Internet access. Otherwise try Kokua Business Center in the Chamber of Commerce building in Lihuʻe, Business Support Services in Kapaʻa, or any number of Internet cafés around the island. Although fees vary, you'll be looking at about $3 per 15 minutes.

TOURIST INFORMATION
Hawaii Visitors Bureau

The Hawaii Visitors Bureau, or HVB (www.gohawaii.com), is a top-notch organization

Signs like this mark important historical sites around the island.

providing help and information to all of Hawaii's visitors. Anyone contemplating a trip to Hawaii should visit a nearby office or check out its website for any specific information that might be required. The HVB's advice and excellent brochures on virtually every facet of living in, visiting, or simply enjoying Hawaii are free. The material offered is too voluminous to list, but for basics, request

BED-AND-BREAKFAST RENTAL AGENCIES

One of the most experienced agencies, **Bed And Breakfast Honolulu (Statewide)** (3242 Kaohinani Dr., Honolulu, HI 96817, 808/595-7533, fax 808/595-2030 or 800/288-4666, www.hawaiibnb.com, rainbow@hawaiibnb.com), owned and operated by Mary Lee and Gene Bridges, began in 1982. Since then, they've become masters at finding visitors the perfect accommodations to match your desires, needs, and pocketbooks. **All Is-** lands Bed and Breakfast (808/263-2342, fax 808/263-0308 or 800/542-0344, www.all-islands.com, inquiries@all-islands.com) can also match your needs up with numerous homes on Kauaʻi. **Hawaii's Best Bed and Breakfast** (P.O. Box 485, Laupahoehoe, HI 96764, 808/962-0100, fax 808/962-6360 or 800/262-9912, http://bestbnb.com, reservations@bestbnb.com) has listings all over the state.

individual island brochures, maps, vacation planners (also on the web at www.hshawaii.com), and an all-island members directory of accommodations, restaurants, entertainment, and transportation. Allow two to three weeks for requests to be answered.

HVB Offices Statewide

Statewide offices include: **HVB Administrative Office** (2270 Kalakaua Ave., Suite 801, Honolulu, 808/923-1811), **O'ahu Visitors Bureau** (733 Bishop St., Suite 1872, Honolulu, 808/524-0722 or 877/525-6242, www.visit-oahu.com), **Big Island HVB, Hilo Branch** (250 Keawe St., Hilo, 808/961-5797 or 800/648-2441, www.bigisland.org), **Big Island HVB, Kona Branch** (250 Waikoloa Beach Dr., Suite B-15, Waikoloa, 808/886-1655), **Kaua'i HVB** (4334 Rice St., Suite 101, Lihu'e, 808/245-3971 or 800/262-1400, www.kauaivisitorsbureau.org), and **Maui HVB** (1727 Wili Pa Loop, Wailuku, 808/244-3530 or 800/525-6284, www.visitmaui.com).

Two other helpful organizations are the **Moloka'i Visitors Association** (808/553-3876 or 800/800-6367 Mainland, www.molokai-hawaii.com) and **Destination Lana'i** (808/565-7600 or 800/947-4774, www.visitlanai.net).

Additional online information pertaining to the island of Kaua'i can be found at the official **County of Kaua'i** tourism website: www.Kauai-hawaii.com.

Free Tourist Literature

Free **tourist literature** and the narrow-format, magazine-style *This Week Kauai, Spotlight's Kauai Gold,* and *Kauai Activities and Attractions* are available at the airport, tourist information stands, and shopping centers around the island. They come out monthly or quarterly and contain money-saving coupons, island maps, and information on local events, activities, shopping, and restaurants. *Kauai Beach Press* has similar content with the addition of stories but is in a newspaper format. Other such magazines and guides appear now and again at the same locations. With a focus on activities and fun things to do, *101 Things to Do on Kauai* is a great resource and also has money-saving coupons. *Menu* is an informative magazine that lists restaurants and details of their menus. *Kauai Drive Guide* is available from the car rental agencies and contains tips, coupons, and good maps. The Hawaii AAA *Tourbook* is also very useful. Other publications of interest are the *Kauai Visitor Magazine* and the in-flight magazines of Aloha and Hawaiian Airlines.

Maps

Aside from the simple maps in the ubiquitous free tourist literature, the Kaua'i Visitors Bureau, Hawaiian Airlines, and other organizations put out folding pocket maps of the island that are available free at the airport and tourist brochure racks around the island. Various Kaua'i island and street maps are available at Borders Books at Kukui Grove Shopping Center in Lihu'e. Perhaps the best and most detailed of these island maps is the University of Hawai'i Press reference map of Kaua'i. These maps can be found at gift and sundries shops around the island, at Borders Books, and at the Kaua'i Museum gift shop. The Kaua'i Museum gift shop also carries USGS maps. If you are looking for detail, the best street map atlas of Kaua'i is *The Ready Mapbook of Kaua'i* by Odyssey Publishing.

Although it has much more detail than would be useful for the average tourist, those planning to spend a good deal of time hiking should consider getting a copy of the *Kaua'i Recreational Trail Map* from the state Division of Forestry and Wildlife office in Lihu'e. This office also has map and trail description handouts for trails in the Na Ala Hele state trail system. Also useful and very detailed is the *Northwestern Kaua'i Recreation Map* by Earthwalk Press, available at Borders Books and some gift shops. This and other hiking maps are also available at the Koke'e Natural History Museum, which is near many of the best hiking trails on the island.

Film and Processing

Photographic film—print and slide, color and

black and white—is available on Kaua'i, but color print film is most widely available. The island's few camera shops carry the widest variety and may be the only ones who carry slide film, but print film can also be found at gift shops, sundries stores, most activity outlets, and general merchandise stores throughout the island. By and large, the cost of film is slightly more expensive in Hawaii than on the Mainland; the cost of developing is roughly the same. There is no camera repair service on Kaua'i. Parts and accessories, aside from new camera bodies and their accompanying lenses, are difficult to come by.

For one-hour service print film developing, see **Longs Drugs, Kmart,** or one of the independent shops listed in the travel chapters of this book. Slide film is sent to Honolulu to be developed.

WEIGHTS AND MEASURES

Hawaii, like all of the United States, employs the "English method" of measuring weights and distances. Basically, dry weights are in ounces and pounds; liquid measures are in ounces, quarts, and gallons; and distances are measured in inches, feet, yards, and miles. The metric system is known but is not in general use.

Electricity

The same electrical current is in use in Hawaii as on the U.S. Mainland and is uniform throughout the islands. The system functions on 110 volts, 60 cycles of alternating current (AC). Appliances from Japan will work, but there is some danger that they will burn out, while those requiring the normal European voltage of 220 will not work.

Time Zones

There is no daylight saving time in Hawaii. When daylight saving time is not observed on the Mainland, Hawaii is two hours behind

the West Coast, four hours behind the Midwest, five hours behind the East Coast, and 11 hours behind Germany. Hawaii, being just east of the International Date Line, is almost a full day behind most Asian and Oceanian cities. Hours behind these countries and cities are: Singapore, 18 hours; Japan, 19 hours; Sydney, 20 hours; New Zealand, 22 hours; Fiji, 22 hours.

LOCAL RESOURCES
Emergencies

For the police, fire department, and ambulance anywhere on Kaua'i, dial **911.**

For **nonemergency police** assistance and information dial 808/241-1711.

The **Coast Guard Search and Rescue** can be reached at 800/552-6458.

In case of **natural disaster** such as hurricanes or tsunami on Kaua'i, call 808/241-6336.

The **Sexual Assault Crisis Line** number is 808/245-4144.

Weather, Surf, and Time

For a recorded message 24 hours a day call: 808/245-6001 for weather; 808/245-3564 for the marine and surf report; or 808/245-0212 for the time of day.

Consumer Protection

If you encounter problems finding accommodations or experience bad service or downright rip-offs, try the following: the Kaua'i Chamber of Commerce (808/245-7363, www.kauaichamber.org), the Office of Consumer Protection on O'ahu (808/274-3141), or the Better Business Bureau of Hawaii on O'ahu (877/222-6551, www.hawaii.bbb.org).

Camping Permits

For state park permits, dial 800/274-3444; for county park permits, dial 800/241-4463.

RESOURCES

Glossary

HAWAIIAN

The following list gives you a "taste" of Hawaiian and provides a basic vocabulary of words in common usage that you are likely to hear. Becoming familiar with them is not a strict necessity, but they will definitely enhance your experience and make talking with local people more congenial. Many islanders spice their speech with certain words and you too can use them just as soon as you feel comfortable. You might even discover some Hawaiian words that are so perfectly expressive they'll become regular parts of your vocabulary. Some Hawaiian words have even been absorbed into the English language and are found in English dictionaries. The definitions given below are not exhaustive, but are generally considered the most common.

'a'a rough clinker lava. 'A'a has become the correct geological term to describe this type of lava found anywhere in the world.

'ae yes

ahupua'a pie-shaped land divisions running from mountain to sea that were governed by *konohiki*, local *ali'i* who owed their allegiance to a reigning chief

aikane friend; pal; buddy

'aina land; the binding spirit to all Hawaiians. Love of the land is paramount in traditional Hawaiian beliefs.

akamai smart; clever; wise

akua a god, or simply "divine"

ali'i a Hawaiian chief or noble

aloha the most common greeting in the islands; can mean both hello and good-bye, welcome and farewell. It can also mean romantic love, affection, or best wishes.

anuenue rainbow

'a'ole no

'aumakua a personal or family god, often an ancestral spirit

auwe alas; ouch! When a great chief or loved one died, it was a traditional wail of mourning.

'awa also known as *kava*, a mildly intoxicating traditional drink made from the juice of chewed *'awa* root, spat into a bowl, and used in religious ceremonies

halakahiki pineapple

halau long house; when used with hula, it means "school"

hale house or building; often combined with other words to name a specific place, such as Haleakala (House of the Sun), or Hale Pa'i at Lahainaluna, meaning Printing House

hana work; combined with *pau* means end of work or quitting time

hanai literally "to feed." Part of the true aloha spirit. A *hanai* is a permanent guest, or an adopted family member, usually an old person or a child. This is an enduring cultural phenomenon in Hawaii, in which a child from one family (perhaps that of a brother or sister, and quite often one's grandchild) is raised as one's own without formal adoption.

haole a word that at one time meant foreigner, but which now means a white person or Caucasian

hapa half, as in a mixed-blooded person being referred to as *hapa haole*

hapai pregnant; used by all ethnic groups when a *keiki* is on the way

haupia a coconut custard dessert often served at a lu'au

he'enalu surfing

heiau A platform made of skillfully fitted rocks, upon which temporary structures were built as temples and offerings made to the gods.

holomu an ankle-length dress that is much more fitted than a mu'umu'u, and which is often worn on formal occasions

hono bay, as in Honolulu (Sheltered Bay)

honu green sea turtle; endangered

ho'oilo traditional Hawaiian winter that began in November

ho'olaule'a any happy event, but especially a family outing or picnic

ho'omalimali sweet talk; flattery

huhu angry; irritated

hui a group; meeting; society. Often used to refer to Chinese businesspeople or family members who pool their money to get businesses started.

hukilau traditional shoreline fish-gathering in which everyone lends a hand to *huki* (pull) the huge net. Anyone taking part shares in the *lau* (food). It is much more like a party than hard work, and if you're lucky you'll be able to take part in one.

hula a native Hawaiian dance in which the rhythm of the islands is captured by swaying hips and stories told by lyrically moving hands. *halau* is a group or school of hula.

huli huli barbecue, as in *huli huli* chicken

i'a fish in general. *I'a maka* is raw fish.

imu underground oven filled with hot rocks and used for baking. The main cooking method featured at a lu'au, used to steam-bake pork and other succulent dishes. The tending of the *imu* was traditionally for men only.

ipo sweetheart; lover; girl- or boyfriend

kahili a tall pole topped with feathers, resembling a huge feather duster. It was used by an *ali'i* to announce his or her presence.

kahuna priest; sorcerer; doctor; skillful person. In old Hawaii *kahuna* had tremendous power, which they used for both good and evil. The *kahuna ana'ana* was a feared individual who practiced "black magic" and could pray a person to death, while the *kahuna lapa'au* was a medical practitioner bringing aid and comfort to the people.

kai the sea. Many businesses and hotels employ *kai* as part of their name.

kalua means roasted underground in an *imu*. A favorite island food is *kalua* pork.

kama'aina a child of the land; an old-timer; a longtime island resident of any ethnic background; a resident of Hawaii or native son or daughter. Hotels and airlines often offer discounts called "kama'aina rates" to anyone who can prove island residency.

kanaka man or commoner; later used to distinguish a Hawaiian from other races. Tone of voice can make it a derisive expression.

kane means man, but actually used to signify a relationship such as husband or boyfriend. Written on a lavatory door it means "men's room."

kapu forbidden; taboo; keep out; do not touch

kupuna a grandparent or old-timer; usually means someone who has gained wisdom. The statewide school system now invites *kupuna* to talk to the children about the old ways and methods.

kaukau slang word meaning food or chow; grub. Some of the best food in Hawaii comes from the *kaukau* wagons, trucks that sell plate lunches and other morsels.

kauwa a landless, untouchable caste once confined to living on reservations. Members of this caste were often used as human sacrifices at *heiau*. Calling someone *kauwa* is still a grave insult.

kava (see *'awa*)

keiki child or children; used by all ethnic groups. "Have you hugged your *keiki* today?"

kiawe an algaroba tree from South America commonly found in Hawaii along the shore. It grows a nasty long thorn that can easily puncture a tire. Legend has it that the trees were introduced to the islands by a misguided missionary who hoped the thorns would coerce natives into wearing shoes. Actually, they are good for fuel, as fodder for hogs and cattle, and for reforestation, none of which you'll appreciate if you step on one of the thorns or flatten a tire on your rental car!

ko'ala any food that has been broiled or barbecued

kokua help. As in "Your kokua is needed to keep Hawaii free from litter."

kolohe rascal

konane a traditional Hawaiian game, similar to checkers, played with pebbles on a large flat stone used as a board

kona wind a muggy subtropical wind that blows from the south and hits the leeward side of the islands. It usually brings sticky hot weather and one of the few times when air-conditioning will be appreciated.

ko'olau windward side of the island

kukui a candlenut tree whose pods are polished and then strung together to make a beautiful lei. Traditionally the oil-rich nuts were strung on the rib of a coconut leaf and used as a candle.

kuleana homesite; the old homestead; small farms. Especially used to describe the small spreads on Hawaiian Homelands on Moloka'i.

Kumulipo ancient Hawaiian genealogical chant that records the pantheon of gods, creation, and the beginning of humankind

la the sun. Often combined with other words to be more descriptive, such as Lahaina (Merciless Sun) or Haleakala (House of the Sun).

lanai veranda or porch. You'll pay more for a hotel room if it has a lanai with an ocean view.

lani sky or the heavens

lau hala traditional Hawaiian weaving of mats, hats, etc., from the prepared fronds of the pandanus (screw pine)

lei a traditional garland of flowers or vines. One of Hawaii's most beautiful customs. Given at any auspicious occasion, but especially when arriving or leaving Hawaii.

lele the stone altar at a heiau

limu edible seaweed of various types. Gathered from the shoreline, it makes an excellent salad. It's used to garnish many island dishes and is a favorite at lu'au.

lolo crazy, as in "lolo buggah" (stupid or crazy guy)

lomi lomi traditional Hawaiian massage; also, raw salmon made into a vinegared salad with chopped onion and spices

lua the toilet; the head; the bathroom

luakini a human-sacrifice temple. Introduced to Hawaii in the 13th century at Waha'ula Heiau on the Big Island.

lu'au a Hawaiian feast featuring poi, imu-baked pork, and other traditional foods. Good ones provide some of the best gastronomic delights in the world.

luna foreman or overseer in the plantation fields. They were often mounted on horseback and were renowned for either their fairness or their cruelty. Representing the middle class, they served as a buffer between plantation workers and white plantation owners.

mahalo thank you. Mahalo nui means "big thanks" or "thank you very much."

mahele division. The "Great Mahele" of 1848 changed Hawaii forever when the traditional common lands were broken up into privately owned plots.

mahimahi a favorite eating fish. Often called a dolphin fish, but a mahimahi is a true fish, not a cetacean.

mahu a homosexual; often used derisively like "fag" or "queer"

maile a fragrant vine used in traditional lei. It looks ordinary but smells delightful.

maka'ainana a commoner; a person "belonging" to the 'aina (land), who supported the ali'i by fishing and farming and as a warrior

makai toward the sea; used by most islanders when giving directions

make dead; deceased

malihini what you are if you have just arrived: a newcomer; a tenderfoot; a recent arrival

malo the native Hawaiian loincloth. Never worn anymore except at festivals or pageants.

mana power from the spirit world; innate energy of all things animate or inanimate; the grace of god. Mana could be passed on from one person to another, or even stolen. Great care was taken to protect the ali'i from having their mana defiled. Commoners were required to lie flat on the ground and cover their faces whenever a great ali'i approached. Kahuna were often employed in the regaining or transference of mana.

manini stingy; tight; a Hawaiianized word

taken from the name of Don Francisco *Marin,* who was instrumental in bringing many fruits and plants to Hawaii. He was known for never sharing any of the bounty from his substantial gardens on Vineyard Street in Honolulu; therefore, his name came to mean "stingy."

manuahi free; gratis; extra

mauka toward the mountains; used by most islanders when giving directions

mauna mountain. Often combined with other words to be more descriptive, such as Mauna Kea (White Mountain)

mele a song or chant in the Hawaiian oral tradition that records the history and genealogies of the *ali'i*

Menehune the legendary "little people" of Hawaii. Like leprechauns, they are said to shun humans and possess magical powers.

moa chicken; fowl

moana the ocean; the sea. Many businesses and hotels as well as places have *moana* as part of their name.

moe sleep

mo'olelo ancient tales kept alive by the oral tradition and recited only by day

mu'umu'u a "Mother Hubbard," an ankle-length dress with a high neckline introduced by the missionaries to cover the nakedness of the Hawaiians. It has become fashionable attire for almost any occasion in Hawaii.

nani beautiful

nui big; great; large; as in *mahalo nui* (thank you very much)

'ohana a family; the fundamental social division; extended family. Now often used to denote a social organization with grassroots overtones.

'okolehau literally "iron bottom"; a traditional booze made from *ti* root. *'Okole* means "rear end" and *hau* means "iron," which was descriptive of the huge blubber pots in which *'okolehau* was made. Also, if you drink too much it'll surely knock you on your *'okole.*

oli chant not done to a musical accompaniment

ono delicious; delightful; the best. *Ono ono* means "extra or absolutely delicious."

'opihi a shellfish or limpet that clings to rocks

and is gathered as one of the islands' favorite *pu pu.* Custom dictates that you never remove all of the *'opihi* from a rock; some are always left to grow for future generations.

'opu belly; stomach

pahoehoe smooth, ropy lava that looks like burnt pancake batter. It is now the correct geological term used to describe this type of lava found anywhere in the world.

pakalolo "crazy smoke"; grass; smoke; dope; marijuana

pake a Chinese person. Can be derisive, depending on the tone in which it is used. It is a bastardization of the Chinese word meaning "uncle."

pali a cliff; precipice. Hawaii's geology makes them quite common. The most famous are the *pali* of O'ahu where a major battle was fought.

paniolo a Hawaiian cowboy. Derived from the Spanish *español.* The first cowboys brought to Hawaii during the early 19th century were Mexicans from California.

papale hat. Except for the feathered helmets of the *ali'i* warriors of old Hawaii, hats were generally not worn. However, once the islanders saw their practical uses and how fashionable they were, they began weaving them from various materials and quickly became experts at manufacture and design.

pa'u long split skirt often worn by women when horseback riding. In the 1800s, an island treat was watching *pa'u* riders in their beautiful dresses at Kapi'olani Park in Honolulu. The tradition is carried on today at many of Hawaii's rodeos.

pau finished; done; completed. Often combined into *pau hana,* which means end of work or quitting time.

pilau stink; bad smell; stench

pilikia trouble of any kind, big or small; bad times

poi a glutinous paste made from the pounded corm of taro, which ferments slightly and has a light sour taste. Purplish in color, it's a staple at lu'au, where it is called "one-, two-, or three-finger" poi, depending upon its thickness.

pono righteous or excellent

pua flower

puka a hole of any size. *Puka* is used by all island residents, whether talking about a pinhole in a rubber boat or a tunnel through a mountain.

punalua a traditional practice, before the missionaries arrived, of sharing mates. Western seamen took advantage of it, leading to the spread of contagious diseases and eventual rapid decline of the Hawaiian people.

pune'e bed; narrow couch. Used by all ethnic groups. To recline on a *pune'e* on a breezy lanai is a true island treat.

pu pu an appetizer; a snack; hors d'oeuvres; can be anything from cheese and crackers to sushi. Oftentimes, bars or nightclubs offer them free.

pupule crazy; nuts; out of your mind

pu'u hill, as in Pu'u 'Ula'ula (Red Hill)

tapa a traditional paper cloth made from beaten bark. Intricate designs were stamped in using beaters, and natural dyes added color. The tradition was lost for many years but is now making a comeback and provides some of the most beautiful folk art in the islands. Also called Kapa.

taro the staple of old Hawaii. A plant with a distinctive broad leaf that produces a starchy root. It was brought by the first Polynesians and was grown on magnificently irrigated plantations. According to the oral tradition, the life-giving properties of taro hold mystical significance for Hawaiians, since it was created by the gods at about the same time as humans.

ti a broad-leafed plant that was used for many purposes, from plates to hula skirts. Especially used to wrap religious offerings presented at the *heiau*.

tutu grandmother; granny; older woman. Used by all as a term of respect and endearment.

ukulele *uku* means "flea" and *lele* means "jumping," so literally "jumping flea" the way the Hawaiians perceived the quick finger movements used on the banjo-like Portuguese folk instrument called a *cavaquinho*. The ukulele quickly became synonymous with the islands.

wahine young woman; female; girl; wife. Used by all ethnic groups. When written on a lavatory door it means "women's room."

wai freshwater; drinking water

wela hot. *Wela kahao* is a "hot time" or "making whoopee."

wiki quickly; fast; in a hurry. Often seen as *wiki wiki* (very fast), as in "Wiki Wiki Messenger Service."

USEFUL PHRASES

Aloha ahiahi Good evening
Aloha au ia 'oe I love you
Aloha kakahiaka Good morning
Aloha nui loa much love; fondest regards
E Komo mai please come in; enter; welcome
Hau'oli la hanau Happy birthday
Hau'oli makahiki hou Happy New Year
Mele kalikimaka Merry Christmas
'Okole maluna bottoms up; salute; cheers; kampai

PIDGIN

The following are a few commonly used words and expressions that should give you an idea of pidgin. It really can't be written properly, merely approximated, but for now, *"Study da' kine an' bimbye it be mo' bettah, brah! OK? Lesgo."*

an' den and then? big deal; so what's next?

auntie respected elderly woman

bad ass very good

bimbye after a while; bye and bye. "Bimbye, you learn pidgin."

blalah brother, but actually only refers to a large, heavy-set, good-natured Hawaiian man

brah all the bros in Hawaii are brahs; brother; pal. Used to call someone's attention. One of the most common words even among people who are not acquainted. After a fill-up at a gas station, a person would say "Tanks, brah."

chicken skin goose bumps.

cockaroach steal; rip off. If you really want to find out what cockaroach means, just leave your camera on your beach blanket when you take a little dip.

da' kine a catchall word of many meanings that epitomizes the essence of pidgin. Da' kine is a euphemism for pidgin and is substituted whenever the speaker is at a loss for a word or just wants to generalize. It can mean: you know? watchamacallit; of that type.

geev um give it to them; give them hell; go for it. Can be used as an encouragement. If a surfer is riding a great wave, the people on the beach might yell, "Geev um, brah!"

grinds food

hana ho again. Especially after a concert the audience shouts "hana ho" (one more!).

hele on let's get going.

howzit? as in "howzit, brah?" what's happening? how's it going? The most common greeting, used in place of the more formal "How do you do?"

huhu angry! "You put the make on the wrong da' kine wahine, brah, and you in da' kine trouble if you get one big Hawaiian blalah plenty huhu."

lesgo Let's go! Do it!

li'dis an' li'dat like this or that; a catch-all grouping especially if you want to avoid details; like, ya know?

lolo buggah stupid or crazy guy (person). Words to a tropical island song go, "I want to find the lolo who stole my pakalolo."

mo' bettah better, real good! great idea. An island sentiment used to be, "mo' bettah you come Hawaii." Now it has subtly changed to, "mo' bettah you visit Hawaii."

ono number one! delicious; great; groovy. "Hawaii is ono, brah!"

pakalolo literally "crazy smoke"; marijuana; grass; reefer.

pakiki head stubborn; bull-headed

pau a Hawaiian word meaning finished; done; over and done with. Pau hana means end of work or quitting time. Once used by plantation workers, now used by everyone.

seestah sister, female

shaka hand wave where only the thumb and baby finger stick out, meaning thank you, all right!

sleepah slipper, flip-flop, zori

stink face (or stink eye) basically frowning at someone; using facial expression to show displeasure. Hard looks. What you'll get if you give local people a hard time.

swell head burned up; angry

talk story spinning yarns; shooting the breeze; throwing the bull; a rap session. If you're lucky enough to be around to hear kupuna (elders) "talk story," you can hear some fantastic tales in the tradition of old Hawaii.

tanks, brah thanks, thank you.

to da max all the way.

waddascoops what's the scoop? what's up? what's happening?)

Suggested Reading

Many publishers print books on Hawaii. Following are a few that focus on Hawaiian topics. **University of Hawai'i Press** (www.uhpress.hawaii.edu) has the best overall general list of titles on Hawaii. The **Bishop Museum Press** (www.bishopmuseum.org/press) puts out many scholarly works on Hawaiiana, as does **Kamehameha Schools Press** (www.kspress.ksbe.edu). Also good, with a more general-interest list, are **Bess Press** (www.besspress.com), **Mutual Publishing** (www.mutualpublishing.com), and **Petrogylph Press** (www.basicallybooks.com). In addition, a websites specifically oriented to books on Hawaii, Hawaiian music, and other things Hawaiian is **Hawaii Books** (www.hawaiibooks.com).

ASTRONOMY

Bryan, E.H. *Stars over Hawaii.* Hilo, HI: Petroglyph Press, 1977. An introduction to astronomy, with information about the constellations and charts featuring the stars filling the night sky in Hawaii, by month. An excellent primer.

Rhoads, Samuel. *The Sky Tonight: A Guided Tour of the Stars over Hawaii.* Honolulu: Bishop Museum, 1993. Four pages per month of star charts one each for the horizon in every cardinal direction. Exceptional!

COOKING

Alexander, Agnes. *How to Use Hawaiian Fruit.* Hilo, HI: Petroglyph Press, 1984. A slim volume of recipes using delicious and different Hawaiian fruits.

Beeman, Judy and Martin Beeman. *Joys of Hawaiian Cooking.* Hilo, HI: Petroglyph Press, 1977. A collection of favorite recipes from Big Island chefs.

Choy, Sam. *Cooking from the Heart with Sam Choy.* Honolulu: Mutual Publishing, 1995.

This beautiful, hand-bound cookbook contains many color photos by Douglas Peebles.

Fukuda, Sachi. *Pupus, An Island Tradition.* Honolulu: Bess Press, 1995.

Margah, Irish and Elvira Monroe. *Hawaii, Cooking with Aloha.* San Carlos, CA: Wide World, 1984. Island recipes, as well as hints on decor.

Rizzuto, Shirley. *Fish Dishes of the Pacific from the Fishwife.* Honolulu: Hawaii Fishing News, 1986. Features recipes using all the fish commonly caught in Hawaiian waters (husband Jim Rizzuto is the author of Fishing, Hawaiian Style).

CULTURE

Dudley, Michael Kioni. *Man, Gods, and Nature.* Honolulu: Na Kane O Ka Malo Press, 1990. An examination of the philosophical underpinnings of Hawaiian beliefs and their interconnected reality.

Hartwell, Jay. *Na Mamo: Hawaiian People Today.* Honolulu: Ai Pohaku Press, 1996. Profiles 12 people practicing Hawaiian traditions in the modern world.

Heyerdahl, Thor. *American Indians in the Pacific.* London: Allen and Unwin Ltd., 1952. Theoretical and anthropological accounts of the influence on Polynesia of the Indians along the Pacific coast of North and South America. Though no longer in print, this book is fascinating reading, presenting unsubstantiated yet intriguing theories.

Kamehameha Schools Press. *Life in Early Hawai'i: The Ahupua'a.* 3rd ed. Honolulu: Kamehameha Schools Press, 1994. Written for schoolchildren to better understand the basic organization of old Hawaiian land use and its function, this slim volume is a good primer for people of any age who wish to understand this fundamental societal fixture.

Kirch, Patrick V. *Feathered Gods and Fish-hooks: An Introduction to Hawaiian Archaeology and Prehistory.* Honolulu: University of Hawai'i Press, 1997. This scholarly, lavishly illustrated, yet very readable book gives new insight into the development of precontact Hawaiian civilization. It focuses on the sites and major settlements of old Hawai'i and chronicles the main cultural developments while weaving in the social climate that contributed to change. A very worthwhile read.

FAUNA

Boom, Robert. *Hawaiian Seashells.* Honolulu: Waikiki Aquarium, 1972. Photos by Jerry Kringle. A collection of 137 seashells found in Hawaiian waters, featuring many found nowhere else on earth. Broken into categories with accompanying text including common and scientific names, physical descriptions, and likely habitats. A must for shell collectors.

Carpenter, Blyth and Russell Carpenter. *Fish Watching in Hawaii.* San Mateo, CA: Natural World Press, 1981. A color guide to many of the reef fish found in Hawaii and often spotted by snorkelers. If you're interested in the fish that you'll be looking at, this guide will be very helpful.

Denny, Jim. *The Birds of Kauai.* Honolulu: University of Hawai'i Press, 1999. Worthy companion for any birder to the island.

Fielding, Ann and Ed Robinson. *An Underwater Guide to Hawai'i.* Honolulu: University of Hawai'i Press, 1987. If you've ever had a desire to snorkel/scuba the living reef waters of Hawaii and to be familiar with what you're seeing, get this small but fact-packed book. The amazing array of marine life found throughout the archipelago is captured in glossy photos with accompanying informative text. Both the scientific and common names of specimens are given. This book will enrich your underwater experience and serve as an easily understood reference guide for many years.

Goodson, Gar. *The Many-Splendored Fishes of Hawaii.* Stanford, CA: Stanford University Press, 1985. This small but thorough "fish-watchers" book includes entries on some deep-sea fish.

Hawaiian Audubon Society. *Hawaii's Birds.* 5th ed. Honolulu: Hawaii Audubon Society, 1997. Excellent bird book, giving description, range, voice, and habits of the over 100 species. Slim volume; good for carrying while hiking.

Hobson, Edmund and E.H. Chave. *Hawaiian Reef Animals.* Honolulu: University of Hawai'i Press, 1987. Colorful photos and descriptions of the fish, invertebrates, turtles, and seals that call Hawaiian reefs their home.

Kay, Alison and Olive Schoenberg-Dole. *Shells of Hawai'i.* Honolulu: University of Hawai'i Press, 1991. Color photos and tips on where to look.

Mahaney, Casey. *Hawaiian Reef Fish, The Identification Book.* Planet Ocean Publishing, 1999. A spiral-bound reference work featuring many color photos and descriptions of common reef fish found in Hawaiian waters.

Nickerson, Roy. *Brother Whale, A Pacific Whalewatcher's Log.* San Francisco: Chronicle Books, 1977. Introduces the average person to the life of earth's greatest mammals. Provides historical accounts, photos, and tips on whalewatching. Well-written, descriptive, and the best "first time" book on whales.

Pratt, H.D. P.L. Bruner, and D.G. Berrett. *The Birds of Hawaii and the Tropical Pacific.* Princeton, N.J.: Princeton University Press, 1987. Useful field guide for novice and expert bird-watchers, covering Hawaii as well as other Pacific Island groups.

Tomich, P. Quentin. *Mammals in Hawai'i.* Honolulu: Bishop Museum Press, 1986. Quintessential scholarly text on all mammal species in Hawaii, with description of distribution and historical references. Lengthy bibliography.

van Riper, Charles and Sandra van Riper. *A Field Guide to the Mammals of Hawaii.* Honolulu: Oriental Publishing. A guide to the surprising number of mammals introduced into Hawaii. Full-color pages document description, uses, tendencies, and habitat. Small and thin, this book makes a worthwhile addition to any serious hiker's backpack.

FLORA

Kepler, Angela. *Hawaiian Heritage Plants.* Honolulu: University of Hawai'i Press, 1998. A treatise on 32 utilitarian plants used by the early Hawaiians.

Kepler, Angela. *Hawai'i's Floral Splendor.* Honolulu: Mutual Publishing, 1997. A general reference to flowers of Hawaii.

Kepler, Angela. *Tropicals of Hawaii.* Honolulu: Mutual Publishing, 1989. This small-format book features many color photos of nonnative flowers.

Kuck, Lorraine and Richard Togg. *Hawaiian Flowers and Flowering Trees.* Rutland, VT: Tuttle, 1960. A classic, though no longer in print, field guide to tropical and subtropical flora illustrated in watercolor. A "to the point" description of Hawaiian plants and flowers with a brief history of their places of origin and their introduction to Hawaii.

Merrill, Elmer. *Plant Life of the Pacific World.* Rutland, VT: Tuttle, 1983. This is the definitive book for anyone planning a botanical tour to the entire Pacific Basin. Originally published in the 1930s, it remains a tremendous work, worth tracking down through out-of-print book services.

Miyano, Leland. *Hawai'i, A Floral Paradise.* Honolulu: Mutual Publishing, 1995. Photographed by Douglas Peebles, this large-format book is filled with informative text and beautiful color shots of tropical flowers commonly seen in Hawaii.

Miyano, Leland. *A Pocket Guide to Hawai'i's Flowers.* Honolulu: Mutual Publishing, 2001. A small guide to readily seen flowers in the state. Good for the backpack or back pocket.

Sohmer, S.H. and R. Gustafson. *Plants and Flowers of Hawai'i.* Honolulu: University of Hawai'i Press, 1987. Sohmer and Gustafson cover the vegetation zones of Hawaii, from mountains to coast, introducing you to the wide and varied floral biology of the islands. They give a good introduction to the history and unique evolution of Hawaiian plantlife. Beautiful color plates are accompanied by clear and concise plant descriptions, with the scientific and common Hawaiian names listed.

Teho, Fortunato. *Plants of Hawaii: How to Grow Them.* Hilo, HI: Petroglyph Press, 1992. A small but useful book for those who want their backyards to bloom into tropical paradises.

Valier, Kathy. *Ferns of Hawaii.* Honolulu: University of Hawai'i Press, 1995. One of the few books that treat the state's ferns as a single subject.

Wagner, Warren L., Derral R. Herbst, and H. S. Sohner. *Manual of the Flowering Plants of Hawai'i,* revised edition, vol. 2. Honolulu: University of Hawai'i Press in association with Bishop Museum Press, 1999. Considered the Bible for Hawaii's botanical world. Scholarly.

HEALTH

Gutmanis, June. *Kahuna La'au Lapa'au.* Honolulu: Island Heritage, rev. ed. 2001. Text on Hawaiian herbal medicines: diseases, treatments, and medicinal plants, with illustrations.

McBride, L.R. *Practical Folk Medicine of Hawaii.* Hilo, HI: Petroglyph Press, 1975. An illustrated guide to Hawaii's medicinal plants as used by the *kahuna lapa'au* (medical healers). Includes a thorough section on ailments, diagnosis, and the proper folk remedy.

Illustrated by the author, a renowned botanical researcher and former ranger at Hawaii Volcanoes National Park.

Wilkerson, James A., M.D., ed. *Medicine for Mountaineering and Other Wilderness.* 4th ed. Seattle: The Mountaineers, 1992. Don't let the title fool you. Although the book focuses on specific health problems that may be encountered while mountaineering, it is the best first-aid and general health guide available today. Written by doctors for the layperson to use until help arrives, it is jampacked with easily understandable techniques and procedures. For those planning extended hikes, it is a must.

HISTORY

Apple, Russell A. *Trails: From Steppingstones to Kerbstones.* Honolulu: Bishop Museum Press, 1965. This "Special Publication #53" is a special-interest archaeological survey focusing on trails, roadways, footpaths, and highways and how they were designed and maintained throughout the years. Many "royal highways" from precontact Hawaii are cited.

Barnes, Phil. *A Concise History of the Hawaiian Islands.* Hilo, HI; Petroglyph Press, 1999. An examination of the main currents of Hawaiian history and its major players, focusing on the important factors in shaping the social, economic, and political trends of the islands. An easy read.

Cameron, Roderick. *The Golden Haze.* New York: World Publishing, 1964. An account of Captain James Cook's voyages of discovery throughout the South Seas. Uses original diaries and journals for an "on the spot" reconstruction of this great seafaring adventure.

Cox, J. Halley and Edward Stasack. *Hawaiian Petroglyphs.* Honolulu: Bishop Museum Press, 1970. The most thorough examination of petroglyph sites throughout the islands.

Daws, Gavan. *Shoal of Time, A History of the Hawaiian Islands.* Honolulu: University of Hawai'i Press, 1974. A highly readable history of Hawaii dating from its "discovery" by the Western world down to its acceptance as the 50th state. Good insight into the psychological makeup of influential characters who helped form Hawaii's past.

Donohugh, Douglas. *The Story of Koloa: A Kauai Plantation Town.* Honolulu: Mutual Publishing, 2001. A short history of the town of Koloa and its role in the history of sugar in Hawaii.

Dorrance, William H. and Francis S. Morgan. *Sugar Islands: The 165-Year Story of Sugar in Hawai'i.* Honolulu: Mutual Publishing, 2000. An overall sketch of the sugar industry in Hawaii from inception to decline, with data on many individual plantations and mills around the islands. Definitely a story from the industry's point of view.

Finney, Ben and James D. Houston. *Surfing, A History of the Ancient Hawaiian Sport.* Los Angeles: Pomegranate, 1996. Features many early etchings and old photos of Hawaiian surfers practicing their native sport.

Fornander, Abraham. *An Account of the Polynesian Race; Its Origins and Migrations, and the Ancient History of the Hawaiian People to the Times of Kamehameha I.* Rutland, VT: C.E. Tuttle Co., 1969. This is a reprint of a three-volume opus originally published 1878–85. It is still one of the best sources of information on Hawaiian myth and legend.

Free, David. *Vignettes of Old Hawaii.* Honolulu: Crossroads Press, 1994. A collection of short essays on a variety of subjects.

Fuchs, Lawrence. *Hawaii Pono.* Honolulu: Bess Press, 1961. A detailed, scholarly work presenting an overview of Hawaii's history, based upon ethnic and sociological interpretations. Encompasses most socio-ethnological groups from native Hawaiians to modern entrepreneurs. This book is a must for obtaining some social historical background.

Handy, E.S. and Elizabeth Handy. *Native*

Planters in Old Hawaii. Honolulu: Bishop Museum Press, 1972. A superbly written, easily understood scholarly work on the intimate relationship of precontact Hawaiians and the *aina* (land). Much more than its title implies, this book should be read by anyone seriously interested in Polynesian Hawaii.

Ii, John Papa. *Fragments of Hawaiian History.* Honolulu: Bishop Museum, 1959. Hawaii's history under Kamehameha I as told by a Hawaiian who actually experienced it.

Joesting, Edward. *Hawaii: An Uncommon History.* New York: W.W. Norton Co., 1978. A truly uncommon history told in a series of vignettes relating to the lives and personalities of the first Caucasians in Hawaii, Hawaiian nobility, sea captains, writers, and adventurers. Brings history to life. Absolutely excellent!

Joesting, Edward. *Kauai: The Separate Kingdom.* Honolulu: University of Hawai'i Press, 1984. The history of Kaua'i through the end of the Hawaiian monarchy. Joesting brings the story of the island to life through the people who shaped it.

Kamakau, S. M. *Ruling Chiefs of Hawaii,* revised edition. Honolulu: Kamehameha Schools Press, 1992. A history of Hawaii from the legendary leader 'Umi to the mid-Kamehameha Dynasty, from oral tales and from a Hawaiian perspective.

Krauss, Robert. *Grove Farm Plantation: The Biography of a Hawaiian Sugar Plantation.* Palo Alto, CA: Pacific Books, 1984. A history of the Grove Farm, the Wilcox family, and the economy of sugar on Kaua'i.

Kurisu, Yasushi. *Sugar Town, Hawaiian Plantation Days Remembered.* Honolulu: Watermark Publishing, 1995. Reminiscences of life growing up on sugar plantations on the Hamakua Coast of the Big Island. Features many old photos.

Lili'uokalani. *Hawaii's Story by Hawaii's Queen.* Reprint, Honolulu: Mutual Publishing, 1990. Originally written in 1898, this moving personal account recounts Hawaii's inevitable move from monarchy to U.S. Territory by its last queen, Lili'uokalani. The facts can be found in other histories, but none provides the emotion or point of view expressed by Hawaii's deposed monarch. This is a must-read to get the whole picture.

McBride, Likeke. *Petroglyphs of Hawaii.* Hilo, HI: Petroglyph Press, 1997. A revised and updated guide to petroglyphs found in the Hawaiian Islands. A basic introduction to these old Hawaiian picture stories.

Nickerson, Roy. *Lahaina, Royal Capital of Hawaii.* Honolulu: Hawaiian Service, 1978. The story of Lahaina from whaling days to present, spiced with ample photographs.

Tabrah, Ruth M. *Ni'ihau: The Last Hawaiian Island.* Kailua, Hawaii: Press Pacifica, 1987. Sympathetic history of the privately owned island of Ni'ihau.

Takaki, Ronald. *Pau Hana: Plantation Life and Labor in Hawaii.* Honolulu, University of Hawaii Press, 1983. The story of immigrant labor and the sugar industry in Hawaii until the 1920s from the worker's perspective.

INTRODUCTORY

Carroll, Rick and Marcie Carroll, ed. *Hawai'i: True Stories of the Island Spirit.* San Francisco: Travelers' Tales, Inc., 1999. A collection of stories by a variety of authors that were chosen to elicit the essence of Hawaii and Hawaiian experiences. A great read.

Cohen, David and Rick Smolan. *A Day in the Life of Hawaii.* New York: Workman, 1984. On December 2, 1983, 50 of the world's top photojournalists were invited to Hawaii to photograph the variety of daily life on the islands. The photos are excellently reproduced, and accompanied by a minimum of text.

Day, A.G. and C. Stroven. *A Hawaiian Reader.* 1959. Reprint, Honolulu: Mutual Publishing, 1984. A poignant compilation of essays, diary entries, and fictitious writings that takes you from the death of Captain Cook through the "statehood services."

Department of Geography, University of Hawai'i, Hilo. *Atlas of Hawai'i*. 3rd ed. Honolulu: University of Hawai'i Press, 1998. Much more than an atlas filled with reference maps, this also contains commentary on the natural environment, culture, and sociology; a gazetteer; and statistical tables. Actually a mini-encyclopedia on Hawai'i.

Michener, James A. *Hawaii*. New York: Random House, 1959. Michener's fictionalized historical novel has done more to inform *and* misinform readers about Hawaii than any other book ever written. A great tale with plenty of local color and information, but read it for pleasure, not facts.

Piercy, LaRue. *Hawaii This and That*. Honolulu: Mutual Publishing, 1994. Illustrated by Scot Ebanez. A 60-page book filled with one-sentence facts and oddities about all manner of things Hawaiian. Informative, amazing, and fun to read.

Steele, R. Thomas: *The Hawaiian Shirt: Its Art and History*. New York: Abbeville Press, 1984.

LANGUAGE

Elbert, Samuel. *Spoken Hawaiian*. Honolulu: University of Hawai'i Press, 1970. Progressive conversational lessons.

Elbert, Samuel and Mary Pukui. *Hawaiian Dictionary*. Honolulu: University of Hawai'i Press, 1986. The best dictionary available on the Hawaiian language. The *Pocket Hawaiian Dictionary* is a less expensive, condensed version of this dictionary, and adequate for most travelers with a general interest in the language.

Pukui, Mary Kawena, Samuel Elbert, and Esther T. Mookini. *Place Names of Hawaii*. Honolulu: University of Hawai'i Press, 1974. The most current and comprehensive listing of Hawaiian and foreign place-names in the state, giving pronunciation, spelling, meaning, and location.

Schutz, Albert J. *All About Hawaiian*. Honolulu: University of Hawai'i Press, 1995. A brief primer on Hawaiian pronunciation, grammar, and vocabulary. A solid introduction.

MYTHOLOGY AND LEGENDS

Beckwith, Martha. *Hawaiian Mythology*. Reprint, Honolulu: University of Hawai'i Press, 1976. Over 60 years after its original printing in 1940, this work remains the definitive text on Hawaiian mythology. Beckwith compiled this book from many sources, giving exhaustive cross-references to genealogies and legends expressed in the oral tradition. If you are going to read one book on Hawaii's folklore, this should be it.

Beckwith, Martha. *The Kumulipo*. 1951. Reprint, Honolulu: University of Hawai'i Press, 1972. Translation of the Hawaiian creation chant.

Colum, Padraic. *Legends of Hawaii*. New Haven: Yale University Press, 1937. Selected legends of old Hawaii, reinterpreted but closely based upon the originals.

Elbert, S.H., ed. *Hawaiian Antiquities and Folklore*. Honolulu: University of Hawai'i Press, 1959. Illustrated by Jean Charlot. A selection of the main legends from Abraham Fornander's great work, *An Account of the Polynesian Race*.

Kalakaua, His Hawaiian Majesty, King David. *The Legends and Myths of Hawaii*. Edited by R.M. Daggett, with a foreword by Glen Grant. Honolulu: Mutual Publishing, 1990. Originally published in 1888, Hawaii's own King Kalakaua draws upon his scholarly and formidable knowledge of the classic oral tradition to bring alive ancient tales from pre-contact Hawaii. A powerful yet somewhat Victorian voice from Hawaii's past speaks clearly and boldly, especially about the intimate role of pre-Christian religion in the lives of the Hawaiian people.

Melville, Leinanai. *Children of the Rainbow.* Wheaton, IL: Theosophical Publishing, 1969. A book on higher spiritual consciousness attuned to nature, which was the basic belief of pre-Christian Hawaii. The appendix contains illustrations of mystical symbols used by the *kahuna.* An enlightening book in many ways.

Pukui, Mary Kawena and Caroline Curtis. *Hawaii Island Legends.* Honolulu: The Kamehameha Schools Press, 1996. Hawaiian tales and legends for the pre-teen.

Pukui, Mary Kawena and Caroline Curtis. *Tales of the Menehune.* Honolulu: The Kamehameha Schools Press, 1960. Compilation of legends relating to Hawaii's "little people."

Pukui, Mary Kawena and Caroline Curtis. *The Waters of Kane and other Hawaiian Legends* Honolulu: The Kamehameha Schools Press, 1994. Tales and legends for the pre-teen.

Thrum, Thomas. *Hawaiian Folk Tales.* 1907. Reprint, Chicago: McClurg and Co., 1950. A collection of Hawaiian tales from the oral tradition as told to the author from various sources.

Westervelt, W.D. *Hawaiian Legends of Volcanoes.* 1916. Reprint, Boston: Ellis Press, 1991. A small book concerning the volcanic legends of Hawaii and how they related to the fledgling field of volcanism in the early 1900s. The vintage photos alone are worth a look.

Wichman, Frederick B. *Kaua'i: Ancient Place Names and Their Stories.* Honolulu: University of Hawai'i Press, 1998. A very readable explanation of stories and legends relating to places on Kaua'i and the meanings of place names.

NATURAL SCIENCE AND GEOGRAPHY

Carlquist, Sherwin. *Hawaii: A Natural History.* National Tropical Botanical Garden, 1984. Definitive account of Hawaii's natural history.

Clark, John. *Beaches of Kaua'i.* Honolulu: University of Hawai'i Press. Definitive guide to beaches, including many off the beaten path. Features maps and black-and-white photos. Also *Beaches of the Big Island, Beaches of O'ahu and Ni'ihau,* and *Beaches of Maui County.*

Hazlett, Richard and Donald Hyndman. *Roadside Geology of Hawai'i.* Missoula, MT: Mountain Press Publishing, 1996. Begins with a general discussion of the geology of the Hawaiian Islands, followed by a road guide to the individual islands offering descriptions of easily seen features. A great book to have in the car as you tour the islands.

Hubbard, Douglass and Gordon Macdonald. *Volcanoes of the National Parks of Hawaii.* 1982. Reprint, Volcanoes, HI: Hawaii Natural History Association, 1989. The volcanology of Hawaii, documenting the major lava flows and their geological effect on the state.

Kay, E. Alison, comp. *A Natural History of the Hawaiian Islands.* Honolulu: University of Hawai'i Press, 1994. A selection of concise articles by experts in the fields of volcanism, oceanography, meteorology, and biology. An excellent reference source.

Macdonald, Gorden, Agatin Abbott, and Frank Peterson. *Volcanoes in the Sea.* Honolulu: University of Hawai'i Press, 1983. The best reference to Hawaiian geology. Well-explained for easy understanding. Illustrated.

Ziegler, Alan C., *Hawaiian Natural History, Ecology, and Evolution.* Honolulu: University of Hawai'i Press. An overview of Hawaiian natural history with treatment of ecology and evolution in that process.

PERIODICALS

Hawaii Magazine. 3 Burroughs, Irvine, CA 92618. This magazine covers the Hawaiian islands like a tropical breeze. Feature articles on all aspects of life in the islands, with special departments on travel, events, exhibits, and restaurant reviews. Up-to-the-minute information, and a fine read.

PICTORIALS

Cook, Chris. *From the Skies of Kauai.* Honolulu: Mutual Publishing, 1991.

La Brucherie, Roger. *Hawaiian World, Hawaiian Heart.* Pine Valley, CA: Imagenes Press, 1989.

Ronck, Ronn. *Kauai: A Many Splendored Island.* Honolulu: Mutual Publishing, 1985.

Tsusumi, Cheryl Chee. *Reflections of Kauai: The Garden Isle.* Honolulu: Island Heritage, 2000.

POLITICAL SCIENCE

Albertini, Jim, et al. *The Dark Side of Paradise, Hawaii in a Nuclear War.* Honolulu: cAtholic Action of Hawaii. Well-documented research outlining Hawaii's role and vulnerability in a nuclear world. This book presents the antinuclear and antimilitary side of the political issue in Hawaii.

Bell, Roger. *Last Among Equals: Hawaiian Statehood and American Politics.* Honolulu: University of Hawai'i Press, 1984. Documents Hawaii's long and rocky road to statehood, tracing political partisanship, racism, and social change.

SPORTS AND RECREATION

Alford, John, D. *Mountain Biking the Hawaiian Islands.* Ohana Publishing, 1997. Good off-road biking guide to the main Hawaiian islands.

Ambrose, Greg. *Surfer's Guide to Hawai'i.* Honolulu: Bess Press, 1991. Island-by-island guide to surfing spots.

Ball, Stuart. *The Hiker's Guide to the Hawaiian Islands.* Honolulu: University of Hawai'i Press, 2000. This excellent guide includes 44 hikes on each of the four main islands.

Cagala, George. *Hawaii: A Camping Guide.* Boston: Hunter Publishing, 1994. Useful.

Chisholm, Craig. *Kauai Hiking Trails.* Lake Oswego, OR: Fernglen Press, 1989. Also *Hawaiian Hiking Trails.*

Cisco, Dan. *Hawai'i Sports.* Honolulu: University of Hawai'i Press, 1999. A compendium of popular and little-known sporting events and figures, with facts, tidbits, and statistical information. Go here first for a general overview.

Lueras, Leonard. *Surfing, the Ultimate Pleasure.* Honolulu: Emphasis International, 1984. One of the most brilliant books ever written on surfing.

McMahon, Richard. *Camping Hawai'i: A Complete Guide.* Honolulu: University of Hawai'i Press, 1997. This book has all you need to know about camping in Hawaii, with descriptions of different campsites.

Morey, Kathy. *Kauai Trails.* Berkeley, CA: Wilderness Press, 1997. Morey's books are specialized, detailed hiker's guides to Hawaii's outdoors. Complete with useful maps, historical references, official procedures, and plants and animals encountered along the way. If you're focused on hiking, these are the best to take along. *Maui Trails, Oahu Trails,* and *Hawaii Trails* are also available.

Rosenberg, Steve. *Diving Hawaii.* Locust Valley, NY: Aqua Quest, 1990. Describes diving locations on the major islands as well as the marine life divers are likely to see. Includes many color photos.

Smith, Robert. *Hawaii's Best Hiking Trails.* Kula, Maui, HI: Hawaiian Outdoor Adventures. Other guides by this author include *Hiking Oahu, Hiking Maui, Hiking Hawaii,* and *Hiking Kauai.*

Sutherland, Audrey. *Paddling Hawai'i,* revised edition. Honolulu: University of Hawai'i

Press, 1998. All you need to know about sea kayaking in Hawaiian waters.

Valeir, Katy. *On the Na Pali Coast; A Guide to Hikers and Boaters.* Honolulu: University of Hawai'i Press, 1988. An invaluable guide to what you encounter along Kaua'i's spec-tacular North Coast. Natural, historical, and cultural references.

Wallin, Doug. *Diving & Snorkeling Guide to the Hawaiian Islands,* 2nd ed. Pisces Books, 1991. A guide offering brief descriptions of diving locations on the four major islands.

Internet Resources

The following list of websites have information about Kaua'i and the state of Hawaii that may be useful in preparation for a trip to the islands and for general interest.

GOVERNMENT

County of Kaua'i
www.kauai.gov
The official website of Kaua'i County. In-cludes, among other items, a calendar of events, information about parks and camp-ing, and island bus schedules.

Hawai'i State Government
www.hawaii.gov
Official website for the state of Hawaii. In-cludes information for visitors, on government organizations, on living in the state, business and employment, education, and many other topics.

TOURISM

Hawaii Visitor and Convention Bureau
www.gohawaii.com
This official site of the Hawaii Visitors and Convention Bureau, the state-run tourism or-ganization, has information about all the major Hawaiian islands: transportation, accommo-dations, eating, activities, shopping, Hawaiian products, an events calendar, a travel planner and resource guide for a host of topics, as well as information about meetings, conventions, and the organization itself.

Kaua'i Visitors Bureau
www.kauaidiscovery.com
The official site of the Kaua'i Visitors Bureau, a branch of the Hawaii Visitors and Conven-tion Bureau, has much the same information as the above website but specific to the island of Hawai'i. A very useful resource.

Best Places Hawaii
www.bestplaceshawaii.com
Produced and maintained by H&S Pub-lishing, this first-rate commercial site has general and specific information about all major Hawaiian islands, a vacation planner, and suggestions for things to do and places to see. For a non-government site, this is a great place to start a search for tourist in-formation about the state or any of its major islands. One of dozens of sites on the inter-net with a focus on Hawaii tourism-related information.

Alternative Hawaii
www.alternative-hawaii.com
Alternative source for eco-friendly general information and links to specific businesses, with some cultural, historical, and events in-formation.

Hawaii Ecotourism Association
www.hawaiiecotourism.org
Official Hawaii Ecotourism Association website. Lists goals, members, activities, and provides links to member organizations and related ecotourism groups.

CULTURAL EVENTS

Hawaii Visitors Bureau Calendar
http://calendar.gohawaii.com

For events of all sorts happening throughout the state, visit the calendar of events listing on the Hawaii Visitors Bureau website. Information can be accessed by island, date, or type.

State Foundation of Culture and the Arts
www.hawaii.gov/sfca

This site of the State Foundation of Culture and the Arts features a calendar of arts and cultural events, activities, and programs held throughout the state. Information is available by island and type.

INTERISLAND AIRLINES

Hawaiian Airlines, Aloha Airlines, and Pacific Wings
www.hawaiianair.com
www.alohaairlines.com
www.pacificwings.com

These websites list all regularly-scheduled interisland commercial air links with Kaua'i.

MUSIC

Hawaiian Music Island
www.mele.com

Check out the Hawaiian music scene at Hawaiian Music Island, one of the largest music websites that focuses on Hawaiian music, books and videos related to Hawaiian music and culture, concert schedules, Hawaiian music awards, and links to music companies and musicians. Others with broad listings and general interest information are: Nahenahenet, **www .nahenahe.net;** and Hawaiian Music Guide, **www.hawaii-music.com.**

BOOKS

University of Hawai'i Press
www.uhpress.hawaii.edu

This University of Hawai'i Press website has the best overall list of titles for books publishes on Hawaiian themes and topics. Other publishers to check for substantial lists of books on Hawaiiana are the Bishop Museum Press, **www.bishopmuseum.org/ press/press.html;** Kamehameha Schools Press, **http://kspress.ksbe.edu;** Bess Press, **www.besspress.com;** Mutual Publishing, **www.mutualpublishing.com;** and Petrogylph Press, **www.basicallybooks .com.**

MUSEUMS

Kaua'i Museum
www.kauaimuseum.org

An introduction to the Kaua'i Museum, its exhibits, events, hours, and services.

Hawai'i Museums Association
www.hawaiimuseums.org

This site is dedicated to the promotion of museums and cultural attractions in the state of Hawaii with links to member sites on each of the islands. A member organization.

Bishop Museum
www.bishopmuseum.org

Site of the premier ethnological and cultural museum dedicated to Hawaiian people, their culture, and cultural artifacts.

NEWSPAPERS

Garden Island News
www.kauaiworld.com

Web presence for Kaua'i's major newspaper, The Garden Island. Good for local news, with some statewide coverage.

Honolulu Star Bulletin and the Honolulu Advertiser
www.starbulletin.com
www.honoluluadvertiser.com

Websites for Hawaii's two main English-language dailies, both published in Honolulu. Both have a concentration of news coverage about Oʻahu yet cover major news from the Neighbor Islands.

ETHNIC HAWAIIAN AFFAIRS

Office of Hawaiian Affairs
www.oha.org
Official site for the state-mandated organization that deals with native Hawaii-related affairs.

Hawaiian Independence
www.hawaii-nation.org

Site of Nation of Hawaiʻi, one of the organizations of native Hawaiians who are advocating for sovereignty and independence. While there are several dozen independent native Hawaiian rights organizations that are pushing for various degrees of sovereignty or independence for native Hawaiian people, some of the major groups are listed below: Reinstated Hawaiian Government, **www.reinstated .org;** Kingdom of Hawaii, **www.freehawaii .org;** (another) Kingdom of Hawaii, **www .pixi.com/~kingdom;** the Hawaiian Kingdom, **www.hawaiiankingdom.org.**

Index

HIKING

Acknowledgments

Since the passing of J.D. Bisignani, the original author of *Moon Handbooks Kaua'i,* I have taken on the great task of revising this book and others in his series of guides to Hawaii. Joe, you have been an inspiration to me and have laid a solid foundation for the subsequent revisions of these books. Even though you are gone, you've been with me with each word. To you, my good friend, a big thank you.

As always, the staff at Avalon Travel Publishing has been professional in every way. A sincere thank you to everyone.

The following individuals require special thanks for their assistance in the revision of this book: Rod Lau, Chris Moore, Javed, Claire Morris-Dobie, Lorraine DeRosa, Michael Orozco, Candy Aluli, George Tandal, Stephanie Kaluahine Reid, Laura Richards, Kathy Lane, and my wife, Linda Nilsen. A sincere *mahalo* to you all.

www.moon.com

For helpful advice on planning a trip, visit www.moon.com for the **TRAVEL PLANNER** and get access to useful travel strategies and valuable information about great places to visit. When you travel with Moon, expect an experience that is uncommon and truly unique.

HANDBOOKS • METRO • OUTDOORS • LIVING ABROAD

MAP SYMBOLS

▨ Expressway	◖ Highlight	✗ Airfield	⚑ Golf Course
▨ Primary Road	○ City/Town	✗ Airport	P Parking Area
── Secondary Road	◉ State Capital	▲ Mountain	⬟ Archaeological Site
‥‥ Unpaved Road	⊛ National Capital	+ Unique Natural Feature	▮ Church
‒ ‒ ‒ Trail	★ Point of Interest		▯ Gas Station
‥‥‥ Ferry	• Accommodation	⬱ Waterfall	◌ Glacier
+─+─+ Railroad	▾ Restaurant/Bar	▲ Park	⬚ Mangrove
▨ Pedestrian Walkway	■ Other Location	◨ Trailhead	▭ Reef
▥ Stairs	Λ Campground	✗ Skiing Area	▭ Swamp

CONVERSION TABLES

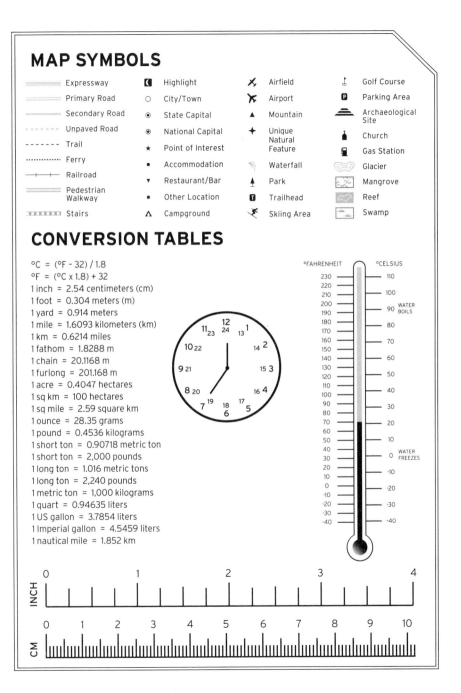

°C = (°F - 32) / 1.8
°F = (°C x 1.8) + 32
1 inch = 2.54 centimeters (cm)
1 foot = 0.304 meters (m)
1 yard = 0.914 meters
1 mile = 1.6093 kilometers (km)
1 km = 0.6214 miles
1 fathom = 1.8288 m
1 chain = 20.1168 m
1 furlong = 201.168 m
1 acre = 0.4047 hectares
1 sq km = 100 hectares
1 sq mile = 2.59 square km
1 ounce = 28.35 grams
1 pound = 0.4536 kilograms
1 short ton = 0.90718 metric ton
1 short ton = 2,000 pounds
1 long ton = 1.016 metric tons
1 long ton = 2,240 pounds
1 metric ton = 1,000 kilograms
1 quart = 0.94635 liters
1 US gallon = 3.7854 liters
1 Imperial gallon = 4.5459 liters
1 nautical mile = 1.852 km

MOON KAUA'I

Avalon Travel Publishing
An Imprint of
Avalon Publishing Group, Inc.

AVALON
publishing group incorporated

1400 65th Street, Suite 250
Emeryville, CA 94608, USA
www.moon.com

Editors: Kay Elliott, Cinnamon Hearst
Series Manager: Kathryn Ettinger
Acquisitions Manager: Rebecca K. Browning
Copy Editor: Valerie Sellers Blanton
Graphics Coordinator: Domini Dragoone
Production Coordinators: Jacob Goolkasian,
    Tabitha Lahr
Cover & Interior Designer: Gerilyn Attebery
Map Editor: Kat Smith
Cartographers: Christine Markiewicz, Kat Bennett
Cartography Manager: Mike Morgenfeld
Indexer: Judy Hunt

ISBN-10: 1-56691-956-8
ISBN-13: 978-1-56691-956-2
ISSN: 1091-3335

Printing History
1st Edition–1989
6th Edition–May 2006
5 4 3 2 1

Text © 2006 by Robert Nilsen.
Maps © 2006 by Robert Nilsen and Avalon Travel
Publishing, Inc.
All rights reserved.

Some photos and illustrations are used by permission
and are the property of the original copyright
owners.

Front cover photo: Heliconia plant © 1997, Ray
Mains/Pacific Stock
Title page photo: Hanalei Valley taro fields and the
Hanalei River © Robert Nilsen

Printed in United States by Worzalla

KEEPING CURRENT

If you have a favorite gem you'd like to see included in the next edition, or see anything
that needs updating, clarification, or correction, please drop us a line. Send your
comments via email to feedback@moon.com, or use the address above.